Historical Dictionaries of Literature and the Arts
Jon Woronoff, Series Editor

Historical Dictionary
of Italian Cinema

Gino Moliterno

*Historical Dictionaries of Literature
and the Arts, No. 28*

The Scarecrow Press, Inc.
Lanham, Maryland • Toronto • Plymouth, UK
2008

SCARECROW PRESS, INC.

Published in the United States of America
by Scarecrow Press, Inc.
A wholly owned subsidiary of
The Rowman & Littlefield Publishing Group, Inc.
4501 Forbes Boulevard, Suite 200, Lanham, Maryland 20706
www.scarecrowpress.com

Estover Road
Plymouth PL6 7PY
United Kingdom

British Library Cataloguing in Publication Information Available

Library of Congress Cataloging-in-Publication Data

Moliterno, Gino, 1951–
  Historical dictionary of Italian cinema / Gino Moliterno.
    p. cm. — (Historical dictionaries of literature and the arts ; no. 28)
  Includes bibliographical references.
  ISBN-13: 978-0-8108-6073-5 (hardcover : alk. paper)
  ISBN-10: 0-8108-6073-2 (hardcover : alk. paper)
  eISBN-13: 978-0-8108-6254-8
  eISBN-10: 0-8108-6254-9
  1. Motion pictures—Italy—Dictionaries. 2. Motion pictures—Italy—History—
Dictionaries. I. Title.
  PN1993.5.I88M56 2008
  791.430945'03—dc22   2008011225

For Patricia, light of my life
too soon extinguished

"Or ho perduta tutta la mia baldanza
che si movea d'amoroso tesoro . . ."

Contents

Editor's Foreword

Italy was one of the first places where cinema emerged, and there are few other countries where it has flourished more spectacularly. Despite crises and being overshadowed by mass production from Hollywood, Italian cinema has constantly reinvented itself in an amazing variety of forms, including neorealism, which has spread worldwide. Its production is amazingly broad, from outright trash to the very finest art films—a steady flow of quite ordinary popular films but also specialties such as *commedia all'italiana* and spaghetti Westerns. Many have gone on to win awards and appear on all-time-great lists, including some that are so universal—and so Italian—that they are known worldwide under their Italian names, such a *La strada*, *La dolce vita*, and *Padre padrone*.

There are more than enough reasons to welcome the *Historical Dictionary of Italian Cinema*, which can serve as an informative guide for both those who simply enjoy watching Italian films and those who study the genre more closely. Italian cinema's long history is charted in the chronology and the introduction, but the dictionary section—with hundreds of entries on directors, producers, and actors; major studios and film companies; characteristic genres and themes; and memorable films—is where readers will spend the most time. The book concludes with an appendix of award winners and a bibliography, which readers can use to find many other sources.

The author, Gino Moliterno, was born in Italy and has had an abiding interest in Italian cinema for several decades. After teaching Italian language and culture at the University of Sydney, the University of Auckland, and the University of Wollongong, he joined the Department of Modern European Languages at the Australian National University. He is presently senior lecturer of its Film Studies Program. He has lectured extensively on Italian cinema and was the general editor and contributing author to the *Encyclopedia of Contemporary Italian Culture* (2000).

In this historical dictionary he presents a broad and deep introduction to one of the most prolific contributors to world cinema.

Jon Woronoff
Series Editor

Preface

Italian cinema has been one of the major cinemas of the world and has been both much admired and extensively studied by numerous scholars in many languages. Italian readers have always been well served by a wealth of authoritative general histories and monographic studies on the Italian cinema in all its aspects, as well as a wide variety of single and multivolume encyclopedias and dictionaries for more specific consultation. For some time now, English readers have also had available a number of excellent overarching histories of the Italian cinema and many outstanding studies of particular aspects and specific directors. However, apart from the valuable but all-too-brief BFI *Companion to Italian Cinema* there exist no comparable dictionaries or encyclopedias of the Italian cinema for quick factual reference or generic consultation for English readers. The present work hopes to go some way toward filling this gap, by offering accurate, up-to-date, and readily accessible entries that cover the entire history of the cinema in Italy from 1895 to the present. Given the limitations of the single-volume format and the need to select from an almost unlimited number of possible inclusions, it too will inevitably have left its own gaps. Nevertheless, the hope is that by strategic selection and cross-referencing of entries, enough of such a vast territory has effectively been covered to be able to provide the non-Italian reader with a useful and accurate guide to one of the truly great cinemas of the world.

Acknowledgments

Many more people have helped to bring this work to completion than can be mentioned by name, not all of whom can be mentioned here. I would like, nevertheless, to express my deepest appreciation to all of them but offer particular thanks to Jon Woronoff for his infinite patience and his invaluable editorial advice; Clara Fossati (Centro Sperimentale di Cinematografia) for facilitating my access to films and printed materials; Paolo Cherchi Usai and Quentin Turnour (Australian National Film and Sound Archive) for help in accessing materials; Luca Giuliani (Cineteca del Friuli) for information and access to films; Peter Delpeut for making available his wonderful documentary on the Italian divas; Roberta Bonalume, Rosie Paris, Joe Di Giacomo, and Dona Di Giacomo for their help in gaining access to many of the films on video; Brigid Maher for her assiduous research assistance; Sarah Lysewycz for her attentive reading of the manuscript; Caren Florance for her typesetting and general wisdom; Roger Hillman for his unfailing encouragement; Paul Eggert for his wise counsel; Vittoria Pasquini for our lively discussions on all aspects of Italian cinema; and Adam Shoemaker for everything. Most of all I would like to thank my wife, Patricia Werlemann, for her forbearance, generosity of spirit, and unstinting support for a project that continued to compete for my time and attention even as she was valiantly battling two major illnesses. This book is dedicated entirely to her.

Reader's Note

For the benefit of non-Italian readers, all Italian film titles are followed in parentheses by their English translation. Where the English title is an official one that already exists in general circulation, it is given in italics. A nonitalicized English title indicates that no previous English version of the title has been found and the translation offered is my own. No translation is given in cases where the Italian title is so well known that it is also used in English or in cases where the title involves an untranslatable play on words, as in Paolo and Vittorio Taviani's *Allonsanfan*.

What is regarded as the official date of a film can often vary according to the source. The date provided here is the one that the majority of the most reliable sources furnish as the year of the film's Italian release.

Throughout the volume if a title, name, or phrase appears in bold it indicates that the dictionary includes an entry on the topic.

Acronyms and Abbreviations

AGIS   Associazione Generale Italiana dello Spettacolo/Italian General Association for Entertainment

ANAC   Associazione Nazionale Autori Cinematografici/National Film Writers' Association

ANEC   Associazione Nazionale Esercenti di Cinema/National Film Exhibitors' Association

ANICA   Associazione Nazionale Industrie Cinematografiche e Affini/National Association of Film and Affiliated Industries

API   Autori e Produttori Italiani/Italian Filmmakers' and Producers' Association

APT   Associazione Produttori Televisivi/Television Producers' Association

BAFTA   British Academy of Film and Television Arts

CDC   Cooperativa Doppiatori Cinematografici/Cooperative of Film Dubbers

CSC   Centro Sperimentale di Cinematografia/Experimental Center for Cinematography (National Film School)

EAGC   Ente Autonomo di Gestione per il Cinema/Independent Authority for Cinema Management

ENIC   Ente Nazionale per le Industrie Cinematografiche/National Film Industries Authority

FEDIC   Federazione Italiana dei Cineclub/Italian Cineclub Federation

LUCE   L'Unione Cinematografica Educativa/Union of Educational Cinematography

OCIC   Office Catholique International du Cinéma/The International Catholic Organization for Cinema and Audio-Visual

ODI   Organizzazione Doppiatori Cinematografici/Organization of Film Dubbers

RAI   Radiotelevisione Italiana/Italian National Radio and Television

SAFFI   Società Anonima Fabbricazione Films Italiane/Italian Film-making Company Limited

SIGLA   Società Italiana Gustavo Lombardo Anonima/The Italian Gustavo Lombardo Company Limited

SNCCI   Sindacato Nazionale Critici Cinematografici Italiani/ National Union of Italian Film Critics

SNGCI   Sindacato Nazionale Giornalisti Cinematografici Italiani/ National Union of Screenwriters

UCI   Unione Cinematografica Italiana/Italian Cinematographic Union

Chronology

1895   11 November: In Florence, Filoteo Alberini applies for a patent for his Kinotografo Alberini, a device for "recording, projecting and printing moving images on film." The patent is officially granted on 21 December, too late to scoop the Lumière brothers, who have already patented, and extensively exhibited, their own *cinématographe* during that year.

1896   12 March: A demonstration of the Lumière invention is held in Rome in the studio of Henri Le Lieure. **29 March:** Vittorio Calcina organizes the first Italian exhibition of the Lumière cinematograph in Milan. Screenings in other Italian cities follow. **20 November:** Calcina shoots the first Italian newsreel: *Umberto e Margherita di Savoia a passeggio per il parco* (*King Umberto and Margherita of Savoy Strolling in the Park*).

1898   Italo Pacchioni begins making films in Italy with his own version of the Lumière cinematograph. Transformist Leopoldo Fregoli also adapts the Lumière invention to create his own Fregoligraph, which he uses to film himself in sequences that are then projected as part of his stage performances. The first permanent movie houses are opened in Rome and other Italian cities.

1901   In Naples, Menotti Cattaneo opens the Sala Iride. Father Ferdinando Rodolfi (later bishop of Vicenza) publishes a long essay on the new art of moving pictures.

1904   Gustavo Lombardo sets up a film distribution company in Naples. In Rome, Alberini inaugurates the cinema Moderno. In Turin, Arturo Ambrosio sets up a workshop for the manufacture of film stock.

1905   In Rome, Alberini and Dante Santoni establish the first Italian film production company, Alberini & Santoni. Soon after Alberini directs *La presa di Roma* (*The Taking of Rome*), widely acknowledged as the first Italian feature film. Permanent movie houses are now present in all the major Italian cities. In Naples the Troncone brothers begin making films. In Venice the brothers Almerigo and Luigi Roatto begin making films that they screen in their small chain of theaters.

1906 The Alberini & Santoni company is transformed into the Cines. In Turin, Arturo Ambrosio founds the Ambrosio Film company and, with the help of photographer Roberto Omegna, begins producing documentaries and fiction films. Also in Turin, Carlo Rossi founds Carlo Rossi & C., which two years later will become Itala Film.

1907 The Cines opens a distribution office in New York. In Milan, Luca Comerio founds the Comerio production company, which soon merges with SAFFI to become SAFFI-Comerio. The first Italian film magazines begin to be published. Philosopher Giovanni Papini publishes one of the first theoretical articles on the cinema in the Turin daily, *La Stampa*.

1908 Ambrosio Film scores its first international success with the historical superspectacle *Gli ultimi giorni di Pompei* (*The Last Days of Pompeii*), directed by Luigi Maggi. In Naples Lombardo begins publication of the film magazine *Lux*.

1909 In Naples, Elvira and Nicola Notari found the Dora Film company. In Milan SAFFI-Comerio becomes Milano Films. André Deed begins making his Cretinetti films for *Itala* in Turin.

1910 An estimated 500 permanent movie houses are now operating throughout the peninsula. Lombardo establishes the SIGLA film distribution company in Naples.

1911 Roberto Omegna wins first prize in the documentary film section of the Turin International Exhibition with his *La vita delle farfalle* (The Life of Butterflies). Milano Films release *Inferno*, acknowledged as the first Italian full-length feature film (70 minutes). In Paris Ricciardo Canudo publishes his first essay on the cinema, styling it the "Sixth Art."

1912 Enrico Guazzoni directs *Quo vadis?* for the Cines company. Films are now granted the legal protection of copyright.

1913 Giovanni Pastrone directs *Cabiria*, which, when released in 1914, achieves unprecedented box office success and international critical acclaim. Lyda Borelli, appearing in *Ma l'amor mio non muore* (*But My Love Does Not Die*), becomes the first diva, thus inaugurating the Italian star system. The first national film censorship regulations are introduced.

1914 Ninety full-length feature films are produced in Italy. Highest point of Italian silent film penetration of the American market. Release of Nino Martoglio's *Sperduti nel buio* (*Lost in the Dark*), later to be revered as an early milestone of cinematic realism.

1915 Release of *Maciste* (*Marvelous Maciste*), the first of a long line of films produced by Itala and featuring the "good giant" who had first appeared in *Cabiria*. Francesca Bertini gives one of her most acclaimed performances in Gustavo Serena's *Assunta Spina*. She becomes the highest-paid film actress in Europe.

1916 Publication of the Manifesto of Futurist cinema. *Maciste alpino* (*The Warrior*) is severely cut by the censors in order not to offend Austria, Italy's ally in World War I.

1917 Ambrosio Film produces *Cenere* (*Ashes*), Eleonora Duse's only film, directed by Febo Mari. The film is only moderately successful. In Naples Lombardo expands from distribution to production by creating Lombardo Film.

1918 Francesca Bertini creates her own film production company, Bertini Film.

1919 Formation of the consortium Unione Cinematografica Italiana (UCI, Italian Cinematographic Union), uniting most of the major production houses. In Turin Enrico Fiori founds Fert, a production company independent of the UCI.

1920 Stefano Pittaluga establishes his film distribution company, Societa Anonima Stefano Pittaluga (SASP). Tighter film censorship regulations are introduced, to be enforced by a film censorship board.

1921 Crisis of the UCI following the collapse of the Banca di sconto.

1923 Fascist law confirming and strengthening previous regulations regarding film censorship. Most of the American majors open subsidiaries in Italy.

1924 Creation of L'Unione Cinematografica Educativa (LUCE). MGM begins shooting *Ben-Hur* in the Cines studios in Rome. Pittaluga expands from distribution to film production by buying the Fert studios.

1925 LUCE nationalized; becomes the Istituto Nazionale LUCE, with exclusive responsibility for the production of all documentary and educational films in Italy.

1926 Law requiring all cinemas to screen a LUCE newsreel before any feature film. Pittaluga buys all of the UCI's exhibition and distribution networks. Blasetti founds the cinema journal *Lo schermo*, soon renamed *Cinematografo*.

1927 After a long crisis the UCI is liquidated and most of its properties are bought by Stefano Pittaluga's SASP. Law requiring first-run cinemas to devote 10 percent of screening time to Italian films.

1928 Gustavo Lombardo moves from Naples to Rome, where he founds the Titanus production company. Alessandro Blasetti directs *Sole* (*Sun*), released the following year. The government creates the Ente Nazionale per la Cinematografia (ENAC, National Authority for Cinematography).

1929 Pittaluga takes over the Cines studios and equips them for sound. Mario Camerini directs *Rotaie* (*Rails*), subsequently also released in a sound version in 1931. **19 April:** First screening of *The Jazz Singer* at the Supercinema in Rome.

1930 Sound films begin to be produced at the Rome Cines studios. The first film released is Gennaro Righelli's *La canzone d'amore* (*The Song of Love*), adapted from a short story by Luigi Pirandello.

1931 First law providing state subsidies to Italian film producers. **5 April:** Death of Stefano Pittaluga. Founding of the satirical magazine *Marc'Aurelio*.

1932 The inclusion of film screenings at the Venice Biennale inaugurates the Venice International Film Festival. Emilio Cecchi appointed artistic director at Cines. Alessandro Blasetti opens the first film school in Italy under the auspices of the Conservatory of Saint Cecilia in Rome. First dubbing studio opened in Rome.

1933   Law requiring all feature-length foreign films to be dubbed into Italian. Exhibitors required to show at least one Italian film for every three non-Italian films screened during the year. Ivo Perilli's *Ragazzo* (*Boy*) becomes the only film to be banned outright by the Fascist regime, prohibited by express order of Mussolini himself.

1934   Formation of the Direzione Generale per la Cinematografia (General Directorate of Cinematography), a government department for the management of the film industry, under the direction of Luigi Freddi. Signing of the Ciano-Hays accord to regulate the importation of American films into Italy. Giovacchino Forzano founds the Pisorno studios at Tirrenia. Renato Gualino sets up the LUX Film production company.

1935   Formation of the Ente Nazionale per le Industrie Cinematografiche (ENIC, National Film Industries Authority). A decree establishes a special fund to finance film production at the Banca Nazionale del Lavoro. Opening of a national film school, the Centro Sperimentale di Cinematografia, under the direction of Luigi Chiarini. **26 September:** Fire mysteriously destroys the Cines studios in Rome.

1936   29 January: Work begins on the construction of Cinecittà. Founding of the journal *Cinema*, soon to come under the direction of Vittorio Mussolini.

1937   28 April: In Rome the Cinecittà studio complex is opened by Mussolini. The Centro Sperimentale begins publishing its journal *Bianco e nero*. Carmine Gallone directs *Scipione l'Africano* (*Scipio the African*), the most expensive film produced under Fascism and financed largely by government funds.

1938   The Alfieri law establishes significant financial incentives for Italian films that do well at the box office. Decree granting ENIC a monopoly over the importation and distribution of all foreign films in Italy. In protest the American majors withdraw from Italy.

1939   Decree strengthening state censorship over all film production and exhibition. Publication of Francesco Pasinetti's *Storia del cinema*.

1940   Vittorio De Sica directs his first film, *Rose scarlatte* (*Red Roses*).

1941   The Cines is resurrected a third time, with Luigi Freddi as head. After working with Francesco De Robertis on the fictional documentary *Uomini sul fondo* (*Men on the Bottom*), Roberto Rossellini directs his first film, *La nave bianca* (*The White Ship*).

1942   Law prohibiting Jews from working in any branch of the film industry. Blasetti directs *Quattro passi fra le nuvole* (*A Stroll through the Clouds*), Luchino Visconti directs *Ossessione* (*Obsession*), and Vittorio De Sica directs *I bambini ci guardano* (*The Children Are Watching Us*), all three films later regarded as forerunners of neorealism.

1943   Following the declaration of the armistice in September, the Cinecittà studios are dismantled and facilities are taken north by retreating Fascists with the intention of founding a Cinevillage in Venice. Much of the equipment ends up in Germany.

1944   In Rome the founding of the Associazione Nazionale Industrie Cinematografiche e Affini (ANICA, National Association of Film and Affiliated Industries). Following the liberation of Rome the studios of Cinecittà are used as a camp for displaced persons.

1945   Rossellini directs *Roma città aperta* (*Rome Open City*). Birth of the Associazione Generale Italiana dello Spettacolo (AGIS, Italian General Association for Entertainment). The abrogation of Fascist laws restricting importation of foreign films opens the way for a massive return of Hollywood films to Italy.

1946   Rossellini directs *Paisà* (*Paisan*), the second of his war trilogy. The Sindacato Nazionale Giornalisti Cinematografici Italiani (SNGCI, National Union of Screenwriters) establishes the annual Nastro d'argento prize.

1947   Cinecittà and the Centro Sperimentale reopen. Creation of the Central Office for Cinematography within the Prime Minister's Department, headed by undersecretary Giulio Andreotti. New law to regulate film subsidy and censorship. Pietro Germi's *Gioventù perduta* (*Lost Youth*) censored by Andreotti for its "pessimism," provoking a public letter of protest from Rossellini and 34 other directors.

1948   **22 February:** Manifesto of the Movimento per la difesa del cinema italiano (Movement for the Defense of Italian Cinema) against state censorship of films. De Sica directs *Ladri di biciclette* (*Bicycle Thieves*). Giuseppe De Santis directs *Riso amaro* (*Bitter Rice*), released the following year. In spite of the growing recovery, three-quarters of all new films screened in Italy are American.

1949 First accord governing coproductions with France. A copy of every Italian film produced from now on to be lodged with the National Film Library. De Sica's *Ladri di biciclette* wins the Academy Award for Best Foreign Film. MGM begins shooting *Quo vadis?* in Rome.

1950 New (Andreotti) law governing film subsidy, censorship, and distribution. Producers Carlo Ponti and Dino De Laurentiis form a joint production company. Antonioni directs his first feature film, *Cronaca di un amore* (*Story of a Love Affair*). Pietro Germi's *Il cammino della speranza* (*Path of Hope*) suffers cuts due to censorship.

1951 ANICA and the American MPAA sign their first accord. A manifesto for the defense of Italian cinema is issued and signed by 18 leading directors and screenwriters.

1952 Andreotti publicly criticizes De Sica's *Umberto D.* Fellini directs his first solo film, *Lo sceicco bianco* (*The White Sheik*). Steno and Mario Monicelli direct the first Italian film in color, *Totò a colori* (*Toto in Color*).

1953 Guido Aristarco and Renzo Renzi are jailed for publishing a film script that allegedly defames the armed forces. Monicelli's *Totò e Carolina* (*Toto and Carolina*) is blocked by the censors and released only two years later after a host of cuts and changes. The long-awaited inauguration of the Museo Nazionale del Cinema (National Cinema Museum) in Turin. Introduction of Cinemascope.

1954 Fellini directs *La strada*, awarded the Oscar for Best Foreign Film in 1956. ANICA institutes a board of self-censorship. Ponti and De Laurentiis dissolve their joint company. Introduction of television in Italy.

1955 ANICA and AGIS institute the David di Donatello prize. Highest point of cinema attendance in Italy (819 million).

1956 Angelo Rizzoli founds Rizzoli Film. Cinema attendance begins to decline.

1957   ENIC dissolved.

1958   Mario Monicelli makes *I soliti ignoti* (*Big Deal on Madonna Street*), which inaugurates the *commedia all'italiana* (comedy Italian style). Law creating the Ente Autonomo di Gestione per il Cinema (EAGC, Independent Authority for Cinema Management). Carlo Ponti moves to Hollywood. The Cines is definitively wound up.

1959   Creation of the Ministero del Turismo e Spettacolo (Ministry for Tourism and Spectacle). Rossellini directs Vittorio De Sica in *Il generale Della Rovere* (*General della Rovere*). Mario Monicelli makes *La grande guerra* (*The Great War*).

1960   Fellini's *La dolce vita* wins the Palme d'or at Cannes but in Italy provokes widespread scandal and protests. Visconti's *Rocco e i suoi fratelli* (*Rocco and His Brothers*) is initially granted a release but is subsequently impounded by the censors.

1961   Pasolini makes his directorial debut with *Accattone*. Vittorio De Seta makes *Banditi a Orgosolo* (*Bandits of Orgosolo*). Francesco Rosi directs *Salvatore Giuliano*. The first university course on the history of cinema is instituted at the University of Pisa and taught by Luigi Chiarini. Sophia Loren wins an Oscar for her performance in De Sica's *La ciociara* (*Two Women*). Germi directs *Divorzio all'italiana* (*Divorce Italian Style*).

1962   New censorship regulations proclaimed as part of a long-awaited new law on the cinema. De Laurentiis initiates construction of rival studio complex to be called Dinocittà. Dino Risi makes *Il sorpasso* (*The Good Life*).

1963   Fellini releases *Otto e mezzo* (*8½*). Visconti directs *Il gattopardo* (*The Leopard*). A new agreement is signed between ANICA and the MPAA.

1964   The overwhelming success of Sergio Leone's *Per un pugno di dollari* (*A Fistful of Dollars*) initiates the spaghetti Western genre. Pasolini makes *Il vangelo secondo Matteo* (*The Gospel According to Matthew*). LUX Film withdraws from film production. First Mostra Internazionale del Nuovo Cinema (International Exhibition of New Cinema) at Pesaro.

1965   New law (legge Corona) regulating production and subsidy of films by the Italian state. Marco Bellocchio directs his first film, *I pugni in tasca* (*Fists in the Pocket*).

1966   RAI TV moves into film production with Liliana Cavani's *Francesco d'Assisi* (*Francis of Assisi*). Agreement between ANICA and RAI regarding the screening of films on television. Creation of *Italnoleggio* to improve national production and international distribution of Italian films. Golden Lion at Venice awarded to Gillo Pontecorvo's *La Battaglia di Algeri* (*The Battle of Algiers*).

1967   At Cannes, Antonioni wins the Palme d'or with *Blowup*. Paolo and Vittorio Taviani direct their first solo film, *I sovversivi* (*The Subversives*).

1968   Pasolini makes *Teorema* (*Theorem*). ANICA members withdraw from all state film boards as a protest against government policy. Demonstrations disrupt the Venice Film Festival, leading to a decision to discontinue the awarding of prizes for the next decade.

1969   Workers occupy the offices of the Instituto LUCE. Rossellini appointed head of the Centro Sperimentale.

1970   Dario Argento directs his first film, *L'uccello dalle piume di cristallo* (*The Bird with the Crystal Plumage*). Marcello Mastroianni wins the Best Actor award at Cannes for his role in Ettore Scola's *Dramma della gelosia—tutti i particolari in cronaca* (*The Pizza Triangle*).

1971   Pasolini makes *Il Decameron* (*The Decameron*), the first of his Trilogy of Life. Elio Petri's *Indagine su un cittadino al di sopra di ogni sospetto* (*Investigation of a Citizen Above Suspicion*) is awarded the Oscar for Best Foreign Film. LUCE and Cinecittà in grave financial debt. New law to provide more credit for national film production. Italian films achieve the historic record of 65 percent of the home market.

1972   Bernardo Bertolucci's *Ultimo tango a Parigi* (*Last Tango in Paris*) is granted a release by the censorship board but immediately impounded by local authorities. De Sica's *Il giardino dei Finzi Contini* (*The Garden of the Finzi-Continis*) wins the Oscar for Best Foreign Film. Francesco Rosi's *Il caso Mattei* (*The Mattei Affair*) receives the Palme d'or at Cannes.

1973   Death of Anna Magnani.

1974   Dino De Laurentiis moves to America. Fellini's *Amarcord* wins the Oscar for Best Foreign Film. The Mostra Internazionale del Nuovo Cinema at Pesaro is dedicated to a reevaluation of neorealism.

1975   1 November: Pasolini is murdered at Ostia, Rome. His last film, *Salò*, is confiscated by the censors and its producer, Alberto Grimaldi, is given a two-month jail sentence.

1976   Bertolucci makes *Novecento (1900)*. A tribunal orders all copies of Bertolucci's *Ultimo tango* to be destroyed and director and producer receive a two-month jail sentence. **17 March:** Death of Luchino Visconti.

1977   Nanni Moretti makes *Io sono un autarchico (I Am Self-Sufficient)* in Super 8, which immediately achieves cult status. Paolo and Vittorio Taviani's *Padre padrone (My Father My Master)* receives the Palme d'or at Cannes. **3 June:** Roberto Rossellini dies. Appearance in Italy of the first red-light cinemas.

1978   Ermanno Olmi's *L'albero degli zoccoli (The Tree of the Wooden Clogs)* is awarded the Palme d'or at Cannes. Marked decrease in cinema attendance in Italy. Italian films' share of the home market falls to 42 percent while American films increase to 41.5 percent. The New York Museum of Modern Art hosts a retrospective of Italian films, Before Neorealism: Italian Cinema 1929–1944.

1980   A large retrospective of Italian postwar cinema broadcast on the TV network Canale 5.

1981   Massimo Troisi directs his first film, *Ricomincio da tre (I'm Starting from Three)*.

1982   Ermanno Olmi establishes Ipotesi Cinema, an independent film school at Bassano del Grappa. Inauguration of Le giornate del cinema muto (Pordenone Silent Film Festival), soon to become the most internationally renowned of silent-film festivals in the world. The Tavianis' *La notte di San Lorenzo (Night of the Shooting Stars)* wins the Grand Jury Prize at Cannes.

1983 Roberto Benigni directs himself in his first feature, *Tu mi turbi* (*You Disturb Me*). A fire at the Statuto cinema in Turin kills 64.

1984 Italnoleggio is wound up and its functions absorbed by LUCE. Silvio Berlusconi's Reteitalia TV network moves into film production.

1985 Fewer than 90 films produced in Italy; lowest level since 1950. Law instituting a new unitary fund for the finance of film and theater.

1987 Mario Cecchi Gori establishes the Cecchi Gori Group for film production. Nanni Moretti and Angelo Barbagallo found Sacher Film. Bertolucci's *L'ultimo imperatore* (*The Last Emperor*) wins nine Oscars. **1 February:** Death of Alessandro Blasetti.

1988 The Odeon cinema in Milan opens as Italy's first multiplex. Film attendance in Italy reaches the record low of 93 million.

1989 Giuseppe Tornatore's *Nuovo cinema Paradiso* (*Cinema Paradiso*) wins the Oscar for Best Foreign Film.

1990 Fellini directs what will be his last film, *La voce della luna* (*The Voice of the Moon*). Daniele Luchetti makes *Il portaborse* (*The Yes Man*), a film that uncannily anticipates the revelations of the *Mani pulite* (Clean Hands) investigations two years later. Sophia Loren receives an Oscar for her career.

1991 Nanni Moretti opens the Nuovo Sacher, an independent cinema in Rome.

1992 Mario Martone makes his directorial debut with *Morte di un matematico napoletano* (*Death of a Neapolitan Mathematician*). Gabriele Salvatores's *Mediterraneo* awarded the Oscar for Best Foreign Film. Gianni Amelio's *Ladro di bambini* (*The Stolen Children*) wins the Grand Jury Prize at Cannes. Lowest level of cinema attendance in Italian postwar history.

1993 **31 October:** Death of Fellini. Italian films' share of home market falls to a record low (14.5 percent).

1994 New law to encourage production and provide credit for the film industry. Antonioni receives an Oscar for lifetime achievement.

1996   Creation of the Istituzione Roberto Rossellini to restore and preserve all of the director's work. Deaths of Giuseppe De Santis and Marcello Mastroianni. Vittorio Gassman receives the Golden Lion for his career.

1997   Cinema attendance increases to 120 million.

1998   Cinecittà privatized. Ciprì and Maresco's *Totò che visse due volte* (*Toto Who Lived Twice*) is refused a release by the censorship board on grounds of blasphemy but is subsequently absolved on appeal. Left-wing government proposes to abolish film censorship altogether.

1999   Roberto Benigni's *La vita è bella* (*Life Is Beautiful*) wins Oscars for Best Actor, Best Musical Score, and Best Foreign Film. Legislation enacted officially transforming the Centro Sperimentale into the Scuola Nazionale del Cinema. Cinecittà divided into Cinecittà Holding and Cinecittà Studios.

2000   The National Cinema Museum in Turin is reopened at the Mole Antonelliana. Italia Cinema is instituted to help promote and distribute Italian films abroad.

2001   Nanni Moretti wins the Palme d'or at Cannes with *La stanza del figlio* (*The Son's Room*).

2003   Marco Tullio Giordana's *La meglio gioventù* (*The Best of Youth*) wins the *Un certain regard* section at Cannes. Giulio Pontecorvo's 1966 *The Battle of Algiers* is screened at the Pentagon as a study in how to combat terrorist insurgence.

2004   Comprehensive new law (Legge Urbani) on cinema and the Internet. In Rome the official opening of the Casa del Cinema on the grounds of the Villa Borghese. Establishment of the Massimo Troisi Prize for best short comic film of the year.

2005   Death of Alberto Lattuada. First-ever comprehensive white paper on the state of the Italian film and audiovisual industry is commissioned and published by Cinecittà Holding. The Association of Italian Documentarists (DOC/IT) institutes an annual prize for best feature documentary. Fellini's memory is honored with his image on the Italian five euro coin.

2006   Death of Alida Valli. Cristina Comencini's *La bestia nel cuore* (*The Beast in the Heart*) nominated for the Academy Award for Best Foreign Language Film. The New York Museum of Modern Art hosts a retrospective of the films of Paolo Virzì.

2007   Ennio Morricone awarded an honorary Oscar for his lifetime achievement. Deaths of Michelangelo Antonioni and Luigi Comencini.

2008   Matteo Garrone's *Gomorra* wins the Grand Prix at Cannes. Paolo Sorrentino's *Il divo* receives the Jury Prize.

Introduction

Italian cinema is now justly regarded as one of the great cinemas of the world. Historically, however, its fortunes have varied. Following a brief moment of glory in the early silent era, Italian cinema appeared to descend almost into irrelevance in the early 1920s, as screens in Italy came to be dominated largely by the advancing Hollywood machine. A strong revival of the industry throughout the 1930s was abruptly truncated by the advent of World War II. The end of the war, however, initiated a wholesale renewal as films such as *Roma città aperta* (*Rome Open City*), *Sciuscià* (*Shoe-Shine*, 1946), and *Ladri di biciclette* (*Bicycle Thieves*, 1948), flag bearers of what soon came to be known as neorealism, attracted unprecedented international acclaim and a reputation that only continued to grow in the following years as Italian films were feted worldwide. Ironically, they were feted nowhere more than in the United States, where Italian films consistently garnered the lion's share of the Oscars, with Lina Wertmüller becoming the first woman to ever be nominated for the Best Director award.

It was during this period, then, that Italian cinema achieved something of an apotheosis, with the names of directors like Federico Fellini, Michelangelo Antonioni, and Pier Paolo Pasolini becoming international bywords for cinematic daring and innovation and the release of their next films being eagerly awaited everywhere. At the same time, in a wide variety of personal styles, other filmmakers extensively explored social and political themes, using the cinema to reflect Italy back on itself, while other directors like Sergio Leone, Mario Bava, and Dino Risi also played with the genres and expanded the boundaries of popular cinema.

Such glory could not last forever, of course, and by the mid-1970s much of the vitality that had characterized postwar cinema had begun to wane. With remarkable resilience, however, and defying all rumors of its demise, Italian cinema revived in the early 1990s as a younger generation of auteurs again embraced the cinema in order to explore both private concerns and public vices in a postmodern Italy.

Thus, for over a century, with all its waxing and waning fortunes, Italian cinema has retained its position as a key social and cultural institution. The real miracle has been that while drawing primarily on its own cultural and artistic heritage, and thus being in many ways so thoroughly Italian, it has also so frequently produced films whose cinematic artistry, humor, and deep humanity have resonated well beyond their local context to appeal to audiences worldwide. Images such as Anna Magnani cut down by gunfire as she chases the army truck in *Rome Open City* or Anita Ekberg swanning through the Trevi fountain in *La dolce vita* have thus remained indelibly imprinted in the minds of spectators everywhere, as icons of cinematic art at its most moving and most exhilarating.

THE EARLY YEARS

But for a simple twist of fate, the history of Italian cinema might well have coincided with the invention of cinema itself. Indeed, the records show that in the same year in which the Lumière brothers patented their *cinématographe* in France, a young technical officer named Filoteo Alberini filed a patent for a very similar device, "for the recording, printing and projecting of moving images," in Florence. By the time Alberini's patent was granted, however, the Lumière brothers had already begun holding public screenings using their device in Paris and were manufacturing it in large numbers in their factory at Lyon. Within only a few months the Lumière *cinématographe* reached Italy, where it was first shown in Rome in March 1896 before screenings in all the other major Italian cities.

Given the immediate and overwhelming success of the Lumière invention, it hardly seems surprising that Alberini would abandon the idea of marketing his own *kinetografo*. Nevertheless, he clearly remained interested in the new medium and by 1901 had opened one of the first permanent movie houses in Florence. Three years later he moved to Rome and opened the cinema Moderno before joining in partnership with Dante Santoni in establishing the first Italian company "for the manufacture of films."

While undoubtedly not the very first film ever to be shot in Italy, the first film produced by the Alberini & Santoni company (a year later renamed Cines) can nevertheless be regarded as marking the beginning of the Italian feature film industry. Directed by Alberini himself, *La presa di Roma—20 settembre 1870* (*The Capture of Rome—20 September 1870*) was an imaginative if rather hagiographic re-creation of the culminating event of Italian unification: the battle in which the Piemontese army breached the walls of Rome and annexed the city (against the wishes of the pope) to the United Kingdom of Italy. Rather appropriately, then, Italian cinema came to be born in a filmic reenactment of the birth of the modern Italian nation itself. While the film's choice of subject and its mode of production (filmed partly in a studio and partly on external locations, using both professional actors and hundreds of extras lent by the Italian army) already betrayed the propensity for grand historical reconstructions that would soon come to characterize Italian cinema, its national theme significantly also prefigured the role that the cinema would continue to play in establishing and reflecting notions of Italian identity.

Projected on a giant screen at Porta Pia where the event had taken place exactly 45 years earlier, the film proved to be an enormous success and firmly established Alberini and his company at the forefront of filmmaking in Italy. At the same time other filmmakers were also beginning to emerge throughout the peninsula. In Naples the Troncone brothers had already graduated from screening to making films and in Turin Arturo Ambrosio, an enterprising photographer and optical equipment supplier, was also busy establishing his own Ambrosio Film company and equipping it with its own studios. Thus, by 1907 there were at least nine companies operating in Italy, distributed throughout the peninsula in the major cities of Rome, Turin, Naples, and Milan. In that same year the Cines opened the first of its many international subsidiaries in New York, where it proceeded to market its films under the rubric of "the matchless splendour of Italian Art." A year later the enormous popularity in the United States of Ambrosio's *Gli ultimi giorni di Pompei* (*The Last Days of Pompeii*, 1908) effectively opened up the American market to Italian films.

The industry in Italy continued to flourish with new companies being set up by the day. In 1909 the Film d'Arte Italiana, following the model of its parent, the French Pathé's Film d'Art, began to employ well-known actors to make "quality" films of famous plays, beginning with a version of Shakespeare's *Othello*. In the same year the newly formed

Milano Films company, whose management board included some of the most august members of the Milanese nobility, embarked on the production of a full-length feature film of Dante's *Inferno*. Taking three years to complete, the 70-minute film was released in 1911 to tremendous acclaim both in Italy and abroad, where it was seen as establishing a new benchmark for the length and artistic quality of feature films. By this time Giovanni Pastrone, the enterprising head of the Itala company, had also succeeded in luring the foremost French film comic, André Deed, to work for him at Turin. For the next few years Deed continued to churn out hundreds of slapstick comedies at Itala, all featuring the anarchic character of Cretinetti (Foolshead), who became so popular worldwide that Pastrone was able to sell his films sight unseen from Moscow to Rio de Janeiro.

Especially in the early days most of the Italian studios produced a wide variety of films, including "actualities," documentaries, comedies, historical costume dramas, and myriad adaptations of literary and theatrical works. The major studios, however, came to achieve their greatest commercial successes with a number of monumental Greco-Roman epics with which they established a strong presence in the international market and particularly in the United States. In the wake of the acclaim lavished on Ambrosio's early version of *The Last Days of Pompeii*, Itala scored a huge hit in America with *La caduta di Troia* (*The Fall of Troy*, 1910) and Cines achieved an even greater triumph with its *Quo vadis?* (1912), a spectacular extravaganza directed by painter-turned-director Enrico Guazzoni, who now specialized in the genre. However, by far the most impressive and commercially successful of all these early sword-and-sandal epics was Pastrone's *Cabiria* (made 1913, released 1914), a film whose technical brilliance and extraordinary scope impressed even D. W. Griffith, who paid homage by imitating it in his own *Intolerance* (1916).

During this period the Italian studios also came to make a great deal of what came to be known as *cinema in frac* (cinema in white tie). Influenced by late decadent romanticism and the works, and more particularly the style, of Italian literary superstar Gabriele D'Annunzio, these were frenetically passionate melodramas set in elegant upper-class salons featuring the femmes fatales of the Italian screen (the divas) in doomed and deadly love affairs. Beginning with Mario Caserini's *Ma l'amor mio non muore* (*But My Love Does Not Die*, 1913), the film that launched the career of the foremost diva of the period, Lyda Borelli, the genre continued to flourish for almost a decade, making the reputation of actresses such as Francesca Bertini and Pina Menichelli, who came to be venerated as screen goddesses throughout Europe.

The years leading up to World War I thus marked the first golden age of Italian cinema when production boomed and Italian films were in great demand both at home and abroad. Surprisingly, Italy's entry into the war in 1915 provoked only a momentary and minimal disruption in film production, which continued unabated during the war years. The end of the war, however, brought a rude shock to the industry as it confronted a radically changed situation. As the war had dragged on, the foreign markets had all closed their doors; the American industry had organized itself into a more efficient and aggressive supplier of attractive films; and at home, the diva phenomenon had pushed production costs up to absurd and unsustainable levels. In 1919, in an attempt to remedy an ever-deteriorating situation, the major companies and their staff banded together under the leadership of the president of the Cines, Baron Fassini, to form the Unione Cinematografica Italiana (UCI, Italian Cinematographic Union). High hopes were short lived, however, as poor management practices, internal conflicts between some of the major players, technical and artistic inertia, and finally the declared bankruptcy in 1921 of UCI's principal financial backer, the Banca di sconto, inexorably led to the syndicate's collapse, and with it the greater part of the Italian film industry itself. Thus in 1922, even as Benito Mussolini and his black-shirted followers were marching on Rome to install their new Fascist regime, the Italian film industry, which had known such glories only a decade earlier, appeared to be entering a phase of terminal decline. By the mid-1920s, when more Italians than ever were going to the cinema, the Italian industry had largely dissolved, with many of the leading actors and directors having either abandoned the industry or moved to France or Germany, where film production was still flourishing.

THE FASCIST PERIOD

Given the cinema's obvious potential for propaganda and Fascism's nationalistic profile, one might well have expected the Fascist regime to immediately initiate measures to attempt to salvage the national film industry as soon as it took power in 1922, even if only to bend the cinema to its own purposes. However, apart from confirming, and indeed strengthening, film censorship regulations in 1923, the regime showed little interest in feature film production during its first few years and did little to stem the flow of American films flooding into Italy in response to an ever-growing popularity of the cinema with Italian audiences. Where it showed a great deal of interest, however, was in newsreel and documentary filmmaking.

In 1924, even as the American majors were setting up branches in Italy and MGM was preparing to shoot a version of *Ben-Hur* in Rome, the regime was offering strong encouragement for the proposed formation of L'Unione Cinematografica Educativa (Union of Educational Cinematography), an organization set up to promote the use of film for scientific and educational purposes, and sponsored by the loosely constituted Syndicate of Cinematographic Instruction. The organization was essentially private but Mussolini showed his own personal support for it by providing the acronym under which it would come to be universally known, LUCE (Light). A year later the body was nationalized. Renamed the Istituto Nazionale LUCE, it was placed under the direct control of Mussolini himself and henceforth had the official function of recording and broadcasting the achievements of the regime through newsreels and documentaries. The crucial role that the government was reserving for this sort of filmmaking was confirmed by a decree in 1926 that obliged all cinemas (now likely to be showing foreign, and in all probability American, films) to screen a LUCE newsreel or documentary before every feature.

The major part of the handful of feature films still being made in Italy during this period, such as the strongman, or Maciste, films, were coming from the studios of Stefano Pittaluga. An veteran distributor and cinema manager who had wisely avoided joining the UCI, Pittaluga had in fact prospered during the crisis, in large part by distributing and exhibiting foreign films. He had consequently been in a position to buy up most of what remained of the old production houses, including the historic Cines studios, and had thus, by the mid-1920s, actually become the industry. Indeed, being a distributor, a producer, and an exhibitor at the same time, Pittaluga was the closest Italy ever came to having an American-style film tycoon. As the president of the film producers' association, Pittaluga began to lobby the government for stronger support for the industry, but as an astute operator he also read the signs and began to equip both his cinemas and his studios for sound.

At the same time Alessandro Blasetti, a young film critic and passionate advocate for a revival of the national cinema, succeeded in setting up an independent production company, Augustus. With it he produced his first feature film, *Sole* (*Sun*, 1928), a powerful, epic rural drama set in the Roman Pontine marshes, showing the strong influence of Russian cinema. Around the same time, another young director, Mario Camerini, having already impressed the authorities with his colonial epic, *Keff Tebbi* (1927), also put together an independent production company to make *Rotaie* (*Rails*, 1929), a brooding existential drama bearing all the stylistic markers of the German *Kammerspiel* film. In very different ways during the next decade, Blasetti and Camerini would come to be the two most representative Italian directors of Italian cinema under Fascism.

With its officiating presence at the inauguration of Pittaluga's revived Cines studios in May 1930, the Fascist government signaled its willingness to provide greater support for the national feature film industry. In October of that year the Pittaluga-Cines studios released Italy's first sound film, *La canzone d'amore* (*The Song of Love*, 1930), directed by a veteran from the early silent days, Gennaro Righelli, who had been enticed back to Italy after several years of working abroad. In June 1931 the government finally offered its first tangible support to the industry by enacting a law providing to film producers a rebate of 10 percent of a film's box office takings in its first year of Italian release. As well as the financial incentive itself, the measure was meant to encourage the production of popular Italian films that could compete successfully at the box office against foreign imports. A more systematic regulation of the industry came in 1933 via a law that replaced the previous financial rebate with a series of cash prizes for films that could demonstrate a high level of artistic or technical excellence. The new law also attempted to address the issue of foreign competition by requiring all foreign films to be dubbed into Italian and by levying a tax on the dubbing that would be used to provide more financing of national production. The strongest support for the local industry, however, lay in the new legal requirement for exhibitors to screen at least one national film for every three imports.

Such overt government support helped to revive feature film production, especially at the Cines where, following Pittaluga's untimely death in 1931, artistic directorship had been wisely passed into the hands of writer and literary scholar Emilio Cecchi. Under Cecchi's enlightened leadership and strong encouragement, directors such as Blasetti and Camerini came to be joined by many others returning from self-imposed exile in other European countries in making both fiction films and quality documentaries. By the time Cecchi decided to retire from the Cines in late 1933 in order to pursue his literary interests, feature film production in Italy had doubled. This still proved hardly enough to undermine Hollywood's dominance of Italian screens, which continued uninterrupted until the monopoly law of 1938, but it did go some way toward allowing exhibitors to fulfill their Italian screen quota.

At the same time a number of other measures were also contributing to a national revival. In 1932 a film festival was introduced as part of the already flourishing Venice Biennale. Although initially intended as a biennial showcase of world cinema, the festival's extraordinary and immediate success led to its becoming transformed, from its second occasion, into an annual international filmmaking competition.

In 1934, with the setting up of the Direzione Generale per la Cinematografia (General Directorate of Cinematography) under the direction of Luigi Freddi, the regime effectively took control over all aspects of filmmaking in Italy, from the approval of financing from a special fund with the Banca di Lavoro to the final granting of a censorship release. Film treatments and screenplays were required to be submitted to the directorate for approval before work on any project was started, although few films were rejected outright since Freddi's film policy proved to be relatively enlightened. Before being appointed director, Freddi had visited both Hollywood and Nazi Germany and had written a report for the government in which he praised the former and severely criticized the latter for what he regarded as counterproductive indoctrination. Within a year of taking up his post, Freddi also created the Centro Sperimentale di Cinematografia, a world-class national film school that would soon be training many of the actors and directors who would go on to play a major role in the cinema of the immediate postwar period.

These same years also witnessed the spread of a network of progressive university cinema clubs (the cine-GUF), strongly supported by Freddi, and the birth of prestigious specialized journals such as *Bianco e nero*, the official journal of the Centro Sperimentale, and *Cinema*, which would soon come under the editorship of the Duce's son, Vittorio Mussolini. After a mysterious fire destroyed the Cines studios in September 1935, Freddi proposed the building of a new and much larger cinema studio complex, to be financed by the government but administered, at least in the first instance, by the then head of the Cines, Carlo Roncoroni. Built in record time, the new complex, named Cinecittà (Cinema City), was officially inaugurated by Mussolini himself on 28 April 1937 under a banner that proclaimed, "Il cinema è l'arma più forte" (Cinema is the strongest weapon).

In spite of the increased national production made possible by the new studios, American films nevertheless continued to dominate Italian screens, with foreign films generally accounting for 85 percent of the internal market at a time when cinema-going was attracting 70 percent of all money spent on leisure and entertainment. In 1938 the so-called Alfieri law significantly raised the government rebate on Italian feature films and, at the same time, established a virtual government monopoly over the importation and distribution of all foreign films. Affronted by a measure they feared would reduce their profits, the American majors withdrew from Italy altogether, leaving the field free to Italian producers. Predictably, the number of feature films made in Italy continued to increase, soon reaching the quota of 100, which had been set by the regime itself.

Curiously enough, however, a decade of strong financial support and institutional control of the industry by the regime produced few openly Fascist films. Indeed, one of the most accomplished, Blasetti's *Vecchia guardia* (*Old Guard*, 1934), a film that sought to provide some justification for the violence of the Fascist street gangs in the old days, was actually one of the very few films that Freddi ever attempted to censor, convinced as he was that it would be counterproductive at this point for the regime to have its previous history brought back into the limelight. The big-budget and highly rhetorical *Scipione l'Africano* (*Scipio the African*, 1937), financed almost completely from government coffers, also proved to be a complete flop, both critically and at the box office. In the wake of Mussolini's Ethiopian campaign of 1935 a number of heroic war films were produced, such as Augusta Genina's *Lo squadrone bianco* (*White Squadron*, 1936) and Goffredo Alessandrini's *Luciano Serra pilota* (*Luciano Serra, Pilot*, 1938), a film nominally supervised by Vittorio Mussolini on which the young Roberto Rossellini collaborated as a scriptwriter. Especially after the withdrawal of the American companies, there was also a prolific production of sentimental comedies and light melodramas that came to be known as the *cinema dei telefoni bianchi*, or white telephone films. Modeled in part on the Hollywood screwball comedy but often based on popular middle European, and in particular Hungarian, theater, these films were largely escapist fare. After the war, however, they would consistently be accused of having been functional to the interests of the regime by distracting Italians from the realities around them.

The frivolity and artificiality of these films was especially decried at the time by writers connected with the journal *Cinema*. Although nominally edited by Vittorio Mussolini, the journal was relatively progressive and became something of a haven for left-leaning critics and even clandestine members of the Italian Communist Party. From the pages of the journal critics like Giuseppe De Santis called for a greater sense of realism in Italian films, and in 1942 the group around De Santis was given the opportunity of putting ideas into practice when they came together to work on Luchino Visconti's *Ossessione* (*Obsession*, 1943). Visconti's film would later be canonically cited as the direct forebearer of postwar neorealism, but it is important to note that a call for greater realism in the cinema was rather widespread at the time and not confined to left-wing or anti-Fascist circles.

Despite all the difficulties that naturally arose with Italy's entry into World War II, film production not only continued unabated but actually increased, reaching 120 films in 1942. Film production was continuing apace in 1943 when, in the wake of the armistice that Italy signed with the Allies, Cinecittà was closed and much of its equipment looted by the retreating Germans and die-hard Fascists. Freddi and a small number of others who had worked in the industry attempted to revive national film production in Venice under the aegis of the so-called Republic of Salò, but of the 20 or so films actually made, few were widely seen and even fewer survived.

NEOREALISM AND THE POSTWAR REVIVAL

While particular aspects of neorealism have continued to be debated to the present day, there has never been any real doubt that neorealist films played the central role in the rebirth of Italian cinema in the immediate postwar period. Made almost as the smoke was still clearing, films like Rossellini's *Roma città aperta* (*Rome Open City*, 1945) and Vittorio De Sica's *Sciuscià* (*Shoe-Shine*, 1946) immediately won worldwide acclaim and brought Italian cinema an international reputation and prestige that it had not enjoyed since the early silent days. At the same time it is important to note that neorealist films were always more appreciated abroad than in Italy itself where, with only a small number of notable exceptions, they failed to attract anything like the same amount of viewer interest. Furthermore, in Italy, as a result of the annulment in 1945 of all Fascist legislation regarding cinema imports, neorealist films found themselves forced to compete against literally hundreds of films that the American studios had not been able to distribute in Italy since 1938 and which they now dumped, almost with a vengeance, on what had always been their most lucrative overseas market. At the same time, after a first flush of enthusiasm for the rawness and honesty with which neorealist films presented the harsh reality around them, Italian audiences soon turned away from neorealism and toward the less committed but more entertaining fare offered by the commercial cinema. It is instructive to note that the highest-grossing film in Italy in 1946 was not Rossellini's neorealist classic *Paisà* (*Paisan*, 1946), which only took sixth place, nor De Sica's *Sciuscià*, which, with an honorary Oscar to its credit, did not even earn enough to make it into the top 10, but rather Riccardo Freda's remake of a 1925 Rudolph Valentino adventure fantasy, *Aquila nera* (*Return of the Black Eagle*), starring heartthrob Rossano Brazzi. Moreover, once the center-right Christian Democrat Party had installed itself in power and created the Central Office for Cinematography, which in many ways reproduced all the powers and functions of the Direzione Generale of the Fascist period, neorealist filmmakers also found themselves having to contend with a certain hostility from government authorities regarding the image of a poor and downtrodden Italy that their films were allegedly presenting to the world. Given all these pressures, it is not surprising that many neorealist directors gradually reverted to the more traditional elements of cinematic spectacle and genre in order to produce more palatable films.

Alongside this "rosy" or "pink" neorealism, as it came to be called, the traditional genres themselves made a strong comeback. Comedy, a great staple of Italian cinema from its earliest days, returned massively in the films of Erminio Macario and the great Totò, whose legion of films would stretch out to the early 1960s and end up constituting a genre of their own. In 1949 Raffaele Matarazzo revived the classic form of the sentimental melodrama with *Catene* (*Chains*), the first of what became a long series of enormously popular old-style heart-tuggers featuring the regular couple of Yvonne Sanson and Amedeo Nazzari. With the Cold War intensifying in the early 1950s, the petty squabbles in a provincial town between a parish priest and the town's Communist mayor became the big attraction of the Don Camillo films, with the first in the series, *Il piccolo mondo di Don Camillo* (*The Little World of Don Camillo*), topping the box office in 1952 and its sequel, *Il ritorno di Don Camillo* (*The Return of Don Camillo*, 1953) earning almost as much in the following year. A year later Luigi Comencini scored his first big success with the highest-grossing film of that year, the "pink neorealist" *Pane amore e fantasia* (*Bread, Love and Dreams*, 1953), quickly followed the next year by its equally popular sequel, *Pane, amore e gelosia* (*Bread, Love and Jealousy*). Thus, thanks perhaps even more to the genres than to neorealism, by the early 1950s the Italian film industry had not only returned to health but was positively thriving. By 1954, the year in which Federico Fellini released his Oscar-winning *La strada*, Italy was producing over 200 films a year. At the same time, in spite of the continuing dominance of Hollywood, the Italian share of the home market had grown from 13 percent in 1946 to 36 percent in 1954. During the same period cinema attendance had also doubled, reaching a peak of 820 million in 1955 at a time when audiences worldwide had already drastically declined; in America, in fact, they had declined by almost half.

The overflowing health of Italian cinema in the 1950s came to be embodied in the *maggiorate*, buxom starlets like Gina Lollobrigida and Sophia Loren who were soon conquering not only Italian screens but Hollywood itself. At the same time, making a virtue of currency regulations that severely limited the amount of money they were allowed to repatriate from their films in Italy, some of the American majors began to produce their biggest-budget films in Rome, thus creating the Hollywood on the Tiber so brilliantly depicted in Fellini's *La dolce vita* (1960). Ironically, while the aim of the American studios was to exploit the fact that production costs were lower in Italy, the net result for the local industry was a leg up in terms of increased function and capacity.

Soon, with films such as *Le fatiche di Ercole* (*Hercules*, 1957) and *Le legioni di Cleopatra* (*Legions of the Nile*, 1959), enterprising Italian directors were making homegrown but highly marketable versions of the big-budget historical superspectacles that Hollywood had come to make in Rome, but making them at a fraction of the price. Then, in 1958 the remarkable critical and commercial success of Mario Monicelli's *I soliti ignoti* (*Big Deal on Madonna Street*) marked the birth of what would become the most prolific and commercially viable genre of the next two decades, the *commedia all'italiana* (comedy Italian style).

TRIUMPH AND DECLINE: THE 1960s

After its steady revival during the previous decade, Italian cinema achieved what was a virtual apotheosis in the 1960s. A key year for a number of national cinemas was 1960, but in Italy itself it proved to be the *annus mirabilis*. Released that year, Fellini's *La dolce vita*, Visconti's *Rocco e i suoi fratelli* (*Rocco and His Brothers*), and De Sica's *La ciociara* (*Two Women*) all received huge international acclaim but even more tellingly, as a sign of a new level of film culture in Italy itself, they were also the three highest-grossing films on the home market. The year also bristled with the impressive debuts of many new directors like Ermanno Olmi, Florestano Vancini, and Damiano Damiani, who would soon rise to the front ranks. They were joined less than a year later by others also destined to make their mark, among them Pier Paolo Pasolini, Elio Petri, Giuliano Montaldo, and Vittorio De Seta.

With some justification, this enormous flowering of filmmaking talent would later be characterized as an Italian New Wave, except that in Italy the sheer number of new directors who either emerged or reached their artistic maturity during the next 15 years was so huge as to suggest a tide. The roll call of emerging directors included many who would soon go on to achieve an international reputation, such as Bernardo Bertolucci, Lina Wertmüller, Sergio Leone, and Paolo and Vittorio Taviani, as well as a host of others, such as Marco Ferreri, Ettore Scola, and Tinto Brass, whose no-less-considerable reputations would be more confined to the European sphere. This enormous recruitment to the film industry was strongly supported by a number of major production companies, chief among them Goffredo Lombardo's Titanus, which had set down solid foundations during the revival of the 1950s and was thus in a position to underwrite much of the growth. But the increase was also due to the arrival of adventurous new producers like Alfredo Bini, Alberto Grimaldi, and Gaetano G. De Negri, all of whom believed strongly enough in the young directors to take chances in supporting their artistic experimentation.

One factor that undoubtedly contributed to the richness and depth of the film culture of this period was that the young auteurs who continued to emerge throughout the decade—by contrast, for example, with the French New Wave—appeared able to carry out their innovative experiments in film form and language without needing to explicitly reject their cinematic fathers. It thus became a time when several generations of filmmakers worked side by side, with established directors like Rossellini, Visconti, Fellini, and Antonioni producing some of their most assured and mature work while alongside them young directors like Marco Bellocchio were making their angry and iconoclastic debuts.

It is important to note, however, that the huge increase in recruitment and production during this period occurred not only at the level of "quality" or art house cinema but also, and indeed more spectacularly, in the realm of the popular genres. The peplum, or sword-and-sandal film, which had already begun to flourish in the latter part of the 1950s, reached its peak in the early 1960s with over 30 peplums released in 1961 alone. The horror genre, which had also witnessed a number of tentative attempts in the previous decade, began invading the screens in 1960, with Mario Bava's *La maschera del demonio* (*Black Sunday*) only the first of five horror films released that year, and those only the first of hundreds that would proliferate throughout the decade. Even as Fellini and De Sica were collecting their Oscars for art films like *Otto e mezzo* (*8½*, 1963) and *Ieri, oggi, domani* (*Yesterday, Today and Tomorrow*, 1963), Sergio Leone, under the pseudonym Bob Robertson, was giving birth to the spaghetti Western, a genre that would dominate both Italian and international screens for the next decade. Most significant of all, however, was the flowering of the *commedia all'italiana*, a sort of supergenre that, in all its prolific manifestations, managed to continually blur distinctions between high art and popular cinema.

If the creative energies of individual directors and producers were undoubtedly a determining factor in all this growth, the real basis of the commercial viability of Italian cinema during this period was the extensive network of second- and third-run cinemas that had grown up throughout the peninsula in the early 1950s and that allowed films to continue generating a return for several years after their first release. Genre films, the staple of this network, were also able to benefit from generous government subsidies for coproductions with other European countries. From 1965 onward, through the provisions of Article 28 of the so-called Corona law, the government also provided a significant contribution to films being financed or cofinanced by the personnel concerned. All of these factors contributed to helping the industry both develop its export potential and claw back a major share of the home market from foreign (American) imports. Thus by the mid-1960s, thanks in part to the continuing international popularity of the genres, for the first time since the early silent days Italy had become a net exporter of films. In 1971, as Petri's *Indagine su un cittadino al di sopra di ogni sospetto* (*Investigation of a Citizen Above Suspicion*) brought home yet another Oscar, the industry had achieved the almost unthinkable, with Italian films supplying 65 percent of the home market.

The triumph, however, was relatively short lived. By the mid-1970s, through an aggressive policy of blockbuster production and saturation booking, Hollywood had begun to reimpose its dominance over Italian screens. At the same time, the deaths of veteran directors like Visconti, De Sica, Rossellini, and Pasolini inevitably depleted the production ranks. As costs escalated, fewer films were made, with annual film production falling by almost a third in five years. In an effort to maintain profits, exhibitors continued to increase admission prices. A combination of demographic changes and a lowering of attendance provoked by higher ticket prices resulted in the progressive closure of the second- and third-run cinemas. Then, beginning in 1975, cinema-going, which had been declining only slowly for two decades, began to plummet. Thus, by the end of the 1970s, Italian cinema was, once again, in crisis.

CINEMA AND TELEVISION

In the following years, television would often be apportioned the lion's share of blame for what appeared to many at the time to be cinema's terminal decline. As already suggested, the factors involved were undoubtedly many but the allegation regarding television's responsibility for reducing cinema attendance was, at least partially, justified. With the introduction of American-style commercial television, following the total liberalization of broadcasting in 1976, the small screen became attractive enough to keep audiences away from the cinemas in droves. At the same time, the absence for a number of years of any legal regulatory framework allowed the newly established commercial and private networks to screen any number of films, however acquired and whenever they chose. As a result, commercial television not only drastically emptied the cinemas but effectively took over the role previously played by the second- and third-run theaters, thus putting further pressure on even the few that remained.

However, the relations between the cinema and the public television broadcaster, Radiotelevisione Italiana (RAI), had always been more complex and less antagonistic. In the early 1960s the RAI had regularly produced its own fiction programs, and its screening of a very limited number of commercial feature films had continued to be strictly regulated by both state legislation and agreements with the filmmakers' association, ANICA. In the late 1960s a more progressive administration that had been installed at RAI initiated a policy of inviting both established and emerging directors to make films destined eventually for the small screen but which could first be shown in theatrical release. Very few directors declined such an attractive offer, which provided them with opportunities to make films they might not otherwise have been able to produce. Among the first, and far from negligible, results of this policy were Fellini's *I clowns* (*The Clowns*, 1970), Bertolucci's *La strategia del ragno* (*The Spider's Stratagem*, 1970), and Luigi Comencini's *Le avventure di Pinocchio* (*The Adventures of Pinocchio*, 1972), made in both a longer five-hour multiepisode version for television and as a standard-length feature for theatrical release. In 1977 RAI's policy bore even more significant fruit when the Taviani brothers' *Padre padrone* (*My Father My Master*) became the first film produced by and for television to be awarded the Palme d'or at Cannes, a feat repeated a year later when the Golden Palm was awarded to Olmi's *L'albero degli zoccoli* (*The Tree of the Wooden Clogs*).

As over 250 million Italians deserted the cinemas in the next five years and conditions for filmmakers inexorably worsened, RAI continued to hold out a lifeline to many directors, financing or cofinancing a host of films for many of the established auteurs, among them

Francesco Rosi's *Cristo si è fermato a Eboli* (*Christ Stopped at Eboli*, 1980), Carlo Lizzani's *Fontamara* (1980), Michelangelo Antonioni's *Il mistero di Oberwald* (*The Oberwald Mystery*, 1981), and the Taviani brothers' *Kaos* (*Chaos*, 1984). In 1982 RAI's Paolo Valmarana also collaborated with directors Ermanno Olmi and Mario Brenta in setting up the independent cooperative film school Ipotesi Cinema. Thus even as the crisis in the film industry continued to deepen in the early 1980s and as many talked openly of the death of Italian cinema, the relationship between cinema and television had already radically changed from rivalry and hostility to substantial interaction and collaboration. Indeed by the mid-1980s it had become clear that only by cultivating this new relation could Italian cinema ensure its own survival.

REVIVAL AND RENEWAL IN THE 1990s

In 1989, following almost a decade during which it had become ever more common to talk about Italian cinema as a thing of the past, the award of the Grand Jury Prize at Cannes and, a year later, the Oscar for Best Foreign Film to Giuseppe Tornatore's *Nuovo cinema Paradiso* (*Cinema Paradiso*, 1988) seemed to many to signal not only a revival of the cinema in Italy but also the return of Italian cinema to the world stage. Three years later that return appeared to be amply confirmed when the Oscar for Best Foreign Film was awarded to Gabriele Salvatores's *Mediterraneo* (1990), and the Grand Jury Prize and the European Film Award to Gianni Amelio's *Il ladro di bambini* (*The Stolen Children*, 1992). By the time Roberto Benigni's *La vita è bella* (*Life Is Beautiful*, 1998) also collected the Grand Jury Prize at Cannes and three Oscars, including the awards for Best Actor and Best Foreign Film, it was clear that reports of the death of Italian cinema had indeed been exaggerated and that a new generation of filmmakers had been active in Italy for some time.

This renewed flowering of cinematic talent was soon dubbed the New Italian Cinema but continued to fit uneasily within generic characterizations. Indeed the most distinctive trait of this new cinematic production turned out to be precisely its extreme heterogeneity. Furthermore, although it became common, especially in the early years, to also refer to it as the "young" Italian cinema, quite a number of those who would soon be regarded as its most representative figures, directors such as Amelio and Nanni Moretti, were really not so young and in fact had been making films since the 1970s. It was, nevertheless, true that the greater part of the directors (but also screenwriters and actors) who made their debut during this period were of a younger generation. Some came from cabaret or the dramatic theater, some from the National or other film schools; many had worked, to a greater or lesser extent, in television and advertising. Yet while all displayed a high level of professional competence and a deep devotion to cinema as a form of artistic expression, none subscribed to any particular aesthetic program nor shared any artistic creed.

Many of the films of this new cinema did show a tendency to focus on the personal, often confining themselves to exploring domestic spaces and private concerns. The family, relationships, adolescence, and coming of age reappeared often as themes. The road movie began to appear frequently as a form. But alongside this focus on the private there was also an attempt to observe and reflect on the Italy that had emerged from what many called the "stupid years" of the 1980s, with some films of directors like Amelio, Marco Risi, Ricky Tognazzi, and Antonio Capuano demonstrating such a level of social commitment and critique that critics were prompted to talk about a "neo-neorealism." Emblematic of this cinema's reengagement with the social and the political was Daniele Luchetti's *Il portaborse* (*The Yes Man*, 1990), whose uncanny perspicacity was brought out when the *Mani pulite* investigations confirmed the real extent of the political and social corruption that the film had sought to portray half in jest. Other films tackled even more difficult issues such as the legacy of the political terrorism of the 1970s, the continuing power of the Mafia, and the problems associated with the new immigration.

One noticeable commonality of this new cinema was an abandonment of Rome as a primary geographical setting and a readiness on the part of these younger directors to locate their stories in different parts of the peninsula: Carlo Mazzacurati in the Italian northeast, Paolo Virzì and Benigni in Tuscany, Mario Martone and Capuano in Naples, Tornatore returning often to his native Sicily. Furthermore, if this new cinema appeared to have no canonical center, it did have one major point of reference in Nanni Moretti. A maverick filmmaker who had emerged in the 1970s, Moretti became, in the 1990s, not only a major presence through his own films and his appearance in the films of others, but also, through his fierce independence and his production company, Sacher, a mentor and a model for many younger directors making their debuts.

THE NEW MILLENNIUM

Despite widespread fears and expectations of a natural downturn after the revival of the 1990s, Italian cinema has continued to flourish in the new millennium. Although the situation is very different, in some ways the generational mix has come to resemble that of the 1960s. Alongside the films of now-veteran "new" cinema directors, such as Nanni Moretti's *La stanza del figlio* (*The Son's Room*, 2001), which won the International Film Critics' Prize and the Palme d'or at Cannes in 2002, and Tullio Marco Giordana's *La meglio gioventù* (*The Best of Youth*, 2003), whose six-hour length has not prevented it from being one of the most watched Italian films outside Italy in recent years, there have continued to be the impressive debuts of younger directors such as Vincenzo Marra, Daniele Gaglianone, Saverio Costanzo, and Daniele Vicari. Paolo Sorrentino has attracted much attention, both in Italy and abroad, with three of his first four films, *Le consequenze dell'amore* (*The Consequences of Love*, 2004), *L'amico di famiglia* (*The Family Friend*, 2006), and *Il divo* (2008), all being nominated for the Palme d'or at Cannes.

   The last five years have also witnessed a very strong resurgence of interest in documentary filmmaking. This has been marked not only by an enormous increase in production but also by the formation of a national association of Italian documentarists (Doc/It) and the institution of numerous eagerly awaited annual documentary film festivals such as RomaDocFest, not to mention a higher visibility for the documentary within the Venice Festival itself. The short film has also come into its own. Losing the stigma of being a mere preparatory exercise for feature filmmaking, the short film now has its own major festivals and is officially recognized with the award of annual prizes.

   As the end of the first decade of the new millennium approaches, film production and film culture in Italy appear extremely vibrant even if cinema-going has been reduced to almost a tenth of its record levels in the mid-1950s. An average of 100 feature films, consistently supported by substantial government subsidies, continue to be produced annually. The major problem since the 1990s has remained that of visibility. Both distribution and exhibition in Italy have come to be concentrated in fewer hands with a general tendency to privilege American and foreign imports, thus providing little opportunity for Italian films to be actually seen on Italian screens. Nevertheless, the most recent news from the reporting agencies appears to be positive. In the first half of 2007, cinema attendance increased considerably with, moreover, national films accounting for almost 40 percent of the market. These are figures not seen since the 1970s, so their appearance is indeed encouraging. And so the adventurous story of Italian cinema continues.

The Dictionary

ABATANTUONO, DIEGO (1955–). Actor. One of the new generation of young actors to emerge in the late 1970s, Abatantuono came to films and television after having been immersed from an early age in Milanese cabaret culture. He became particularly well known for his impersonation on stage of an ebullient wild-haired young lout (a so-called terrunciello or country boy) with lots of attitude and an incomprehensible speech that jumbled together the dialects of Lombardy and Puglia. The character's notoriety led to small roles in satirical films such as *Fantozzi contro tutti* (*Fantozzi against the Wind*, 1980), directed by Neri Parenti, and Renzo Arbore's *Il pap'occhio* (*The Pope's Eye*, 1980). After starring in a number of extremely popular low-grade farces, films commonly referred to as "demented comedies" or "cinema trash," Abatantuono abandoned the screen for a period in order to work in theater again, attracting much praise for his interpretation of Sganarelle in a production of Molière's *Don Giovanni*. He returned to the cinema in 1986 working with **Pupi Avati** in *Regalo di Natale* (*Christmas Present*, 1986) and in **Giuseppe Bertolucci**'s *Strana la vita* (*The Strangeness of Life*, 1987) although he scored his greatest successes with roles in a handful of films directed by **Gabriele Salvatores**, in particular *Marrakech Express* (1989), *Turnè* (1990), and the Oscar-winning *Mediterraneo* (1991). With an obvious propensity for comedy, he has also continued to prove himself in more dramatic roles in **Carlo Mazzacurati**'s *Il toro* (*The Bull*, 1994), **Ettore Scola**'s *Concorrenza sleale* (*Unfair Competition*, 2001), and Avati's more recent *La rivincita di Natale* (*Christmas Rematch*, 2004).

ACCORSI, STEFANO (1971–). Actor. One of the most charismatic of the new generation of actors who emerged in the Italian cinema of the 1990s, Accorsi landed a supporting role in **Pupi Avati**'s *Fratelli e sorelle* (*Brothers and Sisters*, 1991) soon after graduating from high school. He then moved to Bologna and joined the Teatro Stabile dell'Arena del Sole. While working in the theater he came to national prominence through a television advertisement for a well-known brand of ice cream, directed by the young **Daniele Luchetti**. His reputation was enhanced by a subsequent appearance in Enza Negroni's popular generational film *Jack Frusciante è uscito dal gruppo* (*Jack Frusciante Left the Band*, 1995).

After more work on the stage, Accorsi returned to the cinema in a very moving interpretation of a young **Resistance** fighter's coming of age in Luchetti's *Piccoli maestri* (*Little Teachers*, 1998). This was followed by the lead role in Luciano Ligabue's *Radiofreccia* (*Radio Arrow*, 1998), which earned him a **David di Donatello** and the Premio Amidei. Following his appearance in the enormously popular television miniseries *Come quando fuori piove* (*Hens, Ducks, Chicken and Swine*, 2000), directed by **Mario Monicelli**, he played the young homosexual lover in **Ferzan Ozpetek**'s *Le fate ignoranti* (*The Ignorant Fairies*, 2001), a demanding role that was recognized with a **Nastro d'argento**. A year later he was awarded the Volpi Cup at Venice for his interpretation of the poet Dino Campana in **Michele Placido**'s *Un viaggio chiamato amore* (*A Journey Called Love*, 2002). After a two-year break he returned to the big screen in **Carlo Mazzacurati**'s sentimental love story *L'amore ritrovato* (*An Italian Romance*, 2004) and more recently has taken the lead in Placido's romantic crime drama, *Romanzo criminale* (*Crime Novel*, 2005).

AGE E SCARPELLI. Screenwriting team. *See* INCROCCI, AGENORE; SCARPELLI, FURIO.

ALBERINI, FILOTEO (1865–1937). Widely regarded as the founding father of Italian cinema, Alberini patented an apparatus for shooting, printing, and projecting film in Italy in late 1895, only a month before the Lumière brothers began screening films in Paris using the *cinématographe*, which they had patented earlier that year. Although the Kinetografo Alberini was never built, Alberini maintained his interest in the new medium and by 1904 had opened a number of permanent movie houses in Florence and Rome.

Early in 1905, together with Dante Santoni, he established the first Italian company "for the manufacture of films" and subsequently directed what is generally regarded as the first Italian feature film, *La presa di Roma 20 settembre 1870* (*The Capture of Rome, 20 September 1870*). The film employed experienced stage actors and was made with the collaboration of the army, which supplied the soldiers and the cannons. First screened outdoors at Porta Pia where the crucial breach of the walls had taken place and on the anniversary of the event, it demonstrated Alberini's talents not only as director but also as producer and entrepreneur. A year later the Alberini and Santoni company was transformed into the **Cines**. The company would continue, even if through a number of crises and interruptions, to be one of the pillars of the Italian film industry from the silent era into the 1950s, although Alberini himself would soon lose effective control of the company to others.

In the following years Alberini continued to experiment with cinematography, patenting a number of technical innovations, including a panoramic device and a pocket-size movie camera. His last patent, filed in 1935, two years before his death, was for a stereoscopic camera.

ALDO, G. R. (1902–1953). (Born Aldo Graziati.) Having moved to France in his late teens, Aldo briefly tried stage acting before working for many years as a still photographer in the French film studios. In the early 1940s he graduated to camera operator on a number of films directed by Christian-Jacque. Returning to Italy in 1947 for on-location shooting of Christian-Jacque's *La Chartreuse de Parme* (*The Charterhouse of Parma*, 1948), he met **Luchino Visconti**, who engaged him as director of photography for *La terra trema* (*The Earth Trembles*, 1948). He subsequently served as cinematographer on a number of **Vittorio De Sica**'s films, including *Miracolo a Milano* (*Miracle in Milan*, 1951), *Umberto D* (1952), and *Stazione Termini* (*Indiscretion of an American Wife*, 1953); photographed **Augusto Genina**'s *Cielo sulla palude* (*Heaven over the Marshes*, 1949); and also worked with Orson Welles on *The Tragedy of Othello: The Moor* *of Venice* (1952). Tragically, still at the peak of his career, Aldo was killed in a car crash during the filming of Visconti's *Senso* (*The Wanton Countess*, 1954), which was eventually completed by fellow cinematographer **Giuseppe Rotunno**.

ALESSANDRINI, GOFFREDO (1904–1978). Director. Born in Cairo to Italian parents, Alessandrini abandoned an engineering degree at Cambridge University in order to pursue his passion for the cinema. In between working as assistant to **Alessandro Blasetti** on *Sole* (*Sun*, 1928) and *Terra madre* (*Earth Mother*, 1932), he produced an impressive **documentary** on the making of the Nag Hamadi Dam (*La diga di Nag Hamadi*, 1929). His first fictional feature, *La segretaria privata* (The Private Secretary, 1931), the Italian version of a light comedy that had already been shot in German, French, and English, proved extremely popular and established his professional reputation. After several years in Hollywood as a consultant for bilingual versions at MGM, Alessandrini returned to Italy to direct *Seconda B* (1934), another light sentimental comedy set in a girls' college (the title refers to a high school class), scripted by **Umberto Barbaro**.

A biography of the Silesian saint Don Bosco was followed by *Cavalleria* (*Cavalry*, 1936), a historical melodrama much admired for its period re-creation and for **Amedeo Nazzari**'s portrayal of the self-sacrificing cavalry officer. Romantic military heroism returned as a theme in *Luciano Serra pilota* (*Luciano Serra, Pilot*, 1938), a film nominally supervised by Vittorio Mussolini but on which the young **Roberto Rossellini** also worked as scriptwriter. *Abuna Messias* (*Cardinal Messias*, 1939) and *Giarabub* (1941) were both epic stories set in Africa—the latter recounting the heroic resistance of Italian troops besieged by the English at the oasis of Giarabub—and suggested to some that Alessandrini was supporting the colonialist aspirations of the Fascist regime. However, his next film, *Noi vivi* (*We the Living*, 1942), adapted from a novel by Ayn Rand, although ostensibly directed against the Russian Communist system, appeared to denounce the corruption at the heart of all totalitarianism.

In the postwar period Alessandrini's putative closeness to the regime counted against him and he worked mostly abroad. The most impressive of the few films he directed in Italy was *Camicie Rosse* (*Redshirts*, also known as *Anita Garibaldi*, 1952), a film about the

Risorgimento hero Giuseppe Garibaldi and his partner Anita, played by a fiery **Anna Magnani**. For a number of reasons, including ill health but also tension between the director and Magnani, who were in the middle of a marriage breakup at the time, the film was eventually completed by the young **Francesco Rosi**.

ALLASIO, MARISA (1936–). Actress. With her slightly mischievous upturned nose and her pretty girl-next-door looks, Alassio seemed destined to become one of the major starlets of the Italian screen in the mid-1950s. She played small parts in **Mario Camerini**'s *Gli eroi della domenica* (*Sunday Heroes*, 1952) and Mario Costa's *Perdonami* (Forgive Me, 1953), before her curvaceous figure and modest acting talents were showcased in **Luigi Zampa**'s *Ragazze d'oggi* (*Girls of Today*, 1955) and Luigi Capuano's *Maruzzella* (1956). She then appeared in her most famous role, as Giovanna, in **Dino Risi**'s box office hit *Poveri ma belli* (*Poor, but Handsome*, 1956), which was quickly followed by its equally successful sequel, *Belle ma povere* (*Pretty but Poor*, 1957). With her popularity at its peak, she played similar roles in **Mauro Bolognini**'s *Marisa la civetta* (*Marisa*, 1957) and **Steno**'s *Susanna tutta panna* (Susanna Whipped Cream, 1957) before starring with legendary Italian American tenor Mario Lanza in *Arrivederci Roma* (*Seven Hills of Rome*, 1957). A year later, however, she met and married Count Pier Francesco Calvi di Bergolo, a nobleman related to the House of Savoy, and retired from the cinema, never to return. Her last appearance on the screen was opposite **Nino Manfredi** in Risi's romantic comedy *Venezia, la luna e tu* (*Venice, the Moon and You*, 1958).

AMATO, GIUSEPPE (1889–1964). Actor, director, producer. After having worked for many years in various capacities in the Neapolitan film industry, Amato emigrated to America where, for a time, he tried unsuccessfully to become a Hollywood film producer. Returning to Italy in 1932, he produced *Cinque a zero* (*Five to Nil*, 1932), a film directed by **Mario Bonnard** that employed the talents of veteran Sicilian stage actor Angelo Musco. This was followed by a string of popular comedies, among them *Tre uomini in frac* (*I Sing for You Alone*, 1932) and *Il cappello a tre punte* (*The Three-Cornered Hat*, 1934), two of the first films to star **Eduardo** and **Peppino De Filippo**.

In the following years Peppino, as he was universally known, produced many of **Mario Camerini**'s films, among them *Batticuore* (*Heartbeat*, 1939), *I grandi magazzini* (*Department Store*, 1939), and *Una romantica avventura* (*A Romantic Adventure*, 1940), as well as **Alessandro Blasetti**'s *La cena delle beffe* (*The Jester's Supper*, 1940) and *Quattro passi fra le nuvole* (*A Stroll through the Clouds*, 1942).

In the postwar period he distinguished himself further as producer of several of the great classics of **neorealism** including **Vittorio De Sica**'s *Sciuscià* (*Shoe-Shine*, 1946), *Ladri di biciclette* (*Bicycle Thieves*, 1948), and *Umberto D* (1952). He was also associate producer (usually uncredited) for **Roberto Rossellini**'s *Roma città aperta* (*Rome Open City*, 1945) and for *Francesco, giullare di Dio* (*Francis, God's Jester*, 1950). His final, and perhaps greatest, triumph as a producer was **Federico Fellini**'s landmark *La dolce vita* (1960).

Remembered affectionately as one of the Italian film industry's most colorful characters, Amato also directed a handful of films, among them *Yvonne la nuit* (*Yvonne of the Night*, 1949) and *Donne proibite* (*Angels of Darkness*, 1954).

AMBROSIO, ARTURO (1882–1960). Filmmaker and producer. One of the founding fathers of the Italian film industry, Ambrosio was a photographer who owned an optical equipment and photographic supply shop in Turin in the early years of the 20th century. In 1904 he returned from Paris with a French camera and, together with fellow photographers and film enthusiasts **Roberto Omegna** and **Giovanni Vitrotti**, began experimenting with the new medium in documenting current events. Two years later, buoyed by the success of these short documentaries and with the foresight of an astute entrepreneur, he founded the **Ambrosio Film** company, providing it with its own well-equipped studios and other appropriate facilities.

The company quickly grew, continuing to make actualities and documentaries under the supervision of Omegna, but also soon expanded into fiction films of a wide variety of genres. In 1908 its production of *Gli ultimi giorni di Pompei* (*The Last Days of Pompeii*) gave birth to the grand epic spectacles that would distinguish Italian cinema for the next five years.

A good businessman and an able manager, Ambrosio steered the company through a long series of award-winning films and innovative strategies throughout the 1910s, successfully penetrating the American market and setting up partnerships with German and Russian film companies. However, in the crisis that gripped the industry in the period immediately following World War I, Ambrosio sold his stock in the company to Milanese industrialist Armando Zanotto and joined the ill-fated consortium **Unione Cinematografica Italiana** (UCI, Italian Cinematographic Union), for which he produced a number of films in the early 1920s. Following the spectacular critical and financial failure of the big-budget *Quo vadis?* (1925), Ambrosio retired from the industry, returning only briefly to head production at Scalera Film from 1939 to 1943.

AMBROSIO FILM. Production company. Founded in Turin by **Arturo Ambrosio** in 1906 (originally Film Ambrosio e C., then transformed into a public stock company and renamed in 1907), Ambrosio Film quickly grew into one of the major production houses of the early Italian cinema, contributing significantly to making Turin the capital of the Italian film industry during this early period. By the end of its first year of operation the company could boast a catalog of 80 films, including a short feature by **Giovanni Vitrotti**, *Il cane riconoscente* (*The Grateful Dog*), which was awarded the first prize for a feature film by the Lumière brothers. In addition to other award-winning documentaries and actualities, mostly shot by Vitrotti and **Roberto Omegna**, the company produced comedies—its resident comic Marcel Fabre made over 150 films featuring the character of Robinet—and also initiated what would become the great success of the epic superspectacle with its 1908 production of *Gli ultimi giorni di Pompei* (*The Last Days of Pompeii*). Ambrosio became particularly renowned for its quality literary adaptations, releasing, among many others, seven films based on the works of the then reigning literary superstar Gabriele D'Annunzio in just two years (1911–1912), followed by an internationally acclaimed adaptation of Alessandro Manzoni's historical novel *I promessi sposi* (*The Betrothed*, 1913). In 1913 the company also opened the Cinema Ambrosio in Turin, one of the first luxury picture palaces in Italy.

As well as maintaining a major presence on the Italian scene, Ambrosio coproduced films with German and Russian companies and was one of the few Italian companies to export into the American market, opening an affiliate in New York in 1912. After a glorious decade of successful production, however, the company began to falter in the general crisis that engulfed the Italian film industry in the period immediately after World War I. Having reduced its production to only a few modestly successful films in the early 1920s, the company was liquidated in 1924.

AMELIO, GIANNI (1945–). Director and screenwriter. Having migrated to Rome from a small village in Calabria in 1965, Amelio began his career in cinema as assistant director to **Vittorio De Seta** on *Un uomo a metà* (*Half a Man*, 1966). He served a further apprenticeship as assistant director to, among others, **Gianni Puccini**, **Lina Wertmüller**, and **Liliana Cavani** while also making a number of short films and television advertisements. Having joined the RAI in 1970, he directed his first television feature, *La fine del gioco* (*The End of the Game*, 1970). His next major work, also made for television and financed by the RAI, was *La città del sole* (*The City of the Sun*, 1973), a meditation on the social utopia imagined by the sixteenth-century monk Tommaso Campanella, in his book of the same name. Amelio next produced and directed *Bertolucci secondo il cinema* (*The Cinema According to Bertolucci*, 1975), a **documentary** on the making of *Novecento*, before making *La morte al lavoro* (*Death at Work*, 1978), a telefilm imbued with cinephilia that took its title from Jean Cocteau's remark, "Cinema is Death working on the actor." *Il piccolo Archimede* (*The Little Archimedes*, 1979), the adaptation of a short story by Aldous Huxley about a child musical prodigy, is regarded as the most accomplished of these early films made largely with television audiences in mind.

Amelio's first work made specifically for the big screen came three years later with *Colpire al cuore* (*Blow to the Heart*, 1982), a film that tackled the theme of political terrorism through the exploration of a troubled father-son relationship. Although the film brought Amelio the recognition of a **Nastro d'argento** for Best Story, he returned to making shorts for several years before directing *I ragazzi di via Panisperna* (*The Boys from Via Panisperna*, 1988). Adapted from a work by Sicilian writer Leonardo Sciascia, *I ragazzi* was originally made as a three-hour television miniseries and suffered somewhat when it was cut by an hour for its theatrical release. However, *Porte aperte* (*Open Doors*, 1990), adapted from another work by Sciascia and exploring the moral quandaries of capital punishment, won Amelio both a Nastro d'argento and an Oscar nomination for Best Foreign Film. It was followed two years later by what is still widely regarded as his best film and, for many, the finest Italian film of the 1990s, *Il ladro di bambini* (*The Stolen Children*, 1992). A powerful portrayal of the tenuous relationship that develops between a young *carabiniere* and the two children whom he has been charged to escort from Milan to Sicily, *Ladro* brought Amelio much international acclaim, including a nomination for the Palme d'or and the Grand Jury Prize at Cannes, and in Italy two Silver Ribbons and a **David di Donatello**. This stunning achievement was followed by the equally impressive *Lamerica* (1994), a powerful and complex film set in the context of the downfall of the Communist regime in Albania, inherently juxtaposing what America had meant for Italian migrants in the 1950s with what Italy had come to mean for Albanians in the 1990s.

Così ridevano (*The Way We Laughed*, 1998), the story of two Sicilian brothers who migrate to Turin with tragic consequences in the late 1950s, was awarded the Golden Lion at Venice and compared favorably, in spirit if not quite in scope, with **Luchino Visconti**'s *Rocco e i suoi fratelli* (*Rocco and His Brothers*, 1960). Returning to one of his favorite themes, the exploration of the father-son relationship, Amelio then made *Le chiavi di casa* (*The Keys to the House*, 2004), although, unusually for Amelio, the father's encounter with his handicapped child in this film is played out in Germany rather than Italy. This willingness to move outside Italy while retaining a commitment to a cinema of social conscience has been confirmed by Amelio's most recent film, *La stella che non c'è* (*The Missing Star*, 2006), adapted from a novel by Ermanno Rea but filmed almost entirely in China.

AMENDOLA, FERRUCCIO (1930–2001). Actor and dubber. Widely regarded as one of the finest male dubbers in Italy in the postwar period, Amendola began his career in pictures by playing a number of small roles in films such as **Mario Monicelli**'s *La grande Guerra* (*The Great War*, 1960) before becoming the regular Italian voice of

American superstars Al Pacino, Dustin Hoffman, Sylvester Stallone, Peter Falk, and Bill Cosby, among others. Amendola's voicing of Robert De Niro in the Italian versions of Martin Scorsese's *Taxi Driver* (1976) and *Raging Bull* (1980) and Michael Cimino's *The Deer Hunter* (1978) were highly praised, and there was something of a scandal when he was not chosen to dub De Niro again in 1996 in the Italian version of Scorsese's *Casino* (the part was done by veteran stage and television actor Gigi Proietti). Amendola also played substantial roles in films for television such as *Storia d'amore e di amicizia* (*Story of Love and Friendship*, 1982), directed by Franco Rossi, and in a number of very popular television miniseries, among them *Quer pasticciaccio brutto de Via Merulana* (*That Awful Mess on Via Merulana*, 1982), *Little Roma* (*Little Rome*, 1988), and *Pronto soccorso* (*Medical Emergency*, 1990 and 1992).

AMIDEI, SERGIO (1904–1981). Screenwriter. Although probably most remembered for his collaboration on **Roberto Rossellini**'s *Roma città aperta* (*Rome Open City*, 1945, also known as *Open City*), Amidei was a prolific and versatile screenwriter who scripted more than a hundred films in a long and varied career.

As a student in the 1920s, Amidei began acting as an extra at the Fert studios in Turin, his first role being one of the many devils in **Guido Brignone**'s *Maciste all'Inferno* (*Maciste in Hell*, 1926). He subsequently served as assitant to Brignone on some of the other **Maciste** films and worked in a variety of other capacities at the Fert studios before moving to France where he was, among other things, assistant to Russian director Alexis Granowski on *Les aventures du roi Pausole* (*The Adventures of King Pausole*, 1933) and *Les nuits moscovites* (*Moscow Nights*, 1934). After returning to Rome in 1936 he took up screenwriting in earnest, ranging across a wide variety of genres, from **Aldo Vergano**'s historical drama *Pietro Micca* (1938) to **Carlo Campogalliani**'s playful comedy *La notte delle beffe* (*The Night of Tricks*, 1940). He even scripted Camillo Mastrocinque's *L'ultimo ballo* (*The Last Ball*, 1941), usually regarded as one of the **white telephone films**. However, it would be his encounter with Rossellini in 1944 that would prove decisive for his career, with his screenplay for Rossellini's *Open City* earning him the first of the four Oscar nominations of his career.

In the following years, Amidei came to work with all the major directors of the postwar period, writing or cowriting films for Rossellini, **Vittorio De Sica**, **Luigi Zampa**, **Luciano Emmer**, **Mario Monicelli**, and **Ettore Scola**, among others. His screenplay for Rossellini's *Il Generale della Rovere* (*General della Rovere*, 1959) earned him another Oscar nomination. For a short period in the 1950s he also worked as a producer for Colonna Films, a company that he had founded but that folded after producing only a handful of films. Two of the last films he worked on were Scola's *Il mondo nuovo* (*That Night in Varennes*, 1982) and **Marco Ferreri**'s *Storie di ordinaria follia* (*Tales of Ordinary Madness*, 1981), for which he was awarded a **David di Donatello**.

Following his death, an annual prize was instituted in 1982 to honor his memory and to recognize the contribution of screenwriters to the film industry.

ANTONIONI, MICHELANGELO (1912–2007). Director, critic, screenwriter. Universally acknowledged as the foremost representative of cinematic modernism in Italy, Antonioni nurtured an early passion for music and drawing but drifted into a degree in economics at the University of Bologna. He nevertheless continued to cultivate his artistic interests and took an active part in student theater while also publishing fiction and film reviews in the Ferrara daily *Corriere padano*. In 1939 he moved to Rome, where he became part of the editorial committee of the prestigious journal *Cinema* and briefly attended the **Centro Sperimentale di Cinematografia**. In 1942, in between carrying out his military service, he was able to serve as an assistant on Enrico Fulchignoni's *I due Foscari* (The Two Foscaris, 1942) and to collaborate on the screenplay of **Roberto Rossellini**'s *Un pilota ritorna* (*A Pilot Returns*, 1942) before spending a short period in France as an assistant to Marcel Carné on *Les visiteurs du soir* (*The Devil's Envoys*, 1942). On his return to Italy he began work on his first **documentary**, *Gente del Po* (*People of the Po*, begun 1943, but finished and first screened in 1947).

Following the interruption of the war, he worked on the screenplay of **Giuseppe De Santis**'s *Caccia tragica* (*Tragic Hunt*, 1947) and made a handful of short award-winning documentaries, among them *N.U.-Nettezza Urbana* (N.U., 1948), a portrait of Roman street sweepers, and *L'amorosa menzogna* (*Loving Lie*, 1949), a look at the current Italian fad for photoromances, before directing his first feature, *Cronaca d'un amore* (*Story of a Love Affair*, 1950), a noir narrative echoing some of the elements of **Luchino Visconti**'s *Ossessione* (*Obsession*, 1943). This was followed two years later by *I vinti* (*The Vanquished*, 1952), three unconnected stories of juvenile delinquency in the cities of Rome, Paris, and London. Originally financed by a Catholic production company, the film came under strong pressure from the censors both in Italy, where the Italian episode was forced to be modified almost beyond recognition, and in France, where, on the strength of the French episode, the film was banned for over a decade. Antonioni's third feature, *La signora senze camelie* (*The Lady without Camelias*, 1953), a wry exposé of the Italian film industry starring ex-Miss Italia **Lucia Bosé**, was followed by *Tentato suicidio* (Attempted Suicide), an episode for **Cesare Zavattini**'s portmanteau film *L'amore in città* (*Love in the City,* 1953). Then came *Le amiche* (*The Girlfriends*, 1955), a loose adaptation of a novel by Cesare Pavese that proved to be Antonioni's first real critical success, winning the Silver Lion at the **Venice Festival** and two **Nastri d'argento**.

In spite of the recognizable presence of some of the hallmarks of Antonioni's mature style in these earlier films, it is generally agreed that *Il grido* (*The Cry*, 1957) marks the beginning of a new stage in Antonioni's filmmaking, a phase characterized by more intense formal and stylistic experimentation and a strong, and almost exclusive, focus on the themes of social disconnectedness and existential alienation. This phase comes to full maturity with the three films usually grouped as his "trilogy of alienation": *L'avventura* (*The Adventure*, 1960), *La notte* (*The Night*, 1961), and *L'eclisse* (*The Eclipse*, 1962). Many would also include his first film in color, *Il deserto rosso* (*Red Desert*, 1964), as part of a tetralogy in which Antonioni succeeded in forging a new cinematic language with which to communicate the profound social and psychological dislocations provoked by modernity.

Antonioni's international stature, now firmly established, was reconfirmed with *Blowup* (*Blow-Up*, 1966). Set in the swinging London of the 1960s and made entirely in English, the film follows the unsuccessful attempts of a British fashion photographer to utilize all the technical resources of photography to uncover the truth of what appears to be a murder in a city park. The film won overwhelming international acclaim, being nominated for a Golden Globe, three BAFTA, and two Academy Awards, and winning the Palme d'or at Cannes. Ironically, given that it was made completely in English with a British crew, it also received the Nastro d'argento in Italy for Best Foreign Film. *Zabriskie Point* (1970), also made completely in English and filmed in the United States, received a more qualified critical response and, in spite of its countercultural themes, proved to be a commercial flop, especially in the United States, where it received wide public criticism for what was seen as its anti-Americanism. Antonioni then returned to his roots in documentary filmmaking with *Chung-Kuo Cina* (*China*, made in 1972 but first shown on Italian television in 1973) before making what many regard as one of the finest of his later films, *Professione reporter* (*The Passenger*, 1975). Starring Jack Nicholson in the story of a misguided attempt to assume a new identity, *The Passenger* was nominated for the Golden Palm and was awarded the Nastro d'argento for both direction and cinematography.

Unable to get a number of other film projects financed, Antonioni then withdrew from the cinema for several years to indulge his earlier passions of painting and writing before returning in 1979 to make *Il mistero di Oberwald* (*The Oberwald Mystery*, 1980). Adapted from a play by Jean Cocteau and shot completely on video and then converted to film, *Oberwald* was a courageous experiment by a director who had been praised for his spirit of experimentation. However, when first screened at Venice in 1980 it received a very tepid response, being regarded as little more than a minor exercise in an inferior format. Two years later, *Identificazione d'una donna* (*Identification of a Woman*, 1982) was much more warmly received both at home and abroad, especially in France, where it was widely hailed as a return to form by the old master. Nevertheless, with a number of projects stalled due to lack of funding, Antonioni returned once more to writing and painting. He published *Quel bowling sul Tevere* (*That Bowling Alley on the Tiber*), a collection of short stories with Einaudi, and mounted a large exhibition of his paintings in Venice in 1983 before also directing *Fotoromanza* (1984), a four-minute music video for Italian singer Gianna Nannini.

A year later, with several projects still on hold, Antonioni suffered a major stroke that left him severely paralyzed and unable to speak.

While this effectively appeared to end his filmmaking career, in 1995, with the help and support of German director Wim Wenders, he was able to adapt several of his own stories from *That Bowling Alley on the Tiber* to make *Al di là delle nuvole* (*Beyond the Clouds*, 1995). While the film itself received a mixed critical response, later in the same year his enormous contribution to world cinema was recognized with an Academy Award for Lifetime Achievement.

ARATA, UBALDO (1895–1947). Cinematographer. Arata began his career in films as a cameraman on **Augusto Genina**'s *Il principe dell'impossibile* (The Prince of the Impossible, 1918) and subsequently struck up a 10-year partnership with Mario Almirante, with whom he collaborated on a dozen films beginning with *Zingari* (Gypsies, 1920) and ending with *Napoli che canta* (Naples Sings, 1930). At the same time he also worked with **Baldassare Negroni** on *Gli ultimi zar* (The Last Tsars, 1926) and *Giuditta e Oleferne* (Judith and Holofernes, 1928), and with **Guido Brignone** on *Maciste all'Inferno* (*Maciste in Hell*, 1926), and he helped to create the strikingly expressionist atmosphere of **Mario Camerini**'s *Rotaie* (*Rails*, 1929). After serving as director of photography on what is generally regarded as the first Italian sound film, *La canzone dell'amore* (*The Song of Love*, 1930), directed by **Gennaro Righelli**, he collaborated with Max Ophüls on *La signora di tutti* (*Everybody's Woman*, 1936), after which he teamed up with fellow cinematographer **Anchise Brizzi** to photograph **Carmine Gallone**'s ill-fated Roman epic, *Scipione l'Africano* (*Scipio the African*, 1937).

In the postwar period Arata achieved what was perhaps the highest point in his career, working as the cinematographer of **Roberto Rossellini**'s legendary *Roma città aperta* (*Rome Open City*, 1945, also known as *Open City*). He subsequently worked on a number of minor films before teaming up again with Anchise Brizzi on what would be his last film, Gregory Ratoff's *Black Magic* (1949).

ARCHIBUGI, FRANCESCA (1960–). Actress, screenwriter, director. One of the most prominent of the young Italian directors who emerged in the late 1980s, Archibugi studied at the **Centro Sperimentale di Cinematografia** before also attending **Ermanno Olmi**'s film school, Ipotesi Cinema, where she made a number of short films, among them *Il sogno truffato* (The Betrayed Dream, 1984). After appearing in a small supporting role in **Giuseppe Bertolucci**'s *Segreti segreti* (*Secrets Secrets*, 1985) and honing her screenwriting skills on Bruno Cortini's *L'estate sta finendo* (Summer Is Ending, 1987), she wrote and directed her first feature, *Mignon è partita* (*Mignon Has Come to Stay*, 1988). An affectionate and moving story of male adolescence and first love, the film proved to be something of a revelation, winning six **David di Donatello** awards, including Best New Director, and two **Nastri d'argento**. Archibugi's next feature, *Verso sera* (Towards Evening, 1990), highlighting the generation gap that had opened up in Italy with the social upheavals of the 1970s, also won the David for Best Film, as did her third feature, *Il grande cocomero* (*The Great Pumpkin*, 1993), a film that centered on the treatment of a young girl with epilepsy and was inspired by the alternative psychiatric practices of Marco Lombardo Radice. *Con gli occhi chiusi* (*With Closed Eyes*, 1994), an elegant adaptation of a novel by 19th-century writer Federico Tozzi, was less warmly received, but *L'albero delle pere* (*Shooting the Moon,* 1998), which tackled the complex problem of drug addiction with great sensitivity, was nominated for the Golden Lion at the **Venice Festival** and awarded the prize of the Office Catholique International du Cinéma. After exploring the shattered lives of people caught up in the 1997 Umbria earthquake in *Domani* (*Tomorrow*, 2000), Archibugi provided an interesting variation on Alessandro Manzoni's 19th-century novel in the television miniseries *Renzo e Lucia* (2004). She returned to the big screen with *Lezioni di volo* (*Flying Lessons*, 2006), another contemporary generational film, this time set in India.

ARGENTO, ASIA (1975–). Actress, writer, director. Daughter of cult horror director **Dario Argento**, Asia began acting at the age of nine in the television miniseries *Sogni e bisogni* (Dreams and Needs, 1985). Following minor parts in several horror films, she distinguished herself playing the lead role in **Cristina Comencini**'s *Zoo* (1988). After costarring in **Michele Placido**'s moving coming-of-age-film *Le amiche del cuore* (*Close Friends*, 1992), she appeared in *Trauma* (*Dario Argento's Trauma*, 1992), the first of several of her father's horror films, which would also include *La sindrome di Stendhal* (*Stendhal's Syndrome*, 1996) and *Il fantasma dell'opera* (*The*

Phantom of the Opera, 1998). Although by this time she had acquired a reputation as the "dark woman" of Italian cinema, Argento nevertheless went on to play the part of a young disabled woman in **Carlo Verdone**'s *Perdiamoci di vista!* (*Let's Not Keep in Touch*, 1994), for which she was awarded a **David di Donatello**, and earned another David for her leading role in Peter Del Monte's *Compagna di viaggio* (*Traveling Companion*, 1996). Having by now built an international reputation for tough female roles, she was called to star in Michael Radford's taut crime thriller, *B. Monkey* (1998), and Abel Ferrara's futuristic commercial spy movie, *New Rose Hotel* (1998). At this point she decided to try her hand at directing, beginning with the short music video *La tua lingua sul mio cuore* (*Your Tongue on My Heart*, 1998), and a brief interview-**documentary** on Abel Ferrara, *Abel/Asia* (1998). These shorts were soon followed by the full-length fictional autobiography *Scarlet Diva* (2000), and a powerful adaptation of J. T. Leroy's short-story anthology *The Heart Is Deceitful Above All Things* (2004).

Argento subsequently appeared in George Romero's *Land of the Dead* (2005) and as Madame Du Barry in Sofia Coppola's *Marie Antoinette* (2006).

ARGENTO, DARIO (1940–). Screenwriter, director, producer. Internationally renowned for his stylish **horror films** (*gialli*), Argento has often been called the Italian Alfred Hitchcock, while the brilliant visual style of his films has also earned him the title of "the Fellini of Horror."

After writing film reviews for the Roman daily *Paese sera*, Argento moved to screenwriting in the mid-1960s, first collaborating with veteran writer **Sergio Amidei** on **Alberto Sordi**'s comedy *Scusi, lei è favorevole o contrario?* (Pardon Me but Are You For or Against, 1966), and later working with **Bernardo Bertolucci** and others on the script of **Sergio Leone**'s *C'era una volta il West* (*Once upon a Time in the West*, 1968). He achieved immediate fame, however, with his directorial debut, *L'uccello dalle piume di cristallo* (*The Bird with the Crystal Plumage*, 1969), a *giallo* clearly influenced by the films of **Mario Bava** and the popular German Edgar Wallace crime films, but already displaying Argento's own inimitable style. His second film, *Il gatto a nove code* (*The Cat o' Nine Tails*, 1971), another sleek mix of horror thriller and detective fiction, firmly established all the Argento hallmarks: the black-gloved, almost supernatural killer, the gruesome and long, drawn-out murder scenes, and the obsession with eyes and sharp objects. These trademarks all appeared again, to great effect, in the third of the "animal trilogy," *Quattro mosche di velluto grigio* (*Four Flies on Grey Velvet*, 1971).

After *Le cinque giornate* (*Five Days*, 1973), an uncharacteristic film set in the **Risorgimento** period and dealing with political themes, Argento made what many regard as his best and most unnerving horror thriller, *Profondo rosso* (*Deep Red*, 1975). Two years later with *Suspiria* (*Dario Argento's Suspiria*, 1977), loosely based on a work on witches by Thomas De Quincey, Argento moved more decidedly into the supernatural horror genre. Having by this stage set up his own production company, SEDA Spettacoli Produzioni, Argento coproduced and collaborated on George A. Romero's *Dawn of the Dead* (1978). After the film was finished Argento reedited it, added a musical score by Goblin, and released the film in Europe as *Zombi* (*Zombie: Dawn of the Dead*, 1978), which achieved huge box office success and spawned a host of imitations. His next film, *Inferno* (*Dario Argento's Inferno*, 1980), with a number of sequences designed and shot by Mario Bava, was a hallucinatory excursion into pure nightmare but curiously did very poorly worldwide, prompting Argento to return to the *giallo* format for his next film, *Tenebre* (*Tenebrae*, 1982, also known as *Unsane* in the United States). Argento's next effort, *Phenomena* (1985), a gory thriller that revolves around a young girl who has a psychic affinity with insects, was cut by almost 30 minutes when it was released in America under the title *Creepers*.

After a number of other projects, which included filming a fashion show for Trussardi and an advertisement for Fiat cars in Australia, Argento teamed up with Lamberto Bava to produce and cowrite the gruesome supernatural horrorfest *Demoni* (*Demons*, 1985) and its sequel, *Demoni 2: L'incubo ritorna* (*Demons 2: The Nightmare Is Back*, 1986). *Opera* (1987), the story of a musical understudy stalked by a murderous psychopath under the influence of too many viewings of *A Clockwork Orange*, performed very poorly in theatrical release in Italy and in most other countries was released only on video. Nevertheless, in the next two years Argento cohosted a television program for *giallo* afficionados and produced 15 episodes of *Turno di notte* (Night Shift, 1988), a series of short films about the dark adventures that befall cab drivers at night.

After teaming up again with George A. Romero to codirect *Due occhi diabolici* (*Two Evil Eyes*, 1990), Argento directed *Trauma* (1993), the first of his films to be made completely in the United States and starring his daughter, **Asia Argento**. *La sindrome di Stendahl* (*Stendhal Syndrome*, 1996) again used Asia to play a young policewoman afflicted with this condition who is brutally raped a number of times before taking a gruesome revenge on the psychopath. Two years later, *Il fantasma dell'opera* (*The Phantom of the Opera*, 1998), a fairly brutal retelling of Gaston Leroux's classic story, flopped miserably at the box office and was generally panned even by afficionados. More recently, however, *Nonhosonno* (*Sleepless*, 2001) and *Il cartaio* (*The Card Player*, 2004) have revived Argento's reputation as the undisputed master of the Italian horror thriller.

ASSOCIAZIONE NAZIONALE AUTORI CINEMATOGRAFICI (ANAC). (National Film Writers' Association.) Founded in Rome in 1950, ANAC brought together directors and screenwriters with the aim of promoting cinema as a means of cultural expression. In the following years, the association was active in attempting to influence government policy regarding the industry and the management of important events such as the **Venice Festival**. The heated atmosphere of 1968 prompted a division in the association between those who wanted it to function along the lines of a trade union to protect the rights of workers in the industry, and who thus broke away to form the Associazione Autori Cinematografici Italiani (AACI), and others who preferred to be part of a looser cultural association and who remained part of ANAC.

The association continued to be active in the 1970s and became one of the founding members of the Fédération Européenne des Réalisateurs de l'Audiovisuel (FERA). It also worked closely with the Associazione Nazionale Industrie Cinematografiche e Affini (ANICA, National Association of Film and Affiliated Industries, now the **Associazione Nazionale Industrie Cinematografiche Audiovisive e Multimediali**) to continue to lobby for a better regulatory framework for the film industry in Italy. As well as promoting the general interests of Italian cinema, the association now organizes a week of screenings and a forum within the Venice Film Festival.

ASSOCIAZIONE NAZIONALE INDUSTRIE CINEMATOGRA-FICHE AUDIOVISIVE E MULTIMEDIALI (ANICA). (National Association of Film and Affiliated Industries.) Officially founded in Rome on 10 July 1944 as the Associazione Nazionale Industrie Cinematografiche e Affini (National Association of Cinematographic and Related Industries), ANICA is the umbrella organization that brings together the various unions representing the major areas and activities of the Italian film industry, including production, promotion, distribution, exhibition, and technical services. As such, it publishes the trade magazine *Cinema oggi* (*Cinema Today*) and represents the industry on government boards and commissions. As the officially designated representative of the American Academy of Motion Picture Arts and Sciences, it organizes the Italian nomination in the Best Foreign Film category of the Oscars. Since 1958 it has also been the official cosponsor of the **David di Donatello** awards.

ASTI, ADRIANA (1933–). Actress. One of Italy's most respected actresses, whose prolific career has spanned the entire postwar period, Asti made her acting debut in 1951 at the Teatro Stabile of Bolzano. Four years later she achieved her first major triumph playing the female lead in a production of Arthur Miller's *The Crucible*, directed by **Luchino Visconti**. While pursuing her acting career on stage, she also began appearing in films in the late 1950s. After small parts in Visconti's *Rocco e i suoi fratelli (Rocco and His Brothers*, 1960) and **Pier Paolo Pasolini**'s *Accattone* (*Accattone!* 1961), she provided one of her most memorable performances as Gina, the protagonist's neurotic aunt and lover, in **Bernardo Bertolucci**'s *Prima della Rivoluzione* (*Before the Revolution*, 1964). She subsequently appeared, among other roles, as the wife in Susan Sontag's *Duett foör kannibaler* (*Duet for Cannibals*, 1969), as the daughter in **Mauro Bolognini**'s *L'eredità Ferramonti* (*The Inheritance*, 1970), as Lila Von Buliowski in Visconti's *Ludwig* (1973), and as Felicita in Giorgio Ferrara's adaptation of Gustave Flaubert's novella *Un cuore semplice* (*A Simple Heart*, 1977).

After playing Ennia in **Tinto Brass**'s *Caligola* (*Caligula,* 1979), she largely withdrew from the cinema in the 1980s to again work mostly in theater, both in Italy and in France. With her stage career continuing to flourish, in the 1990s she wrote and directed several of her own plays and appeared in a number of Italian and French television series. She returned to the big screen playing a mischievous comic role in Giorgio Ferrara's *Tosca e altre due* (*Tosca and the Women,* 2003) before giving a very moving performance as the mother in **Marco Tullio Giordana**'s *La meglio gioventù* (*The Best of Youth,* 2003), for which she shared the **Nastro d'argento** for Best Actress. More recently, while continuing to win much acclaim for her work on the stage, she also played the mother in Giordana's *Quando sei nato non puoi più nasconderti* (*Once You're Born You Can No Longer Hide,* 2005).

AVATI, PUPI (1938–). Director, producer, screenwriter. A prolific and popular but extremely eclectic director, Pupi (short for Giuseppe) Avati has directed over 30 feature films, which have ranged widely across a variety of genres to include everything from gothic horror to musicals, from historical dramas to romantic comedies.

After graduating in political science from the University of Bologna, Avati played clarinet in a jazz band for a number of years before directing his first film, *Balsamus, l'uomo di Satana* (*Blood Relations,* 1968), a bizarre and rather surreal tale about a dwarf with presumed magical powers. In both subject and style, the film, now apparently lost, displayed that propensity for the absurd and the grotesque which would frequently reappear in Avati's subsequent films. It was quickly followed by the equally quirky gothic fantasy *Thomas—gli indemoniati* (*Thomas and the Bewitched,* 1969), which, however, was never released in Italy. Avati then achieved a wider following with his irreverent satirical comedy, *La mazurka del barone, della santa e del fico fiorone* (The Mazurka of the Baron, 1974), and *Bordella* (*House of Pleasure for Women,* 1976), a provocative musical set in a brothel for women; the film was severely attacked by the censors for its alleged affront to public morals.

After collaborating with **Pier Paolo Pasolini** on the screenplay of *Salò o le 120 gionate di Sodoma* (*Salò, or the 120 Days of Sodom,* 1975), and several other successful forays into the gothic and horror genres with *La casa dalle finestre che ridono* (*The House with Laughing Windows*, 1976), *Tutti defunti . . . tranne i morti* (All Deceased Except for the Dead, 1977), and *Le strelle nel fosso* (The Stars in the Ditch, 1978), Avati returned to two of his old passions with the extended television miniseries *Jazz Band* (1978) and *Cinema!!!* (1979). He produced another classic horror thriller, *Zeder* (1982), before changing direction and style completely with *Una gita scolastica* (*A School Outing*, 1983), the nostalgic re-creation of a romantic school outing in an idealized Tuscan countryside at the beginning of World War I. Subsequent films continued to alternate between the past and the present with *Noi tre* (*The Three of Us*, 1984), depicting the short period that the young Mozart spent in Bologna in 1770, being followed by *Impiegati* (Personnel, 1985), a caustic portrayal of Italian yuppie culture in the early 1980s. Set in the 1950s, *Festa di laurea* (*Graduation Party*, 1985) pitilessly recounts an unmitigated fiasco in place of the celebration announced in the title, while the similarly ironically titled *Regalo di Natale* (*Christmas Present*, 1986) focuses on a harrowing all-night poker game set in contemporary times.

The late 1980s brought one of Avati's best-known films, *Storia di ragazzi e di ragazze* (*Story of Boys and Girls*, 1989). Reliving all the stages of an extended engagement dinner prepared by the girl's rural family for the urban middle-class family of the groom-to-be, the film received the **Nastro d'argento** for Best Direction and both the Nastro and the **David di Donatello** for Best Screenplay. Two years later *Bix—un ipotesi leggendaria* (*Bix: An Interpretation of a Legend*, 1991), Avati's affectionate portrait of legendary American jazz musician Leon "Bix" Beiderbecke, was similarly awarded a David for its meticulous production design as well as being nominated for the Golden Palm at Cannes. Avati's long-held fascination with the Middle Ages produced *Magnificat* (1993) before he returned to the gothic genre with *L'arcano incantatore* (*Mysterious Enchanter*, 1996) and to his native countryside of Emilia at the end of the 19th century with his charming romantic comedy *Il testimone dello sposo* (*The Best Man*, 1997), which was nominated for a Golden Globe and presented as Italy's submission to the 1998 Academy Awards.

Avati's subsequent films have continued to range widely, from another foray into the Middle Ages in *I cavallieri che fecero l'impresa* (*The Knights of the Quest*, 2001) to *Il cuore altrove* (*The Heart Is*

Elsewhere, 2003), an unusual love story set in Bologna in the early 1900s. More recently he has filmed an effective sequel to his earlier *Il regalo di Natale* in *La rivincita di Natale* (*Christmas Rematch*, 2004) and found a way of bringing together all his favorite themes of friendship, music, and coming of age in *Ma quando arrivano le ragazze?* (When Will the Girls Arrive? 2005). At the same time with *La seconda notte di nozze* (*The Second Wedding Night*, 2005) he furnished mature opera star Katia Ricciarelli with an opportunity to make her film acting debut in a zany love story set in the immediate postwar period. The film, as eccentric as any Avati has ever produced, was nominated for the Golden Lion Award at Venice, with Ricciarelli herself being awarded a Nastro d'argento for her performance. Avati's most recent film, *La cena per farli conoscere* (*The Get-Together Dinner*, 2007), is a bittersweet comedy in which a middle-aged man (**Diego Abatantuono**), deep in the throes of a midlife crisis and on the brink of suicide, is rehabilitated through a dinner organized by his three daughters.

– B –

BARAGLI, NINO (1926–). Editor. One of the most respected editors in the Italian film industry, Baragli learned his craft while working as assistant to Eraldo Da Roma before graduating to full editor in the early 1950s on a number of light comedies directed by Giorgio Simonelli. He subsequently collaborated with all the major Italian directors on over 200 films. Beginning with *Accattone* (*Accattone!* 1961), he supervised the editing of all the films of **Pier Paolo Pasolini**, worked with **Sergio Leone** on all his films from *Il buono, il brutto, il cattivo* (*The Good, the Bad and the Ugly*, 1966) to *C'era una volta in America* (*Once upon a Time in America*, 1984) and collaborated with **Mauro Bolognini** on all his major works. After editing **Federico Fellini**'s *Ginger e Fred* (*Ginger and Fred*, 1986) and *Intervista* (*Fellini's Intervista*, 1987), Baragli also began working with many of the younger generation of directors, winning the **David di Donatello** award for Best Editing for **Gabriele Salvatores**'s *Turnè* (Tour, 1990) and *Mediterraneo* (1991). In 1998 he was given a special **Nastro d'argento** in recognition of his career achievement.

BARATTOLO, GIUSEPPE (1882–1949). Lawyer, politician, financier, producer. An influential presence in the Italian film industry during the silent period, Barattolo began as a distributor but in 1913 founded the production company Caesar Film, which quickly succeeded in attracting rising star and soon-to-be diva **Francesca Bertini** into its ranks, and went on to produce some of the most significant films of the silent period, including the first of the **Za-la-Mort** films, *Nelly la gigolette* (*Nelly*, 1914), and **Gustavo Serena**'s *Assunta Spina* (1915). During the crisis that developed in the film industry in the period following World War I, Barattolo became one of the most enthusiastic promoters of the ill-fated **Unione Cinematografica Italiana** (UCI, Italian Cinematographic Union), and his viability as a producer declined with its fading fortunes. Between 1931 and 1934 he tried, but ultimately failed, to reestablish Caesar Film as a force in Italian film production. In 1937 he joined the Scalera Film company and in 1942 was instrumental in setting up a branch of the Scalera studios in Venice. After the war, in partneship with his brother, Gaetano, he worked briefly as an independent producer.

BARBAGALLO, ANGELO (1958–). Producer. After working as production manager on **Marco Bellocchio**'s *Gli occhi, la bocca* (*The Eyes, the Mouth*, 1982), Barbagallo teamed up with actor-director **Nanni Moretti** to establish **Sacher Film**, with which he has produced not only all of Moretti's own films but also the directorial debuts of several of the most promising of the younger directors, among them **Carlo Mazzacurati**'s *Notte italiana* (*Italian Night*, 1987) and **Mimmo Calopresti**'s *La seconda volta* (*The Second Time*, 1995). Having already won the **Nastro d'argento** four times, he has most recently been awarded the **David di Donatello** for producing both one of the most acclaimed films of recent years, **Marco Tullio Giordana**'s *La meglio gioventù* (*The Best of Youth*, 2003) and Nanni Moretti's *Il caimano* (*The Caiman*, 2006).

BARBARO, UMBERTO (1902–1959). Film theorist, playwright, screenwriter, **documentary** filmmaker. A self-taught Marxist writer and intellectual active in a wide variety of cultural fields, Barbaro was deeply influenced by the film theories of Belá Balázs, Rudolf

Arnheim, and Vsevolod Pudovkin, whose work he was the first to translate and make known in Italy.

While working as a literary critic, editor, translator, novelist, and playwright, in the late 1920s Barbaro also developed a passionate interest in film and so became part of the group of writers and intellectuals that had formed around **Alessandro Blasetti**'s film journal, *Cinematografo*. With Blasetti and others he joined the reborn **Cines** studios during Emilio Cecchi's period as artistic director there in the early 1930s. With Cecchi's encouragement he made two labor documentaries, *Una giornata nel cantiere di Monfalcone* (*A Day at the Monfalcone Shipyard*, 1932) and *Cantieri dell'Adriatico* (*Shipyards of the Adriatic Coast*, 1932), both demonstrating the strong influence of Sergei Eisenstein and the Russian school. While at the Cines he also worked as a screenwriter, most notably on **Goffredo Alessandrini**'s charming light comedy *Seconda B* (1934).

In 1935, in spite of his Marxist orientation, he was called to teach at the **Centro Sperimentale di Cinematografia** by its first director, **Luigi Chiarini**. Together with Chiarini he founded the Centro's official journal, ***Bianco e nero***, and produced a number of teaching documentaries related to different aspects of filmmaking. Between 1944 and 1947 he served as director of the Centro, following which he also taught at the Polish Film Institute. More of a theorist than a practitioner, he only ever directed one feature film, *L'ultima nemica* (*The Last Enemy*, 1937).

BAVA, LAMBERTO (1944–). Director, screenwriter, producer. Son of cinematographer and director **Mario Bava**, Lamberto Bava followed in his father's footsteps to become a prolific director and producer in the **horror film** genre. After assisting his father on a host of films and working as assistant director on Mario Lanfranchi's *Il bacio* (*The Kiss*, 1974) and **Ruggero Deodato**'s *Ultimo mondo cannibale* (*Last Cannibal World*, 1977) and *Cannibal Holocaust* (1980), he directed his first feature, *Macabro* (1980), cowritten with **Pupi Avati**. He subsequently made over 20 horror thrillers and *gialli*, coming to be best known among aficionados of the genre for *La casa con la scala nel buio* (*A Blade in the Dark*, 1983), *Le foto di Gioia* (*Gioia's Photograph*, 1987), *Demoni* (*Demons*, 1985), and its equally frightening sequel, *Demoni 2: L'incubo ritorna* (*Demons 2: The Nightmare Is*

Back, 1986). In the 1990s he became better known to mainstream audiences for his rather more traditional fairy-tale *Fantaghirò* series, made for television (1991–1996).

BAVA, MARIO (1914–1980). Writer, cinematographer, director. Now internationally acknowledged as the master of Italian B-grade **horror films**, Bava learned the craft of special effects photography from his father, Eugenio, a set and special effects designer and cinematographer of the silent era. By the early 1930s Bava had joined his father at the Istituto **LUCE** and helped to photograph two of **Roberto Rossellini**'s earliest shorts, *La vispa Teresa* (*Lively Theresa*, 1939) and *Il tacchino prepotente* (*The Bullying Turkey*, 1939). He subsequently joined the Scalera studios and worked as a camera operator on Francesco De Robertis's *Uomini sul fondo* (*Men on the Sea Floor*, 1941) and Rossellini's *La nave bianca* (*The White Ship*, 1941) before graduating to cinematographer on Luigi Menardi's *L'avventura di Annabella* (*Annabella's Adventure*, 1943).

In the immediate postwar period he made a number of documentaries before initiating a partnership with director **Pietro Francisci**, for whom he photographed *Natale al campo 119* (*Christmas at Camp 119*, 1948) and *Antonio di Padova* (*Anthony of Padua*, 1949). After also working with, among others, **Steno** and **Mario Monicelli** on *Vita da cani* (*A Dog's Life*, 1950) and *Guardie e ladri* (*Cops and Robbers*, 1951) and **Mario Camerini** on *Gli eroi della domenica* (*Sunday Heroes*, 1954), he provided sets, special effects, cinematography, and codirection for **Riccardo Freda**'s seminal *I vampiri* (*The Devil's Commandment*, 1957). He then worked with Francisci again on *Le fatiche di Ercole* (*Hercules*, 1957), the film that initiated the **peplum** genre, before making his solo directorial debut with *La maschera del demonio* (*Black Sunday*, 1960), the film with which he is generally regarded as having laid the foundation for all subsequent Italian horror films.

There followed *Ercole al centro della terra* (*Hercules and the Haunted World*, 1961), an interesting mixture of the peplum and horror genres, and the Viking adventure fantasy *Gli invasori* (*Erik the Conqueror*, 1961) before *La ragazza che sapeva troppo* (*The Evil Eye*, 1962), regarded by many as the first true *giallo*. This was quickly followed by several more accomplished, if small-budget, exercises in gothic horror: *I tre volti della paura* (*Black Sabbath*, 1963), three separate stories, one of which stars the legendary actor Boris Karloff; and *La frusta e il corpo* (*The Whip and the Body*, 1963), made under the pseudonym John M. Old. A year later, *Sei donne per l'assassino* (*Blood and Black Lace*, 1963) confirmed Bava's unequalled mastery of the *giallo*. Ever resourceful and versatile, Bava then tried his hand at a Western, *La strada per Fort Alamo* (*The Road to Fort Alamo*, 1964), before merging science fiction with horror in *Terrore nello spazio* (*Planet of the Vampires*, 1965), a film that in many ways anticipated Ridley Scott's *Alien* (1979). After the hilarious spy-film spoof *Le spie vengono dal semifreddo* (*Dr. Goldfoot and the Girl Bombs*, 1966), Bava returned to the supernatural horror genre with *Operazione paura* (*Kill, Baby, Kill*, 1966), which he followed with the stylish, if rather kitschy, adaptation of the exploits of the comic-book master criminal, *Diabolik* (1968).

After another foray into the Western genre, Bava returned to the *giallo* with *5 bambole per la luna d'agosto* (*Island of Terror*, 1970), a remake of Agatha Christie's *Ten Little Indians*, which was quickly followed by *Ecologia del Delitto* (*Twitch of the Death Nerve*, 1971) and *Gli orrori del castello di Norimberga* (*Baron Blood*, 1972), both of which were generally regarded as disappointing. *Lisa e il diavolo* (*Lisa and the Devil*), made in 1972 but only released internationally in 1975 in a much reedited version (and retitled *La casa dell'esorcismo* [*The House of Exorcism*] in order to cash in on the release of William Friedkin's *The Exorcist*), also proved to be something of a flop. His final feature, *Shock* (*Beyond the Door II*, 1977), the story of an apparently possessed child, similarly failed to restore his stocks. After codirecting an episode of a television compilation film, *Il giorno del diavolo* (*The Day of the Devil*, 1978), with his son, Lamberto, Bava's last contribution to film was as cinematographer and special effects director on **Dario Argento**'s *Inferno* (1980).

BELLOCCHIO, MARCO (1939–). Screenwriter and director. The most prominent representative of a confrontational cinema that voiced the revolt of the immediate postwar generation against what they regarded as the moral bankruptcy of their fathers, Bellocchio graduated in philosophy from the Catholic University of Milan before moving to Rome in 1959 to study acting and directing at the

Centro Sperimentale di Cinematografia. After a further year of study at the London Slade School of Art, during which he came into contact with the Angry Young Man movement, he returned to Italy to make his first feature film, *I pugni in tasca* (*Fists in His Pocket*, 1965), a provocative film in which Alessandro, a surly young epileptic, kills three members of his own family. The film outraged the Italian establishment but received a host of prizes, including a **Nastro d'argento** for Best Original Story, and thus established Bellocchio's reputation as an uncompromising young director. Two years later his second feature, *La Cina è vicina* (*China Is Near*, 1967), was equally provocative but more expressly political in its iconoclasm. Bellocchio subsequently joined the 1968 movement, directing two militant political documentaries, *Paola* (1969) and *Viva il Primo Maggio rosso e proletario* (*Long Live Red May Day*, 1969). After directing a strongly politicized production of Shakespeare's *Timon of Athens* at the Teatro Piccolo of Milan, Bellocchio abandoned the movement but went on to make *Nel nome del padre* (*In the Name of the Father*, 1972), a fierce and full-frontal attack on the Catholic boarding school system in which he himself had spent his adolescence.

Following *Sbatti il mostro in prima pagina* (*Slap the Monster on Page One*, 1972), a caustic critique of the conservative press that was a project he had taken over from screenwriter-director Sergio Donati, Bellocchio joined forces with Silvano Agosti and screenwriters **Francesco Rulli** and **Sandro Petraglia** to make *Matti da slegare* (*Fit to Be Untied*, 1974), a critical examination of the treatment of the mentally insane in Italy. This was followed by *Marcia trionfale* (*Victory March*, 1976), a ferocious attack on the Italian military system, before he turned to television, for which he produced an unconventional but highly praised version of *Il gabbiano* (*The Seagull*, 1977) and *La macchina cinema* (*The Cinema Machine*, 1978), a five-episode series on the cinema itself. He returned to the big screen with *Salto nel vuoto* (*Leap into the Void*, 1980), another study of a decadent middle-class family, and *Gli occhi, la bocca* (*The Eyes, the Mouth*, 1982), before another highly praised television adaptation, this time of Luigi Pirandello's *Enrico IV* (*Henry IV*, 1984). Again for the big screen he directed *Il diavolo in corpo* (*The Devil in the Flesh*, 1986) and *La condanna* (*The Conviction*, 1991), two highly contested films, not least for the strong influence on both of them of the controversial anti-Freudian psychoanalyst Massimo Fagioli. *Il sogno della farfalla* (*The Butterfly's Dream*, 1994), the story of an actor who recites words on stage but renounces the use of language in his everyday life, won the Silver Lion at Berlin and was followed by the polished period piece *Il principe di Homburg* (*The Prince of Homburg*, 1996) and *La balia* (*The Nanny*, 1999), loosely adapted from a short story by Pirandello. His reputation as a first-rate director was strongly revived by *L'ora di religione—il sorriso di mia madre* (*The Religion Hour—My Mother's Smile*, 2002), another pitiless family drama that received six **David di Donatello** nominations and the Special Mention at Cannes, and *Buongiorno notte* (*Good Morning, Night*, 2003), a deeply moving but unsentimental film about the kidnapping of Italian politician Aldo Moro. Bellocchio's most recent film is *Il regista di matrimoni* (*The Wedding Director*, 2006).

BELLUCCI, MONICA (1964–). Model and actress. Bellucci began modeling while studying law at the University of Perugia and soon abandoned her legal studies in favor of the fashion catwalk. Her acting career began in 1990 when she appeared on Italian television in the miniseries *Vita coi figli* (*Life with the Children*, 1990), directed by veteran **Dino Risi**. Her first film role was as the raffled wife in Francesco Laudadio's *La riffa* (*The Raffle*, 1991), which was followed by a small part in Francis Ford Coppola's *Bram Stoker's Dracula* (1992).

Her subsequent appearance in a number of Italian films failed to bring out her real talent, but her role as Lisa in the French thriller *L'appartement* (*The Apartment*, 1996) earned her a prestigious César nomination. She appeared in mostly French films from then on, frequently with Vincent Castell, whom she would later marry. She was called to Hollywood again in 2000 to play opposite Gene Hackman in the crime thriller *Under Suspicion* (2000) and in the same year she also achieved greater international renown in the title role of **Giuseppe Tornatore**'s *Malèna* (2000). Bellucci went on to play what was perhaps the most demanding role of her career as the woman severely raped and beaten in Gaspar Noé's *Irréversible* (*Irreversible*, 2002). More recently she has returned to Hollywood to play opposite Bruce Willis in Antoine Fuqua's big-budget action movie *Tears of the Sun* (2003) and also taken on the role of Mary Magdalene in Mel Gibson's *The Passion of the Christ* (2004).

BENE, CARMELO (1937–2002). Actor, writer, theater and film director. The unrivaled *enfant terrible* of Italian postwar theater, Bene studied briefly at the National Academy for Dramatic Art in Rome before abandoning it to form his own theater company. Beginning with an adaptation of Albert Camus's *Caligula* (1959), he became the foremost representative of an uncompromisingly iconoclastic and experimental form of theater, cultivating an extravagant baroque tendency both on and off the stage. He made his first appearance in film playing the character of a priest in Franco Indovina's *Lo scatenato* (*Catch as Catch Can*, 1967), followed by the role of Creon in **Pier Paolo Pasolini**'s *Edipo re* (*Oedipus Rex*, 1967). A year later, after making the short *Hermitage* (1968), he directed himself in an adaptation of his own novel, *La signora dei turchi* (*Our Lady of the Turks*, 1968), which was nominated for the Golden Lion at the **Venice Festival** but in the event was awarded the Special Jury Prize. This was followed by *Capricci* (1969), *Don Giovanni* (1971), which interwove Shakespearean sonnets with a short story by Barbey d'Aurevilly, and a version of Oscar Wilde's *Salomè* (1972). A year later, *Un Amleto di meno* (*One Hamlet Less*, 1973) brilliantly combined elements of Shakespeare's play with the poetry of Jules Laforgue, earning the work a nomination for the Palme d'or at Cannes.

After this frenetic series of visually baroque "antifilms," Bene abandoned the cinema in order to devote himself to theater, writing, and music. He returned to the small screen in the late 1990s with *Macbeth horror suite di Carmelo Bene da William Shakespeare* (*Macbeth Horror Suite*, 1996), and an iconoclastic version of the children's classic *Pinocchio ovvero lo spettacolo della providenza* (Pinocchio, 1999).

BENIGNI, ROBERTO (1952–). Actor and director. One of the most prominent of the new generation of actor-directors who emerged in the 1980s, Benigni had already begun to make his mark in the mid-1970s as a cabaret performer. Following the success of his lively comic monologues on national television, he made his first appearance on the big screen in **Giuseppe Bertolucci**'s *Berlinguer, ti voglio bene* (*Berlinguer, I Love You*, 1977), which attempted to bring to the screen the character Cioni Mario that had been so popular on stage and on television. A tepid reception to the film prompted a retreat back to television, where he gained a following as the zany film critic on Renzo Arbore's *L'altra domenica* (The Other Sunday). He returned to the cinema in 1979, taking small parts in Costa-Gavras's *Clair de femme* (*Womanlight*, 1979) and **Bernardo Bertolucci**'s *La luna* (*Luna*, 1979) before finding his mark as the lovable nursery school teacher in **Marco Ferreri**'s *Chiedo asilo* (*Seeking Asylum*, 1980). He subsequently appeared in major roles in Sergio Citti's *Il minestrone* (1981), Jim Jarmusch's *Down by Law* (1986) and *Night on Earth* (1991), **Federico Fellini**'s *La voce della luna* (*The Voice of the Moon*, 1990), and Blake Edwards's *The Son of the Pink Panther* (1993). By this time he was directing himself in his own films, beginning with *Tu mi turbi* (*You Disturb Me*, 1982), a four-episode film that toyed gently with religious themes, before teaming up with fellow comic actor and director **Massimo Troisi**, in *Non ci resta che piangere* (*Nothing Left to Do but Cry*, 1984). With *Il piccolo diavolo* (*The Little Devil*, 1988), Benigni initiated a fruitful long-term partnership with screenwriter **Vincenzo Cerami**, who has collaborated on all of Benigni's subsequent films, including *Johnny Stecchino* (*Johnny Toothpick*, 1991) and *Il mostro* (*The Monster*, 1994).

Already something of a national hero, Benigni achieved international fame with his *La vita è bella* (*Life Is Beautiful*, 1998), which broke box office records and received a plethora of awards, including three Oscars, nine **David di Donatello**, and the Grand Jury Prize at Cannes. *Pinocchio* (*Roberto Benigni's Pinocchio*, 2002) was less successful, both with critics and with audiences, but the more recent *La tigre e la neve* (*The Tiger and the Snow*, 2005), a romantic comedy set in war-torn Baghdad, has been better received, winning a **Nastro d'argento** for Best Original Story and David di Donatello nominations for Best Music and Best Special Effects.

BENTIVOGLIO, FABRIZIO (1957–). Actor, screenwriter, director. One of the most accomplished of the younger actors who emerged in the 1980s, Bentivoglio studied at the school of the Piccolo Teatro of Milan and worked on the stage before making his film debut as the young Dumas in **Mauro Bolognini**'s *La storia vera della signora delle camelie* (*The True Story of Camille*, 1980). After appearing in a handful of minor parts and then taking major roles in **Gabriele Salvatores**'s *Marrakech Express* (1989) and *Turnè* (1990), which he cowrote, he won the Volpi Cup at the **Venice Festival** in 1993 for his powerful performance in **Silvio Soldini**'s *Un'anima divisa in due* (*A Soul Split in Two*). He subsequently became one of the best-known faces on the Italian screen, appearing in, among a host of others, Giacomo Campiotti's *Come due coccodrilli* (*Like Two Crocodiles*, 1994), **Michel Placido**'s *Un eroe borghese* (*Ordinary Hero*, 1995), **Paolo and Vittorio Taviani**'s *Le affinità elettive* (*The Elective Affinities*, 1996) and Pasquale Pozzessere's *Testimone a rischio* (*An Eyewitness Account*, 1997), where his role as the courageous witness willing to testify to a Mafia killing earned him his first **David di Donatello**. He was awarded a second David for his supporting role in Placido's *Del perduto amore* (Of Lost Love, 1999) and a year later his first attempt at directing himself in *Tipota* (1999) earned him a nomination for the David for Best Short Film. His most memorable recent appearances have been as the father in **Gabriele Muccino**'s enormously popular *Ricordati di me* (*Remember Me, My Love*, 2003) and as the older brother in **Sergio Rubini**'s *La terra* (*The Land*, 2006).

BENVENUTI, LEO (1923–2000). Screenwriter. After studying classics at university, Benvenuti teamed up with Piero De Bernardi and they began a long-term partnership working on the screenplays of **Valerio Zurlini**'s *Le ragazze di San Frediano* (*The Girls from San Frediano*, 1954), **Alberto Lattuada**'s *Guendalina* (1957) and **Pietro Germi**'s *L'uomo di paglia* (*Man of Straw*, 1958).

Having established a solid reputation with these early films and always as a team, Benvenuti and De Bernardi then went on to write the screenplay for **Vittorio De Sica**'s *Matrimonio all'italiana* (*Marriage Italian Style*, 1964) and **Alessandro Blasetti**'s mordant comedy, *Io io io . . . e gli altri* (*Me, Me, Me . . . and the Others*, 1966) before also working with **Alberto Sordi** on his *Finchè c'è guerra c'è speranza* (*While There's War There's Hope*, 1974). Together they scripted the first of what would eventually be 10 films featuring the hapless character of Fantozzi for **Luciano Salce**, *Fantozzi* (*White Collar Blues*, 1975) and the truculent but now legendary *Amici miei* (*My Friends*, 1975), originally written for **Pietro Germi** but, in the event, directed after Germi's death by **Mario Monicelli**. In the early 1980s, while continuing their collaboration with Monicelli on *Il marchese del Grillo* (The Marquis Del Grillo, 1981), they also began working regularly with emerging young comic director **Carlo Verdone**, for whom they would write seven films, including *Un sacco bello* (*Fun Is Beautiful*, 1980), *Bianco, Rosso e verdone* (White, Red and Green, 1981), and *Io e mia sorella* (*My Sister and I*, 1987), the last earning them a shared **David di Donatello**. It was during this period that they made one of their rare excursions away from comedy when they collaborated with veteran director **Sergio Leone** on the screenplay of the epic gangster saga *C'era una volta in America* (*Once upon a Time in America*, 1984).

In the 1990s they continued their partnership, writing several more of the Fantozzi films, adapting Marcella D'Orta's book for **Lina Wertmüller**'s *Io speriamo che me la cavo* (*Ciao, Professore*, 1994) and working with Monicelli again on *Cari fottuttissimi amici* (*Dear Goddamned Friends*, 1994) and the popular television miniseries *Come quando fuori piove* (*Hens, Ducks, Chicken and Swine*, 2000). Benvenuti's last work, still together with De Bernardi, was the directorial debut of popular television satirist Piero Chiambretti, *Ogni lasciato è perso* (*Every Dumped Boyfriend Is Lost*, 2000).

BENVENUTI, PAOLO (1946–). Painter, screenwriter, director. One of Italy's most resolutely independent filmmakers, Benvenuti initially trained as a painter at the Florence Art Institute, but a strong sense of social commitment soon led him to exchange his paintbrushes for a film camera. Beginning in 1968, he produced short films and **documentaries** before working as a voluntary assistant for **Roberto Rossellini** on *L'età dei Medici* (*The Age of the Medici*, 1972). After also assisting Jean-Marie Straub and Danièle Huillet on *Moses und Aaron* (*Aaron and Moses*, 1974), he made several historical documentaries before directing his first full-length feature, *Il bacio di Giuda* (*The Kiss of Judas*, 1988), a reexamination of the relationship between Judas and Christ, which was received warmly when screened in competition at the **Venice Festival**. There followed three rigorously researched historical features, *Confortorio* (1992), revolving around the official execution of two Jewish men in Rome in 1736; *Tiburzi* (1996), an inquiry into the capture and killing of the Tuscan bandit Domenico Tiburzi in 1896; and *Gostanza da Libbiano* (*Gostanza of Libbiano*, 2000), a meticulous re-creation (in black and white) of the trial of a woman accused of being a witch in San Miniato in 1594. Strongly praised and favorably compared with Carl Theodore Dreyer's *La Passion de Jeanne D'Arc* (*The Passion of Joan of Arc*, 1928), Gostanza was nominated for the Golden Leopard at the Festival of Locarno but received the Special Jury Prize. Benvenuti's more recent *Segreti di stato* (*Secret File*, 2003) was an attempt to re-examine all the disparate evidence regarding the violent incident at Portella della Ginestra in Sicily on May Day 1951, in which 11 Communists were shot dead and dozens wounded, allegedly by the band of the brigand Salvatore Giuliano. The film was widely praised for its rigor and civic courage and was nominated for the Golden Lion at Venice.

BERTINI, FRANCESCA (1892–1985). (Born Elena Seracini Vitiello.) One of the greatest divas of the Italian silent cinema, Bertini served a brief apprenticeship on the Neapolitan stage before being recruited by the Film D'Arte Italiana in 1910 to appear in a number of theatrical adaptations of the classics, including playing Cordelia in an early production of *King Lear*. Two years later she moved to the **Cines** and its affiliated Celio Film company, where she distinguished herself in a handful of films, mostly light comedies and melodramas, playing opposite leading men Alberto Collo and **Emilio Ghione**. Her first steps to stardom, however, appear to have been taken with her delicate and moving performance as Pierrot in the highly acclaimed pantomime *Histoire d'un Pierrot* (*Pierrot, the Prodigal*, 1913), directed by **Baldassare Negroni** and featuring Emilio Ghione as Pochenet and another future diva, Leda Gys, as Louisette.

Although her acting style in emotionally charged melodramas such as *Sangue Bleu* (*Blue Blood*, 1914), *Odette* (1915), and *La signora delle camelie* (*The Lady of the Camelias*, 1915) could be excessively gestural and highly rhetorical, Bertini undoubtedly had a wider acting range than **Lyda Borelli**, with whom she was often compared, and some of her most acclaimed performances were in the more naturalistic style. She received special praise for her nuanced and realistic portrayal of the poor laundress of *Assunta Spina* (1915), a film that later would be widely regarded, both for its acting and its mise-en-scène, as a forerunner of **neorealism**.

Having achieved an extraordinary national and international renown for her physical beauty, her acting, and her glamorous lifestyle, in 1918 she was able to form her own production company, Bertini Film, for which she produced and starred in a number of films, including *Mariute* (1918), a film that cleverly integrated a reflection on the life and role of the diva herself into its plot. However, a series of seven films on each of the capital sins, *I sette peccati*, made over two years but released all together in 1919 in order to achieve a greater impact, received a very poor critical and box office response and thus appeared to signal the beginning of a decline. In 1919 Bertini and her company joined the **Unione Cinematografica Italiana** (UCI) but were caught up in the ever-deepening crisis that was engulfing the Italian film industry at this time, a crisis to which, ironically, the astonomical salaries paid to divas like Bertini were contributing in no small measure.

In 1921, revoking a million-dollar contract that she had signed with Fox to make films in Hollywood, Bertini married the Swiss count Paul Cartier and retired from the cinema altogether, except for a brief but unsuccessful attempt at a comeback in Paris in the late 1920s. In 1938 she published a set of memoirs, which liberally mixed truth and fancy, and in the postwar period appeared sporadically in a number of very small supporting roles, the last and most significant, perhaps, being the part of a nun, Sister Desolata, in **Bernardo Bertolucci**'s *Novecento* (*1900*, 1976). At the same time she published a second version of her autobiography, *Il resto non conta* (*The Rest Doesn't Matter*), in 1973. Before dying, however, she was once again able to recount her remarkable experiences as a silent-film goddess in Gianfranco Mingozzi's celebratory television **documentary**, *L'ultima diva: Francesca Bertini* (*The Last Diva*, 1982).

BERTOLUCCI, BERNARDO (1941–). Poet, screenwriter, director. Son of the renowned Italian poet Attilio Bertolucci, Bernardo was born into a cultured middle-class family and initially appeared destined to follow in his father's artistic footsteps. From early on, however, he also developed a passion for the cinema and at 16 had already made several amateur short films. In 1959, while on a visit to Paris, he became acquainted with the emerging directors of the French New Wave and was particularly struck by the work of Jean-Luc Godard. After returning to Italy and still only 20, he abandoned literary studies at the university in order to work as assistant to **Pier**

Paolo Pasolini on Pasolini's first attempt at filmmaking, *Accattone* (*Accattone!* 1961). The film proved to be a formative experience for both of them and so, in spite of winning the prestigious Viareggio Prize with his first published collection of poems that year, Bertolucci turned his back on a literary career and seized the opportunity he was offered to direct his own first film, *La commare secca* (*The Grim Reaper*, 1962).

Demonstrating an already impressive command of film language and technique, Bertolucci's debut feature also betrayed the strong influence of both Pasolini and Godard, who consequently featured as the two "fathers" whom he would eventually feel forced to exorcise in order to affirm his own artistic autonomy. Two years later he began to find his own style with *Prima della rivoluzione* (*Before the Revolution*, 1964). Although the film still bore strong traces of the influence of Godard and the French New Wave, the conflict at the core of the film between the comfortable bourgeois existence of its young protagonist and his felt need to engage in revolutionary politics introduced those autobiographical and political elements that would characterize the films of Bertolucci's early period. However, in spite of being praised at Cannes, where it won the special Young Critics prize, the film fared very poorly with Italian audiences, leading the young cinephile to abandon the big screen for a period in order to make commercial documentaries for the RAI. After also working on the screenplay of **Sergio Leone**'s *C'era una volta il West* (*Once upon a Time in the West*, 1968), Bertolucci returned to feature filmmaking with *Partner* (1968), an unsettling film loosely based on Fyodor Dostoyevsky's *The Double* and strongly influenced by both Godard and the radical ideas of the New York Living Theater. The film's intentionally anticommercial style ensured its lack of popular appeal but both Bertolucci's style and fortunes would change dramatically with his next feature, *La strategia del ragno* (*The Spider's Stratagem*, 1970). Financed by RAI television, the film was conceptually difficult and openly displayed Bertolucci's now obsessive interest in psychoanalysis, but it was visually and aurally stunning. Shown twice on national television in a single week, it had already attracted an audience of millions of viewers by the time it was presented to loud critical acclaim at the **Venice Festival** that year.

La strategia thus marked a crucial turn in Bertolucci's filmmaking, away from a cinema of ideas that spoke only to a small elite and toward quality films that would appeal to a mass audience. This new direction was confirmed that same year by what is still widely regarded as his most artistically accomplished film, *Il conformista* (*The Conformist*, 1970). Adapting a novel by Alberto Moravia set during the Fascist period, the film ably mixed politics, psychoanalysis, and cinephilia in a consummate exercise of virtuosic filmmaking. *The Conformist*'s enormous critical and commercial success, however, was far surpassed two years later by the film that made his international reputation, *Ultimo tango a Parigi* (*Last Tango in Paris*, 1972). Starring Marlon Brando and Maria Schneider in a profound study of existential alienation and sexual politics, the film won international acclaim and a host of awards, including two Oscar nominations. In Italy, however, the film quickly became embroiled in a long series of censorship battles that kept it in the courts and officially banned from Italian screens for over a decade.

In the wake of the enormous international success of *Last Tango*, Bertolucci was easily able to attract financing from three of the major American studios for his monumental five-and-a-half-hour historical epic, *Novecento* (*1900*, 1976). Nevertheless, in spite of its wide historical sweep and its extraordinary visual lyricism, the film was criticized from many quarters for both its ambivalent left-wing politics and its romantic approach to Italian history. It also suffered, especially in the United States, from circulating in a variety of shortened versions. Bertolucci returned to smaller-scale filmmaking with *La luna* (*Luna*, 1979), in which he emphatically brought together two of his major interests, opera and psychoanalysis, but the film was greeted with only a tepid critical response. Two years later, *La tragedia d'un uomo ridicolo* (*Tragedy of a Ridiculous Man*, 1981), a courageous attempt to explore the issue of political terrorism, which was still rife in Italy at the time, was also generally dismissed. After collaborating with a number of other directors on a documentary on the death of Italian Communist Party leader Enrico Berlinguer in 1984, Bertolucci directed *L'ultimo imperatore* (*The Last Emperor*, 1987), the first of the English-language megaproductions that would characterize his mature period. The most successful film of his entire career, *The Last Emperor* attracted a legion of national and international awards including nine **David di Donatello**, the César for Best Foreign Film, four Golden Globes, and nine Oscars, thus elevating Bertolucci to a world superstar status unmatched by any postwar Italian director, with the possible exception of **Federico Fellini**. However, while he continued, with the help of his regular cinematographer, **Vittorio Storaro**, to produce films of extraordinary visual beauty, none of his subsequent works received the same attention or acclaim. *The Sheltering Sky* (1990), adapted from a novel by American writer Paul Bowles, was ironically more appreciated in Italy than in the United States, and *Little Buddha* (1993) received some critical praise but did poorly at the box office. For all its warmth and color, *Stealing Beauty* (1996) failed to impress, and *Besieged* (1998), the story of a relationship that develops in an apartment in Rome between a white American musician and a black African housekeeper, was also widely dismissed, when not attacked as implicitly racist. A warmer critical reception has greeted Bertolucci's most recent celebration of sex, politics, and cinephilia in Paris in the 1960s, *The Dreamers* (2003), though perhaps not quite enough to fully restore him to the rank of Italy's greatest international director, a position that he managed to occupy for a large part of his extraordinary career.

BERTOLUCCI, GIUSEPPE (1947–). Director and screenwriter. Younger brother of more famous director **Bernardo Bertolucci**, Giuseppe began his career in cinema as assistant to his brother on *La strategia del ragno* (*The Spider's Stratagem*, 1970), in which he also appeared in a small part. After a number of shorts and documentaries made for television, he directed his first feature film, *Berlinguer, ti voglio bene* (*Berlinguer, I Love You*, 1977), adapting a comic stage show Bertolucci had written for then cabaret artist and future actor-director **Roberto Benigni**. This was followed by two films dealing with much more serious themes and interestingly utilizing a largely female perspective, *Oggetti smarriti* (*Lost and Found*, 1980) and *Segreti segreti* (*Secrets Secrets*, 1984), the latter being one of the few films to openly confront the issue of political terrorism at the time. *Tutto Benigni* (All Benigni, made in 1983, released 1986), essentially an attempt to record some of Benigni's liveliest stage performances for a wider audience, was followed by *Strana la vita* (*The Stangeness of Life*, 1987) and the quirky, fragmented comedy *I cammelli* (1988), which featured the popular stand-up comedian Paolo Rossi in the lead role. *Amori in corso* (*Love in Progress*, 1988), set almost completely in a country house in Bertolucci's native Emilia region and played out between two young women who await the arrival of a male lover, is generally regarded as Bertolucci's most accomplished film to date. He subsequently directed more shorts and documentaries for television and three other feature films: *Troppo sole* (*Too Much Sun*, 1993), a satire on celebrity and modern mass-media society in which impersonator Sabina Guzzanti plays over a dozen different roles; *Il dolce rumore della vita* (*The Sweet Sounds of Life*, 1999); and *L'amore probabilmente* (*Probably Love*, 2000), the last made exclusively with digital video.

BETTI, LAURA (1934–2004). Singer and actress. Betti began, under the name of Laura Sarno, as a jazz singer in musical revues but soon graduated to more demanding roles in dramatic theater, giving a particularly strong performance in an Italian production of Arthur Miller's *The Crucible* in 1956. In the early 1960s she appeared on radio and television and performed in a series of solo recitals (*Giro a vuoto*) in which she sang texts written by established writers such as Alberto Moravia and **Pier Paolo Pasolini** and set to music composed by **Piero Umiliani** and **Piero Piccioni**.

After small parts in **Federico Fellini**'s *La dolce vita* (1960) and **Roberto Rossellini**'s *Era notte a Roma* (*Escape by Night*, 1960), she appeared ever more frequently, and in more substantial roles, in the films of Pasolini, eventually winning the Coppa Volpi for her role as Emilia, the enigmatic serving girl in *Teorema* (*Theorem*, 1968). She would play the more cheerful character of the Wife of Bath in Pasolini's *I racconti di Canterbury* (*The Canterbury Tales*, 1972).

Never averse to interpreting hard and often unsympathetic women, she played Fulvio's reactionary sister, Esther, in **Paolo and Vittorio Taviani**'s *Allonsanfan* (1973) and the pro-Fascist Regina in **Bernardo Bertolucci**'s *Novecento* (*1900*, 1976). Ferociously devoted to Pasolini and to celebrating his memory, in 2000 she produced and directed *Pier Paolo Pasolini e la ragione di un sogno* (*Pasolini and the Reason for a Dream*, 2001).

BIANCO E NERO. Film journal. Official organ of the **Centro Sperimentale di Cinematografia**, *Bianco e nero* began monthly publication in January 1937, edited by the Centro's founding director, **Luigi Chiarini**, and **Umberto Barbaro**. The journal quickly presented its scholarly credentials by publishing not only the editors' own pedagogical essays and film reviews but also informed discussion of theoretical works such as Roger Spottiswoode's *A Grammar of Film* and Ricciotto Canudo's *L'usine aux images*. With its reputation well established, the journal was nevertheless forced to cease publication between 1944 and 1946 but resumed with the reopening of the Centro in 1947.

In 1999, following legislation that changed the Centro's status from a state body to an autonomous foundation, the journal also changed its name to *Bianco & Nero* and became a bimonthly with a double summer edition. In December 2003, under the editorship of Leonardo Quaresima, it was given a new look to initiate its third series. It remains the oldest and most prestigious film publication in Italy.

BIGAZZI, LUCA (1958–). Cinematographer. One of the most prolific and respected of the new generation of cinematographers to emerge in Italy in the last twenty years, Bigazzi worked on television commercials before making his debut as director of photography on **Silvio Soldini**'s *Paesaggio con figure* (*Landscape with Figures*, 1983). In the years that followed, he photographed practically all of Soldini's subsequent films, including the extremely successful *Pane e tulipani* (*Bread and Tulips*, 2000), as well as collaborating with most of the young directors of the New Italian Cinema, in particular with **Mario Martone** on *Morte d'un matematico napolitano* (*Death of a Neapolitan Mathematician*, 1992) and *L'amore molesto* (*Nasty Love*, 1995), with **Michele Placido** on *Un eroe borghese* (*Ordinary Hero*, 1995) and *Un viaggio chiamato amore* (*A Journey Called Love*, 2002), and with the iconoclastic duo **Daniele Ciprì** and **Franco Maresco** on *Lo zio did Brooklyn* (*The Uncle from Brooklyn*, 1995) and the controversial *Totò che visse due volte* (*Toto Who Lived Twice*, 1998). Some of his most impressive work has been done on the films of **Gianni Amelio**, with Bigazzi's cinematography on Amelio's *Lamerica* (*America*, 1993) being particularly praised and recognized with the award of both a **Nastro d'argento** and a **David di Donatello**.

BINI, ALFREDO (1926–). Producer. After dabbling in journalism and theatrical management, Bini began his career as a film producer in 1960, founding Arco Film to make **Mauro Bolognini**'s *Il bell'Antonio* (*Bell'Antonio*, 1960). A year later, in addition to financing Bolognini's subsequent *La viaccia* (*The Lovemakers*, 1961) and Ugo Gregoretti's first film, *I nuovi angeli* (*The New Angels*, 1961), he also took on producing **Pier Paolo Pasolini**'s first feature, *Accattone* (*Accattone!* 1961), when **Federico Fellini**, who had originally agreed to produce the film, decided to pull out of the project. Bini then produced all of Pasolini's films up to and including *Edipo re* (*Oedipus Rex*, 1967), for which he received his second **Nastro d'argento** for Best Producer. Discerning rather than prolific, Bini was responsible for a number of interesting productions before retiring from the industry in the 1970s, among them **Alberto Lattuada**'s *La mandragola* (*The Mandrake*, 1965), Ugo Liberatore's *Bora Bora* (1968), and, although usually uncredited, for Robert Bresson's *Lancelot du Lac* (*Lancelot of the Lake*, 1974).

BLASETTI, ALESSANDRO (1900–1987). Critic, screenwriter, director. Sometimes affectionately called the father of Italian cinema in recognition of the crucial role he played in the rebirth of Italy's film industry in the late 1920s, Blasetti graduated in law but subsequently chose to work as a journalist and film critic. In 1925, at a time when Italian cinema had reached its lowest historical ebb, Blasetti initiated a regular film column in the Roman daily *L'Impero*.

He soon also founded several dedicated film magazines, beginning with *Lo schermo* (which would later become *Cinematografo*), in which he carried out a passionate campaign to revive national film production. In 1928, together with a number of other film enthusiasts, including **Aldo Vergano**, **Umberto Barbaro**, and **Goffredo Alessandrini**, he founded the Augustus company to finance his first feature, *Sole* (*Sun*, 1929), a powerful portrayal of harsh peasant life in the Pontine marshes that displayed the distinctive influences of the new Soviet cinema. Following the film's critical success, **Stefano Pittaluga**, the only film producer still working in Italy, invited Blasetti to join him at the newly restored **Cines** studios, which Pittaluga had equipped for sound. Blasetti accepted and in 1930 made *Resurrectio*, although, for a number of bureaucratic reasons, the film was not released until a year later, by which time **Gennaro Righelli**'s *La canzone dell'amore* (*Song of Love*, 1930) had already crossed the line to become the first Italian sound film. Again at the urging of Pittaluga, Blasetti then directed *Nerone* (*Nero*, 1931), essentially a recording of one of the most famous stage revues of the celebrated comedian **Ettore Petrolini**. This modest exercise in filmed theater was followed by a return to the more marked style and rural themes of Blasetti's first film in *Terra madre* (*Earth Mother*, 1932).

In the wake of Pittaluga's untimely death in 1931 and with **Emilio Cecchi** as the new artistic director at **Cines**, Blasetti produced a **documentary** on Assisi and a much-admired adaptation of Cesare Viviani's Neapolitan comedy *La tavola dei poveri* (The Table of the Poor, 1932) before directing what is generally regarded as his finest film, *1860* (also known as *Gesuzza, the Garibaldian Wife*, 1933). An epic re-creation of Garibaldi's expedition to Sicily and his military triumph at Calatafimi, the film employed largely nonprofessional actors and a realistic style that would later lead many to see it as an early forerunner of postwar **neorealism**. Motivated by an idealistic faith in Fascism, which he abandoned after the invasion of Ethiopia a year later, Blasetti then made his only openly Fascist film, *Vecchia guardia* (*Old Guard*, 1934). Presenting a heroic picture of the historic march on Rome in 1922, the film also provided a measure of moral justification for the violent methods the Fascist gangs had used at the time. Ironically, however, Blasetti's film found very little favor with the party hierarchy, which was concerned at the time with projecting a much more respectable image of itself.

Disappointed and frustrated, Blasetti turned to making more commercially viable films, beginning with the navy melodrama *Aldebaran* (1935), followed by the film that Blasetti himself would describe as his only **white telephone film**, *La contessa di Parma* (*The Duchess of Parma*, 1936). Then, after two elegant and feisty historical costume dramas, *Ettore Fieramosca* (1938) and *Un'avventura di Salvator Rosa* (*An Adventure of Salvator Rosa*, 1940), Blasetti produced the extraordinary *La corona di ferro* (*The Iron Crown*, 1941). A strange blend of fairy tale, historical fantasy, action adventure, and romantic melodrama, the film won the Mussolini Prize at the **Venice Festival** that year in spite of its openly antimilitaristic and antiwar sentiments. Indeed, Joseph Goebbels, who was present at the screening, is said to have remarked that if a German director had made such a film at the time he would have been immediately shot. Unperturbed, Blasetti had already gone on to make another historical costume drama, *La cena delle beffe* (*The Jester's Supper*, 1941), an adaptation of a dramatic poem about a family feud in Renaissance Florence that became famous, above all, for a scene in which **Clara Calamai** was shown, momentarily, bare breasted. Blasetti then returned to a contemporary setting in *Quattro passi fra le nuvole* (*A Stroll through the Clouds*, 1942), the charming story of a day in the life of a traveling salesman; the film, on the basis of its representation of everyday life and its adoption of a realist style, would later be numbered among the forerunners of **neorealism**.

In the immediate postwar period, Blasetti was able to square accounts with his earlier involvement with Fascism by paying homage to the **Resistance** movement in *Un giorno nella vita* (A Day in the Life, 1946). He then went on, always with consummate professional competence, to direct an extraordinary variety of different sorts of films, ranging from the big-budget Roman-Christian sword-and-sandal epic *Fabiola* (1948) to *Prima comunione* (*Father's Dilemma*, 1950), a modest but well-crafted neorealist comedy about a father trying to find a suitable dress for his daughter's first communion ceremony. After playing himself as the established director at **Cinecittà** in **Luchino Visconti**'s *Bellissima* (1951), Blasetti also initiated the vogue for multiple-episode film with *Altri tempi* (*Times Gone By*, 1952) and *Tempi nostri* (*The Anatomy of Love*, 1953), the biting social comedy in many of the episodes prefiguring the coming trends of the ***commedia all'italiana***. Then, demonstrating his habitual professional acumen, he brought **Sophia Loren** and **Marcello Mastroianni** together in *Peccato che sia una canaglia* (*Too Bad She's Bad*, 1955) and *La fortuna di essere donna* (*Lucky to Be a Woman*, 1956), two slightly scurrilous comedies that highlighted the considerable acting talents of both future stars. In 1959, with *Europa di notte* (*Europe by Night*, 1959), Blasetti also delineated the form of the exotic pseudo-documentary that would soon be taken up in the Mondo films of Gualtiero Jacopetti and others.

From the late 1960s, however, having provided his own trenchant critique of the newly affluent Italian society in *Io, io, io . . . e gli altri* (*Me, Me, Me . . . and the Others*, 1965), he began to move away from the big screen in order to work mostly for television, where he came to be best known for his nine-episode series, *Racconti di fanta-scienza di Blasetti* (Science Fiction Stories by Blasetti, 1978–1979).

BOLOGNINI, MAURO (1922–2001). Screenwriter and director. A filmmaker whose work is characterized by a propensity for visual elegance and literary themes, Bolognini studied architecture and design in Florence before moving to Rome, where he spent a year at the **Centro Sperimentale di Cinematografia**. After a short period in France working with Jean Delannoy and Yves Allégret, he returned to Italy and served as assistant to **Luigi Zampa** before making his directorial debut with the musical melodrama *Ci troviamo in galleria* (Let's Meet at the Gallery, 1953), a film that provided **Sophia Loren** with one of her first significant roles. This was followed by *Gli innamorati* (*Wild Love*, 1955), a tangle of love stories set in the lower-class quarters of Rome, and several social comedies, among them *I giovani mariti* (*Young Husbands*, 1957) and *Arrangiatevi* (*You're on Your Own*, 1959), one of the many films starring the popular comic actor **Totò**.

By this time Bolognini had also initiated a close collaboration with **Pier Paolo Pasolini**, who would help to write the screenplays of five of Bolognini's subsequent films, including *La notte brava* (*On Any Street*, 1959), *La giornata balorda* (*From a Roman Balcony*, 1960), and *Il Bell'Antonio* (*Bell'Antonio*, 1960), the first of what would become a long series of fine literary adaptations and Bolognini's first real critical and box office success. With Pasolini leaving to direct his own films in 1961, Bolognini turned to other writers for inspiration and adapted Vasco Pratolini's turn-of-the-century novel, *La viaccia* (*The Lovemakers*, 1961), which was nominated for the Palme d'or at Cannes.

Many of the feature films that followed, in between shorter sketches produced for compilation films such as *La donna è una cosa meravigliosa* (*Woman Is a Wonderful Thing*, 1964), *I tre volti* (*The Three Faces*, 1965), *Le fate* (*The Queens*, 1966), *Le Streghe* (*The Witches*, 1967), and *Capriccio all'italiana* (*Caprice Italian Style*, 1968), were also literary adaptions: *Senilità* (*Careless*, 1962), *Agostino* (1962), *Madamigella di Maupin* (1965), and *Un bellissimo novembre* (*That Splendid November*, 1968), with Bolognini turning to Vasco Pratolini again in 1969 for what became his most critically acclaimed film, *Metello* (1969). The story of a young, handsome working-class hero set in a meticulously re-created late-19th-century Florence, the film was showered with awards, among them three **David di Donatello**, two **Nastri d'argento**, and two nominations for the Palme d'or.

Bolognini's production during the 1970s was marked by a greater variety and included *Imputazione di omicidio per uno studente* (*A Student Charged with Murder*, 1972), a film that attempted to reflect the social and political chaos in Italy at the time, and an unusual foray into the **horror film** genre with the macabre *Gran bollito* (*Black Journal*, 1977). He returned to literary adaptations in the 1980s with an explicitly erotic version of Alexandre Dumas' novel in *La storia vera della signora delle camelie* (*The True Story of Camille*, 1980) and a similarly erotically charged adaptation of the anonymous 16th-century comedy *La Venexiana* (*The Venetian Woman*, 1986). Having at times received a greater appreciation abroad than in Italy itself, Bolognini's body of work was officially recognized in 1999 when he was awarded a David di Donatello for his whole career.

BONNARD, MARIO (1889–1965). Actor, screenwriter, director. One of the leading male actors of the Italian silent period, Bonnard joined **Ambrosio Film** in 1911. After a number of light roles that showcased his cultivated and refined looks, he took on the more difficult role of Satan in Ambrosio's much-acclaimed triptych of evil, *Satana* (Satan, 1912), a film that anticipated, and in all probability influenced, D. W. Griffith's *Intolerance* (1914). His most renowned performance during this period, however, was in the role of the elegant but sickly young nobleman in ***Ma l'amor mio non muore*** (*But My Love Will Not Die*, 1913), the film that launched **Lyda Borelli** as the first diva of the Italian silver screen and Bonnard with her as the leading male star.

Like many actors during this period, Bonnard soon graduated to directing, beginning in 1917 with *L'altro io* (*The Other Me*), a loose adaptation of Robert Louis Stevenson's *The Strange Case of Dr. Jekyll and Mr. Hyde*. He continued to both act and direct in the 1920s, producing, among others, a creditable two-part adaptation of Manzoni's classic historical novel *I promessi sposi* (*The Betrothed*, 1922) before working for a period in France and Germany, where he directed several Bergfilme (mountain films). One of the first sound films he made upon returning to Italy was *Tre uomini in frac* (*I Sing for You Alone*, 1932), the film in which both the De Filippo brothers and starlet-to-be **Assia Noris** made their big-screen debuts.

Of the other films he directed in subsequent years, the ones most remembered are the two popular working-class melodramas *Avanti c'è posto* (*Before the Postman*, 1942), notable, in part, for the collaboration of **Cesare Zavattini** and **Federico Fellini** on the script and as **Aldo Fabrizi**'s first time on the screen, and *Campo de' Fiori* (*Peddler and the Lady*, 1943), which provided **Anna Magnani** with one of her first significant film roles. Bonnard's foray into the **peplum** genre at the end of his career, a remake of the classic *Gli ultimi giorni di Pompei* (*The Last Days of Pompeii*, 1961), was competent enough as a genre film but is remembered mostly for having been completed by the young **Sergio Leone**.

BORELLI, LYDA (1884–1959). Actress. The most renowned of all the Italian divas of the silent period, Borelli was already one of the most famous theatrical actresses of her day, acclaimed above all for her intense portrayals of the femmes fatales in the plays of Gabriele D'Annunzio (and Oscar Wilde's *Salome*), before coming to the silver screen in 1913. However, her appearance that year in *Ma l'amor mio non muore* (*But My Love Will Not Die*, 1913), a highly charged melodrama directed by **Mario Caserini** for Gloria Films, immediately launched her to superstardom. Her highly stylized and expressionistic form of acting, which was characterized by exaggerated physical movements and dramatic poses and gestures, led to the creation of the neologism *borelleggiare*, meaning "to act in the style of Borelli."

Thanks to a remarkable ability to use her body to mime the torment of a soul in the throes of an overwhelming passion, Borelli was able to command astronomical fees for her appearance in films such as *La donna nuda* (*The Naked Woman*, 1914), *Rapsodia satanica* (*Satanic Rhapsody*, 1915), *Fior di male* (*Flower of Evil*, 1915), *Malombra* (1916), *Carnevalesca* (*Carnivalesque*, 1917), and the 10-minute intermezzo *La leggenda di Santa Barbara* (*The Legend of Saint Barbara*, 1918). After having scaled the Olympic heights of stardom and becoming a screen legend in spite of appearing in no more than a dozen films, Borelli brought it all to an abrupt end in 1918 by marrying the Ferrarese nobleman Count Vittorio Cini and retiring from the cinema, never to return.

BOSÉ, LUCIA (1931–). (Born Lucia Borloni.) Actress. Bosé entered films after winning the Miss Italia title in 1947, playing a young peasant girl in **Giuseppe De Santis**'s *Non c'è pace tra gli ulivi (Under the Olive Tree*, 1950). Cast more appropriately, she was able to give much more convincing performances in **Michelangelo Antonioni**'s *Cronaca d'un amore (Story of a Love Affair*, 1950) and *La signora senza camelie (The Lady without Camelias*, 1953), and in two charming comedies directed by **Luciano Emmer**, *Parigi è sempre Parigi (Paris Is Always Paris*, 1951) and *Le ragazze di Piazza di Spagna (Three Girls from Rome*, 1952). Much in demand, she reached an early peak in her career in 1955 when she appeared in **Francesco Maselli**'s *Gli sbandati (Abandoned*, 1955), Luis Buñuel's *Cela s'appelle l'aurore (This Is the Dawn*, 1955), and Juan Antonio Bardem's *La muerte de un ciclista (The Death of a Cyclist*, 1955), on the set of which she met the flamboyant Spanish bullfighter Luis Dominguin. A year later, having married Dominguin, she announced her retirement from the cinema.

She returned to the silver screen in the late 1960s in a number of Spanish films, beginning with *Nocturno 29 (Nocturne 29*, 1968), directed by Catalan director Pedro Portabella, and in Italy where she appeared in **Paolo and Vittorio Taviani**'s *Sotto il segno dello scorpione (Under the Sign of Scorpio*, 1969), **Federico Fellini**'s *Satyricon (Fellini Satyricon*, 1969), and **Mauro Bolognini**'s *Metello* (1970). She also appeared in a number of French films, notably as the mother in Marguerite Duras's *Nathalie Granger* (1972).

After playing Donna Violanta in Donald Schmid's *Violanta* (1976), she again retired from the screen until the late 1980s, when she returned to play the mother in **Francesco Rosi**'s adaptation of the novel by Gabriel García Márquez, *Cronaca di una morte annunciate (Chronicle of a Death Foretold*, 1987) and Dona Elvira in Tonino Cervi's Molière adaptation *L'avaro (The Miser*, 1990). After appearing in the television miniseries *Alta società (Surviving at the Top*, 1994), she rather appropriately played the role of Old Safiye in **Ferzan Ozpetek**'s *Harem suaré* (1999).

BOZZETTO, BRUNO (1938–). Director, cartoonist, animator. Widely regarded as Italy's leading animator, in 1958 Bozzetto created by hand in his home his first 13-minute animated short film, *Tapum: La storia delle armi* (*A History of Weapons*, 1958). Following the critical acclaim the film received, Bozzetto was able to access better facilities in order to produce *La storia delle invenzioni* (*History of Inventions*, 1959) and soon to establish his own company, Bruno Bozzetto Film. With *Un Oscar per il Signor Rossi* (*An Award for Mr. Rossi*, 1960), Bozzetto gave birth to the distinctive little man with the red hat who would become the Bozzetto trademark and who would subsequently reappear in many stories such as *Il Signor Rossi compra l'automobile* (*Mr. Rossi Buys a Car*, 1967), *Il Signor Rossi al camping* (*Mr Rossi Goes Camping*, 1970), and the full-length feature *I sogni del Signor Rossi* (*Mr. Rossi Dreams*, 1977). In 1976, together with actor-animator **Maurizio Nichetti**, Bozzetto made *Allegro non troppo* (1976), which mixed live action and animation to illustrate six pieces of classical music in something of a parody of Disney's *Fantasia*. *Sotto il ristorante cinese* (*Under the Chinese Restaurant*, 1987) also mixed live action and animation in a charming modern fable partly based on Shakespeare's *The Tempest*.

Having already collected numerous prizes and awards, Bozzetto received the Golden Bear at the 1990 Berlin Film Festival for *Mistertao* (*Mr. Tao*, 1989) and a year later an Oscar nomination for *Cavallette* (*Grasshoppers*, 1990). In the following years he produced, among other things, an acclaimed animated short for Hanna Barbera, *HELP?* (1995), and in 1996, in coproduction with RAI television and with the support of Cartoon, the Media Programme of the European Union, he created the 26-episode cartoon serial *The Spaghetti Family*. One of Bozzetto's most amusing subsequent creations was the two-dimensional computer animation *Europe & Italy* (1999), which graphically illustrated how Italian social habits differed from the European norm. Among Bozzetto's many delightful creations is his own animated website: www.bozzetto.com.

BRAGAGLIA, ANTON GIULIO (1890–1960). Photographer, journalist, writer, film and theater director. Brother of photographer and director **Carlo Ludovico Bragaglia**, Anton Giulio began working as a journalist in Rome in 1906 when his father, Francesco, was managing director at the **Cines**. An active interest in all the arts led to his involvement with the futurist movement and he produced two experimental films, *Perfido incanto* (*Wicked Enchantment*, 1916) and *Thais* (1916) before turning to the theater in 1922 and founding the Teatro degli Indipendenti with his brother. After touring America with his theatrical troupe in the late 1920s, he returned to Italy and directed *Vele ammainate* (*Lowered Sails*, 1931) at the new Cines-Pittaluga studios. Following the film's singular lack of success, Anton Giulio abandoned the cinema altogether and henceforth dedicated himself to writing and the theater.

BRAGAGLIA, CARLO LUDOVICO (1894–1998). Photographer, screenwriter, theater and film director. Son of the first managing director of the **Cines**, Francesco Bragaglia, and brother of writer and director **Anton Giulio** and painter Alberto, Carlo Ludovico Bragaglia nurtured a passion for photography from a very young age. In 1922, together with brother Anton Giulio, he founded the experimental theater company, Il Teatro degli Indipendenti. With the coming of sound he began working at the Cines, first as set photographer and then as film editor. He then served as assistant director to his brother, Anton Giulio, on *Vele ammainate* (*Lowered Sails*, 1931), before directing his first solo film, *O la borsa o la vita* (*Either the Stock Exchange or Life*, 1933), a surrealistic comedy adapted from a popular radio play. After another handful of undistinguished comedies, he made *Animali pazzi* (*Mad Animals*, 1939), the first film to feature master comic **Totò**. He subsequently directed the popular stage duo **Eduardo** and **Peppino De Filippo** in *Casanova farebbe così!* (*After Casanova's Fashion*, 1942) and *Non ti pago!* (*I'm Not Paying!* 1942) and made another series of comedies featuring Totò, including the extremely popular *Totò le Moko* (1949) and *Le sei mogli di Barbablù* (*Bluebeard's Six Wives*, 1950). In the early 1960s, before retiring from the cinema altogether, he also directed a number of colorful sword-and-sandal epics that included *Gli amori did Ercole* (*The Loves of Hercules*, 1960), *Annibale* (*Hannibal*, 1960), and *Ursus nella valle dei Leoni* (*Ursus in the Valley of the Lions*, 1961).

BRANCATI, VITALIANO (1907–1954). Novelist, playwright, screenwriter. Although better known for his novels and plays, Brancati also worked in the film industry as a screenwriter during the last decade of his life, beginning with his collaboration on the screenplay of **Luigi Chiarini**'s *La bella addormentata* (*Sleeping Beauty*, 1943). His involvement with the cinema continued in the postwar period with a series of films that he wrote or cowrote for **Luigi Zampa,** including *Anni difficili* (*Difficult Years*, 1947), which he adapted from one of his own short stories, *Anni facili* (*Easy Years*, 1953), and *L'arte di arrangiarsi* (*The Art of Getting Along*, 1955). At the same time, he also worked on **Mario Monicelli**'s *Guardie e ladri* (*Cops and Robbers*, 1951), **Alessandro Blasetti**'s *Altri tempi* (*Times Gone By*, 1952), and **Roberto Rossellini**'s *Dov'è la libertà* (*Where Is Freedom?* 1954). After his premature death in 1954, two of his novels were also adapted for the screen: *Il bell'Antonio* (*Bell' Antonio*, 1960), directed by **Mauro Bolognini** and starring **Marcello Mastroianni**, and *Paolo il caldo* (*The Sensuous Sicilian*, 1973), directed by Marco Vicario. In 1975 his play *La governante* (*The Governess*), which had drawn the ire of the censors in 1952 due to its references to female homosexuality, was also adapted for the screen in a film directed by Giovanni Grimaldi.

BRASCHI, NICOLETTA (1960–). Actress. Braschi studied acting at the National Academy of Dramatic Art in Rome before making her film debut in **Roberto Benigni**'s *Tu mi turbi* (*You Disturb Me*, 1982) where, in one of the four episodes, she played the part of the Virgin Mary. She subsequently appeared in **Giuseppe Bertolucci**'s *Segreti segreti* (*Secrets Secrets*, 1985) and as Benigni's love interest in Jim Jarmusch's *Down by Law* (1986). After playing a female devil in Benigni's *Il piccolo diavolo* (*The Little Devil*, 1988) and the Italian tourist in Memphis in the second story of Jarmusch's *Mystery Train* (1989), she again appeared as Benigni's love interest in *Johnny Stecchino* (1991) and indeed married Benigni that year. After a strong supporting role in **Roberto Faenza**'s *Sostiena Pereira* (*According to Pereira*, 1995) and appearing as Pasolini's niece in **Marco Tullio Giordana**'s *Pasolini, un delitto italiano* (*Pasolini, an Italian Crime*, 1995), Braschi played the part of Dora, the wife and mother, in Benigni's Oscar-winning *La vita è bella* (*Life Is Beautiful*, 1997). In the same year she was awarded the **David di Donatello** for Best Supporting Actress for her interpretation of the school teacher Giovanna in **Paolo Virzì**'s coming-of-age film, *Ovosodo* (*Hardboiled Egg*, 1997). While continuing her professional partnership with her husband—she has acted in and also produced both Benigni's *Pinocchio* (*Roberto Benigni's Pinocchio*, 2002) and his more recent *La tigre e la neve* (*The Tiger and the Snow*, 2005)—she has also distinguished herself playing the lead role in **Francesca Comencini**'s powerful workplace drama, *Mi piace lavorare—mobbing* (*I Like to Work—Mobbing*, 2004), for which she received a nomination for the **Nastro d'argento**.

BRASS, TINTO (1933–). (Born Giovanni Brass.) Actor, screenwriter, director. Despite what would become his characteristic association with soft-porn films, Brass began his career as a passionate cinephile, working for a number of years as an archivist at the Cinémathèque Française in Paris. Returning to Italy in the late 1950s, he served as assistant director to **Roberto Rossellini** on *India: Matra Bhumi* (*India*, 1959) and *Il Generale della Rovere* (*General della Rovere*, 1959) before making his directorial debut with the anarchistic social satire *Chi lavora è perduto* (*Who Works Is Lost*, 1963), a film well received at the **Venice Festival** but immediately attacked by the censors. A similar strong sense of social commitment was evident in *Ça ira—Il fiume della rivolta* (*Tell It Like It Is*, 1963), a powerful documentation of revolutions throughout the world, edited from stock footage. He returned to truculent social satire in the two episodes he contributed to the compilation film *La mia signora* (*My Wife*, 1964), starring **Silvana Mangano** and **Alberto Sordi**, and with the science fiction spoof *Il disco volante* (*The Flying Saucer*, 1965). He then experimented with the **spaghetti Western** in *Yankee* (1966) before moving to London to make *Col cuore in gola* (*I Am What I Am*, 1967), an erotic thriller adapted from a novel by Sergio Donati that exploited split-screen and animation techniques.

The provocative eroticism already present in Brass's earlier works became more pronounced in his subsequent films *Nerosubianco* (*Black on White*, 1967), *L'urlo* (*The Howl*, 1968), and *Dropout* (1970), all made in England and all held up for long periods by the censors. The sexual dimension per se appeared to move ever more to center stage in *Salon Kitty* (1975), *Caligola* (*Caligula*, 1977), and the films that followed: *La chiave* (*The Key*, 1983), adapted from the novel by Junikiro Tanizaki and scored by **Ennio Morricone**, *Miranda* (1985), *Snack Bar Budapest* (1988), *Paprika* (*Paprika, Life in a Brothel*, 1991), *L'uomo che guarda* (*The Voyeur*, 1994), and, more recently, *Trasgredire* (*Transgressions*, 2000), *Fallo!* (*Do It!* 2003), and *Monamour* (2005), all of which have served to locate him very firmly in the area of soft-core pornography.

BRAZZI, ROSSANO (1916–1994). Actor and director. A keen sportsman in his youth, Brazzi became interested in theater while studying law at the University of Florence. In 1937 he moved to Rome and began acting professionally in the company of Emma Grammatica. While making a name for himself onstage, he also began to appear in films, playing his first lead role in **Guido Brignone**'s *Kean* (1940) before appearing as Cavaradossi in Carl Koch's *Tosca* (1940) and then as the Russian nobleman Leo Kovalenski in **Goffredo Alessandrini**'s two-part epic, *Noi vivi* (*We the Living*, 1942). After the war he continued to alternate between the Italian stage and screen before being drawn to Hollywood in the late 1940s to play Professor Bhaer in Mervyn LeRoy's production of *Little Women* (1949). His real fame, however, came in the next decade when—in films such as Jean Negulesco's *Three Coins in a Fountain* (1954), Joseph L. Mankiewicz's *The Barefoot Countessa* (1954), David Lean's *Summertime* (1955), and Joshua Logan's *South Pacific* (1958)—he came to incarnate the Hollywood ideal of the suave Latin lover.

Indeed, he became so identified with the image of the irresistible Mediterranean playboy that he was featured as himself, being literally mobbed by hundreds of women, in Gualtiero Jacopetti's "shockumentary" *Mondo cane* (*A Dog's World*, 1962).

From the late 1960s, in addition to appearing in a wide variety of films ranging from **spaghetti Westerns** like *Il giorno del giudizio* (*Day of Judgment*, 1971) to sexy horror thrillers such as *Terror! Il castello delle donne maledette* (*Dr. Frankenstein's Castle of Freaks*, 1974), Brazzi was also often seen on both European and American television, making guest appearances in episodes of popular long-running series such as *The Survivors* (1969), *Hawaii Five-O* (1977), *Charlie's Angels* (1979), and *The Love Boat* (1982). At the same time he also tried his hand at directing, producing a charming children's fantasy, *The Christmas That Almost Wasn't* (1966), the heist film

Sette uomini e un cervello (*Criminal Affair*, 1968), and the taut and stylish **giallo** *Salvare la faccia* (*Psychout for Murder*, 1969). His last appearance on the big screen was as the counterespionage chief Marini in **Pasquale Squitieri**'s Vatican spy thriller, *Russicum, i giorni del diavolo* (*The Third Solution*, 1989).

BRENTA, MARIO (1942–). Director. Following a degree in engineering at the Politecnico of Milan, Venetian-born Brenta began working in advertising before moving to films. After serving as assistant to a number of directors, including **Luigi Zampa**, he produced a remarkable first film, *Vermistat* (1974), the portrait of a man so poor and socially marginal that he survives by selling worms to fishermen. A slow-paced film of austere beauty and profound compassion, it was hailed, especially in France, as an extraordinary first work. In 1982, while continuing to make documentaries and short films for French and Italian television, Brenta joined **Ermanno Olmi** in setting up the alternative film school Ipotesi Cinema at Bassano di Grappa, where he has subsequently taught.

In 1989 he directed his second feature, *Maicol*, a powerful film that documents the plight of Maicol, a withdrawn five-year-old child who lives alone with his mother in a relationship of near neglect. The film charts the odyssey of the child one night when he is carelessly abandoned on a train by a mother who is more concerned with tracking down her sometime lover than with paying attention to her son. A moving but unsentimental study of child neglect and emotional deprivation, the film is all the more powerful in its studied avoidance of moralistic condemnation. Brenta's third film, made in 1994, was a stunningly beautiful adaptation of the novel by Dino Buzzati, *Barnabo delle montagne* (*Barnabo of the Mountains*), the story of an introverted forest ranger who seeks expiation and solitude among the craggy peaks and eternal silences of the Dolomites. Between feature films, and in keeping with his great love of the natural environment, Brenta has continued to make nature documentaries, among them the remarkable *Robinson in Laguna* (1985), a 25-minute film about a man who has rowed across the Venetian lagoon every morning for the last 50 years in order to cultivate a small plot of land on an island within sight of but a world away from the city that the tourists see.

BRIGNONE, GUIDO (1887–1959). Actor and director. Belonging to
a theatrical family—his father Giuseppe was a distinguished stage actor and his sister Mercedes acted for both the stage and screen—
Brignone joined the Film d'Arte Italiana as an actor in 1913. Within
three years he had graduated to directing and for the next decade he
worked for all the major Italian studios. During the downturn in the
industry in the early 1920s he continued to direct the only successful
films that were being made at the time, the Fert-Pittaluga films featuring the legendary **Maciste**, which included the famous *Maciste al-
l'Inferno* (*Maciste in Hell*, 1926). Brignone then worked in France
and Germany for several years before being enticed back to the modernized **Cines** studios in Rome by **Stefano Pittaluga** at the beginning
of the sound era.

A prolific and highly professional director who could work across
many genres with ease and who acquired a particular reputation for
being able to get the best out of actors, Brignone made over 30 features in the following years, ranging from the legal thriller *Corte
d'Assise* (*Court of Assizes*, 1930), through sophisticated comedies
such as *Paradiso* (*Paradise*, 1933) to historical melodramas such as
Teresa Confalonieri (*Loyalty of Love*, 1934), which received much
acclaim at the **Venice Festival** that year. His most popular film during this period, however, was undoubtedly *Vivere* (*To Live*, 1937), an
unashamedly heart-tugging melodrama built around the famous tenor
Tito Schipa, with a catchy title song penned by Cesare Bixio. After
the war Brignone continued to work in popular genres such as the
musical and the Neapolitan melodrama. He concluded his career with
Nel segno di Roma (*Sign of the Gladiator*, 1959), a sword-and-sandal
epic in which Anita Ekberg as Zenobia, queen of Palmira, battles for
love against the military might of Rome.

BRIZZI, ANCHISE (1887–1964). Cinematographer. Brizzi began his
career as a director of photography in the mid-1920s working on two
of the later **Maciste** films, *Maciste e il nipote d'America* (*Maciste
and the American Nephew*, 1924), directed by Eleuterio Rodolfi, and
Guido Brignone's *Maciste nella gabbia dei leoni* (*Maciste in the Lions' Cage*, 1926). He first distinguished himself, however, with his
cinematography on **Alessandro Blasetti**'s **Risorgimento** epic, *1860*
(also known as *Gesuzza, the Garibaldian Wife*, 1933). Three years

later Brizzi collaborated with fellow cinematographer **Ubaldo Arata** on **Carmine Gallone**'s ill-fated Roman epic, *Scipione l'Africano* (*Scipio, the African*, 1937), before photographing two of **Mario Camerini**'s finest films of the 1930s, *Il signor Max* (*Mister Max*, 1937) and *I grandi magazzini* (*Department Store*, 1939). In the early 1940s he worked with **Mario Soldati** on his first solo film, *Dora Nelson* (1939), and on several of **Carmine Gallone**'s musical films.

In the immediate postwar period, Brizzi achieved what was perhaps the greatest success of his career with the grainy newsreel feel he gave to **Vittorio De Sica**'s neorealist classic, *Sciuscià* (*Shoe-Shine*, 1945). In the following years he collaborated with Russian American actor-director Gregory Ratoff on several minor films, the most interesting of which was *Black Magic* (1949), a fictional biography of the 18th-century magician-adventurer Cagliostro that starred Orson Welles in the lead role. Brizzi then went on to photograph Welles's own *The Tragedy of Othello: The Moor of Venice* (1952). He subsequently worked mostly on popular genre films including two of the **Don Camillo** films, *Il ritorno di Don Camillo* (*The Return of Don Camillo*, 1953) and *Don Camillo e l'onorevole Peppone* (*Don Camillo's Last Round*, 1955), as well as one of the most popular of the **Totò** films, *Totò, Peppino e le fanatiche* (*Totò, Peppino and the Fanatics*, 1958). Perhaps rather appropriately for someone who had begun his career working on the Maciste films, Brizzi's last credited cinematography was for the **peplum** *Ursus e la ragazza tartara* (*Ursus and the Tartar Princess*, 1962).

BRUSATI, FRANCO (1922–1993). Playwright, screenwriter, director. More interested in theater than in cinema, Brusati nevertheless began working in the film industry in the late 1940s, first as assistant to **Renato Castellani** and **Roberto Rossellini** and soon as screenwriter for many other directors, including **Mario Camerini**, **Luciano Emmer**, and **Alberto Lattuada**.

After cowriting Camerini's *Ulisse* (*Ulysses*, 1954), Brusati was given the opportunity to direct his first film, *Il padrone sono me* (*I'm the Owner*, 1955), from an elegiac novel by Alfredo Panzini. A tepid response to the film led Brusati to turn to the theater and write his first play, *Il benessere* (*Affluence*, 1959). The critical success of the play prompted a return to the big screen with *Il disordine* (*Disorder*,

1963), but the film's very mixed reception led him to turn once again to the stage and write *La fastidiosa* (1963) and *Pietà di novembre* (1966), both judged best plays of the year by the Instituto del Dramma Italiano. Again encouraged by this success, Brusati wrote and directed *Il suo modo di fare* (also known in Italy as *Tenderly* but in the United States as *The Girl Who Couldn't Say No*, 1968), a Capraesque comedy that paired George Segal with Virna Lisi, which he followed with *I tulipani di Haarlem* (*Tulips of Haarlem*, 1970), a profoundly heart-wrenching but thoroughly unsentimental love story that was nominated for the Golden Palm at Cannes. He then made the film for which he is perhaps best remembered, *Pane e cioccolata* (*Bread and Chocolate*, 1973), a tragicomic portrayal of the trials and tribulations of an Italian migrant worker in Switzerland. The film was both a huge commercial and critical success, earning Brusati a **David di Donatello** for direction and a **Nastro d'argento** for Best Story. Although poorly distributed internationally, the film eventually received great acclaim in France, where it was nominated for a César, and in America, where in 1978 it received the New York Film Critics award for Best Foreign Film.

A year later *Dimenticare Venezia* (*To Forget Venice*, 1979), a lesbian-gay drama set in the 1920s, brought Brusati a second David di Donatello, with the film also receiving an Oscar nomination for Best Foreign Language Film. In the 1990s, while adding to his reputation as a playwright with several more critically acclaimed plays, Brusati also directed *Il buon soldato* (*The Good Soldier*, 1982) and his final film, *Lo zio indegno* (*The Sleazy Uncle*, 1989), an ebullient and irreverent comedy that brought **Vittorio Gassman** a Nastro d'argento for his performance in the title role.

BUY, MARGHERITA (1962–). Actress. One of the most prominent of the young actresses to emerge in the **New Italian Cinema** of the 1990s, Buy studied at the Academia d'Arte Drammatica before beginning to work in television and on the stage. After her appearance in Nino Bizarri's *La seconda notte* (*The Second Night*, 1988) and **Daniele Luchetti**'s *Domani accadrà* (*It's Happening Tomorrow*, 1988), her acting talents really came to the fore in *La stazione* (*The Station*, 1990), the first film she made with her sometime husband, actor-director **Sergio Rubini**, and for which she received both the

David di Donatello and the **Nastro d'argento** for best actress in a leading role. She subsequently starred in a number of films directed by **Giuseppe Piccioni** including *Chiedi la luna* (*Ask for the Moon*, 1991), *Cuori al verde* (*Penniless Hearts*, 1996), and *Fuori dal mondo* (*Not of This World*, 1999), in the last playing the role of a young nun in an interpretation that brought her a second David. Although competent enough in erotic and comic roles, as in Rubini's *Prestazione straordinaria* (*Working Overtime*, 1994), Buy's strengths have continued to emerge more clearly in the difficult dramatic characterizations that she has taken on, such as that of the distraught wife forced to come to terms not only with her husband's death in a car accident but also his previous homosexual double life in **Ferzan Ozpetek**'s *La fate ignoranti* (*The Ignorant Fairies*, 2000). In more recent times she has been very convincing as the timid and subdued mother in **Paolo Virzi**'s highly acclaimed coming-of-age comedy *Caterina va in città* (*Caterina in the Big City*, 2003) and the psychologically scarred and abandoned wife and mother in **Roberto Faenza**'s *I giorni dell'abbandono* (*The Days of Abandonment*, 2005).

– C –

CABIRIA (**1914**). Silent film. The most financially successful and critically acclaimed of all the Greco-Roman superspectacles that characterized Italian cinema during the silent period, *Cabiria* was not only a masterpiece of silent filmmaking (realistic three-dimensional sets, use of tracking shots, artificial lighting, and external sequences shot on location) but also a masterstroke of entrepreneurship and marketing.

Set in the third century BC against the backdrop of the Second Punic War, *Cabiria* tells the story of a young Roman girl and her nurse who are kidnapped by pirates and taken to Carthage, where the girl is destined to be sacrificed to the fire god Moloch. Fulvio Axilla, a Roman spy in Carthage, responds to the pleas of Cabiria's nurse and, with the help of his powerful and faithful African slave **Maciste**, attempts to liberate the girl. The attempt only half succeeds; Cabiria is left with Queen Sofinisba and Maciste is eventually overpowered and chained to a millstone, but Fulvio Axilla escapes to help Rome fight the war against Carthage. Years later he returns to liberate

Maciste and, with his help, Cabiria, who in the meantime has grown into a beautiful young woman who now falls in love with her rescuer.

The script was, for the most part, a loose adaptation of a pulp novel by Italian adventure writer Emilio Salgari, but the head of **Itala Film**, **Giovanni Pastrone**, who had already directed the hugely popular *La caduta di Troia* (*The Fall of Troy*, 1910), had meticulously researched the historical details, hired the remarkable Segundo de Chomón as cinematographer, and clearly planned the most spectacular historical epic to date. With the film already well into production, Pastrone traveled to Paris to meet with the leading Italian writer at the time, Gabriele D'Annunzio, and engage his collaboration. In essence D'Annunzio was offered, and gladly accepted, 50,000 lira to rewrite the intertitles, revise the title of the film and the names of the characters, and to publicly assume paternity of the work, which then would be "realized" by Piero Fosco, the pseudonym Pastrone proposed for himself. The film (whose name D'Annunzio changed from *Il romanzo delle fiamme* to *Cabiria*), was thus explicitly marketed as an excursion into the seventh art by the illustrious writer himself.

Described in the publicity as a "cinematographic opera," with the intertitles sold as "libretti" in the theater foyers, the film was premiered in Turin at the prestigious Teatro Vittorio Emmanuele on 18 April 1914. Its screening was accompanied by a specially written musical score by Ildebrando Pizzetti, which was performed by an orchestra of 80 and a choir of 70. Its premiere in Rome four days later was equally grandiose, with the added element of an airplane dropping flyers over the center of the city on the afternoon of the opening to advertise the event. The film was an instant and overwhelming success, not only in Italy, where it was hailed as the fruit of D'Annunzio's genius, but also in the United States, where it screened in all the major cities for many months on end. It also must have impressed D. W. Griffith, since the Babylonian episode of *Intolerance* seems to bear all the signs of direct influence. In the 21st century perhaps more talked about than seen, *Cabiria* nevertheless continues, justifiably, to be regarded as the highest point reached by the Italian silent cinema in its golden age.

CALAMAI, CLARA (1915–1998). Actress. One of the major Italian female film stars of the interwar period, Calamai first appeared (as

Clara Mais) in **Aldo Vergano**'s historical costume drama *Pietro Micca* (1938). Her first major role was in **Ferdinando Maria Poggioli**'s elegiac melodrama about student life in turn-of-the-century Turin, *Addio giovinezza* (*Goodbye Youth*, 1940), where she played the part of the seductive older woman. She was again the temptress in **Raffaele Matarazzo**'s **white telephone** comedy *L'avventuriera del piano di sopra* (*The Adventuress from the Floor Above*, 1941) but achieved national notoriety for a scene in **Alessandro Blasetti**'s *La cena delle beffe* (*The Jester's Supper*, 1941) in which she appeared, for a moment, bare breasted. While this undoubtedly contributed to her erotic pinup image at the time, her real place in Italian film history was earned by her much more nuanced interpretation of the character of the adulteress wife, Giovanna, in **Luchino Visconti**'s *Ossessione* (*Obsession*, 1943), a role that had been marked originally for **Anna Magnani**.

Although slightly compromised by association with the previous regime, Calamai's career continued into the immediate postwar period with very creditable performances in **Mario Camerini**'s **Resistance** drama *Due letter anonime* (*Two Anonymous Letters*, 1945) and Duillio Coletti's *L'adultera* (*The Adulteress*, 1945), for which she received the **Nastro d'argento** for Best Actress. From this point, however, her career quickly declined and she subsequently only appeared in a handful of minor films. Perhaps in homage to her brilliant work in *Ossessione*, Visconti gave her cameo roles in *Le notti bianche* (*White Nights*, 1957), where she played the part of a passing prostitute, and as an ex-starlet in *La strega bruciata viva* (*The Witch Burned Alive*), an episode Visconti made for the compilation film *Le streghe* (*The Witches*, 1967). Ironically, for someone who had been regarded as one of the foremost beauties of the Italian screen, her very last appearance on film was as the old and crazed murderess in **Dario Argento**'s **horror film** classic, *Profondo rosso* (*Deep Red*, 1975).

CALCINA, VITTORIO (1847–1916). Photographer, cameraman. A professional photographer with a successful practice in Turin in the 1890s, Vittorio Calcina was also the Italian concessionary agent of the Société anonyme des plaques et papiers photographiques A. Lumière & ses fils. Being thus among the first to have access to the Lumière *cinématographe*, he organized some of the very first demonstrations of the invention in Italy, beginning with a screening in Milan on 29 March 1896 and soon spreading to other Italian cities. In addition to actively promoting the new invention for its **documentary** and educational potential, Calcina began to shoot films himself. He soon succeeded in attracting the interest of members of the royal house, who not only requested numerous private screenings but also conferred on him the status of royal documentarist, a position that allowed him to use the *cinématographe* to record all major state and royal occasions. One of his most famous newsreels from this period, and thus one of the earliest pieces of film shot in Italy, catches the king and queen as they descend the steps of the royal palace at Monza.

In 1899, Calcina and a partner opened one of the first permanent movie houses in Turin, but in 1901 Calcina sold his share and returned to his photographic practice. His interest in cinema continued, however, and between 1908 and 1911 he worked on, and eventually patented, a 16 mm camera that he called the Cine Parvus. Unfortunately, circumstances continued to delay commercial production of the apparatus and Calcina died before he could see the project realized.

CALOPRESTI, MIMMO (1955–). Screenwriter, actor, producer, director. After producing several prize-winning videos and a number of historical documentaries for the Democratic Workers Movement and RAI television, Calopresti directed his first feature film, *La seconda volta* (*The Second Time*, 1995), an exploration of the personal consequences of the political terrorism of the 1970s, which was immediately nominated for the Golden Palm in Cannes and earned its female lead, Valeria Bruni Tedeschi, a **David di Donatello**. This was followed by *La parola amore esiste* (*Notes of Love*, 1998), the bittersweet tale of a dysfunctional infatuation, and *Preferisco il Rumore del Mare* (*I Prefer the Sound of the Sea*, 1999). In 2002 Calopresti brought his acting talents to the fore, playing the male lead in **Francesca Comencini**'s *Le parole di mio padre* (*My Father's Words*, 2002), an elegant and sensitive adaptation of a novel by Italo Svevo, while also directing himself in his fourth feature, *La felicità non costa niente* (*Happiness Costs Nothing*, 2002). He subsequently produced actress Valeria Bruni Tedeschi's directorial debut, *È più facile per un cammello . . .* (*It's Easier for a Camel . . .*, 2003), which was followed by *Volevo solo vivere* (*I Only Wanted to Live*, 2005), a **documentary** bringing together the testimonies of nine Italian concentration camp survivors, coproduced by RAI cinema and Steven Spielberg's Shoah Foundation Institute.

CAMERINI, MARIO (1895–1981). Screenwriter and director. One of the foremost directors of Italian cinema in the interwar years, Camerini started writing subjects for films while still in high school. After serving as an infantry officer during World War I, he began working in the cinema as assistant to **Augusto Genina**, and then for his own brother, Augusto, who helped him to finance his first solo film, *Jolly, clown da circo* (*Jolly, the Circus Clown*, 1923). With national film production in decline during this period, Camerini found work at **Stefano Pittaluga**'s Fert studios in Turin, where he directed a number of films on commission, including two of the popular strongman films, *Saetta principe per un giorno* (*Saetta, Prince for a Day*, 1924) and *Maciste contro lo sceicco* (*Maciste against the Sheik*, 1925). Disagreements with Pittaluga led him to join with a number of other directors to create the independent production company Autori Direttori Italiani Associati, with which he produced *Kiff Tebbi* (1927), a love story filmed on location in Africa that attracted the sizable sum of 50,000 lire from the Ministry for Education as encouragement. Camerini then directed what is generally regarded as his first major film, *Rotaie* (*Rails*, 1929), a powerful, moody melodrama clearly influenced by contemporary German cinema, recounting the redemptive journey of a suicidal young couple. Made silent but rereleased in a sound version in 1931, the film was enormously successful and firmly established Camerini's credentials both at home and abroad. Indeed, on the strength of the film's success, Camerini was invited to Paramount's Joinville studios in Paris to work on a multiple-language adaptation of Joseph Conrad's *Victory*, and it was here that he was able to familiarize himself with the new sound technology.

Returning to Italy, he began to work at the new **Cines** studios, directing *Figaro e la sua gran giornata* (*Figaro and His Big Day*, 1931) and *Gli uomini che mascalzoni* (*What Scoundrels Men Are!* 1932), the first of a series of well-crafted romantic comedies featuring **Vittorio De Sica** and **Assia Noris** for which he would come to be favorably compared with directors like René Clair and Ernst Lubitsch.

Two years later, however, *Il cappello a tre punte* (*Three-Cornered Hat*, 1934) brought him into conflict with the authorities. A historical costume drama set in Naples under Spanish domination, and adapted from a novel by Pedro de Alarcón, the film included a number of sequences that Benito Mussolini himself judged as too openly critical of constituted authority, and so the film was obliged to be cut before it could be released commercially in 1935. Whether by accident or design, *Il grande appello* (*The Last Roll-Call*, 1936), set and photographed in East Africa just after the Italian invasion of Ethiopia, appeared to offer at least moral support to the regime's practice of militant colonialism. Generally avoiding politics, however, Camerini returned to the winning formula of his earlier comedies and achieved a huge success with *Il signor Max* (*Mister Max*, 1937) and *I grandi magazzini* (*Department Store*, 1939), both again starring Noris and De Sica. This was followed by *I promessi sposi* (*The Spirit and the Flesh*, 1941), an elegant adaptation of Alessandro Manzoni's 19th-century novel that is still regarded by many as the definitive cinematic version of this classic text.

After the disruption caused by World War II, Camerini returned to the cinema and produced a considerable body of work, but he was never able to regain either the critical or popular success of his earlier period. Immediately after the war he made *Due lettere anonime* (*Two Anonymous Letters*, 1945), one of the first films to be set within the context of the **Resistance**. This was followed by *Molti sogni per le strade* (*Woman Trouble*, 1948) and *Il brigante Musolino* (*Outlaw Girl*, 1950), a dark melodrama starring **Amedeo Nazzari** and **Silvana Mangano** about a man falsely convicted of a crime returning to wreak revenge on those responsible for his imprisonment. Following *Gli eroi della domenica* (*Sunday Heroes*, 1953), a film about soccer that starred not only an athletic **Raf Vallone** and a very young **Marcello Mastroianni** but also the entire A. C. Milan team, Camerini directed the big-budget American-Italian coproduction *Ulisse* (*Ulysses*, 1954), with Kirk Douglas playing the lead. After *La bella mugnaia* (*The Miller's Beautiful Wife*, 1956), a remake of *Il cappello a tre punte* that restored the jibes against the authorities that had been originally cut by Fascist censorship, and the heart-tugging melodrama *Suor Letizia* (*The Awakening*, 1957), Camerini directed *Crimen* (1960), a contorted crime comedy set in Montecarlo that, despite the presence of actors of the caliber of **Vittorio Gassman**, **Nino Manfredi**, **Alberto Sordi**, and **Franca Valeri**, achieved only a very lukewarm success.

Camerini continued to make a variety of films in the early 1960s including *I briganti italiani* (*The Italian Brigands*, 1962), a bandit film set in the **Risorgimento** period that chose to use American actor Ernest Borgnine in the lead role, and two adventure fantasies set in India, *Kali Yug, la dea della vendetta* (*Vengeance of Kali*, 1963) and its sequel, *Mistero del tempio indiano* (Mystery of an Indian Temple, 1963). However, by the end of the decade he had largely retired from the industry, his last film being one of the **Don Camillo** series, *Don Camillo e i giovani d'oggi* (*Don Camillo and Today's Youth*, 1971).

CAMPOGALLIANI, CARLO (1885–1974). Actor and director. Campogalliani began as an actor during the early silent period, first appearing as the Fool in Giuseppe De Liguoro's adaptation of *King Lear* made for **Milano Films** in 1910. After roles in a number of major silent films, including **Luigi Maggi**'s *Satana* (*Satan*, 1912) and **Mario Caserini**'s *Gli ultimi giorni di Pompei* (*The Last Days of Pompeii*, 1913), he played the lead in Edoardo Bencivenga's *Napoleone, epopea napoleonica* (Napoleon, 1914), before graduating to directing on *Il violino di Ketty* (Ketty's Violin, 1914), in which he also acted with his wife, Letizia Quaranta. He directed his wife in another half a dozen crime thrillers and made several of the **Maciste** films before founding his own production company, Campogalliani Film, in 1920. In 1922 he and Quaranta moved to South America, where he made films in Argentina and Brazil while also touring with his own theater company. Having returned to Europe in 1927, he worked in Germany for several years before returning to Italy at the beginning of the sound era to direct *Cortile* (*Courtyard*, 1930) and *Medico per forza* (The Doctor in Spite of Himself, 1931), two of the very few films to feature the renowned comic stage actor **Petrolini**. After making an animated version of *The Four Musketeers* (*I quattro moschettieri*, 1936), which reputedly involved the construction and manipulation of more than 3,000 marionettes, he made what many regard as his finest film, *Montevergine* (also known as *La grande luce* [*The Great Light*], 1939), which was awarded the Fascist Cup at the **Venice Festival** in 1939.

In the postwar period, he worked across a range of the popular genres, from light comedies and gothic mysteries to a number of sentimental melodramas adapted from the novels of Carolina Invernizio. Before retiring from the industry altogether in the early 1960s, he produced two well-respected sword-and-sandal epics, *Maciste nella valle dei re* (*Son of Samson*, 1960) and *Ursus* (*Ursus, Son of Hercules*, 1961). His last film, *Rosmunda e Alboino* (*Sword of the Conqueror*, 1961), was a historical adventure fantasy set in the early Middle Ages.

CAPUANO, ANTONIO (1940–). Painter, set designer, and theater, television, and film director. After a period of working extensively in theater and television, Capuano made his directorial film debut with *Vito e gli altri* (*Vito and the Others*, 1991), a gritty depiction of delinquent children in the poorer quarters of Naples that was awarded the International Critics Award at the 1992 **Venice Festival** and won the **Nastro d'argento** for Best New Director. However, his second feature, *Pianese Nunzio 14 anni a maggio* (*Pianese Nunzio Fourteen in May*, 1996), severely divided the critics at Venice in 1996 for its depiction of a sexual relationship between a young street urchin with a beautiful voice and a courageous priest battling the Neapolitan Mafia. After *Sofialorén*, a half-hour episode made as part of the omnibus film *I Vesuviani* (*The Vesuvians*, 1997), Capuano's third feature, *Polvere di Napoli* (Dust of Naples, 1998), ironically updated the picture-postcard portrait of Naples provided in **Vittorio De Sica**'s *L'oro di Napoli* (*Gold of Naples*, 1954). Two years later Naples was again the setting for the violent implosion of a Mafia family depicted with all the intensity of a Greek tragedy in *Luna rossa* (*Red Moon*, 2001). Capuano's most recent film, *La guerra di Mario* (*Mario's War*, 2005), sensitively tackled the vexing issue of temporary adoption.

CARDINALE, CLAUDIA (1939–). Actress. Born in Tunisia of Italian parents, Cardinale moved to Italy in 1958 and studied briefly at the **Centro Sperimentale di Cinematografia** before securing a long-term contract with producer **Franco Cristaldi**, whom she would later marry. After covering minor roles in **Mario Monicelli**'s *I soliti ignoti* (*Big Deal on Madonna Street*, 1958) and **Luchino Visconti**'s *Rocco e i suoi fratelli* (*Rocco and His Brothers*, 1960), she was able to display her acting abilities to the full in **Valerio Zurlini**'s *La ragazza* *con la valigia* (*Girl with a Suitcase*, 1960). Two years later her portrayal of Mara in **Luigi Comencini**'s *La ragazza di Bube* (*Bebo's Girl*, 1963) earned her a **Nastro d'argento**. **Federico Fellini** perceptively cast her as the director's muse in his *Otto e mezzo* (*8½*, 1963), but her most impressive appearance during this period was undoubtedly as the radiant Angelica in Luchino Visconti's *Il gattopardo* (*The Leopard*, 1963).

Having achieved international status by this time, she began appearing in Hollywood films such as Blake Edwards's *The Pink Panther* (1963) and Henry Hathaway's *Circus World* (1964), although her talents continued to be better showcased in Italian films such as **Francesco Maselli**'s *Gli indifferenti* (*Time of Indifference*, 1964) and Visconti's *Vaghe stelle dell'orsa* (*Sandra of a Thousand Delights*, 1965). After acquitting herself brilliantly in the only female role in **Sergio Leone**'s *C'era una volta il West* (*Once upon a Time in the West*, 1968), her interpretation of Carmela, the proxy wife in **Luigi Zampa**'s *Bello, onesto, emigrato Australia sposerebbe compaesana illibata* (*A Girl in Australia*, 1971), brought her her first **David di Donatello** award.

In the 1970s she separated from Cristaldi and married director **Pasquale Squitieri**, with whom she worked extensively from then on. In 1982 she received her second Nastro d'argento for her supporting role in **Liliana Cavani**'s wartime drama, *La pelle* (*The Skin*, 1982), and two years later she was awarded the Pasinetti Prize and a third Nastro d'argento for her portrayal of Mussolini's mistress, Clara Petacci, in Squitieri's *Claretta* (*Claretta Petacci*, 1984). In subsequent years she continued to appear on the big screen, but she did some of her best work for television, as in her portrayal of Jewish schoolteacher Ida Ramado in Comencini's television adaptation of Elsa Morante's *La storia* (*History*, 1987). Still widely regarded as one of the finest actresses of her generation, in 1993 she was awarded a Golden Lion at Venice for lifetime achievement. She has subsequently published an autobiography, *Io Claudia, tu Claudia* (1999).

CASERINI, MARIO (1874–1920). Director. Having joined the Alberini & Santoni company as an actor in 1905, Camerini graduated to directing when it was transformed into the Cines the following year.

Demonstrating a marked predilection for literary and historical subjects, he directed a host of historical dramas and adaptations, among them *Garibaldi* (1908), *Romeo e Giulietta* (*Romeo and Juliet*, 1909), *Giovanna d'Arco* (*Joan of Arc*, 1909), and *Beatrice Cenci* (1909), the last of which he filmed at the Castel Sant'Angelo in order to increase its historical authenticity. He was both prolific and popular; his *Catilina* (1910) was sufficiently in demand to be screened in 14 different cinemas in Rome at the same time.

After a brief period with **Ambrosio Film** where he directed, among others, *Dante e Beatrice* (*Dante and Beatrice*, 1912) and the first long version of *Gli ultimi giorni di Pompei* (*The Last Days of Pompeii*, 1912), he joined the newborn Gloria Film, for which he directed an enormously popular version of *Florette e Patapon* (1913) and the even more acclaimed *Ma l'amor mio non muore* (*But My Love Will Not Die*, 1913), the first film to star **Lyda Borelli** and the one that launched her as a diva. In the wake of the film's enormous success, Camerini left Gloria in order to establish his own production company, with which he produced and directed a number of elegant upper-class melodramas starring **Mario Bonnard** and one of the other reigning divas, Leda Gys. However, when these two stars left, the company folded and Camerini returned to Rome to direct for the Cines until his untimely death in 1920. Among the films of this last period were *Resurrezione* (*Resurrection*, 1917), *Il filo della vita* (The Thread of Life, 1918), *Tragedia senza lagrime* (Tragedy without Tears, 1919), and *La voce del cuore* (The Voice of the Heart, 1920).

CASTELLANI, RENATO (1913–1985). Screenwriter and director. Often labeled a "calligrapher" because of his meticulous attention to the more formal and pictorial aspects of his films, Castellani grew up in Argentina before returning to Italy to study architecture at the Politecnico of Milan. While studying he began experimenting with radio as an artistic medium. In 1936 he served as a military officer in Africa, where he came into contact with **Mario Camerini**, who was filming *Il grande appello* (*The Last Roll-Call*, 1936). After returning to Italy he began working as a screenwriter for a number of established directors, including Camerini and **Alessandro Blasetti**, whom he served as both screenwriter and assistant director on *Un'avventura di Salvator Rosa* (*An Adventure of Salvator Rosa*, 1940) and *La* *corona di ferro* (*The Iron Crown*, 1941). A year later, after having been assistant director for **Mario Soldati**'s *Malombra* (1942), he wrote and directed his first film, *Un colpo di pistola* (*A Pistol Shot*, 1942), a highly composed and very elegant adaptation of a short story by Alexander Pushkin. This was followed by *Zazà* (1943, but only released in March 1944), a refined variation on the Lady of the Camelias theme to which **Nino Rota** contributed an original score, and *La donna della montagna* (*The Woman of the Mountain*, 1943), which, however, was left unfinished due to the war.

After the war Castellani directed some theatrical reviews (including a production of Noel Coward's *Blithe Spirit*) before embarking on a number of films in a decidedly neorealist vein: *Sotto il sole di Roma* (*Beneath a Roman Sun*, 1948), *È primavera* (*It's Spring*, 1949), and the film for which he is best remembered, *Due soldi di speranza* (*Two Cents' Worth of Hope*, 1952). The story of a young man who returns to his village in southern Italy after the war only to be confronted by dismal job prospects and the infuriating antics of a feisty young woman determined to marry him at any cost, *Due soldi* won the Grand Jury Prize at Cannes and a **Nastro d'argento** for Castellani as director. In 1954 a version of *Romeo and Juliet*, shot in Verona with scenography and costumes meticulously modeled on Italian Renaissance paintings, earned Castellani the Golden Lion at the **Venice Festival**. The tragic love story *I sogni nel cassetto* (*Dreams in a Drawer*, 1957) was followed by *Nella città l'inferno* (*Hell in the City*, 1958), a film that brought **Anna Magnani** and **Giulietta Masina** together in the tough confines of a women's prison. Two years later *Il brigante* (*The Brigand*, 1961), adapted from a novel by Giuseppe Berto, recounted the plight of a left-wing Calabrian peasant forced to become an outlaw. Accompanied by the haunting music of Nino Rota, the film was nominated for the Golden Lion at Venice in 1961. Less-than-memorable episodes in the compilation films *Tre notti d'amore* (*Three Nights of Love*, 1963) and *Controsesso* (*Countersex*, 1964) were followed by *Questi fantasmi* (*Ghosts, Italian-Style*, 1968), an only moderately successful adaptation of Eduardo De Filippo's 1948 play, although well acted by **Sophia Loren** and **Vittorio Gassman**. *Una breve stagione* (*A Brief Season*, 1969) was his last work for the big screen before devoting himself, like **Roberto Rossellini**, to television, for which he wrote and directed a very popular series on the life of Leonardo da Vinci (*Leonardo*, 1971), a three-part fictional recreation of *Il furto della Gioconda* (*The Theft of the Mona Lisa*, 1978) and a miniseries on the composer Giuseppe Verdi (*Verdi*, 1982).

CASTELLITO, SERGIO (1953–). Actor and director. One of the most prominent of the new generation of actors who emerged in Italy in the 1980s, Castellito studied at the Academy of Dramatic Art in Rome and worked extensively in the theater before moving to films with a small part in Luciano Tovoli's *Il generale dell'armata morta* (*The General of the Dead Army*, 1982). He played his first lead in Felice Farina's *Sembra morto ma è solo svenuto* (*He Looks Dead but He Just Fainted*, 1986) before also appearing in **Ettore Scola**'s *La famiglia* (*The Family*, 1987) and **Ricky Tognazzi**'s *Piccoli equivoci* (*Little Misunderstandings*, 1989). After being the piano player afflicted with priapism in **Marco Ferreri**'s *La carne* (*The Flesh*, 1991), he played the young psychiatrist in **Francesca Archibugi**'s *Il grande cocomero* (1993) and the affable photographer and con man in **Giuseppe Tornatore**'s *L'uomo dalle stelle* (*The Star Maker*, 1995). In the same year he also scored a huge success as the legendary Italian cycling champion Fausto Coppi in the television miniseries *Il grande Fausto* (*The Price of Victory*, 1995), a popularity repeated four years later with his portrayal of the recently canonized priest in the two-part telemovie *Padre Pio* (1999). Continuing to display a remarkable versatility, he presented a very nuanced portrayal of a Jewish shopkeeper in Scola's *Concorrenza sleale* (*Unfair Competition*, 2001) before playing Caterina's foolishly self-centered father in **Paolo Virzì**'s *Caterina va in città* (*Caterina in the Big City*, 2003) and a much more psychologically complex father (and son) in **Marco Bellocchio**'s *L'ora di religione, il sorriso di mia madre* (*The Religion Hour—My Mother's Smile*, 2003).

Well known outside of Italy for his appearance in films such as Luc Besson's *Le grand bleu* (*The Big Blue*, 1988), Jacques Rivette's *Va savoir* (*Who Knows?* 2001), and Sandra Nettelbeck's *Bella Martha* (*Mostly Martha*, 2001), for which he won the European Film Award, he has also directed himself in *Libero Burro* (1999) and, more recently, in *Non ti muovere* (*Don't Move*, 2004), for which he received his third **David di Donatello**.

CAVANI, LILIANA (1933–). Director. Cavani began her career in cinema in the early 1960s with a prolific series of television documentaries on a wide variety of historical and social themes. Her first feature film, *Francesco d'Assisi* (*Francis of Assisi*, 1966), displaying the strong influence of **Roberto Rossellini**, was originally made for television on 16 mm film but eventually shown out of competition at Venice in 1967 to warm acclaim. Her next film, *Galileo* (*Galileo Galilei*, 1968), was also made for RAI television but, rather inexplicably, was rejected as unsuitable for general viewing and so was never shown on the small screen. *I cannibali* (*The Year of the Cannibals*, 1969), a provocative modern rendition of the Antigone story, was made with obvious allusion to the student uprisings of 1968. Then *L'ospite* (*The Guest*, 1972) explored mental instability and social marginalization, while *Milarepa* (1974) cast a rather romantic eye on Oriental mysticism. However, it was her highly controversial *Il portiere di notte* (*The Night Porter*, 1974) that brought her to international renown, followed by the similarly disputed *Al di là del bene e del male* (*Beyond Good and Evil*, 1977), a film about Lou Andreas-Salomé's amorous affair with both poet Paul Rée and philosopher Friedrich Nietzsche. She continued to raise controversy with her adaptation of Curzio Malaparte's wartime novel, *La pelle* (*The Skin*, 1981), but returned to more religious themes with *Francesco* (*St. Francis of Assisi*, 1989), made entirely in English and starring Mickey Rourke in an uncharacteristic role. After *Dove siete? Io sono qui* (*Where Are You? I'm Here*, 1993), which highlighted the problems of the hearing impaired, and *Cavalleria rusticana* (1996) and *Manon Lascaut* (1998), two operas for television, she made the internationally successful *Il gioco di Ripley* (*Ripley's Game*, 2001), an adaptation of a popular Patricia Highsmith novel that starred the inimitable John Malkovich.

Cavani returned to television in 2005, directing *De Gasperi, l'uomo della speranza* (*De Gasperi, Man of Hope*, 2005), a miniseries on the life of the influential Italian postwar statesman. In 2005, after many years of being underappreciated as a director, Cavani was awarded the prestigious Fellini Prize for her career in cinema.

CECCHI, EMILIO (1884–1966). Literary critic, translator, poet, novelist, film producer, artistic director, screenwriter. Already a towering figure in Italian 20th-century literary history and widely respected as a fine translator, prose writer, critic, university professor, and art historian, Cecchi also came to make a significant contribution to the history of Italian cinema.

In the wake of the death of **Stefano Pittaluga**, producer and head of the newly reconstituted **Cines** studios in 1931, Cecchi was offered the post of artistic director. Having recently spent a period teaching at the University of California, Berkeley, Cecchi had become very enthusiastic about cinema after a number of visits he had made to Hollywood, and so he readily accepted. He quickly set about improving not only the quantity but also the quality of films at Cines. As a writer himself, he sought to attract more writers and intellectuals into the industry, leading to films such as *Acciaio* (*Steel*, 1933), which saw the collaboration of Luigi Pirandello, author of the short story from which it was adapted, and a musical score especially written by composer Gian Francesco Malipiero. Cecchi also strongly encouraged the making of quality documentaries, which until then had been the exclusive province of the Istituto **LUCE**. **Raffaelo Matarazzo** and **Umberto Barbaro** were among the budding screenwriters and directors who produced some fine documentaries with Cecchi's encouragement. Cecchi also helped to realize such adventurous film projects as **Alessandro Blasetti**'s historical epic, *1860* (also known as *Gesuzza, the Garibaldian Wife*, 1934). Cecchi's influence thus served to generate some real energy and momentum in an industry that had practically ground to a halt in the preceding decade.

Nevertheless, Cecchi's stay at the Cines was relatively brief. He left the studio in September 1933 after having spent only 16 months in the position. However, his enthusiasm and leadership during his period there had been a real boon for the industry. Furthermore, although Cecchi returned to his former literary and art-history studies, he remained sporadically involved with cinema to the end of his life. Among his last contributions were his collaborations on the screenplays of **Renato Castellani**'s *Sotto il sole di Roma* (*Under the Roman Sun*, 1948) and Blasetti's Roman epic *Fabiola* (1949).

CECCHI D'AMICO, SUSO (1914–). (Born Giovanna Cecchi.) Screenwriter. Married to musicologist Fedele D'Amico, and daughter of scholar, writer, and sometime artistic director of the **Cines** studios, **Emilio Cecchi**, Suso Cecchi D'Amico is universally acknowledged as perhaps the greatest, and certainly the most prolific, screenwriter in postwar Italian cinema, having written or collaborated on the screenplays of over 100 films in a career that has spanned six decades.

With a background in literature and translation, Cecchi D'Amico first came to screenwriting working with her father and with director **Renato Castellani** on *Mio figlio professore* (*Professor, My Son*, 1946). A year later her contribution to the script of **Luigi Zampa**'s *Vivere in Pace* (*To Live in Peace*, 1946) attracted a shared **Nastro d'argento** for Best Story. Having thus quickly discovered a natural talent for writing for the cinema, she subsequently contributed to practically all of the key films of the major postwar directors, including **Vittorio De Sica**'s *Ladri di biciclette* (*Bicycle Thieves*, 1948), **Michelangelo Antonioni**'s *La signora senza camelie* (*The Lady without Camelias*, 1953), **Mario Monicelli**'s *I soliti ignoti* (*Big Deal on Madonna Street*, 1958), and **Francesco Rosi**'s *Salvatore Giuliano* (1962). She developed a particularly long and fruitful partnership with **Luchino Visconti**, working with him on most of his films from the 1950s onward, including *Bellissima* (1951), *Senso* (*The Wanton Countess*, 1954), *Rocco e i suoi fratelli* (*Rocco and His Brothers*, 1960), and *Il Gattopardo* (*The Leopard*, 1963), while at the same time also collaborating with Zampa on *Processo alla città* (*The City Stands Trial*, 1952), with Castellani on *È primavera* (*It's Forever Springtime*, 1952) and *Nella città l'inferno* (*Hell in the City*, 1959), and with **Luigi Comencini** on *La finestra sul Luna-Park* (*The Window to Luna Park*, 1956). Her filmography also includes most of **Alessandro Blasetti**'s postwar films, among them *Fabiola* (1949), *Prima comunione* (*Father's Dilemma*, 1950), *Peccato che sia una canaglia* (*Too Bad She's Bad*, 1955) and *Io, io, io . . . e gli altri* (*Me, Me, Me . . . and the Others*, 1966).

Widely respected as the doyenne of Italian screenwriters, she has continued to work with both established and emerging directors. Most recently, while helping Mario Monicelli turn out more caustic social satires such as *Panni sporchi* (*Dirty Linen*, 1999), she also collaborated with Martin Scorsese on his epic **documentary** on Italian cinema, *My Voyage to Italy* (1999). In a brilliant career that has spanned six decades, she has received the Nastro d'argento eight times, the **David di Donatello** twice, the special Luchino Visconti Award, and, in 1994, a special David for lifetime achievement.

CECCHI GORI, MARIO (1920–1993). Producer. One of the leading producers in the Italian film industry for much of the postwar period, Mario Cecchi Gori began working in films as production manager for **Dino De Laurentiis** on **Giuseppe De Santis**'s *Riso amaro* (*Bitter Rice*, 1949). In the late 1950s he founded his own production company, Fair Film, and achieved his first significant box office success with **Dino Risi**'s *Il sorpasso* (*The Easy Life*, 1962). He subsequently worked with directors such as Risi, **Ettore Scola**, **Mario Monicelli**, and others to produce many of the classic films of the *commedia all'italiana*, winning the **David di Donatello** for Best Production with Risi's *La tigre* (*The Tiger and the Pussycat*, 1967). In the 1970s he also moved successfully into the areas of exhibition, cable TV, and home video distribution. In the 1980s, via a number of different companies, the Cecchi Gori Group collaborated on a host of productions with Intercapital and CG Silver Film before forming the Gruppo Penta with Silvio Berlusconi, subsequently dissolved in 1994. In 1990, as well as receiving the David for Best Producer for **Gabriele Salvatores**'s *Turnè* (Tour, 1990), Cecchi Gori was also awarded a David for his career. Among his other production credits were **Federico Fellini**'s *La voce della luna* (*The Voice of the Moon*, 1989) and Gabriele Salvatores's *Mediterraneo* (1991).

CECCHI GORI, VITTORIO (1942–). Producer. Vittorio Cecchi Gori has produced or coproduced over 150 films since he entered the industry in 1980, first working with his father, veteran producer **Mario Cecchi Gori**, and then assuming control of the family company on his father's death in 1993. Although an interest in politics, several television stations, and the difficult financial situation of the Fiorentina soccer team, which the family also owned, have frequently diverted his attention from the cinema, he has continued since his father's death to produce a host of commercially viable films, scoring huge successes in particular with **Leonardo Pieraccioni**'s *Il ciclone* (*The Cyclone*, 1996) and **Roberto Benigni**'s *La vita è bella* (*Life Is Beautiful*, 1997). In 1996 he shared an Oscar nomination and a BAFTA award for his coproduction of Michael Radford's *Il postino* (*The Postman*, 1994) and in 2000 he was awarded a special **David di Donatello** for his general services to Italian cinema.

CELI, ADOLFO (1922–1986). Actor. After graduating from the Rome Academy of Dramatic Art, Celi began his film career playing the kindly priest Don Pietro in **Luigi Comencini**'s *Proibito rubare* (*Stealing Forbidden*, 1948, also known in the United States as *Guagliò*). He then moved to Brazil where, for many years, he directed the Teatro Brasiliero in São Paolo as well as producing and directing a number of films in Portuguese. Having returned to Europe in the early 1960s, he resumed what would become an international film career. He gave proof of his impressive versatility by playing characters as different as clergymen like Monseigneur Radini Tedeschi in **Ermanno Olmi**'s portrait of Pope John XXIII, *E venne un uomo* (*And There Came a Man*, 1965) and Cardinal Giovanni de Medici in Carol Reed's *The Agony and the Ecstasy* (1965), and utter villains like the sadistic commandant Battaglia in Mark Robson's *Von Ryan's Express* (1965) and the ruthless Emilio Largo in the James Bond film *Thunderball* (1965), all in the same year.

After appearing as the evil Valmont in **Mario Bava**'s *Diabolik* (*Danger: Diabolik*, 1967) and as King Boemondo in **Mario Monicelli**'s *Brancaleone alle crociate* (*Brancaleone at the Crusades*, 1970), he gave a finely nuanced performance as Commissioner Rizzuto, the prison administrator in Marco Leto's *La villeggiatura* (*Black Holiday*, 1973). Although he appeared in a host of other films, he is probably best remembered in Italy for his incarnation of the irrepressible doctor turned prankster, Professor Sassaroli, in Monicelli's provocative comedy *Amici miei* (*My Friends*, 1975) and its two equally outrageous sequels, *Amici miei atto II* (*My Friends Act II*, 1982) and *Amici miei atto III* (*My Friends Act III*, 1985).

CENSORSHIP. Film censorship regulations were first introduced in Italy in 1913 by a law that established the requirement for all films to be furnished with an official written release (*nulla osta*) from the Ministry for the Interior, granted on the basis of the film's having been viewed and approved by a designated police commissioner. Henceforth the release of any film, and thus the possibility of its being screened in public, was made conditional on the attested absence of any material that could be deemed offensive to public morality, national decorum, international relations, or any official state institution (including the police). These provisions were reinforced by a new decree in 1919, passed into law in 1920, that reassigned the responsibility for recommending or withholding the award of the *nulla osta* to a commission composed of a magistrate, a teacher, an artist, a publicist, a mother, and two members of the police force. The new law also imposed the further requirement that the subject or screenplay of any prospective film be submitted to, and approved by, the censorship commission before any actual filming was begun.

The incoming Fascist government thus found itself already provided with a fairly strict censorship regime when it came to power in 1922, and the first Fascist law regarding films, promulgated in 1923, merely reaffirmed the provisions of the previous two laws, while stipulating a further prohibition against the inclusion of any scenes that might incite conflict or hatred between the social classes. A number of subsequent Fascist laws and decrees introduced a requirement for the commission to indicate whether a film might be deemed unsuitable for minors (below the age of 16) and progressively modified the makeup of the censorship board itself, which, by 1931, came to be composed of a representative of the Fascist Party, designated members of the police force and of the Ministry for Corporations, a judicial magistrate, and a mother. In addition, from 1933 onward, all foreign films, as well as being subject to normal censorship regulations, were required to be dubbed into Italian (in Italy) in order to obtain a general release. In 1934 the responsibility for preventive censorship over prospective films, together with all other aspects of film production and exhibition, was assumed by the newly formed Direzione Generale per la Cinematografia (General Directorate of Cinematography), headed by **Luigi Freddi**. In the same year the Vatican also established the Centro Cattolico Cinematografico (Catholic Cinema Center, CCC), which regularly published its own moral evaluation of films that might be shown in the church's extensive network of parish cinemas, thus also effectively exercising a censorial function. As war loomed in 1939, further and more restrictive forms of censorship were promulgated, granting the government the power to prohibit and withdraw from circulation any film that might be regarded as in any way "socially dangerous," including films that had already been granted a *nulla osta*.

Immediately following the war, in October 1945, a legislative decree from the new interim government summarily abolished all Fascist regulations relating to the film industry but retained the basic censorship prescriptions of the 1923 law. In 1947 the Constituent Assembly, by the same act with which it instituted a Central Office for Cinematography under the direction of the undersecretary of the Prime Minister's Department, also reconfirmed the censorship provisions of the 1923 law. Although presenting the screenplay before commencement of filming was no longer stipulated as a legal requirement, producers were nevertheless strongly encouraged to do so in order to avoid the risk of the film being eventually refused a general release by the censorship board, which would now be composed of only a member of the Central Office for Cinematography, a judicial magistrate, and a delegated representative of the Ministry for the Interior. As a result, film censorship during the early years of the Italian Republic came to reproduce quite closely the previous situation under Fascism, with the state and its bureaucracy exercising a determining influence over what sorts of films were produced and shown.

One of the first films to fall foul of the new censorship regime was **Pietro Germi**'s *Gioventù perduta* (*Lost Youth*, 1947) due to what was alleged to be its "social pessimism." Three years later the release of Germi's *Il cammino della speranza* (*Path of Hope*, 1950) was similarly held up by the censorship commission on the allegation that a number of the scenes set in Rome presented the police force in an unfavorable light. It was during this period that Undersecretary Giulio Andreotti, in his role as head of the Central Office for Cinematography, frequently took the opportunity publicly to reprimand neorealist directors like **Vittorio De Sica** for their negative portrayal of Italy, with a number of neorealist films consequently having their export permits withheld. At the same time **Mario Monicelli**'s *Totò e Carolina* (*Toto and Carolina,* 1955), a film in which the great comic actor **Totò** played a warmhearted police sergeant willing to bend the rules in order to help a young unmarried pregnant woman, was held up for almost two years and only released after 32 cuts had been made to attenuate its alleged poor reflection on the forces of law and order. By far the most glaring intervention by the censors during this period, however, occurred in 1953 when filmmaker Renzo Renzi and editor and film critic Guido Aristarco were arrested, tried, and given prison sentences for having published the screenplay for a prospective film about the Italian invasion of Greece during World War II, in which the Italian army was shown to be more interested in chasing women than in fighting the enemy. In April 1955 a group of film writers and directors, including **Sergio Amidei**, **Michelangelo Antonioni**, **Alessandro Blasetti**, **Giuseppe De Santis**, **Vittorio De Sica**, **Federico Fellini**, and **Carlo Lizzani**, among others, issued a manifesto calling for an end to repressive film censorship on the part of the Italian state. Nevertheless, the next major law regulating the Italian cinema, passed in 1956, merely reiterated the provisions of the earlier law, and a revision of the entire system of film censorship, frequently promised by the ruling center-right government, was endlessly postponed in all the other film legislation enacted during the following six years.

The long-awaited new law, finally promulgated in April 1962, transferred responsibility for issuing the *nulla osta* to the Ministry for Tourism and Spectacle and provided for a much greater representation on the censorship boards of qualified academics and members of the film industry. More importantly, under the new legislation, films could only be denied a general release on the grounds of seriously offending a generically defined "common sense of decency." In addition, the new law gave the censorship boards the option of classifying a film as either for general release or as unsuitable for minors (under 18 years of age), in which case the film could not be shown on television. These censorship provisions were largely reiterated in the next major piece of legislation on the cinema, the so-called Corona law, passed in 1965. One should note, however, that films granted a general release by the censorship commissions could still be denounced as offensive to common decency by both members of the general public or by police or magistrates in the place where the film was first shown. The most acrimonious censorship struggles of the following decade were all, in fact, the result of such denunciations, the most glaring case being the long-running battle over **Bernardo Bertolucci**'s *Ultimo tango a Parigi* (*Last Tango in Paris*, 1972), a film that had been granted its release by the censorship commission but that was subsequently arraigned and condemned for obscenity by a court of appeal, which took the extraordinary step of ordering all copies of the film in Italy to be burned. After a long legal saga Bertolucci's film was formally exonerated in Italy only in 1987. The abolition of the Ministry for Tourism and Spectacle in 1993 prompted a new law in 1995 that reallocated responsibility for the vetting of films and the granting of the *nulla osta* to the Department of Spectacle, located in the Office of the Prime Minister. The same law restructured the censorship commissions by reducing the representatives from the film industry to two but including a practicing psychologist and two representatives of interested family organizations.

In 1998 responsibility for granting the *nulla osta* was transferred to the newly established Ministry for Culture. In that same year, *Totò che visse due volte* (*Toto Who Lived Twice*), a film by the provocative filmmaking duo Daniele Ciprì and Franco Maresco, was refused a general release on the grounds of obscenity and blasphemy. When the film was finally granted a release on appeal, the ruling center-left government put forward a proposal to withdraw the power of the censorship commissions to block the general release of a film, retaining merely the possibility of awarding either a general release or an unsuitable for under 18, or under 14, classification. The end of film censorship in Italy, however, effectively occurred only in 2007 when a different center-left government abolished the censorship boards altogether in favor of a system of film classification to be carried out by the producers themselves, whereby films should be designated as either suitable for the general public or as unsuitable for either under 18, under 15, or under 10 years of age.

CENTRO SPERIMENTALE DI CINEMATOGRAFIA (CSC). (Experimental Center for Cinematography.) National film institute and film school. Instituted in 1935 with **Luigi Chiarini** as founding director, the Centro Sperimentale was one of the first concrete initiatives taken by the Fascist regime to help revive Italian cinema. In 1937 the Centro began publishing its official journal, *Bianco e nero*, and in 1940 moved to its purpose-built location on the Via Tuscolana, opposite **Cinecittà**. After some disruption during the later part of the war, which saw part of its resources confiscated and dispersed, the Centro was reinstated and in 1949 also took on the function of housing a national film library. In 1965 the Centro's library, named after its first director, was also officially charged with retaining a copy of the script of every national film. In 1997 legislation transformed the Centro into a foundation and officially changed its name to the Scuola Nazionale di Cinema (SNC, National Film School). In 2004, following a concerted campaign of protest, further legislation restored its original name without abrogating its function as both a national film school and film library.

The Centro remains Italy's most prestigious film institute. Teachers and graduates of the Centro over the years have included all the major directors, actors, and technicians of the Italian film industry.

CERAMI, VINCENZO (1940–). Novelist, poet, playwright, actor, and screenwriter. Cerami always expressed his gratitude at having been introduced to literature in high school by **Pier Paolo Pasolini**. He nevertheless enrolled in physics at the University of Rome but soon abandoned it in order to pursue writing. After working as assistant director on Pasolini's *Comizi d'amore* (*Love Meetings*, 1965) and *Uccellacci e uccellini* (*Hawks and Sparrows*, 1966), he collaborated on the scripts of half a dozen **spaghetti Westerns** before writing the screenplay for **Mario Monicelli**'s *Un borghese piccolo piccolo* (*An Average Little Man*, 1977), adapted from his own highly acclaimed novel of the same name.

He subsequently cowrote the screenplays for many important films by major directors, including **Marco Bellocchio**'s *Salto nel vuoto* (*Leap into the Void*, 1980) and *Gli occhi, la bocca* (*The Eyes, the Mouth*, 1982), **Giuseppe Bertolucci**'s *Segreti segreti* (*Secrets Secrets*, 1985) and *I cammelli* (*The Camels*, 1988), and three of **Gianni Amelio**'s early films, *Colpire al cuore* (*Blow to the Heart*, 1982), *I ragazzi di via Panisperna* (*The Kids on Panisperna Road*, 1989), and *Porte aperte* (*Open Doors*, 1990), which received an Oscar nomination for Best Foreign Film. Cerami's closest working relationship to date, however, has been with **Roberto Benigni**, with whom he has cowritten *Il piccolo diavolo* (*The Little Devil*, 1988), *Johnny Stecchino* (*Johnny Toothpick*, 1991), *Il mostro* (*The Monster*, 1994), *La vita è bella* (*Life Is Beautiful*, 1997)—which earned both of them an Oscar nomination for Best Original Screenplay—and, more recently, *Pinocchio* (2002) and *La tigre e la neve* (*The Tiger and the Snow*, 2005).

As well as writing and sometimes acting in his own plays, Cerami has also long collaborated with musician-composer **Nicola Piovani** in the creation and performance of musical drama and operettas.

CERVI, GINO (1901–1974). Actor. A prolific and popular actor who appeared in over a hundred films, Cervi began his career on the stage in 1924 in the company of Alda Borelli (sister of the diva). A decade later he had become the leading male actor in the Tofano-Maltagliati company. His first film appearance was in **Gennaro Righelli**'s *L'armata azzurra* (*The Blue Fleet*, 1932), following which he played the lead role in many of **Alessandro Blasetti**'s most popular films: he was the heroic knight who embodies Italian courage and chivalry in *Ettore Fieramosca* (1938), the dashing righter of wrongs and defender of the ordinary people in *Un'avventura di Salvator Rosa* (*An Adventure of Salvator Rosa*, 1940), the evil king Sedemondo in *La corona di ferro* (*The Iron Crown*, 1941), and the hapless traveling salesman in *Quattro passi fra le nuvole* (*A Stroll through the Clouds*, 1942). He also played a very creditable Renzo in **Mario Camerini**'s adaptation of Manzoni's classic 19th-century historical novel, *I promessi sposi* (*The Betrothed*, 1941).

After the war he became best known for playing Peppone, the Communist mayor, opposite Fernandel in five of the extremely successful **Don Camillo** films, beginning with *Don Camillo* (1952), directed by Julien Duvivier and concluding with *Il compagno Don Camillo* (*Comrade Don Camillo*, 1965), directed by **Luigi Comencini**. By then he was becoming even more popular playing Inspector Maigret in a long-running Italian television series screening between 1964 and 1972 to prime-time audiences. His interpretation of the famous sleuth was praised by no less than the creator of the character Georges Simenon. Cervi's last film was *Il commissario Maigret a Pigalle* (*Maigret at Pigalle*, 1972), directed by Mario Landi.

CHIARI, WALTER (1924–1991). (Born Walter Annichiarico.) Actor. After being a keen sportsman in his teens and showing a great deal of promise as a boxer, Chiari began working in theater in 1946. While displaying a natural talent for stage reviews and musical theater, he also made his first film appearance in Giorgio Pastina's *Vanità* (*Vanity*, 1947), for which he received a **Nastro d'argento** for Best Acting

Debut. From then on he alternated between stage and screen, starring in dozens of light romantic comedies, some written especially for him, but also giving more nuanced performances, as in **Luchino Visconti**'s *Bellissima* (1951).

His popularity continued to grow and by the early 1960s he had achieved something of an international reputation, having appeared in films such as Otto Preminger's *Bonjour tristesse* (1958) as well as on American television on the Steve Allen (1957) and Ed Sullivan (1961) shows. After playing the wryly cynical protagonist of **Alessandro Blasetti**'s *Io, io, io . . . e gli altri* (*Me, Me, Me . . . and the Others*, 1966) and Mr. Silence in Orson Welles's *Chimes at Midnight* (1966), he was memorable as Nino, the hapless Italian journalist who migrates to Australia, in Michael Powell's *They're a Weird Mob* (1966). However, in May 1970, still at the crest of his popularity, he was arrested and jailed for several months on charges of using and supplying cocaine. Although he was eventually acquitted of the supply charge, his career subsequently went into a severe decline. He began making a comeback in the mid-1980s, especially after the screening on national television of a seven-part **documentary** on his life, produced by film critic and historian Tatti Sanguinetti. That same year his performance as the father in Massimo Mazzucco's *Romanzo* (*Romance*, 1986) was highly acclaimed and tipped by many to bring him the Golden Lion at the **Venice Festival**. After playing a minor role in the television miniseries *I promessi sposi* (*The Betrothed*, 1989), he made his final appearance in one of the stories of Peter Del Monte's *Tracce di vita amorosa* (*Traces of an Amorous Life*, 1990).

CHIARINI, LUIGI (1900–1975). Film theorist, teacher, and director. A noted intellectual and a strong advocate of state support for the film industry, Chiarini was appointed as founding director of the **Centro Sperimentale di Cinematografia** in 1935 and was largely responsible for its subsequent success and prestige as a national film school. In 1937 he founded the center's journal, *Bianco e nero*, and continued as its editor for many years. Between 1952 and 1955 he also edited the *Rivista del cinema italiano* and in 1961 was appointed to the first Italian chair of cinema studies at the University of Pisa. From 1963 to 1968 he served as executive director of the **Venice Festival**.

As well as publishing widely on film theory and practice—ideas that he attempted to summarize in the formula "film is an art, cinema is an industry"—Chiarini collaborated with a fellow teacher at the Centro, **Umberto Barbaro**, on training films such as *L'attore* (*The Actor*, 1939). He also directed a handful of feature films that, perhaps unfairly, were then, and have continued to be, generally more coldly respected than warmly admired: *Via delle Cinque Lune* (*Five Moon Street*, 1942), adapted from a novel by Matilde Serrao; *La bella addormentata* (*Sleeping Beauty*, 1942); *La locandiera* (*Mirandolina*, 1944), a realistic adaptation of the 18th-century play by Carlo Goldoni; *Ultimo amore* (*Last Love*, 1947); and *Patto col diavolo* (*Pact with the Devil*, 1949).

CICOGNINI, ALESSANDRO (1906–1995). Trained at the Conservatory of Milan and with an established reputation as a classical composer, Cicognini began working in the cinema in the mid-1930s, his first score being for Amleto Palermi's *Il corsaro nero* (*The Black Corsair*, 1937). He subsequently scored all of **Alessandro Blasetti**'s films from *Ettore Fieramosca* (1938) to *Quattro passi fra le nuvole* (*A Stroll through the Clouds*, 1942), as well as **Augusto Genina**'s *Castelli in aria* (*Castles in the Air*, 1939) and **Mario Camerini**'s *I grandi magazzini* (*Department Store*, 1939). In the immediate postwar period he established a particularly strong association with **Vittorio De Sica**, composing the music for all of De Sica's major films from the Oscar-nominated *Sciuscià* (*Shoe-Shine*, 1946) to *Il tetto* (*The Roof*, 1956), distinguishing himself especially with the score for *Ladri di biciclette* (*Bicycle Thieves*, 1948), which brought him the award of a **Nastro d'argento**.

Versatile and wide ranging, he also collaborated with Julien Duvivier on *Il piccolo mondo di Don Camillo* (*The Little World of Don Camillo*, 1952) and *Il ritorno di Don Camillo* (*The Return of Don Camillo*, 1953), with Camerini again on several films, including the big-budget mythological epic *Ulisse* (*Ulysses*, 1954) and most successfully perhaps on **Luigi Comencini**'s enormously popular *Pane, amore e fantasia* (*Bread, Love and Dreams*, 1953). He also worked with several international directors, notably with David Lean on *Summertime* (1955) and Michael Curtiz on *A Breath of Scandal* (1960) before retiring from composing for film in the early 1960s.

CINECITTÀ. Studio complex. Housing 16 well-equipped studios spread over an area of 400,000 square meters, Cinecittà, or Cinema City, remains the largest and most important film production facility in Italy. Ostensibly built by the owner of the **Cines**, Carlo Roncoroni, as a replacement for the studios in Via Veio that had mysteriously burned down in 1935, the project was largely financed by the Fascist government and officially opened by Benito Mussolini on 28 April 1937 as a sign of state support for the languishing film industry. Originally run privately, the complex was resumed by the state in 1939 under the directorship of **Luigi Freddi**. As expected, the new facility dramatically raised national production, leading to 300 films being made there before the later part of 1943 when, following Italy's declaration of the armistice, the studios were ransacked by retreating Fascist troops with the intention of setting up a *cinevillaggio* (film village) in Venice. Many of the films produced at Cinecittà during the Fascist period were undoubtedly light comedies in the so-called **white telephone** mode, but films like **Alessandro Blasetti**'s *Quattro passi fra le nuvole* (*A Stroll through the Clouds*, 1942) and **Luchino Visconti**'s *Ossessione* (*Obsession*, 1943), both regarded as forerunners of **neorealism**, were also made with the studio's facilities.

The war took its toll on the complex, which was significantly damaged by Allied bombing, and after liberation the studios came to be used as a refugee camp by the Allies. By the early 1950s, however, the studios had been completely restored and both established directors like **De Sica** and **Rossellini** and up-and-coming directors like **Antonioni** and **Fellini** began to make extensive use of its facilities. Taking advantage of an Italian law that obliged foreign film companies to reinvest a portion of their profits in Italy, many American majors also began to produce some of their big-budget spectacles at Cinecittà, thus earning it, for a period, the epithet of Hollywood on the Tiber.

By the late 1970s, however, as a result of a general downturn in the film industry, production at Cinecittà fell alarmingly, leading to rumors of a closure. Fortunately, a reprieve appeared with an increase in production for television, which helped to financially support the complex through the 1980s. In the early 1990s a concerted attempt was made to to revive the flagging fortunes of the studios with the establishment of the state-owned company Cinecittà International, which was meant to promote Italian films in the international market. Nevertheless, the company continued to lose money and so was liquidated in 1996. Two years later Cinecittà itself was privatized but with a majority share reserved for the newly established Cinecittà Holding, a company under the direct control of the Treasury (reassigned a year later to the Ministry for Culture).

Adventurous and well-managed, the new company has been extremely successful in not only stimulating productive use of the studios but also in diversifying its products and services. Its latest initiatives have been the high-tech facility Cinecittà Digital, housed at Cinecittà itself, and Cinecittà Entertainment, an efficient distribution, exhibition, and services company.

CINEMA. Journal. Founded in 1936 and published bimonthly, *Cinema* soon became one of the most important reference points for film culture in Fascist Italy. In spite of being directed from 1938 to 1943 by Benito Mussolini's son, Vittorio, the journal was host to a relatively wide range of opinions and included in its ranks not only left-wing critics but also clandestine members of the banned Italian Communist Party. Although its general tendency was to voice strong support for a national cinema, there was no attempt to hide an obvious admiration for Hollywood films, with Vittorio Mussolini himself expressing opposition to the 1938 monopoly law, introduced by his father, on the grounds that hundreds of American films would no longer find their way to Italian screens. Nevertheless, from 1941 onward, a group of militant young critics, congregating around the figure of **Giuseppe De Santis**, began to use the pages of the journal to call for a greater sense of realism in Italian films, taking as their model the 19th-century Sicilian novelist Giovanni Verga. It was this group that eventually collaborated with **Luchino Visconti** in producing what they regarded as something of a manifesto of this new sort of cinema, *Ossessione* (*Obsession*, 1943).

After being interrupted by World War II, the journal resumed publication in 1948, again providing a range of perspectives on a variety of topics, including cinema and censorship, film audiences, and a number of special issues dedicated to a reappraisal of the work of veteran directors such as **Mario Camerini** and **Alessandro Blasetti**. However, as time went on, it hosted fewer theoretical essays and became more of a film magazine. After initiating a third series in mid-1955, it ceased publication in 1956.

CINES. Production company. The studio that would remain one of the pillars of the Italian film industry during its first half century, albeit with a number of near deaths and resuscitations, Cines was born in April 1906 out of Alberini & Santoni, the company with which **Filoteo Alberini** produced the first Italian feature film, *La presa di Roma* (*The Taking of Rome*, 1905). With the backing of the Bank of Rome and expertise from a number of technicians poached from the French Pathé, Cines rapidly expanded to become the foremost film producer in Italy, turning out a weekly supply of quality films. Under the guidance of **Mario Caserini**, who had joined the company as an actor in 1905 but had quickly taken the reins as artistic director, the company produced films across a wide variety of genres, from "actualities," documentaries, and hundreds of sketches by its resident comic, Ferdinand Guillame, under the name Tontolini, to historical costume dramas and literary and theatrical adaptations. From 1910 onward it achieved a special reputation for colossal Roman epics and ancient world spectacles such as *Brutus* (1910), *Messalina* (1910), *La sposa del Nilo* (*The Bride of the Nile*, 1911), *Quo vadis?* (1912), and *Marcantonio e Cleopatra* (*Mark Anthony and Cleopatra*, 1913), all directed by painter-turned-director **Enrico Guazzoni**. By 1911, run by a board of management headed by Baron Alberto Fassini and that included the cream of Roman nobility and industry, Cines was exporting its films all over the world, with subsidiaries in Paris, London, Barcelona, Moscow, and Berlin, and offices in New York, Buenos Aires, Sydney, Yokohama, and Hong Kong.

Nevertheless, after a decade of almost unmitigated success during which it had produced over 1,500 films and achieved international renown, the Cines suffered, along with all the other companies, in the crisis that engulfed the Italian film industry in the period immediately following World War I. In 1919, together with most of the other major Italian studios, it merged into the ill-fated **Unione Cinematografica Italiana** (UCI), a consortium headed, for a period, by Baron Fassini himself. Poor overall management and a retrograde policy of too many costly remakes of Roman epics, which had made the fortune of the industry a decade earlier but which were no longer viable, led to the collapse of the UCI and of the Cines with it. By the mid-1920s the company's Roman studios in Via Veio were either inactive or hired out to foreign companies.

The company received a new lease on life when entrepreneur **Stefano Pittaluga** bought up the UCI's assets in 1926 and, with great intelligence and foresight, began to renew the old Cines studios, equipping them with Photophone RCA sound recording equipment. The new Cines, with Pittaluga as general manager, was officially inaugurated in May 1930 by the minister for corporations, Giuseppe Bottai, indicating a new willingness by the Fascist government to support the Italian film industry. The farsighted Pittaluga immediately began to invite directors like **Alessandro Blasetti**, who had remained in Italy, and others such as **Guido Brignone** and **Gennaro Righelli**, who had left to work abroad, to join the company and to utilize its studios. Beginning with the first Italian sound film, *La canzone dell'amore* (*The Song of Love*, 1930), directed by Gennaro Righelli—the first sound film actually shot was *Resurrectio*, directed by Blasetti, but it was not released until 1931—the Cines studios became the center of Italian sound film production in the early 1930s.

Pittaluga's untimely death in 1931, at the age of 44, led to the artistic direction of the company being entrusted to **Emilio Cecchi**. A literary critic, poet, translator, and art historian who had become fascinated with cinema while teaching in America, Cecchi encouraged all sorts of quality films at Cines, with a special place reserved for documentaries (which to this point had been the exclusive province of the Istituto **LUCE**). Under Cecchi's guidance the Cines experienced a golden period, producing a long series of fine documentaries and several landmark feature films, the most notable being Blasetti's *1860*, a film about Garibaldi's Sicilian campaign and his decisive victory at the battle of Calatifimi. A number of foreign directors also came to work at the Cines, such as the German director Walter Ruttmann, who directed *Acciaio* (*Steel*, 1933), and Max Ophüls, who made the much-acclaimed *La Signora di Tutti* (*Everybody's Woman*) at the Cines studios in 1934. Nevertheless, by 1934 Cecchi had left the studio to pursue his literary interests. Ludovico Toeplitz had also resigned as general director, and competition from a number of other studios that had set up in the meantime had begun to undermine the Cines' viability. For a brief period control of the company passed into the hands of industrialist Carlo Roncoroni, who nurtured plans for building a larger and more modern studio complex. However, on 26 September 1935 a mysterious fire destroyed much of the studio's facilities. In the wake of the disaster, Roncoroni accepted a proposal from **Luigi Freddi**, head of the government's newly established Direzione Generale della Cinematografia, for a project that would result, only two years later, in the new studio complex of **Cinecittà**, inaugurated by Mussolini in person. With the opening of Cinecittà, Cines and its studios were downgraded and either ceased production or were rented out to other companies.

In 1942 the Cines was reconstituted under state control and its studios used to make a number of films, the most significant being Blasetti's *Quattro passi fra le nuvole* (*A Stroll through the Clouds*, 1942) and **Mario Bonnard**'s *Avanti c'è posto* (*Before the Postman*, 1942). However, following Italy's signing of the armistice in November 1943, many of the facilities were dismantled and appropriated by retreating Fascist forces, with the intention of setting up a new center of film production in Venice.

In the postwar period the Cines was reconstituted as a state-owned company in 1949 and was home to a significant number of productions and coproductions, including **Pietro Germi**'s *Il brigante di Tacca del Lupo* (*The Brigand of Tacca del Lupo*, 1952) and Blasetti's *Altri tempi* (*Times Gone By*, 1952) and *Tempi nostri* (*A Slice of Life*, 1954). However, with increased competition from Cinecittà and a host of new companies and studios, the Cines was definitively closed down in 1956, drawing the curtain on a long and illustrious history.

COLORADO FILM. Production company. An independent production company formed in 1986 by director **Gabriele Salvatores**, actor **Diego Abatantuono**, and independent producer Maurizio Totti, Colorado Film has in its two decades of operation produced, either alone or in partnership, 17 feature films. These have included features by established directors such as Salvatores and **Giuseppe Bertolucci** but also a number of films by younger and relatively unknown directors such as Antonello Grimaldi, Alessandro Cappelletti, and Stefano Reali. In 1997 the company also opened an advertising branch, Colorado Commercials, which became an independent company in 2003. In 2004 Colorado Film established a publishing arm, Colorado

Noir, with the aim of encouraging new crime fiction that could eventually be adapted for cinema. The first novel published by Colorado Noir, Grazia Verasani's *Quo vadis, baby?* (2004), has recently been been directed for the screen by Salvatores, in a coproduction between Colorado and Silvio Berlusconi's Medusa.

COMENCINI, CRISTINA (1958–). Director, novelist, screenwriter. Daughter of veteran director **Luigi Comencini**, Cristina began doing small parts in her father's films as a child and was soon cowriting the screenplays of some of his films, including *Cuore* (*Heart*, 1984) and *La storia* (*History*, 1986). In 1988 she made her own directorial debut with the quirky children's film *Zoo* (1988). This was followed by *I divertimenti della vita privata* (*The Amusements of Private Life*, 1990), an elegant costume drama with feminist undertones set in revolutionary France; *La fine è nota* (*The End Is Known*, 1993), a thriller based on a novel by Geoffrey Holiday Hall; and a very successful adaptation of Susanna Tamaro's best-selling novel *Va' dove ti porta il cuore* (*Follow Your Heart*, 1996). At the same time she pursued her literary interests and published a string of successful novels, among them *Pagine strappate* (*The Missing Pages*, 1991), *Passione di famiglia* (*Family Passion*, 1994), and *Il cappotto del turco* (*The Turk's Overcoat*, 1997). She returned to directing with the bittersweet comedy *Matrimoni* (*Marriages*, 1998), which was followed by what many regard as her finest film, *Il più bel giorno della mia vita* (*The Best Day of My Life*, 2001), an intense family drama filtered through the eyes of a child. Her more recent *La bestia nel cuore* (*The Beast in the Heart/Don't Tell*, 2005), another family drama that Comencini adapted from her own novel of the same name, was nominated for the Golden Lion at the **Venice Festival** in 2005 and put forward as the Italian nominee for the Academy Award for Best Foreign Film at the Oscars in 2006.

COMENCINI, FRANCESCA (1961–). Director and screenwriter. Daughter of veteran director **Luigi Comencini** (and sister of **Cristina** and Paola, who also work in the film industry), Francesca Comencini abandoned her university studies in Italy and moved to France, where she soon directed her first feature, *Pianoforte* (1984). A love story afflicted with all the problems of drug addiction, the film earned her the De Sica Prize for young directors at the **Venice Festival**. After collaborating with her father on the screenplay of *Un ragazzo di Calabria* (*The Boy from Calabria*, 1987), she directed two more features, *La lumière du lac* (*The Light of the Lake*, 1988) and *Annabelle partagée* (*Annabelle Divided*, 1991), before again working with her father on his remake of the children's classic *Marcellino pane e vino* (*Miracle of Marcellino*, 1991). She subsequently made a number of documentaries for French television before directing *Le parole di mio padre* (*The Words of My Father*, 2001), a loose but interesting adaptation of Italo Svevo's *La coscienza di Zeno*. This was followed by *Carlo Giuliani, ragazzo* (*Carlo Giuliani, Boy*, 2002), a **documentary** portrait of the young man killed by police at Genoa in 2002 during the violent protests against globalization. She subsequently directed a fifth feature, *Mi piace lavorare—Mobbing* (*I Like to Work—Mobbing*, 2004), a very socially committed film in which **Nicoletta Braschi** plays a single mother working in the corporate environment, subjected to the practice of "mobbing." The film was strongly praised, earning Nicoletta Braschi a nomination for the **Nastro d'argento** for Best Actress and itself winning the Special Prize of the Ecumenical Jury at the Berlin International Festival.

COMENCINI, LUIGI (1916–2007). Director and screenwriter. Although often characterized almost exclusively as one of the leading practitioners of the ***commedia all'italiana***, Comencini was an eclectic and versatile director whose production ranged widely from murder mysteries and family dramas to the farcical comedies of **Totò**. The two most constant features of his filmmaking, however, were a wry sense of humor and an abiding interest in children and their view of the world.

Comencini began writing film criticism while an architecture student in Milan. An early passion for collecting and preserving old films led to a conservation project, carried out with fellow students **Alberto Lattuada** and Mario Ferrari, which eventually resulted in the establishment of the Italian Cinematheque. After World War II he again worked as a film critic until he was able to finance *Bambini in città* (*Children in Cities*, 1946), a **documentary** about street kids in Milan living in the midst of the city's war ruins. The work was highly praised when it was screened at both the **Venice Festival** and Cannes and earned him his first **Nastro d'argento**. It also brought an offer from **Carlo Ponti** at **Lux Film** to direct his first feature, *Proibito rubare* (*Stealing Forbidden*, also known as as *Guagliò*, 1948), a sort of *Boys Town* set in Naples. The film's unfortunate lack of either critical or box office success prompted Comencini to accept a commission to direct one of Totò's early films, *L'imperatore di Capri* (*The Emperor of Capri*, 1949). This lighthearted farce was followed by the very different *Persiane chiuse* (*Behind Closed Shutters*, 1951) and *La tratta delle bianche* (*The White Slave Trade*, 1952), two dark social melodramas centered on crime and prostitution, both clearly influenced by American film noir. On the strength of his earlier work with children, Comencini was next invited to Switzerland to direct an adaptation of Johanna Spyri's classic childhood novel, *Heidi* (1953), although the film proved a dismal box office failure.

Comencini's fortunes would improve immeasurably, however, with his next film, *Pane, amore e fantasia* (*Bread, Love and Dreams*, 1953), a rural idyll starring **Vittorio De Sica** and the budding **Gina Lollobrigida** in the role of the beautiful country bumpkin that first brought her to public attention. The film was such an unexpected and overwhelming box office success that it immediately prompted Comencini to make its equally popular sequel, *Pane, amore e gelosia* (*Bread, Love and Jealousy*, 1954, also known as *Frisky*). There followed more gentle social satire in *La bella di Roma* (*The Belle of Rome*, 1955), *Mariti in città* (*Husbands in the City*, 1957), and *Mogli pericolose* (Dangerous Wives, 1958) before Comencini made what many regard as one of his finest films, *Tutti a casa* (*Everybody Go Home*, 1960). In the biting satirical register of what had by now become known as the *commedia all'italiana*, the film presented a disconcerting portrait of the chaotic aftermath of Italy's abrupt armistice with the Allies in September 1943, with **Alberto Sordi** providing one of his most endearing and moving performances as the hapless Lieutenant Innocenzi. After two other caustic comedies set in contemporary Italy, *A cavallo della tigre* (*On the Tiger's Back*, 1960) and *Il commissario* (*The Police Commissioner*, 1962), Comencini returned to the war period in more dramatic terms with his adaption of Carlo Cassola's famous **Resistance** novel *La ragazza di Bube* (*Bebo's Girl*, 1963). He then agreed to direct the fifth in the series of **Don Camillo** films, *Il compagno Don Camillo* (*Don Camillo in Moscow*, 1965), largely in order to be able to finance *L'incompreso* (*Misunderstood*, 1967), another film with children at its center, which earned him his first **David di Donatello** as well as a nomination for the Palme d'or. Bowing once again to commercial pressures, he next produced a spoof of the spy film then so much in vogue with *Italian Secret Service* (1968) and the taut murder thriller *Senza sapere nulla di lei* (Without Knowing Anything about Her, 1969) before returning to the theme of childhood with *Vocazione e prime esperienze di Giacomo Casanova veneziano* (*Giacomo Casanova: Childhood and Adolescence*, 1969). This exploration of the world from a child's point of view was continued even more systematically in a six-episode television documentary, *I bambini e noi* (We and the Children, 1970), and then culminated in the work for which he is perhaps most warmly remembered, *Le avventure di Pinocchio* (*The Adventures of Pinocchio*, 1971). The film Comencini distilled from the original five one-hour episodes made for television has continued to be widely regarded as the best-ever adaptation of Carlo Collodi's children's classic.

In the following years Comencini continued to produce a wide variety of films, from bittersweet social comedies such as *Lo scopone scientifico* (*The Scientific Cardplayer*, 1972) to the classic murder thriller *La donna della domenica* (*The Sunday Woman*, 1976). In the classic style of the *commedia all'italiana*, *L'ingorgo—una storia impossibile* (*Traffic Jam*, 1978) uncovered the social malaise of Italian affluence using the dramatic stratagem of an all-engulfing traffic jam. Comencini's best films from this later period, however, remained those that sought to present the child's point of view, as in *Voltati Eugenio* (*Eugenio*, 1980), *Un ragazzo di Calabria* (*A Boy in Calabria*, 1987), and his television adaptation of the schoolboy classic *Cuore* (*Heart*, 1984). Rather appropriately, his penultimate film, *Buon Natale, Buon anno* (*Merry Christmas, Happy New Year*, 1989) was the story of a contemporary retired couple who secretly elope in order to escape the busy lifestyle of their extended families and live out their last days together as anonymous lighthouse keepers. Comencini's final film, *Marcellino* (*Miracle of Marcellino*, 1992), was a remake of Ladislao Vajda's 1955 film in which an orphaned boy who lives with monks eventually finds true happiness in the arms of the Virgin Mary.

COMERIO, LUCA (1878–1940). Cameraman, director, producer. One of the great pioneers of the Italian film industry, Comerio had already made his mark as an enterprising young photographer when, in 1898, he began to work as cameraman for **Leopoldo Fregoli**. By 1907 he had set up his own film company in Milan, which was producing high-quality literary and theatrical adaptations (including *Hamlet* and the first version of Manzoni's classic novel *I promessi sposi* [*The Betrothed*]) as well as comic sketches and "actualities." In 1909 Comerio merged his company with the Società Anonima Fabbricazione Films Italiane (SAFFI), and a year later SAFFI-Comerio was transformed into **Milano Films**, which Comerio helped to equip with the best studio facilities in Europe at the time. Disagreement with the newly installed board of management, however, led Comerio to abandon the new company and to resurrect Comerio Film, with which he continued to produce newsreels and documentaries.

Comerio's **documentary** zeal led to many exploits and several life-threatening accidents. In 1911 he had himself tied to a plane in order to experiment with aerial action shots. In the same year he followed the Italian troops to Tripoli, risking life and limb in order to record battle scenes, and for most of World War I he served as official documentarist for the Italian army. At the end of the war he attempted to return to feature film production but without much success. Reverting to documentary filmmaking, he recorded, among other things, D'Annunzio's occupation of Fiume in 1919. None of this, however, was enough to keep the company afloat in the general crisis that overtook the Italian film industry in the early 1920s, and Comerio Film was officially liquidated in 1922. Comerio returned to photographic work and to editing the huge mass of documentary material he had filmed in previous years. In the 1930s, impoverished and unemployed, he applied unsuccessfully for work as a cameraman at the **LUCE**. In 1940, destitute and in poor mental health, he was admitted to a mental hospital, where he died.

Having long been forgotten, Comerio and his work were brought to public attention again in 1986 when Yervant Gianikian and Angela Ricci reedited material from the Comerio archives to produce the remarkable compilation film *Dal polo all'equatore* (*From the Pole to the Equator*).

COMMEDIA ALL'ITALIANA. Film genre. Comedy had always occupied a prominent place in Italian cinema, but from the late 1950s Italians began to see on their screens a new and more particular sort of comedy, which soon came to be known as *commedia all'italiana*, "comedy Italian style." This new comedy was characterized above all by a sharper and more caustic wit and a greater and more acknowledged sense of cynicism. Indeed, Italian film historians have repeatedly suggested that what most typifies this new form of comedy is that it comically inflects themes, characters, and situations that could otherwise easily have been treated in a tragic vein. Ebullient and effusive, continually dramatizing hopes and aspirations, the *commedia all'italiana* will nevertheless almost always lack that staple of traditional comedy, the happy ending.

This more incisive form of social comedy is generally taken to begin with **Mario Monicelli**'s *I soliti ignoti* (literally, "The Usual Unknowns," although more generally known in English as *Big Deal on Madonna Street*, 1958), a film about a bungled burglary attempt in Rome by a motley group of petty thieves who in their absurd pretensions and lovable incompetence represent many fundamental aspects of the Italian character in the postwar period. This was followed by a host of films that comically reflected—and, with amused cynicism, reflected on—the way in which the Italian character was both confronting and incorporating the fundamental social changes being wrought by the so-called Italian economic miracle. It is significant that what are thought to be the classics of the genre, films such as **Dino Risi**'s *Una vita difficile* (*A Difficult Life*, 1961), *Il sorpasso* (*The Easy Life*, 1962), and *I mostri* (*15 from Rome*, 1963), **Luciano Salce**'s *La voglia matta* (*Crazy Desire*, 1962), and **Vittorio De Sica**'s *Il boom* (The Boom, 1963), were all produced precisely during the period in which Italians were racing headlong toward consumerism on the back of Italy's economic boom. Having opened the satirical floodgates, however, the genre's corrosive wit and bemused cynicism could also be used to reinterpret Italian history in a less heroic key, as in Monicelli's *La grande guerra* (*The Great War*, 1959), **Luigi Comencini**'s *Tutti a casa* (*Everybody Go Home*, 1960), or Luciano Salce's *Il federale* (*The Fascist*, 1961). The more stolid mores of provincial, and especially southern, Italy were also sharply depicted and satirically derided in several other classics of the genre, particularly in **Pietro Germi**'s *Divorzio all'italiana* (*Divorce Italian Style*, 1961) and *Sedotta e abbandonata* (*Seduced and Abandoned*, 1963).

Regularly produced by the same combination of directors (Risi, Monicelli, Comencini, Salce, **Ettore Scola**) collaborating with screenwriters such as **Age e Scarpelli**, **Suso Cecchi D'Amico**, **Ennio De Concini**, **Rodolfo Sonego**, **Ruggeri Maccari**, and actors such as **Vittorio Gassman**, **Alberto Sordi**, **Nino Manfredi**, **Ugo Tognazzi**, **Marcello Mastroianni**, **Sandra Sandrelli**, and **Monica Vitti**, the genre flourished profusely until the early 1970s when it achieved what many believe to be its finest and most mature incarnation in Scola's *C'eravamo tanto amati* (*We All Loved Each Other So Much*, 1974). Following this high point, however, with Italian society having thoroughly incorporated all the elements which the *commedia all'italiana* had so mischievously sought to satirize, the genre began to grow stale and decline. After offering one last brilliant rogues' gallery in *I nuovi mostri* (*The New Monsters*, 1977), directed collaboratively by Scola, Monicelli, and Risi, the genre presented something like its own epitaph in Scola's *La terrazza* (*The Terrace*, 1980).

CORBUCCI, SERGIO (1927–1990). (Also worked under the names of Stanley Corbett and Gordon Wilson Jr.). Director and screenwriter. A prolific director who chose to work almost exclusively within the confines of the popular genres, Corbucci served an early apprenticeship as assistant to **Aldo Vergano** before beginning to direct melodramas and light musical comedies in the early 1950s. After collaborating on the screenplay of **Mario Bonnard**'s *Gli ultimi giorni di Pompei* (*The Last Days of Pompeii*, 1959), he vigorously embraced the **peplum** in the early 1960s, making several that are regarded as classics of the genre, including *Romolo e Remo* (*Duel of the Titans*, 1961) and *Maciste contro il vampiro* (*Goliath and the Vampires*, 1961). At the same time he also directed six of the films of the great comic actor **Totò**. By the mid-1960s, with *Minnesota Clay* (1963) and *Massacro al Grande Canyon* (*Massacre at Grand Canyon*, 1965), he had also helped to give birth to the **Western *all'italiana***. He would eventually make 14 Westerns in all, the most famous of which were *Django* (1966), with which he helped to launch the career of **Franco Nero**, and *Il grande silenzio* (*The Great Silence*, 1967), which gainfully drew on the talents of both Jean-Louis Trintignant and Klaus Kinsky.

With the **spaghetti Western** on the wane in the mid-1970s, Corbucci turned his attention to other genres. After an isolated attempt at the road movie with *Il bestione* (*The Beast*, 1974), he settled into a series of light comedies featuring popular actor-singers Adriano Celentano and Johnny Dorelli. Following two interesting variations on the *giallo*, *La mazzetta* (*The Payoff*, 1978), adapted from a novel by Attilio Veraldi, and *Giallo napoletano* (*Neapolitan Mystery*, 1979), an offbeat police thriller starring **Marcello Mastroianni**, he also directed one of the funnier **Bud Spencer** and **Terence Hill** movies, *Chi trova un amico trova un tesoro* (*A Friend Is a Treasure*, 1981). Corbucci continued writing and directing comedies throughout the 1980s, reuniting **Giancarlo Giannini** and **Mariangela Melato** in *Bello mio, bellezza mia* (*My Darling, My Dearest*, 1984) and providing **Alberto Sordi** with one of his most bizarre roles in *Sono un fenomeno paranormale* (*I Am an ESP*, 1985). His last film, *Nightclub* (1989), attempted, but with only limited success, to recapture the times and the atmosphere of **Federico Fellini**'s *La dolce vita* (1960).

CORSICATO, PAPPI (1960–). Director, composer, scenographer, video artist. Corsicato studied dance and choreography in the United States before serving his first apprenticeship in filmmaking, working as an uncredited assistant on Pedro Almodóvar's *¡Átame!* (*Tie Me Up! Tie Me Down!* 1990). In 1991 he made a feature short to which, two years later, he added another two episodes to construct his first full-length film, *Libera* (1993). Featuring Iaia Forte, a dynamic actress whom Corsicato would continue to use in most of his subsequent films, *Libera* was shown to great acclaim at the Berlin Festival and in Italy was awarded both a Ciak d'oro and a **Nastro d'argento** as a most promising first work. Two years later *I buchi neri* (*Black Holes*, 1995) mixed realism and fantasy to present an unusual love story between a prostitute and a gay truck driver. At the same time Corsicato produced a number of videos on the work of artists Mimmo Paladino and Jannis Kounellis, as well as *Argento puro* (*Pure Silver*, 1996), a **documentary** on the making of **Marco Ferreri**'s last film, *Nitrato d'argento* (*Silver Nitrate*, 1996). In 1997 Corsicato directed

La stirpe di Iana (Iana's Descendants), an episode of the compilation film *I vesuviani* (*The Vesuvians*, 1997), made in collaboration with four other young Neapolitan directors. After *I colori della città celeste* (*The Colors of the Celestial City*, 1998), a short film focusing on an installation by Italian artist Mario Merz in the Piazza del Plebiscito in Naples, and a series of documentaries on artists Gilberto Zorio, Luigi Ontani, Robert Rauschenberg, Riccardo Serra, and Mimmo Paladino, Corsicato returned to fictional filmmaking with *Chimera* (2001), a complex and multilayered narrative of the chimerical strategies enacted by a couple in order to reignite their flagging sexual passion.

COTTAFAVI, VITTORIO (1914–1998). Director and screenwriter. A prolific director who achieved success working mostly in the popular genres, Cottafavi began his film career as a screenwriter on **Goffredo Alessandrini**'s *Abuna Messias* (*Cardinal Messias*, 1939) before serving as an assistant to several other more established directors, including working with **Vittorio De Sica** on *I bambini ci guardano* (*The Children Are Watching Us*, 1943). He made his directorial debut with *I giorni nostri* (*Our Days*, 1943), an elegant **white telephone** comedy, adapted from a play by Ugo Betti with De Sica acting in the lead role.

In the immediate postwar period he made a number of socially committed melodramas that sympathetically highlighted the condition of women, among them *Una donna ha ucciso* (*A Woman Has Killed*, 1952), *In amore si pecca in due* (*It Takes Two to Sin in Love*, 1954), and *Una donna libera* (*A Free Woman*, 1956). However, Cottafavi achieved much greater popular success with escapist historical fantasy adventures such as *Il boia di Lilla* (*Milady and the Musketeers*, 1952) and *Il cavalliere di Maison Rouge* (*The Glorious Avenger*, 1953), both stylish adaptations of swashbuckling novels by Alexandre Dumas. In the late 1950s he began to specialize in the **peplum** and made half a dozen sword-and-sandal epics, including two that are generally considered to be classics of the strongman genre, *La vendetta di Ercole* (*Hercules' Revenge*, 1960, also known in the United States as *Goliath and the Dragon*) and *Ercole alla conquista di Atlantide* (*Hercules and the Conquest of Atlantis*, 1961). Following the lack of success of what many regard as his best film, *I cento cavalieri* (*Hundred Horsemen*, 1965, also known as *The Son of El Cid*), an adventure fantasy that self-consciously utilized Brechtian techniques to highlight the futility of war and the arrogance of power, he largely retired from the cinema to work in television, where he became well known for his fine adaptations of literary and theatrical works, among them six of G. K. Chesterton's *Father Brown* stories (1970–1971) and a version of Molière's *School for Wives* (1973), and a science fiction series titled *A come Andromeda* (*A for Andromeda*, 1972). His last credited work was a much-admired adaptation of Cesare Pavese's novel *Il diavolo sulle colline* (*The Devil in the Hills*, 1985).

CRETINETTI. Character. With a name meaning, literally, "Little Cretin," Cretinetti was the comic character created by **André Deed** for **Itala Film** in Turin between 1909 and the early 1920s. The character, known as Foolshead in English, Gribouille in French, Toribio in Spanish, and Glupyškin in Russian, became so overwhelmingly popular, both in Italy and abroad, that frequently the company was able to sell the films sight unseen to willing distributors worldwide.

Hilariously innocent and athletic but also manic and pernicious, Cretinetti was, in the words of one film historian, "the gymnast of destruction." In fact, what most characterizes the Cretinetti films is a completely gratuitous sense of explosive anarchy. Cretinetti gleefully destroys everything around him and indeed at times comes to be destroyed himself. In *Cretinetti e le donne* (*Cretinetti and the Women*), made in 1908, Cretinetti is a sharp dresser who ignites the violent desire of every woman he passes. He is thus pursued relentlessly through the countryside by a female mob that eventually reaches him and tears him to pieces. Predictably, as the maenads leave, Cretinetti's body parts come together again. The early series of Cretinetti films were concerted exercises in a wild, surreal humor that in some ways anticipated the hectic chaos of the Keystone Kops, but the comedy of a film like *Cretinetti e gli aeroplani nemici* (*Cretinetti and the Enemy Airplanes*, 1915), made during World War I, is darker and more ominous. Deed attempted to revive the character in the early 1920s with less success, although by then his character's name had entered popular Italian usage as a synonym for idiocy.

CRISTALDI, FRANCO (1924–1992). Producer. One of the most outstanding producers of the Italian postwar cinema, Cristaldi began in the industry in 1946 when he founded the Vides Cinematografica. He had soon produced some 50 high-quality documentaries and short films before helping to write and produce *La pattuglia sperduta* (*The Lost Patrol*, 1953), the interesting first feature by Piero Nelli. Then, during the next four decades, consistently demonstrating foresight and fine judgment, Cristaldi produced the first films of a host of young directors who would become the great names of Italian cinema, among them **Francesco Rosi**, **Gillo Pontecorvo**, **Marco Bellocchio**, **Elio Petri**, and **Francesco Maselli**. As well as actively promoting new talent at all levels—he was responsible for the emergence of **Claudia Cardinale**, whom he would later marry—he also worked with established directors such as **Luchino Visconti** to make *Le notti bianche* (*White Nights*, 1957) and **Federico Fellini** on *Amarcord* (1973). He gained his first great box office success in Italy with **Mario Monicelli**'s *I soliti ignoti* (*Big Deal on Madonna Street*, 1958) but went on to achieve international renown with **Pietro Germi**'s *Divorzio all'italiana* (*Divorce Italian Style*, 1961), which received the comedy prize at Cannes, two Golden Globes, and the Academy Award for Best Screenplay. In 1969 he mounted the first Italo-Soviet coproduction to make Mikhail Kalatozov's *Krasnaya palatka* (*The Red Tent*, 1969) before also producing Louis Malle's *Lacombe Lucien* (1973). In the 1980s, with the Vides renamed Cristaldifilm, he again achieved great box office success with his coproduction of Jean-Jacques Annaud's *The Name of the Rose* (1986) before being responsible for the reedited version of **Giuseppe Tornatore**'s *Nuovo cinema Paradiso* (*Cinema Paradiso*, 1988), which would win the Oscar for Best Foreign Film in 1990. His last production was another first film by an emerging director, Carlo Carlei's *La corsa dell'innocente* (*The Flight of the Innocent*, 1993), nominated for the Golden Globe for Best Foreign Film.

CUCINOTTA, MARIA GRAZIA (1968–). Actress. The very image of the dark-eyed, black-haired, and curvaceous Mediterranean beauty, Cucinotta began her acting career as one of the showgirls in Renzo Arbore's popular television variety show, *Indietro tutta* (*All Behind*, 1987–1988). Her first film experience was a small role in

Enrico Oldoini's *Vacanze di Natale 90* (*Christmas Vacation '90*, 1990). After more television work and a long line of commercials, including one directed by Ridley Scott in which she appeared with Gérard Depardieu, she came to international notice through the huge worldwide success of Michael Radford's *Il postino* (*The Postman*, 1994), in which she played the female lead. She subsequently played more substantial roles in **Leonardo Pieraccioni**'s *I laureati* (*Graduates*, 1995) and **Maurizio Ponzi**'s *Italiani* (*Italians*, 1996), as well as appearing in quite a number of international productions including Alex de la Iglesia's comic **horror** thriller, *El dìa de la bestia* (*The Day of the Beast*, 1995), Michael Aptedt's James Bond adventure, *The World Is Not Enough*, and Alfonso Arau's black comedy, *Picking Up the Pieces* (2000). More recently she has also served as producer for the multistory film *All the Invisible Children* (2005).

– D –

DAMIANI, DAMIANO (1922–). Screenwriter and director. After studying painting at the Brera Academy, Damiani made documentaries and worked as a screenwriter before directing his first feature film, *Il rossetto* (*Lipstick*, 1960), a tense and very effective police thriller, which he quickly followed with *Il sicario* (*The Hit Man*, 1960). He subsequently scripted and directed several fine literary adaptations, including *L'isola di Arturo* (*Arturo's Island*, 1961), from a novel by Elsa Morante, and *La noia* (*The Empty Canvas*, 1962), before dabbling in most of the major genres, with comedies such as *La rimpatriata* (*The Reunion*, 1963) and **spaghetti Westerns** such as *Quién sabe?* (*A Bullet for the General*, 1967). Forays into the gothic, as in *La strega in amore* (*The Witch in Love*, 1966), and a strong affinity with American cinema eventually led to his directing *Amityville II: The Possession* (1982) in the United States.

Although his production continued to be varied, he became best known for taut police and Mafia thrillers such as *Confessioni di un commissario di polizia al procuratore della repubblica* (*Confessions of a Police Captain*, 1971) and *Un uomo in ginocchio* (*A Man on His Knees*, 1978), and especially for the first series of the enormously popular television miniseries on the Mafia, *La piovra* (1983). Subsequent films, such as the historical drama *Quel treno per Pietrogrado* (*Lenin: The Train*, 1992) and *L'angelo con la pistola* (*Angel with a Gun*, 1992), were also done for television. In the early 1970s Damiani also distinguished himself as an actor, playing a significant supporting role in **Florestano Vancini**'s historical drama *Il delitto Matteotti* (*The Assassination of Matteotti*, 1973).

DAVID DI DONATELLO. Prize. Instituted in 1955 under the aegis of the Open Gate Club and the Club Internazionale del Cinema (International Cinema Club)—voluntary associations formed in the early 1950s with the aim of encouraging Italian cinema and raising its profile abroad—the David di Donatello prize has effectively become the Italian equivalent of the American Academy Awards. The name of the award derives from the golden replica of the young David sculpted by Donatello that is given each year to winners across a number of categories. The first Davids awarded in 1956 in Rome, under the patronage of the President of the Republic, were awarded to Gianni Franciolini as Best Director for *Racconti romani* (*Roman Stories*), **Vittorio De Sica** as Best Actor in *Pane, amore e . . .* (*Scandal in Sorrento*), and **Gina Lollobrigida** as Best Actress in *La donna più bella del mondo* (*The World's Most Beautiful Woman*). The first David for Best Foreign Film went to the Walt Disney studios for its *Lady and the Tramp*.

The award ceremony was shifted to Taormina in 1957, and in 1958 the strong but unofficial support that had been shown for the awards by the Associazione Generale Italiana dello Spettacolo (AGIS, General Italian Association for Entertainment) and the **Associazione Nazionale Industrie Cinematografiche e Affini** (ANICA, National Association of Cinematographic and Affiliated Industries) was ratified, with both associations becoming the official promoters of the David, which from then on has been legally administered by the Ente David (the David Authority).

In subsequent years a number of new categories were added: between 1973 and 1983 a David was awarded for the best European film and between 1976 and 1995 a Premio David "Luchino Visconti" was also presented to distinguished directors. In any particular year any number of Special Davids may be awarded, over and above the usual categories, as was done in 1999 when **Sophia Loren** was given a Career David in recognition of lifetime achievement.

DE BENEDETTI, ALDO (1892–1970). Playwright and screenwriter. Already an established playwright, De Benedetti began working as a screenwriter in 1923 when he scripted the first Italian-Indian coproduction, *Savitri Satyavan* (*Savitri*, 1923), directed by Giorgio Mannini. He subsequently worked on the screenplays of dozens of films, many adapted from his own stage comedies, although his contributions after 1938 were often uncredited due to the race laws that prohibited Jews from working in the industry. One outstanding achievement during this period was his collaboration with Piero Tellini and **Cesare Zavattini** on the screenplay of **Alessandro Blasetti**'s *Quattro passi fra le nuvole* (*A Stroll through the Clouds*, 1942).

At the end of the war he returned officially to the industry with the story and screenplay of the aptly titled *La vita ricomincia* (*Life Begins Anew*, 1945), directed by **Mario Mattoli**. After adapting Vittorio Bersezio's play for **Mario Soldati**'s *Le miserie del Signor Travet* (*His Young Wife*, 1945), and collaborating with the very young **Suso Cecchi D'Amico** on **Renato Castellani**'s *Mio figlio professore* (*Professor, My Son*, 1947), he went on to work on the extremely successful series of tear-jerking melodramas directed by **Raffaele Matarazzo**, which included *Catene* (*Chains*, 1949), *Chi è senza peccato* (Whoever Is Without Sin, 1952) and *L'angelo bianco* (The White Angel, 1955).

Although De Benedetti himself gradually retired from the cinema during the 1960s, some of his stage comedies and stories continued to be adapted for the screen by both Italian and European directors. In the course of his long writing career he also directed one film, *Anita o il romanzo d'amore dell'eroe dei due mondi* (*Anita*, 1927), a costume drama that featured the diva Rina De Liguoro as the companion and lover of Italian **Risorgimento** hero Giuseppe Garibaldi.

DE CONCINI, ENNIO (1923–). Screenwriter. One of the most prolific and versatile of Italian screenwriters, De Concini began his career in films as assistant director and cowriter of **Vittorio De Sica**'s *Sciuscià* (*Shoe-Shine*, 1946). He subsequently wrote or cowrote the screenplays of approximately 150 films, moving easily between the commercialism of the popular genres and the artistic demands of auteurist cinema. He was particularly prolific in the **peplum**, helping to write many of the classics of the genre, including **Pietro Francisci**'s *Le fatiche di Ercole* (*Hercules*, 1957) and *Ercole e la regina di Lidia*

(*Hercules Unchained*, 1958) and **Riccardo Freda**'s *Maciste all'inferno* (*Maciste in Hell*, 1962). He also helped to launch the **horror** genre by writing **Mario Bava**'s seminal *La maschera del demonio* (*Black Sunday*, 1960) and the film that is regarded as marking the birth of the *giallo*, *La ragazza che sapeva troppo* (*The Girl Who Knew Too Much*, 1962). At the same time he also worked with many of the up-and-coming auteurs, collaborating with **Michelangelo Antonioni** on *Il grido* (*The Cry*, 1957), with **Gillo Pontecorvo** on *La grande strada azzurra* (*The Wide Blue Road*, 1957), and with **Pietro Germi** on *Un maledetto imbroglio* (*The Facts of Murder*, 1959), for which he shared a **Nastro d'argento**. He scored his greatest triumph, however, with the story and screenplay of Germi's *Divorzio all'italiana* (*Divorce Italian Style*, 1961), for which he received both a Silver Ribbon and an Academy Award.

He continued to turn out scripts in subsequent years, working with **Luciano Salce** on *La pecora nera* (*The Black Sheep*, 1968) and *Colpo di stato* (*Coup d'État*, 1968) and **Dino Risi** on *Operazione San Gennaro* (*The Treasure of San Gennaro*, 1966). He also coscripted Edward Dmytryk's *Bluebeard* (1972), which starred Richard Burton and Raquel Welch. From the mid-1980s he began to work extensively for Italian television, writing, among other things, three of the enormously popular *Piovra* (*Octopus*) series on the Mafia. Concini also directed two films himself, *Daniele e Maria* (*Daniele and Maria*, 1972), a film that attempted to highlight the plight of the mentally handicapped, and *Hitler, gli ultimi dieci giorni* (*Hitler: The Last Ten Days*, 1973), which starred Alec Guiness as a close approximation of the führer.

DE FILIPPO, EDUARDO (1900–1984). Playwright, actor, and director. Illegitimate son of the the much-renowned Neapolitan actor and director Eduardo Scarpetta, De Filippo first appeared on stage at the age of four. He continued to play small parts with the Scarpetta Company until he was sent away to study in college. Having completed his studies, he joined the Scarpetta Company again until 1920, when he was called up for military service. Following his discharge, he gained experience working with many of the other established theater companies in Naples before joining with his brother **Peppino** and his sister **Titina** in forming their own family company in 1931.

Appropriately, De Filippo made his debut in cinema playing a theatrical impressario in **Mario Bonnard**'s *Tre uomini in frac* (*I Sing for You Alone*, 1932), which also featured the famed tenor Tito Schipa. The film was not a great success but Eduardo and Peppino then went on to star in the extremely popular *Il cappello a tre punte* (*The Three-Cornered Hat*, 1934), a Neapolitan transposition of the novella by Pedro de Alarcon, directed by **Mario Camerini**. Eduardo acted, once again with Peppino, in **Gennaro Righelli**'s *Quei due* (*Those Two*, 1935), adapted from one of his own plays, and then the brothers were joined by Titina in **Raffaello Matarazzo**'s *Sono stato io!* (*It Was I!* 1937).

After a first and unsuccessful attempt at directing *In campagna è caduta una stella* (*In the Country Fell a Star*, 1939), Eduardo appeared on the screen again, together with his brother, in two films directed by **Carlo L. Bragaglia**: *Non ti pago!* (I'm Not Paying, 1942) and *Casanova farebbe così* (*After Casanova's Fashion*, 1942). He tried his hand at directing again in 1944 with *Ti conosco mascherina!* (You Can't Fool Me! 1944) but once more met with a tepid response. In the immediate postwar period, Eduardo appeared in many films, beginning as the kind professor in **Mario Mattoli**'s *La vita ricomincia* (*Life Begins Anew*, 1945) and then playing the violent, jealous lover in Mattoli's remake of the silent classic melodrama *Assunta Spina* (*Scarred*, 1948). There followed what many regard as his best films as director: *Napoli milionaria* (*Side Street Story*, 1950), *Filumena Marturano* (1951), and *Questi fantasmi* (*These Phantoms*, 1954), all successful transpositions of his own stage plays. His direction began to wane with *Fortunella* (1958), scripted by **Ennio Flaiano** and **Tullio Pinelli** from a story written by **Federico Fellini** and starring **Giulietta Masina**, but which, in the event, only succeeded, in the words of one critic, in being "Fellinian without Fellini." When *Spara forte, più forte . . . non ti sento* (*Shoot Loud, Louder . . . I Don't Understand*, 1966), which had been adapted from one of his own plays, was also savaged by the critics, De Filippo abandoned the big screen in order to return to the stage. He did, however, subsequently direct a series of very popular television adaptations of all his major plays.

DE FILIPPO, PEPPINO (1903–1980). Actor and playwright. Illegitimate son of renowned Neapolitan actor Eduardo Scarpetta, and younger brother of **Eduardo** and **Titina**, Peppino began acting at the age of six in the company of Vincenzo Scarpetta in Rome, playing the part of Peppeniello in *Miseria e nobiltà* (*Poverty and Nobility*). For the next two decades he worked with many of the leading theatrical companies in both Rome and Naples. In 1931 he joined Eduardo and Titina in forming the Compagnia Teatro Umoristico i De Filippo (The De Filippo Comic Theater Company), which became one of the most successful dialect theater companies in Italy during the interwar period, performing a repertoire composed mostly of plays written by Peppino and Eduardo themselves. A falling-out between the brothers led to the dissolution of the family company in 1944, following which Peppino formed his own troupe with which he performed and toured widely throughout Europe and South America until the mid-1970s.

Peppino made his debut in cinema together with brother Eduardo in *Tre uomini in frac* (*I Sing for You Alone*, 1932), directed by **Mario Bonnard**, soon followed by **Mario Camerini**'s *Il capello a tre punte* (*The Three-Cornered Hat*, 1934), where he played the major role of Luca, the miller. He subsequently appeared, usually in strong supporting parts, in dozens of films, including **Raffaele Matarazzo**'s *Il Marchese di Ruvolito* (*The Marquis of Ruvolito*, 1938) and Mario Bonnard's *Campo de' Fiori* (1943). In the postwar period he continued to alternate between stage and screen. He played the male lead in **Federico Fellini**'s first film (codirected with **Alberto Lattuada**), *Luci del varietà* (*Variety Lights*, 1950), and gave a brilliant performance as the repressed and moralistic bigot of *Le tentazioni del dottor Antonio* (*The Temptations of Dr. Antonio*, 1962), the episode Fellini contributed to *Boccaccio '70* (1962). He is probably remembered most fondly, however, for consistently playing the foil to the great comic actor **Totò**, appearing in no fewer than 14 films, including *Totò, Peppino e . . . la malafemmina* (*Totò, Peppino, and the Hussy*, 1956), *Totò, Peppino e la dolce vita* (*Totò, Peppino and La Dolce Vita*, 1961), and *Totò, Peppino e . . . i fuorilegge* (*Totò, Peppino and the Outlaws*, 1956), for which he received a **Nastro d'argento** as best supporting actor.

In the 1960s he was also frequently seen on television, appearing as "Peppino cuoco sopraffino" (Peppino the most refined cook) in a very popular advertisement shown on *Carosello* between 1959 and

1963, and as Gaetano Pappagone, a comic character in the variety show *Scala Reale* (*Royal Straight*), broadcast in 1966. His final appearance on the big screen was as **Marcello Mastroianni**'s gambling-addicted father in **Sergio Corbucci**'s comic murder mystery *Giallo napoletano* (*Neapolitan Thriller*, 1978).

DE FILIPPO, TITINA (1898–1965). Actress and playwright. Illegitimate daughter of renowned Neapolitan actor Eduardo Scarpetta, and elder sister of **Eduardo** and **Peppino De Filippo**, Titina (Annunziata) began acting on stage at the age of seven. She was soon a member of the Teatro Nuovo di Napoli, performing regularly in its musical revues and variety shows. In 1931 she united with her two brothers to form the Compagnia Teatro Umoristico i De Filippo (The De Filippo Comic Theater Company), and in partnership with Peppino wrote many of the plays in the company's repertoire, the best known being *Quaranta ma non li dimostra* (Forty Years Old but It Doesn't Show) and *Ma c'è papà* (But Daddy's Here). Together with the two brothers she also appeared in films in the late 1930s, but her first significant film role was as **Totò**'s fiery wife, Concetta, in Amleto Palermi's *San Giovanni Decollato* (*St. John the Baptist Beheaded*, 1940). After World War II, while continuing to work to great acclaim on the stage, she appeared in some 30 films, usually in strong supporting roles. However, she also gave a memorable performance playing the lead in *Filumena Marturano* (1951), a film adaptation of the stage play that her brother Eduardo had written for her several years earlier. In addition to playing her character roles, she also worked as a screenwriter and shared a **Nastro d'argento** in 1952 for her collaboration on the screenplay of **Renato Castellani**'s *Due soldi di speranza* (*Two Cents' Worth of Hope*, 1952).

DE LAURENTIIS, DINO (1919–). The son of a pasta manufacturer, Dino (originally Agostino) De Laurentiis studied acting at the **Centro Sperimentale di Cinematografia** before playing a number of small parts in **Mario Camerini**'s *Batticuore* (*Heartbeat*, 1939) and *I grande magazzini* (*Department Store*, 1939). In 1940, having founded Realcine, he produced his first film, *L'ultimo combattimento* (*The Last Fight*), directed by Pietro Ballerini.

After the war he moved to **Lux Film** and scored his first major success as executive producer of **Giuseppe De Santis's** *Riso amaro* (*Bitter Rice*, 1949), whose female star, **Silvana Mangano**, he would marry in 1949. In 1950 he teamed up with **Carlo Ponti** to create the Ponti-De Laurentiis company, whose studios produced the first Italian color film, *Totò a colori* (*Totò in Color*, 1952). De Laurentiis subsequently oversaw the production of some of the most notable films of the immediate postwar period including **Vittorio De Sica's** *L'oro di Napoli* (*The Gold of Naples*, 1954) and **Federico Fellini's** *La strada* (1954) and *Le notti di Cabiria* (*The Nights of Cabiria*, 1957), both of which won Oscars for Best Foreign Film.

The partnership with Ponti dissolved in the mid-1950s, prompting De Laurentiis to set up on the outskirts of Rome his own studios, which he named, with only a touch of hubris, Dinocittà. The studio achieved some success with blockbusters such as John Huston's *The Bible* (1966) and Edward Dmytryk's *Anzio* (1968) but eventually became economically unviable and De Laurentiis was forced to sell. Consequently, in 1973, he moved to the United States, where he produced a series of critically acclaimed films that included *Three Days of the Condor* (directed by Sidney Lumet, 1975), *Ragtime* (directed by Milos Forman, 1981), and *Blue Velvet* (directed by David Lynch, 1986). He was also responsible, however, for a number of expensive flops, such as *Hurricane* (directed by Jan Troell, 1979) and *Dune* (directed by David Lynch, 1984). In 1984 he attempted once again to set up a new megastudio, this time under the name of De Laurentiis Entertainment Group (DEG), but the venture was short lived and the studio soon folded.

After the death of Mangano, with whom he had four children, De Laurentiis married Martha Schumaker in 1990 and together they continued to produce films, the most notable of which has been Ridley Scott's *Hannibal* (2001). Having already garnered a host of international prizes and much recognition during his 60-year career, in 2001 De Laurentiis was awarded an Oscar for lifetime achievement.

DE SANTIS, GIUSEPPE (1917–1997). Critic, screenwriter, director. Widely acknowledged as one of the founding fathers of **neorealism**, De Santis enrolled in directing at the **Centro Sperimentale di Cinematografia** in 1941 and was soon one of the leading critical voices in the journal *Cinema*, which advocated a greater sense of realism in Italian films. This advocacy was put into practice in 1942 when he collaborated on the script and served as assistant director on the film that is generally regarded as the immediate forebearer of neorealism, **Luchino Visconti**'s *Ossessione* (*Obsession*, 1943).

In the immediate postwar period De Santis collaborated with **Mario Serandrei**, Luchino Visconti, **Gianni Puccini**, and others on the partisan **documentary** *Giorni di Gloria* (*Days of Glory*, 1945). He then made his directorial debut with *Caccia tragica* (*Tragic Hunt*, 1947), a film about the last days of the **Resistance** movement financed by the National Partisan Association (ANPI). A year later he achieved what would remain the greatest success of his career with *Riso amaro* (*Bitter Rice*, 1949), a film that daringly mixed a neorealist preoccupation with contemporary social conditions with the more popular elements of the American crime film and tragic melodrama. The film broke all box office records, launched the career of **Silvana Mangano**, and introduced a new upfront eroticism into Italian cinema. Despite his strongly theoretical background as a critic, De Santis proved to be an extremely eclectic director, making a wide range of films that included pastoral melodramas such as *Non c'è pace tra gli ulivi* (*No Peace under the Olive Tree*, 1950), urban neorealist chronicles such as *Roma ore 11* (*Rome 11:00*, 1952), the romantic rural fable of *Giorni d'amore* (*Days of Love*, 1954), and the epic *Italiani brava gente* (*Attack and Retreat*, 1964), a masterful re-creation of the disastrous rout of the Italian army in Russia at the end of World War II. After this extraordinary film, and despite a host of projects, De Santis was strangely but consistently marginalized within the film industry. His only subsequent film, *Un apprezzato professionista di sicuro avvenire* (A Qualified Professional with an Assured Future, 1972), was very poorly received and generally panned. Nevertheless, after a long period of silence and neglect, his significant contribution to Italian cinema was finally recognized in 1995 when he was presented with a Golden Lion at the **Venice Festival** for his lifetime achievement.

DE SANTIS, PASQUALINO (1927–1996). Cinematographer. Brother of director **Giuseppe De Santis**, Pasquale (or Pasqualino, as he was most often known) studied at the **Centro Sperimentale di**

Cinematografia before working as assistant cameraman for Piero Portalupi on a number of **Giuseppe De Santis**'s films during the early 1950s. He then worked as camera operator for **Gianni Di Venanzo** until Di Venanzo's death in 1966. His first solo film as director of photography was **Francesco Rosi**'s *Once upon a Time . . . (More Than a Miracle*, 1967) but only a year later he received an Academy Award for Best Cinematography for his work on **Franco Zeffirelli**'s *Romeo e Giulietta (Romeo and Juliet*, 1968).

In the years that followed he worked again with Rosi on all Rosi's major films, including *Il caso Mattei (The Mattei Affair*, 1972), *Lucky Luciano* (1974), and *Cadaveri eccellenti (Illustrious Corpses*, 1976) and photographed **Federico Fellini**'s *Block-notes d'un regista (Fellini: A Director's Notebook*, 1969). However, he appeared to provide the best proof of his brilliance as a cinematographer in the films he did with **Luchino Visconti**: *La caduta degli dei (The Damned*, 1969), *Morte a Venezia (Death in Venice*, 1971), *Gruppo di famiglia in un interno (Conversation Piece*, 1974), and *L'Innocente (The Innocent*, 1976). Internationally he also worked on a number of films with Robert Bresson, including *Lancelot du Lac* (1974) and *Le diable, probablement (The Devil, Probably*, 1977), and with Joseph Losey on *The Assassination of Trotsky* (1972). In 1995, together with his brother, Giuseppe, and fellow cinematographer **Giuseppe Lanci**, De Santis founded the Nuova Università del Cinema e della Televisione with a special scholarship established for cinematography. After a successful and prolific career, crowned with many prizes and awards, including the **Nastro d'argento** four times and two **David di Donatello**, De Santis died in Ukraine in 1996 on the set of Francesco Rosi's *La tregua (The Truce*, 1996).

DE SETA, VITTORIO (1923–). Director and screenwriter. Following an apprenticeship as assistant to French filmmaker Jean-Paul Le Chanois, in 1954 De Seta began making a series of prize-winning **documentary** films on the lives of fishermen and shepherds of both his native Sicily and Sardinia, which included *Lu tempu de li pisci spata (Swordfish Season*, 1954), *Sulfarara (Sulphur Mine*, 1955), *Pasqua in Sicilia (Easter in Sicily*, 1955), *Contadini del mare (Farmers of the Sea*, 1955), and *Pastori di Orgosolo (Shepherds of Orgosolo*, 1958). Socially committed but also highly lyrical documentaries, they demonstrate the strong influence of Robert Flaherty. This influence was carried over into his first fictional feature, *I banditi di Orgosolo* (*Bandits at Orgosolo*, 1961), made in collaboration with his wife but produced, photographed, and edited by De Seta himself. The film presents, with compassion but without sentimentality, the tragic plight of a poor shepherd forced by circumstances to become a bandit and to lose all his sheep, one by one. The film's austere lyricism earned De Seta the prize for a first work at the **Venice Festival** in 1961 and a **Nastro d'argento** for photography.

In 1965 he made his second fictional feature, *Un uomo a metà* (*Almost a Man*), the moving portrayal of a young writer's descent into madness. After a third feature, *L'invitata* (*The Uninvited*, 1969), he produced *Diario di un maestro* (*A Teacher's Diary*, 1973), a four-episode miniseries for television that ignited great discussion and controversy regarding the Italian school system. There followed two other documentaries for Italian television, *Hong Kong, città di profughi* (*Hong Kong, City of Refugees*, 1980) and *In Calabria*, a three-part documentary for Raidue made in 1993. After a long absence, De Seta returned to Sicily in 2002 to make a documentary on the life and work of anthropologist Antonino Uccello.

DE SICA, VITTORIO (1902–1974). Stage and screen actor, director, and screenwriter. One of Italy's most prolific but also best-loved actor-directors, De Sica was born in Sora, a small town south of Rome, but spent his earliest years in Naples, hence his lifelong affinity for the city. In 1914 the De Sica family moved to Rome, where the young Vittorio studied to become an accountant. In 1923, while working at the Bank of Italy and largely at the urging of a close friend, he applied to fill a vacancy with the theater company of Tatiana Pavlova and, to his own surprise, was accepted. Having served his stage apprenticeship covering a wide range of character parts, including clowns and old men, in 1925 he transferred to the company of Luigi Almirante, where he specialized in playing the romantic lead in sentimental comedies, before moving, in 1927, to play similar roles in the company of Almirante-Rissone-Tofano. From 1931 to 1933 he appeared in many of the musical revues staged by the Za Bum company under the direction of **Mario Mattoli**. In 1933, together with Umberto Melnati and actress Giuditta Rissone, whom he would eventually marry, he formed his own theater company, which produced comic revues and melodramas but also hosted up-and-coming young guest directors such as **Luchino Visconti**.

By this time De Sica had also begun to act in films. After an isolated early appearance in Edoardo Bencivenga's *L'Affaire Clémenceau* (*The Clémenceau Affair*, 1918) and some undistinguished supporting parts in several minor films in the late 1920s, he achieved almost instant star status playing the male lead in **Mario Camerini**'s *Gli uomini che mascalzoni* (*What Scoundrels Men Are!* 1932), a role that established the nice boy-next-door image that would characterize him in the following years. The song "Parlami d'amore Mariù" ("Sing to Me of Love, Maria"), which he casually sang in the film, was released separately and became a big hit on the radio, generating an even wider popularity. He subsequently appeared in a host of films, the most memorable being the handful of light comedies and social melodramas directed by Camerini, where he was frequently paired with the most prominent female star of the time, **Assia Noris**, as in *Darò un milione* (*I'll Give a Million*, 1936), *Il signor Max* (*Mister Max*, 1937), and *I grandi magazzini* (*Department Store*, 1939).

In the early 1940s, while continuing to divide his time between stage and screen, De Sica started to direct films, beginning with several sentimental comedies in the **white telephone** vein, *Rose scarlatte* (*Red Roses*, 1940), *Maddalena zero in condotta* (*Maddalena, Zero for Conduct*, 1940), and *Teresa Venerdì* (*Mademoiselle Friday*, 1941), and the historical romantic melodrama, *Un garibaldino al convento* (*A Garibaldian in the Convent*, 1942). His next film, *I bambini ci guardano* (*The Children Are Watching Us*, 1943), initiated an entirely new phase in his artistic development. A profoundly moving but wholly unsentimental study of a family breakup seen through the eyes of an eight-year-old child, *I bambini* was filmed in a more realistic style and, moreover, marked the beginning of De Sica's long and fruitful collaboration with screenwriter **Cesare Zavattini**. Their next film, *La porta del cielo* (*The Gate of Heaven*, 1945), the story of a pilgrimage to the Catholic shrine of Loreto, was made in Rome under considerable difficulty during the period of German occupation. Financed by the Vatican and produced by the Centro Cattolico di Cinematografia, the film continued in the more realistic style of the previous film but it also served the purpose of helping De Sica (and others) to avoid being forced to join the new studios that were being set up in Venice under the aegis of the Republic of Salò.

In the immediate postwar period, developing further the socially committed and realistic approach that by now had become his characteristic style, De Sica, always flanked by Zavattini, directed two films that would come to be regarded as landmarks of **neorealism**: *Sciuscià* (*Shoe-Shine*, 1946) and *Ladri di biciclette* (*Bicycle Thieves*, 1948), the latter universally hailed as a masterpiece of world cinema and winning, among a host of other prizes and awards, six **Nastri d'argento** and the Special Academy Award for Best Foreign Film. This, however, did not prevent De Sica's next film, *Miracolo a Milano* (*Miracle in Milan*, 1951), from being severely criticized by many left-wing Italian critics for its mix of fable and social realism, while *Umberto D* (1952), now generally recognized as one of the most perfect expressions of neorealist cinema, was pilloried by the Italian government itself for its unflattering portrayal of social conditions in postwar Italy.

Stazione Termini (*Indiscretion of an American Wife*, 1953), which De Sica directed and coproduced with David O. Selznick, was both a critical and box office flop, but the affectionate portrait of Naples in *L'oro di Napoli* (*The Gold of Naples*, 1954) revived De Sica's reputation and popularity as a director. By this stage, however, he had revived his star status as an actor with his portrayal of the comic philandering officer of the carabinieri in **Luigi Comencini**'s enormously popular *Pane, amore e fantasia* (*Bread, Love and Dreams*, 1953) and its similarly successful sequels *Pane, amore e gelosia* (*Bread, Love and Jealousy*, 1954, also known as *Frisky*) and *Pane, amore e . . .* (*Scandal in Sorrento*, 1955). He continued to appear in a host of both major and minor roles, often as a duplicitous but lovable old rogue, but his greatest performance during this period was undoubtedly as the title character of **Roberto Rossellini**'s Oscar-nominated *Il Generale della Rovere* (*General della Rovere*, 1959). The 1960s saw several more directorial triumphs, beginning with *La ciociara* (*Two Women*, 1960), the adaptation of a novel by Alberto Moravia that earned De Sica a nomination for the Golden Palm at Cannes and **Sophia Loren** an Oscar for her stirring performance. De Sica would direct Loren again, together with **Marcello Mastroianni**, in his two other triumphs of the 1960s, *Ieri, oggi, domani* (*Yesterday, Today and*

Tomorrow, 1963), which was awarded the Oscar for Best Foreign Film in 1965, and *Matrimonio all'italiana* (*Marriage Italian Style*, 1964), which received two Oscar nominations and the Golden Globe award for Best Foreign Film. After a handful of films that were generally judged inferior to what he had been able to achieve at his peak, De Sica regained his former brilliance with *Il giardino dei Finzi-Contini* (*The Garden of the Finzi-Continis*, 1970), an elegant and very moving adaptation of the elegiac novel by Giorgio Bassani that won, among a host of other prizes, the Oscar for Best Foreign Film and the Berlin Golden Bear Award. His last film, widely regarded as below par for a director who had made some of the greatest masterpieces of world cinema, paired Sophia Loren with Richard Burton in the romantic melodrama *Il viaggio* (*The Voyage*, 1974).

DEED, ANDRÉ (1879–1938). Actor, writer, director. Following an early career as a stage performer and sometime actor in the films of Georges Méliès, Deed (whose real name was André Chapuis or De Chapais) had become one of the Pathé studios' greatest stars with his creation of the popular comic character Boireau. Still at the peak of his fame, Deed was lured to Turin by a lucrative contract from **Giovanni Pastrone**, head of **Itala Film**. At Itala, Deed created the even more popular character of **Cretinetti**, the overwhelming success of which did much to solidify Itala's financial position (and thus help it, only a few years later, to finance *Cabiria*).

Deed assembled an energetic team around him that included actors Alberto Collo, **Emilio Ghione**, and Valentina Frascaroli (whom he later married), and was able to produce a film a week for over two years, films that were so popular they were bought sight unseen by distributors throughout Europe and America. In 1912 Deed broke his contract with Itala and returned to Paris to work for Pathé again but in 1914 was induced by legal threat to return to Turin, where he continued to make feature-length Cretinetti films, which included *La paura degli aeromobili nemici* (The Fear of the Enemy Airplanes, 1915) and the extremely popular *Cretinetti e gli stivali del brasiliano* (Foolshead and the Brazilian Boots, 1916). Following another brief period in France he returned in 1919 to Italy, where, after several other Cretinetti films, he made *L'uomo meccanico* (*The Mechanical*

Man, 1922), a much more ominous and curious mixture of comedy, crime, and science fiction that, with its two dueling robots, appears to anticipate certain elements of Fritz Lang's *Metropolis* (1927). Deed returned to Paris in 1923 and thereafter played small parts in a number of otherwise unremarkable films. With the coming of sound he retired completely from the film industry, preferring to work as a night watchman at the Pathé studios.

DEL POGGIO, CARLA (1925–). (Born Maria Luisa Attanasio.) Actress. Still in her teens, Del Poggio studied acting for a year at the **Centro Sperimentale di Cinematografia**, during which she came to the notice of **Vittorio De Sica**, who immediately cast her as the spirited young schoolgirl in *Maddalena zero in condotta* (*Maddalena, Zero for Conduct*, 1940) and then in a similar role in *Un garibaldino al convento* (*A Garibaldian in the Convent*, 1942). In 1945 she met, and soon after married, director **Alberto Lattuada**, who cast her in the role of the prostitute-sister of the protagonist of his gangster melodrama *Il bandito* (*The Bandit*, 1946). Del Poggio continued to take on dramatic roles in several of Lattuada's subsequent films, *Senza pietà* (*Without Pity*, 1948) and *Il mulino del Po* (*The Mill on the Po*, 1948), but reverted to a lighter vein in *Luci del varietà* (*Variety Lights*, 1951), which Lattuada coproduced and codirected with **Federico Fellini** and in which Del Poggio plays a pretty, aspiring stage actress who lures an infatuated **Peppino De Filippo** away from the plainer **Giulietta Masina**.

After strong performances in **Giuseppe De Santis**'s *Caccia tragica* (*Tragic Hunt*, 1947) and *Roma ore 11* (*Rome 11:00*, 1952), she also tried her hand at acting in stage revues, with a measure of success. However, her film career seemed to falter after this. She appeared in several minor French films and in *Cose da pazzi* (*Craziness*, 1953), a rather lackluster comedy directed by Georg Wilhelm Pabst, before making what would be her last film for the silver screen, Hugo Fregonese's *I girovaghi* (*The Wanderers*, 1956), where she shared top billing with Peter Ustinov. In the following years she appeared only in a small number of films made for televison, including a remake of the classic *Piccolo mondo antico* (*Old-Fashioned World*, 1957), and an Italian version of *David Copperfield* (1965).

DELLI COLLI, TONINO (1923–2005). Cinematographer. Delli Colli began his long career at **Cinecittà** in 1938, initially working as cameraman and assistant to **Ubaldo Arata** and **Anchise Brizzi**. His first film as director of photography was *Finalmente sì* (Finally Yes, 1944), a Titanus production in the line of the so-called **white telephone films**, directed by László Kish.

In the postwar period he photographed a number of otherwise unremarkable films before shooting the first Italian color film, *Totò a colori* (*Totò in Color*, 1952), directed by **Steno** and **Marie Monicelli**. After a host of undistinguished Italian-American productions, Delli Colli was recruited by **Pier Paolo Pasolini** for his first film, *Accattone* (*Accattone!* 1961). He subsequently served as director of photography on all of Pasolini's major films (12 in all) while at the same time also working with **Sergio Leone** on *Il buono, il brutto, il cattivo* (*The Good, the Bad and the Ugly*, 1966), *C'era una volta il West* (*Once upon a Time in the West*, 1968) and *C'era una volta in America* (*Once upon a Time in America*, 1982); with **Federico Fellini** on *Intervista* (*Interview*, 1986), *Ginger e Fred* (*Ginger and Fred*, 1985), and *Le voci della luna* (*The Voices of the Moon*, 1989); with **Lina Wertmüller** on *Pasqualino Settebellezze* (*Seven Beauties*, 1975); with **Mario Monicelli** on *I nuovi mostri* (*The New Monsters*, 1977); and with **Marco Ferreri** on *Storie di ordinaria follia* (*Tales of Ordinary Madness*, 1981). In 1994 he photographed **Roberto Benigni**'s Oscar-winning international success, *La vita è bella* (*Life Is Beautiful*, 1994). He also collaborated with many distinguished foreign directors, photographing Luis Malle's *Lacombe Lucien* (1974), Roman Polanski's *Bitter Moon* (1992) and *Death and the Maiden* (1994), and Jean-Jacques Annaud's *The Name of the Rose* (1986).

In a career that spanned more than 60 years, Delli Colli won four **David di Donatello** and six **Nastro d'argento** awards. In 2005, in recognition of his international standing, the American Society of Cinematographers also gave him their International Life Achievement Award.

DEODATO, RUGGERO (1939–). Screenwriter and director. After serving as assistant director for **Roberto Rossellini** on *Il Generale della Rovere* (*General della Rovere*, 1959) and *Era notte a Roma* (*Escape by Night*, 1960), Deodato worked across most of the popular genres, frequently collaborating as assistant or codirecting with **Antonio Margheriti** on films as different as the **peplum** *Ursus il terrore dei Kirghizi* (*Hercules, Prisoner of Evil*, 1964) and the minibudget science fiction fantasy *I criminali della galassia* (*Wild, Wild Planet*, 1965). On his own he directed (at times under the pseudonym Roger Rockefeller) exotic adventures, jungle films, musical comedies, Westerns, and police thrillers. He made his greatest mark, however, in the splatter-horror genre, achieving international cult status as "Mr. Cannibal" for his controversial and highly censored *Ultimo mondo cannibale* (*The Last Cannibal World*, 1977) and *Cannibal Holocaust* (*Ruggero Deodato's Cannibal Holocaust*, 1980), described as "the most savage and brutal film in modern history." From the late 1980s he has worked on much milder television fare, but in 2005 a *Cannibal Holocaust 2* was announced as being in preproduction.

DI GIANNI, LUIGI (1926–). Documentary filmmaker. Widely regarded as one of Italy's leading documentarists, Di Gianni graduated from the **Centro Sperimentale di Cinematografia** in 1954 with the short film *L'arresto* (The Arrest), a free adaptation of Franz Kafka's *The Trial* (*Der Prozess*), which was screened out of competition at the **Venice Festival** that year. He subsequently embarked on a series of evocative ethnographic documentaries focusing on life and customs in some of the poorer regions of southern Italy, beginning with *Nascita e morte nel meridione—San Cataldo* (Birth and Death in Southern Italy—San Cataldo, 1958), followed by *Magia lucania* (*Lucania Magic*, 1958), *Frana in Lucania* (*Landslide in Lucania*, 1959), *Donne di Bagnara* (*Women of Bagnara*, 1959), and *La punidura* (*The Punidura*, 1959).

In the 1960s, while continuing to document magical and ritual practices in provincial Italy, he also extended his sights to more historical and contemporary subjects, as in *Via Tasso* (*Tasso Street*, 1961), a documentary on the Nazi occupation of Rome, and *La tragedia del Vajont* (*The Tragedy of the Vajont*, 1964), an investigation into the 1963 dam disaster in northern Italy that caused close to 2,000 deaths. At the same time he directed a number of theatrical adaptations for television, among them versions of Samuel Beckett's *Krapp's Last Tape* and *Act without Words*, while his disturbing and oneiric *La tana* (The Lair, 1967) was nominated for the Palme d'or for Best Short Film at Cannes. His even more provocative full-length fictional feature *Il tempo dell'inizio* (*The Time of the Beginning*, 1974), a recounting (in black and white) of the dreams of an inmate of an insane asylum, earned him the **Nastro d'argento** for Best New Director. In 1988, while teaching at the Centro Sperimentale, he was awarded his second Nastro d'argento for his short documentary *L'arte del vetro* (*The Art of Glass*, 1987) and two years later he celebrated the memory of one of his old masters, **Cesare Zavattini**, in a one-hour documentary made for the **LUCE**. More recently he has documented the survival of maternal cults in *La madonna in cielo, la "matre" in terra* (The Madonna in Heaven, the Mother on Earth, 2006) while he himself has become the subject of *La malattia dell'arcobaleno* (The Rainbow Sickness, 2006), a documentary on his work directed by Simone Del Grosso.

DI PALMA, CARLO (1925–2004). Cinematographer. Widely regarded as one of the leading cinematographers of the entire postwar period, Di Palma studied at the **Centro Sperimentale di Cinematografia** while working as camera operator and assistant to **Aldo Tonti** on a number of films, including **Luchino Visconti**'s *Ossessione* (*Obsession*, 1943). After the war he served a further apprenticeship with many of the established cinematographers, including **Ubaldo Arata**, **Carlo Montuori**, and **Gianni Di Venanzo** before graduating to director of photography himself on **Florestano Vancini**'s remarkable first film, *La lunga notte del '43* (*The Long Night of '43*, 1960).

After establishing a solid reputation for his black-and-white photography on films such as **Elio Petri**'s *L'assassino* (*The Assassin*, 1961) and **Giuliano Montaldo**'s *Tiro al Piccione* (*Pigeon-Shoot*, 1961), Di Palma soared to international fame with his work on **Michelangelo Antonioni**'s first color film, *Il deserto rosso* (*The Red Desert*, 1964), reaffirmed two years later with *Blow-up* (1966). He subsequently contributed a very distinctive look to many of the films of the *commedia all'italiana*, working on, among others, **Mario Monicelli**'s *La ragazza con la pistola* (*Girl with a Pistol*, 1968), **Ettore Scola**'s *Dramma della gelosia* (*Jealousy, Italian Style*, 1970), and **Dino Risi**'s *Noi donne siamo fatte così* (*That's How We Women*

Are, 1971), before directing three films himself, all starring his then partner **Monica Vitti**: *Teresa la ladra* (*Teresa, the Thief*, 1972), adapted from a novel by Dacia Maraini; *Qui comincia l'avventura* (*Blonde in Black Leather*, 1975), a female road movie that in many ways uncannily anticipated Ridley Scott's *Thelma and Louise* (1991); and *Mimì Bluette, fiore del mio giardino* (*Mimì, Flower of My Garden*, 1977). Nevertheless, Di Palma will probably be best remembered for his stunning cinematography on many Woody Allen films, beginning with *Hannah and Her Sisters* (1984) and continuing through *Radio Days* (1986) and *Shadows and Fog* (1991) to *Mighty Aphrodite* (1995) and *Deconstructing Harry* (1996). During a distinguished career that spanned half a century and over 50 films, Di Palma won many prizes, including four **Nastri d'argento** and a BAFTA nomination. In 2003 he was also honored with the European Film Award for Achievement in World Cinema.

DI VENANZO, GIANNI (1920–1966). Cinematographer. One of the most respected cinematographers of the postwar period, Di Venanzo served an early apprenticeship as camera assistant to **Aldo Tonti** on **Luchino Visconti**'s landmark film, *Ossessione* (*Obsession*, 1943), and in the immediate postwar period was assistant to **Otello Martelli** and **G. R. Aldo** on many of the classic neorealist films, including **Roberto Rossellini**'s *Paisà* (*Paisan*, 1946) and Visconti's *La terra trema* (*The Earth Trembles*, 1948). He graduated to director of photography on **Carlo Lizzani**'s *Achtung! Banditi!* (*Attention! Bandits!* 1951) and thereafter worked on over 40 films with most of the leading Italian directors including **Luigi Comencini**, **Lina Wertmüller**, **Federico Fellini**, and **Mario Monicelli**, for whom he photographed the famous *I soliti ignoti* (*Big Deal on Madonna Street*, 1958). He developed an especially strong partnership with **Michelangelo Antonioni**, with whom he worked on all the latter's early black-and-white films, with the exception of *L'avventura* (*The Adventure*, 1960), and with **Francesco Rosi**, for whom he photographed all the films up to and including *Le mani sulla città* (*Hands over the City*, 1963), earning the **Nastro d'argento** for *I magliari* (*The Magliari*, 1959) and again for *Salvatore Giuliano* (1961).

A particularly innovative and creative cinematographer, Di Venanzo experimented with lighting and new techniques to develop a highly distinctive personal style that was nevertheless flexible enough to serve both the austerity of Antonioni's *La notte* (*The Night*, 1961) and the sumptuousness of Fellini's *Otto e mezzo* (*8½*, 1963). Following his premature death from cancer in 1966, he was awarded a posthumous Nastro d'argento for his color photography on Fellini's *Giulietta degli spiriti* (*Juliet of the Spirits*, 1965).

DOCUMENTARY. Although subsequently often relegated to the status of poor cousin of the fictional feature film, the documentary held pride of place in the early years of the Italian cinema. Indeed it would appear to have been the commercial success in 1904 of his first two documentaries, *La prima corsa automobilistica Susa-Moncenisio* (The First Car Race between Susa and Moncenisio) and *Le manovre degli alpini* (The Alpine Maneuvers), that prompted the Milanese optical equipment merchant **Arturo Ambrosio** to establish **Ambrosio Film**, the production company that would soon become one of the major pillars of the Italian film industry in the early silent period. Other early film pioneers like **Luca Comerio** remained firmly devoted to the documentary even during the full bloom of the fiction film. Ambrosio's close collaborator and cinematographer, **Roberto Omegna**, directed dozens of fictional features at the Ambrosio studios, but he became best known for exotic nature and ethnographic documentaries such as *La caccia al leopardo* (The Leopard Hunt, 1908), *Usi e costumi abissini* (Abyssinian Customs, 1908), and *Elefanti al lavoro* (Elephants at Work, 1911). In 1911 Omegna's remarkable nature study, *La vita delle farfalle* (The Life of Butterflies), was awarded first prize in the documentary film section of the Turin International Exhibition by a jury that included Louis Lumière and Paul Nadar. In the same period another Ambrosio cinematographer and collaborator, **Giovanni Vitrotti**, also produced numerous documentaries while traveling extensively through Russia and the East.

The documentary came to be somewhat marginalized during the golden age of the Italian silent cinema when it was overshadowed by the grandeur of the historical Roman epics and the passionate melodramas. However, as the Italian feature film industry initiated its steep decline in the early 1920s, there was a marked resurgence of interest in using the cinema for informational and educational purposes. The result was the establishment in 1924 of **L'Unione Cine-**

matografica Educativa (Union of Educational Cinematography), better known by its acronym **LUCE**. In 1925 LUCE was nationalized and thereafter functioned as the chief instrument for propaganda and consensus building of the Fascist regime, especially through its newsreels and reports, which, from 1926 onward, were required by law to be screened before every feature. Nevertheless, LUCE also hosted a number of technical departments, including a science unit directed by none other than Roberto Omegna and which thus continued to turn out first-rate and award-winning scientific documentaries throughout the years of the regime.

LUCE remained the exclusive producer of documentaries in Italy until the early 1930s when, following the death of **Stefano Pittaluga**, **Emilio Cecchi** took over as artistic director at the **Cines** studios and began to encourage artistic and experimental documentary filmmaking alongside the production of fiction films. During Cecchi's brief reign, 17 documentaries were made at the Cines, including **Aldo Vergano**'s *I fori imperiali* (*The Imperial Forums*, 1932), **Umberto Barbaro**'s *Una giornata nel cantiere di Monfalcone* (*A Day in the Monfalcone Shipyard*, 1932), **Alessandro Blasetti**'s *Assisi* (1932), and Francesco di Cocco's *Il ventre della città* (*The Belly of the City*, 1932), a remakable exploration of Rome's abattoir and its central fruit and vegetable market. In 1938, LUCE's dominance over documentary filmmaking in Italy was eroded further with the birth of Industria Cortometraggi (Short Film Industry), which soon became well known for its *La Settimana INCOM* (*INCOM Weekly*). The heightened competition prompted a rise in the quality of documentaries during this period, resulting in first-rate works such as Giacomo Pozzi Bellini's *Il pianto delle zitelle* (The Spinsters' Cry, 1939), Francesco Pasinetti's *Venezia minore* (Venice in a Minor Key, 1942), and Fernando Cerchio's *Comacchio* (1942). It was also during this period that **Luciano Emmer** made the first of what would become a long series of acclaimed art documentaries with *Racconto di un affresco* (*Story of a Fresco*, 1938–1941), and **Michelangelo Antonioni** began filming his *Gente del Po* (*People of the Po*), a stunning portrait of hardship and misery in the Po delta, which was interrupted by the war but eventually completed and released in 1947.

In the immediate postwar period a widespread desire to bear witness to recent history produced a number of documentaries celebrating the **Resistance** movement, foremost among them the collaboratively directed *Giorni di gloria* (*Days of Glory*, 1945). The documentaristic tendency also naturally spread and found a place in the fictional features that came under the banner of **neorealism**. However, the greatest boost to medium- and full-length documentary filmmaking was provided by the Italian government itself, which in 1947 passed a law that introduced both a significant financial subsidy to documentary film producers and a legal obligation on exhibitors to screen nationally produced documentaries together with feature films on at least 80 days each year. The immediate result was a massive increase in the annual number of documentaries, rising from approximately 250 in 1948 to 1,150 in 1955, the year in which the law was due to expire (it was, in fact, extended until 1962). This vast expanse of production was uneven in quality, and some of it was undoubtedly motivated by largely commercial considerations on the part of fly-by-night producers. Nevertheless, many of the short and medium-length documentaries made under this dispensation also represented the first testing ground and apprentice work of future auteurs like **Valerio Zurlini**, **Florestano Vancini**, **Gillo Pontecorvo**, and **Paolo and Vittorio Taviani**, not to mention two filmmakers who would remain dedicated documentarists, **Vittorio De Seta** and **Luigi Di Gianni**. By the end of the 1950s **Roberto Rossellini** also turned to the documentary, beginning his move away from film to television with the 10-episode *L'India vista da Rossellini* (India Seen by Rossellini, made 1957–1958, broadcast 1959). Indeed, with the abandonment of the screen quota for documentaries in the early 1960s, the greater part of documentary production inevitably came to gravitate toward the small screen.

The genre continued to flourish in Italy in the early 1960s, not only in the more traditional forms of the nature and travel documentaries of Folco Quilici but also in the more hybrid forms of Ugo Gregoretti's *I nuovi angeli* (*The New Angels*, 1962) and **Pier Paolo Pasolini**'s *Comizi d'amore* (*Love Meetings*, 1964). An even more audacious transformation of the genre into what came to be known as the "shockumentary" was enacted in the crowded series of "mondo" films, beginning with Gualtiero Jacopetti's *Mondo cane* (*A Dog's World*, 1962) and continuing through his *La donna nel mondo* (*Women of the World*, 1962), *Africa addio* (*Africa Blood and Guts*,

1966), and *Addio zio Tom* (*Goodbye Uncle Tom*, 1971), as well as in the plethora of other "show and shock" films, such as Gianni Proia's *Mondo di notte 3* (*Ecco*, 1963), Marco Vicario's *Il Pelo nel mondo* (*Go! Go! Go! World*, 1964), Paolo Cavara's *L'occhio selvaggio* (*The Wild Eye,* 1967), and Luigi Scattini's *Svezia: Inferno e paradiso* (*Sweden: Heaven and Hell*, 1965).

After a host of small-budget pro-labor and agitprop films made in the wake of the 1968 uprisings, and auteurist documentaries such as Antonioni's *Chung-Kuo Cina* (*China*, made in 1972 but first broadcast on Italian television in 1973), documentary production in Italy declined to a trickle by the end of the 1970s. After two decades of relative neglect, however, the documentary returned in force to Italian screens in the mid-1990s. In 1994, the year that marked the beginning of the undeniable resurgence of the form in Italy, the Fondazione Libero Bizzarri instituted an annual film festival and prize in order to showcase and encourage documentary filmmakers. In the same year, the **Centro Sperimentale di Cinematografia** also established its first course in documentary cinema and the influential National Syndicate of Italian Film Critics (SNCC) united with the Florence-based Festival dei popoli (Festival of Peoples) in publishing a white paper on the state of Italian documentary. An even greater boost to documentary filmmaking was provided by the pay satellite television channel Telepiù, which from 1998 onward bought and broadcast the work of both established and up-and-coming Italian documentarists such as **Daniele Segre**, Daniele Incalcaterra, Gianfranco Pannone, Alessandro Rossetto, Daniele Vicari, and Stefano Missio.

Interest in, and production of, documentary films has continued to grow in Italy in the new millennium to the point where many critics have taken to speaking about a vogue. In the year 2000 Stefano Missio and Francesco Gottardo established the dedicated website www.ildocumentario.it, which has continued to grow and flourish ever since, and three years later over 250 Italian documentarists came together to form their own professional association, Doc/it., which has become an influential lobbying group with both government film authorities and RAI television. With annual documentary film festivals such as the RomaDocFest now as eagerly awaited as Venice or Cannes, the documentary has never been in better health in Italy since perhaps the very earliest days of silent cinema.

DON CAMILLO. Film series. A French-Italian coproduction directed by Julien Duvivier, *Don Camillo* (*The Little World of Don Camillo*, 1951) was the first of a series of five films made between 1951 and 1965 based on the comic stories of journalist and humorist Giovanni Guareschi. Recounting endless variations on a never-ending tussle in a small town in the Po Valley between the hotheaded but lovable parish priest, Don Camillo, and his eternal adversary and the town's Communist mayor, Peppone, the films all starred veteran French actor Fernandel (Fernand Contandin) as the irrepressible priest and **Gino Cervi** as his bullheaded nemesis. The enormous and unexpected box office success, both in Italy and aboad, of the first film, which had ended with Don Camillo being exiled from the village by the bishop because of his irascible behavior, led to the pugnacious priest's being brought back almost immediately in *Il ritorno di Don Camillo* (*The Return of Don Camillo*, 1953), also directed by Duvivier and scoring a similar worldwide success. The popularity of the characters was renewed with the next two films of the series, *Don Camillo e l'onorevole Peppone* (*Don Camillo's Last Round*, 1955) and *Don Camillo monsignore ma non troppo* (*Don Camillo: Monsignor*, 1961), both directed by **Carmine Gallone**, and again with *Il compagno Don Camillo* (*Don Camillo in Moscow*, 1965), directed by **Luigi Comencini**, in which the fiercely anti-Communist Don Camillo goes so far as to undertake a trip to Soviet Russia in order to thwart what he regards as Peppone's evil plans.

A sixth film in the series, also to feature the winning Fernandel-Cervi combination, was begun in late 1969 but abandoned when Fernandel retired from the project due to ill health. In 1971 veteran director **Mario Camerini** took up the challenge and made *Don Camillo e i giovani d'oggi* (*Don Camillo and Today's Youth*, 1971), with Gastone Moschin and Lionel Stander as Don Camillo and Peppone respectively, but the resulting film provoked little interest. A last attempt to revive the character was made in the early 1980s by **Terence Hill**, who directed himself in the lead of *Don Camillo* (*The World of Don Camillo*, 1983), with Colin Blakeley playing Peppone. Made completely in English, the film more resembled Hill's *Trinity* Westerns than the earlier Don Camillo films and consequently sank without a trace.

DONATI, DANILO (1926–2001). Costume, art, and production designer. Widely regarded as the foremost costume designer of Italian postwar cinema, Donati studied at the Academy of Fine Arts in Florence before beginning his career by designing the costumes of a dozen operas and plays directed by **Luchino Visconti**, including productions of *La traviata* and Arthur Miller's *The Crucible*, both staged in 1955. Only a few years later he moved into film with costumes for **Mario Monicelli**'s *La grande guerra* (*The Great War*, 1960). He subsequently provided the period costumes for **Roberto Rossellini**'s *Vanina Vanini* (1961) before beginning a long and fruitful collaboration with **Pier Paolo Pasolini**, all of whose major films he would work on, winning his first **Nastro d'argento** for the costumes for *Il Vangelo secondo Matteo* (*The Gospel According to St. Matthew*, 1964). He also worked with **Franco Zeffirelli**, winning the Academy Award for Best Costume Design for Zeffirelli's production of *Romeo and Juliet* (1968), but perhaps most closely with **Federico Fellini**, providing the costumes as well as art direction and production design for *Satyricon* (*Fellini Satyricon*, 1968), *Roma* (*Fellini's Roma*, 1972), *Amarcord* (1974), and *Casanova* (*Fellini's Casanova*, 1976), the last bringing him not only two Nastri d'argento for both Costume and Production Design but also two BAFTA awards and his second Oscar. Having also designed the costumes for the science fiction fantasy *Flash Gordon* (1980), which earned him a further two BAFTA awards, Donati crowned what had been a truly illustrious career with four more **David di Donatello** awards for costume and production design on **Roberto Benigni**'s *La vita è bella* (*Life Is Beautiful*, 1997) and *Pinocchio* (*Roberto Benigni's Pinocchio*, 2003).

DUBBING. Ever since the arrival of sound, Italians have watched (or rather heard) all foreign-language films in their own language. The practice of dubbing foreign films, now not only accepted but generally demanded by Italian audiences themselves, was first imposed on the industry by a decree, signed by Mussolini in 1927, that prohibited the screening of foreign films in their original languages. As more and more films came to be made in sound and the stock of silent films dwindled, the government's intransigence created a crisis in the supply of films for exhibition. The only version of Hollywood films shown in Italy during the early sound period were either Italian-version films already dubbed by the major studios themselves in Hollywood (Paramount had established a facility at Joinville in Paris for the purpose), the quality of which was usually execrable due to the poor language abilities of the Italian American actors employed, or muted versions in which the dialogue had been removed from the soundtrack, leaving only music and sounds, with the meaning of the dialogue conveyed by intertitles. Given the dearth of films being produced in Italy at the time, Italian cinemas faced a desertion by cinema-goers. Dubbing thus came to be the industry's solution to this intricate problem.

A further Fascist law in 1933 prohibited even the projection of foreign films dubbed outside Italy. By this time, however, a dubbing unit had already been set up within the revived **Cines** studios in Rome under the directorship of Mario Almirante, an actor and screenwriter who had also directed some 20 films during the silent period. Among the first films to be dubbed at the Cines facility were René Clair's *À nous la liberté* (*Liberty for Us*, 1931, although the Italian title changed the plural "us" to the singular "me") and Georg Wilhelm Pabst's *Kameradschaft* (*Comradeship*, 1931) and *Die Herrin von Atlantis* (*Queen of Atlantis*, 1932). The first group of dubbers included Mario Ferrari, Olinto Cristina, Tina Lattanzi, Ugo Cesari, Gero Zambuto (later to direct **Totò** in his first film), Augusto Marcacci, and Camillo Pilotto (later to star in, among other significant films, **Mario Camerini**'s *Il grande appello* [*The Last Roll-Call*], 1936). There soon followed the establishment of other dubbing studios such as Fotovox, under the directorship of Franco Schirato, Fono Roma under Salvatore Persichetti, and Itala-Acustica, headed by Vincenzo Sorelli. In 1932 MGM set up its own Italian dubbing unit in Rome under Augusto Galli. After establishing the unit Galli returned to the United States in 1935, leaving its management in the hands of Franco Schirato. Other American majors also established their own Italian dubbing units: Paramount, under the direction of Luigi Savini, Warner Brothers under Nicola Fausto Neroni, and Twentieth Century Fox under Vittorio Malpassuti.

Given how widespread the practice had become, most critics came to accept dubbing as a necessary evil and many reviews, even in specialized and academic journals such as *Bianco e nero*, regularly commented on the quality of the dubbing as part of their appraisal of the film in question. Nevertheless, some disquiet about the practice remained. In 1936 **Luigi Chiarini** spoke out against it in the pages of the film journal *Lo Schermo*, and soon thereafter **Michelangelo Antonioni** also criticized the practice in several articles published in the journal *Cinema*. In 1941, a survey promoted by *Cinema* found deep-seated and widespread opposition to the practice from many quarters. However, dubbing had by now taken firm root and it was clear that audiences, at least, were unwilling to forego the easy option it offered in contrast to subtitles.

With the withdrawal of the American majors from Italy in the wake of the promulgation of the 1938 law giving monoply control over distribution of all foreign films to the Ente Nazionale Industrie Cinematografiche (ENIC, National Film Industries Authority), there was a marked decrease in the number of foreign films circulating in Italy and thus in the need to dub. The small number of American films that did screen in Italy during the war had been mostly dubbed in Hollywood and exhibited the same deficiences as previous attempts in the early days of sound. The practice returned in earnest, together with the massive presence of the American majors, at the end of the war. In 1944, immediately following the liberation of Rome, a number of actors who had worked as dubbers before the war joined together to form the Cooperativa Doppiatori Cinematografici (Cooperative of Film Dubbers, CDC), soon followed by the Organizzazione Doppiatori Cinematografici (Organization of Film Dubbers, ODI). Ironically, a strong boost to the dubbing industry was provided not only by the huge influx of Hollywood films into Italy during this period but also by Italian-language neorealist films themselves, since on-location shooting and the use of nonprofessional actors meant that most neorealist films required the soundtrack and dialogue to be added in postproduction. All this experience led to Italian dubbing units becoming among the best in the world. Although films were now dubbed as a matter of course, the question of "to dub or not to dub" continued to be raised sporadically in film circles in the following years. In 1956 the journal *Cinema* took up the issue again in a two-part inquiry in which directors such as **Vittorio De Sica** declared their firm opposition to it in principle, in spite of having practiced it themselves out of necessity (Lamberto Maggiorani in De Sica's

Bicycle Thieves had been dubbed by a professional actor). In February 1968 the authoritative journal *Filmcritica* carried the so-called Manifesto of Amalfi in which most of the major directors, among them Michelangelo Antonioni, **Marco Bellocchio**, **Bernardo Bertolucci**, **Pier Paolo Pasolini**, **Alberto Lattuada**, and **Paolo and Vittorio Taviani**, called for the complete abolition of the practice as the only way to ensure the survival of Italian cinema. This was followed by another extensive survey of major directors in *Filmcritica* in July–August 1970, which again reported strong opposition to the practice. None of this served to stem the tide, however, and by the 1980s dubbing was such an inescapable feature of Italian cinema that the *Rivista del cinematografo* ran a dossier in its September–December issue of 1982 that demonstrated, with extensive documentation, the absolute professionalism and creativity of the practice, which had always been regarded as the Cinderella of the Italian film industry. The continuing, indeed increased, dominance over the Italian market by foreign films in the following two decades ensured that dubbing gained complete respectability. In certain cases during the 1990s, producers began to include the names of dubbers in the film's credits. Consequently, dubbers in Italy have now achieved a status, if not a visibility, comparable to that of film actors themselves. Among the most respected names in Italian dubbing are Gualtiero De Angelis, Emilio Cigoli, Oreste Lionello (the Italian voice of Woody Allen), Tina Lattanzi, Maria Pia Di Meo, and **Ferruccio Amendola** (the Italian voice of, among others, Robert De Niro, Dustin Hoffman, and Al Pacino). Among the famous Italian actors who have also worked as dubbers are **Alberto Sordi** (voice of Oliver Hardy and Robert Mitchum) and **Gino Cervi** (the voice of Sir Laurence Olivier, Orson Welles, Clark Gable, and James Stewart).

– E –

EMMER, LUCIANO (1918–). Documentarist, screenwriter, director. A passionate art lover, Emmer began what would become a lifelong engagement with the art **documentary** in the late 1930s with *Racconto di un affresco* (*Story of a Fresco*, 1938), a study of Giotto's work in the Cappella degli Scrovegni. After a host of acclaimed documentaries, including *Isole nella laguna* (*Islands of the Laguna*, 1948), for which he was awarded a **Nastro d'argento** for Best Documentary, in 1950 he directed his first fictional feature, *Una domenica d'agosto* (*Sunday in August*, 1950), a charming set of intertwining stories of Romans going to the beach on Sunday. In the next decade he alternated documentaries on artists such as Goya and Picasso with half a dozen well-structured and generally lighthearted feature films, among them *Parigi è sempre Parigi* (*Paris Is Always Paris*, 1951), *Le ragazze di Piazza di Spagna* (*Three Girls from Rome*, 1952), *Terza liceo* (*High School*, 1954), and *Il momento più bello* (*The Most Wonderful Moment*, 1957). After being forced by the censors to cut some key sequences from his *La ragazza in vetrina* (*Girl in the Window*, 1960), Emmer decided to abandon cinema for television, where he achieved wide renown for his creative and innovative segments for the national advertising program *Carosello*, one of which involved filming contemporary Italian artists such as Renato Guttuso in their studios while they executed a drawing in two minutes.

After almost three decades of successful television advertisements and high-quality documentaries, Emmer returned to the big screen with *Basta! Ci faccio un film* (Enough! I'll Make a Film about It, 1990), which in some ways reprised the high-school setting of his earlier *Terza liceo*. He has recently directed two more features, *Una lunga lunga lunga notte d'amore* (*A Long Long Long Night of Love*, 2001) and *L'acqua . . . il fuoco* (*The Water . . . the Fire*, 2003).

– F –

FABRIZI, ALDO (1905–1990). Actor and director. Of modest working-class origins, Fabrizi began acting in stage revues and cabaret in the 1930s, soon becoming famous for his endearing characters and vaudeville routines. His first foray into cinema was in *Avanti c'è posto* (*Before the Postman*, 1942), directed by **Mario Bonnard**, which allowed him to transfer one of his stage personas to the screen. He played similar roles in Bonnard's *Campo de' Fiori* (*Peddler and the Lady*, 1943), set in the very working-class area of Rome where Fabrizi was born, and **Mario Mattoli**'s *L'ultima carozzella* (*The Last*

Wagon, 1943). Although he had already become widely known in Italy, he then came to international renown as the character of Don Pietro, the courageous priest who lends his support to the **Resistance** movement and pays the price, in **Roberto Rossellini**'s *Roma città aperta* (*Rome Open City*, 1945, also known as *Open City*). After more leading roles in neorealist films such as **Luigi Zampa**'s *Vivere in pace* (*To Live in Peace*, 1946), he also tried his hand at directing, with *Emigrantes* (*Immigrants*, 1949), *La famiglia Passaguai* (*The Passaguai Family*, 1951), and with what is generally regarded as his best self-directed film, *Il Maestro* (*The Teacher and the Miracle*, 1957).

He returned to comedy in a number of films with **Totò** but also continued to do stage comedy and revues. In 1964 he scored a great triumph on Broadway when he was hailed as a comic genius for his interpretation of the role of Mastro Titta in Pietro Garinei and Sandro Giovannini's musical comedy *Rugantino*. His last film appearances were as the Governor in an adaptation of the *Tosca* story directed by Luigi Magni in 1974, and as the grotesquely overweight wealthy father-in-law in **Ettore Scola**'s *C'eravamo tanto amati* (*We All Loved Each Other So Much*, 1974), for which he received a **Nastro d'argento** as best supporting actor. Shortly before his death in 1990 he was awarded a **David di Donatello** for career achievement. His iconic status as one of the great actors of the Italian cinema was further confirmed in 1996 when the Italian postal service issued a stamp in his honor.

FAENZA, ROBERTO (1943–). Director and screenwriter. Born in Milan, Faenza moved to Rome to study at the **Centro Sperimentale di Cinematografia**, where he graduated in directing in 1965. In 1968, while still completing a doctorate in political science, he made his first film, *Escalation* (1968), the story of a bitter, no-holds-barred struggle between a wealthy businessman and his nonconformist hippie son, a struggle that eventually escalates into brutal murder. This was quickly followed by an even more ferocious attack on bourgeois conformism, *H2S* (1971), a futuristic dystopic fantasy whose name appropiately alludes to the chemical formula for sulfuric acid. The film's caustic nature provoked the ire of the censors, who delayed its release by almost two years. In the meantime, Faenza moved to the

United States, where he lectured on mass media at the Federal City College, Washington, D.C.

In 1978, having returned to Italy to teach at the University of Pisa, Faenza fired another broadside against the system with his ironically titled *Forza Italia* (*Go Italy*, 1978), a savage attack on the ruling Christian Democrat Party carried out through a careful montage of newsreel footage. This was followed by an even more grotesque critique of the Italian Communist Party in *Si salvi chi vuole* (Whoever Wants Should Save Themselves, 1980). After *Copkiller* (1982), a film shot entirely in English in the United States and starring Harvey Keitel and Johnny Rotten (John Lydon), and *Mio caro dottor Grasler* (*The Bachelor*, 1989), adapted from a short novel by Austrian writer Arthur Schnitzler, Faenza appeared to soften his tone considerably with *Jona che visse nella balena* (*Jonah Who Lived in the Whale*, 1993). The moving adaptation of a biographical novel by Jona Oberski that recounted the experience of a young Jewish boy in the Bergen-Belsen concentration camp, *Jona* earned Faenza much critical acclaim and a **David di Donatello** for direction.

A now-mellowed Faenza followed this up with two further literary adaptations, *Sostiene Pereira* (*Pereira Declares*, 1995), from the best-selling novel by Antonio Tabucchi, and *Marianna Ucrìa* (1997) from a historical novel by Dacia Maraini. *L'amante perduto* (*Lost Lover*, 1999) was also a literary adaptation but this time by Jewish writer Abraham B. Yehoshua, set against the background of the Palestinian-Israeli conflict. *Prendimi l'anima* (*The Soul Keeper*, 2003) was a similarly sensitive portrayal of the ill-fated love affair between psychoanalyst Carl Gustav Jung and his young female patient Sabina Spielrein. Two years later Faenza returned to more socially committed themes with *Alla luce del sole* (*In the Light of the Sun*, 2005), a passionate denunciation of the murder of parish priest Don Giuseppe Puglisi by the Mafia in Palermo in 1993.

FELLINI, FEDERICO (1920–1993). Journalist, cartoonist, screenwriter, director. The most nationally celebrated and internationally renowned of all Italian directors of the postwar period, Fellini was born and raised in the northern Italian coastal town of Rimini. From a very early age he showed a flair for cartoons and as a boy was able to exchange amusing caricatures of Hollywood film stars for free admission to the local cinema.

Having moved to Rome in 1938, ostensibly to study at the university, Fellini hawked his drawings around the city and soon became a regular contributor to the satirical journal *Marc'Aurelio*. The contacts he made at the journal opened up a range of possibilities for extra work, including writing skits for the radio, and it was while working on a radio program that he met the actress **Giulietta Masina**, whom he married in 1943. He was soon also following the example of other writers from *Marc'Aurelio* who moonlighted as assistant screenwriters for films being made in nearby **Cinecittà**, his first acknowledged screenwriting credit being for **Mario Bonnard**'s *Avanti c'è posto* (*Before the Postman*, 1942), during the filming of which he met and befriended the actor **Aldo Fabrizi**. Fellini's real entry into the film industry, however, came only after the liberation of Rome in June 1944 when he was approached by out-of-work director **Roberto Rossellini** to help write a **documentary** on a Catholic priest who had been killed by the Germans for his involvement with the **Resistance**. By this time Fellini was making a good living from selling drawings and caricatures to Allied servicemen, but he accepted the offer and, together with established screenwriter **Sergio Amidei**, wrote what became the founding film of **neorealism**, *Roma città aperta* (*Rome Open City*, also known as *Open City*, 1945). In the wake of the film's international success, he continued to work with Rossellini on the screenplay of *Paisà* (*Paisan*, 1946), parts of which he also directed, and on *L'amore* (*Ways of Love*, 1948), for which he not only wrote the second episode, *Il miracolo* (*The Miracle*), but also acted the role of the Stranger, opposite **Anna Magnani**.

With his screenwriting credentials solidly established, he began to work with a number of other directors, including **Pietro Germi** and **Alberto Lattuada**, before returning to Rossellini to help write *Francesco, giullare di Dio* (*Francis, God's Jester*, 1950). Having already collaborated with Lattuada on *Senza pietà* (*Without Pity*, 1948) and *Il mulino del Po* (*The Mill on the Po*, 1948), Fellini joined forces with the more-established director to form a cooperative company with which to produce *Luci del varietà* (*Variety Lights*, 1950), a film about a motley troupe of traveling players, which they codirected. The film flopped miserably at the box office but provided Fellini with the confidence and experience to direct his first solo feature, *Lo sceicco bianco* (*The White Sheik*, 1952). A broad tongue-in-cheek satire on the photoromances so popular in Italy at this time, the film starred a young **Alberto Sordi** in a role that now seems made to measure, but Sordi's popularity was at a low ebb at the time and the film proved to be another resounding flop. Unperturbed, Fellini then made *I vitelloni* (*Spivs*, 1953). The story of five young middle-class layabouts in a provincial city that greatly resembled Fellini's own native Rimini, *I vitelloni* was the first film to incorporate that dimension of poetic autobiography that would mark so many of his subsequent works. Winning the Silver Lion at the **Venice Festival** that year, it was Fellini's first major success.

While preparing for his next project, Fellini directed an episode for **Cesare Zavattini**'s compilation film, *L'amore in città* (*Love in the City*, 1953). Fellini's *L'agenzia matrimoniale* (*Matrimonial Agency*) was generally judged the best of the film's six segments, but the film itself received scant notice and little acclaim. By this time, however, Fellini had already made what would be his first great international triumph, *La strada* (1954). A charming redemptive fairy tale in modern dress, the film was awarded the Silver Lion when it was first screened at the Venice Festival and soon accrued a veritable host of awards, which included not only the Oscar for Best Foreign Film but also a special prize from the Screen Directors Guild of America that was personally presented to Fellini by John Ford. After *Il bidone* (*The Swindlers*, 1955), a petty-crime drama that suffered from being edited in too much haste in order to be presented at Venice that year, and which was consequently poorly received and soon forgotten, Fellini scored another major international success with *Le notti di Cabiria* (*Nights of Cabiria*, 1957). The story of a warmhearted prostitute who suffers at the hands of a cold-blooded world but whose basic goodness eventually wins out, the film was first shown at Cannes in 1957 to enormous acclaim, with Giulietta Masina winning the Best Actress award. It was also warmly received when later released in Italy as well as in the United States, where it received both the Oscar for Best Foreign Film and the New York Film Critics Award. Fellini's international reputation, already sky-high, was pushed to stratospheric heights with his next film, ***La dolce vita*** (1960). Although the title itself was ironic and the work was essentially a critique of the moral vacuum being created by the increasing affluence in Italy, the film was largely read as a celebration of the hedonistic "good life" of the rich and famous. Initially vilified in Italy by Catholic and conservative elements, who thus helped to make it a cause célèbre, the film eventually proved to be an unprecedented national and international success, winning the Palme d'or at Cannes and earning Fellini yet another Oscar nomination for Best Director.

While searching for a subject for his next major work, Fellini filmed the delightful short *Le tentazioni del dottor Antonio* (*The Temptations of Doctor Antonio*) as his contribution to *Boccaccio '70* (1962), another compilation film organized by Zavattini, before making *Otto e mezzo* (*8½*, 1963). The tragicomic and transparently autobiographical story of a film director in crisis over his next film, *8½* proved to be another international triumph, winning two of its five Oscar nominations, seven **Nastri d'argento** in Italy, and the Grand Prize at the Moscow International Film Festival. Made two years later, Fellini's first film in color, *Giulietta degli spiriti* (*Juliet of the Spirits*, 1965) generated high expectations. In the event, however, despite praising its design, many of the Italian critics voiced disappointment, although the film proved to be very popular in the United States, where it was awarded the Golden Globe for Best Foreign Film and received two Oscar nominations. While again exploring a number of projects for his next major work, Fellini made a brief excursion into the **horror** genre with *Toby Dammit*, his contribution to the omnibus film *Tre passi nel delirio* (*Spirits of the Dead*, 1968), and then into television with *Block-notes di un regista* (*Fellini: A Director's Notebook*, 1969), an hour-long program commissioned by the American NBC network. He returned to the big screen with *Satyricon* (*Fellini Satyricon*, 1969), a highly personal and fragmented dream vision of ancient Rome that provoked a varied reaction worldwide but nevertheless earned Fellini another Oscar nomination for Best Director. Following another excursion into television with *I clowns* (*The Clowns*, 1970), Fellini returned to paint an equally personal and impressionistic portrait of a more modern Rome in *Roma* (*Fellini's Roma*, 1972), before making his most autobiographical film, *Amarcord* (1973). With its title meaning, literally, "I remember" in Fellini's native dialect, the film paraded a wonderful series of evocative but largely invented memories of provincial life in a Rimini of the 1930s, all created completely on the sound stages of

Cinecittà. Critically and commercially successful worldwide, *Amarcord* brought Fellini the fifth Oscar of his career. There then followed what are generally, and perhaps unfairly, regarded as minor films in what already comprised an extraordinary body of work: *Casanova* (*Fellini's Casanova*, 1976), his most expensive film up to that time but also one of his least popular; *Prova d'orchestra* (*Orchestra Rehearsal*, 1979); *La città delle donne* (*City of Women*, 1980), which provoked the ire of feminists for what was seen as its caricature of women; and *E la nave va* (*And the Ship Sails On*, 1983). Then, after a hiatus during which he bowed to necessity and filmed eye-catching advertisements for Barilla pasta and Campari liqueurs, Fellini returned to grand form with his mordant satire of Italian television in *Ginger e Fred* (*Ginger and Fred*, 1986). Having now been awarded the Golden Lion at Venice for his lifetime achievement, Fellini turned the limelight squarely back on himself in his next film, *Intervista* (*Fellini's Intervista*, 1987), an amusing, and amused, portrait of himself and of Italian cinema, painted with all the assurance of an old master. Three years later he made what would be his last film, *La voce della luna* (*The Voice of the Moon*, 1990). Adapted from a fantasy novel by Ermanno Cavazzoni and with **Roberto Benigni** playing the young innocent, Ivo, the film re-presented many of the familiar Fellinian motifs in an ever more ethereal setting in order to express the consternation of an innocent before the craziness of a postmodern world. While many critics expressed some reservations about the work and it failed, inexplicably, to find a distributor in the United States, it proved to be Fellini's most popular film in Italy after *Amarcord* and, as such, a fitting conclusion, perhaps, for a director who always seemed to be looking at cinema through the eyes of an awed child.

In 1993, shortly before his death, Fellini made the journey to Hollywood, where he was presented with an honorary Academy Award for his remarkable lifetime achievement.

FERRERI, MARCO (1928–1997). Actor, producer, and director. One of the most iconoclastic directors of Italian postwar cinema, Ferreri began his film career in the early 1950s by collaborating on the production of current affairs documentaries. After acting as executive producer for **Cesare Zavattini**'s compilation film, *L'amore in città*

(*Love in the City*, 1953), Ferreri moved to Spain, where he began his long association with writer Rafael Azcona, making three films that anticipated the anarchistic black humor of his major films to follow, *El pisito* (The Apartment, 1958), *Los Chicos* (The Boys, 1959), and *El cochechito* (*The Little Coach*, 1960), the last being nominated for the Golden Lion at the **Venice Festival** that year.

Returning to Italy in 1961, Ferreri contributed a short episode to the Zavattini-inspired compilation film, *Le italiane e l'amore* (*Latin Lovers*, 1961), before making *L'ape regina* (*The Conjugal Bed*, 1963), a caustic satire on sex and marriage that immediately drew the ire of the censors, who forced changes on the film, including its title. Similar hostility from the censors greeted *La donna scimmia* (*The Ape Woman*, 1964), although this did not prevent it from being nominated for the Palme d'or at Cannes and winning a **Nastro d'argento** for Best Original Story. After *Il professore* (*The Professor*), one of the episodes of *Controsesso* (*Countersex*, 1964), and the four-part *Marcia nuziale* (*Wedding March*, 1965), another satire on modern Italian male-female relations, Ferreri ironically reversed the traditional male-female positions in *L'harem* (*The Harem*, 1967), where the harem is made up of men. This provocative take on the gender wars was followed by the sardonic *Dillinger è morto* (*Dillinger Is Dead*, 1969), the apocalyptic *Il seme dell'uomo* (*The Seed of Man*, 1969), *L'udienza* (*The Audience*, 1972), a Kafkaesque tale in which an audience with the pope is forever forestalled, and then the film for which he would become most renowned, *La grande abbuffata* (*The Grande Bouffe*, 1973). The story of four culinary libertines who commit collective suicide by eating themselves to death, the film caused enormous controversy, especially in France, but it was also nominated for the Golden Palm at Cannes and, in the event, received the International Federation of Film Critics prize.

Continuing to play the agent provocateur, Ferreri made *Non toccare la donna bianca* (*Don't Touch the White Woman*, 1974), a burlesque revisitation of the Western genre that restaged Custer's Last Stand as a confrontation between the first and third worlds in the hollowed-out building site of Les Halles in Paris, before returning to the sex wars with *L'ultima donna* (*The Last Woman*, 1976) and the more surreal and apocalyptic *Ciao Maschio* (*Bye Bye Monkey*, 1978). The milder *Chiedo asilo* (*Seeking Asylum*, 1979), in which **Roberto Be-**

nigni plays a lovable nursery-school teacher, was followed by an adaptation of Charles Bukowsky's semiautobiographical novel, *Storie di ordinaria follia* (*Tales of Ordinary Madness*, 1981), before Ferreri's taste for the absurd returned to the fore in *I Love You* (1986), a portrait of modern alienation presented through the story of a man's fetishistic sexual attachment to a talking keyring. The ironically titled *Come sono buoni i bianchi* (*How Good the Whites Are*, 1987) excoriated the well-meaning but ultimately self-serving stratagems of Western food aid to Africa while *La casa del sorriso* (*The House of Smiles*, 1991), a love story between an elderly couple set in an old people's home, was refused a screening at Venice but awarded the Golden Bear when shown at Berlin. After *La carne* (*The Flesh*, 1991), another excessive love story, this time involving priapism and anthropophagy, Fererri's final film, *Nitrato d'argento* (*Nitrate Base*, 1996), was an affectionate celebration of silent cinema.

A competent actor as well as director, Ferreri appeared in Luigi Malerba's *Donne e soldati* (*Women and Soldiers*, 1954) and in **Mario Monicelli**'s *Casanova '70* (*Casanova 70*, 1965), and played Dr. Salamoia in **Ugo Tognazzi**'s *Il fischio al naso* (*The Seventh Floor*, 1967), but he is probably best remembered as the sardonic Hans Guenther in **Pier Paolo Pasolini**'s *Porcile* (*Pigpen*, 1969).

FERRETTI, DANTE (1943–). Art director and production designer. One of Italy's most nationally respected and internationally renowned designers, Ferretti graduated in architecture from the University of Rome before embarking on a career in the cinema. Still in his early 20s, he began working as an assistant designer on **Pier Paolo Pasolini**'s *Il Vangelo secondo Matteo* (*The Gospel According to St. Matthew*, 1964) and *Uccellacci e uccellini* (*Hawks and Sparrows*, 1966) before becoming the principal production designer for *Medea* (1969) and for all of Pasolini's subsequent films. In the following years he worked with many of the other major Italian directors, including **Elio Petri**, **Luigi Comencini**, and **Marco Ferreri**. In 1978 he initiated a very fruitful collaboration with **Federico Fellini** by creating the sets for *Prova d'orchestra* (*Orchestra Rehearsal*) and thereafter designed all of Fellini's films. With his national reputation firmly established, in the 1980s he also began to work internationally and received a **David di Donatello** for his design of Jean-Jacques

Annaud's *The Name of the Rose* (1986) and Oscar nominations for his work on Terry Gilliam's *The Adventures of Baron Munchausen* (1988) and **Franco Zeffirelli**'s *Hamlet* (1990). In the 1990s he worked regularly as art director and production designer for Martin Scorsese and received Oscar nominations for his work on Scorsese's *Age of Innocence* (1994), *Kundun* (1997), and *Gangs of New York* (2002). In 2004, having already been nominated for an Academy Award six times, he finally received the Oscar for his work on Scorsese's *The Aviator*.

FLAIANO, ENNIO (1910–1972). Novelist, playwright, journalist, and screenwriter. Flaiano began writing for films in the early 1940s and achieved an early success with the award of a **Nastro d'argento** for the screenplay of Marcello Pagliero's *Roma città libera* (*Rome Free City*, 1946). While continuing to pursue a literary career—he won the prestigious Premio Strega in 1947 with his novel *Tempo di uccidere* (*Time to Kill*)—he also collaborated on numerous screenplays with many of the major directors, from **Roberto Rossellini**, for whom he helped to write *Dov'è la libertà?* (*Where Is Freedom*, 1954) to **Michelangelo Antonioni**, for whom he wrote *La notte* (*The Night*, 1960). His greatest screenwriting successes, however, came from his long association with **Federico Fellini**, with whom he worked on almost a dozen films, including *La dolce vita* (1960) and *Otto e mezzo* (8½, 1963), the latter earning him two Nastri d'argento as well as an Oscar nomination. In 1989 **Giuliano Montaldo** adapted Flaiano's *Tempo di uccidere* for the screen.

FONDATO, MARCELLO (1924–). Screenwriter and director. Fondato began his career in films as a screenwriter, collaborating with **Luigi Comencini** on a number of films, including *Mogli pericolose* (Dangerous Wives, 1958), *Tutti a casa* (*Everybody Go Home*, 1960), and *La ragazza di Bube* (*Bebo's Girl*, 1963). After also working on a number of the **Totò** films and cowriting several of **Mario Bava**'s **horror** classics, including *I tre volti della paura* (Black Sabbath, 1963) and *Sei donne per l'assassino* (*Blood and Black Lace*, 1964), he made his directorial debut with *I protagonisti* (*The Protagonists*, 1968), a film about five wealthy tourists who pay to spend time with a notorious Sardinian bandit and which earned him a **Nas-**

tro d'argento for Best Original Story. *Certo certissimo . . . anzi probabile* (*Diary of a Telephone Operator*, 1969), adapted from a short story by Dacia Maraini, is usually regarded as his finest work as a director. However, he continued to write and direct a number of other successful films in the 1970s, including *Causa di divorzio* (*Cause of Divorce*, 1972), which reflected a burning issue in Italy at the time; *Altrimenti ci arrabbiamo* (*Watch Out, We're Mad*, 1974), one of the films featuring the comic duo **Bud Spencer** and **Terence Hill** (Mario Girotti); and *A mezzanotte va la ronda del piacere* (*The Immortal Bachelor*, 1975), which took its title from a popular song of the 1930s. In the 1980s he worked mostly in television, directing several miniseries, among them the six-episode *Affari di famiglia* (*Family Affairs*, 1989).

FRANCHI, FRANCO (1922–1992). (Born Francesco Benenato.) Actor. An amateur singer and performer at country fairs, Franchi met comic actor **Ciccio Ingrassia** in 1957 and thereby initiated the most successful comic partnership in Italy of the 1960s. The duo originally did stage revues and musical theater but soon graduated to television and film, through which they gained enormous popularity. Beginning with minor appearances in **Mario Mattoli**'s *Appuntamento ad Ischia* (Rendezvous at Ischia, 1960) and **Vittorio De Sica**'s *Il giudizio universale* (*The Last Judgement*, 1961), Franchi and Ingrassia went on to star in over 120 films of varying quality, mostly knockabout farces and often hastily concocted parodies of other well-known and successful films. Although hugely popular with audiences, the duo was generally maligned by the critics, who often found the humor of the films too lowbrow. Franchi's talents emerged more clearly, however, in films such as *Che cosa sono le nuvole?* (What Are the Clouds?), the episode directed by **Pier Paolo Pasolini** for the compilation film *Capriccio all'Italiana* (*Caprice Italian Style*, 1968), and in his role of the Cat to Ingrassia's Fox in **Luigi Comencini**'s much-loved television adaptation *Le avventure di Pinocchio* (*The Adventures of Pinocchio*, 1972). From the late 1970s, while not abandoning the cinema altogether, Franchi appeared mostly on television, although he returned to the big screen in the mid-1980s to give what is probably his most memorable performance in the role of Zi' Dima in **Paolo and Vittorio Taviani**'s *Kaos* (*Chaos*, 1984).

FRANCISCI, PIETRO (1906–1977). Director. Although a lawyer by training, Francisci embarked on a career in cinema in the mid-1930s with *Rapsodie di Roma* (*Roman Rhapsodies*, 1934), the first of many quality documentaries that he would make on commission for the Istituto **LUCE**. In the postwar period he chose to devote himself to fiction, beginning with the melodrama *Io ti ho incontrato a Napoli* (*I Met You in Naples*, 1945). There followed *Natale al campo 119* (*Christmas in Camp 119*, 1947), a sentimental musical comedy set in a prisoner-of-war camp in California where Italians, waiting to be repatriated, reminisce about life at home. After a fictional biography of Saint Anthony of Padua (*Antonio di Padova*, 1949), he began to specialize in historical adventure fantasies such as *Il leone di Amalfi* (*The Lion of Amalfi*, 1950) and *Orlando e i paladini di Francia* (*Roland the Mighty*, 1956). Then in 1957 he made *Le fatiche di Ercole* (*Hercules*, 1957), the film by which he is generally credited with initiating the **peplum** genre and launching the film career of American bodybuilder Steve Reeves. The film was hugely successful, both in Italy and abroad. After making what are regarded by aficionados as several other classics of the genre, such as *Ercole e la regina di Lidia* (*Hercules Unchained*, 1958) and *Ercole sfida Sansone* (*Hercules, Samson and Ulysses*, 1963)—and with the genre itself now definitely on the wane—Francisci tried his hand at science fiction with the oddly titled and minibudgeted *2+5: Missione Hydra* (*2+5: Mission Hydra*, 1967), which, however, failed to stir much interest or acclaim. His last film was the Oriental adventure *Simbad e il califfo di Bagdad* (*Sinbad and the Caliph of Bagdad*, 1973).

FREDA, RICCARDO (1909–1999). Screenwriter and director. Born in Alexandria, Egypt, of Neapolitan parents, Freda joined the film industry in 1934, working originally as a screenwriter. He made his directorial debut with *Don Cesare di Bazan* (1942), a swashbuckling costume drama set in 17th-century Spain, cowritten with **Sergio Amidei** and **Cesare Zavattini** and starring **Gino Cervi**.

In the immediate postwar period Freda began to specialize in the adventure genre, beginning with *Aquila nera* (*Return of the Black Eagle*, 1946), an exotic costume drama set in czarist Russia, and then *I miserabili* (1948), an adaptation of Victor Hugo's novel *Les misérables*, which was released in two parts, *Caccia all'uomo* (Man

Hunt) and *Tempesta su Parigi* (Storm over Paris). This was followed by *Il cavaliere misterioso* (*The Mysterious Rider*, 1948), a Casanova adventure thriller that starred **Vittorio Gassman** in one of his first lead roles, and *Il conte Ugolino* (*Count Ugolino*, 1949), a gothic rendering of one of the most famous episodes from Dante's *Inferno*.

In the 1950s Freda made a number of low-budget historical epics before laying down what is regarded as the cornerstone of the revival of the Italian **horror** genre with *I vampiri* (*The Devil's Commandment*, 1957, made under the pseudonym Robert Hampton), which was photographed by **Mario Bava**. He subsequently worked with some success in most of the popular genres, from more sword-and-sandal films such as *Maciste alla corte del Gran Khan* (*Samson and the Seven Miracles of the World*) and *Maciste all'inferno* (*Maciste in Hell*, 1962, as Robert Hampton), to Westerns such as *La morte non conta i dollari* (*No Death without Dollars*, 1967, credited as George Lincoln). However, he achieved his greatest renown internationally for his stylish exercises in gothic horror, such as *L'orribile segreto del dottor Hichcock* (*The Horrible Secret of Dr. Hichcock*, 1962) and *Estratto dagli archivi segreti della polizia di una capitale europea* (*Tragic Ceremony*, 1972). In the early 1980s he made a final horror thriller, *L'ossessione che uccide* (*Murder Syndrome*, 1981) before retiring from filmmaking altogether. He returned briefly to the industry in the early 1990s to direct *La fille de d'Artagnan* (*The Daughter of D'Artagnan*, 1994), but the film was eventually finished by Bernand Tavernier and Freda's name was removed from the credits.

FREDDI, LUIGI (1895–1977). Journalist, producer, administrator. Much maligned in the postwar period due to his close association with Fascism, Freddi served as the director of the Direzione Generale per la Cinematografia (General Directorate of Cinematography) from its inception in 1934 until 1939, when he relinquished this all-important position in favor of becoming the head of both **Cinecittà**, which he had been instrumental in creating, and the revived **Cines** studios. After the fall of Fascism in 1943, Freddi pledged his allegiance to the Republic of Salò and consequently moved to Venice, where he was part of the ill-fated attempt to establish a new center for film production, in lieu of the bombed and now-unusable Cinecittà studios in Rome. In the last days of the war, while attempting to reach Switzerland, he was captured by **Resistance** fighters and imprisoned. He was eventually put on trial in May 1946 on charges of having unlawfully profited from his official position under the Fascist regime, but he was promptly acquitted and released. Given his past history and association, he was unable ever to work again in the film industry, except for a brief collaboration in 1954 with producer **Angelo Rizzoli**. Before fading into obscurity, he wrote and published *Il cinema* (Cinema), a two-volume memoir detailing his involvement with the Italian film industry. Although long neglected, the book contains such a wealth of information about the Italian cinema during the Fascist period that it has recently been republished in an abridged form by the **Centro Sperimentale di Cinematografia** under the title of *Il cinema: Il governo dell'immagine* (*Cinema: The Government of the Image*, 1994).

FREGOLI, LEOPOLDO (1867–1936). Illusionist, comic actor, singer, and director. A remarkably gifted mime and impersonator who had already achieved international fame for his ability to change in and out of myriad characters, Fregoli was also one of the first to grasp the potential of the Lumière *cinématographe* for the purposes of theatrical spectacle. After visiting the Lumière brothers at Lyon in 1896 to learn how to work the apparatus, he returned to Italy with a modified version of their machine, which he dubbed the Fregoligraph. With the help of **Luca Comerio**, another pioneer of Italian cinema, he used the device to shoot footage, often of his own performances, and then project these short films as part of his stage act. He experimented with splicing short films together to create longer sequences and with projecting films in reverse to create greater amazement in his audiences. He also made several films that unveiled the techniques he used to effect his transformations and projected these too as part of his act. Surprisingly, rather than demystifying the process, this seemed only to increase the audience's appreciation of his remarkable skill.

Fregoli toured extensively throughout Europe and the Americas and continued to appear onstage to great acclaim until 1925. However, he was primarily a stage performer and his dalliance with film was short lived. By 1905 when feature films were beginning to be made in Italy, Fregoli had already ceased to include films in any of his performances.

FRUSTA, ARRIGO (1875–1965). (Born Augusto Sebastiano Ferraris.) Poet and scriptwriter. Although a qualified lawyer, Frusta had chosen to practice journalism and also earned a reputation as a poet in his native Piedmontese dialect before being recruited in 1908 by **Arturo Ambrosio** to head **Ambrosio Film**'s scriptwriting department. It was Frustra's writing talents that were largely responsible for the quality and success of Ambrosio's films, in particular its legion of literary adaptations. When the famous writer-poet Gabriele D'Annunzio, after accepting a sizable advance for six adaptations of his works, failed to deliver any of them, Ambrosio delegated the task to Frusta, who scripted all six in less than two years (the films were all released in 1911–1912). Frusta was also responsible for the spectacularly successful *Nozze d'oro*, which won first prize for a feature film (and 25,000 lire) at the International Exhibition of Turin in 1911. The film was remarkable for, among other things, narrating its story through the use of flashback.

In all, Frustra was responsible for close to 300 films. A keen mountaineer, he also used the talents of cameraman **Giovanni Vitrotti** to make three feature-length travelogues set in the Italian Alps, and he directed several adaptations of Shakespeare, among them *La bisbetica domata* (*The Taming of the Shrew*, 1913) and *Otello* (*Othello*, 1914). After a short but prolific career, briefly interrupted by the war, Frusta left the film industry in 1921 and never returned. However, in the 1950s, in a series of articles in the film journal *Bianco e nero*, Frusta was happy to recount his experiences and the part he had played in the industry's earliest days.

FULCI, LUCIO (1927–1996). Screenwriter and director. Regarded as one of the foremost directors of Italian **horror** and honored among aficionados with the title "the godfather of Italian gore," Fulci studied at the **Centro Sperimentale di Cinematografia** before making documentaries and working as a screenwriter. He learned the art of directing screen comedy by working as an assistant to **Steno** on such classic comedies as *Un giorno in pretura* (*A Day in Court*, 1954) and *Un americano a Roma* (*An American in Rome*, 1954) as well as many of the **Totò** films, such as *Totò e le donne* (*Totò and the Women*, 1952) and *Totò a colori* (*Totò in Color*, 1952). In fact, he made his solo directorial debut with *I ladri* (*The Thieves*, 1959), a crime comedy starring

Totò and **Giovanna Ralli**. He subsequently directed a wide variety of films ranging from teen rock musicals like *I ragazzi del juke-box* (*The Jukebox Kids*, 1959) and *Urlatori alla sbarra* (*Howlers of the Dock*, 1960), which featured then up-and-coming young Italian pop singers Adriano Celentano and Mina, to **spaghetti Westerns** like *Tempo di massacro* (*Massacre Time*, 1966). He achieved his best box office successes, however, with a dozen exceptionally popular screwball comedies featuring the popular comic duo **Franco Franchi** and **Ciccio Ingrassia**.

His move to the darker side began in 1969 with *Una sull'altra* (*One on Top of the Other*), a thriller set in San Francisco with distinct similarities to Hitchcock's *Vertigo*. This was soon followed by *Una lucertola con la pelle di donna* (*A Lizard in a Woman's Skin*, 1971) and the more famous *Non si sevizia un paperino* (*Don't Torture a Duckling*, 1972), a dark *giallo* revolving around a series of gruesome child murders in a backward region of southern Italy. For a period he continued to alternate between genres but from the late 1970s Fulci devoted himself almost exclusively to horror, producing the many zombie and slasher films that would earn him worldwide notoriety, among them *Zombi 2* (*Zombie Flesh Eaters*, 1979), *Paura nella città dei morti viventi* (*City of the Living Dead*, 1980), *Lo squartatore di New York* (*The New York Ripper*, 1982), and *Zombi 3* (*Zombie Flesh Eaters 2*, 1988). Having played cameos in quite a number of his films, Fulci rather appropriately chose to appear in his final film, *Voci dal profondo* (*Voices from the Deep*, 1994), as a doctor carrying out an autopsy on the decaying body of the protagonist.

– G –

GAGLIANONE, DANIELE (1966–). Screenwriter and director. A very distinctive presence in the most recent generation of Italian directors, Gaglianone began working at the Archivio Nazionale Cinematografico della Resistenza (National Film Archive of the Resistance) in 1991, where he produced a number of documentaries on historical topics. At the same time he began making videos and award-winning short films, often addressing social problems in a very personal key. After collaborating as cowriter and assistant director on **Gianni Amelio**'s *Così ridevano* (*The Way We Laughed*, 1998), he directed his first feature, *I nostri anni* (*The Years of Our Lives*, 2000), a powerful exploration of the **Resistance** and its long personal legacy for the people who lived through it. The film received strong acclaim at Cannes in 2001, and in Italy was nominated for a **Nastro d'argento**. After several more interesting documentaries, including *Storie di calcio: Le domeniche del signor Mantaut* (*Football Stories: Mr. Mantaut's Sundays*, 2003), the portrait of an elderly blind man who insists on going to "watch" his favorite soccer team play every Sunday, Gaglianone directed his similarly much-acclaimed second feature, *Nemmeno il destino* (*Changing Destiny*, 2004), a harsh but moving coming-of-age narrative, adapted from an autobiographical novel by Gianfranco Bettin.

GALLONE, CARMINE (1886–1973). Director. Frequently unfairly remembered merely as the author of that great flop of Fascist cinema, *Scipione l'Africano* (*Scipio the African*, 1937), Gallone was a prolific and widely acclaimed director responsible for over 100 films in a career that stretched from the silent era to the early 1960s.

Having already achieved some success as an actor and playwright, Gallone joined **Cines** in 1913, bringing with him his wife, Stanislawa Winaver, who, as Soava Gallone, would become a celebrated actress and one of the major divas. A year later he made his directorial debut with *La donna nuda* (*The Naked Woman*, 1914), initiating an artistic partnership with the already-famous diva **Lyda Borelli**, whom he would subsequently also direct in *Marcia nuziale* (*Wedding March*, 1915), *Fior di male* (*Flower of Evil*, 1915), *La Falena* (*The Moth*, 1916), and *Malombra* (1916). In the following years he worked extensively with novelist, scriptwriter, and director Lucio D'Ambra to produce a host of sophisticated comedies and elegant melodramas. He widened his scope to the historical film in 1925 with *La cavalcata ardente* (*The Fiery Cavalcade*), a romantic costume drama set against the backdrop of the **Risorgimento**, and a year later a remake of *Gli ultimi giorni di Pompei* (*The Last Days of Pompeii*).

In the severe crisis afflicting the Italian film industry during that time, Gallone, like many others, left to work abroad, directing films in Germany, Austria, England, and especially France, where he was influenced by René Clair and made several films scripted by

Henri-Georges Clouzot. He returned to Italy in 1936 to direct one of the few films directly financed and sponsored by the Fascist regime and, although *Scipione L'Africano* was officially feted at Venice with the Mussolini Prize, it has come to be generally regarded as an artistic low point in his career. Subsequently Gallone concentrated on what was undoubtedly his most congenial interest, namely music, and followed a direction he had already begun to explore in 1935 with *Casta diva* (*The Divine Spark*), a romanticized biography of composer Vincenzo Bellini. In the following years Gallone would pursue his musical interests through fictional biographies of great composers like Verdi (*Giuseppe Verdi*, 1938), Mozart (*Melodie eterne* [*Eternal Melodies*], 1940), and *Puccini* (1953) and films of canonical operas such as *Manon Lescaut* (1940), *Rigoletto* (1947), *Il trovatore* (1949), and *Madama Butterfly* (1954). Quite interesting experiments in the postwar period were *Avanti a lui tremava tutta Roma* (*Before Him All Rome Trembled*, 1949), which married *Tosca* and the **Resistance** movement, and *Carmen in Trastevere* (1963), which set the story of the opera in contemporary times in one of the poorer quarters of Rome.

Gallone was lured back briefly to the Roman epic with *Cartagine in fiamme* (*Carthage in Flames*, 1959), which became his contribution to the flowering of the **peplum** at that time. Before retiring he also directed two of the popular Don Camillo films, *Don Camillo e l'onorevole Peppone* (*Don Camillo and Deputy Peppone*, 1955) and *Don Camillo monsignore ma non troppo* (*Don Cammillo: Monsignor*, 1961).

GARRONE, MATTEO (1968–). Director, screenwriter, cameraman. One of the most impressive young directors to emerge in the late 1990s, Garrone studied art before working for several years as an assistant camera operator. His first short film, *Silhouette* (1995), a semifictional presentation of the lives of Nigerian prostitutes in Italy, won first prize at the 1996 Sacher Festival. *Silhouette* formed the basis for the opening episode of his first feature, *Terra di mezzo* (*Middle Ground*, 1997), a film that forcefully highlighted the hinterland experience of illegal migrants in Italy and which was awarded the Jury Special Prize at the Turin International Festival of Young Cinema. Garrone's next film, *Ospiti* (*Guests*, 1998), the tragicomic portrayal of two young Albanian immigrants who come to live as "guests" in one of the wealthier parts of Rome, won the Italian Cineclub Federation (FEDIC) award and special mention at the **Venice Festival**. After *Estate romana* (*Roman Summer*, 2000), another tragicomic portrayal of existential dislocation in modern-day Rome, Garrone made the film that many have considered his best to date, *L'imbalsamatore* (*The Embalmer*, 2002), a slightly surreal and macabre black comedy that was well received both in Italy and abroad and that was nominated for nine **David di Donatello** awards, eventually winning for Best Screenplay and Best Supporting Actor. After *Primo amore* (*First Love*, 2004), the story of a goldsmith's obsessive attempt to reduce the body of the woman he loves to his ideal dimensions, Garrone has recently achieved his greatest triumph to date with *Gomorra* (2008), a powerful adaptation of Roberto Savianio's best-selling novel about the Neapolitan mafia, which was awarded the Grand Prize at Cannes.

GASSMAN, VITTORIO (1922–2000). Actor. Celebrated as Italy's greatest stage and screen actor of the postwar period, Gassman was born in Genoa but grew up in Rome. As a teenager he showed great promise as a basketball player but eventually the lure of the stage won out and he enrolled to receive classical training in theater at the National Academy of Dramatic Art. His talent was soon recognized and even before formally graduating from the academy he was called to work with the prestigious company of Alda Borelli in Milan. By 1944 he had formed his own touring company and by 1946 he was not only appearing on stage but had also, in collaboration with **Luciano Salce**, published a handbook on acting, *L'educazione teatrale* (Training for the Theater). Following a successful tour of Paris and London, in 1948 he was called to work with director **Luchino Visconti** and won high praise, particularly for his interpretation of Stanley Kowalski in Tennessee Williams's *A Streecar Named Desire* and as Troilus in Shakespeare's *Troilus and Cressida*. After three years as principal actor for the National Theater, in 1952 he joined with director Luigi Squarzina to give birth to the Teatro d'Arte Italiano (Italian Art Theater), in which he performed many of the classics to great acclaim.

By this time he had, almost naturally, also begun to appear in films, his first role being one of the male leads in Giovanni Paolucci's romantic melodrama *Preludio d'amore* (*Shamed*, 1946). There followed several other romantic leads in **Mario Soldati**'s *Daniele Cortis* (1947) and **Mario Camerini**'s *La figlia del capitano* (*The Captain's Daughter*, 1947), but, especially in the wake of his performance as the evil Walter in **Giuseppe De Santis**'s *Riso amaro* (*Bitter Rice*, 1949), he was frequently cast as the melodramatic villain, as in **Alberto Lattuada**'s *Anna* (1951) or **Luigi Comencini**'s *La tratta delle bianche* (*The White Slave Trade*, 1952). Following his marriage in 1952 to the American actress Shelley Winters, he began appearing in a number of American films, including Maxwell Shane's *The Glass Wall* (1952), in which he played an illegal immigrant to the United States who eventually commits suicide from desperation, and Joseph H. Lewis's *Cry of the Hunted* (1952), in which he is an escaped convict on the run. Overall, however, and in spite of appearing with American actresses of the caliber of Elizabeth Taylor and Audrey Hepburn, Gassman's career in Hollywood remained a relatively modest affair.

Back in Italy (and having divorced Winters) he was slightly more successful directing his first film, *Kean: Genio e sregolatezza* (*Kean: Genius or Scoundrel*, 1956), in which he himself played the role of the famous 19th-century English actor Edmund Kean. The real break in his film career, however, came with his appearance as the stuttering ex-boxer, Peppe, in **Mario Monicelli**'s *I soliti ignoti* (*Big Deal on Madonna Street*, 1958), a role that finally revealed his extraordinary propensity for comedy and which was recognized with the award of his first **Nastro d'argento**. The critical and box office triumph of *I soliti ignoti* was then repeated in Monicelli's *La grande guerra* (*The Great War*, 1960), in which Gassman's performance as the reluctant infantryman Giovanni Busacca won him his first **David di Donatello**. With the fundamental parameters of his comic persona firmly established, there followed a host of films in which he played variations on a basic characterization, a superficial bragadoccio and a loud can-do-anything attitude masking a more basic wiliness and feeling of insecurity. It was thus as something of a personification of an Italy nervously riding the wave of the so-called economic miracle that Gassman came to appear in so many of the key films of the ***commedia all'italiana***, from **Dino Risi**'s *Il sorpasso* (*The Easy Life*, 1962) and *I mostri* (1963) to **Ettore Scola**'s *C'eravamo tanto amati*

(*We All Loved Each Other So Much*, 1973). Perhaps his most nuanced performance of this characterization, the retired and blind military officer in Risi's *Profumo di donna* (*Scent of a Woman*, 1974), earned him not only another Nastro and a David but also the prize for Best Actor at Cannes. The film's widespread international success also prompted a number of further appearances in American films in the late 1970s, the most notable being in Robert Altman's *A Wedding* (1978) and *Quintet* (1978).

Although he continued to alternate between stage and screen, as he had done throughout his career, Gassman reduced his involvement in films during the 1980s while still providing many memorable performances, the most outstanding being in the role of the patriarch in Scola's *La famiglia* (*The Family*, 1987), for which he was awarded the sixth David of his career, and as the zany but lovable uncle in **Franco Brusati**'s *Lo zio indegno* (*The Sleazy Uncle*, 1989). Having collected a host of honors and prizes throughout his career, in 1993 he was awarded an honorary degree from the University of Urbino for his contribution to Italian culture. In 1996 he received a Career David and a Golden Lion at the **Venice Festival** for his extraordinary lifetime achievement.

GEMMA, GIULIANO (1938–). Actor. After being a keen sportsman in his teenage years, Gemma began his career in films working as a stuntman at **Cinecittà**. Following a number of tiny roles, including a momentary (and uncredited) appearance in William Wyler's *Ben-Hur* (1959), he scored a substantial part in Duccio Tessari's **peplum** *Arrivano i Titani* (*The Titans*, 1961). More prestigious was his appearance as Garibaldi's General in **Luchino Visconti**'s *Il gattopardo* (*The Leopard*, 1963), following which he did several more sword-and-sandal epics before launching into a host of **spaghetti Westerns**, often under the pseudonym Montgomery Wood. He thereafter alternated between playing the facile characters of popular B-grade films such as Pasquale Festa Campanile's prehistoric sex comedy, *Quando le donne avevano la coda* (*When Women Had Tails*, 1970), and the gangster spoof, *Anche gli angeli mangiano fagioli* (*Even Angels Eat Beans*, 1973), and taking on more significant roles in auteur films, such as the heroic **Resistance** fighter Silvio Corbari in **Valentino Orsini**'s *Corbari* (1970) or the character of Mattis in **Valerio Zurlini**'s adaptation of the Dino Buzzati novel *Il deserto dei Tartari*

(*The Desert of the Tartars*, 1976), a finely nuanced interpretation that earned him a **David di Donatello**. A year later he provided a similarly convincing personification of Cesare Mori, the police prefect sent to Sicily by Mussolini to clean up the Mafia, in **Pasquale Squitieri**'s *Il prefetto di ferro* (*The Iron Prefect*, 1977).

After appearing as the detective, Germani, in **Dario Argento**'s **horror** classic *Tenebre* (*Tenebrae*, 1982), and as the Western comic book hero Tex in Duccio Tessari's *Tex Willer e il signore degli abissi* (*Tex and the Lord of the Deep*, 1985), Gemma gravitated more toward playing supporting roles in television miniseries. This permitted him to indulge in what had always been another of his passionate interests, sculpture. Gemma's most recent television appearance has been as Judge Concato in the two-episode crime drama *La bambina dalle mani sporche* (*The Little Girl with Dirty Hands*, 2005), directed by Renzo Martinelli.

GENINA, AUGUSTO (1892–1957). Director and screenwriter. A prolific director whose career spanned four decades and over 100 films, Genina entered the silent-film industry in 1912 as a story writer, intially supplying subjects for the Film D'Arte Italiana and the Celio Film company. A year later he made his directorial debut with an Italian-Spanish coproduction, *La moglie di Sua Eccellenza* (*His Excellency's Wife*, 1914), filmed on location in Barcelona. During the next decade Genina worked for most of the major Italian studios, writing and directing a host of sophisticated comedies and dark melodramas full of love and betrayal, intrigues and disguises, nobles and paupers, foundlings, and femmes fatales. Having thus acquired a reputation for unerring professional competence, he was hired by the **Unione Cinematografica Italiana** (UCI) in 1919 to head one of their studios in Turin, where he produced, among others, a very effective adaptation of Edmond Rostand's *Cyrano De Bergerac*, which won first prize at the Turin Film Festival in 1923 and much praise in France some time before its Italian release.

Following the collapse of the UCI and the Italian film industry generally by the mid-1920s, Genina migrated to Germany in 1927, where he made several films with the UFA. In 1929 he moved to Paris, where he worked with René Clair, directing the outstanding *Prix de beauté* (released in Italy in 1930 as *Miss Europa*), a film starring Louise Brooks and coscripted by Genina and Clair, from a story by G. W. Pabst. Although shot silent, the film was dubbed into six languages and released to great acclaim.

With the industry slowly beginning to recover in Italy in the early 1930s, Genina returned and, in spite of lacking any strong personal commitment to Fascism, directed several films that appeared to echo the regime's militaristic rhetoric and to support its colonialistic aspirations: *Squadrone bianco* (*White Squadron*, 1936), *L'assedio dell'Alcazar* (*The Seige of Alcazar*, 1940), and *Bengasi* (1942). Although the considerable aesthetic achievement of these films was always acknowledged—indeed, Alcazar was highly praised by both **Luigi Chiarini** and **Michelangelo Antonioni**—their ideological basis counted strongly against Genina in the immediate postwar period. This negative evaluation of the director was redeemed to some extent by *Il cielo sulla palude* (*The Sky above the Swamp*, 1949), an effective, quasi-neorealist biography of the modern saint Maria Goretti, a young girl who had allowed herself to be murdered rather than compromise her virginity. The film received the award for Best Film and Best Director at the **Venice Festival** in 1949 and the **Nastro d'argento** for best direction in 1950. Genina's last film, *Frou-Frou*, filmed in Paris in 1955, was a well-made and colorful romantic melodrama not dissimilar in style and spirit to many of the films that he had produced in his early silent period.

GERMI, PIETRO (1914–1974). Actor, director, and screenwriter. Born into a family of very modest means, Germi held ambitions to become an officer and so enrolled in the Naval Institute of his native Genoa. Within three years, however, he had abandoned his plan in favor of attempting a career in the cinema. In 1937 he moved to Rome to study at the **Centro Sperimentale di Cinematografia**, where he proved to be a somewhat disruptive student, but not enough to be prevented from soon working as an assistant to **Alessandro Blasetti** on *Retroscena* (*Backstage*, 1939), and with Amleto Palermi on *La peccatrice* (*The Sinner*, 1940).

After appearing as an extra in Blasetti's *La corona di ferro* (*The Iron Crown*, 1941) and **Goffredo Alessandrini**'s *Nozze di sangue* (*Blood Wedding*, 1941), Germi made his directorial debut in 1945 with *Il testimone* (*The Witness*, released 1946), from a story that he had written himself and which was financed by the Catholic production company Orbis. Although superficially identified with **neorealism**, it was dark and expressionistic in tone and displayed, above all, the strong influence of American crime films, as did *Gioventù perduta* (*Lost Youth*, 1947) and *In nome della legge* (*In the Name of the Law*, 1948), which was set in Sicily and explored the influence of the Mafia but was also clearly indebted to the Westerns of John Ford. Germi came closer to the social commitment of neorealism with *Il cammino della speranza* (*Path of Hope*, 1950) and *Il brigante di Tacca Del Lupo* (*The Bandit of Tacca del Lupo*, 1952), but these were followed by two minor films, made on commission, which Germi himself would later dismiss: *La presidentessa* (*Mademoiselle Gobete*, 1952) and *Gelosia* (*Jealousy*, 1953). There was a return to a more socially committed style of filmmaking with *Il ferroviere* (*The Railroad Man*, 1956) and *L'uomo di paglia* (*A Man of Straw*, 1958), in both of which he also played the lead, and he continued to direct himself in *Un maledetto imbroglio* (*The Facts of Murder*, 1959), an interesting if not altogether successful attempt to adapt Carlo Emilio Gadda's complex murder mystery, *Quer pasticciaccio brutto de Via Merulana*.

Germi's most famous film, however, and the one that brought him to international notice, was *Divorzio all'italiana* (*Divorce Italian Style*, 1961), which won two **Nastri d'argento** and two Golden Globes, was nominated for three Oscars, and won the Oscar for Best Screenplay. The film has continued to be regarded by many as one of the high points of the *commedia all'italiana* and certainly one of **Marcello Mastroianni**'s finest performances. After another biting satire of Sicilian marriage customs and notions of honor in *Sedotta e abbandonata* (*Seduced and Abandoned*, 1963), which brought him the **David di Donatello** for direction, Germi turned his satirical sights north to the Veneto region in the three-episode *Signori e signore* (*The Birds, the Bees and the Italians*, 1965), which was poorly received in Italy but was awarded the Palme d'or at Cannes. There followed several other comedies: *L'Immorale* (*Climax*, 1966), which was thought by many to be a refracted portrait of **Vittorio De Sica** and his complicated love life, *Serafino* (1968), *Le castagne sono buone* (*A Pocketful of Chestnuts*, 1970), and *Alfredo, Alfredo* (1972), universally regarded as one of his least successful films in spite of the presence of Dustin Hoffman in the leading role. His last film would have been *Amici miei* (*My Friends*, 1975), which he had written and was preparing to shoot when he died, the film eventually being directed, to great acclaim, by **Mario Monicelli**.

GHERARDI, PIERO (1909–1971). Art director and production and costume designer. Originally trained as an architect, Gherardi gravitated toward the cinema after World War II, working first as a set decorator on **Mario Soldati**'s *Daniele Cortis* (1947) and *Fuga in Francia* (*Flight into France*, 1948) and then as art director for **Luigi Zampa**'s *Anni facili* (*Easy Years*, 1953). Quick to recognize Gherardi's enormous talents, **Mario Monicelli** employed him as production designer for a number of his films, including *Proibito* (*Forbidden*, 1954), *Totò e Carolina* (*Totò and Carolina*, 1955), *Padri e figli* (*A Tailor's Maid*, 1955), and Monicelli's landmark comedy, *I soliti ignoti* (*Big Deal on Madonna Street*, 1958). By this time Gherardi had also initiated what would be a close and fruitful association with **Federico Fellini**, designing both the sets and costumes for *Le notti di Cabiria* (*Nights of Cabiria*, 1957), *La dolce vita* (1960)—Gherardi was the one responsible for re-creating the Via Veneto at **Cinecittà**—and *Otto e mezzo* (*8½*, 1963), his contribution to the last two films earning him the two Oscars of his relatively short career. His production design for Fellini's *Giulietta degli spiriti* (*Juliet of the Spirits*, 1965) brought him the second **Nastro d'argento** of his career, the first having already been conferred on him for his production design for *La dolce vita* and the third being awarded for his costume design for Monicelli's *L'armata Brancaleone* (*For Love and Gold*, 1966). His most interesting later work was probably the costume design for **Mario Bava**'s *Diabolik* (*Danger: Diabolik*, 1968).

GHIONE, EMILIO (1872–1930). Actor and director. Trained as a miniaturist, Ghione came to the cinema by chance when, unexpectedly, in 1908, he was asked to work as a stuntman and extra for **Itala Film** in Turin. After also playing supporting roles in several of Itala's **Cretinetti** films, he moved to Rome in 1911, where he scored major parts in a number of films with the **Cines**. In 1913 he transferred to the newly established Celio Film company and appeared in several films directed by **Baldassare Negroni**, including the landmark film pantomime, *Historie d'un Pierrot* (*Pierrot the Prodigal*, 1913). This led to his directorial debut, *Idolo infranto* (*Broken Idol*, 1913), which starred the diva **Francesca Bertini**. Ghione's most famous films, however, were the ones in which he directed himself as **Za-la-Mort**, a gentleman thief and dark moral avenger, whom he fashioned on the French models of Victorin Jasset and Louis Feuillade. The films used stark, expressionistic lighting to further hollow out the gaunt and cadaverous features of the mysterious protagonist as he pursued his vengeance in a dark and shadowy underworld.

Ghione produced a dozen feature films and several series featuring the Za-la-Mort character, the most famous being the eight-episode *Topi grigi* (*Gray Mice*). The series (and the character) were extremely popular for a time and Ghione figured as one of the *divi* of the period, earning fabulously and spending all of it on living the high life. By the 1920s, however, the popularity of Za-la-Mort was fading. Ghione acted in a number of other films, including **Carmine Gallone**'s *La Cavalcata ardente* (*The Fiery Cavalcade*, 1926), but his star was waning. He turned to the theater for a time but with little success. In 1929 he migrated to Paris, where he lived a destitute existence and eventually fell ill. Repatriated with the financial help of friends, he died in Turin in 1930.

GIALLO. Film genre. The Italian use of the term *giallo* for mystery or detective fiction derives from the distinctive yellow covers of the cheap paperback editions of translations of authors such as Edgar Wallace, Agatha Christie, and Arthur Conan Doyle, which began to be published in Italy in the late 1920s. As applied to films, however, the *giallo* is an extremely wide-ranging and permeable generic category that can include anything from the simple whodunit or police procedural to the psychological thriller and the **horror** and slasher film.

Some historians have seen early antecedents of the modern *giallo* in a number of murder mystery and crime detection films produced in Italy in the interwar years, films such as **Guido Brignone**'s *Corte d'Assise* (1930), Nunzio Malasomma's *L'uomo dall'artiglio* (*The Man with the Claw*, 1931), **Mario Camerini**'s *Giallo* (1933), and Gentile Gentilomo's *Cortocircuito* (Short Circuit, 1943). In the immediate postwar period, films such as **Pietro Germi**'s *Il testimone* (*The Testimony*, 1947) and *Un maledetto imbroglio* (*The Facts of*

Murder, 1958) also appear to foreshadow some of the later develop-
ments of the genre. Nevertheless, the *giallo* proper is usually regarded as beginning with **Mario Bava**'s *La ragazza che sapeva
troppo* (*The Evil Eye*, 1962), which laid down the narrative framework that would become one of the staples of the genre, namely, the
story of an innocent eyewitness to a violent murder who takes on the
role of amateur detective in order to track down the killer and, in the
process, becomes one of the killer's main targets. Two years later,
Bava's *Sei donne per l'assassino* (*Blood and Black Lace*, 1964) also
established what would become the genre's most distinctive visual
tropes: the killer's ubiquitous black leather gloves and trench coat,
wide-brimmed hat and masked face, graphic and drawn-out killings
staged as spectacular set pieces, the liberal use of knives and other
slashing weapons, and a complicit subjective camera that places the
spectator in the position of the killer.

At first overshadowed by the more flourishing genres of the
spaghetti Western and the horror film, the *giallo* began to gather real
momentum in the late 1960s, emerging in a distinctly erotic version
in films such as **Umberto Lenzi**'s *Orgasmo* (*Paranoia*, 1969) and
Così dolce così perversa (*So Sweet . . . So Perverse*, 1970), Romolo
Guerrieri's *Il dolce corpo di Deborah* (*The Sweet Body of Deborah*,
1968), and **Lucio Fulci**'s *Una sull'altra* (*One on Top of the Other*,
1969). The form received its greatest boost with **Dario Argento**'s
L'uccello dalle piume di cristallo (*The Bird with the Crystal
Plumage*, 1969), which effectively modernized the genre by characterizing the killer's irrepressible impulse to murder as determined by
an earlier, usually childhood, trauma. With his subsequent *Il gatto a
nove code* (*The Cat o' Nine Tails*, 1971) and *Quattro mosche di velluto grigio* (*Four Flies on Grey Velvet*, 1971), Argento confirmed his
mastery of the genre, which then exploded frenetically over the next
five years in a plethora of slasherfests that included Fulci's *Una
lucertola con la pelle di donna* (*A Lizard in a Woman's Skin*, 1971)
and *Non si sevizia un paperino* (*Don't Torture a Duckling*, 1972),
Sergio Martino's *Lo strano vizio della signora Wardh* (*Blade of the
Ripper*, 1971), Paolo Cavara's *La tarantola dal ventre nero* (*Black
Belly of the Tarantula*, 1971), Aldo Lado's *La corta notte delle bambole di vetro* (*Short Night of the Glass Dolls,* 1972), Mario Caiano's
L'occhio nel labirinto (*The Eye in the Labyrinth*, 1972), Giuliano

Carnimeo's *Perché quelle strane gocce di sangue sul corpo di Jennifer?* (*What Are Those Strange Drops of Blood Doing on Jennifer's Body?* 1972), and Umberto Lenzi's *Spasmo* (*The Death Dealer*, 1974). While these films could vary in their (often improbable) stories and settings, they generally worked according to a recognizable formula and tended to employ a limited number of character actors such as George Hilton, Jean Sorel, Luigi Pistilli, Edwige Fenech, Carroll Baker, and Ivan Rassimonov, who thus came to be especially associated with the genre. Although critically dismissed as exploitative and misogynist, many of the films were also graced with effective and memorable musical scores by composers of the caliber of **Ennio Morricone** and Bruno Nicolai. In 1975 Argento took the *giallo* to new heights with *Profondo rosso* (*Deep Red*) before moving to the supernatural horror genre with *Suspiria* (*Dario Argento's Suspiria*, 1977). Veteran directors such as **Luigi Comencini** and **Steno** also took up the genre during this period, albeit in its more traditional form of the police investigation, and **Francesco Rosi** provided a political version of the *giallo* with his *Cadaveri eccellenti* (*Illustrious Corpses*, 1976). Nevertheless, by the late 1970s the *giallo's* fortunes had clearly begun to wane, with many of the directors who had practiced it extensively moving to related genres like the police action thriller and the zombie-cannibal movie. At the same time, much of its taste for spectacular gore and violence was taken up by the budding American stalk-and-slasher film.

The genre reappeared only sporadically over the next two decades, with Argento returning to it with his own *Tenebre* (*Tenebrae*, 1982) and *Nonhosonno* (*Sleepless*, 2001) and its sexy version making a reappearance in films such as Carlo Vanzina's *Sotto il vestito niente* (*Nothing Underneath*, 1985) and **Lamberto Bava**'s *Le foto di Gioia* (*Delirium*, 1987). More recently the continuing popularity of the literary *giallo* has led to two acclaimed films, Alex Infascelli's *Almost Blue* (2000), adapted from Carlo Lucarelli's novel of the same name, and Eros Puglielli's *Occhi di cristallo* (*Eyes of Crystal*, 2004), from Luca di Fulvio's *L'impagliatore* (The Taxidermist).

GIANNINI, GIANCARLO (1942–). Actor. Born at La Spezia, Giannini grew up in Naples but moved to Rome to study at the National Academy of Dramatic Art. He made his professional theatrical debut in 1963 as Puck in an Italian production of Shakespeare's *Midsummer Night's Dream*. He soon acquired a strong reputation for his performances both on stage and on television, distinguishing himself particularly in the lead role of a much-praised television adaptation of Charles Dickens's *David Copperfield* (1965). By this time he was also appearing in films, beginning with Gino Mancini's police thriller *Fango sulla metropoli* (Mud on the City, 1965) and then playing the love interest of popular singer Rita Pavone in **Lina Wertmüller**'s *Rita la zanzara* (*Rita the Mosquito*, 1966) and *Non stuzzicate la zanzara* (*Don't Sting the Mosquito*, 1967). After being noticed for his performance in **Ettore Scola**'s *Dramma della gelosia: Tutti i particolari in cronaca* (*The Pizza Triangle*, 1970) and his strong supporting role in **Valerio Zurlini**'s *La prima notte di quiete* (*Indian Summer*, 1972), he achieved both national and international renown as the ebullient Mimì in Wertmüller's *Mimì metallurgico ferito nell'onore* (*The Seduction of Mimi*, 1972), for which he received both the **David di Donatello** and the **Nastro d'argento**. He subsequently starred, most often paired with the fiery **Melangela Melato**, in another half dozen of Wertmüller's social farces, earning an Oscar nomination for his performance in *Pasqualino Settebellezze* (*Seven Beauties*, 1975).

In the following years Giannini worked with many of the major Italian and international directors, playing the lead in **Luchino Visconti**'s *L'innocente* (*The Innocent*, 1976) and one of the main roles in Rainer Werner Fassbinder's *Lili Marleen* (1981). His exceptionally fine performance as the Neapolitan scrounger and fix-it man in **Nanni Loy**'s *Mi manda Picone* (*Picone Sent Me*, 1984), brought him his second Nastro d'argento, and he received a third for his dubbing of Al Pacino in the Italian version of *Carlito's Way* (1994). He continued to work prolifically throughout the 1990s, often appearing in several films a year. Most recently he was awarded his fourth Silver Ribbon for his role as the Italian police inspector in Ridley Scott's *Hannibal* (2001).

GIORDANA, MARCO TULLIO (1950–). Director and screenwriter. After an intense involvement with left-wing politics during his student years, Giordana worked with **Roberto Faenza** on the feature-length political documentary *Forza Italia* (1978). Three years later he wrote and directed his first fictional feature, *Maledetti vi amerò* (*To*

Love the Damned, 1980), a bitter reflection on the failure of the 1968 movement to achieve its utopian goals. This was followed by *La caduta degli angeli ribelli* (*The Fall of the Rebel Angels*, 1981), which recounted an ill-fated liaison between a middle-class wife and mother and a terrorist on the run, and *Notti e nebbie* (Nights and Fog, 1984), a two-part television adaptation of a wartime novel by Carlo Castellaneta. In the wake of the tragedy at the Heysel soccer stadium in Brussels in 1985, Giordana made *Appuntamento a Liverpool* (Rendezvous at Liverpool, 1988), a thriller in which a young woman attempts to track down the person responsible for her father's death. After a period spent directing opera and lyric theater in the early 1990s and also publishing a novel, *Vita segreta del signore delle macchine* (Secret Life of the Lord of Machines, 1990), Giordana returned to the big screen in 1995 with *Pasolini, un delitto italiano* (*Pasolini, an Italian Crime*), a fictional investigation of the many still-unexplained circumstances surrounding the brutal murder of **Pier Paolo Pasolini**.

This was followed by the similarly socially committed *I cento passi* (*The Hundred Steps*, 2000), which recounted the life and death of Peppino Impastato, a passionate young left-wing organizer blown up by the Mafia in Sicily in 1978. The film was widely praised and received a host of prizes, including the Scholars Jury **David di Donatello** and the **Venice Festival** Pasinetti Award. Giordana's greatest triumph, however, came with *La meglio gioventù* (*The Best of Youth*, 2003) a moving six-hour family saga set within the context of 40 years of recent Italian history. Originally made for RAI television, the film was shown in two parts at Cannes, where it won the *Un certain regard* section and thereafter achieved spectacular international box office success. Giordana's most recent work, *Quando sei nato non puoi più nasconderti* (*Once You're Born You Can No Longer Hide*, 2005), a film highlighting the plight of illegal immigrants to Italy, seen from the viewpoint of a young Italian boy, has also been strongly acclaimed, confirming Giordana's standing as one of the most socially conscious of contemporary Italian filmmakers.

GIROTTI, MARIO (1939–). Actor. Born in Italy of an Italian father and a German mother, Girotti was first enticed into the film industry at the age of 12 by **Dino Risi**, who gave him a small part in *Vazanze* *col gangster* (*Vacation with a Gangster*, 1951). He then went on to study classics at the University of Rome but soon abandoned academic studies in order to act in films.

After minor roles in **Mauro Bolognini**'s *La vena d'oro* (*The Golden Vein*, 1955) and **Gillo Pontecorvo**'s *La grande strada azzurra* (*The Wide Blue Road*, 1957), he appeared as Count Cavriaghi in **Luchino Visconti**'s *Il gattopardo* (*The Leopard*, 1963). There followed a drift toward the European Western, first with parts in a number of the German Westerns adapted from the novels of Karl May, which included *Winnetou 2. Teil* (*Winnetou: Last of the Renegades*, 1964), directed by Harald Reinl, and *Der Ölprinz* (*Rampage at Apache Wells*, 1965), directed by Harald Philipp, and then with a small role in the Italian musical Western *Rita nel West* (*Crazy Westerners*, 1967). This led to the role of Cat Stevens in *Dio perdona . . . io no* (*God Forgives . . . I Don't*, 1967), the first film in which he adopted the Anglo-Saxon pseudonym **Terence Hill**, and teamed up with **Bud Spencer**. As Hill, and with Spencer, he went on to make a long series of knockabout comedies beginning with *Lo chiamavano Trinità* (*My Name Is Trinity*, 1971) and continuing with . . . *continuavano a chiamarlo Trinità* (*Trinity Is Still My Name*, 1972), and *Altrimenti ci arrabbiamo* (*Watch Out! We're Mad*, 1974).

Having achieved an international reputation with the Trinity films, in the mid-1970s Girotti moved to Hollywood, where he made *March or Die* (1977) with Gene Hackman and *Mr. Billion* (1977), directed by Jonathan Kaplan. After directing himself in an updated version of *Don Camillo* (*The World of Don Camillo*, 1983) and following the death of his teenage son in a car accident, Hill largely withdrew from the cinema for a number of years but returned to prominence playing the popular priest-detective in the long-running Italian television series *Don Matteo* (2000–2006).

GIROTTI, MASSIMO (1918–2003). Actor. After university studies in engineering, Girotti embarked on a career as an athlete, becoming one of the star swimmers of the Lazio team. By chance the swimming coach, Fulvio Jacchia, also worked as a scenographer at **Cinecittà** and so introduced Girotti to **Mario Soldati**, who gave him a small part in *Dora Nelson* (1939). Girotti's physique and good looks soon brought him to the attention of **Alessandro Blasetti**, who cast him as the good king Licinio and his son, Arminio, in *La corona di ferro* (*The Iron Crown*, 1941), following which **Roberto Rossellini** gave him the lead in *Un pilota ritorna* (*A Pilot Returns*, 1942). Then came what would remain Girotti's defining performance, that of Gino, the handsome young tramp, in **Luchino Visconti**'s *Ossessione* (*Obsession*, 1943).

After the war Girotti took the lead in a number of significant neorealist films, appearing as Michele, the just-married husband whose wife is kidnapped, in **Giuseppe De Santis**'s *Caccia tragica* (*Tragic Hunt*, 1947) and as the determined young magistrate in **Pietro Germi**'s *In nome della legge* (*In the Name of the Law*, 1949), a powerful performance that earned him the **Nastro d'argento**. A year later he played Guido in **Michelangelo Antonioni**'s *Cronaca di un amore* (*Story of a Love Affair*, 1950) followed by the role of the patriotic marquis, Roberto Ussoni, in Visconti's *Senso* (*The Wanton Countess*, 1954).

His career then faded somewhat with not much more than appearances in a number of sword-and-sandal epics but was revived when, with his usual acumen, **Pier Paolo Pasolini** cast him as the father in *Teorema* (*Theorem*, 1968) and **Bernardo Bertolucci** had him play Rosa's lover, Marcel, in *Ultimo Tango a Parigi* (*Last Tango in Paris*, 1972). In the following years he continued to appear in a number of minor supporting roles, as in **Giuliano Montaldo**'s *L'Agnese va a morire* (*And Agnes Chose to Die*, 1976) and Joseph Losey's *Monsieur Klein* (*Mr. Klein*, 1976). He then gave a very creditable performance as the Colonel in **Ettore Scola**'s *Passione d'amore* (*Passion of Love*, 1981) and played the part of the distinguished resident in **Roberto Benigni**'s *Il monstro* (*The Monster*, 1994). A decade later, just before passing away, he crowned a career of solid achievement with his very powerful and sensitive portrayal of the elderly amnesiac survivor of the death camps in **Ferzan Ozpetek**'s *La finestra di fronte* (*Facing Windows*, 2003).

GRIMALDI, AURELIO (1957–). Novelist, screenwriter, director. Grimaldi began as a writer in the late 1980s recounting his experience as a teacher in a Palermo juvenile prison. He subsequently adapted one of his novels set in a Sicilian reformatory as the screenplay of **Marco Risi**'s *Mery per sempre* (*Forever Mary*, 1989), which received the Special Grand Jury Prize at Cannes that year. This was followed by *Ragazzi fuori* (*Boys on the Outside*, 1990), effectively a sequel to *Mery*, which followed the lives of the young juveniles once they had been discharged.

After scripting *Uomo di rispetto* (*Man of Respect*, 1992), one of **Damiano Damiani**'s films on the Mafia, and providing the subject for Felice Farina's *Ultimo respiro* (*The Last Breath*, 1992), Grimaldi began writing and directing his own films, beginning with *La discesa di Aclà a Floristella* (*Aclà's Descent into Floristella*, 1992), a story about child labor and exploitation, and *La ribelle* (*The Rebel*, 1993), a portrait of Enza, a streetwise but sexually innocent 16-year-old juvenile, convincingly played by a young Penelope Cruz. After *Le Buttane* (*The Whores*, 1994), another hard-edged portrayal of the life of a group of Sicilian prostitutes, Grimaldi went even further with the provocative *Nerolio. Sputerò su mio padre* (*Blackoil: I Will Spit on My Father*), a fictional portrait of the last days of **Pier Paolo Pasolini** (made in 1996 but only released in Italy two years later). There followed *Il macellaio* (*The Butcher*, 1998) and *La donna lupo* (*The Man-Eater*, 1999) before Grimaldi returned to Pasolini with *Un mondo d'amore* (*A World of Love*, 2001), this time focusing on an earlier period of Pasolini's life. A year later, still obsessed with Pasolini, as he himself admitted, Grimaldi produced a contemporary Neapolitan remake of Pasolini's *Mamma Roma* (1962) with his *Rosa Funzeca* (2002). The erotic-libertine dimension present in the earlier films was made more explicit in Grimaldi's most recent film, *L'educazione sentimentale di Eugenie* (*The Sentimental Education of Eugenie*, 2005), loosely adapted from the Marquis de Sade.

GUAZZONI, ENRICO (1876–1949). Painter, director. With a degree in fine arts and a background in painting, Guazzoni began his career in films as a scenographer for the Alberini & Santoni company in Rome in 1906. In 1909 he joined **Cines**, originally as set designer for **Mario Caserini**, but he soon became one of the company's most prolific and high-profile directors. Although he would make films in a wide variety of genres, he became best known for his grand historical epics, especially those set in Roman times, which demonstrated a real flair for the spectacular and consistently created a strong sense of three-dimensional space absent from earlier films of the genre. The moderate acclaim won by Guazzoni's early Roman films like *Agrippina and Brutus*, released in 1911, paled before the overwhelming international success a year later of *Quo vadis?*, a film that catapulted him to world fame and set the benchmark for epic spectacle from then on. Guazzoni lifted that benchmark himself a year later with the colossal (and colossally budgeted) *Giulio Cesare* (*Julius Caesar*), a film that required not only the accurate miniature reconstruction of the entire city of Rome but also the employment of 20,000 extras for the crowd scenes.

Having set up his own production company in 1918, he continued to produce large-canvas films such as the medieval epic *Gerusalemme Liberata* (*The Crusaders*, 1918), adapted from Torquato Tasso's poem, and *Clemente VII e il sacco di Roma* (*The Sack of Rome*, 1920), but the company soon collapsed in the general crisis that gripped the industry in the early 1920s. In 1923, however, again for the Cines, he directed what many regard as his most spectacular film, *Messalina*, which raised the sword-and-sandal epic to new heights and included a splendid chariot race that would be closely imitated, two years later, in the Hollywood production of *Ben-Hur*. Nevertheless, the cost of the film helped to bankrupt the company and Guazzoni left the industry to return only briefly in the 1930s with a small number of lighthearted and humorous films, the best known being *Re burlone* (*The Joker King*, 1935).

GUERRA, TONINO (1920–). (Born Antonio Guerra.) Poet, painter, novelist, installation artist, screenwriter. While establishing a strong reputation as a dialect poet and fiction writer in the late 1950s, Guerra also began to write for the cinema, his first collaborations being with **Giuseppe De Santis** on *Uomini e lupi* (*Men and Wolves*, 1956) and *La strada lunga un anno* (*The Year Long Road*, 1958). Two years later, with his screenplay for *L'avventura* (*The Adventure*, 1960), he initiated what would become a lifelong partnership with **Michelangelo Antonioni,** which would see him writing all of Antonioni's subsequent films (with the exception of *The Passenger* [1975]) and sharing an Oscar nomination with the director for the screenplay of *Blowup* (*Blow-Up*, 1966). By the mid-1960s, while continuing to publish poetry and fiction, he had also instituted a similarly long and fruitful partnership with **Francesco Rosi**, for whom he would write all the major films from *C'era una volta* (*More Than a Miracle*, 1967) to *La tregua* (*The Truce*, 1997). Only a few years later his contribution to **Federico Fellini**'s *Amarcord* (1973) earned him his second Oscar nomination for screenwriting.

During the 1980s he continued to write for Antonioni and Fellini while also collaborating with **Paolo and Vittorio Taviani** on several of their most acclaimed films, including *La notte di San Lorenzo* (*Night of the Shooting Stars*, 1982), *Kaos* (*Chaos*, 1984), and *Good morning Babilonia* (*Good Morning, Babylon*, 1987). In 1983, having acquired an international reputation, Guerra was sought out by legendary Russian director Andrei Tarkovsky to help write the screenplay for *Nostalghia* (1983). Soon after, he also began working with eminent Greek director Theodoros Angelopoulos, with whom he would eventually make seven films, beginning with *Taxidi sta Kithira* (*Voyage to Cythera*, 1984), for which he received the Best Screenplay award at Cannes, and continuing through to the most recent *Trilogia I: To Livadi pou dakryzei* (*Trilogy: The Weeping Meadow*, 2004), which was nominated for the Golden Bear at Berlin.

After receiving a host of prizes and awards during his long career, in 2004 Guerra was also honored with the title of Best European Screenwriter at the first Festival of European Screenwriters at Strasbourg.

– H –

HILL, TERENCE. Actor. *See* GIROTTI, MARIO.

HORROR FILM. Film genre. With the significant exception of **Carmine Gallone**'s gothic mystery tale *Malombra* (1917) and Eugenio Testa's *Il Mostro di Frankenstein* (*Frankenstein's Monster*, 1920), Italian silent cinema appears to have shown little interest in the horror genre. In the early sound years **Alessandro Blasetti** made a version of the Jekyll and Hyde story, *Il Caso Haller* (The Haller Case, 1933), but it is generally agreed that the horror genre really only began in Italy in the late 1950s with **Riccardo Freda**'s *I vampiri* (*The Devil's Commandment*, 1957) and *Caltiki, il mostro immortale* (*Caltiki, the Immortal Monster*, 1959), both photographed and codirected by **Mario Bava**. The genre exploded, however, in 1960 when

Mario Bava made his landmark *Maschera del Demonio* (*Black Sunday*, 1960), flanked by Giorgio Ferroni's *Il mulino delle donne di pietra* (*Mill of the Stone Women*, 1960), Renato Polselli's *L'amante del vampiro* (*The Vampire and the Ballerina*, 1960), Piero Regnoli's *L'ultima preda del vampire* (*The Playgirls and the Vampire*, 1960), and Anton Giulio Majano's *Seddok, l'erede di Satana* (*Atom Age Vampire*, 1960).

The genre continued to flourish throughout the 1960s in films such as Freda's *L'orribile segreto del dottor Hichcock* (*The Horrible Secret of Dr. Hichcock*, 1962) and *Lo spettro* (*The Ghost*, 1963); **Antonio Margheriti**'s *La danza macabra* (*The Castle of Terror*, 1963), *La vergine di Norimberga* (*Horror Castle*, 1963), *I lunghi capelli della morte* (*The Long Hair of Death*, 1964), and *Contronatura* (*Unnaturals*, 1969); Camillo Mastrocinque's *La cripta e l'incubo* (*Terror in the Crypt*, 1964) and *Un angelo per Satana* (*An Angel for Satan*, 1966); and Massimo Pupillo's *Il boia scarlatto* (*Bloody Pit of Horror*, 1965), *Cinque tombe per un medium* (*Terror Creatures from the Grave*, 1966), and *La vendetta di Lady Morgan* (*The Vengeance of Lady Morgan*, 1966). The borders between the horror film proper and the emerging *giallo* were not always clear as the same directors often worked in both, and the spectacular aspects of horror also easily migrated to genres like the **peplum** in films such as Bava's *Ercole al centro della terra* (*Hercules in the Haunted World*, 1961) and Giacomo Gentilomo's *Maciste contro il vampiro* (1961), and to science fiction as in Bava's *Terrore nello spazio* (*Terror in Space*, 1965). The genre flourished so much during this period that it also spawned numerous parodies, such as **Steno**'s *Tempi duri per vampiri* (*Hard Times for Vampires*, 1959) and *Un mostro e mezzo* (*A Monster and a Half*, 1964).

In the 1970s the genre dissipated into a number of subgenres such as the zombie and cannibal films of **Lucio Fulci** and **Umberto Lenzi** but received new life in the work of **Dario Argento**, who came to be internationally renowned as the master of Italian horror for classics such as *Profondo rosso* (*Deep Red*, 1975), *Suspiria* (*Dario Argento's Suspiria*, 1976), and *Inferno* (*Dario Argento's Inferno*, 1980). A notable contribution to the genre was also made by the more art house director **Pupi Avati** with his *La casa dalle finestre che ridono* (*The House with Laughing Windows*, 1976), *Zeder* (*Revenge of the Dead*, 1983), and *L'arcano incantatore* (*The Arcane Enchanter*, 1996).

Although the genre was critically disregarded, it attracted collaboration from musicians such as **Ennio Morricone**, Roman Vlad, and **Riz Ortolani**, screenwriters such as **Ennio De Concini** and Bernardino Zapponi, and cinematographers like **Vittorio Storaro**, Luciano Tovoli, and Luigi Kuveiller, all of whom contributed to the spectacular quality of this genre.

– I –

I SOLITI IGNOTI (1958). (*BIG DEAL ON MADONNA STREET.*) Film. Directed by **Mario Monicelli** from a screenplay written by **Age e Scarpelli** and **Suso Cecchi D'Amico**, *I soliti ignoti* (literally "The Usual Unkowns") is widely acknowledged as the film that initiated the prolific genre of the *commedia all'italiana*. A sort of comic version of Jules Dassin's *Rififi* (1955) and an implicit parody of the American crime film, it recounts the story of a bungled attempt by a motley group of Roman petty thieves to break into a pawnbroker's shop in Via delle madonne (Madonna Street) to steal the valuables from its safe. The plan calls for the gang first to make their way at night into an empty apartment adjacent to the shop and then to break through its (supposedly) paper-thin wall to reach the room with the safe. Although nothing goes quite according to plan from the very beginning and complications result all along the way, the gang does manage finally to enter the apartment and, after a great deal of comic business, succeeds in breaking through the wall. They discover, however, to their jaw-dropping surprise, that they have chosen the wrong wall; instead of breaking into the pawnshop next door, they have only managed to break through to the apartment's own kitchen. Resigning themselves to the fact that the plan has misfired, they do the only thing they can do in the situation, which is to settle down at the table and finish off a pot of pasta and chickpeas that the owners have left behind on the stove. The newspaper headlines the next day will read: "The usual unknowns—thieves knock down a wall to steal a plate of pasta and chickpeas."

With stunning black-and-white photography by master cinematographer **Gianni Di Venanzo**, and a boisterous jazz score from **Piero Umiliani**, the film has become legendary in the annals of Italian cinema, not least for being a revelation of **Vittorio Gassman**'s previously unsuspected talent for comedy as well as being the film in which **Claudia Cardinale** made her screen debut. The film's comedy is multifaceted and draws on slapstick and farce for its verbal and visual gags and on situation comedy for its characterizations. A strikingly effective use is also made of the silent-film technique of intertitles. The greater part of the humor, however, derives from the characters themselves and the way in which they are incisively portrayed: Peppe (Gassman), a failed boxer with a stutter who has self-delusions about being "scientific" in his approach; Tiberio (**Marcello Mastroianni**), an unemployed photographer eternally playing mother to his infant child while his wife is in prison for selling contraband cigarettes; Mario (**Renato Salvatori**), the young thief always concerned about his mother; Ferribotte (Tiberio Murgia), the swarthy Sicilian who keeps his sister under lock and key in order to safeguard her virtue; and, perhaps the funniest and most unlikely of them all, Capanelle (Carlo Pisacane), a toothless old codger with a squeaky voice always ready to pounce on any food in the vicinity. The inclusion of **Totò** as Dante Cruciani, the retired master safecracker who lectures the boys on the finer points of the art, is an inspired touch, playing a crucial role in the film itself but also paying homage to the comedian's brilliant performance as a poor thief in Monicelli's own earlier *Guardie e ladri* (*Cops and Robbers*, 1951).

The film's extraordinary box office success prompted two sequels and a number of imitations. In *Audace colpo dei soliti ignoti* (*Fiasco in Milan*, 1959), directed a year later by **Nanni Loy**, the same gang of incompetents (minus Mastronianni's Tiberio but with the addition of **Nino Manfredi**) is drawn into a plan to rob the proceeds of a soccer match at the Milan stadium. Against all odds and in spite of all sorts of complications, they finally succeed in getting their hands on the money but are forced in the end to abandon it all in a public park. *I soliti ignoti vent'anni dopo* (*Big Deal after 20 Years*, 1985), directed by Amanzio Todini, brings back Mastroianni's Tiberio (but with only Ferribotte and Peppe from the old gang) in a plan that appears to involve smuggling currency across the Italian border for a syndicate of Yugoslav gangsters. In the end, Tiberio and his gang discover that they have been used as drug couriers. While Loy's more immediate sequel was judged almost as good as the original, Todini's film was generally dismissed as a much paler imitation.

INCROCCI, AGENORE (1919–2005). Screenwriter. For almost four decades, and always known simply as "Age," Incrocci teamed up with **Furio Scarpelli** to form the most productive screenwriting duo in Italian postwar cinema. Their prolific partnership began in the immediate postwar period when they both collaborated on the script of **Mario Monicelli**'s *Totò cerca casa* (*Totò Looks for an Apartment*, 1949), which became the first of over a dozen films they would help pen for the great comic actor **Totò**. After having worked together on over 30 films ranging from romantic comedies to action adventures, in 1958 they initiated the so-called *commedia all'italiana* with the story and screenplay of Monicelli's *I soliti ignoti* (*Big Deal on Madonna Street*, 1958), for which they shared their first **Nastro d'argento**. They subsequently wrote many of the great classics of the genre including *La grande guerra* (*The Great War*, 1960), *Tutti a casa* (*Everybody Go Home*, 1960), *Il sorpasso* (*The Easy Life*, 1962), *I mostri* (*15 from Rome*, 1963), and *C'eravamo tanto amati* (*We All Loved Each Other So Much*, 1974). In 1965 they received an Oscar nomination for their work with Monicelli on *I compagni* (*The Organizer*, 1963) and in 1980 their script for **Ettore Scola**'s *La terrazza* (*The Terrace*) received the award for Best Screenplay at Cannes. They were both also credited with helping to write **Sergio Leone**'s *Il buono, il brutto, il cattivo* (*The Good, the Bad and the Ugly*, 1966), although it appears that much of what they wrote was ultimately too comic and so not included in the final shooting script.

After separating amicably from Scarpelli in the mid-1980s, Incrocci collaborated with **Suso Cecchi d'Amico** on Amanzio Todini's *I soliti ignoti vent'anni dopo* (*Big Deal after 20 Years*, 1985) and worked on a number of minor films but gradually reduced his involvement in the industry in favor of teaching screenwriting privately. In 1990 he published his own screenwriting manual, *Scriviamo un film* (*Let's Write a Film*).

INDAGINE SU UN CITTADINO AL DI SOPRA DI OGNI SOSPETTO (1970). (*INVESTIGATION OF A CITIZEN ABOVE SUSPICION.*) Film. One of the most entertaining as well as disturbing police-political thrillers of the the early 1970s, *Investigation* was directed by **Elio Petri** and starred **Gian Maria Volontè** in one of his most impressive performances. Stylishly photographed by Luigi Kuveiller and punctuated by a whimsically ironic musical score by

Ennio Morricone, the film tells the story of an unnamed police inspector, recently promoted from head of homicide to the Political Division, who kills his beautiful lover in cold blood, intentionally leaving numerous and obvious clues. In the investigation that follows, he plays a cynical game of cat and mouse with his former colleagues by both prompting them toward the truth and, at the same time, using his new position in the Political Division to point them in the direction of a young left-wing activist who lived in the same building as the woman. He clearly enjoys his feeling of power and invulnerability when the other detectives follow the clues along their logical path but then, deferential to his status and authority, refuse to draw the obvious conclusion. In the end he appears to tire of the game and disdainfully confesses to the crime. However, in the (imagined?) meeting with his political superiors that closes the film, he is exonerated rather than punished and they clasp him to their bosom as one of their own. A quotation from Franz Kafka introduces the credits: "Whatever impression he makes on us, he is the servant of the Law. He belongs to the Law and is not answerable to human judgment."

The film's truculent caricature of the police and its openly voiced cynicism toward politicians well reflected the widespread mistrust of constituted authority in Italy at the time, a distrust that would only increase in the following so-called leaden years. However, the film also found a warm reception abroad, being nominated for two Oscars, a Golden Globe, and the Palme d'or. In the event it won the Oscar for Best Foreign Film and received the International Federation of Film Critics Prize and the Grand Prize of the Jury at Cannes.

INGRASSIA, CICCIO (1922–2003). (Ciccio, short for Francesco.) Actor. A vaudeville performer from a very young age, Ingrassia met **Franco Franchi** while touring in the mid-1950s and together they formed what would soon become one of the most successful comic acts in postwar Italian cinema. After making a name for themselves with their variety shows onstage, the duo appeared in very small roles in **Mario Mattoli**'s *Appuntamento a Ischia* (*Rendezvous at Ischia*, 1960). Then, during the next decade and a half, they came to star in over 100 films of varying quality, many of them hastily concocted farces and parodies of other well-known films, such as *Il bello il brutto e il cretino* (*The Handsome, the Ugly and the Stupid*, 1967) and *Indovina chi viene a merenda?* (*Guess Who's Coming to After-noon Tea*, 1968).

Loved by the audiences who flocked to see the films but generally maligned by the critics, the duo were able to give better proof of their abilities in **Pier Paolo Pasolini**'s *Che cosa sono le nuvole?*, an episode of the compilation film *Capriccio italiano* (*Caprice Italian Style*, 1968), and as the Fox and the Cat in **Luigi Comencini**'s adaptation of *Pinocchio* (1972) for Italian television. Ingrassia also appeared on his own: he played the eccentric uncle who shouts, "I want a woman" from the treetops in **Federico Fellini**'s *Amarcord* (1973), and won a **Nastro d'argento** for his supporting role in **Elio Petri**'s political satire *Todo modo* (1976). In 1991 he was also awarded a **David di Donatello** for his supporting role in Felice Farina's *Condominio* (*Condominium*, 1991). Nevertheless, Ingrassia's most memorable performance probably remains his interpretation of Don Lollò, the antagonist of Zì Dima, played by Franchi, in the *La giara* episode of **Paolo and Vittorio Taviani**'s *Kaos* (*Chaos*, 1984). Ingrassia also directed two films: *Paolo il freddo* (Paolo, the Cold-Blooded, 1974) and *L'esorciccio* (*The Exorcist: Italian Style*, 1975).

ITALA FILM. Production company. Founded in 1905 by Carlo Rossi and William Remmert as Carlo Rossi & C., the company recruited a number of technicians from the French Pathé to become one of the first film manufacturing companies in Turin. Two years later it was joined by **Giovanni Pastrone**, who helped to reorganize its management procedures on a much firmer commercial basis. In 1908, with Rossi leaving to work for the **Cines** in Rome, the company was transformed into Itala Film, adopting *Fixité* as its motto and principle.

For the next decade the company's growth and development was ably guided by Pastrone, who demonstrated remarkable skills as manager, producer, director, and technician. One of Pastrone's shrewdest moves was to entice the Pathé's most successful comedian, **André Deed**, to Itala's well-outfitted new studios in Turin, where Deed was able to turn out hundreds of the extremely popular **Cretinetti** films. At the same time, *La caduta di Troia* (*The Fall of Troy*, 1910), directed by Pastrone himself, broke box office records in the United States, allowing Itala to set up a subsidiary in New York in 1913 and thus pave the way for the stellar success of Pastrone's

Cabiria there in 1914. Under Pastrone's firm guidance, Itala distinguished itself for the quality of its literary adaptations and its costume melodramas while also exploiting the character of **Maciste**, the mucleman with a heart of gold who had first appeared in *Cabiria*, in a string of very popular films bearing his name. Segundo De Chomón's remarkable talents for special effects, also first seen in *Cabiria*, were further showcased in the brilliant animation of *La guerra e il sogno di Momi* (*The War and the Dream of Momi*, 1917).

Nevertheless, by 1918 Pastrone had lost financial control of the company, which in 1919, in the general crisis that began to engulf the industry, was absorbed into the ill-fated **Unione Cinematografia Italiana** (UCI). In 1927 the derelict Itala studios in Turin were bought up by **Stefano Pittaluga**.

– L –

LA DOLCE VITA. Film. Directed by **Federico Fellini** in 1959, released in 1960. The most renowned Italian art film of the 1960s, *La dolce vita* was Fellini's acerbic, if rather fascinated, take on the glamorous, media-soaked, but ultimately empty lifestyle that had developed around Rome's Via Veneto district in the wake of Hollywood's colonization of the Tiber during the 1950s. The title, meaning literally "the sweet life," was clearly inflected ironically, but many mistakenly interpreted the film as an endorsement and a celebration of that new celebrity worship and media consciousness that was becoming part of the new Italy of the so-called economic miracle.

The plot is willfully disconnected and episodic. Tabloid journalist Marcello Rubini, inimitably played by **Marcello Mastroianni**, flits around Rome for most of the film, usually accompanied by his photographer, Paparazzo, returning frequently to the Via Veneto to catch up with the latest events. Nurturing aspirations to being a serious writer but with neither the discipline nor the inspiration to realize it, Marcello drifts between sexual dalliances and journalistic assignments that include, among other things, showing a visiting international starlet, played by Anita Ekberg, the sights of Rome (prompting the legendary scene in which they both splash about in the Fountain of Trevi), and reporting on the "miraculous" apparition of the Virgin

Mary to two children in a field on the outskirts of the city. In the course of his meanderings he also visits an intellectual writer friend whose professed love of music and literature masks a more deep-seated existential malaise that abruptly emerges when he kills his two small children before shooting himself. Running as a thread through most of the episodes is Marcello's attempt to escape from what he obviously feels is a cloying relationship with his official fiancée, Emma. In the final episode, in what was judged to be one of the most scandalous and immoral scenes of the whole film, Marcello attends a wild party thrown by a recent divorcée, during which the hostess performs a self-conscious striptease and Marcello rides one of the female partygoers like a horse.

Stylistically the film was something of a turning point for Fellini, who here abandoned forever any vestiges of his involvement with **neorealism**, which still persisted in his previous *Le notti di Cabiria* (*The Nights of Cabiria*, 1957), embracing an unashamedly modernist idiom that would soon metamorphose into the postmodern self-referentiality of *Otto e mezzo* (*8½*, 1963). At the same time, in spite of being shot mostly in a studio—the Via Veneto itself was meticulously reconstructed in the **Cinecittà** studios by **Piero Gherardi**—the film managed to convey the pulse of a changing, and changed, Italy rapidly careening into its own chaotic future. At its first gala screening in Milan in February 1960, the film caused a major furor, with many of the invited guests booing and hissing, and Fellini himself being spat upon. In the days that followed the film was vehemently attacked by the Catholic and conservative press, and a number of right-wing politicians even presented a proposal to ban it in Parliament. However, good sense eventually prevailed and the film, having already received its certificate of release from the censorship board, was allowed to circulate freely. Due, at least in part, to all the publicity generated by the heated controversy, *La dolce vita* achieved unprecedented box office success, both in Italy and abroad, and was enthusiastically awarded the Palme d'or when presented at Cannes. In the United States it subsequently received the New York Film Critics Prize for Best Foreign Film and four Oscar nominations, winning the Academy Award for Best Costume Design. As part of the film's enduring legacy, the name of the photographer, Paparazzo, came to be widely used internationally from then on to designate any member of that race of invasive and aggressive celebrity photographers that has unfortunately continued to flourish to the present day.

LABATE, WILMA (1949–). Director and screenwriter. After studying philosophy at the University of Rome, Labate began working for the national RAI television network. In 1990, with a number of documentaries already to her credit, she made *Ciro il piccolo* (Little Ciro), a sort of **documentary** on the city of Naples, seen through the eyes of a young boy who wanders the streets for most of the night on his way to work at the fish markets in the early morning. Two years later Labate directed her first feature, *Ambrogio* (1992), the story of a young girl in Italy in the late 1950s who joins the Naval Academy in order to fulfill her aspirations of becoming a ship's captain. Following a number of other commercial documentaries, Labate's second feature, *La mia generazione* (*My Generation*, 1996), tackled the difficult theme of political terrorism in Italy in the early 1980s. Still regarded by many as her best work to date, it won the International Federation of Film Critics Prize and was put forward as the Italian nominee for the Oscar for Best Foreign Film. After several other short films she directed *Domenica* (*Sunday*, 2001), the moving story of a rebellious 12-year-old street girl in Naples (named Domenica) and the relationship that develops between her and the terminally ill policeman charged with bringing her in to make a statement. Two years later, after collaborating on the group documentary *Lettere dalla Palestina* (*Letters from Palestine*, 2002), Labate produced and directed *maledetta Mia* (Cursed Be Mia, 2003), a documentary portrait of five anarchic young people all attempting to present their objections to the established social system. Still passionately left-wing in her political orientation, in 2005 Labate published *Il ragazzo con la maglietta a strisce* (*The Boy with the Striped Jumper*), a book-length interview with the former leader of the Communist Refoundation Party, Fausto Bertinotti.

LANCI, GIUSEPPE (1942–). Cinematographer. Better known as Beppe (short for Giuseppe), Lanci studied at the **Centro Sperimentale di Cinematografia** before serving an apprenticeship as assistant cameraman with **Tonino Delli Colli**, Mario Montuori, and Franco Di Giacomo. From 1979 he became the preferred cinematographer of

Marco Bellocchio, photographing eight of his major films, worked with **Paolo and Vittorio Taviani** on *Kaos* (*Chaos*, 1984) and *Good Morning Babilonia* (1986), with **Mauro Bolognini** on *La Veneziana* (*The Venetian Woman*, 1985) and *La villa del venerdì* (*Husbands and Lovers*, 1992), and with **Nanni Moretti** on *Palombella Rossa* (*Red Lob*, 1988), *Caro diario* (*Dear Diary*, 1993), *Aprile* (*April*, 1996), and *La stanza del figlio* (*The Son's Room*, 2001). He also collaborated extensively with the younger generation of directors who emerged in the 1990s, working on, among others, **Francesca Archibugi**'s *Con gli occhi chiusi* (*With Closed Eyes*, 1994) and **Daniele Luchetti**'s *I piccoli maestri* (*Little Teachers*, 1997). Internationally he served as director of photography for Margarethe Von Trotta's *Fürchten und Lieben* (*Three Sisters*, 1988) and, memorably, for Andrei Tarkovsky, for whom he produced the stunning images of *Nostalghia* (*Nostalgia*, 1984). Among his many awards is the **David di Donatello** he won in 1986 for his work on **Lina Wertmüller**'s *Un complicato intrigo di donne, vicoli e delitti* (*Camorra: A Story of Streets, Women and Crime*, 1986).

LATTUADA, ALBERTO (1914–2005). Photographer, writer, director, screenwriter. A director of extraordinary versatility often characterized as merely eclectic, Lattuada was born into a cultured Milanese family and was exposed to all the arts from a very young age. His father, a composer and musician who often took his son to the opera at La Scala, also scored a number of films for **Alessandro Blasetti** and **Mario Camerini**. While still in high school, Lattuada began writing and editing literary magazines and later, as an architecture student at the Politecnico of Milan, he also contributed art criticism and film reviews to several cultural journals.

He began his career in the film industry in 1933 as a set decorator and designer. In 1938, together with fellow enthusiasts **Luigi Comencini** and Mario Ferrari, he founded the Cineteca (Film Library) of Milan while at the same time publishing a book of arresting photographs of the poorer quarters of the city titled *Occhio quadrato* (*Square Eye*). After working as screenwriter and assistant director to **Mario Soldati** on *Piccolo mondo antico* (*Old-Fashioned World*, 1941) and **Ferdinando Maria Poggioli**'s *Sissignora* (*Yes, Madam*, 1942), he made his directorial debut with *Giacomo l'idealista*

(*Giacomo the Idealist*, 1943), a stylish adaption of Emilio De Marchi's 19th-century novel. The film's elegant formal composition and visual beauty immediately located him within the camp of the so-called calligraphers.

Displaying a versatility that would become his trademark, in the immediate postwar period he made a number of films in the neorealist mold: *Il bandito* (*The Bandit*, 1946), the story of a returned soldier that was clearly influenced by American gangster films; *Il delitto di Giovanni Episcopo* (*Flesh Will Surrender*, 1947), which earned him his first **Nastro d'argento**; *Senza pietà* (*Without Pity*, 1948); and *Il mulino del Po* (*The Mill on the Po*, 1949), a lyrical story of peasant struggles set in the 19th century. In 1950 he joined forces with a young **Federico Fellini** in producing and directing *Luci del varietà* (*Variety Lights*, 1950), which was received with positive critical interest but proved a financial disaster for both of them. The situation for Lattuada was redeemed by the international box office success of *Anna* (1951), an erotic melodrama starring **Silvana Mangano** as a nightclub singer who becomes a nun to atone for her previous selfishness, and then *Il cappotto* (*The Overcoat*, 1952), the adaptation of a tragicomic short story by Nikolai Gogol. A year later Lattuada made *Gli italiani si voltano* (*Italians Turn to Look*) for **Cesare Zavattini**'s compilation film *L'amore in città* (*Love in the City*, 1953). By this time he had already directed *La lupa* (*She Wolf*, 1952), adapted from a novel by Giovanni Verga. A refined eroticism, already present in his earlier work, now came to characterize his films, and he began to become almost as famous for his discovery of a number of beautiful young actresses as for the films in which he showcased their talents.

Nevertheless, many of his films also continued to carry out a mild social critique as in the highlighting of middle-class hypocrisies in *La spiaggia* (*Riviera*, 1954) or in the many social satires that he produced in parallel to the ***commedia all'italiana***, such as *Il Mafioso* (*Mafioso*, 1962) and *Don Giovanni in Sicilia* (*Don Juan in Sicily*, 1967). He also received high praise for his adaptation of Machiavelli's 16th-century comedy *La mandragola* (*The Mandrake*, 1965), in which he employed the comic actor **Totò** to play the key role of Fra' Timoteo. Ever eclectic, he then produced an amusing parody of the then popular spy film in *Matchless* (1967), which he followed with the epic antiwar film *Fräulein Doktor* (1969). In the 1970s he became increasingly identified with films with an explicit erotic content, such as *Le farò da padre* (*Bambina*, 1974), *Oh Serafina!* (1976), and *La cicala* (*The Cricket*, 1980), the last one impounded by the censors on charges of obscenity, although it was eventually released.

In the 1980s Lattuada largely abandoned the big screen in favor of television, for which he directed, among others, a four-part miniseries on Christopher Columbus (*Cristoforo Colombo*, 1985) and another miniseries, *Due fratelli* (Brothers, 1988). Having occasionally acted in small roles in his own films, he also made a final cameo appearance in **Carlo Mazzacurati**'s *Il toro* (*The Bull*, 1996).

One of Italy's most popular and critically respected directors, in 1994 Lattuada was recognized at the **David di Donatello** Awards with the **Franco Cristaldi** prize for career achievement.

LENZI, UMBERTO (1931–). Screenwriter and director. A cult director working mostly in genre films (and under a number of aliases, Humphrey Humbert, Harry Kirkpatrick, and Hank Milestone among them), Lenzi abandoned legal studies at university in order to train in film at the **Centro Sperimentale di Cinematografia**. Having worked as assistant director on Domenico Paolella's pirate fantasy, *Il terrore dei mari* (*Guns of the Black Witch*, 1961), Lenzi directed his own female pirate adventure, *Le avventure di Mary Read* (*Queen of the Seas*, 1961), which was followed by a host of other swashbuckling adventure fantasies such as *Sandokan, la tigre della Mompracem* (*Sandokan, the Great*, 1963) and *I pirati della malesia* (*The Pirates of Malaysia*, 1964). After *Attentato ai tre grandi* (*Desert Commandos*, 1967), a desert war drama portraying an attempt by German commandos to assassinate Churchill, Roosevelt, and Stalin at their meeting in Casablanca, several spy films, and a number of **spaghetti Westerns**, Lenzi made the first of his erotic psychological thrillers, *Orgasmo* (*Orgasm*, but released in the United States as *Paranoia*, 1968), followed by *Così dolce . . . così perversa* (*So Sweet . . . So Perverse*, 1969). In the 1970s he became particularly renowned for his mastery of the police-crime thriller genre while also achieving international cult status with *Il paese del sesso selvaggio* (*Sacrifice!* 1972), the film that launched the cannibal **horror** cycle in Italy, to which Lenzi would contribute several classics of the genre, including *Mangiati vivi* (*Eaten Alive*, 1980) and the notorious *Cannibal ferox* (*Make Them Die Slowly*, 1981), advertised as "the most violent film ever made!"

In the 1980s he continued to dabble in most of the major genres but came back to prominence with the voodoo horror *Demoni 3* (*Black Demons*, 1991). His last film was the police thriller *Hornsby and Rodriguez—sfida criminale* (*Mean Tricks*, 1992).

LEONE, SERGIO (1929–1989). Director, screenwriter, producer. The son of silent film director Roberto Roberti (Vincenzo Leone) and actress Bice Walerian, Leone entered the film industry at a very young age, serving as an unpaid assistant and appearing in a small role in one of his father's last films when he was only 12. In the immediate postwar period, he worked in various capacities on a host of films, including making an appearance as one of the German seminarians in **Vittorio De Sica**'s *Ladri di biciclette* (*Bicycle Thieves*, 1948). In the 1950s he served as assistant director on many of the big-budget American productions being shot at **Cinecittà**, including Mervyn Le Roy's *Quo vadis?* (1950), Robert Wise's *Helen of Troy* (1955), and William Wyler's *Ben-Hur* (1959). Having also, during this period, regularly served as assistant director to **Mario Bonnard**, he took over directing Bonnard's remake of *Gli ultimi giorni di Pompei* (*The Last Days of Pompeii*, 1959) at short notice but subsequently chose to go back to working as assistant director to Robert Aldrich on the ill-fated *Sodom and Gomorrah* (1961) before writing and directing his own sword-and-sandal epic, *Il colosso di Rodi* (*The Colossus of Rhodes*, 1961).

Real success, however, came with *Per un pugno di dollari* (*A Fistful of Dollars*, 1964, released in the United States in 1967), the film with which Leone is credited as having given birth to the **Western al-l'italiana**, or as it often disparagingly came to be known outside of Italy, the **spaghetti Western**. Made on a shoestring budget and under the pseudonym Bob Robertson, the film proved to be an unexpected but enormous commercial success, prompting Leone to make the four other Westerns that confirmed his mastery of the genre, *Per qualche dollaro in più* (*For a Few Dollars More*, 1965), *Il buono, il brutto, il cattivo* (*The Good, the Bad and the Ugly*, 1966), *C'era una* *volta il West* (*Once upon a Time in the West*, 1968), and *Giù la testa* (*Duck, You Sucker*, 1971).

For the next decade Leone limited himself to producing films for other directors, including Tonino Valerii's *Il mio nome è nessuno* (*My Name Is Nobody*, 1973) and **Carlo Verdone**'s directorial debut, *Un sacco bello* (*Fun Is Beautiful*, 1980), while preparing to make what many regard as his most accomplished film, *C'era una volta in America* (*Once upon a Time in America*, 1984), the magnificent gangster epic that finally brought him the recognition of a **Nastro d'argento** as well as nominations for both BAFTA and Golden Globe awards. This was to have been followed by an even more spectacular film on the German siege of Leningrad during World War II, which was apparently in the final stages of preparation at the time of Leone's untimely death in 1989.

LETO, MARCO (1931–). Critic, screenwriter, director. After graduating from university with a degree in law, Leto enrolled at the **Centro Sperimentale di Cinematografia**. He subsequently worked as a film critic for *Il Globo*, while also serving as an assistant to directors **Mario Monicelli**, **Florestano Vancini**, and **Renato Castellani**. In 1963 he began working for state television and for a period also held the post of artistic director at the Istituto **LUCE** before directing his first feature, *La villeggiatura* (*Black Holiday*, 1972), a perceptive analysis of Fascism widely regarded as his best film and for which he received numerous awards, including a **Nastro d'argento** and the Mario Gromo Award for Best Director. While continuing to produce a host of award-winning programs for television, he directed his second feature film, *Al piacere di rivederla* (*Till We Meet Again*, 1976). He taught at the Centro Sperimentale between 1983 and 1987 and coauthored several novels before directing *Una donna spezzata* (*The Woman Destroyed*, 1988), closely followed by *L'uscita* (*The Exit*, 1989) and *A proposito di quella strana ragazza* (*About That Foreign Girl*, 1989), both of which tackled the difficult theme of political terrorism. He subsequently directed *L'inchiesta* (*The Investigation*, 1991), adapted from one of his earlier novels, and worked as a director of dubbing while also publishing another novel, a neo-noir titled *L'intrattenimento* (*Entertainment*, 2001).

LIZZANI, CARLO (1922–). Director, screenwriter, film historian, critic. A passionate cinephile from a very early age, Lizzani began attending the **Centro Sperimentale di Cinematografia** in his late teens while also contributing articles to film journals, including the prestigious *Cinema*. After participating in the **Resistance** movement during the war, he acted the role of a parish priest killed by the Germans in **Aldo Vergano**'s Resistance film, *Il sole sorge ancora* (*Outcry*, 1946) before serving as assistant director to **Roberto Rossellini** on *Germania anno zero* (*Germany Year Zero*, 1947). At the same time he worked with **Giuseppe De Santis** on the screenplays of *Caccia tragica* (*Tragic Hunt*, 1947) and *Riso amaro* (*Bitter Rice*, 1949) and made a number of socially committed documentaries before directing his first feature, *Achtung! Banditi!* (*Attention! Bandits!* 1951), a film on the Resistance movement in northern Italy; because the film was strongly opposed by the ruling center-right Christian Democrat authorities, it was financed autonomously through a film workers' cooperative.

After *Ai margini della metropoli* (*At the Edge of the City*, 1952) and *L'amore che si paga* (*The Love One Pays For*), one of the five episodes of the compilation film *L'amore in città* (*Love in the City*, 1953), Lizzani directed *Cronache di poveri amanti* (*Chronicle of Poor Lovers*, 1954), the adaption of an anti-Fascist novel by Florentine writer Vasco Pratolini, which was again produced by an independent cooperative and again strongly opposed by the authorities on the grounds of alleged left-wing bias. Despite concerted pressure from the Italian authorities, who blocked the film's international release for several years, the film was highly acclaimed at Cannes, where it was awarded the Grand Jury Prize.

Having by this time also published an authoritative history of Italian cinema, Lizzani then veered more toward the mainstream with *Lo svitato* (*Screwball*, 1955), a comedy featuring the then little-known Dario Fo, before journeying to China, still largely closed to Westerners, to make the feature **documentary** *La muraglia cinese* (*Behind the Great Wall*, 1958). After *Esterina* (1959) Lizzani returned to the war years and to the Resistance movement with *Il gobbo* (*The Hunchback of Rome*, 1960), *L'oro di Roma* (*Gold of Rome*, 1961), and *Il processo di Verona* (*The Verona Trial*, 1963), films that confirmed both his directorial professionalism and his social commitment. In the following years he continued to make films with a historical or political focus, among them *Mussolini ultimo atto* (*Last Days of Mussolini*, 1974) and *Caro Gorbaciov* (*Dear Gorbachev*, 1988), but also worked extensively within many of the more popular genres, making Westerns such as *Un fiume di dollari* (*River of Dollars*, 1966) and *Requiescant* (*Kill and Pray*, 1967)—the latter memorable not least for the appearance of **Pier Paolo Pasolini** as a revolutionary Mexican priest—and urban crime and gangster thrillers such as *Banditi a Milano* (*Bandits in Milan*, 1968), *Torino nera* (*Black Turin*, 1972), and *Crazy Joe* (1974). In 1980, while serving a four-year term as director of the **Venice Festival**, he returned to a cinema of strong social commitment with *Fontamara* (1980), a moving adaptation of a novel by Ignazio Silone about the plight of peasants in southern Italy, set during the Fascist period. In 1996 Lizzani's passion for both history and the cinema came together in *Celluloide* (*Celluloid*, 1996), a fictional re-creation of the making of Rossellini's landmark film *Roma città aperta* (*Rome Open City*, 1945, also known as *Open City*). In more recent times he has worked largely for television, directing, among others, *Maria Josè, l'ultima regina* (*Maria Josè, the Last Queen*, 2001), an enormously popular miniseries on the life of the daughter-in-law of King Victor Emmanuel III, and *Le cinque giornate di Milano* (*The Five Days of Milan*, 2004), a two-part telefilm on the revolutionary uprising in Milan in 1848.

LO VERSO, ENRICO (1964–). Actor. One of the most distinctive young actors to emerge in the **New Italian Cinema** of the early 1990s, Lo Verso studied at the **Centro Sperimentale di Cinematografia** before making his first screen appearance in Antonello Grimaldi's *Nulla ci puo fermare* (Nothing Can Stop Us, 1988). After playing strong supporting roles in **Pasquale Squitieri**'s *Atto di dolore* (*Act of Sorrow*, 1991) and **Michele Placido**'s *Le Amiche del cuore* (*Close Friends*, 1992), he achieved international renown as the young policeman charged with escorting the children to Sicily in **Gianni Amelio**'s *Il ladro di bambini* (*The Stolen Children*, 1992). He subsequently acted in several other major films by Amelio, including *Lamerica* (1994) and *Così ridevano* (*So They Laughed*, 1999), while also providing strong performances in, among others, **Ricky Tognazzi**'s *La scorta* (*The Escort*, 1993), Carmine Amoroso's *Come mi vuoi* (*As You Want Me*, 1997), Michele Placido's *Del perduto amore*

(*Of Love Lost*, 1998), and Giovanni Davide Maderna's *L'amore imperfetto* (Imperfect Love, 2001). He has also worked extensively outside of Italy, appearing in films such as Gérard Corbiau's baroque extravaganza *Farinelli* (1994), Philippe Bérenger's *Méditerranées*, and Ridley Scott's horror classic *Hannibal* (2001).

LOLLOBRIGIDA, GINA (1927–). Actress. One of the most popular and internationally renowned Italian actresses of the postwar Italian cinema, Gina (short for Luigina) Lollobrigida began appearing in films as an extra in order to pay for her singing lessons. After doing small parts in a number of minor films, her stunning looks and her acting abilities began to emerge more clearly in Giorgio Pastina's *Alina* (1950) and Duillio Coletti's *Miss Italia* (*Miss Italy*, 1950), the latter bringing her an offer of a seven-year contract in Hollywood from American magnate Howard Hughes, an offer that she originally accepted but soon reneged under pressure from her husband and manager, Milko Skofic.

Having returned to Europe, she scored her first major success in France in the title role of Christian-Jacque's *Fanfan la Tulipe* (*Fan-Fan the Tulip*, 1952), which led to her being known in France simply as Le Lollo. Back in Italy she distinguished herself in **Mario Soldati**'s *La provinciale* (*The Wayward Wife*, 1953) before scoring an even bigger hit as the sweet but wild young country girl in **Luigi Comencini**'s *Pane, amore e fantasia* (*Bread, Love and Dreams*, 1953), a role that earned her a **Nastro d'argento** and a BAFTA nomination for Best Foreign Actress. The success was then repeated by her reprise of the role in the equally popular sequel, *Pane, amore e gelosia* (*Bread, Love and Jealousy*, 1954, also known as *Frisky*). Much in demand, both in Italy and abroad, she subsequently starred in a host of both European and Hollywood productions, including Carol Reed's *Trapeze* (1956), King Vidor's *The Queen of Sheba* (1959), and Jean Delannoy's *Venere imperiale* (*Imperial Venus*, 1962), in which she played Napoleon's sister, Paulina Borghese, in an interpretation that brought her both a **David di Donatello** and a second Nastro d'argento. After appearing opposite Sean Connery in Bill Dearden's *Woman of Straw* (1963) and in **Alessandro Blasetti**'s *Io, io, io . . . e gli altri* (*Me, Me, Me . . . and the Others*, 1966), she received a David di Donatello and a Golden Globe nomination for her role in the film for which she is probably best re-membered in America, *Buonasera signora Campbell* (*Buona Sera, Mrs. Campbell*, 1968), a Hollywood comedy directed by Melvin Frank.

Following a serious highway accident in 1969 and although still very much in demand, she began to withdraw from the cinema in the early 1970s. She played the Blue Fairy in **Luigi Comencini**'s highly acclaimed television miniseries *Le avventure di Pinocchio*, later re-leased as a film (*Pinocchio*, 1972), and appeared with David Niven in Jerzy Skolimowski's adaptation of Vladimir Nabokov's novel *King, Queen, Knave* (1972), but thereafter retired from cinema to fol-low her passion for photography.

After having published many books of photographs, organized art exhibitions, and, more recently, been appointed ambassador for the Food and Agriculture Organization of the United Nations, in 2006 she was awarded a David di Donatello for her career.

LOMBARDO, GOFFREDO (1920–2005). Producer. Son of the founder of the Titanus film company, **Gustavo Lombardo**, and silent diva Leda Gys, Lombardo graduated in law from the University of Rome before joining the film industry as a scene painter in the late 1930s. After the war he joined his father as an assistant producer and on his father's death in 1951 took over the company, greatly improv-ing its fortunes through the production of a series of enormously pop-ular melodramas directed by **Raffaele Matarazzo**. With a keen eye for what would be successful at the box office, Lombardo also pro-duced *Pane, amore e fantasia* (*Bread, Love and Dreams,* 1953) and its two sequels, *Pane, amore e gelosia* (*Bread, Love and Jealousy,* 1954, also known as *Frisky*) and *Pane, amore e . . .* (*Scandal in Sor-rento,* 1955), the latter showcasing both the looks and talents of a still little-known **Sophia Loren**. For Lombardo, however, commercial success was not an end in itself, and he used the profits from these and other popular films to support auteurist cinema, distributing and promoting the films of emerging young directors like **Ermanno Olmi** and **Valerio Zurlini**, and producing **Federico Fellini**'s *Il bidone* (*The Swindle*, 1955), **Luchino Visconti**'s *Rocco e i suoi fratelli* (*Rocco and His Brothers*, 1960), and **Vittorio De Sica**'s *La ciociara* (*Two Women*, 1960).

However, budget overruns on Visconti's *Il gattopardo* (*The Leopard*, 1963) and Robert Aldrich's *Sodom and Gomorrah* (1962) put the company into serious financial difficulties and Lombardo was soon forced to sell the Titanus studios, although he succeeded in keeping the production arm of the company intact. Continuing to display courage and foresight, he financed **Dario Argento**'s directorial debut, *L'uccello dalle piume di cristallo* (*The Bird with the Crystal Plumage*, 1970) as well as **Giuseppe Tornatore**'s first film, *Il camorrista* (*The Professor*, 1986). Nevertheless, after a long and productive career during which he was awarded the **Nastro d'argento** twice and the **David di Donatello** three times, in 1989, in the wake of a disappointing response to **Luigi Comencini**'s *Buon Natale . . . Buon Anno* (*Merry Christmas and a Happy New Year*, 1989), Lombardo decided to retire from the industry, leaving the company in the hands of his son Guido.

LOMBARDO, GUSTAVO (1885–1951). Producer and distributor. A key figure in the history of the Italian film industry, Lombardo established one of the first film distribution companies in Naples in 1904. In 1908 he founded the monthly magazine *Lux* to publicize films and their availability and a year later his Società italiana Gustavo Lombardo anonima (SIGLA) had become the official distributor for most of the major Italian and foreign companies, including Gaumont, Éclair, Comerio, Vitagraph, **Itala**, and Aquila. At a time when cinema owners still bought their films outright from producers, Lombardo strongly championed the idea of exhibitors' hiring films from distributors. In 1911, as both a distributor and exhibitor himself, he achieved a major coup with his effective launch of **Milano Films**' milestone film, *L'Inferno*, a feat he repeated with the spectacular Roman premiere of Itala's *Cabiria* in 1914. In 1915, still in Naples, he greatly extended his distribution network with the creation of Monopolio grandi films (Monopoly Great Films).

In 1917 he moved into production by forming Lombardo Film, one of the few companies that declined to join the ill-fated **Unione Cinematografica Italiana** (UCI, Italian Cinematographic Union) and which thus managed to weather the crisis that engulfed the industry in the early 1920s. In 1928 Lombardo moved his operations to Rome and founded the production company Titanus, providing it with its own studios at the Farnesina. Although the number of films Lombardo produced himself during this period was relatively small, two of them, *Fermo con le mani* (*Hands Off Me!*, 1937) and *Animali pazzi* (*Crazy Animals*, 1939), were historically significant since they effectively launched the film career of the great comic actor **Totò**. In the immediate postwar period Lombardo remained a major presence in the industry. Again he produced very few films but among them was *Catene* (*Chains*, 1949), the first of a long line of teary but extremely popular melodramas directed by **Raffaello Matarazzo**, which would sustain the company's fortunes in the 1950s when it would be managed by his son, Goffredo.

LOREN, SOPHIA (1934–). (Born Sofia Villani Scicolone.) Actress. The most nationally celebrated and internationally renowned Italian actress of the postwar period, Loren was born illegitimately in Rome and grew up in one of the poorer quarters of Naples, where her mother had taken refuge at the beginning of World War II. After the war she and her mother both returned to Rome with hopes of a career in the movies. Under the name of Sofia Lazzaro she posed for magazines and photoromances before being runner-up in a beauty contest where her looks caught the attention of film producer **Carlo Ponti**, who soon became both her mentor and her husband. Alternatively under the names Scicolone and Lazzaro, she appeared in small parts in a dozen films made at **Cinecittà** in the early 1950s before being induced by veteran Italian producer **Gustavo Lombardo** to change her name to Sophia Loren.

She was soon playing more substantial roles and even graduated to the lead in minor films such as **Mario Mattoli**'s *Due notti con Cleopatra* (*Two Nights with Cleopatra*, 1953), in which she played both the Queen of the Nile and her lookalike slave girl, opposite the up-and-coming **Alberto Sordi**. By 1954 she had begun to make her mark in quality films like **Vittorio De Sica**'s *L'oro di Napoli* (*The Gold of Naples*, 1954) and a year later substituted for **Gina Lollobrigida** in the third of the extremely popular *Pane e amore* films, *Pane, amore e . . .* (*Scandal in Sorrento*, 1955). By this time she was also frequently being paired with **Marcello Mastroianni** in films such as **Alessandro Blasetti**'s *Peccato che sia una canaglia* (*Too Bad She's Bad*, 1955) and **Mario Camerini**'s *La bella mugnaia* (*The Miller's*

Beautiful Wife, 1955). Thus, in a few years she had taken her place, alongside the reigning Lollobrigida, as one of the two leading ladies of the Italian silver screen.

At this point Ponti, with whom Loren was now living, decided she was ready for a career in Hollywood. In her first American film, Stanley Kramer's *The Pride and the Passion* (1957), Loren shared star billing with Cary Grant and Frank Sinatra. In the host of films that followed, among them *Legend of the Lost* (1957), *Boy on a Dolphin* (1957), *Desire under the Elms* (1958), *Black Orchid* (1958), *Houseboat* (1958), and *Heller in Pink Tights* (1960), she appeared with all of Hollywood's leading men, including John Wayne, Alan Ladd, William Holden, and Anthony Quinn. Having become a celebrity as well as a star in the United States, Loren returned to Italy, where she achieved her first great critical triumph playing the role of the mother in De Sica's *La Ciociara* (*Two Women*, 1960), a part that originally had been earmarked for **Anna Magnani**. Her brilliant performance in the demanding role earned her worldwide acclaim and a plethora of awards, including the **Nastro d'argento** at home, Best Actress at Cannes, and the first Academy Award given to an actress in a foreign-language film. In the following years she continued to alternate between appearing in big-budget Hollywood and international spectaculars and working in Italy, mostly with De Sica, who, in films such as *Ieri, oggi e domani* (*Yesterday, Today and Tomorrow*, 1963) and *Matrimonio all'italiana* (*Marriage Italian Style*, 1964), continued to pair her with Marcello Mastroianni. Many of the roles that she undertook in international productions, such as Peter Ustinov's *Lady L* (1965) or Charles Chaplin's *A Countess from Hong Kong* (1967), successfully promoted her as an icon of feminine glamour and beauty but seldom exploited her true strengths as an actress. These would only really return to the fore in **Ettore Scola**'s *Una giornata particolare* (*A Special Day*, 1977), where she again appeared with Mastroianni in a moving performance that earned her both the Nastro d'argento and the **David di Donatello**.

Although her international reputation for beauty and glamour continued to flourish, her image in Italy was considerably tarnished in the late 1970s by allegations of and then a conviction for tax fraud. She subsequently largely withdrew from the cinema and during the 1980s appeared only as the mother in a number of television mini series and in **Dino Risi**'s television version of *La ciociara* (*Running Away*, 1988). Loren returned triumphantly to the big screen at the beginning of the 1990s in **Lina Wertmüller**'s *Sabato, domenica e lunedì* (*Saturday, Sunday and Monday*, 1990), a film which, as the adaptation of a stage play by **Eduardo De Filippo**, brought her back to her Neapolitan roots. This was followed by a cameo appearance and a final reunion with Mastroianni in Robert Altman's satire of the fashion industry, *Prêt-à-Porter* (*Ready to Wear*, 1994), where she was able to reprise her famous striptease from *Ieri, oggi e domani* to great effect. After playing the much more difficult role of a Jewish mother of five living in Algiers during World War II in Roger Hanin's *Soleil* (Sun, 1997), she worked again with Wertmüller in the made-for-television *Francesca e Nunziata* (2001) before giving a very touching performance as an older woman in *Between Strangers* (2002), a Canadian production directed by her son Edoardo.

Having already been showered with numerous prizes and awards, in 1990 she received an honorary Oscar for lifetime achievement. In 1998 at the **Venice Festival** she was awarded the Golden Lion for her entire career.

LOY, NANNI (1925–1995). (Giovanni Loy.) Actor, director, screenwriter. Born into an aristocratic family in Sardinia, Loy moved to Rome in his teens and attended the **Centro Sperimentale di Cinematografia** while studying at university for his law degree. After serving an apprenticeship as assistant director on a number of films, including **Luigi Zampa**'s *Processo alla città* (*The City Stands Trial*, 1952) and *Anni facili* (*Easy Years*, 1953), he collaborated with **Gianni Puccini** on the direction of *Parola di ladro* (*Honor among Thieves*, 1957) and *Il marito* (*The Husband*, 1957) before directing his first solo film, *Un audace colpo dei soliti ignoti* (*Fiasco in Milan*, 1959), a sequel to **Mario Monicelli**'s enormously popular *I soliti ignoti* (1958) that many judged to be almost as good as the original. The success of the film allowed Loy to make two films on the war, *Un giorno da leoni* (*A Day as Lions*, 1961) and *Le quattro giornate di Napoli* (*The Four Days of Naples*, 1962), the latter a remarkably realistic re-creation of a popular uprising staged by the people of Naples against the occupying German forces in 1943. The film was widely acclaimed, winning three **Nastri d'argento** as well as two

Academy Award nominations, and brought a number of offers from Hollywood, which Loy declined in favor of working for Italian television and producing *Specchio segreto* (*Secret Mirror*, 1965), a program inspired by the American *Candid Camera* format. He nevertheless also soon returned to the big screen with the multiepisode *Made in Italy* (1965), a satirical look at Italian attitudes and habits, and *Il padre di famiglia* (*The Head of the Family*, 1967), a portrait of the dashed expectations of an entire generation told through the history of one particular family. He took up the theme of the war again, although in a decidedly comic vein, in *Rosolino Paternò soldato* (*Situation Normal: All Fouled Up*, 1970) followed by a Kafkaesque voyage through the Italian judicial and penal system in *Detenuto in attesa di giudizio* (*Why*, 1971), which earned **Alberto Sordi** a **David di Donatello** for his acting and the film a nomination for the Golden Bear at Berlin. After *Sistemo l'America e torno* (*I Fix America and Return*, 1973) Loy turned again to television to make *Viaggio in seconda classe* (Traveling in Second Class, 1977), a program that examined changes in Italian society using a *Candid Camera* format similar to the earlier *Specchio segreto*.

Café Express (1980), a caustic comedy celebrating the Italian propensity for making do, was followed by *Mi manda Picone* (*Picone Sent Me*, 1984), which highlighted the extensive social problems in a Naples ever more infiltrated by the camorra. Loy's fascination with Naples, which he regarded as his adopted city, blossomed again in the delightful musical drama *Scugnizzi* (*Streetkids*, 1989) and in his final film, *Pacco, doppio pacco e contropaccotto* (*Package, Double Package and Counterpackage*, 1993). In the 1990s, as well as making films and producing television programs, Loy directed a number of stage productions, including Italian versions of Neil Simon's *Last of the Red Hot Lovers* and Beth Henley's *Crimes of the Heart*.

LUCE. *See* L'UNIONE CINEMATOGRAFICA EDUCATIVA.

LUCHETTI, DANIELE (1960–). Director and screenwriter. After studying at the Gaumont Film School in Rome, where he directed *Nei dintorni di mezzanotte* (Around Midnight) as an episode of the group film *Juke Box* (1983), Luchetti worked in advertising before assisting

Cabiria (1914), directed by Giovanni Pastrone. Photo courtesy of the Kobal Collection.

Massimo Girotti and Clara Calamai in *Ossessione* (1943), directed by Luchino Visconti. Photo courtesy of Photofest.

Roberto Rossellini and Ingrid Bergman on the set of *Stromboli* (1950). Photo courtesy of Photofest.

Anna Magnani in *Bellissima* (1951), directed by Luchino Visconti. Photo courtesy of Photofest.

Vittorio De Sica on the set of *Umberto D* (1952). Photo courtesy of the Kobal Collection.

Alberto Sordi in *I vitelloni* (1953), directed by Federico Fellini. Photo courtesy of Photofest.

Big Deal on Madonna Street (1958), directed by Mario Monicelli. Photo courtesy of Photofest.

Marcello Mastroianni in *La dolce vita* (1960), directed by Federico Fellini. Photo courtesy of Photofest.

Luchino Visconti directing Delon and Cardinale in *The Leopard* (1963). Photo courtesy of the Kobal Collection.

Pier Paolo Pasolini interviewing girl in *Love Meetings* (1964). Photo courtesy of Photofest.

Sophia Loren in *Yesterday, Today, and Tomorrow* (1964), directed by Vittorio De Sica. Photo courtesy of Photofest.

Gian Maria Volontè in *Investigation of a Citizen* (1970), directed by Elio Petri. Photo courtesy of Photofest.

Bernardo Bertolucci directing Marlon Brando in *Last Tango in Paris* (1972). Photo courtesy of Photofest.

Michelango Antonioni directing Jack Nicholson on the set of *The Passenger* (1975). Photo courtesy of Photofest.

Marcello Mastroianni and Sophia Loren in *A Special Day* (1977), directed by Ettore Scola. Photo courtesy of Photofest.

Directors Paolo and Vittorio Taviani on the set of *The Meadow* (1979). Photo courtesy of Photofest.

Federico Fellini manhandling Marcello Mastroianni on the set of *The City of Women* (1980). Photo courtesy of the Kobal Collection.

Nanni Moretti directing. Photo courtesy of the Kobal Collection.

Gianni Amelio on the set of *The Stolen Children* (1992). Photo courtesy of Photofest.

Paolo Sorrentino on the set of *The Consequences of Love* (2003). Photo courtesy of Photofest.

Nanni Moretti on *Bianca* (*The Sweet Body of Bianca*, 1984) and *La messa è finita* (*The Mass Is Ended*, 1985). In 1987, with the financial backing of Moretti's newly formed **Sacher Film** company, he was able to make his directorial debut with *Domani accadrà* (*Tomorrow It Will Happen*), a witty historical costume drama that earned him the **David di Donatello** for Best New Director. After the less convincing *La settimana della sfinge* (*The Week of the Sphinx*, 1990), he directed what many still regard as his best work to date, *Il portaborse* (*The Yes Man*, 1991), a film that uncannily anticipated the revelations of systematic political corruption in Italy that were brought to light only a year later by the *Mani pulite* (Clean Hands) investigations. A further attempt to unveil political corruption and collusion in *Arriva la bufera* (The Storm Arrives, 1993) was followed by an affectionate, though not uncritical, portrait of the Italian educational system in *La scuola* (*School*, 1995), before another return to the past in *I piccoli maestri* (*Little Teachers*, 1998), the story of several young and idealistic intellectuals who join the **Resistance** movement in 1943. Luchetti's more recent *Mio fratello e' un figlio unico* (*My brother Is an Only Child*, 2007) dramatically reexamines the 1968 generation.

L'UNIONE CINEMATOGRAFICA EDUCATIVA (LUCE). (Union of Educational Cinematography.) National Film Institute. Founded originally in 1919 as the Sindacato Istruzione Cinematografica, a trade union of **documentary** filmmakers, L'Unione Cinematografica Educativa was officially constituted in 1924 to coordinate the use of film for public instruction on scientific and cultural matters as well as national and international affairs. In 1925 the body was nationalized and officially renamed Istituto Nazionale LUCE. Answerable directly to Mussolini, it was charged with the specific mission of spreading popular culture and disseminating information on the government's various projects and initiatives. In 1926 a decree, later to become law, required at least one LUCE newsreel or documentary to accompany every screening of feature films in all cinemas. In addition, to overcome the scarcity of theaters in many parts of Italy, LUCE developed a fleet of "auto-cinemas" whereby vehicles outfitted with screens and projection facilities would tour country areas to bring cinema to the most remote towns and villages. Since LUCE newsreels and documentaries often focused on Mussolini himself and Il Duce personally scrutinized anything that was to be broadcast, the institute's major role became ever more explicitly that of transmitting Fascist propaganda or, as film historian Gian Piero Brunetta famously put it, to construct a cinematographic monument to Mussolini himself. Nevertheless, the institute also covered other areas and included a science unit, which from 1927 was headed by the pioneer scientific documentary filmmaker **Roberto Omegna**. Omegna had worked for the **Ambrosio Film** company in Turin in the earliest days of Italian cinema, making numerous prize-winning documentaries, and he continued this educational activity at LUCE until his retirement in 1942.

Having made a successful transition to sound, the institute was used by the government to establish a new state body in 1935, the Ente Nazionale Industrie Cinematografiche (National Film Industry Authority). Soon after, it was transferred administratively from the Head of Government's department to the Ministry for Popular Culture and, following the construction of **Cinecittà**, the institute's headquarters were also physically relocated to the new complex. After the war, given its close affiliation with the fallen regime, LUCE was provisionally put into liquidation in 1947 but was reinstated two years later with a mission similar in many ways to its original aim, namely, that of providing education and instruction through films, although clearly in a more democratic context. After being restructured a number of times from the mid-1960s onward, in line with changes in government policies regulating the rest of the film industry, in 1982 it was merged with Italnoleggio Cinematografico, a state company for film distribution. In the 1990s it was given greater autonomy to allow it to collaborate on projects funded by private investment. In 1998, as Istituto Luce spa., it became a subsidiary of Cinecittà Holding, a stock company controlled by the Ministry for Culture. Since then, in addition to its other activities, it has pursued a very active and successful strategy of marketing its huge store of historical material on DVD.

LUX FILM. Production company. Founded as a film distribution company in Turin in 1934 by philanthropic (and anti-Fascist) industrialist-entrepreneur Riccardo Gualino, Lux soon became one of Italy's foremost film production companies. In the following two decades, with Gualino as president and musicologist Guido Gatti as director (joined in 1942 by a young **Dino De Laurentiis**), Lux produced more than 100 features directed by Italy's most significant filmmakers. The long list of films produced by Lux during its golden period includes **Goffredo Alessandrini**'s *Don Bosco* (1935), **Alessandro Blasetti**'s *La corona di ferro* (*The Iron Crown*, 1941), **Mario Camerini**'s *I promessi sposi* (*The Spirit and the Flesh*, 1941), **Giuseppe De Santis**'s *Riso amaro* (*Bitter Rice*, 1949), **Alberto Lattuada**'s *Senza Pietà* (*Without Pity*, 1948), and **Luchino Visconti**'s *Senso* (*The Wanton Countess*, 1954).

In the immediate postwar period, between 1945 and 1954, in addition to funding feature films, the company also employed the talents of writers and directors such as **Rodolfo Sonego**, **Luciano Emmer**, **Michelangelo Antonioni**, **Valerio Zurlini**, and **Riccardo Freda** to make dozens of high-quality art historical documentaries. From 1956 onward, however, with Riccardo's son Renato now at the helm, the company reduced its activities mostly to distribution and coproduction. Then, in 1964, following the death of its founder and after almost three decades as one of the beacons of the Italian film industry, the company was wound up.

– M –

MA L'AMOR MIO NON MUORE. (*But My Love Will Not Die.*) Film. With the possible exception of **Giovanni Pastrone**'s *Cabiria* (1914), *Ma l'amor mio non muore* undoubtedly stands as the most famous of all Italian early silent films. Directed by **Mario Caserini** for Gloria Film in Turin in 1913, it starred **Lyda Borelli**, **Mario Bonnard**, and Gianpaolo Rosmino. Its plot was pure melodrama.

In order to pay for his rich and idle lifestyle, the villainous young adventurer Moise Sthar undertakes to steal valuable military documents from the house of Col. Julius Holbein, head of the military forces of the Granduchy of Wallenstein. As part of his evil plan he courts the colonel's beautiful daughter, Elsa, and soon declares his love to her. Her acceptance of his suit furnishes him with the opportunity to take the documents and flee. When the theft is discovered the colonel is accused of treason and so, shamed and dishonored, he commits suicide. Suspected of complicity in the matter, Elsa is also banished from the realm. Alone and defenseless in a foreign land, she assumes a new identity and, as Diana Candouleur, embarks on a successful career as an opera singer. Having achieved great fame and fortune, she is courted by many but the sadness that continues to afflict her leads her to fall in love with a similarly sad and wistful young man who, unbeknown to all, is actually Prince Maximilien, son of the Grand Duke, traveling incognito and tarrying in warmer climes to recover from a serious illness. With neither of them knowing the other's true identity, the couple enjoy their idyll of love until one day the evil Sthar reappears, recognizes Elsa, and again declares his love for her. When she forcefully rejects his advances he promises to reveal all to the Grand Duke, who will undoubtedly recall the young prince and end the couple's relationship. Distraught, Elsa returns to the stage to give one last performance but only after having drunk a poison draft. As Elsa/Diana collapses on the stage, she is caught in the arms of Maximilien, who has thrown all to the winds just to be with her forever. As she dies, outstretched beneath his loving gaze, she whispers, "*Ma l'amor mio non muore.*"

With its elaborate sets, elegant, high-class costumes, and relatively assured photography, in addition to its unashamedly melodramatic story line, the film topped the Italian box office in 1913. It launched the short but brilliant career of Lyda Borelli and was instrumental in establishing her reputation as the foremost diva of the Italian screen, with her heavily stylized gestures and Pre-Raphaelite poses becoming the model for a whole generation of actresses that followed. The film's overwhelming success and its theme of dying for love also initiated a vogue for decadent sentimental melodramas in the D'Annunzian vein that would last into the early 1920s.

MACARIO, ERMINIO (1902–1980). Actor. Having already achieved wide renown in Italy and abroad as a comic stage actor, Macario made his film debut as a Chaplinesque innocent in Eugenio De Liguoro's *Aria di paese* (*Country Air*, 1933). His first real success on the silver screen, however, came with the enormously popular *Imputato alzatevi* (Let the Accused Rise, 1939), a film directed by **Mario Mattoli** and widely regarded as something of a landmark in Italian screen comedy. Macario's popularity was cemented further in subsequent slightly surreal comedies such as *Non me lo dire* (*Don't Tell Me*, 1940) and spoofs such as *Il pirata sono io!* (*The Pirate's Dream*,

1940) and *Il fanciullo del West* (*The Boy from the West*, 1943), a far-cical early Italian Western with a Romeo and Juliet theme, directed by Giorgio Ferroni.

After the war he continued to be popular in films such as *Come persi la guerra* (*How I Lost the War*, 1947) and *L'eroe della strada* (*Street Hero*, 1948), a multiepisode film created as a tribute to Charlie Chaplin. In the 1950s he was more visible on stage than on screen but did venture into more dramatic territory, playing the lead in **Mario Soldati**'s melodrama *Italia piccola* (*Little Italy*, 1957). He subsequently appeared in a dozen other comedies, including a handful of films with **Totò**, but his popularity continued to decline inexorably during the 1960s as his more innocent brand of zany humor seemed to belong to a bygone era.

MACCARI, RUGGERI (1919–1989). Screenwriter. After working as a journalist and editing a number of satirical magazines, Maccari began writing for films in 1948 when he collaborated on the screenplay of Giorgio Simonelli's *Undici uomini e un pallone* (Eleven Men and a Ball, 1948). In the early 1950s he cowrote and codirected four films with Mario Amendola but with rather disappointing results. He subsequently concentrated on screenwriting and contributed to many of the key films of directors such as **Antonio Pietrangeli**, **Mario Monicelli**, **Luigi Zampa**, **Alberto Lattuada**, **Luigi Comencini**, and **Dino Risi**. He formed an especially close partnership with **Ettore Scola**, with whom he cowrote over a dozen films and shared the **Nastro d'argento** award for the screenplays of *Io la conoscevo bene* (*I Knew Her Well*, 1965), *Una giornata particolare* (*A Special Day*, 1977), *Passione d'amore* (*Passion of Love*, 1981), and *La Famiglia* (*The Family*, 1987). After having also worked extensively with Dino Risi on close to 15 films, in 1975 Maccari received an Oscar nomination for his screenplay of Risi's *Profumo di donna* (*Scent of a Woman*, 1975).

MACISTE. Film character. Played by the barrel-chested **Bartolomeo Pagano**, a Genoese dockworker with no previous acting experience, Maciste is the powerful but faithful African slave who helps rescue the young Roman girl from the jaws of Moloch in **Giovanni Pastrone**'s epic blockbuster *Cabiria* (1914). The perceived popular appeal of the character led to a long line of films in which Maciste appeared in a variety of guises and in different times and settings, playing roles as different as an Alpine trooper, an emperor, or a policeman, and yet always fundamentally the same "good giant" who had delighted audiences in the earlier film. After some 15 films for the **Itala Film** company in Italy, Pagano was enticed to make a further four Maciste films in Germany before returning to Italy to make several more for **Stefano Pittaluga**, including the surreal and at times hilarious *Maciste all'Inferno* (*Maciste in Hell*, 1926).

While the character's popular appeal undoubtedly derived from his uncomplicated moral values and his role as a natural defender of the weak against the bullying of the strong, many of the Itala films also demonstrated a more complex self-awareness of the medium on the part of the filmmakers. In the very first Maciste film (*Marvelous Maciste*, 1915), for example, a young girl mistreated by an evil uncle who is attempting to appropriate her inheritance sees *Cabiria* in a movie theater and decides to seek Maciste's help. She goes to the Itala studios in Turin where Maciste is in the middle of making a new film but he immediately accedes to her plea for help and embarks on setting things right.

Fading from the screens with Pagano's retirement and the coming of sound, the character was revived in the late 1950s in many of the sword-and-sandal epics, or so-called **peplums**, produced at **Cinecittà**. By this time, however, Maciste had lost his individuality and had become indistinguishable from the many Herculeses, Atlases, and other assorted neomythological strongmen, all played by a host of American bodybuilders.

MAGGI, LUIGI (1867–1946). Director. Having joined **Ambrosio Film** as an actor in 1906, Maggi quickly graduated to being one of the studio's most prominent and accomplished directors. His first great triumph was with *Gli ultimi giorni di Pompei* (*The Last Days of Pompeii*, 1908), the first of what would become numerous adaptations of Edward Bulwer-Lytton's novel in that long stream of spectacular historical epics that would constitute such a large part of Italian silent cinema. In 1911 the historical drama *Nozze d'oro* (*Golden Wedding*), in which he also starred alongside the rising diva Mary Cleo Talarini, was awarded first prize in the film section of the International Exhibition of Turin by a panel that included one of the Lumière brothers. Still for Ambrosio, in 1912 Maggi made *Satana* (*Satan*), a three-part portrait of the prince of evil in different historical settings and manifestations, an ambitious and complex work that, although now lost, is thought to have deeply influenced both the conception and structure of D. W. Griffith's *Intolerance*. Maggi's participation in World War I interrupted his flourishing career and when he returned he worked mainly as an actor. He abandoned the film industry altogether in the early 1920s.

MAGNANI, ANNA (1908–1973). Actress. The most celebrated actress of the Italian cinema in the immediate postwar period, Magnani was born illegitimately and grew up in one of the poorer quarters of Rome in the care of her maternal grandmother. An early interest in music— she studied piano at the Academy of Santa Cecilia—gave way to a stronger passion for the theater and she enrolled in the Eleanor Duse Acting School in Rome in 1927. Even before graduating she began working in the theater company of Dario Niccodemi and toured South America with the company in 1928. By 1930 she was becoming well known for her appearances in revues and musical theater. While continuing to work extensively on the stage she began to play small roles in films, her first appearance being in Nunzio Malasomma's *La cieca di Sorrento* (*The Blind Woman of Sorrento*, 1934). She subsequently played Fanny, the *chanteuse*, in **Goffredo Alessandrini**'s *Cavalleria* (*Cavalry*, 1936), a role that she repeated with slight variation in **Vittorio De Sica**'s *Teresa Venerdì* (*Mademoiselle Friday*, 1940). Forced to abandon the part of Giovanna in **Luchino Visconti**'s *Ossessione* (*Obsession*, 1943) due to an advanced state of pregnancy, she then went on to play Elide in **Mario Bonnard**'s *Campo de' Fiori* (*Peddler and the Lady*, 1943), the first of many incarnations of the forceful, down-to-earth Roman working-class woman that would characterize her acting repertoire from then on. Indeed it was as a variation on this role, playing Pina, the Roman housewife and mother mercilessly gunned down by German fire in **Roberto Rossellini**'s *Roma città aperta* (*Rome Open City*, 1945, also known as *Open City*), that she would score the greatest triumph of her entire career, earning a first **Nastro d'argento** for her moving interpretation and being catapulted to international fame by the film's worldwide success.

She subsequently appeared in a wide variety of films that ranged from dramas such as **Carmine Gallone**'s *Davanti a lui tremava tutta Roma* (*Before Him All Rome Trembled*, 1946) and **Alberto Lattuada**'s *Il bandito* (*The Bandit*, 1946) to more lighthearted comedies such as **Gennaro Righelli**'s *Abbassa la ricchezza* (*Peddlin' in Society*, 1947). Her splendid performance in **Luigi Zampa**'s *L'Onorevole Angelina (Angelina, MP*, 1947), again playing a Roman housewife and mother forced by circumstances to become a political agitator, earned her a second Nastro d'argento and the Volpi Cup at the **Venice Festival**. She then played the lead in **Mario Mattoli**'s remake of *Assunta Spina* (*Scarred*, 1947), a role that had originally been played by silent diva **Francesca Bertini** in 1915, before Rossellini devotedly showcased the range of Magnani's dramatic abilities in the two episodes of *L'amore* (*Ways of Love*, 1948).

After a number of other films in Italy, including her very convincing and moving performance as the self-deluded mother in Visconti's *Bellissima* (1951) and as the stage actress Camilla in Jean Renoir's *La carrozza d'oro* (*The Golden Coach*, 1952), she was enticed to America to star opposite Burt Lancaster in a screen adaptation of Tennessee Williams's *The Rose Tattoo* (1955), a performance that brought her the further recognition of an Academy Award. Her reputation as an international star now established and her participation much in demand, she appeared in several other American productions, including George Cukor's *Wild Is the Wind* (1958), where she starred opposite Anthony Quinn and Anthony Franciosa, and Sydnet Lumet's *The Fugitive Kind* (1960), where she was paired with Marlon Brando. However, both films were relative flops and she returned to Italy where, after appearing with **Totò** in **Mario Monicelli**'s bittersweet comedy *Risate di gioia* (*Joyful Laughter*, 1960), she came to play the other role for which she is most remembered, the ex-prostitute and tragic mother in **Pier Paolo Pasolini**'s *Mamma Roma* (1962).

From this high point, Magnani's film career rapidly declined. After an unimpressive performance in Claude Autant-Lara's lackluster *La magot de Josefa* (*Josefa's Loot*, 1964), done as part of a deal between producers, she was lured back to the stage and shone in an adaptation of Giovanni Verga's *La lupa* (*She Wolf*, 1965) and in a production in Italian of Jean Anouilh's *Medea* (1966), both directed by **Franco Zeffirelli**. Enticed once more back to the big screen, she gave a frothy performance as the wife of the drunken vintner played by Anthony Quinn in Stanley Kramer's *The Secret of Santa Vittoria* (1969) and then made four modest films for television directed by Alfredo Giannetti. Rather appropriately, her final appearance in film was a cameo role where she played herself closing the door of her house and wishing **Federico Fellini** good night in the concluding sequence of Fellini's *Roma* (*Fellini Roma*, 1972).

MANFREDI, NINO (1921–2004). Actor and director. An extremely popular actor who appeared in over 100 films in a career that spanned the entire postwar period, Nino (short for Saturnino) Manfredi graduated in law while also studying at the Rome Academy of Dramatic Art. A born and very versatile entertainer, he was soon appearing on stage with some of the most prestigious theatrical companies as well as creating comic characters on the radio and dubbing films, including being the voice of **Marcello Mastroianni** in **Luciano Emmer**'s *Parigi è sempre Parigi* (*Paris Is Always Paris*, 1951) and *Le ragazze di piazza di Spagna* (*Three Girls from Rome*, 1952). His first film appearance was in the otherwise undistinguished *Monastero di Santa Chiara* (*Monastery of Saint Clare*, 1949). While continuing to work in revues and musical theater he played supporting roles in a handful of other minor films while also beginning to achieve a solid popularity through his appearances on television.

Following more significant roles in comedies such as *Guardia, ladro e cameriera* (*Maid, Thief and Guard*, 1958) and **Nanni Loy**'s *Audace colpo dei soliti ignoti* (*Fiasco in Milan*, 1959), Manfredi's film career blossomed during the 1960s when he became one of the regular and much-loved faces in many of the films of the ***commedia all'italiana***. His multiple performances in **Lina Wertmüller**'s caustic satire of Italian masculinity, *Questa volta parliamo di uomini* (*This Time Let's Talk about Men*, 1965), brought him his first **Nastro d'argento**, which was soon followed by a second one for his role in Luigi Magni's *Nell'anno del Signore* (*The Conspirators*, 1969). His greatest cinematic triumphs, however, came in the 1970s with his portrayal of Geppetto in **Luigi Comencini**'s much-loved made-for-television *Pinocchio* (1972), his interpretation of the hapless Italian immigrant in Switzerland in **Franco Brusati**'s *Pane e cioccolata* (*Bread and Chocolate*, 1973), and his most endearing performance as Antonio in **Ettore Scola**'s *C'eravamo tanto amati* (*We All Loved Each Other So Much*, 1974). Having already tried his hand at directing with an episode of the compilation film *L'amore difficile* (*Of Wayward Love*, 1963), in 1971 he also cowrote and directed himself in *Per grazia ricevuta* (*Between Miracles*, 1971), an irreverent satire on religion that earned him a nomination for the Palme d'or at Cannes, a **David di Donatello** for his direction, and two Nastri d'argento for Best Story and Screenplay.

His popularity continued unabated throughout the 1980s and 1990s when, alongside a host of successful films for the big screen, he starred in a number of extremely popular television miniseries including *Un commissario a Roma* (*Police Commissioner in Rome*, 1993) and the even longer-running *Linda e il brigadiere* (*Linda and the Police Sergeant*, 1997–1999).

MANGANO, SILVANA (1930–1989). Actress. One of the first of the so-called *maggiorate*, or generously proportioned starlets of Italian postwar cinema, Mangano (Miss Rome, 1946) had been a model and had played small supporting parts in a number of minor films before skyrocketing to international stardom as the feisty, black-stockinged rice worker in **Giuseppe De Santis**'s *Riso amaro* (*Bitter Rice*, 1949). In the same year she married producer **Dino De Laurentiis** in a civil ceremony and subsequently had four children by him before seeking a legal separation in 1983. (Their son Federico died in a plane accident in 1981.)

Although De Laurentiis sought to exploit Mangano's strongly erotic image in the early 1950s in films such as **Alberto Lattuada**'s *Anna* (1951), in which she played a troubled nightclub singer who eventually becomes a nun, and **Mario Camerini**'s *Ulisse* (*Ulysses*, 1954), in which she played both Circe and Penelope, Mangano would earn a much more exalted and enduring reputation for the ethereal, almost abstract, femininity that she came to exemplify in the mother figures she played in **Pier Paolo Pasolini**'s *Edipo re* (*Oedipus Rex*, 1966) and *Teorema* (*Theorem*, 1968) and **Luchino Visconti**'s *Morte a Venezia* (*Death in Venice*, 1968), *Ludwig* (1972), and *Gruppo di famiglia in un interno* (*Conversation Piece*, 1974). Always more interested in her family than in international stardom, she chose her roles very carefully in the later part of her career and drastically reduced her screen appearances to a minimum. Her last role was as Elisa, the wife of Romano (played by her friend **Marcello Mastroianni**), in Nikita Mikhalkov's *Oci ciornie* (*Dark Eyes*, 1987), following which she retired to battle a long, and eventually fatal, illness.

MANNINO, FRANCO (1924–2005). Composer and musician. A prolific and wide-ranging composer who published over 500 musical works during his lifetime, Mannino also scored the music for a host of films. He initiated his association with the cinema in the early 1950s by composing the music for Lèonide Moguy's *Domani è un altro giorno* (*Tomorrow Is Another Day*, 1950). He then worked extensively with **Luchino Visconti**, scoring or arranging the music for *Bellissima* (1951), *Morte a Venezia* (*Death in Venice*, 1968), *Ludwig* (1972), *Gruppo di famiglia in un interno* (*Conversation Piece*, 1974), and *L'innocente* (*The Innocent*, 1976), the last being awarded the **David di Donatello** for Best Musical Score. At the same time he also composed the music for **Carlo Lizzani**'s *Ai margini della metropoli* (*At the Edge of the City*, 1952), **Mario Soldati**'s *La provinciale* (*The Wayward Wife*, 1953), John Huston's *Beat the Devil* (1953, known in Italy as *Il tesoro dell'Africa*), and **Luigi Zampa**'s *La romana* (*Woman of Rome*, 1954). Beginning in the mid-1950s he also collaborated with directors of the more popular genres such as **Antonio Margheriti** and **Riccardo Freda,** for whom he scored *I vampiri* (*The Devil's Commandment*, 1957), the film that initiated the Italian **horror** genre. Mannino's last credited film score was in fact for Freda's *L'ossessione che uccide* (*Murder Syndrome*, 1981).

MARGADONNA, ETTORE MARIA (1893–1975). Writer, journalist, screenwriter. After successfully pursuing a career in journalism and publishing one of the earliest Italian histories of the cinema, Margadonna turned to screenwriting in the late 1930s, working with many of the most significant directors of the period, including **Alessandro Blasetti**, **Mario Bonnard**, **Gennaro Righelli**, **Mario Soldati**, and **Carlo Ludovico Bragaglia**. In the immediate postwar period he collaborated with **Alberto Lattuada** on *Il bandito* (*The Bandit*, 1946) and with **Renato Castellani** on both *Sotto il sole di*

Roma (*Beneath a Roman Sun*, 1948) and *Due soldi di speranza* (*Two Cents' Worth of Hope*, 1952), the subject for the last film earning him a **Nastro d'argento**. In 1950 he published an anthology of short stories and two years later also provided a creditable performance as Ivan's uncle in **Federico Fellini**'s *Lo sceicco bianco* (*The White Sheik*, 1952). His greatest triumph, however, came in 1953 when he wrote the story and screenplay for **Luigi Comencini**'s enormously popular *Pane, amore e fantasia* (*Bread, Love and Dreams*, 1953), which brought him a nomination for an Academy Award. He subsequently provided the story and screenplay for both the sequels, *Pane, amore e gelosia* (*Bread, Love and Jealousy*, 1954, also known as *Frisky*) and *Pane, amore e . . .* (*Scandal in Sorento*, 1955) and worked on another half a dozen minor films before retiring from films altogether in the early 1960s. His last contribution to the Italian cinema was the subject of *Il monaco di Monza* (*The Monk of Monza*, 1963), one of the **Totò** films directed by **Sergio Corbucci**.

MARGHERITI, ANTONIO (1930–2002). Screenwriter and director. One of the masters of Italian (and international) low-budget B-grade films, Margheriti worked in, and across, all the major genres, producing more than 50 films in a career that spanned almost half a century.

After working mostly as a screenwriter in the early 1950s, Margheriti made his directorial debut with *Spacemen* (also known as *Assignment Outer Space*, 1960), one of the first examples of Italian science fiction. Thereafter, usually under the pseudonym Anthony M. Dawson, Margheriti dabbled freely in all the genres, making more apocalyptic science fiction fantasies like *Il pianeta degli uomini spenti* (*The Battle of the Worlds*, 1961) and *I Diafanoidi vengono da Marte* (*Diaphanoids, Bringers of Death*, 1966), sword-and-sandal epics like *Il crollo di Roma* (*The Collapse of Rome*, 1962) and *Ursus, il terrore di Kirghisi* (*Hercules, Prisoner of Evil*, 1964), **spaghetti Westerns** such as *Joko invoca Dio . . . e muori* (*Vengeance*, 1968) and parodic spy thrillers in the James Bond mold: *Operaciòn Goldman* (*Lightning Bolt*, 1966) and *A007, sfida ai killers* (*Bob Flemming, Mission Casablanca*, 1966). He achieved a strong international reputation, particularly in the **horror** genre, with films such as *La vergine di Norimberga* (*Horror Castle*, 1963), *Danza macabra* (*Castle of*

Blood, 1964), *Apocalypse domain* (*Cannibal Apocalypse*, 1980), and the two films he codirected with Paul Morrissey, *Flesh for Franken-stein* (1973) and *Blood for Dracula* (1974). He also had a special propensity for creating hybrid genres such as the bizarre supernatural Western, *Whisky & Fantasmi* (*Whiskey and Ghosts*, 1976), where a young man on the run from Mexican bandits is protected by the ghosts of Davy Crockett, Pecos Bill, and Johnny Appleseed.

Appropriately, his last film, *Virtual Weapon* (1996), filmed entirely in Miami, Florida, and made under his usual pseudonym, is a blend of police thriller, buddy movie, and dystopic science fiction.

MARRA, VINCENZO (1972–). Screenwriter and director. One of the most promising of the younger generation of contemporary Italian filmmakers, Marra studied law and worked as a sports photographer before beginning to make short films in 1998. After working as assistant to **Mario Martone** on *Teatri di guerra* (*Rehearsals for War*, 1998), and with Chilean Italian director Marco Bechis on *Garage Olimpo* (1999), a film that highlighted the use of torture during the Argentinian regime, Marra directed his own first feature, *Tornando a casa* (*Sailing Home*, 2001). A complex drama about Neapolitan fishermen forced by necessity into illegal activities, the film was screened to great acclaim at a host of festivals, including the **Venice**, where it was awarded the first prize for a debut feature. There followed the feature-length documentary *Estanei alla massa* (Separate from the Rest, 2002), which closely observed the daily lives of seven fanatical Neapolitan soccer fans, and a shorter documentary on Sicily, *Paesaggio a sud* (2003), before Marra's similarly acclaimed second feature, *Vento di terra* (*Land Wind*, 2004). The moving but unsentimental story of a young Neapolitan boy who becomes ill through exposure to depleted uranium while on voluntary military service in Kosovo, the film won both the International Film Critics Prize and the Pasinetti Award for most innovative film. Marra's most recent work is *L'udienza è aperta* (*The Session Is Open*, 2006), a full-length documentary on the trial of members of the camorra in Naples.

MARTELLI, OTELLO (1902–2000). Cinematographer. Martelli began working as a cameraman at Caesar Film in 1916 and graduated to director of photography on a number of films directed by Roberto

Roberti before joining the Istituto **LUCE** in the mid-1920s. In 1928 he followed and recorded Umberto Nobile's hapless expedition to the North Pole in his feature-length **documentary** *Le gesta dell'Artide* (Exploits in the Arctic Region, 1928). On his return, he joined the newly revived **Cines**, where he worked as cinematographer on a host of films that included **Alessandro Blasetti**'s *Vecchia guardia* (1933), **Mario Camerini**'s *Darò un milione* (*I'll Give a Million*, 1935), and the first film to star comic actor **Totò**, *Fermo con le mani* (*Hands Off Me!* 1936), directed by Gero Zambuto.

After the war he collaborated with **Roberto Rossellini** on *Paisà* (*Paisan*, 1946), *Stromboli, terra di Dio* (*Stromboli*, 1949), and *Francesco, giullare di Dio* (*Francis, God's Jester*, 1950), on many of **Giuseppe De Santis**'s films, including the extremely successful *Riso amaro* (*Bitter Rice*, 1949), and with **Federico Fellini** on *I vitelloni* (*Spivs*, 1953), *La strada* (1954), *Il bidone* (*The Swindlers*, 1955), *Le notti di Cabiria* (*The Nights of Cabiria*, 1957), and ***La dolce vita*** (1960). Although not unduly enthusiastic about color, he photographed **Vittorio De Sica**'s *La riffa* (*The Raffle*) and Fellini's *Le tentazioni del dottor Antonio* (*The Temptations of Dottor Antonio*), and two episodes of *Boccaccio '70* (*Boccaccio 70*, 1962), as well as Abel Gance's final film, *Cyrano et D'Artagnan* (*Cyrano and D'Artagnan*, 1964), before retiring from the industry in 1966.

MARTOGLIO, NINO (1870–1921). Journalist, poet, playwright, film director. Already a prolific and highly renowned poet, playwright, and theater director, Martoglio also came to earn an honored place in the history of early Italian cinema by directing three films for the short-lived Morgana Film company, which he had helped to found in Sicily: *Sperduti nel buio* (*Lost in the Dark*, 1914), *Capitan Blanco* (1914), and *Teresa Raquin* (1915). The meticulously realistic sets and the naturalistic acting in these films were in very strong contrast to the artificial scenography and the more stylized acting in the historical superspectacles and costume dramas that were monopolizing so much Italian film production at the time. This has prompted many to see Martoglio's films as distant forebearers of **neorealism**. Indeed, the only known existing copy of *Sperduti nel buio* continued to be used for teaching at the **Centro Sperimentale di Cinematografia** as a consummate example of cinematic realism until 1943, when it was destroyed while being transported to Germany.

MARTONE, MARIO (1959–). Actor, screenwriter, film and theater director. Martone began acting onstage in 1976. Two years later he founded the experimental theater group Falso movimento (False Movement), with which he staged a series of critically acclaimed theatrical spectacles, the most renowned of which was *Tango glaciale* (Glacial Tango, 1982).

While continuing to work in live theater, Martone began experimenting with video art and in 1984 made his first short film, *Nella città barocca* (*In the Baroque City*, 1984), a lyrical **documentary** on 17th-century Naples. His first full-length feature, *Morte di un matematico napolitano* (*Death of a Neapolitan Mathematician*, 1992), recounting the last days of internationally renowned Neapolitan mathematician Renato Caccioppoli before he committed suicide in 1959, was immediately hailed as a brilliant first work, winning the Special Grand Jury Prize at **Venice**, as well as a **Nastro d'argento** and a **David di Donatello** for Best New Director. Following the medium-length *Rasoi* (*Razors*, 1993), a series of reflections on Naples, and the documentary *Lucio Amelio/Terrae Motus* (1993), Martone directed *Amore molesto* (*Nasty Love*, 1995), a dark, erotic thriller that was nominated for the Palme d'or at Cannes and which brought him another David di Donatello for Best Director. After *Una storia sahawari* (*A Story of the Sahawari*, 1996), a documentary made for television focusing on the plight of children living in a refugee camp, he directed *La salita* (*The Climb*), one episode of the compilation film *I vesuviani* (1997), made in collaboration with four other young Neapolitan directors. A year later, *Teatro di guerra* (*Rehearsals for War*, 1998) was built around a theatrical production of Aeschylus's *Seven against Thebes* but provocatively set against the backdrop of war in Sarajevo. After having been drawn away from cinema by his appointment as director of the Theater of Rome in 1999, Martone returned to the big screen with *L'odore del sangue* (*The Smell of the Blood*, 2004), another dark, erotic work adapted from a novel by Goffredo Parise.

MASELLI, FRANCESCO (1930–). Director and screenwriter. During a career that has spanned half a century, Maselli has remained one of the most politically vocal and socially committed of all Italian directors. After taking part in the **Resistance** movement during World War II, Maselli enrolled at the **Centro Sperimentale di Cinematografia**, graduating in 1949. At the same time he served as assistant on some of **Michelangelo Antonioni**'s early documentaries and made a number of his own, which were shown to strong acclaim at Venice. He subsequently worked as codirector with **Cesare Zavattini** on *La storia di Caterina* (*Caterina's Story*), one of the six episodes of the compilation film *Amore in Città* (*Love in the City*, 1953). He would collaborate again with Zavattini in the early 1960s, when he would contribute the episode *Le adolescenti e l'amore* (The Adolescents and Love) to Zavattini's *Le italiane e l'amore* (*Latin Lovers*, 1961).

His first feature, *Gli sbandati* (*Abandoned*, 1955), examined the issue of political responsibility among the younger generation at the time of the events of 1943. After a number of minor works, including *Bambini al cinema* (*Children at the Cinema*, 1956), a delightful short film about a small cinema for children in Rome's Villa Borghese, he made *I delfini* (*The Dauphins*, 1960), a scathing portrait of the bored and wealthy younger generation in a provincial city at the beginning of Italy's economic boom. This was followed by a finely crafted adaptation of Alberto Moravia's novel *Gli Indifferenti* (*A Time of Indifference*, 1964), beautifully photographed in black and white by master cinematographer **Gianni Di Venanzo**. Maselli played an active part in the protests of 1968 including the occupation and boycott of the **Venice Festival** that year, following which he made *Lettera aperta a un giornale della sera* (*Open Letter to an Evening Daily*, 1970), a highly polemic and provocative film shot on 16 mm film in cinema verité style. This was followed by *Il sospetto* (*The Suspect*, 1975), a taut and highly charged political thriller set in the mid-1930s, written with Marxist screenwriter **Franco Solinas** and starring **Gian Maria Volontè** in what was perhaps one of his finest performances. For the next decade Maselli largely produced films made for television, among them *Avventura di un fotografo* (*The Adventure of a Photographer*, 1984), which he adapted from a short story by Italo Calvino. He returned to the big screen with *Storia d'amore* (*Love Story*, 1986), a penetrating psychological study of female breakdown that earned the film the Grand Jury Prize at Venice as well as the Volpi Cup for lead actress, Valeria Golino. As an active member of the Communist Refoundation Party and president of ANAC, Maselli organized a number of directors to film the antiglobalization demonstration at the G8 meeting in Rome in 2002. His most recent works have been documentaries: *Lettere dalla Palestina* (*Letters from Palestine*, 2002) and *Firenze, nostro domaini* (*Florence, Our Tomorrow*, 2003).

MASINA, GIULIETTA (1921–1994). Actress. An accomplished and versatile actress who appeared in some 30 films in a career that spanned five decades, Masina is nevertheless probably best remembered for the roles she played in the films of her husband, **Federico Fellini**. After achieving some popularity on the radio in the early 1940s playing the main female character in a comic program written by the then unknown Fellini, Masina made her screen debut in **Alberto Lattuada**'s *Senza pietà* (*Without Pity*, 1948) in a strong supporting role that earned her the **Nastro d'argento**. Two years later she received her second Nastro for her performance as Melina Amour, the plainer variety actress abandoned by her man for the more beautiful **Carla Del Poggio** in *Luci del varietà* (*Variety Lights*, 1950). After a minor role in **Roberto Rossellini**'s *Europa '51* (*The Greatest Love*, 1952) and a fleeting appearance as a prostitute named Cabiria in Fellini's *Lo sceicco bianco* (*The White Sheik*, 1952), she came to international prominence as the endearing waif, Gelsomina, in *La strada* (1954), with the film winning the Academy Award for Best Foreign Film and Masina being nominated for the BAFTA award for Best Actress. Three years later her captivating performance as the warm-hearted prostitute in *Le notti di Cabiria* (*The Nights of Cabiria*, 1957) brought her a third Nastro d'argento as well as the Best Actress prize at Cannes. In the following years she appeared in a number of films by other directors, including alongside **Anna Magnani** in **Renato Castellani**'s prison drama *Nella città l'inferno* (*Hell in the City*, 1958), but her most memorable subsequent performances were undoubtedly those Fellini elicited from her in *Giulietta degli spiriti* (*Juliet of the Spirits*, 1965) and *Ginger e Fred* (*Ginger and Fred*, 1986). Her final appearance on the big screen was as Bertille, a 70-year-old mother attempting to bring her family together for a last meal, in Jean-Louis Bertucelli's *Aujourd'hui peut-être* (*A Day to Remember*, 1991).

MASTROIANNI, MARCELLO (1924–1996). Actor. Undoubtedly *the* actor who most came to represent Italian cinema in the postwar period, Mastroianni began acting in films from a relatively young age, making early appearances as an uncredited extra in **Alessandro Blasetti**'s *La corona di ferro* (*The Iron Crown*, 1941) and **Vittorio De Sica**'s *I bambini ci guardano* (*The Children Are Watching Us*, 1943). After carrying out his military service during World War II, he returned to Rome and entered the theater, where he worked with **Luchino Visconti**. By the early 1950s he had returned to films, at first doing minor parts, as in **Luciano Emmer**'s *Domenica d'agosto* (*A Sunday in August*, 1950) and *Le ragazze di Piazza di Spagna* (*Three Girls from Rome*, 1952), but soon taking on more significant supporting roles, as in **Carlo Lizzani**'s *Cronache di poveri amanti* (*Chronicle of Poor Lovers*, 1954). His interpretation of the male romantic lead in **Giuseppe De Santis**'s *Giorni d'amore* (*Days of Love*, 1954) earned him his first **Nastro d'argento**. Thanks to Alessandro Blasetti he was soon paired with **Sophia Loren** in the first of many films they would make together, beginning with Blasetti's *Peccato che sia una canaglia* (*Too Bad She's Bad*, 1954) and *La fortuna di essere donna* (*Lucky to Be a Woman*, 1955). Two years later his moving portrayal of Mario in Visconti's *Le notti bianche* (*White Nights*, 1957) earned him another Nastro d'argento. Having conquered drama, his considerable talent for comedy was then fully brought to the fore in **Mario Monicelli**'s hilarious *I soliti ignoti* (*Big Deal on Madonna Street*, 1958).

With his reputation now securely established, in the early 1960s he appeared in most of the key films of both established and up-and-coming directors, including **Mauro Bolognini**'s *Il bell'Antonio* (*Bell'Antonio*, 1960), **Michelangelo Antonioni**'s *La notte* (*Night*, 1961), **Valerio Zurlini**'s *Cronaca familiare* (*Family Diary*, 1962), and, perhaps most memorably, as the lovable scoundrel of a husband in **Pietro Germi**'s *Divorzio all'italiana* (*Divorce Italian Style*, 1961), a finely modulated interpretation that earned him his first Oscar nomination. By this time, however, he had already become well known to international audiences playing the wayward journalist Marcello in **Federico Fellini**'s landmark film, *La dolce vita* (1960), for which he had received another Nastro d'argento. He subsequently became Fellini's onscreen alter ego in the Oscar-winning *Otto e mezzo* (*8½*, 1963). At the same time he continued to garner both national and international acclaim playing opposite a fiery Sophia Loren at the peak of her prowess in De Sica's *Ieri, oggi e domani* (*Yesterday, Today and Tomorrow*, 1963), which was awarded the Academy Award for Best Foreign Film in 1965, and *Matrimonio all'italiana* (*Marriage Italian Style*, 1964), also nominated for an Oscar.

In the next decade he continued to work with all the major directors, appearing in, among others, Visconti's *Lo straniero* (*The Stranger*, 1967), **Ettore Scola**'s *Dramma della gelosia—tutti i particolari in cronaca* (*Drama of Jealousy*, 1970), **Paolo and Vittorio Taviani**'s *Allonsanfan* (1973), **Marco Ferreri**'s *La grande abbuffata* (*The Grande Bouffe*, 1973), and **Luigi Comencini**'s *La donna della domenica* (*The Sunday Woman*, 1976). Arguably his best performance during this period was as Gabriele, the homosexual radio journalist in Scola's *Una giornata particolare* (*A Special Day*, 1976), a role that saw him again paired with Sophia Loren and that brought out the very best in both of them. In the 1980s he again worked with Fellini in *La città delle donne* (*The City of Women*, 1980) and *Ginger e Fred* (*Ginger and Fred*, 1986) and gave a magisterial performance as Casanova in Scola's *La nuit de Varennes* (*That Night in Varennes*, 1982). By the end of the 1980s, however, he was tending toward more fatherly roles as in Scola's *Che ora è?* (*What Time Is It?* 1989) and **Giuseppe Tornatore**'s *Stanno tutti bene* (*Everybody's Fine*, 1990). Nevertheless, in 1994 he was induced by Robert Altman to team up again with Sophia Loren in a reprise of their legendary performance in *Marriage Italian Style* for Altman's satire on the fashion industry, *Prêt-à-Porter* (*Ready to Wear*, 1994). After playing the title role in **Roberto Faenza**'s *Sostiene Pereira* (*According to Pereira*, 1996) and a man with four personalities in Raul Ruiz's *Trois vies et une seule mort* (*Three Lives and Only One Death*, 1996), Mastroianni made his final film appearance in Manoel de Oliviera's *Viagem ao Principio do Mundo* (*Voyage to the Beginning of the World*, 1997), where, rather fittingly perhaps, after a life devoted to the cinema, he played the part of an aging film director traveling with a film crew through Portugal in search of the origins of a famous French actor.

Having already received innumerable prizes for his appearances in some 140 films, in 1997 Mastroianni was awarded both a Special Nastro d'Argento and a David di Donatello for his career in cinema. Before dying he recounted his life story in *Marcello Mastroianni: Mi ricordo, sì mi ricordo* (*Marcello Mastroianni: I Remember*, 1997), a three-hour **documentary** directed by his long-time companion, Anna Maria Tatò.

MASTROIANNI, RUGGERO (1929–1996). Editor. Younger brother of **Marcello Mastroianni**, Ruggero was as widely respected as a film editor as his brother was an actor. Beginning with **Giuseppe De Santis**'s *Giorni d'amore* (*Days of Love*, 1954), Mastroianni served as assistant editor on a number of films before graduating to editor on Enzo Provenzale's *Vento del sud* (*South Wind*, 1959). He subsequently worked extensively with both established and up-and-coming directors, including **Luchino Visconti**, **Francesco Maselli**, **Nanni Loy**, **Lina Wertmüller**, and **Mario Monicelli**, and he formed a special relationship with **Elio Petri**, all of whose major films he edited. In 1965 with *Giulietta degli spiriti* (*Juliet of the Spirits*) he also initiated a long and fruitful collaboration with **Federico Fellini**, for whom he would edit all the films from the Toby Dammit episode in *Tre passi nel delirio* (*Spirits of the Dead*, 1968) to *Ginger e Fred* (*Ginger and Fred*, 1986). At the same time, beginning with *Uomini contro* (*Many Wars Ago*, 1970), he also worked extensively with **Francesco Rosi** and in fact died while preparing to edit Rosi's *La tregua* (*The Truce*, 1996). In a long career that saw him edit over 150 films, he received many honors and awards, including the **David di Donatello** five times and a **Nastro d'argento** for his editing of Monicelli's *Speriamo che sia femina* (*Let's Hope It's a Girl*, 1986).

MATARAZZO, RAFFAELLO (1906–1966). Director and screenwriter. Probably best remembered for the series of extremely popular heart-tugging melodramas he directed in the 1950s, Matarazzo had begun his career in cinema as a film critic writing for, among others, **Alessandro Blasetti**'s journal, *Cinematografo*. Together with Blasetti and others who were connected with the journal, Matarazzo joined the revived **Cines** studio during **Emilio Cecchi**'s period as artistic director and with Cecchi's encouragement began working as a screenwriter while also making several documentaries in the Cines series, among them *Mussolinia di Sardegna* (1933) and *Littoria* (1933). His first solo feature was *Treno popolare* (*People's Train*, 1933), a charming fictional travelogue to Orvieto, often regarded as a distant forerunner of **neorealism**, also notable as the first film scored by composer **Nino Rota**. This promising debut was followed by a number of light situation comedies and what came to be known as **white telephone films**, the best of which was *L'Avventuriera del piano di sopra* (*The Adventuress from the Floor Above*, 1941), which ably employed the talents of **Vittorio De Sica** and **Clara Calamai** in the leading roles.

After the war, Matarazzo directed *Fumeria d'oppio* (*Opium Den*, 1947), a promising but ultimately unsuccessful attempt at reviving the **Za-la-Mort** character who had been made so famous by **Emilio Ghione** during the silent era (Ghione's son starred in the film). This was followed by *Paolo e Francesca* (*Paolo and Francesca*, 1949), a competent enough adaptation of one of the most famous episodes from Dante's *Inferno*. In the same year, however, Matarazzo finally struck box office gold with *Catene* (*Chains*, 1949), the first of a long line of enormously popular tear-jerking melodramas featuring the romantic couple **Amedeo Nazzari** and **Yvonne Sanson**. Over the next decade he continued his run of box office successes with *Figli di Nessuno* (*Nobody's Children*, 1951), *Chi è senza peccato* (*Whoever Is Without Sin*, 1952), *Angelo Bianco* (*The White Angel*, 1955), and *Malinconico autunno* (*Melancholic Autumn*, 1959). By the early 1960s, however, with interest in the genre fading, his own star also waned and his last film, *Amore mio* (*My Love*, 1964), passed largely unnoticed.

MATTOLI, MARIO (1898–1980). Director and screenwriter. A popular genre director who came to be associated mainly with comedy and melodrama, Mattoli graduated in law before working as a legal administrator for the Suvini-Zerboni theater company. In 1927 he founded Spettacoli Za-bum, a theatrical revue company whose productions attracted the participation of many fine actors, including the young **Vittorio De Sica**. In 1934 Mattoli initiated what would be an extraordinarily prolific film career by writing and directing *Tempo massimo* (*Full Speed*, 1934), a romantic comedy that starred De Sica and Milly and which included future star **Anna Magnani** in a minor role.

From then until the war years Mattoli directed a host of light comedies and melodramas, sometimes as many as six films in one year. His first real success, however, came with *Imputato alzatevi* (Let the

Accused Rise, 1939), a film now regarded as something of a landmark in Italian comedy and that also definitively launched the screen career of popular comedian **Erminio Macario**. In the immediate postwar period Mattoli directed *La vita ricomincia* (*Life Begins Anew*, 1945) followed by a remake of the classic silent melodrama *Assunta Spina* (1948), with Anna Magnani in the role of the Neapolitan laundress that had originally been played by the silent diva **Francesca Bertini**. By this time Mattoli had also begun directing **Totò** in *I due orfanelli* (*The Two Orphans*, 1947), the first of 16 films Mattoli would make with the great comedian and which would include such classics as *Un turco napoletano* (*Neapolitan Turk*, 1953), *Miseria e nobiltà* (*Poverty and Nobility*, 1954), and *Totò, Fabrizi e i giovani d'oggi* (Totò, Fabrizi and the Young People of Today, 1960). Still directing at the rate of three or four films a year, in the early 1960s Mattoli helped to launch the film career of the comic duo **Franco Franchi** and **Ciccio Ingrassia** with *Appuntamento a Ischia* (Rendezvous at Ischia, 1960), while at the same time injecting some comedy into the **peplum** genre with his *Maciste contro Ercole nella valle dei guai* (*Hercules in the Valley of Woe*, 1961). After making close to 90 films in 30 years, Mattoli directed his last film in 1966, a spoof on the then flourishing genre of the **spaghetti Western** titled *Per qualche dollaro in meno* (*For a Few Dollars Less*, 1966).

MAZZACURATI, CARLO (1956–). Director and screenwriter. One of the first directors to be hailed as a representative of the **New Italian Cinema**, Mazzacurati studied at the DAMS (Faculty of Comunication) in Bologna before self-financing his first short film, *Vagabondi* (Vagabonds, 1979). After working for television and collaborating on the screenplay of what would later become **Gabriele Salvatores**'s *Marrakech Express* (1989), he secured the support of **Nanni Moretti**'s newly established **Sacher Film** company for his first feature, *Notte Italiana* (*Italian Night*, 1987). An atmospheric tale of crime and corruption set in the Po delta area of the Italian northeast, the film was highly praised and earned Mazzacurati the **Nastro d'argento** for Best New Director. His second feature, *Il prete bello* (The Handsome Priest, 1989), was generally regarded as lackluster and disappointing, but his talent appeared to be reconfirmed with *Un'altra vita* (*Another Life*, 1992) and *Il toro* (*The Bull*, 1994), an interesting variation on the road movie that recounted the story of two male friends attempting to transport a stolen stud bull to Hungary in hopes of making a huge profit. The bittersweet comedy was awarded the Silver Lion at the **Venice Festival** that year, and two years later his *Vesna va veloce* (*Vesna Goes Fast*, 1996), the tragic story of a Czech girl's attempts to remain in Italy, was also nominated for the Golden Lion. *L'estate di Davide* (*David's Summer*, 1998), a powerful but unsentimental coming-of-age film originally made for television, was followed by the tragicomic *La lingua del santo* (*Holy Tongue*, 1999) and *A cavallo della tigre* (*Riding the Tiger*, 2002), in which Mazzacurati continued to explore the life of eccentric individuals living on the social fringes. His most recent film, *L'amore ritrovato* (*An Italian Romance*, 2004), is a more conventional love story adapted from a novel by Carlo Cassola.

MELATO, MARIANGELA (1943–). Actress. After studying painting at the Academy of Brera, Melato served an apprenticeship with a number of minor theater companies before being accepted into the company directed by Dario Fo. Her career was greatly boosted in 1967 when she was selected to play the lead in **Luchino Visconti**'s production of *La Monaca di Monza* (The Nun of Monza) at the Piccolo Teatro of Milan. She subsequently played the role of Olimpia in Luca Ronconi's groundbreaking production of *Orlando Furioso* (1969) before making her film debut in **Pupi Avati**'s first film, *Thomas—gli indemoniati* (*Thomas and the Bewitched*, 1969). Avati's film sank without a trace but Melato's film career continued with small parts in **Nino Manfredi**'s *Per grazia ricevuta* (*Between Miracles*, 1971), **Luciano Salce**'s *Basta Guardarla* (Just Look at Her, 1971), and the much more significant role of Lidia, the wife of the manic factory worker played by **Gian Maria Volontè**, in **Elio Petri**'s *La classe operaia va in paradiso* (*The Working Class Goes to Heaven*, 1971). She soon became internationally famous, however, particularly in the United States, playing opposite **Giancarlo Giannini** in a series of social farces directed by **Lina Wertmüller**. After also demonstrating her talents as a dancer in Avati's *Aiutami a sognare* (*Help Me Dream*, 1981) and **Maurizio Nichetti**'s *Domani si balla* (Tomorrow We Dance, 1982), she returned to the stage, where she worked again with Ronconi and with Giorgio Strehler. From the

early 1990s she appeared frequently on television, with her interpretation of the role of Marianna in the first two episodes of *Una vita in
gioco* (A Life on the Line) earning her the Best European Actress
award. She returned to the big screen at the end of the 1990s in Maurizio Zaccaro's *Un uomo per bene* (A Respectable Man, 1999).

In addition to numerous prizes and awards for her work in the theater, Melato received the **Nastro d'argento** five times and collected
eight **David di Donatello** awards, including the Special Medal of the
City of Rome in 1986 and the David Golden Plate in 2000.

MENICHELLI, PINA (1890–1984). Actress and diva. Born of a Sicilian couple who were both actors, Pina (short for Giuseppina)
Menichelli made her screen debut in 1913 playing small parts in
comic sketches produced by the **Cines**. She was soon taking on more
substantial roles in films such as **Baldassare Negroni**'s *Zuma* (1913)
and **Enrico Guazzoni**'s *Scuola d'eroi* (*School for Heroes*, 1914), in
which Menichelli played a patriotic and self-sacrificing young drum-
mer in the Napoleonic wars. Already popular as an actress and a frequent cover girl of the various film magazines of the time, she was
consecrated to stardom by her appearance in **Giovanni Pastrone**'s *Il
fuoco* (*The Fire*, 1915), where she played a mysterious noblewoman
who lures a young painter to her castle with her morbid beauty and
languid sensuality only to destroy him. Although severely cut by the
censors, as were a number of Menichelli's subsequent films, *Il fuoco*
was extremely popular and elevated her to the same status as the
reigning divas **Lyda Borelli** and **Francesca Bertini**. Her superstar
status was reinforced by her appearance in Pastrone's next film, *Tigre
Reale* (*Royal Tigress*, 1916), adapted from a novel by realist writer
Giovanni Verga, but which Menichelli saturated with a decadent sensuality far beyond the original.

Menichelli utilized her highly gestural style to consistently convey
a certain perverse insouciance and an aggressive sensuality that distinguished her from the morbid Pre-Raphaelitism of her fellow divas
and kept her popular into the 1920s. She was still having an electrifying effect on both critics and the public in 1921 with her portrayal
of a precocious 17-year-old in *L'età critica* (*The Critical Age*), directed by Amleto Palermi. Having married Baron Carlo Amato, head
of Rinascimento Film, in 1920, she acted exclusively for that production house until she retired from the cinema in 1924.

MILANO FILMS. Production company. Formed in 1908 as a further transformation of the SAFFI-Comerio (*see* COMERIO, LUCA), Milano Films quickly developed into one of the principal Italian production companies of the silent era. Run largely by a board of aristocrats with high moral principles and pedagogic ideals, Milano pursued a declared policy of making films of high cultural and aesthetic value. Its first major production, three years in the making, was the first full-length (1,000 meters) adaptation of the most revered of all Italian literary works, Dante's *Inferno*. Closely based on the well-known illustrated edition of the poem by Gustave Doré, the film was hailed both at home and abroad as a landmark achievement of cinematic art. Writer and theorist Ricciotto Canudo delivered a public lecture on the film at the École des Hautes Études directly after its first public screening in Paris to underscore his thesis that cinema was, in fact, the seventh art.

Employing many of the major directors of the period, among them **Baldassare Negroni** and **Augusto Genina**, and the attraction of divas such as **Pina Menichelli**, Mercedes Brignone, and Lina Millefleurs, the company continued its prolific production of relatively high-quality films until the early 1920s, when it too succumbed to the general crisis that engulfed the Italian film industry. One of the few companies not to join the **Unione Cinematografica Italiana** in 1919, it chose to reduce its production of films in favor of providing printing and postproduction services to other companies until it closed at the end of the 1920s. A shadow of its former self, it was apparently the best in Europe when set up originally by Luca Comerio in 1909. Milano's studios at the Bovisa were used sporadically during the 1930s, and again in the late 1950s, by other companies.

MONICELLI, MARIO (1915–). Screenwriter and director. One of Italy's most prolific and consistently popular directors, Monicelli has worked in many genres but has come to be regarded above all as a master practitioner of the ***commedia all'italiana***.

Interested in cinema from a very young age, Monicelli began making 16 mm films while still a student in Milan. *I ragazzi di via Paal* (*The Boys of Via Paal*, 1935), a full-length feature shot in 16 mm and financed by his cousin, Alberto Mondadori, won first prize at the **Venice Festival** in 1935, allowing Monicelli to begin serving an apprenticeship at the Tirrenia film studios, where he acted as assistant to established filmmakers such as Gustav Machatý, **Mario Camerini**, Giacomo Gentilomo, and **Augusto Genina**. By the early 1940s he had also begun screenwriting, an activity he continued in the immediate postwar period, working on the scripts for a host of films that included **Gennaro Righelli**'s *Il corriere del re* (*The King's Courier*, 1947), Mario Camerini's *La figlia del capitano* (*The Captain's Daughter*, 1947), and **Raffaele Matarazzo**'s unsuccessful attempt to revive the **Za-la-Mort** character, *La fumeria dell'oppio* (*The Opium Den*, 1947). He also collaborated on the screenplay of **Giuseppe De Santis**'s hugely successful *Riso amaro* (*Bitter Rice*, 1949) and on **Pietro Germi**'s *Gioventù perduta* (1947) and *In nome della legge* (*In the Name of the Law*, 1948). While working on a number of films with **Riccardo Freda**, Monicelli met fellow scriptwriter and future director **Steno** (**Stefano Vanzina**), with whom he began writing and codirecting a series of films that included some of the very popular social farces featuring **Totò**, among them *Guardie e ladri* (*Cops and Robbers*, 1951), which received the prize at Cannes for scriptwriting. Then with *Totò e Carolina* (*Toto and Carolina*, made in 1953 but not released till 1955 due to problems with censorship) Monicelli began his long-term collaboration with the screenwriters **Age e Scarpelli** and **Rodolfo Sonego**, with whom he would produce many of the key films of the *commedia all'italiana*.

National box office success and international renown came with *I soliti ignoti* (*Big Deal on Madonna Street*, 1958), a funny heist-gone-wrong movie that masterfully brought to the fore the considerable comic talents of both a young **Marcello Mastroianni** and **Vittorio Gassman**. The film was a huge hit and marked the birth of what from then on became known as "comedy Italian style." Monicelli repeated his enormous success with *La grande guerra* (*The Great War*, 1959), a powerful tragicomic antiwar film that paired Gassman with **Alberto Sordi** and that came to share the Golden Lion at Venice that year with **Roberto Rossellini**'s *Il Generale della Rovere* (*General della Rovere*, 1959). In 1963 *I compagni* (*The Organizer*, 1963), a film recounting the birth of the Socialist movement in Turin in the 1890s, found a lukewarm response in Italy but was nominated for an Academy Award for Best Screenplay.

There followed a host of clever bittersweet comedies including the picaresque misadventures of *L'armata Brancaleone* (*For Love and Gold*, 1966), and *Brancaleone alle crociate* (*Brancaleone at the Crusades*, 1970). The political satire *Vogliamo i colonnelli* (*We Want the Colonels*, 1973) was followed by the extremely popular *Amici miei* (*My Friends*, 1975) and *Caro Michele* (*Dear Michael*, 1976), a successful adaptation of a popular novel by Natalia Ginzburg that was awarded the Silver Bear at Berlin. However, Monicelli's most significant and provocative film during this period was undoubtedly *Un borghese piccolo piccolo* (*An Average Little Man*, 1977). Adapted from a novel by Vincenzo Cerami and starring Alberto Sordi in what was perhaps one of the most powerful roles of his crowded career, the film recounts the story of a meek and mild public servant who turns into something of a monster as he seeks to exact revenge for the accidental shooting of his teenage son during a botched bank robbery. Although misunderstood by some as an apology for vigilante violence, the film earned Monicelli a **David di Donatello** for his direction.

In the 1980s, again with Sordi, Monicelli made *Il marchese del Grillo* (*Marquis Del Grillo*, 1981), which won the Silver Bear at Berlin, but his attempt to repeat the extraordinary popularity of the earlier *Amici miei* with the sequel, *Amici miei atto II* (*My Friends, Act II*, 1982), was less successful. *Le due vite di Mattia Pascal* (*The Two Lives of Mattia Pascal*, 1985), an adaptation of Pirandello's novel made in separate versions for television and the big screen, also proved to be something of a flop, but in the same year *Speriamo che sia femmina* (*Let's Hope It's a Girl*, 1985) both was popular at the box office and won seven David di Donatello awards and three **Nastri d'argento**. In recognition of his extraordinary contribution to Italian cinema, in 1991 he was awarded a Golden Lion at Venice for career achievement. In the following years he has continued to turn out caustic social satires like *Parenti serpenti* (*Dearest Relatives, Poisonous Relations*, 1992) and *Panni sporchi* (*Dirty Linen*, 1999) and in 2000 returned to the small screen with the popular miniseries *Come quando fuori piove* (*Hens, Ducks, Chicken and Swine*, 2000). More recently he has collaborated with a number of other committed filmmakers on the social **documentary** *Un altro mondo è possibile* (Another World Is Possible, 2001), before braving the desert sands to film *Le rose del deserto* (*Roses of the Desert*), a bittersweet satire about Italy's invasion of Libya during World War II.

MONTALDO, GIULIANO (1930–). Actor and director. Montaldo began his film career as an actor, playing the role of a partisan leader in
Carlo Lizzani's **Resistance** drama *Achtung! Banditi! (Attention!
Bandits!* 1951). While appearing in small roles in other films he began working as assistant to **Gillo Pontecorvo** and **Elio Petri** and
made a number of shorts before directing his first feature, *Tiro al piccione (Pigeon Shoot,* 1960). Adapted from a novel by Giose Rimanelli, the film caused controversy for what was seen as its unduly
sympathetic treatment of those who had been foolish enough to em-
brace the Fascist cause. His next feature, however, *Una bella grinta
(Reckless,* 1964), the story of a ruthless social climber in an Italy riding the wave of the economic miracle, was more warmly received
and was nominated for the Golden Bear at Berlin. After several other
films, including the international crime action drama *Ad ogni costo
(Grand Slam,* 1967) and *Gli intoccabili (Machine Gun McCain,*
1969), another gangster-heist film shot in the United States and starring John Cassavetes and Peter Falk, Montaldo returned to more socially committed filmmaking with *Sacco e Vanzetti (Sacco and
Vanzetti,* 1971), a powerful indictment of the legal execution of two
Italian anarchists in the United States in 1927, which earned him the
nomination for the Palme d'or at Cannes.

After a convincing portrait of the renowned Neapolitan Renaissance philosopher in *Giordano Bruno (Revolt of the City,* 1973), Montaldo returned to engage with the theme of the Resistance again in his
adaptation of Renata Viganò's popular novel *L'Agnese va a morire
(And Agnes Chose to Die,* 1976). In the early 1980s he moved to television and spent two years preparing an epic and much-acclaimed
miniseries on Marco Polo that was broadcast internationally, including in the United States, where it was nominated for eight Emmy
Awards. Soon thereafter he was commissioned to direct a production
of Giacomo Puccini's *Turandot* at the Arena Theater of Verona, the
success of which led him to divide his efforts between the stage and
screen for the next two decades. He returned to the silver screen in
1987 with *Gli occhiali d'oro (The Gold Rimmed Glasses),* an adaptation of Giorgio Bassani's elegiac novel that won the Golden Osella at
the **Venice Festival** for its elegant set design and costumes. After a
somewhat less successful attempt to adapt **Ennio Flaiano**'s novel
Tempo di uccidere (A Time to Kill, 1990), Montaldo edited hundreds

of hours of the holdings of the Istituto **LUCE** in order to produce the stunning feature documentary *Le stagioni dell'aquila* (The Seasons of the Eagle, 1997). In 2001, while serving as president of RAI Cinema, he was awarded the Flaiano Prize for career achievement.

MONTELEONE, ENZO (1954–). Screenwriter and director. One of the most prominent of the younger generation of screenwriters to emerge during the 1980s, Monteleone scripted several films for **Gabriele Salvatores** including *Kamikazen, ultima notte a Milano* (Kamikazen, Last Night in Milan, 1987) and the Oscar-winning *Mediterraneo* (1991). After also collaborating with Spanish director Carlos Saura on the screenplay of the revenge thriller *¡Dispara!* (*Outrage*, 1993), he ventured into directing with *La vera vita di Antonio H* (*The True Life of Antonio H*, 1994), a clever self-reflexive film performed as one continuous monologue delivered by veteran actor Antonio Haber. This was followed by *Ormai è fatta* (*Outlaw*, 1999) and *El Alamein* (*El Alamein: The Line of Fire*, 2002), a powerful war film that won much critical acclaim but that was also attacked by conservative critics for its less-than-heroic portrayal of Italian soldiers. Most recently Monteleone wrote and directed for television *Il tunnel della libertà* (The Tunnel of Freedom, 2004), the story of two Italians who dug their way to freedom under the Berlin Wall in 1961.

MONTUORI, CARLO (1883–1963). Cinematographer. Active in the Italian film industry from its earliest days, Montuori began working as a camera operator in 1908 and by 1912 had developed an improved system of arc lighting for filming indoors. His skills as a cinematographer received international recognition when in 1925 he helped to film the American production of *Ben-Hur*, directed in Rome by Fred Niblo. He subsequently worked with many of the major Italian directors of the interwar period, including **Alessandro Blasetti**, for whom he photographed *Sole* (*Sun*, 1929), *Resurrectio* (*Rebirth*, 1931), and *Terra madre* (*Earth Mother*, 1931); **Gennaro Righelli**, with whom he made the aviation epic *L'armata azzurra* (*The Blue Fleet*, 1932); and **Carlo Ludovico Bragaglia**, for whom he created the remarkable expressionistic lighting of *O la borsa o la vita* (Your Money or Your Life, 1933).

In the immediate postwar period he collaborated with **Luigi Zampa** on *Vivere in pace* (*To Live in Peace*, 1946) and *Anni difficili* (*Difficult Years*, 1948), with Blasetti again on *Altri tempi* (*Times Gone By*, 1952), with **Pietro Germi** on *Gioventù perduta* (*Lost Youth*, 1947) and *La città si difende* (*Four Ways Out*, 1951), and with **Luigi Comencini** on *Pane, amore e gelosia* (*Bread, Love and Jealousy*, 1954, also known as *Frisky*). He is best remembered during this period, however, for his cinematography on the films of **Vittorio De Sica**, in particular *Ladri di biciclette* (*Bicycle Thieves*, 1948), *L'oro di Napoli* (*The Gold of Naples*, 1954), and *Il tetto* (*The Roof*, 1956).

MORETTI, NANNI (1953–). Actor, director, screenwriter, producer. For three decades Moretti has engaged in a highly personal and defiantly independent form of filmmaking that has made him a unique presence within the panorama of contemporary Italian cinema.

Born in Bolzano while his parents were on vacation, Moretti grew up in Rome and during his teens developed two passions: water polo and cinema. After active involvement in the left-wing student movement of the late 1960s, he bought a Super 8 camera and began making short films. That peculiar mix of the personal and the political, and a willingness to put himself on show, so characteristic of all his later films, are already present in his first two shorts, *La sconfitta* (The Defeat, 1973) and *Paté de bourgeois* (1973). His truculent iconoclasm also surfaces early in *Come parli, frate?* (How Speak You, Brother? 1974), an hour-long parody of Alessandro Manzoni's canonical 19th-century novel *I promessi sposi* (*The Betrothed*), in which Moretti plays the evil Don Rodrigo, who, however, in this upended version of the story is the victim rather than the perpetrator of the violence.

Two years later, having found it impossible to make a feature film through the normal channels, Moretti self-financed *Io sono un autarchico* (*I Am Self-Sufficient*, 1976), again adopting the Super 8 format. Featuring for the first time his alter ego–persona, Michele Apicella, played by Moretti himself, the film was an unexpected, and enormous, commercial success. After screening to packed houses for five consecutive months at the Filmstudio Cineclub in Rome, it was bought and broadcast by RAI state television and thus seen by literally millions of viewers. As a result, after the parenthesis of playing a small part in **Paolo and Vittorio Taviani**'s *Padre padrone* (*My Father My Master*, 1977), Moretti directed his first mainstream feature, *Ecce bombo* (1978), a film that appeared, accurately and ironically, to be taking the pulse of a now directionless 1968 generation. It too proved to be an extraordinary commercial and critical success, winning a host of awards and confirming Moretti's status as one of Italy's most distinctive young auteurs.

Nevertheless, it would be three years before he would make his next film, *Sogni d'oro* (*Sweet Dreams*, 1981). Using Moretti's now regular alter ego, Michele Apicella, *Sogni d'oro* dramatized something of a creative crisis not unlike **Federico Fellini**'s *8½*, while also carrying out a playful critique of Sigmund Freud and psychoanalysis. However, in spite of the critical acclaim it received that year at the **Venice Festival**, where it won the Grand Jury Prize and a special commendation, it did very poorly at the box office. Unperturbed, Moretti brought Apicella back as a high school teacher in *Bianca* (*Sweet Body of Bianca*, 1984), a typically eccentric take on the murder thriller, and then as a young but disillusioned Catholic priest in *La messa è finita* (*The Mass Is Ended*, 1985), the latter winning both the Silver Bear and the International Confederation of Art Cinemas prize at Berlin. In 1987, with his artistic reputation firmly established, Moretti took a further step toward independence by establishing his own production company, **Sacher Film**, with which he produced the debut films of two promising young directors, **Carlo Mazzacurati**'s *Notte italiana* (*Italian Night*, 1987) and **Daniele Luchetti**'s *Domani accadrà* (*It's Happening Tomorrow*, 1988). His own next film, *Palombella rossa* (*Red Wood Pigeon*, 1989), made in a period when the Italian Communist Party appeared to be in terminal decline, was a hilarious reflection on the crisis afflicting the party carried out through the stratagem of a long-running water polo competition. This was followed by a more serious examination of the Communist Party and its future prospects in the one-hour **documentary** *La cosa* (*The Thing*, 1990). Having by this time become a mentor for many of the younger directors forming part of the **New Italian Cinema**, Moretti next produced and acted in Luchetti's *Il portaborse* (*The Yes Man*, 1991), giving one of his most memorable performances as the cynical Socialist minister Cesare Botero.

The personal dimension of Moretti's cinema reached a new level in what many still regard as his most perfect film, *Caro diario* (*Dear Diary*, 1993), where the Apicella persona is dispensed with altogether and the film is recounted simply as a series of diary entries in the first person. Critically acclaimed and widely distributed, the film finally brought Moretti well-deserved international recognition. After producing and acting in **Mimmo Calopresti**'s *La seconda volta* (*The Second Time*, 1995), Moretti returned to the diary form in *Aprile* (*April*, 1998), a bright film that celebrated the birth of his son but in the context of a more general consternation at the electoral victory in Italy of the center-right forces led by Silvio Berlusconi. Contrasting sharply with many of his other films but stunning in its expressive intensity, Moretti's next film, *La stanza del figlio* (*The Son's Room*, 2001), left politics to the side in order to examine the effect of a son's death on a well-to-do Italian family, with Moretti himself playing the role of the father. The film was showered with numerous awards, including the International Film Critics Prize and the Palme d'or at Cannes, and the **David di Donatello** and a **Nastro d'argento** at home.

The personal and the political blended again in Moretti's most recent film, *Il caimano* (*The Caiman*, 2006), an amusing recounting of an ill-fated attempt to make a fictional film about a wily entrepreneur and politician with all the features of Silvio Berlusconi. Nominated for the Golden Palm at Cannes and winning six Davids at home, the film confirmed Moretti's standing as one of the most significant directors of Italian cinema in the third millennium.

MORRICONE, ENNIO (1928–). Musician and film composer. The most prolific film composer in the history of cinema, Morricone has written the scores of over 500 films and television series, in addition to more than 100 other musical compositions, including sonatas, symphonies, chamber pieces, music for theatrical productions, radio plays, and arrangements of popular songs.

Morricone received his musical training at the Conservatory of Santa Cecilia in Rome, which he entered at the age of 14 and where he studied trumpet, orchestration, choral music, and composition under renowned composer Goffredo Petrassi. While completing his academic studies he also played second trumpet in the musical ensemble of Alberto Flamini. Having earned his diploma in trumpet in 1946, he began experimenting with compositions for piano and voice while also writing music for theatrical productions. In the early 1950s he expanded his activities to include writing music for radio plays while continuing to experiment with original compositions and avant-garde music. By the late 1950s he was working as a musical arranger for RAI television while conducting and arranging popular songs for performers such as Gianni Morandi, Charles Aznavour, and Mario Lanza.

He began composing for films in the early 1960s, with a score for **Luciano Salce**'s *Il federale* (*The Fascist*, 1961). His first resounding success, however, came with the innovative musical track for **Sergio Leone**'s *Per un pugno di dollari* (*For a Fistful of Dollars*, 1964), which he had written under the pseudonym Don Savio and for which he received his first **Nastro d'argento**. He subsequently scored all of Leone's films, including the gangster epic *Once upon a Time in America* (1983), and worked with all the major Italian directors from **Gillo Pontecorvo** and **Marco Bellocchio** to **Pier Paolo Pasolini** and **Bernardo Bertolucci**. Indeed, as Bertolucci himself once remarked in an interview, there was a period during the 1970s when practically every Italian film, with the possible exception of those of **Federico Fellini**, carried the name of Morricone.

Although he had previously also worked with American and British directors on films as different as John Boorman's *Exorcist II* (1977) and Terence Malick's *Days of Heaven* (1978), for which he had received his first Oscar nomination, Morricone became especially well known in America for his haunting and moving soundtrack to Roland Joffe's *The Mission* (1986), a score that earned him his second Oscar nomination as well as a Golden Globe and a BAFTA Award. He then went on to work on a multitude of other international films, including Brian De Palma's *The Untouchables* (1987), Roman Polanski's *Frantic* (1988), and Pedro Almodóvar's *¡Átame!* (*Tie Me Up! Tie Me Down!* 1990), as well as further contributing to Italian cinema with the scores of films such as **Giuseppe Tornatore**'s Oscar-winning *Nuovo cinema Paradiso* (*Cinema Paradiso*, 1988) and **Roberto Faenza**'s *Jona che visse nella balena* (*Jonah Who Lived in the Whale*, 1993), for which he received his fourth **David di Donatello**.

In subsequent years his prolific output remained matched only by its extraordinary variety as he continued to move freely between art house and popular cinema, from **Dario Argento**'s **horror** thrillers like *Il sindrome di Stendhal* (*The Stendhal Syndrome*, 1996) to an American satirical comedy like Warren Beatty's *Bulworth* (1998), whose score earned him yet another Grammy nomination. Since the beginning of the 1990s he has also been particularly active on Italian television, writing everything from the music to the never-ending series on the Mafia, *La piovra* (*Octopus*), to scoring the hagiographic telefilm *Padre Pio, tra cielo e terra* (*Father Pio, between Heaven and Earth*, 2000).

A great musical experimenter, freely able to combine popular and classical idioms, Morricone has remained the most widely recognized and sought-after film composer in the world. In 1995 he was awarded the Golden Lion at the **Venice Festival** for his career achievement and in 2003 he personally conducted a long list of his most famous film scores at a special sellout concert at London's Albert Hall. In 2007, after five previous nominations, he was awarded an honorary Oscar for lifetime achievement.

MUCCINO, GABRIELE (1967–). Director and screenwriter. After serving an apprenticeship as assistant to directors **Pupi Avati** and **Marco Risi**, Muccino enrolled at the **Centro Sperimentale di Cinematografia** and studied screenwriting with **Leo Benvenuti**. He made several short features for RAI television before directing *Ecco fatto* (*That's It*, 1998), a frothy generational comedy that received the nomination for the Prize of the City at the Turin International Festival of Young Cinema. His second feature, *Come te nessuno mai* (*But Forever in My Mind*, 1999), a portrayal of the trials and tribulations of adolescence in contemporary Italy, was also well received and nominated for the Grand Prix at the Paris Film Festival. His greatest commercial and critical success, however, came with *L'ultimo bacio* (*The Last Kiss*, 2001), another engaging generational comedy that was nominated for 10 **David di Donatello** awards, in the event winning five, and three **Nastri d'argento**. The film also became a huge international hit, receiving the Audience Award at the Sundance Film Festival and rated among the top 10 films of the year by the American *Entertainment Weekly*. Muccino's next feature, *Ricordati di me*

(*Remember Me*, 2003), a portrait of the contemporary Italian family in crisis, was similarly acclaimed, if less commercially successful, prompting a number of offers to work in Hollywood, where Muccino directed *The Pursuit of Happyness* (2006). Being awarded what is, perhaps, Hollywood's ultimate accolade, Muccino's *L'ultimo bacio* was remade in the United States as *The Last Kiss* (2006), directed by Tony Goldwyn.

– N –

NASCIMBENE, MARIO (1913–2002). Musical director and composer. One of the most respected and versatile of Italian film composers, Nascimbene is credited with the musical scores of over 300 films.

After graduating from the Conservatory of Milan in 1935, Nascimbene indulged an early passion for cinema by scoring **Ferdinando Maria Poggioli**'s *L'Amore canta* (*Love Song*, 1941). In the immediate postwar period he increased his involvement in the cinema, working with many directors on a wide variety of films ranging from socially committed neorealist works such as **Giuseppe De Santis**'s *Roma ore 11* (*Rome 11:00*, 1952) to **peplums** like **Carmine Gallone**'s *Cartagine in fiamme* (*Carthage in Flames*, 1960). He scored a number of films for **Valerio Zurlini**, beginning with *Estate Violenta* (*Violent Summer*, 1959), for which he received the **Nastro d'argento**, and also collaborated with **Franco Brusati** on *Il disordine* (*Disorder*, 1962) and **Carlo Lizzani** on *Il processo di Verona* (*The Verona Trial*, 1963). In the late 1960s he initiated a long and fruitful partnership with **Roberto Rossellini**, scoring many of his films for television including *Atti degli Apostoli* (*Acts of the Apostles*, 1969), *Socrate* (*Socrates*, 1970), *Blaise Pascal* (1971), *Agostino d'Ippona* (*Augustine of Hippo*, 1972), and *Cartesius* (*Descartes*, 1974) as well as Rossellini's last work for the big screen, *Il Messia* (*The Messiah*, 1976).

One of the few Italian directors to have worked extensively in Hollywood, Nascimbene also scored dozens of big-budget American productions, among them Joseph L. Mankiewicz's *The Barefoot Contessa* (1954) and *The Quiet American* (1958), Robert Rossen's

Alexander the Great (1956), Charles Vidor's *A Farewell to Arms* (1957), and King Vidor's *Solomon and Sheba* (1959). Having already received the **Nastro d'argento** three times, in 1992 he was given a special **David di Donatello** for his entire career. After his death in 2002 an annual prize was instituted in his name to recognize other fine film composers.

NASTRO D'ARGENTO. Award. Meaning, literally, "Silver Ribbon," the Nastro d'argento is a prestigious award conferred annually by the **Sindacato Nazionale Giornalisti Cinematografici Italiani** (SNGCI, National Union of Italian Film Journalists). Awarding of the Nastri is decided by a general vote of all union members. The award was instituted in 1946 when the ribbon for Best Film went to **Roberto Rossellini**'s *Roma città aperta* (*Rome Open City*, 1945, also known as *Open City*) and Best Direction was shared between **Vittorio De Sica** for *Sciuscià* (*Shoe-Shine*, 1946) and **Alessandro Blasetti** for *Un giorno nella vita* (*A Day in the Life*, 1946).

The Nastri are specifically intended to acknowledge and reward the achievement of Italians in the national industry, although one of the 16 ribbons is reserved for the Best Foreign Film of the year and one for Best European Production. The other categories include Best Director, Best Film, Best Actor, Best Actress, Best First Direction, Best Song, and Best Dubbing of a Foreign Film. From year to year special ribbons may be awarded, as in 2003 when a Nastro d'argento speciale was presented to actor-director **Carlo Verdone** for his achievements during his first 25 years in the industry. Traditionally the awards were made in the Sicilian city of Taormina but since 2005 the ceremony for the awarding of the prizes has taken place in Rome.

NAZZARI, AMEDEO (1907–1979). Actor. Born in Cagliari, Sardinia, as Salvatore Amedeo Buffa, Nazzari had already distinguished himself as a stage actor before moving to films in the mid-1930s. Tall and handsome, and frequently compared in bearing and looks to Errol Flynn, he was often cast in the role of the courageous and principled adventurer with a big heart. His first important role was as the self-sacrificing young cavalry officer in **Goffredo Alessandrini**'s 19th-century costume drama *Cavalleria* (*Cavalry*, 1936), which was followed by the similarly heroic self-sacrificing father in *Luciano Serra Pilota* (1939), also directed by Alessandrini. More dashing but also more villainous was the role of Neri Chiaramontesi that Nazzari played in **Alessandro Blasetti**'s *La cena delle beffe* (*The Jester's Supper*, 1941), but the part allowed Nazzari to rip Clara Calamai's bodice in order to expose the first naked bosom in Italian cinema history.

After the war Nazzari starred in a number of neorealist films including **Alberto Lattuada**'s *Il Bandito* (*The Bandit*, 1946), where he played a war veteran forced by circumstances to become a gangster, and Blasetti's *Un giorno nella vita* (*A Day in the Life*, 1946), where he was the leader a group of partisans who take refuge in a convent, resulting in tragedy when the Germans take reprisals. In spite of appearing in a wide variety of films during this period, he came to be characterized by his role in a series of weepy melodramas directed by **Raffaele Matarazzo**, which included *Catene* (*Chains*, 1950), *Figli di Nessuno* (*Nobody's Children*, 1951), and *L'angelo bianco* (*The White Angel*, 1955). In 1957, with typical whimsy, **Federico Fellini** enticed him to play Alberto Lazzari, an aging and veteran film star much like himself, in *Le notti di Cabiria* (*The Nights of Cabiria*, 1957). Nazzari continued to work both in Italy and abroad throughout the 1960s, appearing memorably as the Italian émigré become successful Argentinian cattle baron in **Dino Risi**'s *Il gaucho* (*The Gaucho*, 1964). As time went on, however, he came to be cast mostly in supporting roles, often in B-grade crime films. Fittingly, perhaps, his final appearance was in the glaringly titled *Melodrammore* (1978), a parody of film melodramas written and directed by Maurizio Costanzo, in which Nazzari played himself giving lessons to a younger actor on how to do melodrama.

NEGRONI, BALDASSARE (1877–1948). Director. Descended from a noble Roman family and bearing the title of count, Negroni studied law and worked in finance until 1911 when he joined the **Cines**, first as cameraman and then as a scriptwriter. In 1912, together with Gioacchino Mecheri, he founded the Celio Film Company, for which he directed a series of elegant melodramas featuring **Francesca Bertini**, Alberto Collo, and **Emilio Ghione**. After making four films starring Hesperia, a diva with whom he would work extensively and then marry in 1923, he codirected (with **Gustavo Serena**) the much-acclaimed musical pantomime *Histoire d'un Pierrot* (*Pierrot, the Prodigal*, 1913). He subsequently transferred to **Milano Film**, where he directed Hesperia in another dozen films, including a version of *La signora delle camelie* (*The Lady of the Camelias*, 1915). After being part of the ill-fated trust the **Unione Cinematografica Italiana** (UCI) in the early 1920s, Negroni joined the **Stefano Pittaluga** company, for which he directed, among others, *Il vetturale di Moncenisio* (The Courier of Moncenisio, 1927) and *Giuditta e Oloferne* (*Judith and Holofernes*, 1928), both of which starred **Bartolomeo Pagano** (**Maciste**) in two of his last roles. From the early 1930s Negroni worked mostly as production manager, the last film he produced being **Mario Mattoli**'s *La vita ricomincia* (*Life Begins Anew*, 1945).

NEOREALISM. The most celebrated movement in the history of Italian cinema, neorealism was in fact always more of a common socially committed approach to filmmaking embraced by a number of directors in the immediate postwar period than a structured artistic movement. Nevertheless, while its formal status as a movement has long been questioned and its precise nature, extent, and defining characteristics have continued to be debated, there has never been any doubt about neorealism's crucial role in the revival of the Italian cinema in the immediate postwar period.

Since what came to be regarded as neorealist films were created more from a spontaneous desire to use cinema to engage with social reality rather than to follow the dictates of a manifesto or a set of rules, the precise features of neorealist cinema have always proven difficult to define. However, at least some of the elements that characterized this new cinema, which in its turn to reality implicitly sought to reverse two decades of Fascist mystification and evasion, were: a stronger sense of realism, a focus on the everyday life of ordinary people, an attitude of social commitment and human solidarity, the use of quasi-documentary techniques and nonprofessional actors, on-location shooting, natural lighting, long takes, and unobtrusive editing.

The three directors most closely associated with the movement and widely regarded as its founding fathers were **Roberto Rossellini**,

Vittorio De Sica, and **Luchino Visconti**. Rossellini, in particular, having already directed three relatively realistic films during the Fascist period, is considered to have founded neorealism proper with *Roma città aperta* (*Rome Open City*, 1945, also known as *Open City*), subsequently consolidating this new approach to filmmaking with the two other films of his so-called war trilogy, *Paisà* (*Paisan*, 1946) and *Germania anno zero* (*Germany Year Zero*, 1947). De Sica, whose earlier *I bambini ci guardano* (*The Children Are Watching Us*, 1943) would often be hailed as a forerunner to the full-fledged neorealism of the postwar period, created, in partnership with screenwriter **Cesare Zavattini**, what are considered to be three of the movement's key films: *Sciuscià* (*Shoe-Shine*, 1946), *Ladri di biciclette* (*Bicycle Thieves*, 1948), and *Umberto D* (1952). **Luchino Visconti**, whose first film, *Ossessione* (*Obsession*, 1943), is canonically cited as the movement's most immediate precursor, offered what was perhaps the purest possible version of neorealism in *La terra trema* (*The Earth Trembles*, 1948), a loose adaptation of Giovanni Verga's 19th-century novel filmed entirely on location in a small Sicilian fishing village, employing only the local people as actors and all speaking in their own dialect. Unfortunately, even if now regarded as one of the movement's most exemplary films, *La terra trema* was also the least successful at the box office. Among the other directors most closely associated with the movement in the immediate postwar period were **Giuseppe De Santis**, **Luigi Zampa**, **Aldo Vergano**, **Pietro Germi**, and **Renato Castellani**. However, even such celebrated neorealist films as De Santis's *Riso amaro* (*Bitter Rice*, 1949) and Germi's *In nome della legge* (*In the Name of the Law*, 1948) have often been seen by historians of the movement as already moving away from the social concerns of "pure" neorealism toward a more entertaining cinema of genre and spectacle, inaugurating what would later come to be known pejoratively as "pink" or "rosy" neorealism. Other historians suggest, however, that it might be more accurate to talk of "neorealisms" in the plural and to see these directors and others, at least in their films of the immediate postwar period, as all creating their own valid versions of a cinema engaging with reality rather than striving to evade it.

It is instructive to note, however, that while Italian neorealism was universally honored as an artistic movement and internationally acclaimed, in Italy itself neorealist films only ever formed a very small part of national production and exhibition. Furthermore, although they were critically praised at home, neorealist films were not particularly popular either with the Italian authorities, who objected to the poor image of Italy generally presented, or with Italian audiences, who showed a distinct preference for the entertaining melodramas and action-adventures being turned out by the more commercially oriented film industry. Consequently, while the ethical approach and the technical innovations that neorealism had introduced in its short flowering would continue to influence filmmakers for many years to come, it is generally agreed that by the early 1950s the movement itself had already passed into history.

NERO, FRANCO (1941–). (Born Francesco Sparanero.) Actor. Abandoning a university degree in economics, Nero studied acting at the Piccolo Teatro of Milan before moving to Rome to make his screen debut in a small part in Alfredo Gianetti's *La ragazza in prestito* (*Engagement Italiano*, 1964). A year later he began appearing in a wide variety of films, from B-graders like **Antonio Margheriti**'s *I criminali della galassia* (*Wild, Wild Planet*, 1965) to art films like **Carlo Lizzani**'s *La Celestina P. R.* (*Celestial Maid at Your Service*, 1965) and **Antonio Pietrangeli**'s *Io la conoscevo bene* (*I Knew Her Well*, 1966). He soon made his mark in what would remain one of his most famous roles, as the deadly tongue-in-cheek gunslinger in **Sergio Corbucci**'s *Django* (1966). He subsequently played Abel in John Huston's production of *The Bible: In the Beginning* (1966) and his rugged good looks and flashing blue eyes made him a natural choice for the part of Lancelot in Joshua Logan's *Camelot* (1967). While filming *Camelot* he met English actress Vanessa Redgrave, who became his long-term partner. A year later, with a growing international reputation, he received the **David di Donatello** for his interpretation of Captain Bellodi in **Damiano Damiani**'s adaptation of Leonardo Sciascia's mafia novel, *Il giorno della civetta* (*The Day of the Owl*, 1968).

Nero continued to appear in a host of films in the 1970s, alternating with ease between Italian and foreign productions, and between popular genre and auteur cinema. Alongside Westerns like *Viva la muerte . . . tua!* (*Don't Turn the Other Cheek*, 1971) and crime thrillers such as *Il cittadino si ribelle* (*The Citizen Rebels*, 1973), he also appeared in Luis Buñuel's *Tristana* (1970) and played the ill-fated Socialist deputy, Giacomo Matteotti, in **Florestano Vancini**'s *Il delitto Matteotti* (*The Assassination of Matteotti*, 1973). For the next two decades he continued to exhibit an enormous versatility as he moved between international action thrillers like *Enter the Ninja* (1981) and *Die Hard 2* (1990) and auteur films like Rainer Werner Fassbinder's *Querelle* (1982) and **Pupi Avati**'s *Fratelli e sorelle* (*Brothers and Sisters*, 1992). The 1990s, however, saw him less on the big screen and more on European television, featuring in everything from German telefilms such as *Das Babylon Komplott* (The Babylon Conspiracy, 1993) to Italian miniseries such as *Desideria e l'anello del drago* (*The Dragon Ring*, 1994). In 2003, after appearing in almost 150 films, he was given a Lifetime Achievement Award at the Milano Film Festival. Still much in demand as an actor, he also tried his hand at producing and directing in *Forever Blues* (2005), a much-praised effort that was awarded the Fregene Fellini Prize for direction.

NEW ITALIAN CINEMA. New Italian Cinema was a rubric that came to be used ever more frequently from the mid-1990s onward to characterize what was widely seen as a resurgence of creative energies after the period of relative stagnation that had followed the crisis of the film industry in the mid-1970s. Although the expression had been used earlier in a tentative way to indicate the work of a number of younger filmmakers who had made their debut in the early 1980s, it was the overwhelming success of **Giuseppe Tornatore**'s *Nuovo cinema Paradiso* (*Cinema Paradiso*, 1988) in winning both the Grand Jury Prize at Cannes and the Academy Award for Best Foreign Film that appeared to set the seal on the return of Italian cinema to the world stage. Soon after, the similar international success of **Gabriele Salvatores**'s *Mediterraneo* (1991) and **Gianni Amelio**'s *Il ladro di bambini* (*The Stolen Children*, 1992) confirmed that Italy was indeed producing a new generation of world-class filmmakers who were, in fact, creating a new Italian cinema.

Although the signs of this renaissance were undeniable, the precise features of the new cinema continued to prove difficult to define. The many directors who came to be grouped under its umbrella—**Nanni**

Moretti, Gianni Amelio, Maurizio Nichetti, Mario Martone, Francesca Archibugi, Silvio Soldini, and others—were of widely varying ages and backgrounds and their films often seemed to have little in common with each other. Nevertheless, even if they displayed no common ethical or political vision or any shared aesthetic project, these films all appeared to be responding in their own particular way to the more complicated and fragmented social reality around them, to an Italy where the old political ideologies had crumbled and with them a great part of all the previous certainties. The early films of Salvatores in particular voiced the profound disillusionment of the now-adult members of a 1968 generation who continued to dream of flight from that intolerable society that they had so fiercely contested but into which they had ultimately become firmly integrated. Other films such as **Marco Risi**'s *Mery per sempre* (*Forever Mary*, 1989), **Aurelio Grimaldi**'s *La ribelle* (*The Rebel*, 1993), and **Vito Capuano**'s remarkable first film, *Vito e gli altri* (*Vito and the Others*, 1991), attempted to report in an honest and almost dispassionate way the institutionalized marginalization and the social degradation of the big cities, especially as they affected the younger generation, without, however, being able to propose any solutions. Amelio's own *Il ladro di bambini*, one of the high points of this new cinema, successfully renewed the aesthetic paradigm of **neorealism** while at the same time recording the defeat of its aspirations to social justice and human solidarity. On the other hand, **Daniele Luchetti**'s *Il portaborse* (*The Yes Man*, 1991) was able to use caricature to present a fictional portrait of the inbred corruption that had become such a regular feature of Italian political life and which only a year later the *Mani pulite* (Clean Hands) investigations would confirm in detail.

Although the New Italian Cinema appeared to have no center—indeed, a dislocation away from the traditional center of Rome was a characteristic feature of these films—Nanni Moretti came to be one of its major points of reference, not only for his eccentric and always independent filmmaking but also for his willingness to act in the films of other younger directors. More importantly, his initiative in setting up his independent production company, **Sacher Film**, allowed him to exercise complete control over his own work as well as to facilitate the entry into the industry of other promising young directors. The founding of other small but solid independent production companies in the late 1980s, such as Salvatores's **Colorado Film** and Domenico Procacci's Fandango, also helped to construct a firm financial basis for the new cinema, leading to a proliferation of films by both established and new directors in the late 1990s. Although the very existence of a New Italian Cinema had been challenged by some skeptics in the early part of the decade, the three Oscars awarded to **Roberto Benigni**'s *La vita è bella* (*Life Is Beautiful*, 1997) and the Palme d'or at Cannes for Moretti's *La stanza del figlio* (*The Son's Room*, 2001) dispelled all doubts that Italian cinema had indeed gone through a renaissance and emerged into what is now simply called the cinema of the third millennium.

NICHETTI, MAURIZIO (1948–). Actor, director, animator. An architecture graduate with a background in mime, Nichetti joined the **Bruno Bozzetto** Film company in the early 1970s, working as cartoonist and animator and appearing as the harried animator in the charming live action-animated feature, *Allegro non troppo* (1977). Having founded Quellidigrok, an independent mime school, in 1974, he left the Bozzetto company in 1978 in order to make his first independent feature film, *Rataplan* (1979), an almost silent comedy that received high praise at the **Venice Festival** and was hugely successful at the box office. This was followed by *Ho fatto splash* (*I Made a Splash*, 1980), an amusing variation of the Rip Van Winkle theme in which a boy, played by Nichetti himself, wakes up after a 20-year sleep and finds himself needing to adapt to contemporary society. Two years later, *Domani si balla* (*Tomorrow We Dance*, 1982), again starring Nichetti himself, was part tribute to Méliès and part satire on the television industry, and moreover showcased **Mariangela Melato**'s considerable talents as a dancer.

After a variety of other shorts and extensive television work, Nichetti founded his own film production company, Bambu, to make *Ladri di saponette* (*Icicle Thieves*, 1989), a playful homage to **Vittorio De Sica**'s neorealist classic *Ladri di biciclette* (*Bicycle Thieves*, 1948), but done as another satire on television and the encroachment of advertising. The film attracted international acclaim with Nichetti winning his second **Nastro d'argento** for Best Original Story. There followed a host of internationally acclaimed films that mixed animation and live actors: *Volere Volare* (*To Want to Fly*, 1991), the amusing trials of a man turning into a cartoon character, which was awarded a **David di Donatello** for its screenplay; *Stefano Quantestorie* (1993), in which a young man of the 1960s lives out a number of possible alternative lives; and *Luna e l'altra* (*Luna and the Other*, 1996), where shadows live out independent existences. More recently, as well as continuing to make screwball comedies such as *Honolulu Baby* (2001), he has also widened his artistic activities to include directing opera and lyric theater, beginning with a much-praised production of Gioacchino Rossini's *Barber of Seville* at Trento in 1999.

NINCHI, AVE (1915–1997). Actress. After studying at the Academy of Dramatic Art in Rome, Ninchi distinguished herself working with a number of important theater companies. She moved to the cinema in the immediate postwar period with small parts in films such as **Guido Brignone**'s *Canto, ma sottovoce . . .* (I'm Singing but Quietly, 1945) and **Carmine Gallone**'s *Avanti a lui tremava tutta Roma* (*Before Him All Rome Trembled*, 1946). She began taking on more substantial roles in **Alberto Lattuada**'s *Il delitto di Giovanni Episcopo* (*Flesh Will Surrender*, 1947) and **Luigi Zampa**'s *Vivere in pace* (*To Live in Peace*, 1946), for which she received a **Nastro d'argento** for best supporting female interpretation. Although undoubtedly a talented dramatic actress, in the 1950s she was most often seen in comedies, among them **Aldo Fabrizi**'s *La famiglia Passaguai* (*The Passaguai Family*, 1951) and its two sequels, **Pietro Germi**'s *La presidentessa* (*Mademoiselle Gobete*, 1952), and many of the **Totò** films, including *Totò cerca moglie* (Toto Looks for a Wife, 1950), *Guardie e ladri* (*Cops and Robbers*, 1951), *Totò e le donne* (*Toto and the Women*, 1952), and *Totò cerca pace* (*Toto Wants Peace*, 1954). During the 1960s, while not abandoning screen comedy, she moved progressively more toward television, appearing not only in a number of serials, telefilms, and a famous advertisement, but also as the presenter of a cooking program and the hostess of the popular variety show *Speciale per noi* (Special for Us, 1971).

Her last appearance on the big screen was in a small supporting role in Louis Malle's *Lacombe Lucien* (*Lacombe, Lucien*, 1973).

NORIS, ASSIA (1912–1998). Actress. Born in St. Petersburg, Russia, but raised in France, Anastasia von Gerzfeld, under the stage name of

Assia Noris, became one of the leading Italian divas of the interwar period.

A chance encounter with maverick Italian producer **Giuseppe Amato** led to her acting debut in **Mario Bonnard**'s *Tre uomini in frac* (*I Sing for You Alone*, 1932), where she played the part of a rich and spoiled American schoolgirl who wants to have her own tenor. Having been drawn into the world of cinema, she soon became romantically involved with a young **Roberto Rossellini** and they were (reputedly) married, although the marriage was quickly annulled. Noris's cinematic career, however, continued to blossom, particularly due to her leading role in a number of elegant romantic comedies directed by **Mario Camerini**, in which she was paired with debonair leading man **Vittorio De Sica**, among them *Darò un milione* (*I'll Give a Million*, 1936), *Il signor Max* (*Mister Max*, 1937), and *I grandi magazzini* (*Department Store*, 1939). She subsequently took on more dramatic roles as in **Mario Soldati**'s directorial debut, *Dora Nelson* (1939), where she played both a spoiled Russian princess and a lowly worker, and in **Renato Castellani**'s "calligraphic" *Un colpo di pistola* (*A Pistol Shot*, 1942), adapted from a short story by Alexander Pushkin. Outside Italy she appeared in Abel Gance's remake of *Le capitaine Fracasse* (*Captain Fracasse*, 1943) and Louis Daquin's lackluster adaptation of a Georges Simenon novel, *Le Voyageur de la Toussaint* (The Traveler on All Saints' Day, 1943). She subsequently reappeared in Italy in a number of **white telephone** comedies, which included Mario Bonnard's *Che distinta famiglia!* (What a Distinguished Family! made 1943, released 1945), in which she was paired with veteran male heartthrob **Gino Cervi**.

Although long regarded as the sweetheart of Italy and something of a pinup girl for Italian soldiers during World War II, Noris only surfaced in two films in the postwar period: *Amina* (1950), made in Egypt by **Goffredo Alessandrini**, and **Carlo Lizzani**'s *La Celestina P.R.* (1965), a less-than-brilliant film that Noris herself both wrote and produced, and in which she played the madam of a brothel.

NOTARI, ELVIRA (1875–1946). Director, producer, scriptwriter, editor. Born in Salerno in 1875, Elvira Coda moved to Naples in 1902, where she married painter and freelance photographer Nicola Notari. Both were passionately interested in the new medium of moving pictures and by 1906 were making short actualities and newsreels together, which they were able to screen in the growing number of Neapolitan movie houses. In 1910 they founded the Film Dora production company (changed in 1915 to Dora Film) and began making fictional feature films. Many of these were violent and passionate melodramas with a very distinctive Neapolitan inflection, often adapted from popular novels, such as those of Carolina Invernizio, or from folk songs and local stories. Hugely popular in Naples, these films were less appreciated in other parts of Italy, but Dora Film soon opened an office in New York, where the films found greatest favor among the expatriate Neapolitan community. Having remained an artisanal and family business, the company survived the general crisis that affected the Italian film industry in the early 1920s, but political pressure against manifestations of regional culture from the Fascist authorities and the coming of sound eventually led to its closure in 1930. Still devoted to cinema, Notari continued to run a film acting school in Naples, where she championed the naturalistic style.

Most of Notari's films have been lost but it is estimated that, along with many shorts and actualities, she directed close to 60 features, among them *Il nano rosso* (*The Red Dwarf*, 1917, based on a novel by Invernizio) and *Piange Pierrot* (*Pierrot Cries*, 1924, based on a song by Cesare Andrea Bixio). In 1987, to recognize Notari's often overlooked contribution to Italian cinema, the Casa Internazionale delle Donne established the Elvira Notari Prize, awarded each year as part of the **Venice Festival** to the film that best exemplifies women's achievements.

NUTI, FRANCESCO (1955–). Actor, screenwriter, director. One of a number of actor-directors who emerged on Italian screens in the 1980s after an apprenticeship in cabaret theater, Nuti had achieved a great deal of success on both stage and television as part of the trio I Giancattivi before appearing with them in the zany comedy *Ad ovest di paperino* (*West of Paperino*, 1982), directed by Alessandro Benvenuti. Branching out on his own as an actor, Nuti then starred in three extremely popular films directed by **Maurizio Ponzi**: *Madonna che silenzio c'è stasera* (What a Ghostly Silence There Is Tonight, 1982), *Io, Chiara e lo Scuro* (*The Pool Hustlers*, 1983), and *Son contento* (I'm Happy, 1983), creating a lovable if slightly narcissistic comic persona that would earn him something of a cult following. He subsequently directed himself in a string of clever and successful comedies that included *Casablanca, Casablanca* (1985), which played with the classic film by Michael Curtiz, *Stregati* (*Bewitched*, 1986), *Caruso Pascoski di padre polacco* (*Caruso Paskoski, Son of a Pole*, 1988), *Occhio Pinocchio* (1995), and *Il signor Quindicipalle* (*Mr. Fifteen Balls*, 1998), which showcased Nuti's favorite game, snooker.

– O –

OLMI, ERMANNO (1931–). Director and scriptwriter. With a continuing strong attachment to his peasant origins and his rural Catholic background, both of which are amply reflected in his major works, Olmi has come to occupy a unique position within mainstream Italian cinema through a series of films that have been remarkable for their honesty and their profound commitment to validating the ordinary lives and daily experiences of common people.

Having moved to Milan from his native Bergamo at the end of World War II, Olmi began working for the Edison Volta company for which, from 1953 onward, he produced over 30 educational and scientific documentaries. From this extensive experience came his first feature, *Il tempo si è fermato* (*Time Stood Still*, 1959), a slow-paced but intensely moving portrayal of a brief encounter between a veteran watchman and a temporary young recruit at an isolated hydroelectric dam in the mountains of northern Italy. Filmed entirely on snowbound location and with nonprofessional actors, the film displays an unflinching devotion to documenting the most minute of everyday events without extraneous artificial drama. Olmi's next feature film, *Il posto* (*The Job*, 1961), was a similarly understated account of the Kafkaesque trials of a young man seeking a place in the office of a large and anonymous Milanese company. The film, a penetrating study of modern urban alienation, again acted by nonprofessionals and filmed in the offices of the Edison Volta where Olmi had worked, was awarded the Film Critics Award at the **Venice Festival** and brought Olmi to worldwide attention. His next film, *I fidanzati* (*The Fiances*, 1962), the story of a young couple forced into temporary separation by a company requirement for the man to move to Sicily, was also an acute study of loneliness and isolation. The distinctive style that Olmi developed in these early works explored a communication of human emotions through a relay of looks and silences rather than words and dramatic gestures.

Subsequent works such as *E venne un uomo* (*A Man Named John*, 1965), a respectful biography of Pope John XXIII, met with a more mixed reception, but Olmi returned to international prominence with *L'albero degli zoccoli* (*The Tree of the Wooden Clogs*, 1978). A loving re-creation of poor rural life in the peasant communities of Olmi's native Bergamo region in the late 1800s, the film won the Palme d'or at Cannes and a host of other national and international awards. In 1982, together with **Mario Brenta** and Paolo Valmarana, Olmi founded an alternative film school at Bassano del Grappa. Called Ipotesi Cinema, it was structured more as a communal cooperative than a traditional school, and had the explicit aim of helping younger directors successfully make their first films. After *Cammina cammina* (*Keep Walking*, 1983), a genial retelling of the biblical story of the Magi set in rural Lombardy, Olmi retired from filmmaking due to serious illness. He returned in 1987 with *Lunga vita alla Signora* (*Long Live the Lady!* 1987), a merciless look at the sclerotic stultification of upper-middle-class rituals, seen through the eyes of a young boy training in the hospitality industry. The film's success at Venice (Silver Lion, 1987) was repeated a year later when *La leggenda del santo bevitore* (*The Legend of the Holy Drinker*, 1988), a contemporary adaptation of an early 20th-century novel by Joseph Roth, received the Golden Lion. By contrast, *Il Segreto del bosco vecchio* (*The Secret of the Old Woods*, 1993), an animistic fable adapted from a novel by Dino Buzzati, divided critics for its open ecological didacticism and for a style that was pejoratively characterized as "Bambi meets *National Geographic*."

However, after extensive work with RAI television, for which he produced *Genesi* (*Genesis, the Creation and the Flood*, 1994), an epic retelling of the first seven books of the Bible, Olmi returned to the large screen with the austere but visually stunning *Il mestiere delle armi* (*The Profession of Arms*, 2001). A chronicle of the final days of the legendary Renaissance military leader Giovanni delle Bande Nere, it documents with extreme dignity his slow and painful death provoked ignominiously by a newly invented firearm. The implicit antiwar message of *Mestiere* was echoed in the charming *Cantando dietro i paraventi* (*Singing behind Screens*, 2003), a fablelike and highly theatrical adaptation of a 19th-century Chinese poem in which Madame Ching, the wife of a treacherously murdered admiral, comes to lead a pirate band to avenge her husband's death, but eventually, with victory assured, offers her enemies the palm of peace rather than death and defeat. For Olmi, ever the champion of a compassionate humanism, such a pacifist gesture is the only possible response to what has become the ongoing age of terror in the early 21st century.

OMEGNA, ROBERTO (1876–1948). Cinematographer and documentarist. Generally regarded as the father of Italian scientific and **documentary** filmmaking, Omegna began making films in 1904 using a camera supplied by **Arturo Ambrosio**. His first "actualities" recorded the running of a historic automobile race (*La prima corsa automobilistica Susa-Moncenisio*) and military maneuvers of the Italian Alpine regiment. After helping Ambrosio to establish **Ambrosio Film** as a production company in 1906, Omegna became head of its technical department and sometime director. He supervised the making of over 100 films for the company, ranging all the way from simple comic sketches and psychological dramas to highly successful sword-and-sandal epics like *Nerone* (*Nero*, 1909) and *Lo schiavo di Cartagine* (*The Slave of Carthage*, 1910). In 1914 he directed a number of films for the Centauro Film company, in particular the much-acclaimed *Chiavi d'oro e chiavi di ferro* (*Keys of Gold and Keys of Iron*). His strongest passion, however, remained documentary filmmaking and in particular the nature documentary, which he helped to pioneer. Extensive travel throughout Africa and India resulted in dozens of fascinating documentaries, among them *La caccia al leopardo* (*The Leopard Hunt*, 1908), *Usi e costumi abissini* (*Abyssinian Customs*, 1908), and *Elefanti al lavoro* (*Elephants at Work*, 1911). In 1911 his remarkable *La vita delle farfalle* (*The Life of Butterflies*) was awarded first prize in the documentary film section of the Turin International Exhibition.

In 1926, after the demise of Ambrosio Film, Omegna became the head of the scientific department of the newly formed Istituto **LUCE**, where he spent the next two decades producing scores of award-winning educational films until his retirement in 1942.

ORLANDO, SILVIO (1957–). Actor. One of the new generation of actors who emerged in the 1990s, Orlando graduated to film after working onstage with **Gabriele Salvatores** at the Teatro dell'Elfo, making his first appearance on the big screen in Salvatores's *Kamikazen ultima notte a Milano* (*Last Night in Milan*, 1987). After distinguishing himself in a strong supporting role in **Nanni Moretti**'s *Palombella rossa* (*Red Wood Pigeon*, 1989), he starred as the affable and honest schoolteacher forced to turn speechwriter for a corrupt politician in **Daniele Luchetti**'s *Il portaborse* (*The Yes Man*, 1991), a characterization he would reprise in Luchetti's *La scuola* (*School*, 1995). Following the film's extraordinary success, not least for the way in which it anticipated all the revelations of systematic corruption in Italian politics subsequently revealed by the *Mani pulite* investigations, Orlando came to work with all the directors of the **New Italian Cinema**, with Salvatores again in *Sud* (*South*, 1993) and *Nirvana* (1994), with **Carlo Mazzacurati** in *Un'altra vita* (*Another Life*, 1992) and *Vesna va veloce* (*Vesna Moves Quickly*, 1995), with **Paolo Virzì** in *Ferie d'agosto* (*Summer Holidays*, 1996), and with **Giuseppe Piccioni** in *Fuori dal mondo* (Not of This World, 1999) and *Luce dei miei occhi* (Light of My Eyes, 2000).

In the late 1990s he also often returned to the stage, playing Caliban in Giorgio Barberio Corsetti's 1999 production of Shakespeare's *The Tempest* and directing himself in several comedies by **Peppino De Filippo**. Having already won a **Nastro d'argento** for his lead role in **Mimmo Calopresti's** *Preferisco il rumore del mare* (*I Prefer the Sound of the Sea*, 2000), he was more recently awarded the **David di Donatello** and nominated for the European Film Award for his brilliant performance in Nanni Moretti's *Il caimano* (*The Caiman*, 2006).

ORSINI, VALENTINO (1927–2001). Director. A filmmaker of unwavering social and political commitment as well as a courageous experimenter with filmic techniques, Orsini never succeeded in receiving the critical and popular recognition that he undoubtedly deserved.

Still in his teens, Orsini fought in the **Resistance** movement. After the war he began organizing film clubs and writing film criticism. His early films were written and directed in close collaboration with **Paolo and Vittorio Taviani**, beginning with *Un uomo da bruciare* (*A Man for Burning*, 1962), a film about the union activist Salvatore

Carnevale (played masterfully by **Gian Maria Volontè**), who was eventually murdered by the Mafia for his social activism. Further collaboration with the Taviani bothers resulted in *I fuorilegge del matrimonio* (*Marriage Outlaws*, 1963), a film in six episodes that attempted to deal with the fraught question of divorce. In 1969, inspired by the militant ideas of West Indian psychoanalyst and social philosopher Franz Fanon, Orsini directed his first solo film, *I dannati della terra* (*The Wretched of the Earth*, 1969). This was followed by *Corbari* (1970), the realistic, if heroic, portrayal of the maverick Resistance fighter Silvio Corbari, who was such a thorn in the side of the Fascists that, when caught, he was executed twice as an example to others. Two years later *L'amante dell'Orsa Maggiore* (*The Smugglers*, 1972) was a more mainstream and conventional story of love and intrigue adapted from a novel by Polish writer Sergiusz Piasecki. Its lackluster reception led Orsini to a period of silence until *Uomini e no* (*Men and Not Men*, 1980), another very competent literary adaptation but this time of the famous Resistance novel by Elio Vittorini. Five years later Orsini's last film, *Figlio mio infinitamente caro* (*My Dearest Son*, 1985), movingly presented the plight of a loving father attempting to save his son from advanced drug addiction. At this point, discouraged by what appeared to be a continuing lack of popular and critical reaction to his films, Orsini retired from active filmmaking, although he continued to teach at the **Centro Sperimentale di Cinematografia** (National Film School) for a number of years.

ORTOLANI, RIZ (1931–). (Full name Rizerio Ortolani; at times also worked under the name Roger Higgins.) Musician, songwriter, film composer. One of the most prolific and versatile composers of Italian cinema, Ortolani graduated from the Gioacchino Rossini Conservatory in his native Pesaro before moving to Rome to work as a pianist and arranger for the national RAI radio. After writing a great deal of music for theater and television, in the mid-1950s he began composing for films, achieving his first major triumph with the soundtrack of Gualtiero Jacopetti's *Mondo cane* (*A Dog's Life*, 1962). The film's theme song, *More*, sung by Katyna Ranieri, became an international best seller, and Ortolani was nominated for both a Grammy and an Academy Award. He subsequently scored all of Jacopetti's "shockumentaries" while also collaborating with a wide variety of Italian and foreign directors, among them **Vittorio De Sica**, **Dino Risi**, **Franco Zeffirelli**, Anthony Asquith, Jerzy Skolimowski, and Robert Siodmak. He worked prolifically in all the popular genres but became especially identified with the *giallo*, providing memorable soundtracks for such classics as **Umberto Lenzi**'s *Così dolce così perversa* (*So Sweet . . . So Perverse*, 1970) and Lucio Fulci's *Non si sevizia un paperino* (*Don't Torture a Duckling*, 1972). In the early 1980s, after having written the music for **Ruggero Deodato**'s controversial *Cannibal Holocaust* (*Ruggero Deodato's Cannibal Holocaust*, 1980), he began a long and fruitful collaboration with **Pupi Avati**, for whom he scored all the major films from *Zeder* (1982) to *La cena per farli conoscere* (*The Get-Together Dinner*, 2007). At the same time he also worked extensively for Italian television, writing the music for popular miniseries like *La piovra* (*The Octopus*, 1984), *Cristoforo Colombo* (*Christopher Columbus*, 1984), and *Ama il tuo nemico* (*Love Your Enemy*, 1999).

With over 200 film scores to his credit, Ortolani has been nominated twice for the Oscar and four times for the Golden Globe. At home he has received three **Nastri d'argento** and four **David di Donatello** awards, the most recent for his score of Avati's *Ma quando arrivano le ragazze?* (*When Will the Girls Arrive?* 2005).

OSSESSIONE (1943). (*OBSESSION.*) Film. Made in 1942, *Ossessione* marked **Luchino Visconti**'s directorial debut. Provisionally titled *Palude* (Swamp), it was a free (and unauthorized) adaptation of James M. Cain's novel *The Postman Always Rings Twice*, which transposed Cain's story of marital infidelity, lust, and murder from California during the Depression era to the Po Valley in Fascist Italy. Although it undoubtedly demonstrated a surprising maturity for a director on his first attempt, the film itself emerged as something of a collaborative project between Visconti and a number of young left-wing critics and aspirant filmmakers associated with the journal *Cinema*, with the screenplay being cowritten by Visconti, **Giuseppe De Santis**, **Antonio Pietrangeli**, Mario Alicata, and **Gianni Puccini**.

From their own later accounts, Visconti and this extended group saw the film as a vital opportunity to give a new truth and direction to an Italian cinema that they regarded as having become sclerotic and unreal. In order to carry out this project of renewal, Visconti had originally engaged the relatively unknown **Massimo Girotti** and stage star **Anna Magnani** to play the lead roles, but the discovery of Magnani's advanced state of pregnancy forced Visconti to substitute **Clara Calamai** in the role of Giovanna.

The story, with a number of significant additions and with changes necessitated by the Italian context, follows the general lines of Cain's narrative. Penniless and drifting, Gino (Girotti) arrives at a highway roadhouse run by the older and boorish Bragana (Juan de Landa) and soon meets his sultry young wife, Giovanna. Sensing immediately Giovanna's mutual physical attraction, Gino readily accepts Bragana's invitation to remain and work at the roadhouse and, as a result, he and Giovanna are soon engaged in a torrid love affair behind Bragana's back. They decide to leave and start a new life together elsewhere, but along the way Giovanna changes her mind and returns home to her husband. Adrift again on his own, Gino is befriended by Lo Spagnolo (The Spaniard), a young freewheeling vagabond who has lived for a period in Spain (hence his name) but who now travels around Italy making his living as a fairground fortune-teller. Given that Lo Spagnolo tries to get Gino to forget Giovanna and that he later also betrays Gino to the police, it is important to note that the character does not appear in Cain's novel but is one of the major additions by the screenwriters to the original text.

According to the screenwriters' own later account, the character's free-spirited attitude and the allusion to the Spanish Civil War in his connection with Spain was intended to make him a cipher for a rejection of the claustrophobic conformism demanded by the Fascist regime. It is doubtful whether such an interpretation emerges quite so clearly in the version of the film as we have it today, with most contemporary viewers being more likely, perhaps, to be simply confused by the character's sexual and moral ambivalence. In any case, Gino and Lo Spagnolo begin to work the fairgrounds together, which is where one day Gino meets the Bragana couple again. While the husband, who is an opera buff, takes part in a singing competition, Gino and Giovanna renew their earlier bond, with the result that Gino accepts Bragana's offer to return with them to the roadhouse. On the way, exploiting the opportunity of Bragana's drunkenness, Gino and Giovanna stage a road accident in which the husband dies. Although the police appear to remain suspicious of the incident, the couple should now be able to live happily together at the roadhouse, but Gino continues to be haunted by a mixture of remorse and restlessness, which is further exacerbated by a chance visit from Lo Spagnolo. The strained rapport between the couple deteriorates further when, during a visit they make to Ferrara, Gino learns that Giovanna has collected life insurance on Bragana's death. Suspecting that he has been used as a pawn for her purposes, Gino aggressively abandons Giovanna and takes refuge with a young prostitute, to whom he contritely confesses the murder. Noticing, however, that he is being followed by the police, he concludes that Giovanna has denounced him to the authorities and so he returns to the roadhouse to confront her with the accusation. His anger turns to tenderness when he discovers that not only has she not denounced him, but she is carrying his baby. Emotionally reconciled, they prepare to leave the roadhouse and begin another life elsewhere. As fortune would have it, however, as they drive hopefully toward a future together, their car veers off the road in heavy fog and Giovanna is killed. The police, who have been following all along, soon arrive and Gino is arrested.

Although filmed, largely on location, in late 1942, the eagerly awaited film had its premiere in Rome only in May 1943. There have always been conflicting accounts of how the film was received. An often-repeated version suggests that Vittorio Mussolini, who was present at the screening, knocked over chairs as he walked out in disgust, shouting, "This is not Italy." Giuseppe De Santis, however, in his account reports that the film was not only well received but that Vittorio Mussolini spoke warmly to Visconti and reaffirmed the positive judgment of the film given by his father, Il Duce, who had apparently seen it earlier in a private screening. Whatever the truth of either version, what seems undeniable is that the film was never widely distributed and where it was shown it often received a hostile reception from local civil and religious authorities who objected to what they regarded as its immorality. It only began to be screened in Italy after 1945, when it came to be widely acclaimed as an immediate precursor of neorealism. In the United States, copyright problems prevented it from being widely screened until the mid-1960s, by which time Hollywood had already made its own version of Cain's novel.

OZPETEK, FERZAN (1959–). Director. Born in Istanbul, in 1977 Ozpetek moved to Rome, where he studied cinema at the university and theater direction at the National Academy of Dramatic Art. He then joined Julian Beck and the Living Theater troupe for a short period before abandoning the stage in order to work as an assistant for a number of the younger Italian directors, including **Massimo Troisi**, **Maurizio Ponzi**, and **Ricky Tognazzi**. In 1997 he directed his first feature, *Hamam, il bagno turco* (*Steam: The Turkish Baths*, 1997), an intense drama of self-discovery that was well received at Cannes and brought its producers a **Nastro d'argento**. This was followed by *Harem suaré* (1999), an exotic tale that allowed a now-elderly **Lucia Bosé** to reminisce about her days as the sultan's favorite concubine in the late years of the Ottoman Empire, and *Le fate ignoranti* (*The Ignorant Fairies*, 2000), the story of a wife painfully coming to terms with the discovery of her husband's homosexuality after his death in a car accident. *La finestra di fronte* (*Facing Windows*, 2002), a similarly intense drama of interpersonal relationships and unexpected discoveries, also provided **Massimo Girotti** with his last major film role. Ozpetek's most recent film is *Cuore sacro* (*Sacred Heart*, 2005), the inspiring fable of an impossible altruism set against the backdrop of modern consumer culture.

– P –

PACCHIONI, ITALO (1872–1940). Cameraman and film pioneer. Owner of a photographic studio in Milan in the early 1890s, Pacchioni was greatly excited by the Lumière *cinématographe* but was unable to acquire one for himself. Consequently, with the help of his brother Enrico, he built his own version of a Lumière-style movie camera and began taking films. Pacchioni's footage of a train arriving at the station in Milan is thus probably the first film shot in Italy with an Italian camera. This was followed by some basic comic sketches such as *Il finto storpio al Castello Sforzesco di Milano* (*The Sham Cripple at the Sforza Castle in Milan*, 1896) and a number of other attempts at short filmic narratives, some reputedly shot on the terrace of his own house with his relatives as actors. At the same time, again in partnership with his brother, he opened and managed some of the earliest movie houses in the cities of Modena and Ravenna. Soon after, however, he and his brother took to the road in an elaborate traveling pavilion in which they screened films regularly at provincial fairs throughout northern Italy. In 1901 Pacchioni filmed the elaborate funeral of the great Italian composer Giuseppe Verdi, which he screened in March that year. For unknown reasons, however, after such a flurry of activity, by 1902 Pacchioni appears to have returned to his photographic studio and never been involved with the cinema again.

PAGANO, BARTOLOMEO (1878–1947). Actor. A Genoese dock-worker with no previous acting experience, Pagano was chosen by director **Giovanni Pastrone**, largely on the basis of his powerful physique and gentle disposition, to play the part of the faithful slave **Maciste** in the spectacular historical epic *Cabiria* (1914). The over-whelming success of the film and Pagano's sympathetic portrayal of the good-natured strongman who helps to rescue Cabiria from the fire god Moloch led to the character's acquiring a life of its own. Pagano went on to play "the good giant," as he was affectionately known, in a long and very popular series of Maciste films, first in Italy with Pastrone's **Itala Film** company and then, during the downturn of the Italian film industry in the early 1920s, in Germany, making four Maciste films there between 1922 and 1924. He subsequently returned to Italy to make another series of Maciste films for the Fert-Pittaluga company, the most famous of which was *Maciste all'Inferno* (*Maciste in Hell*, 1926). In the late 1920s Pagano attempted to break out of the Maciste mold by accepting roles in films like *Gli ultimi zar* (*The Last Tzars*, 1926) and *Il vetturale di Moncenisio* (The Courier of Moncenisio, 1927) but the films were only moderately successful and, in any case, their publicity continued to exploit the Maciste connection. At this point, as good-natured as the character he had played in all those films, Pagano declared his intention to make only one film from then on: *Maciste in Retirement*.

PAMPANINI, SILVANA (1925–). Actress. One of the first of the large-bosomed starlets who came to dominate the Italian screen in the immediate postwar period, Pampanini briefly studied singing at the Conservatorium of Santa Cecilia in Rome but was drawn to acting in films following her win in the 1946 Miss Italia contest. After a small part in Giuseppe Maria Scotese's *L'Apocalisse* (Apocalypse, 1946), her first significant role was in **Camillo Mastrocinque**'s *Il segreto di Don Giovanni* (*When Love Calls*, 1947), which was followed by a host of popular films that attempted to exploit her pinup qualities. In the early 1950s she extended herself in a number of more dramatic roles, as in **Luigi Zampa**'s *Processo alla città* (*The City Stands Trial*, 1952), **Giuseppe De Santis**'s *Un marito per Anna Zaccheo* (*A Husband for Anna*, 1953), and **Luigi Comencini**'s *La tratta delle bianche* (*The White Slave Trade*, 1955) and also appeared in French films such as Abel Gance's *La Tour de Nesle* (*Tower of Nesle*, 1954) and in the Mexican melodrama *Sed de amor* (*Thirst for Love*, 1958), directed by Alfonso Corona Blake. However, unlike other *maggiorate* such as **Gina Lollobrigida** and **Sophia Loren**, Pampanini's career declined sharply in the early 1960s, and one of her last substantial roles was, ironically, that of a fading Italian fim starlet in **Dino Risi**'s *Il gaucho* (*The Gaucho*, 1964). After appearing sporadically in the odd lightweight comedy during the 1970s, she has reappeared more recently on the small screen, playing the role of a mother in the television miniseries *Tre stelle* (Three Stars, 1999) and hosting the variety program *Domenica In* in 2002.

PASOLINI, PIER PAOLO (1922–1975). Poet, playwright, novelist, painter, essayist, film director. Although he would become one of the foremost directors to emerge in the second wave of postwar Italian cinema in the early 1960s, Pasolini came to cinema relatively late in life, after having already established a strong reputation as an innovative poet, novelist, and radical cultural critic, in search of an alternative medium for self-expression.

Having been expelled from both his teaching post and the Communist Party for alleged homosexual activities, in 1950 Pasolini moved from the northern Italian town of Casarsa, where he had lived with his mother since the end of World War II, to one of the poorer outlying districts of Rome. Despite continuing financial hardship, he quickly became part of the city's bustling literary scene and published several acclaimed collections of poetry before also beginning to work in the cinema, his first involvement being a collaboration on the screenplay of **Mario Soldati**'s *La donna del fiume* (*The River*

Girl, 1954). In the wake of the publication of his controversial novel *Ragazzi di vita* (1955), which presented a vivid portrait of the precarious existence lived by so many in the *borgate* (shantytowns) that he had come to know so well, Pasolini was approached more frequently to work on the screenplays of films that were set in the seamier side of Rome. He thus contributed to writing the dialogue of **Federico Fellini**'s *Le notti di Cabiria* (*The Nights of Cabiria*, 1956) before also working with **Mauro Bolognini** on the screenplays of half a dozen films, including *La notte brava* (*On Any Street*, 1959), *Il bell'Antonio* (*Bell'Antonio*, 1960), and *La giornata balorda* (*A Crazy Day*, 1960).

After playing a small role in **Carlo Lizzani**'s *Il gobo di Roma* (*The Hunchback of Rome*, 1960), an experience that allowed him to become familiar with the more technical aspects of filmmaking, he finally wrote and directed his first film, *Accattone* (*Accattone!* 1961), the story of a truculent layabout in one of the Roman *borgate* whose wayward existence and baneful ordeals nevertheless mark him out as a sort of negative Christ figure. The film's nonmoralistic portrayal of prostitutes and petty thieves, coupled with its use of Christological imagery in a profane context, immediately drew censure from the authorities who originally sought to ban the film outright but eventually allowed its release under an R rating. Pasolini's second film, *Mamma Roma* (1962), also set in the Roman *borgate* and featuring **Anna Magnani** in one of the most forceful roles of her career, was also denounced for obscenity at its first screening but later absolved of the charge. An even harsher reaction attended *La ricotta* (The Curd Cheese), a short self-contained episode that Pasolini contributed to the compilation film *Ro.Go.Pa.G.* (*Let's Have a Brainwash*, 1963), with the film's being impounded by the authorities for its alleged offense to the Catholic religion and Pasolini himself receiving a four-month suspended jail sentence.

Almost as a rejoinder, Pasolini then made a powerful but iconoclastic adaptation of what he regarded as the most socially committed of the Gospels, *Il vangelo secondo Matteo* (*The Gospel According to St. Matthew*, 1964). The film, screened to great acclaim at the **Venice Festival** that year, received both the Special Jury Prize and the Office Catholique International du Cinéma (OCIC) Award, and also went on to win three **Nastri d'argento** and three nominations for

Academy Awards. Following *Comizi d'amore* (*Love Meetings*, 1964), an illuminating documentary-inquest into the sexual attitudes of contemporary Italians, filmed largely while Pasolini was scouting locations for *Il vangelo*, he directed *Uccellacci e uccellini* (*Hawks and Sparrows*, 1966), a surreal road movie that utilized the great acting talents of **Totò** to construct what was effectively a filmic essay on the death of political ideologies in the guise of a picaresque adventure. A bizarre filmic concoction but typical of Pasolini's way of using the cinema to present his provocative ideas, *Uccellacci* was nominated for the Golden Palm at Cannes and won two Nastri d'argento at home. Totò would also feature in two subsequent short films, *La terra vista dalla luna* (*The Earth Seen from the Moon*), which was Pasolini's contribution to the compilation film *Le streghe* (*The Witches*, 1967), and *Che cosa sono le nuvole?* (*What Are the Clouds?*), a charming existential fable that became one of the episodes of *Capriccio all'italiana* (*Caprice Italian Style*, 1968).

After playing the part of a revolutionary Mexican priest in Lizzani's political Western, *Requiescant* (*Kill and Pray*, 1967), Pasolini made the first of his screen adaptations of ancient tragedies, *Edipo Re* (*Oedipus Rex*, 1967). Stunning in its creation of an archaic mythopoetic setting that avoided all the usual iconography of ancient Greek culture (the film was, in fact, shot mostly in Morocco), *Edipo* was also remarkable for the way in which it succeeded in faithfully adapting Sophocles' text while also subjectively expressing Pasolini's oedipal conflict with his own father.

Pasolini's next film, *Teorema* (*Theorem*, 1968), adapted from a book he had already published the same year, profoundly divided the critics at Venice and again put Pasolini at the center of controversy. A highly ambivalent allegory that could be read both as a profanity and as a spiritual epiphany, the film was given the OCIC Award but at the same time also strongly attacked by other religious authorities. Following what had by now become a pattern, the film was impounded by the authorities on the usual charges of obscenity but eventually acquitted of the charges and released. Following *Appunti per un film sull'India* (Notes for a Film on India, 1968), a short documentary eventually shown on television, Pasolini made *Porcile* (*Pigpen*, 1969), another highly idiosyncratic and ambiguous allegory that appeared purposely structured to resist univocal interpretation.

This was followed by the second of Pasolini's adaptations of ancient Greek tragedy, *Medea* (1969), which was memorable for, among other elements, a brilliant performance in the lead role by opera diva Maria Callas. After so many difficult works, Pasolini lightened up with his next three films, *Il Decameron* (*The Decameron*, 1971), *I racconti di Canterbury* (*The Canterbury Tales*, 1972), and *Il fiore delle mille e una notte* (*A Thousand and One Nights*, 1974). United under the rubric of what he called his Trilogy of Life, all three were creative but relatively transparent adaptations of major literary works and all celebrated the body and human sexuality. Pasolini's own appearance as a fresco painter in one of the frame stories of *Il Decameron* and as Geoffrey Chaucer himself in *The Canterbury Tales* also added a self-reflexive and personal dimension to the films. This lightness of tone, however, was short lived. In 1975, largely in response to what he had come to see as an ever more degraded Italian reality around him, Pasolini made his bleakest and most nihilistic cinematic statement, *Salò o le 120 giornate di Sodoma* (*Salo, or the 120 Days of Sodom*, 1975). In the event, the film was first screened at the Paris Festival on 23 November 1975, three weeks after Pasolini himself was brutally murdered. An unflinching representation of naked power at its worst, the film was so confrontational that it was completely banned in Italy and in most other countries until quite recently, its dark shadow at times succeeding in obscuring the extraordinary overall achievement of Pasolini's remarkable body of work.

PASQUINI, ANGELO (1948–). Screenwriter. After being one of the animators and writers of the notorious satirical journal *Il Male*, Pasquini began working in films as a cowriter for **Daniele Luchetti**'s *Domani accadrà* (*It's Happening Tomorrow*, 1988). He collaborated again with Luchetti on *La settimana della sfinge* (The Week of the Sphinx, 1990) and on *Il portaborse* (*The Yes Man*, 1991), for which he supplied the story. He subsequently worked with **Gabriele Salvatores** on *Sud* (*South*, 1993), with **Michele Placido** on *Le amiche del cuore* (*Close Friends*, 1992) and *Un eroe borghese* (*Ordinary Hero*, 1995), with **Mario Brenta** on *Barnabò delle montagne* (*Barnabo of the Mountains*, 1994), and with **Sergio Rubini** on *Prestazione straordinaria* (*Working Overtime*, 1994). In the late 1990s, after writing and directing his first feature film, *Santo Stefano* (1997), he also worked extensively for Italian television, writing, among other things, one of the popular Inspector Montalbano series, *Il commissario Montalbano: la voce del violino* (*Inspector Montalbano: The Sound of the Violin*, 1999). He has most recently collaborated on the screenplay of Rubini's *La terra* (*The Land*, 2006), sharing a nomination for the **David di Donatello** for Best Screenplay.

PASTRONE, GIOVANNI (1883–1959). Producer and director. Long known as merely the producer and director of *Cabiria* (1914), Pastrone has continued to grow in stature as more recent research has revealed his major role in, and contribution to, the Italian film industry during its golden silent period.

A gifted child with a talent for both music and languages, Pastrone was soon forced to abandon music in favor of accounting. It was as a bright junior accountant and factotum that he joined the Turin film company of Carlo Rossi & C. in 1907. Within six months he had risen through the ranks and become a full partner. When Rossi left to work for the **Cines** in Rome, Pastrone and fellow partner, Carlo Sciamengo, formed **Itala Film**. Pastrone soon reorganized the company on a firm business basis, introducing stricter management, planning, and accounting practices as well as technical innovations. Recognizing the popularity of comic sketches at the time, he lured Pathé's most successful resident comic, **André Deed**, to come to Turin to work for Itala. Deed's **Cretinetti** films, turned out for a time at the rate of one a week, were a gold mine for the company and kept it solvent. At the same time Pastrone produced and directed the epic spectacle *La caduta di Troia* (*The Fall of Troy*, 1910). Poorly received at home, the film broke box office records in the United States, allowing Pastrone to open up an American subsidiary. It also prompted him to plan the greatest film made to date, *Cabiria*, a film that would require almost a year and an astronomical budget to make. Taking out a patent on what would become known as the *dolly*—Hitchcock would later attest that in his early days it was known in the trade as the *cabiria*—Pastrone also shrewdly recruited the best special effects cinematographer of the day, Segundo De Chomón, to work for Itala. With the film meticulously planned and partly completed, Pastrone conceived the masterstroke of approaching the current greatest literary name in Italy, Gabriele D'Annunzio, and paying him a huge fee to accept paternity of the film, an offer that D'Annunzio gleefully accepted.

D'Annunzio's name helped to make what was an extraordinary cinematic achievement even more spectacularly successful at the box office and thus allowed Pastrone to proceed to other projects. In the following years, as well as initiating the long line of films featuring **Maciste**, the musclebound strongman from *Cabiria*, he also directed (under the pseudonym Piero Fosco) the diva **Pina Menichelli** in *Il Fuoco* (*The Fire*, 1915) and *Tigre reale* (*Royal Tigress*, 1916) and his own discovery, Itala Almirante Manzini, in a fine adaptation of Ibsen's *Hedda Gabbler* (1919). Nevertheless, by the end of World War I, with the onset of the crisis that would soon decimate the Italian film industry, Pastrone had lost financial control of Itala. He briefly joined the **Unione Cinematografia Italiana** (UCI) under duress, but following the trust's refusal to fund a major project he had proposed, he left the industry to carry on scientific and other studies in private for many years. His only real connection with the cinema was the reissue of a version of *Cabiria* with a coordinated musical track in the early 1930s and his strong support for the setting up of the National Film Museum in Turin. He died in 1959 just as the new golden age of Italian cinema was beginning.

PEDERSOLI, CARLO (1929–). Actor. After working at a wide variety of occupations and having been at various times a champion Olympic swimmer, an assembly line worker, a film extra, and a songwriter, in 1967 Pedersoli was offered one of the lead roles in the **spaghetti Western** *Dio perdona . . . io no!* (*God Forgives, I Don't*, 1967), playing alongside another little-known actor, **Mario Girotti**. Following what had become something of a tradition in the Italian Western, both actors adopted anglicized stage names, Girotti becoming Terence Hill and Pedersoli taking on the name of Bud Spencer (in homage to his preferred brand of American beer and his favorite American actor, Spencer Tracy). Their appearance in a handful of other films made them a popular duo but they then gained an overwhelming, and international, cult following with the knockabout comic Western *Lo chiamavano Trinità* (*They Call Me Trinity*, 1970), a popularity that was confirmed and augmented by its immediate sequel, *Continuavano a chiamarlo Trinità* (*Trinity Is Still My Name!*

1971). They continued to appear together in a dozen subsequent films, but Pedersoli (always as Bud Spencer) also branched out on his own, achieving his own cult following playing a limited number of character roles, the most famous in Italy being that of Inspector "Flatfoot" Rizzo in a series of comic police dramas directed by **Steno**. He became especially renowned in Germany, where in 1979 he received the Jupiter Prize as most popular actor, and *Lo chiamavano Bulldozer* (*Uppercut*, 1978), a film in which he played one of his most typical roles, was given the Golden Screen Award.

After 30 years of playing an amiable hulk who uses his fists to bring evildoers back to the straight and narrow, Pedersoli has recently taken on more demanding roles and in 2003 (as Bud Spencer) was nominated for a **Nastro d'argento** as best supporting actor in **Ermanno Olmi**'s *Cantando dietro i paraventi* (*Singing behind Screens*).

PEPLUM. Genre. Derived from the Latin term for the small over-the-shoulder tunic often worn in these films, peplum was the name given to the popular sword-and-sandal genre that flourished in Italy in the late 1950s. Some 180 such films were made in Italy between 1957 and 1965, when the genre rapidly waned and was replaced by an even more prolific genre, the Italian, or so-called **spaghetti Western**.

The distant origins of the peplum were undoubtedly in the historical superspectacles, or "kolossals," of the silent period, and it was no coincidence that the names of Ursus and **Maciste**, the muscular strongmen who had first made their appearance in **Enrico Guazzoni**'s *Quo vadis?* (1912) and **Giovanni Pastrone**'s *Cabiria* (1914), reappeared so frequently in the titles of many classics of the genre. Its more immediate forerunners, however, were the spate of American historical and biblical spectaculars produced at **Cinecittà** in the early 1950s, as well as several homegrown big-budget epics such as **Alessandro Blasetti**'s *Fabiola* (1949) and **Mario Camerini**'s *Ulisse* (*Ulysses*, 1954). The peplums themselves, however, were far from big-budget productions, and the film usually credited with giving birth to the genre, **Pietro Francisci**'s *Le fatiche di Ercole* (*Hercules*, 1957), was made for $120,000 but eventually earned $18 million. Francisci tried to repeat his winning formula, which included the hiring of a relatively inexpensive bodybuilder rather than a costly star to play the part of the muscleman superhero and concentrating on the hero's action-filled adventures rather than the rise and fall of civilizations, in *Ercole e la regina di Lidia* (*Hercules Unchained*, 1958) but by this time many others were also attempting to follow his example, with four other muscleman epics produced in 1959, 15 in 1960, and 31 in 1961.

The directors who came to be most closely associated with the genre, in addition to Francisci himself, were **Vittorio Cottafavi**, who made two classics of the genre, *La vendetta di Ercole* (*Hercules' Revenge*, 1960, also known in the United States as *Goliath and the Dragon*) and *Ercole alla conquista di Atlantide* (*Hercules and the Conquest of Atlantis*, 1961, also known in the United States as *Hercules and the Captive Women*); **Riccardo Freda**, who directed five muscleman epics including *Maciste alla corte del Gran Khan* (*Maciste at the Court of the Great Khan*, 1961, also known as *Samson and the Seven Miracles of the World*) and *Maciste all'Inferno* (*Maciste in Hell*, 1962, also known as *The Witch's Curse*); and **Carlo Campogalliani**, who contributed *Il terrore dei barbari* (*Goliath and the Barbarians*, 1959), *Maciste nella valle dei re* (*Son of Samson*, 1960), and *Ursus* (*Ursus, Son of Hercules*, 1961). Among other practitioners of the genre were Domenico Paolella, **Sergio Corbucci**, and Duccio Tessari. **Mario Mattoli** inflected the genre with comedy in his *Maciste contro Ercole nella valle dei guai* (*Hercules in the Valley of Woe*, 1961) and **Mario Bava** with horror in *Ercole al centro della terra* (*Hercules in the Haunted World*, 1961). **Sergio Leone**, who would be responsible for the birth of the Western genre that would soon replace the peplum, was called in to complete **Mario Bonnard**'s foray into the genre, *Gli ultimi giorni di Pompei* (*The Last Days of Pompeii*, 1959), before making his own highly regarded *Il colosso di Rodi* (*The Colossus of Rhodes*, 1961).

The musclemen who were enlisted to impersonate the superhero, who could be called, quite interchangeably, Maciste, Hercules, Ursus, Goliath, Samson, or Colossus, were for the most part American bodybuilders, including Steve Reeves, Reg Park, Gordon Scott, Mark Forrest, Kirk Morris, Ed Fury, Dan Vadis, and Alan Steel (Sergio Ciani). And just as the hero's name could vary, the stories themselves could also be set in widely differing times and places, from Greek and Roman mythological times to the "barbaric" Middle Ages, and from Greece, Rome, Egypt, China, and the Orient to the very center of the Earth.

Generally dismissed by serious critics and relatively short lived, the genre was nevertheless both popular and lucrative, exploiting the extensive network of Italian second- and third-run cinemas and easily accessing markets outside Italy due to the fact that many of the films were made as European or American coproductions. Despite its extraordinary success, however, the genre was already substantially on the wane in 1964 when the enormous box office receipts of *Per un pugno di dollari* (*For a Fistful of Dollars*, 1964), a **Western all'Italiana** directed by Bob Robertson (Sergio Leone), were already indicating a different way forward for Italian popular cinema.

PERILLI, IVO (1902–1994). Screenwriter and director. After working in the theater as a set designer during the 1920s, at the beginning of the sound era Perilli joined the new **Cines**, where he served as production designer and then as assistant director to **Mario Camerini**. In 1933 he directed his first feature film, *Ragazzo* (*Boy*). In spite of recounting the edifying story of a street kid whose criminal behavior is eventually reformed by time in a Fascist youth camp, *Ragazzo* became one of the few films to be completely banned by the Fascist authorities, its total prohibition coming from Benito Mussolini himself. Perilli directed two other minor films in the early 1940s, *Margherita fra i tre* (*Margherita and Her Three Uncles*, 1942) and *La primadonna* (The First Soprano, 1943), but for the most part he worked as a regular screenwriter (and sometimes assistant director) on a dozen of Camerini's subsequent films including *Il cappello a tre punte* (*Three-Cornered Hat*, 1934), *Darò un milione* (*I'll Give a Million*, 1936), *I grandi magazzini* (*Department Store*, 1939), and *I promessi sposi* (*The Spirit and the Flesh*, 1941). In the period following World War II he collaborated with many of the major directors: with Camerini again on a half dozen films including *Due lettere anonime* (*Two Anonymous Letters*, 1945), *La bella mugnaia* (*The Miller's Beautiful Wife*, 1956), and *I briganti italiani* (*The Italian Brigands*, 1962); with **Roberto Rossellini** on *Europa '51* (*The Greatest Love*, 1952); with **Giuseppe De Santis** on *Riso amaro* (*Bitter Rice*, 1949); and with **Alberto Lattuada** on *Anna* (1952). He also worked with American directors such as Martin Ritt on *5 Branded*

Women (*Jovanka e le altre*, 1960) and Richard Fleisher on *Barabbas* (1961). Following his collaboration on the screenplay of John Huston's *The Bible: The Beginning* (1966), however, he largely retired from the cinema, returning only to supply the story and screenplay for **Luigi Comencini**'s *Mio dio come sono caduta in basso* (*How Long Can You Fall?* 1974).

PETRAGLIA, SANDRO (1947–). Screenwriter. For much of his professional career Petraglia has worked with Franco Rulli to form the most prolific and respected screenwriting team in the Italian cinema of the last two decades. With a background in film criticism, Petraglia collaborated with **Marco Bellocchio**, Silvano Agosti, and Rulli in writing and directing *Nessuno o tutti—Matti da slegare* (*Fit to Be Untied*, 1975), a three-hour documentary on Italian mental asylums, and *La macchina cinema* (*The Cinema Machine*), a five-part documentary on the seamier aspects of the Italian film industry screened on Italian television in 1979. He subsequently worked on the screenplays of **Nanni Moretti**'s *Bianca* (*Sweet Body of Bianca*, 1983) and *La messa è finita* (*The Mass Is Ended*, 1985) before teaming up again with Rulli to write several successful television miniseries including *Attentato al papa* (Attempt on the Pope's Life, 1986) and the popular and long-running series on the Mafia, *La piovra* (*Octopus*, 1987–1994). Regularly working together from then on, Petraglia and Rulli scripted many of the key films of the emerging directors of the **New Italian Cinema**, including **Marco Risi**'s *Mery per sempre* (*Mary Forever*, 1989), **Daniele Luchetti**'s *Il portaborse* (*The Yes Man*, 1991), and **Gianni Amelio**'s *Il ladro di bambini* (*The Stolen Children*, 1992). While continuing to write for the big screen and furnishing the screenplays of films such as **Marco Tullio Giordana**'s *Pasolini un delitto italiano* (*Pasolini, an Italian Crime*, 1995) and **Francesco Rosi**'s *La tregua* (*The Truce*, 1997), they also worked extensively for television in the late 1990s, on quality miniseries such as *Don Milani—Il priore di Barbiana* (*Don Milani, the Prior of Barbiana*, 1997) and *La vita che verrà* (The Life to Come, 1999). In 2003 Petraglia and Rulli achieved their greatest triumph with Marco Tullio Giordana's much-acclaimed six-hour epic, *La meglio gioventù* (*The Best of Youth*, 2003), for which they received both the **David di Donatello** and the **Nastro d'argento**.

PETRI, ELIO (1929–1982). (Born Eraclio Petri.) Screenwriter and director. A journalist and film reviewer for the Communist Party daily *L'unità*, Petri graduated to writing for the cinema in 1951 when he was invited by director **Giuseppe De Santis** to collaborate on the screenplay of *Roma ore 11* (*Rome 11:00*, 1952). While continuing to work as a screenwriter for De Santis and others, Petri also made several documentaries before directing his first feature, *L'assassino* (*The Assassin*, 1961), an intriguing police thriller starring **Marcello Mastroianni** that was nominated for the Golden Bear at Berlin. This was followed by *I giorni contati* (*Numbered Days*, 1962), an interesting portrayal of an existential midlife crisis, and *La decimal vittima* (*The Tenth Victim*, 1965), a science fiction story set in the 21st century that appeared to be part James Bond, part Hitchcock, and part George Orwell. *A ciascuno il suo* (*We Still Kill the Old Way*, 1967), adapted from a novel by Leonardo Sciascia and ostensibly about the Mafia but effectively exploring wider legal and illegal power networks, was hailed as a major work and won four **Nastri d'argento** and a nomination for the Palme d'or at Cannes. Then, after the ironically titled *Un tranquillo posto di campagna* (*A Quiet Place in the Country*, 1969), the portrait of a disturbed artist tormented by both ghosts and hallucinations, Petri made what is generally regarded as his best film, ***Indagine su un cittadino al di sopra di ogni sospetto*** (*Investigation of a Citizen Above Suspicion*, 1970). The first of a series of strongly committed political works displaying an open distrust, and often outright cynicism, toward all established authority, the film was both commercially and critically successful and went on to win the Oscar for Best Foreign Film. The caricatural and slightly hysterical style that had characterized *Indagine* returned in *La classe operaia va in paradiso* (*The Working Class Goes to Heaven*, 1971), a film that was fiercely attacked for what appeared to be its very confused pro-labor ideology but which nevertheless was awarded the Palme d'or at Cannes and the **David di Donatello** for Best Film. The same mixture of caricature and black humor reappeared in *La proprieta non è più un furto* (*Property Is No Longer a Theft*, 1973) and then *Todo modo* (1976), a mercilessly grotesque and transparent portrait of the ruling Christian Democrat Party, again adapted from a work by Sciascia. After *Le mani sporche* (Soiled Hands, 1978), a production of Jean-Paul Sartre's play for Italian television, Petri's last film before his untimely death from cancer at the age of only 53 was *Le buone notizie* (*Good News*, 1979), another grotesque social satire, this time directed at the Italian television industry.

PETROLINI, ETTORE (1886–1936). Actor and playwright. Taking to the stage at the age of 14, Petrolini achieved enormous national and international renown as a performer of cabaret and musical theater, touring extensively throughout Europe and the Americas. In spite of his huge popularity over three decades, he appeared only twice in films during the silent period: in a brief comic sketch for Latium films in 1913 and in **Mario Bonnard**'s *Mentre il pubblico ride* (*While the Public Laughs*, 1919). However, in 1930 **Alessandro Blasetti** filmed a performance of his stage show *Nerone* (*Nero*, 1930) and a year later **Carlo Campogalliani** also recorded theatrical performances of *Cortile* (*Courtyard*, 1931) and *Medico per forza* (1931), an Italian version of Molière's *Le médecin malgré lui* (*The Doctor in Spite of Himself*). Although Petrolini's lampoon of the Roman emperor in *Nerone* appeared to many as thinly veiled references to Mussolini, such was his overwhelming popularity that the film was allowed to circulate freely and Mussolini himself is said to have been amused by it.

PICCIONI, GIUSEPPE (1953–). Director and screenwriter. Piccioni began making short films in the early 1980s while studying at the Gaumont Film School in Rome. In 1985, after working for a period in advertising, he helped found the Vertigo Film production company, with which he produced his first feature, *Il grande Blek* (The Mighty Blek, 1987). A warm-hearted if melancholic coming-of-age film, *Blek* was much acclaimed when presented in competition at the Berlin Film Festival and in Italy received both a **Nastro d'argento** and the De Sica Prize for Young Cinema. There followed the romantic road movie *Chiedi la luna* (*Ask for the Moon*, 1991), the more cynical *Condannato a nozze* (*Condemned to Wed*, 1993), and *Cuori al verde* (*Penniless Hearts*, 1996), a bittersweet comedy about midlife crisis. In 1999 *Fuori dal mondo* (*Not of This World*, 1999), a moving tale about the profound spiritual transformation wrought on the lives of several people by the discovery of an abandoned baby, won five **David di Donatello** and four Ciak d'oro awards and became the Italian nominee for Best Foreign Film at that year's Oscars. Two years later the intense love story *Luce dei miei occhi* (*Light of My Eyes*, 2001) deeply divided the critics but was nevertheless nominated for the Golden Lion at the **Venice Festival**, with both its leads also being awarded the prestigious Volpi Cup. Piccioni's most recent effort, *La vita che vorrei* (*The Life I Want*, 2004), a romantic melodrama that cleverly blurs the boundaries between cinema and real life, was also nominated for five David di Donatello awards.

PICCIONI, PIERO (1921–2004). Jazz musician, orchestra director, film composer. Piccioni was launched on a musical career in his teens when he was hired as a solo pianist to play live on a weekly program on national Italian radio. Profoundly influenced by the music of Duke Ellington, he soon formed his own jazz orchestra which, as the "013" Big Band, was the first orchestra to play live on Italian radio after the announcement of the fall of Fascism. At the end of the 1940s he lived for a period in the United States, where he met and played with jazz musicians such as Charlie Parker and Max Roach. Back in Italy he worked briefly as a lawyer before beginning to compose music for films in the early 1950s, originally under the stage name of Piero Morgan. His first feature film score was for Gianni Franciolini's *Il mondo le condanna* (The World Condemns Them, 1952), which was soon followed by music for **Alberto Lattuada**'s *La spiaggia* (*The Beach*, 1953). After scoring, among others, **Dino Risi**'s two popular teen comedies, *Poveri ma belli* (*Poor, but Handsome*, 1956) and *Belle ma povere* (*Pretty but Poor*, 1957), he began to use his own name while working on **Francesco Rosi**'s *I magliari* (*The Magliari*, 1959). He subsequently scored all of Rosi's films, winning the **Nastro d'argento** for the stark and unnerving sound design of Rosi's *Salvatore Giuliano* (1962).

For the next 25 years, Piccioni worked extensively in both commercial and auteur cinema, moving easily between sword-and-sandal epics such as *Il figlio di Spartaco* (*The Son of Spartacus*, 1963) and auteur films such as **Luchino Visconti**'s *Lo straniero* (*The Stranger*, 1967). He formed an especially close professional relationship with **Alberto Sordi** and scored practically all the films that Sordi appeared in or directed, from the early *Fumo di Londra* (*Smoke Over London*,

1966) to Sordi's final film, *Incontri proibiti* (*Forbidden Encounters*, 1998). In the 1970s, beginning with *Mimì metallurgico ferito nell'onore* (*The Seduction of Mimi*, 1972), he also frequently worked with **Lina Wertmüller** and received the **David di Donatello** for his score of Wertmüller's *Travolti da un insolito destino nell'azzurro mare d'agosto* (*Swept Away*, 1975). Having composed music for over 150 films, in 1996 he was awarded the Flaiano International Prize for his career.

PIERACCIONI, LEONARDO (1965–). Actor, director, screenwriter. After doing cabaret in his teens and small roles in minor films in the early 1990s, Pieraccioni was presented with the opportunity to make a feature film and so directed *I laureati* (*Graduates*, 1995), the story of the hopes and loves of four self-indulgent students who share an apartment in Florence, the lead being played by Pieraccioni himself. The film was critically panned but its unexpected and enormous box office success allowed Pieraccioni to go on to make *Il ciclone* (*The Cyclone*, 1996), a racy comedy focused on a small troupe of beautiful Spanish flamenco dancers who descend on a sleepy town in Tuscany, thereby provoking the storm of excited reactions that gives the film its title. As before, the film was not only popular but broke all previous Italian box office records and thus confirmed Pieraccioni's reputation as a bankable director.

Always in partnership with screenwriter Giovanni Veronesi, Pieraccioni subsequently made *Fuochi d'artificio* (*Fireworks*, 1997), *Il mio West* (*Gunslinger's Revenge*, 1998), an amusing if rather familiar take on the Western exploiting the well-known faces of Harvey Keitel and David Bowie, *Il pesce innamorato* (*The Fish in Love*, 1999), and *Il principe e il pirata* (*The Prince and the Pirate*, 2001), a road movie about two childhood friends who eventually discover that they are actually siblings. After *Il Paradiso all'improvviso* (*Suddenly Paradise*, 2003), again critically panned but enormously successful at the box office, Pieraccioni has most recently directed *Ti amo in tutte le lingue del mondo* (*I Love You in Every Language*, 2005).

PIETRANGELI, ANTONIO (1919–1968). Critic, screenwriter, director. Pietrangeli graduated in medecine but preferred to write literary and film criticism and so became one of the militant young cineastes associated with the journal *Cinema* who came to assist **Luchino Visconti** in making *Ossessione* (*Obsession*, 1943). After the war, he continued to contribute to film journals but also collaborated as screenwriter on a number of films including **Pietro Germi**'s *Gioventù perduta* (*Lost Youth*, 1947) and **Alessandro Blasetti**'s *Fabiola* (1949) before directing his first solo film, *Il sole negli occhi* (*Empty Eyes*, 1953), the first of many of his works to privilege female characters and to highlight the position of women in Italian society. After several well-constructed light comedies such as the amusing saga of foreign girls finding love and romance in Italy, *Souvenir d'Italie* (*It Happened in Rome*, 1957), and *Fantasmi a Roma* (*Ghosts of Rome*, 1960), which cleverly used the setting of a haunted Roman palace to highlight the issue of real estate speculation, he made *Adua e le sue compagne* (*Adua and Her Friends*, 1960), a film that examined the life prospects of four prostitutes after the brothels were closed by law in Italy in 1958. This was followed by a number of other finely crafted female portraits in *La visita* (*The Visitor*, 1963), *La parmigiana* (*The Girl from Parma*, 1963), and what is generally regarded as his most powerful and moving film, *Io la conoscevo bene* (*I Knew Her Well*, 1965), for which he received the **Nastro d'argento** for both direction and writing. Tragically, while still at the peak of his creative powers, he was killed in a boating accident off the island of Gaeta while filming *Come, quando, perchè* (*How, When, and with Whom*, 1969), which was then completed by **Valerio Zurlini**.

PINELLI, TULLIO (1908–). Playwright and screenwriter. After graduating in jurisprudence, Pinelli alternated between practicing as a lawyer and writing plays, becoming, by the early 1940s, one of Italy's most respected contemporary playwrights. At this time he also began working as a screenwriter, one of his first efforts being the screenplay of **Mario Bonnard**'s *Campo de' Fiori* (*Peddler and the Lady*, 1943), which he cowrote with **Federico Fellini**.

In the immediate postwar period, Pinelli collaborated extensively with **Alberto Lattuada**, helping to write *Il bandito* (*The Bandit*, 1946), *Senza pietà* (*Without Pity*, 1948), and *Il Mulino del Po* (*The Mill on the Po*, 1948) and worked with **Pietro Germi** on *In nome della legge* (*In the Name of the Law*, 1949) and *Il cammino della speranza* (*Path of Hope*, 1950) before collaborating with both Fellini and Lattuada on *Luci del varietà* (*Variety Lights*, 1950). From then on, usually together with **Ennio Flaiano**, he was Fellini's regular screenwriter on all the latter's major films up to *Giulietta degli spiriti* (*Juliet of the Spirits*, 1965), which included *La dolce vita* (1960), for which he shared an Oscar nomination for Best Screenplay and a **Nastro d'argento** for Best Original Story, a success repeated with *Otto e mezzo* (8½, 1963). After a number of years away from Fellini, during which he worked again with Pietro Germi as well as with **Antonio Pietrangeli**, **Liliana Cavani**, and **Mario Monicelli**, he returned to write Fellini's last two films, *Ginger e Fred* (*Ginger and Fred*, 1986) and *La voce della luna* (*The Voice of the Moon*, 1990). He subsequently retired from screenwriting but in 1998 published his first novel, *La casa di Robespierre* (*Robespierre's House*).

PIOVANI, NICOLA (1946–). Pianist, orchestra director, film and theater composer. After graduating from the Conservatory of Milan in 1967, Piovani worked as a pianist and song arranger before studying composition under Manos Hadjidakis. He began composing for film in the early 1970s, writing his first scores for Silvano Agosti's *N.P. il segreto* (*NP*, 1970) and **Marco Bellocchio**'s *Nel nome del padre* (*In the Name of the Father*, 1972). He subsequently scored six other films for Bellocchio, including *Marcia trionfale* (*Victory March*, 1976) and *Salto nel vuoto* (*Leap into the Void*, 1980) while also working regularly on the films of **Mario Monicelli** and **Nanni Moretti**, his scores for Moretti's *Caro diario* (*Dear Diary*, 1993) and *La stanza del figlio* (*The Son's Room*, 2001) both receiving the **David di Donatello**. Piovani also collaborated extensively with **Paolo and Vittorio Taviani**, creating the haunting soundtracks of all the Tavianis' films from *La notte di San Lorenzo* (*Night of the Shooting Stars*, 1982) to *Tu ridi* (*You're Laughing*, 1998), and proved to be a worthy successor to **Nino Rota** in providing the music for Fellini's *Ginger e Fred* (*Ginger and Fred*, 1986), *Intervista* (*Fellini's Intervista*, 1987), and *La voce della luna* (*The Voice of the Moon*, 1990).

He has also worked with a host of foreign directors including Dusan Makavejev, Bigas Luna, and Ben Verbong. In addition to film music he has written songs, chamber music, musical comedy, and ballet and orchestra suites and has also been prolific in music for theatrical productions. In 1991, together with writer **Vincenzo Cerami**,

Piovani founded the musical theater company La Compagnia della Luna (The Company of the Moon), which has continued to tour widely, performing his compositions. A recipient of numerous honors and prizes, his greatest triumph to date has been the Oscar he received for the score of **Roberto Benigni**'s *La vita è bella* (*Life Is Beautiful*, 1998).

PIRRO, UGO (1920–2008). Journalist, novelist, playwright, screenwriter. A respected and socially committed writer who continued to alternate between literature and cinema throughout his career, Pirro began in films with a collaboration on the story and screenplay of **Carlo Lizzani**'s *Achtung! Banditi!* (*Attention! Bandits!* 1951). He subsequently worked extensively with Lizzani, writing or cowriting six more films for him, including *Il gobbo* (*The Hunchback of Rome*, 1960), *Il processo di Verona* (*The Verona Trial*, 1963), and *Celluloide* (*Celluloid*, 1996), which he adapted from his own novel of the same name. At the same time he also worked with a host of other leading Italian directors, among them **Antonio Pietrangeli**, **Giuseppe De Santis**, **Luciano Emmer**, **Mauro Bolognini**, **Gillo Pontecorvo**, and **Luigi Comencini**. With his screenplay for *A ciascuno il suo* (*We Still Kill the Old Way*, 1967) he initiated a strong professional partnership with **Elio Petri**, for whom he wrote several more key films, including *Indagine su un cittadino al di sopra di ogni sospetto* (*Investigation of a Citizen Above Suspicion*, 1970), which was awarded the **Nastro d'argento** for best story as well as an Oscar nomination for best screenplay. In 1972 he received a second Oscar nomination for his work on the screenplay of Vittorio De Sica's *Il giardino dei Finzi-Contini* (*The Garden of the Finzi-Continis*, 1970).

He also worked with directors outside Italy, adapting his own novel *Jovanka e le altre* for Martin Ritt's *5 Branded Women* (1960) and helping to write Veljko Bulajic's epic war movie *Bitka na Neretvi* (*The Battle of the River Neretva*, 1969). After publishing the screenwriting manual *Per scrivere un film* in 1982, he gradually reduced his involvement in films in order to pursue his literary activities and in the late 1980s worked more regularly for television. He returned to writing for the big screen with his screenplay for Alessandro De Robilant's *Il giudice ragazzino* (*The Boy Judge*, 1994), a film about the young judge Rosario Livatino, murdered by the Sicilian Mafia in 1990.

In 2004, in recognition of his contribution to Italian cinema, Pirro was presented with the Vittorio De Sica Prize by the president of the Italian Republic.

PITTALUGA, STEFANO (1887–1931). Distributor, exhibitor, producer. Beginning in the period immediately prior to World War I as just one more entrepreneur jostling for a place in the sun of a booming Italian film industry, Pittaluga would go on to become the single most important figure in the development of the Italian cinema during the 1920s. Indeed, the very shape of the Italian film industry in the 1930s may have looked very different had the plans and projects carefully prepared by Pittaluga not been brought to an abrupt end by his untimely death in 1931.

Pittaluga first emerged in the industry in 1914 as an enterprising young film distributor holding exclusive rights over the Piemonte region for the films of several major Italian companies (Celio, **Cines**, **Milano Films**, and Aquila) as well as the French Pathé and other foreign companies. At the same time, showing a keen awareness of the importance of controlling exhibition, he acquired a number of cinemas in Genova. By 1920 he had a chain of over 200 theaters throughout northern and central Italy. His firm remained outside the **Unione Cinematografica Italiana** (UCI) and, by a clever policy of distribution of foreign films, especially American, continued to flourish even as the fortunes of most of the members of the UCI declined. In 1924 as many of the other companies either severely reduced their production or ceased it altogether, Pittaluga bought up Fert, a small company that had remained independent of the UCI, and began to produce a closely calculated number of films, including the last series of popular films featuring **Maciste** (*Maciste all'Inferno* [*Maciste in Hell*, 1926], *Maciste e il nipote d'America* [*Maciste and the Nephew from America*, 1926], *Maciste e lo sceicco* [*Maciste and the Sheik*], 1927), which, astutely, he had already presold abroad. In 1926, as the UCI was being liquidated, Pittaluga's company secured all of UCI's assets, including cinemas, distribution networks, and studios (including the Roman studios of the Cines), thus bringing under its control almost all that remained of the Italian film industry at that time. In 1927, with great foresight, he began to equip his theaters for sound and the Roman Cines studios with Photophone RCA sound recording equipment. The Pittaluga cinemas were consequently the first to screen *The Jazz Singer* in 1929, and the first Italian sound film, *La canzone dell'amore* (*The Love Song*, 1930), was made at the Rome Cines studios, which henceforth became the major center of film production in the country. By this stage, having achieved a significant degree of vertical integration, Pittaluga's company was beginning to approach the model of an American major. Also by this time, as the head of the industry in Italy, Pittaluga had begun to lobby the government for some real support for the industry, to which Mussolini assented and then effectively provided by means of a decree in 1930. Before the law was proclaimed in 1931, however, Pittaluga died, leaving a vacuum that would only begin to be filled several years later with the Fascist government's creation of a unified bureau for cinematography (Direzione Generale per la Cinematografia) under the headship of **Luigi Freddi**.

PLACIDO, MICHELE (1946–). Actor and director. After graduating from the Italian National Academy for Dramatic Art, Placido made his stage debut in Luca Ronconi's landmark production of *Orlando Furioso* in 1969. While continuing to work in the theater in the early 1970s, he also began appearing in films, one of his first notable roles being that of the young man recruited to the Mafia in the telefilm *Il piccioto* (*The Young Man*, 1973). He then appeared as **Ugo Tognazzi**'s handsome young rival in **Mario Monicelli**'s *Romanzo popolare* (*Come Home and Meet My Wife*, 1974) before playing the more demanding lead role in Marco Bellocchio's *Marcia trionfale* (*Victory March*, 1976), for which he received both a **Nastro d'argento** and a special **David di Donatello**. After strong performances in, among others, **Carlo Lizzani**'s *Fontamara* (1980) and **Francesco Rosi**'s *Tre fratelli* (*Three Brothers*, 1981), he became one of the best-recognized and most loved faces in Italy playing the part of Inspector Cattani in the popular and long-running television series on the Mafia, *La piovra* (*Octopus*, 1984–1989).

While providing powerful performances in socially committed films such as **Marco Risi**'s *Mery per sempre* (*Forever Mary*, 1983) and **Gianni Amelio**'s *Lamerica* (1994), he also made his own directorial debut in 1990 with *Pummarò* (Tomato, 1990), one of the first films to focus on the plight of clandestine immigrants in Italy. This was followed by *Le amiche del cuore* (*Close Friends*, 1992), which courageously tackled the difficult theme of incest, and *Un eroe borghese* (*Ordinary Hero*, 1995), a portrait of financial lawyer Giorgio Ambrosoli, who was killed in 1979 while investigating links between politics and organized crime in the so-called Sindona Affair. The film's expression of a strong sense of civic duty earned Placido a second special David di Donatello. After *Del perduto amore* (*Of Lost Love*, 1998) and *Un viaggio chiamato amore* (*A Journey Called Love*, 2002), the story of the tortured love affair between poet Dino Campana and writer Sibilla Aleramo, Placido directed what remains his most impressive work to date, *Romanzo criminale* (*Crime Novel*, 2005). A long but fast-paced gangster epic detailing the rise and fall of the notorious Magliana Gang in Rome in the 1970s, it won eight David di Donatello and seven Nastri d'argento as well as a nomination for the Berlin Golden Bear.

POGGIOLI, FERDINANDO MARIA (1897–1945). Director, editor, screenwriter. Having begun as an assistant editor at the newly revamped **Cines** studios, Poggioli soon contributed to the **documentary** series initiated by **Emilio Cecchi** with *Il presepio* (*The Nativity*, 1932) and *Paestum* (1932). At the same time he served as assistant director to **Baldassare Negroni** on the very popular *Due cuori felici* (*Two Happy Hearts*, 1932) and thereafter worked as editor on a number of films including Max Ophüls's *La signora di tutti* (*Everybody's Lady*, 1934).

Poggioli's first solo direction was *Arma bianca* (*Bayonet*, 1936), the adaptation of a play on the life of Giacomo Casanova by Alessandro De Stefani. This was followed three years later with *Ricchezza senza domani* (*Wealth without a Future*, 1939), which told the rather curious story of an industrialist who resolves his marital crisis by donating his factory to his workers. His third feature was *Addio giovinezza!* (*Farewell, Youth*, 1940), a lively but melancholic evocation of student life and first love in Turin in the early years of the 20th century, adapting a popular play by Sandro Camasio and Nino Oxilia that had already been filmed three times during the silent period. Poggioli's close attention to the formal qualities of the film's visual composition immediately placed him in the camp of the so-called calligraphers.

There followed *Sissignora* (*Yes, Madam*, 1941), *La morte civile* (*Civil Death*, 1942), and *La bisbettica domata*, an inventive adaptation of Shakespeare's *Taming of the Shrew* set in contemporary Rome. *Le sorelle Materassi* (*Materassi Sisters*, 1943), a fine adaptation of one of Aldo Palazzeschi's best-known novels, was followed by what many believe was Poggioli's most stylistically mature film, *Gelosia* (*Jealousy*, 1943), adapted from a novel by Luigi Capuana. His last film, *Il cappello da prete* (*The Priest's Hat*, 1944), a dark drama of murder and remorse also adapted from a 19th-century novel, was not shown until after the end of the war. By that time, what promised to be a most fruitful career had been unexpectedly brought to an end by Poggioli's tragic death in February 1945 in an accident involving gas. The field remains divided between those who claim it was a domestic accident and those who assert that it was willful suicide.

PONTECORVO, GILLO (1919–2006). Director. One of Italy's most politically committed filmmakers, Pontecorvo was born into a large and wealthy Jewish family in Pisa. He began studying chemistry at the local university but, following the proclamation of race laws in 1938, he went to Paris, where he took up journalism and cultivated an interest in photography. In 1941, having become a member of the Italian Communist Party (PCI), he returned to Italy to join the **Resistance** movement in northern Italy where, from 1943 to 1945, he was a commander in the Garibaldi brigade.

After the war he continued to work as an organizer and journalist for the PCI, but a viewing of **Roberto Rossellini**'s *Paisà* (*Paisan*, 1946) inspired him to take up cinema as a tool for political and social change. His first film experience was as third assistant and supporting actor in **Aldo Vergano**'s film on the Partisan movement, *Il sole sorge ancora* (*Outcry*, 1946). Having acquired his own camera in the early 1950s, he began making documentaries while continuing to work as assistant director for Yves Allégret and **Mario Monicelli**. In 1955 he initiated what would be a long and fruitful collaboration with Marxist screenwriter **Franco Solinas**, and together they made "Giovanna," the Italian segment of *Die Windrose* (*Rose of the Winds*, 1955), a five-episode international film exploring the position of women in postwar European society, coordinated by Dutch political filmmaker Joris Ivens. Continuing his partnership with Franco Solinas, in 1957 Pontecorvo made his first feature, *La grande strada azzura* (*The Wide Blue Road*), a French-Italian-German coproduction that starred Yves Montand and Alida Valli in an adaptation of Solinas's own novel, *Squarciò*. The story of a poor fisherman who refuses to join a cooperative but is eventually killed by his own unorthodox fishing methods, the film attempts to articulate serious sociopolitical themes but also often sinks into melodrama. (Mildly received at the time, it has been reissued in a restored print on DVD, thanks to the efforts of American filmmaker Jonathan Demme and actor Dustin Hoffman.) In 1959, again in collaboration with Solinas, Pontecorvo made *Kapò*, an Italo-French-Yugoslav production that tells the story of a Jewish girl in the Treblinka death camp forced to become an accomplice of the German guards. A very effective portrayal of the moral dilemma engendered by desperate circumstances, the film is, however, marred, as both Pontecorvo and Solinas themselves later admitted, by the unnecessary inclusion of a love interest at the end. Then followed what is generally regarded as Pontecorvo's greatest film and an undisputed masterwork, *La battaglia di Algeri* (*The Battle of Algiers*, 1966). Filmed on location with nonprofessional actors in a harsh black and white that has all the look of an actual newsreel, the film was a stunningly realistic and largely unbiaised portrayal of the last stages of the Algerian liberation struggle. It received immediate worldwide acclaim, being nominated for the Academy Awards for Best Foreign Film and Best Screenplay, and winning the Golden Lion at Venice and a **Nastro d'argento**. In France, however, it was regarded as too controversial, and not screened publicly until 1971. Pontecorvo (and Solinas) continued to explore the anticolonial theme in *Queimada* (*Burn!* 1969), which starred Marlon Brando and included a stirring soundtrack by **Ennio Morricone**. It was not until a decade later that Pontecorvo directed *Operazione Ogro* (*The Tunnel*, 1980), a film set in Spain and dealing with the assassination of the right-wing Spanish prime minister, Luis Carrero Blanco, by the Basque terrorist group ETA.

Pontecorvo's subsequent cinematic production consisted mostly of shorts and documentaries, among which his *Ritorno ad Algeri* (*Return to Algiers*, 1992), a **documentary** feature commissioned by the Italian RAI television network that allowed him to revisit the country whose struggle for liberation he had documented almost 30 years earlier. It was, he concluded, a very changed country. Pontecorvo's strongest contribution to Italian cinema in subsequent years was his active guidance of the **Venice Festival** in the 1990s.

PONTI, CARLO (1913–2007). Producer. A law graduate from the University of Milan, Ponti practiced as a lawyer before being attracted into the film industry in the early 1940s, his earliest productions being **Mario Soldati**'s *Piccolo mondo antico* (*Old-Fashioned World*, 1941) and **Alberto Lattuada**'s *Giacomo l'idealista* (*Giacomo the Idealist*, 1943). After World War II he worked as an executive producer for **Lux Film** on over a dozen films, among them **Luigi Zampa**'s *Vivere in pace* (*To Live in Peace*, 1946) and Lattuada's *Il mulino del Po* (*The Mill on the Po*, 1948), before leaving in 1950 to join **Dino De Laurentiis** in setting up the Ponti-De Laurentiis company with which, for the next seven years, he produced a host of important films, including **Roberto Rossellini**'s *Europa 51* (*The Greatest Love*, 1951), **Mario Camerini**'s *Ulisse* (*Ulysses*, 1954), **Vittorio De Sica**'s *L'oro di Napoli* (*The Gold of Naples*, 1954), and **Federico Fellini**'s *La strada* (1954). After producing King Vidor's monumental *War and Peace* (1956), the company was dissolved and, due in part to legal problems relating to his Mexican marriage to **Sophia Loren**, Ponti moved to France, where he nevertheless produced some of De Sica's most important films of the 1960s, including *La ciociara* (*Two Women*, 1960), *Ieri, oggi, domani* (*Yesterday, Today and Tomorrow*, 1953), and *Matrimonio all'Italiana* (*Marriage Italian Style*, 1964). At the same time he also lent support to the emerging French New Wave by producing, among others, Jean-Luc Godard's *Une femme est un femme* (*A Woman Is a Woman*, 1961), Agnès Varda's *Cléo de 5 à 7* (*Cleo from 5 to 7*, 1961), and Claude Chabrol's *L'oeil du malin* (*The Third Lover*, 1962). In 1965 he scored one of his greatest critical and box office successes with David Lean's *Dr. Zhivago* (1965), for which he received the Academy Award nomination for Best Picture. Among the most notable of his subsequent productions were **Michelangelo Antonioni**'s first three international films, *Blowup* (*Blow-Up*, 1966), *Zabriskie Point* (1970), and *Profession reporter* (*The Passenger*, 1974), and **Ettore Scola**'s *Una giornata particolare* (*A Special Day*, 1977), which received both the César award and the Golden Globe for Best Foreign Film.

More often remembered as the husband of Sophia Loren than as a major figure in the international film industry, Ponti produced over 140 films in an illustrious career that spanned six decades and which was recognized with a Lifetime Achievement Award at the Milan International Film Festival in 2000.

PONZI, MAURIZIO (1939–). Film critic, director, screenwriter. After working as a film critic and regular writer for journals such as *Filmcritica* and *Cinema 60*, Ponzi graduated to making documentaries for the *Corona Cinematografica* company in the mid-1960s before serving as assistant director to **Pier Paolo Pasolini** on his episode of the omnibus film, *Amore e rabbia* (*Love and Anger*, 1967). A year later Ponzi wrote and directed his first feature, *I visionari* (*The Visionaries*, 1968), a film inspired by the writings of Robert Musil that was awarded the Golden Leopard at the Locarno Film Festival. This was followed by *Equinozio* (Equinox, 1971), an adaptation of a futuristic novel by Anna Banti, and *Il caso Raoul* (*The House of Raoul*, 1975), based on a clinical case study from R. D. Laing's *Self and Others*. Ponzi then worked for a number of years in television, where he directed, among other things, a version of Henrik Ibsen's 19th-century play *Hedda Gabler*, and a **documentary** on **Cinecittà**. He returned to the big screen in the early 1980s with a series of light comedies featuring ex–cabaret actor (and future director) **Francesco Nuti**: *Madonna che silenzio c'è stasera* (What a Ghostly Silence There Is Tonight, 1982), *Io, Chiara e lo Scuro* (*The Pool Hustlers*, 1982), and *Son contento* (I'm Happy, 1983). These were followed by the family melodrama *Qualcosa di biondo* (*Aurora by Night*, 1984), which marked **Sophia Loren**'s return to the screen after a significant absence; *Il Volpone* (*The Big Fox*, 1988), loosely based on Ben Jonson's caustic 17th-century comedy; and *Volevo i pantaloni* (*I Wanted Trousers*, 1990), the adaptation of a best-selling novel by Lara Cardella that denounced the continuing oppression of women in southern Italian families. After the porn-movie spoof *Vietato ai minori* (*Forbidden to Minors*, 1992), and the more sociologically inspired *Italiani* (Italians, 1996), Ponzi's most recent effort was *A luci spente* (With Lights Out, 2004), a film about the making of a film during the last years of World War II that fictionally re-creates the events surrounding **Vittorio De Sica**'s direction of *La porta del cielo* (*The Gate of Heaven*) in 1944.

PUCCINI, GIANNI (1914–1968). Critic, screenwriter, director. A film critic who contributed frequently to specialized journals such as *Bianco e nero* and *Cinema*, Puccini distinguished himself in his collaboration on the screenplay of **Luchino Visconti**'s landmark *Ossessione* (*Obsession*, 1943). After the war he worked closely with **Giuseppe De Santis**, helping to write the screenplays of all of De Santis's early films as well as serving as assistant director on *Riso amaro* (*Bitter Rice*, 1949) and *Non c'è pace tra gli ulivi* (*Under the Olive Tree*, 1950). In the late 1950s Puccini codirected two witty comedies, *Parole di ladro* (*Honor Among Thieves*, 1957) and *Il marito* (The Husband, 1958) with **Nanni Loy**, before directing his first major solo feature, *L'impiegato* (*The Employee*, 1959), another clever comedy with which he also helped to launch the film career of **Nino Manfredi**. Of the dozen subsequent films that Puccini directed or codirected before his untimely death, the best remembered is undoubtedly *I sette fratelli Cervi* (*The Seven Cervi Brothers*, 1967), a recounting of the last days of a family of seven brothers who were all summarily executed by Fascists in December 1943 for taking part in the **Resistance** movement.

– R –

RALLI, GIOVANNA (1935–). Actress. Ralli began acting in films from a very young age, one of her earliest appearances being a walk-on part in **Vittorio De Sica**'s *I bambini ci guardano* (*The Children Are Watching Us*, 1943). After the war she became popular playing roles such as Marcella, the daughter, in **Aldo Fabrizi**'s *La famiglia Passaguai* (*The Passaguai Family*, 1951) and the daughter in **Mario Monicelli**'s *Un eroe dei nostri tempi* (*A Hero of Our Times*, 1955).

Ralli was one of the girls in **Valerio Zurlini**'s *Le ragazze di San Frediano* (*The Girls of San Frediano*, 1955) and then appeared in several films by **Roberto Rossellini**: as Valeria in *Il Generale della Rovere* (*General della Rovere*, 1959), Esperia in *Era notte a Roma* (*Escape by Night*, 1960), and Rosa in *Viva l'Italia* (*Garibaldi*, 1961). After taking the lead role in **Carmine Gallone**'s modern adaptation of the Bizet opera, *Carmen di Trastevere* (*Carmen in Trastevere*, 1963), she received a **Nastro d'argento** for her interpretation of Piera in Paolo Spinola's *La fuga* (*The Escape*, 1964). She played

Anna, a left-wing journalist, in **Carlo Lizzani**'s *La vita agra* (The Bitter Life, 1966) and was in a number of police thrillers before appearing in a key supporting role in **Ettore Scola**'s *C'eravamo tanto amati* (*We All Loved Each Other So Much*, 1974), which earned her another Nastro d'argento. In the late 1970s she tended to appear in light comedies such as *Languidi baci, perfide carezze* (*Languid Kisses, Wet Caresses*, 1976). After a fallow period in the 1980s she returned to the big screen in **Francesca Archibugi**'s *Verso sera* (*Towards Evening*, 1990). In the late 1990s she appeared in a number of popular television series before giving a credible performance as an aging Roman matriarch in **Carlo Vanzina**'s *Il pranzo della domenica* (*Sunday Lunch*, 2003).

RESISTANCE. Movement. The political and military resistance to Fascism and to the Nazi occupying forces that took place in Italy after September 1943 understandably featured prominently in many of the films of the immediate postwar period, beginning with the two films that remained the classic model for representations of the Resistance, **Roberto Rossellini**'s *Roma città aperta* (*Rome Open City*, 1945) and *Paisà* (*Paisan*, 1946). The Resistance, presented as a heroic struggle between good and evil, was also naturally the focus of a number of films produced by the Associazione Nazionale Partigiani d'Italia (ANPI, National Partisan Association), among them *Giorni di gloria* (*Days of Glory*, 1945), a semidocumentary using largely stock footage and produced collaboratively by **Mario Serandrei**, **Giuseppe De Santis**, **Luchino Visconti**, and others, Aldo Vergano's *Il sole sorge ancora* (*Outcry*, 1946), Giulio Ferroni's *Pian delle Stelle* (1946), and Giuseppe De Santis's *Caccia Tragica* (*Tragic Hunt*, 1947). The Resistance, seen as a moral imperative, was also at the center of **Mario Camerini**'s *Due lettere anonime* (*Two Anonymous Letters*, 1945), **Alessandro Blasetti**'s *Un giorno nella vita* (A Day in the Life, 1946), **Carmine Gallone**'s *Avanti a lui tremava tutta Roma* (*Before Him All Rome Trembled*, 1946), and Giacomo Gentilomo's *'O sole mio* (My Sun, 1946).

However, in the wake of the official hostility shown by the center-right authorities toward films such as **Carlo Lizzani**'s *Achtung! Banditi!* (*Achtung! Bandits!* 1951), which attempted to present the Resistance as an aspect of a more generalized class struggle in Italy, the theme of the Resistance largely disappeared from Italian screens for almost a decade. It returned in force at the end of the 1950s in Rossellini's *Il Generale della Rovere* (*General della Rovere*, 1959) and *Era notte a Roma* (*Escape by Night*, 1960) and continued to appear insistently in the following years in a host of films, among them Lizzani's *Il gobbo* (*The Hunchback of Rome*, 1960), **Nanni Loy**'s *Le quattro giornate di Napoli* (*The Four Days of Naples*, 1962), Gianfranco De Bosio's *Il Terrorista* (The Terrorist, 1963), **Luigi Comencini**'s *La ragazza di Bube* (*Bebo's Girl*, 1963), and **Gianni Puccini**'s *I sette fratelli Cervi* (*The Seven Cervi Brothers*, 1968). At the beginning of the 1970s **Bernardo Bertolucci**'s *La strategia del ragno* (*The Spider's Stratagem*, 1970) utilized the Resistance as the stage for a psychoanalytical search for the father, whereas two years later **Marco Leto**'s *La villeggiatura* (*Black Holiday*, 1972) sought to analyze it historically as a struggle against a much more deeply rooted authoritarianism in the Italian political system. The Resistance continued to feature prominently in many films made during the 1970s, among them **Ettore Scola**'s *C'eraramo tanto amati* (*We All Loved Each Other So Much*, 1974), **Francesco Maselli**'s *Il sospetto* (*The Suspect*, 1974), and **Valentino Orsini**'s *Uomini e no* (*Men or Not Men*, 1980), which adapted the classic neorealist Resistance novel by Elio Vittorini. **Mauro Bolognini**'s *Libera, amore mio* (*Libera, My Love,* 1975) and **Giuliano Montaldo**'s *L'Agnese va a morire* (*And Agnes Chose to Die*, 1976) were two of a very small number of films that attempted to portray the Resistance from a female point of view. At the beginning of the 1980s, before fading from sight again for a number of years, the Resistance was given its most poetic and mythical inflection in **Paolo and Vittorio Taviani**'s *La notte di San Lorenzo* (*Night of the Shooting Stars*, 1982).

After being absent from Italian screens for another decade, the Resistance returned in passing in one episode of the Tavianis' generational chronicle *Fiorile* (*Wild Flower*, 1993). By this time, however, there had also developed a historically revisionist reading of the Resistance itself, and the darker side of the movement and its aftermath became the focus for Guido Chiesa's *Il caso Martello* (The Martello Case, 1992) and Massimo Gugliemi's *Gangsters* (1992). Five years later Renzo Martinelli's *Porzus* (1997) portrayed one of the most disturbing episodes of the entire Resistance movement when, in February

1945, a large group of Communist partisans massacred 22 members of the rival Catholic-inspired Osoppo Brigade outside a small village in northern Italy, close to the Yugoslav border. Although the film appeared to be based on firm historical evidence, its depiction of the Resistance was controversial and highly contested. The more traditional interpretation of the Resistance as the heroic struggle for freedom from tyranny returned in **Daniele Luchetti**'s *I piccoli maestri* (*Little Teachers*, 1998), which recounts the story of a number of idealistic university students who follow their professor into the hills in order to fight for a just cause. A heroic view of the Resistance also grounds Guido Chiesa's recent adaptation of Beppe Fenoglio's classic Resistance novel, *Il Partigiano Johnny* (*Johnny the Partisan*, 2000).

RIGHELLI, GENNARO (1886–1949). Director and scriptwriter. After some experience of acting on the Neapolitan stage, Righelli joined the **Cines** studios as a scriptwriter in 1909 and by 1911 had graduated to directing. Soon thereafter he moved to Naples, where for the next decade he directed some 30 films, mostly for the Vesuvio Film Company, many of which featured his wife, diva Maria Jacobini. Best remembered from this period are *L'Innamorata* (*The Woman in Love*, 1920), the story of a dark brooding vamp that was censored for what was regarded as its excessive sensuality, and *Cainà, l'isola e il continente* (*Cainà: The Island and the Mainland*, 1921), a film shot on location in Sardinia.

In the wake of the crisis in the Italian film industry in the early 1920s, Righelli and Jacobini moved to Germany, where he directed some 15 features, including an adaptation of Stendhal's *Le Rouge et le noir* (The Red and the Black, 1928) and *Der Bastard* (*The Bastard*, 1926), a weepy but impressive melodrama in which an unwed mother relentlessly pursues the father of her child literally around the globe. In 1929 Righelli returned to Italy to direct *La canzone dell'amore* (*The Song of Love*, 1930), the first Italian sound film made at the newly restored Cines studios. Another heartstring-tugging melodrama, loosely based on a short story by Luigi Pirandello, the film was shot simultaneously in several different languages. The Italian version achieved an immediate if short-lived popularity, not least for the catchy song "Solo per tu Lucia" ("Only for You, Lucia"), especially composed for the film by Cesare Andrea Bixio.

Among Righelli's many subsequent sound films were Italy's first aviation feature, *L'armata azzurra* (*The Blue Fleet*, 1932), and a number of light comedies that employed the talents of famed Sicilian stage actor Angelo Musco, the best of these being *Pensaci Giacomino* (*Think It Over, Jack*, 1937), adapted from a play by Pirandello.

Righelli's flood of productivity reduced to a trickle after the war. *Abbasso la miseria* (*Down with Misery*, 1945) was followed by *Abbasso la ricchezza* (*Peddlin' in Society*, 1946), both starring **Anna Magnani** in fairly lightweight comic roles. His last film, *Il corriere del re* (*The King's Courier*, 1947), was another adaptation of Stendhal's *The Red and the Black*.

RISI, DINO (1916–2008). Screenwriter, director. The foremost director of that biting social satire that came to be known as ***commedia all'italiana***, Risi (brother of poet and director **Nelo Risi** and father of **Marco Risi**) originally trained as a doctor and specialized in psychiatry but soon abandoned medicine in order to work in the cinema. He served his first apprenticeship as assistant to **Mario Soldati** on *Piccolo mondo antico* (*Old-Fashioned World*, 1941) and to **Alberto Lattuada** on *Giacomo l'idealista* (*Giacomo the Idealist*, 1943). After spending the final years of World War II in Switzerland, where he was able to study with veteran French director Jaques Feyder, Risi returned to Italy in the immediate postwar period to work as a film critic and **documentary** filmmaker. Then, after having also honed his screenwriting skills by collaborating on the scripts of Lattuada's *Anna* (1951) and **Mario Camerini**'s *Gli eroi della domenica* (*Sunday Heroes*, 1952), he directed his first fictional feature, *Vacanze col gangster* (*Vacation with a Gangster*, 1952). There followed a number of other light comedies and an episode made for the compilation film *L'Amore in città* (*Love in the City*, 1953), before he scored his first big commercial success with *Pane, amore e . . .* (*Scandal in Sorrento*, 1955), the third in the series of what had been the hugely popular *Bread and Love* films directed by **Luigi Comencini**. A year later he achieved even greater box office success with *Poveri ma belli* (*Poor, but Handsome*, 1956), a lively and lighthearted romp through the lives and complicated loves of a group of young people in Rome, which was soon followed by its similarly successful sequel, *Belle ma povere* (*Pretty but Poor*, 1957), both the highest-grossing films in Italy in their respective years.

Then, beginning with *Il vedovo* (The Widower, 1959) and continuing through the next decade with *Una vita difficile* (*A Difficult Life*,
1961), *Il sorpasso* (*The Easy Life*, 1962), *I mostri* (The Monsters,
1963, but known in the United States as *15 from Rome*), *Il gaucho*
(*The Gaucho*, 1964), *Il tigre* (*The Tiger and the Pussycat*, 1967), and
Il profeta (*The Prophet*, 1968)—always working with the same team
of screenwriters and utilizing a regular group of comic actors (**Alberto Sordi**, **Ugo Tognazzi**, **Nino Manfredi**, and **Vittorio
Gassman**)—Risi produced a series of mordant social comedies that
bitingly satirized, frequently to the point of caricature, the changing
mores of Italian society as it raced ruthlessly toward affluence on the
back of the so-called economic miracle. Underscoring the serious-
ness of the moral intent beneath the caricature, Risi's comedies often
included tragic deaths, as in *Il vedovo* where, in an attempt to elimi-
nate his rich wife, the financially strapped businessman played by Alberto Sordi actually engineers his own death, or the abrupt and unexpected death of the young coprotagonist in the car accident at the
close of *Il sorpasso*. However, in spite of their extraordinary popularity, Risi's caustic comedies of manners continued to be severely
undervalued by critics, who judged them as mere excercises in commercial cinema, at least until the mid-1970s when *Profumo di donna*
(*Scent of a Woman*, 1974) achieved international recognition, receiving two Oscar nominations in the United States and the César award
for Best Foreign Film in France, and at home two **David di Donatello** awards and the **Nastro d'argento**.

By this time, Risi had begun to extend both the range and depth of
his comic vision to include an exploration of issues such as the
celibacy of priests in *La moglie del prete* (*The Priest's Wife*, 1970),
judicial privileges and the law in *In nome del popolo italiano* (*In the
Name of the Italian People*, 1971), and political terrorism in *Mordi e
fuggi* (*Dirty Weekend*, 1973). Indeed, as the 1970s wore on, while not
foregoing satirical comedy, Risi moved into more dramatic territory
with an effective reworking of a familiar horror motif in *Anima persa*
(*Lost Soul*, 1976) and an elegant playing out of the classic murder
mystery formula in *La stanza del vescovo* (*The Bishop's Bedroom*,
1977). Nevertheless, after a valiant—and largely successful—attempt to reprise some of the fierce social satire of the original *I mostri*
in *I nuovi mostri* (*The New Monsters*, 1977), directed collaboratively

with **Ettore Scola** and **Mario Monicelli**, and another interesting engagement with the theme of political terrorism in *Caro papà* (*Dear Papa*, 1979), Risi's formerly prolific production fell away to a trickle during the 1980s and, with the possible exception of the moving portrait of old age and mental illness in *Tolgo il disturbo* (*I'll Be Going Now*, 1990), never quite regained its former brilliance.

Nevertheless, in 1993 Risi was honored at the Cannes Film Festival with a retrospective of 15 of his most significant films, and at the **Venice Festival** in 2002 he was presented with the Golden Lion for lifetime achievement. In 2004, in recognition of his services to Italian culture, he was also made a Knight of the Great Cross.

RISI, MARCO (1951–). Director, producer, screenwriter. Son of veteran director **Dino Risi**, Marco began his apprenticeship in the cinema as an assistant to his uncle, **Nelo Risi**, on *Una stagione all'inferno* (*A Season in Hell*, 1970). After further experience as second unit director on Duccio Tessari's *Zorro* (1975) and *La madama* (*Cops*, 1976), Risi directed *Appunti su Hollywood* (Notes on Hollywood, 1978), a four-episode television **documentary** on American cinema. He subsequently cowrote the screenplays for *Caro papà* (*Dear Papa*, 1979) and *Sono fotogenico* (*I'm Photogenic*, 1980), both directed by his father, before making his own feature directorial debut with *Vado a vivere da solo* (*I'm Going to Live by Myself*, 1981). After making several other only moderately successful light comedies, he embarked on a series of more socially committed films, beginning with *Soldati, 365 giorni all'alba* (Soldiers, 1987). *Mery per sempre* (*Forever Mary*, 1989), set in a Sicilian reform school for young criminals, won the Special Jury Prize at Cannes, and its sequel, *Ragazzi fuori* (*Boys on the Outside*, 1990), earned Risi the **David di Donatello** for best direction in 1991. In the same year his *Muro di gomma* (*The Invisible Wall*, 1991), an investigative feature on the Ustica air disaster of 1980, was nominated for the Golden Lion at the **Venice Festival**.

In 1992, together with Maurizio Tedesco, he founded the production company Sorpasso Film, with which he financed not only his own films but also the debut films of a number of emerging younger directors, including **Ferzan Ozpetek**'s *Hamam, il bagno turco* (*Steam: The Turkish Baths*, 1997), for which he shared the **Nastro**

d'argento as best producer. Among his subsequent films were *Il branco* (The Pack, 1994), a disturbing film about gang rape; *L'ultimo capodanno* (*Humanity's Last New Year's Eve*, 1998), a grotesque social farce mixing elements of the ***commedia all'italiana*** with American pulp fiction; and *Tre mogli* (*Three Wives*, 2001), a female road movie through South America. Most recently he has directed *Maradona, la mano di Dio* (*Maradona, The Hand of God,* 2006), a celebratory but not uncritical biopic of the legendary soccer player.

RISI, NELO (1920–). Poet, screenwriter, director. Brother of director **Dino Risi** and cinematographer Fernando Risi, Nelo Risi trained as a doctor but never practiced medicine, preferring instead both literature—he came to be widely regarded as one of the leading poets in postwar Italy—and, like his brothers, the cinema.

After some particularly harrowing experiences during World War II, and while beginning to publish his first collections of poetry in the immediate postwar period, Risi assisted John Ferno and Richard Leacock to make their series of human-geography documentaries, filmed in several European countries and in the African Sahara. Returning to Italy in the mid-1950s, he embarked on his own series of documentaries, among them the strongly antifascist *Il delitto Matteotti* (*The Assassination of Matteotti*, 1956) and *I fratelli Rosselli* (*The Rosselli Brothers*, 1959). In 1961 he directed one of the episodes of **Cesare Zavattini**'s compilation film *Le italiane a l'amore* (*Latin Lovers*, 1962), which was followed by *La strada più lunga* (*The Longest Road*, 1965), a television film adaptation of a **Resistance** novel by Davide Lajolo. His first full-length feature for the big screen was *Andremo in città* (*We'll Go to the City*, 1966), a moving Holocaust narrative set and filmed in Yugoslavia. This was soon followed by what many regard as Risi's finest film, *Diario di una schizofrenica* (*Diary of a Schizophrenic Girl*, 1968), which was screened at the **Venice Festival** to wide acclaim. While consolidating his reputation as one of Italy's finest poets, Risi continued to make a number of well-received feature films, including *Ondata di calore* (*Dead of Summer*, 1970); *Una stagione all'inferno* (*A Season in Hell*, 1971), a fictional biography of the extraordinary French poet Arthur Rimbaud; and *La colonna infame* (*The Infamous Column*, 1973), an adaptation of the well-known historical chronicle by Alessandro Manzoni.

In the following years Risi tended to concentrate on his poetry, but he also continued to make a number of fine documentaries for television, among which was *Venezia tra oriente o occidente* (*Venice between East and West*, 1987). After a hiatus of some 15 years, he returned to directing for the big screen with *Un amore di donna* (*Love of a Woman*, 1988), which, however, was generally panned for its sentimentality. His reputation as a filmmaker was slightly restored by the last film he made for television, the mafia melodrama *Per odio, per amore* (For Hatred, For Love, 1990).

RISORGIMENTO. Italy's revolutionary movement for national unification, generally known as the Risorgimento, was one of Italian cinema's favorite themes from its very inception. Indeed, it is no exaggeration to say that Italian cinema was, quite literally, born under the sign of the Risorgimento, for what is historically regarded as the first Italian feature film, **Filoteo Alberini**'s *La presa di Roma* (*The Taking of Rome*, 1905), was nothing less than a grand, celebratory re-creation of the culminating event of the struggle for Italian independence and unity, which was the breaching of the Roman walls at Porta Pia by the armies of the House of Savoy and the subsequent annexation of papal Rome as the capital of a united Italy. Made with the material support of the Italian army, which supplied the men and the armaments, the film was first screened outdoors at the very place where the battle had taken place exactly 35 years earlier, its last and crowning *tableau vivant* explicitly characterizing the event as an apotheosis.

In the years that followed Alberini's foundational film, Italian silent cinema returned often to the Risorgimento, especially as exemplified in the figure of one of its most legendary protoganists, Giuseppe Garibaldi. Only two years after *La presa di Roma*, **Mario Caserini** directed *Garibaldi* (1907), a brief portrait of the Risorgimento hero, for the Roman **Cines** company. He soon followed this with *Anita Garibaldi* (1910), a similarly heroic portrait of Garibaldi's wife and fellow freedom fighter. A year later, having moved to Turin to work for **Ambrosio Film**, Caserini produced the even grander *I Mille* (*The Thousand*, 1911), one of the first Italian full-length features (40 minutes), which utilized hundreds of extras to re-create the exploits of Garibaldi's Redshirts. **Luigi Maggi**'s *Nozze d'oro*

(*Golden Wedding Anniversary*, 1911), similarly produced at the Ambrosio Film studios and winner of the first prize for a feature film awarded at the International Exhibition of Turin, also narrated the noble battles of the Risorgimento but this time in flashback, as the memories of an old *bersagliere* (light infantryman) recounted on his golden wedding anniversary. Maggi used this narrative stratagem again in a subsequent film he directed for Ambrosio, *La lampada della nonna* (*The Grandmother's Lamp*, 1913), where the birthday gift of an electric lamp prompts a grandmother to recount how things had been during her youth, when she had fallen in love with a young infantryman involved in the Risorgimento struggles.

With the beginning of World War I, what had been a national celebration of the Risorgimento now became nationalistic as a united Italy lined up against the old enemy, Austria. Consequently, a number of films made during this period, such as Augusto Jandolo's *Silvio Pellico* (1915) and *Brescia, leonessa d'Italia* (*Brescia, the Lioness of Italy*, 1915), sought to celebrate the bravery and courage of the specifically anti-Austrian struggles of patriots like Silvio Pellico and Tito Speri.

In the early years of the Fascist period, in addition to the continuing presence of a romantic fascination with the more heroic aspects of the movement, emblematized, as always, by Garibaldi and his redshirted volunteers, there was also an effort to suggest a historical continuity between the Risorgimento and Fascism in films such as Mario Volpe's *Il grido dell'aquila* (*The Cry of the Eagle*, 1923), Umberto Paradisi's *Un balilla del '48* (*A Young Freedom Fighter in 1848*, 1927), and Domenico Gaido's *I martiri d'Italia* (*The Martyrs of Italy*, 1927). A mixture of personal obsession and a pedagogical mission appears to have motivated Silvio Laurenti Rosa's series of films on the Risorgimento: *Dalle cinque giornate di Milano alla breccia di Porta Pia* (*From the Five Days of Milan to the Breaching of Porta Pia*, 1925), *Garibaldi e i suoi tempi* (*Garibaldi and His Times*, 1926), and another *I martiri d'Italia* (*The Martyrs of Italy*, 1928). Although, by all accounts, rather poor films, they attest to a continuing fascination with the movement during this period. **Carmine Gallone**'s *La cavalcata ardente* (*The Fiery Cavalcade*, 1925), one of the most interesting films of what was a low period in Italian cinema, was, for all its nationalistic fervor, largely a historical romance that used the Risorgimento as backdrop. However, in *1860* (1933), **Alessandro Blasetti** succeeded in creating a nationally popular historical epic that fused the private and the public, the personal and the political, in the moving story of a Sicilian shepherd who travels the length of Italy in order to join Garibaldi's forces and return with them to liberate his family, his village, and Sicily from Bourbon tyranny. While *1860* is generally regarded as perhaps the best film ever produced on the Risorgimento, and as something of a forerunner of **neorealism** in its realistic portrayal of the events, on-location shooting, and use of non-professional actors, it is significant that in its original ending, promptly excised after the war, Blasetti explictly reiterated the idea of a continuity between the Redshirts and the Blackshirts, between the nationalistic ideals of the Risorgimento and the ideology of Fascism.

The Risorgimento is again both the setting and theme of **Enrico Guazzoni**'s *Il dottor Antonio* (*Doctor Antonio*, 1937), the adaptation of a novel written in 1855 by revolutionary patriot Giovanni Ruffini (and already adapted several times during the silent period). **Mario Soldati**'s *Piccolo mondo antico* (*Old-Fashioned World*, 1941) returns to using the Risorgimento struggles largely as backdrop for a family melodrama while **Vittorio De Sica**'s *Un garibaldino al convento* (*A Garibaldian in the Convent*, 1942) again utilizes the narrative stratagem of an extended flashback to look back nostalgically on the Risorgimento as a romantic period filled with youthful hopes and idealistic dreams that, in the event, remained unrealized.

A fascination with the Risorgimento continued to animate quite a number of films made in the immediate postwar period. The Risorgimento returned as backdrop in films such as Duilio Coletti's *Cuore* (*Heart*, 1947), an adaptation of Edmondo De Amicis's classic 19th-century educational novel, and **Guido Brignone**'s *La sepolta viva* (*Buried Alive*, 1948). In 1949, to celebrate the centenary of one of the major episodes of the Risorgimento, the foundation of the ill-fated Roman Republic, Mario Costa directed *Cavalcata d'eroi* (*Cavalcade of Heroes*, released 1951). In 1952 **Goffredo Alessandrini**'s *Camicie rosse* (*Red Shirts*, but also known as *Anita Garibaldi*) again sought to celebrate the heroism of both Garibaldi, played by **Raf Vallone**, and his wife, Anita, played with a great deal of fire and passion by **Anna Magnani**. In the same year, however, **Piero Germi**'s *Il brigante della Tacca del Lupo* (*The Bandit of Tacca Del Lupo*, 1952) presented a decidedly less flattering view of the northern army as it attempted to reimpose law and order in the south during the period of unification. A year later, **Luchino Visconti**'s *Senso* (*The Wanton Countess*, 1954) set its story of love and betrayal within the historical context of one of the greatest Italian defeats of the Risorgimento, the routing of forces of the House of Savoy by the Austrians at the Battle of Custoza. To celebrate the centenary of Italy's official unification, **Roberto Rossellini** made *Viva l'Italia* (*Garibaldi*, 1961), a film that, in spite of Rossellini's neorealist heritage, ends up proposing, once again, a relatively hagiographic interpretation of the Risorgimento. Almost as a rejoinder, Visconti returned to the movement with *Il gattopardo* (*The Leopard*, 1963), a sumptuous, faithful adaptation of the novel by Giuseppe Tommaso Di Lampedusa which suggested that, for all the bluster, the Risorgimento would end up providing less a panacea for Italy's social and economic inequalities and more a continuation of its old ills. This more ambivalent attitude to the Risorgimento surfaces again strongly in **Paolo and Vittorio Taviani**'s *Allonsanfan* (1974), and the ostensibly liberating northern forces appear in an even more negative light in **Florestano Vancini**'s *Bronte, cronaca di un massacro che i libri di scuola non hanno raccontato* (*Liberty*, 1972, but more literally Bronte, a Massacre That the History Books Failed to Recount).

Subsequently, the more traditional heroic interpretation of the Risorgimento was again put forward in Luigi Magni's *In nome del papa re* (*In the Name of the Pope King*, 1977), which recounts the story of two of the last patriots to be executed for the cause of unification at the hands of the papal authorities in 1868, and repeated in Magni's subsequent films *Arrivano i bersaglieri* (Here Comes the Infantry, 1980), *'O re* (*The King of Naples*, 1989), *In nome del popolo sovrano* (*In the Name of the Sovereign People*, 1990), and *La carbonara* (*The Coal Woman*, 2000).

RIZZOLI, ANGELO (1889–1970). One of Italy's most successful publishers from the early part of the 20th century, Rizzoli moved into film in the mid-1930s, founding the Novella Film company, with which he produced Max Ophüls's *La signora di tutti* (*Everybody's Woman*, 1934) and **Vittorio De Sica**'s first film as director, *Rose scarlatte* (*Red Roses*, 1940).

In the immediate postwar period Rizzoli was involved extensively in both commercial and art house cinema and generously supported several neorealist films that lost money at the box office, including De Sica's *Umberto D* (1952) and **Roberto Rossellini**'s *Francesco, giullare di Dio* (*Francis, God's Jester*, 1950). He was rewarded, however, by the overwhelming commercial and critical success of two of **Federico Fellini**'s key films, *La dolce vita* (1960) and *Otto e mezzo* (*8½*, 1963).

ROMA CITTÀ APERTA **(1945).** (*Rome Open City*; also known as *Open City*.) Film. Universally acknowledged as the founding film of Italian **neorealism**, *Roma* was **Roberto Rossellini**'s fourth feature film but his first in the postwar period. Among the many myths that have grown up around this legendary film is the idea that Rossellini began shooting it secretly while Rome was still under German occupation. This is, however, merely a myth and Rossellini actually began shooting the film in January 1945, six months after Rome had been liberated by Allied troops.

Provisionally titled *Storie di ieri* (*Stories of Yesterday*), the film resulted from the merger of a number of different projects. These included a **documentary** on a priest who had been executed by the Germans for helping the **Resistance**, for which Rossellini had been commissioned by a pious Roman countess, and a feature on the black market that screenwriter **Sergio Amidei** had been sketching out for maverick producer **Giuseppe Amato**. As a Communist, Amidei objected to the idea of a Catholic priest's representing the entire Resistance and so firmly insisted on incorporating the parallel story of a Communist Resistance leader who is betrayed by his lover and consequently tortured to death by the Germans. Also to be included was a story reported in the newspapers about a Roman housewife and mother who had been killed by the Germans in front of her family for attempting to pass food to her arrested husband. All these strands were eventually merged to create the film's composite narrative, which then became the following: In German-occupied Rome in late 1944, Giorgio Manfredi (Marcello Pagliero), a Communist leader of the Resistance, is being hunted by the Gestapo and takes refuge at the apartment of his friend and fellow Resistance member Francesco (Francesco Grandjacquet). While waiting for his friend's return,

Giorgio meets Francesco's bride-to-be, Pina (**Anna Magnani**), a war widow and mother who, on Giorgio's request, sends her son, Marcello (Vito Annichiarico), to bring back the parish priest, Don Pietro Pellegrini (**Aldo Fabrizi**), who, unbeknownst to Pina and the others around her, also works for the Resistance by forging identity papers. We later learn that Pina's son, too, is part of a group of boys who carry out their own military actions against the occupying Germans.

Don Pietro arrives and agrees to take Giorgio's place in delivering a crucial sum of money to a group of waiting partisans on the outskirts of the city, and there is a short period of calm as everyone prepares for Francesco and Pina's wedding, which has been set for the following day. The next morning, however, as everyone is readying for the occasion, the Germans carry out a raid of the entire quarter and Giorgio, Francesco, and a number of other men are taken away in a truck. In what remains one of the most powerful sequences in the film, and perhaps one of the most indelible moments in film history, Pina desperately chases the vehicle while continually calling out Francesco's name but is abruptly cut down by machine-gun fire. The German convoy with the truck is attacked by partisans and Giorgio and Francesco manage to escape. However, not knowing that his lover, Marina (Maria Michi), has become a pawn of the Germans through her friendship with Major Bergmann's translator, Ingrid (Giovanna Galletti), and her dependence on the drugs that Ingrid procures for her from the major, Giorgio leads Francesco to an appointment with Marina at a restaurant, following which, having nowhere else to spend the night, they take up Marina's offer to sleep at her apartment. At one point in the evening, however, Giorgio and Marina have an argument, during which Giorgio breaks off their relationship. Marina is deeply resentful and, having overheard Giorgio's plans to leave Rome the next day after picking up false documents from Don Pietro, she communicates the information to Ingrid, with the result that on the following day Giorgio and Don Pietro are arrested as they leave the church grounds, with Francesco only narrowly escaping the ambush due to the extra time he has taken to say good-bye to Marcello. The rest of the film takes place at the Gestapo headquarters and is largely taken up with Giorgio's interrogation and torture by Major Bergmann. Heroically steadfast, Giorgio refuses to disclose any sources or contacts and dies under torture. Similarly interrogated by

Major Bergmann, Don Pietro also refuses to provide any information and is subsequently executed by a firing squad. As Don Pietro dies, Marcello and the group of boy partisans, who have been watching from a distance, whistle a defiant tune in unison before turning to walk back toward a city dominated by the dome of the Vatican. Although it has become traditional to praise the film for its quasi-documentary realism, its dependence on fairly conventional melodramatic stratagems is readily apparent. Nevertheless, it is undeniable that what Rossellini managed to create was a very different sort of film from anything that had been seen in Italy up to that time. Undoubtedly part of its immediate appeal was also the way in which it idealistically articulated the possibility of a popular alliance between Catholic and Marxist forces in a post-Fascist Italy, a possibility that was soon laid to rest only the following year with the forcible ejection of the Communist Party from the provisional government. Another oft-repeated myth that has grown up around this legendary film, one mischievously aided and abetted by Rossellini himself, is that it was poorly received when first released in Rome in September 1945. Reviews and newspaper reports suggest the contrary, with the film widely hailed by critics and public alike as a major cinematic achievement and a new beginning for the Italian cinema. The film was seen by almost 3 million Italians in its first four months of screening and became the highest-grossing Italian film of the 1945–1946 season. Its overwhelming national success was repeated abroad, with the film screening for two consecutive years in New York and winning, among others, the New York Film Critics Award, two awards from the National Board of Review, and an Oscar nomination. Shown at Cannes in 1946, the film also won the Grand Festival Prize.

Justifiably regarded as a milestone in both Italian and world cinema, the film, and all the drama that went into its making, was fictionally revisited in **Carlo Lizzani**'s *Celluloide* (*Celluloid*, 1995).

ROSI, FRANCESCO (1922–). Director and screenwriter. After abandoning law studies at university, undertaken only to please his father, and following various unsuccessful attempts at making a living as an illustrator of children's books and a vaudeville actor, Rosi began his film career in earnest as assistant to **Luchino Visconti** on *La terra* *trema* (*The Earth Trembles*, 1948). A year later, when the film had failed dismally at the box office, in part because the authentic Sicilian dialect spoken by the nonprofessional actors was incomprehensible to general Italian audiences, Rosi was given the task of supervising the dubbing of the original film into standard Italian. Having acquitted himself well in the task, he served a further apprenticeship assisting **Raffaele Matarazzo** on two of the latter's most successful melodramas and **Luciano Emmer** on *Domenica d'agosto* (*Sunday in August*, 1950) and *Parigi è sempre Parigi* (*Paris Is Always Paris*, 1951) before returning to work with Visconti again on *Bellissima* (1951). His reputation as an assistant director now well established, he was called to work with **Michelangelo Antonioni** on *I vinti* (*The Vanquished*, 1952) and to complete *Camicie rosse* (*Anita Garibaldi*, 1952) after **Goffredo Alessandrini** had abandoned the project, while at same time writing the story for **Luigi Zampa**'s *Processo alla città* (*The City Stands Trial*, 1952).

After further work as assistant director, screenwriter, and dubber, and having also produced a number of radio plays, he finally directed his first solo feature, *La sfida* (*The Challenge*, 1958). The gritty story of a young tough trying to wrest control of the Neapolitan fruit market from an already-established underworld network, the film was awarded the Special Jury Prize at the **Venice Festival** and a **Nastro d'argento** for Best Original Story. While Rosi's next film, *I magliari* (*The Magliari*, 1959), the story of a group of Italian immigrant workers in Germany in the immediate postwar period, elicited a less-enthusiastic critical reception, *Salvatore Giuliano* (1962), a meticulous fictional reconstruction of the death of the famous Sicilian bandit that brought to the surface all the inadequacies of the official version of events, confirmed Rosi as one of the foremost directors of his generation. Stunningly photographed by **Gianni Di Venanzo**, the film received a host of prizes including the Silver Lion at Berlin. What would become Rosi's characteristic tendency to use cinema to analyze the complex interplay between legal and illegal power networks within social processes again came to the fore in *Le mani sulla città* (*Hands Over the City*, 1963), a brilliant close study of rampant real estate speculation in Naples, which again received a host of tributes, including the Golden Lion at Venice.

After *Il momento della verità* (*The Moment of Truth*, 1965), the portrait of a young man's ill-fated move from the country to the city in search of fame and fortune, set and filmed completely in Spain, and the rather uncharacteristic romantic fable, *C'era una volta* (*More Than a Miracle*, 1967), Rosi returned to a cinema of strong social commitment with *Uomini contro* (*Many Wars Ago*, 1970), a film that deconstructed all the heroic myths regarding Italian participation in World War I. This was followed by another series of major and highly acclaimed films beginning with *Il caso Mattei* (*The Mattei Affair*, 1972), another inquest film, this time into the "accidental" death in the early 1960s of Italian entrepreneur Enrico Mattei; *Lucky Luciano* (1974), a portrait of the Italian American gangster that highlighted the way in which he was as much a tool of greater powers as a crime boss in his own right; and *Cadaveri eccellenti* (*Illustrious Corpses*, 1976), adapted from a speculative novel by Leonardo Sciascia in which a policeman, investigating what on the surface appears to be the revenge killing of a number of judges, comes to find himself enmeshed in a much more complex web of governmental and political machinations.

Rosi's next film, originally made as a four-part television miniseries, was a sensitive and effective adaptation of Carlo Levi's landmark novel about southern Italy, *Cristo si è fermato a Eboli* (*Christ Stopped at Eboli*, 1979). This was followed by a perfect blending of the personal and the political in *Tre fratelli* (*Three Brothers*, 1981), an elegiac but unsentimental examination of Italian society at the beginning of the 1980s that was acclaimed not only in Italy, where it won three Silver Ribbons and four **David di Donatello**, but also abroad, where it was nominated for an Oscar and received the Boston Society of Film Critics award for Best Foreign Film. Less directly political perhaps than Rosi's previous films but nevertheless an electrifying adaptation of Bizet's opera, *Carmen* (1984) was again swamped with prizes and awards, winning no less than seven Davids in Italy, a César in France, and a Golden Globe in the United States. Following a fine adaptation of Gabriel García Márquez's novel, *Cronaca di una morte annunciata* (*Chronicle of a Death Foretold*, 1987), Rosi attempted a return to his more socially committed cinema in the early 1990s with *Dimenticare Palermo* (*The Palermo Connection*, 1990).

Although coscripted by Gore Vidal, the film was generally judged to be less successful in laying bare licit and illicit power networks than many of his earlier films. In the wake of his disappointment at the reception of *Palermo*, he directed only one other major film, a very creditable adaptation of Primo Levi's Holocaust-survivor memoir, *La Tregua* (*The Truce*, 1997).

ROSSELLINI, RENZO (1908–1982). Composer. Younger brother of director **Roberto Rossellini**, Renzo showed an early propensity for musical composition, publishing his first opera with the noted musical firm Ricordi at the age of only 16. After completing his studies at the Conservatory of Santa Cecilia, he became director of the Liceo Musicale at Varese and between 1940 and 1942 taught composition at the Pesaro Conservatory. He began composing for films in the mid-1930s, his first scores being for **Guido Brignone**'s *L'antenato* (*The Ancestor*, 1936) and **Mario Camerini**'s *Il Signor Max* (*Mister Max*, 1937). He wrote the music for another dozen films, including **Vittorio De Sica**'s *Rose scarlatte* (*Red Roses*, 1940), *Maddalena zero in condotta* (*Maddalena, Zero for Conduct*, 1940), and *Teresa Venerdì* (*Mademoiselle Friday*, 1941), before scoring his brother's first feature film, *La nave bianca* (*The White Ship*, 1941). He supplied the background music for all of his brother's subsequent films, up to and including *Vanina Vanini* (1961), and was awarded the **Nastro d'argento** for his score for *Paisà* (*Paisan*, 1947). In 1948 he won his second Nastro d'argento for his music for Giacomo Gentilomo's *I fratelli Karamazoff* (*The Brothers Karamazov*, 1947). Rossellini retired from composing for the cinema in the early 1960s, although, due to a curious set of circumstances, he did contribute some music to one of the several versions of **Tinto Brass**'s *Caligola* (*Caligula*, 1979).

ROSSELLINI, ROBERTO (1906–1977). Director and screenwriter. Universally acknowledged as the father of Italian **neorealism**, Rossellini was born into a wealthy family and a privileged environment. His father was a successful builder-architect with a love of music and a published writer, and the family home was a place of encounter for many local artists and intellectuals. Among the many buildings that Rossellini's father built in Rome was the Corso cinema and it was here that the young Roberto, thanks to a permanent pass provided by his father, was able to watch a multitude of films and to develop a particular love of American cinema.

He had an easy upbringing, avoiding school and doing largely whatever he pleased, which included driving fast cars and chasing women. His extensive womanizing, in fact, led to an early marriage with actress **Assia Noris**, although the marriage was soon annulled. Rossellini would then marry Marcella De Marchis, with whom he would have two sons, but he would also carry on myriad affairs with, among others, **Anna Magnani** and Ingrid Bergman, who also bore him several children. But that was still to come.

In the early 1930s, with much of the family fortune dissipated and confronted with the necessity of finding a job, Rossellini began to work in the film industry, first as a dubbing assistant and then as an uncredited script editor. His first attempts at filmmaking began in 1936 when he made the first of what would be a handful of short animated nature fantasies, two of which, *Il tacchino prepotente* (*The Bullying Turkey*, 1939) and *La vispa Teresa* (*Lively Teresa*, 1939), would be photographed by a young **Mario Bava**. At the same time Rossellini was able to work as fully accredited screenwriter and assistant to **Goffredo Alessandrini** on *Luciano Serra pilota* (*Luciano Serra, Pilot*, 1938), a heroic action melodrama nominally produced and supervised by Il Duce's son, Vittorio Mussolini.

Two years later Rossellini was given his first chance to direct with *La nave bianca* (*The White Ship*, 1941), a film about an Italian hospital ship that he took over from navy commander turned film director Francesco De Robertis. The film, which used stock footage and nonprofessional actors, was highly praised and received a special jury prize, which allowed Rossellini to go on to make the other films that form part of what is commonly called his Fascist trilogy: *Un pilota ritorna* (*A pilot returns*, 1942), from a story written by Vittorio Mussolini and with **Michelangelo Antonioni** collaborating on the screenplay, and *L'uomo dalla croce* (*The Man of the Cross*, completed 1942 but released only in 1943), recounting the deeds of a heroic Italian military chaplain at the Russian front. These films, largely financed and made at the behest of the Italian military, would later be cited by hostile critics as proof of Rossellini's active support of the war and of Fascism, but a more dispassionate view might see them as generically humanist in tone rather than stridently nationalistic.

Rossellini's first major triumph, however, and his elevation to the front ranks of international directors, came with *Roma città aperta* (*Rome Open City*, also known as *Open City*, 1945), a film set during the recent German occupation of the city, recounting the heroism of both **Resistance** fighters and the ordinary Roman populace. The film's relatively rough and improvised style, dictated in part by circumstances, was hailed both at home and abroad as marking the birth of a radically new form of socially committed cinema that came to be labeled **neorealism**. Written by **Sergio Amidei** and **Federico Fellini**, the film was feted everywhere, winning the American Board of Review Award, the Grand Prize at the Cannes Festival, and a nomination for an Academy Award. Its remarkable success turned Rossellini into a celebrity overnight and allowed him to finance the other two films that comprise what is usually referred to as his neorealist trilogy: *Paisà* (*Paisan*, 1946) and *Germania anno zero* (*Germany Year Zero*, 1947), both portraying wartime situations with a very strong sense of realism.

With the war now beginning to recede from memory, Rossellini began to focus more on an exploration of inner psychological conflict, beginning with the two episodes of *L'amore* (*Ways of Love*, 1948), both starring **Anna Magnani**, and continuing with a series of films made with Hollywood star Ingrid Bergman, who had chosen to join him in Italy (and whom he would soon marry): *Stromboli, terra di Dio* (*Stromboli*, 1950), *Europa '51* (*The Greatest Love*, 1952), and *Viaggio in Italia* (*Voyage to Italy*, 1953). However, in spite of their strong realism and their undeniable dramatic power, the Bergman films were received very poorly by most Italian critics for what was seen as an emphasis on the individual and thus a deviation from the more socially oriented concerns of the earlier films. The films were, however, greatly appreciated in France, especially by the young critics who would later become the directors of the French New Wave, for whom Rossellini became something of a mentor. Following the lack of success of other films such as *Dov'è la libertà?* (*Where Is Freedom?* 1954) and *La paura—Non credo più all'amore* (*Fear*, 1954), Rossellini and cinematographer Aldo Tonti spent almost two years in India gathering material for what would become a 10-

episode documentary series for Italian television, as well as a quasi-documentary full feature for the big screen, *India Matri Bhumi* (*India*, 1959), which was enthusiastically acclaimed when shown at Cannes and raised Rossellini's stock at home, where the film was favorably compared with the work of Robert Flaherty. With his reputation slightly restored, Rossellini returned to the theme of the war and the Resistance with *Il Generale della Rovere* (*General della Rovere*, 1959) and *Era notte a Roma* (*Escape by Night*, 1960), before making *Viva l'Italia* (*Garibaldi*, 1961), a film that served to celebrate the centenary of Garibaldi's expedition to southern Italy and which effectively initiated that didactic exploration of the past that would soon become the distinguishing feature of his television productions. And indeed, following *Vanina Vanini* (*The Betrayer*, 1961), another historical costume drama set in the context of the **Risorgimento**, and *Anima nera* (Black Soul, 1961), a modest contribution to the ***commedia all'italiana***, Rossellini turned his attention almost exclusively to television and, for the next decade and a half, attempted to use it as a didactic tool.

La prise de pouvoir par Louis XIV (*The Rise of Louis XIV*, 1966), made originally for French television, is undoubtedly the most accomplished of the television films, but Rossellini continued his exploration of history with the encyclopedic *La lotta dell'uomo per la sua sopravvivenza* (*Man's Struggle for Survival*, made 1967–1969 and shown in twelve episodes, 1970–1971), *Atti degli Apostoli* (*Acts of the Apostles*, made 1968, screened in five episodes, 1969), *Socrate* (*Socrates*, 1970), *Blaise Pascal* (1971), *Agostino d'Ippona* (*Augustine of Hippo*, 1972), *L'età di Cosimo de' Medici* (*The Age of the Medici*, 1973), and *Cartesius* (Descartes, 1973). He returned to the big screen in 1974 with *Anno Uno* (*Year One*, 1974), a film about Christian Democrat leader and long-serving Italian prime minister Alcide De Gasperi, but neither it nor *Il Messia* (*The Messiah*, 1975), Rossellini's attempt to present the life of Christ from a layman's perspective, found anything more than a cordial reception in an Italy that had changed radically since the days of *Rome Open City*. Unperturbed, Rossellini began preparing a film on Karl Marx. Titled *Vivere per l'umanità* (To Live for Humanity), it was apparently in an advanced stage of preparation when Rossellini died suddenly from a heart attack in 1977.

ROTA, NINO (1911–1979). (Born Nini Rinaldi.) Composer. Coming from a long line of musicians, Rota was something of a child prodigy. His first work, the oratorio *L'infanzia di San Giovanni Battista* (*The Childhood of St. John the Baptist*), was written when Rota was eight and performed publicly in Paris and Milan when he was only 12. In the same year he was admitted to the Milan Conservatorium, where he studied with Ildebrando Pizzetti before moving to the Conservatory of Santa Cecilia in Rome to study composition under Alfredo Casella. After graduating in 1930 he spent two years in the United States, studying under Rosario Scalero and Fritz Reiner at the Curtis Institute of Philadelphia. He returned to Italy in 1933 and undertook a degree in literature at the University of Milan. Then, after teaching at the Liceo Musicale of Taranto for a year, he was invited to teach harmony and composition at the Conservatorium of Bari, where he remained for the rest of his life, serving as director of the institute from 1950 onward.

Rota's musical oeuvre is considerable and includes 10 operas, three symphonies, two oratorios, six concertos, a number of ballets, chamber pieces, and a great deal of music for theater and radio. He is, however, best remembered for his numerous and melodic film scores. Beginning with **Raffaello Matarazzo**'s *Treno popolare* (*People's Train*, 1933), Rota composed the music for over 150 films, collaborating with major Italian directors such as **Alberto Lattuada**, **Renato Castellani**, **Mario Monicelli**, **Franco Zeffirelli**, and **Luchino Visconti**, for whom he scored *Senso* (1954), *Rocco e i suoi fratelli* (*Rocco and His Brothers*, 1960), and *Il Gattopardo* (*The Leopard*, 1963). Above all, however, Rota is remembered for his prolific partnership with **Federico Fellini**, having provided the distinctive and often haunting soundtracks of all of Fellini's films from *Lo sceicco bianco* (*The White Sheik*, 1952) to *Prove d'orchestra* (*Orchestra rehearsal*, 1978). Rota also worked with a number of international directors such as King Vidor, Edward Dmytryk, René Clément, and Sergei Bondarchuk, but he achieved his greatest world renown from his extensive collaboration with Francis Ford Coppola on all three of the *Godfather* films, receiving the Oscar for Best Original Dramatic Score for *The Godfather: Part II* (1974). Having already won four **Nastri d'argento** for earlier films, he was also awarded a **David di Donatello** in 1977 for his score for *Il Casanova* *di Federico Fellini* (*Fellini's Casanova*, 1976). In 1995 a foundation was instituted in his name to honor his memory and encourage musical composition.

ROTUNNO, GIUSEPPE (1923–). Cinematographer. Rotunno began in the industry as a still photographer at the age of 17. His career was interrupted in 1942 when he was conscripted and sent to Greece as a film reporter but then captured and interned by the Germans when Italy signed the armistice in 1943. After returning to Italy in 1945 he served an apprenticeship as assistant to **G. R. Aldo** on a number of films, which included **Vittorio De Sica**'s *Umberto D* (1952), before graduating to director of photography on **Dino Risi**'s *Pane, amore e . . .* (*Scandal in Sorrento*, 1955).

In the following years he worked with many of the major Italian directors, among them **Valerio Zurlini**, **Mario Monicelli**, **Lina Wertmüller**, and **Vittorio De Sica**. He was cinematographer for **Luchino Visconti** on *Le notti bianche* (*White Nights*, 1957), *Rocco e i suoi fratelli* (*Rocco and His Brothers*, 1960), *Il gattopardo* (*The Leopard*, 1963), and *Lo straniero* (*The Stranger*, 1967) and for **Federico Fellini** on a host of films that included *Satyricon* (*Fellini Satyricon*, 1969), *Roma* (*Fellini's Roma*, 1972), *Amarcord* (1973), *Casanova* (*Fellini's Casanova*, 1976), *Prova d'orchestra* (*Orchestra Rehearsal*, 1978), and *E la nave va* (*And the Ship Sails On*, 1983). Much respected on both sides of the Atlantic—in 1959 he had already photographed Stanley Kramer's *On the Beach* (1959)—he was also called to work with Mike Nichols on *Carnal Knowledge* (1971) and with Bob Fosse on *All That Jazz* (1979), a contribution that earned him the Oscar nomination for Best Cinematography.

In the late 1990s, with over 70 films to his credit, Rotunno retired from the industry in order to continue teaching at the **Centro Sperimentale di Cinematografia** in Rome. Having already garnered a string of prizes during his career, among them three **David di Donatello** and seven **Nastri d'argento**, in 1999 Rotunno was also recognized with the Camerimage Lifetime Achievement Award and the International Award from the American Society of Cinematographers. Further highlighting his contribution to world cinema, in 2006 he was awarded a special 50th-anniversary David di Donatello.

RUBINI, SERGIO (1959–). Actor, director, screenwriter. After studies at the Academy of Dramatic Art in Rome, Rubini worked on the stage, both as an actor and director, as well as writing and performing plays for radio. He made his acting debut in cinema as the drug-addicted son in **Valentino Orsini's** *Figlio mio infinitamente caro* (*My Dearest Son*, 1985) before also playing the son of kidnapped Italian statesman, Aldo Moro, in Giuseppe Ferrara's *Il caso Moro* (*The Moro Affair*, 1986). His film acting career received its biggest boost, however, when **Federico Fellini** cast him as his young alter ego in *Intervista* (*Fellini's Intervista*, 1987). Rubini thereafter appeared in **Giuseppe Piccioni's** popular coming-of-age saga *Il grande Blek* (The Mighty Blek, 1987) and Andrea Del Carlo's *Treno di panna* (*Cream Train*, 1988) before directing himself and his wife, **Margherita Buy**, in his first feature film, *La stazione* (*The Station*, 1990). Adapted from a play by Umberto Marino, which Rubini had already performed onstage, the film was showered with praise and received both the **David di Donatello** and the **Nastro d'argento** for Best New Director as well as the International Federation of Film Critics Award.

Continuing to display great talent and versatility, he subsequently appeared in a wide variety of films, including **Carlo Verdone's** *Al lupo al lupo* (*Wolf, Wolf*, 1992), **Giuseppe Tornatore's** *Una pura formalità* (*A Pure Formality*, 1994), **Gabriele Salvatores's** *Nirvana* (1997), and **Francesca Archibugi's** *L'albero delle pere* (*Shooting the Moon*, 1998) while also directing himself in *Prestazione straordinaria* (*Working Overtime*, 1994) and *Il viaggio della sposa* (*The Bride's Journey*, 1997). With his reputation extending beyond Italy, he has also appeared in international productions including Anthony Minghella's *The Talented Mr. Ripley* (1999), in which his interpretation of the police inspector earned him a Silver Ribbon nomination for Best Supporting Actor, and Mel Gibson's *The Passion of the Christ* (2002), where he played the Good Thief. His most recent film as director, *La terra* (*The Land*, 2006), a taut family drama set in southern Italy in which Rubini himself played a loan shark, was nominated for six David di Donatello awards.

RULLI, STEFANO (1949–). Film historian and screenwriter. After convening a historic conference on **neorealism** at the Pesaro Young

Cinema Festival in 1974, Rulli collaborated with **Marco Bellocchio**, Silvano Agosti, and **Sandro Petraglia** in writing and directing *Nessuno o tutti—Matti da slegare* (*Fit to Be Untied*, 1975), a three-hour **documentary** on Italian mental asylums, and *La macchina cinema* (*The Cinema Machine*, 1979), a five-part television documentary on the seamier aspects of the Italian film industry. He subsequently teamed up regularly with Petraglia to write several popular television series, including the long-running *La piovra* (*Octopus*, 1987–1994) and many of the key films made by the directors of the so-called **New Italian Cinema**, among them **Daniele Luchetti**'s *Il portaborse* (*The Yes Man*, 1991) and **Gianni Amelio**'s *Il ladro di bambini* (*The Stolen Children*, 1992). Together Rulli and Petraglia achieved their greatest success scripting **Marco Tullio Giordana**'s six-hour epic, *La meglio gioventù* (*The Best of Youth*, 2003), for which they received both the **David di Donatello** and the **Nastro d'argento**. In 2004 Rulli's own *Un silenzio particolare* (A Particular Silence), a documentary fiction about autism, was awarded the prize for digital film at the **Venice Festival**. Rulli has since collaborated once again with Petraglia on the screenplays of Giordana's *Quando sei nato non puoi più nasconderti* (*Once You're Born You Can No Longer Hide*, 2005) and Michele Placido's *Romanzo criminale* (*Crime Novel*, 2005), the latter earning them both another David di Donatello award.

RUSTICHELLI, CARLO (1916–2004). Musician and composer. A versatile and prolific composer with over 250 original film scores to his credit, in addition to his arrangements for many others, Rustichelli studied piano in Bologna and then composition at the Academy of Santa Cecilia in Rome. In the 1930s and 1940s he composed mostly operas and theater music but also made a first foray into writing for film with his collaboration on the score of **Mario Bonnard**'s *Papà per una notte* (Dad for a Night, 1939). However, his more regular involvement with cinema came in the postwar period, beginning with his music for **Pietro Germi**'s *Gioventù perduta* (*Lost Youth*, 1947). He subsequently wrote the music for all of Germi's films, including the Oscar-winning *Divorzio all'italiana* (*Divorce Italian Style*, 1961), although he received his first **Nastro d'argento** for his score of Germi's lesser-known *L'uomo di paglia* (*A Man of Straw*, 1959). He also came to work with all the other, both major and minor, Italian directors across a wide variety of genres, moving easily from **spaghetti Westerns** and **peplums** to social comedies and the classic **horror** thrillers of **Mario Bava**. He collaborated extensively with Mario Monicelli, earning another Nastro d'argento for his score of Monicelli's *L'armata Brancaleone* (*For Love and Gold*, 1966), and with **Pier Paolo Pasolini**, for whom he arranged the music for *Accattone* (*Accattone!* 1961), *Mamma Roma* (1962), and *Il Vangelo secondo Matteo* (*The Gospel According to St. Matthew*, 1964). After an intense involvement that saw him sometimes score over 20 films in a single year, he began to reduce his participation in films in the early 1980s, his last major contribution being the score for **Nanni Loy**'s *Amici miei atto III* (*My Friends Act III*, 1985).

– S –

SACHER FILM. Production company. Founded in Rome in 1987 by **Angelo Barbagallo** and actor-director **Nanni Moretti**. In its first years Sacher produced or coproduced (often in partnership with RAI television) **Carlo Mazzacurati**'s *Notte Italiana* (*Italian Night*, 1987), **Daniele Luchetti**'s *Domani accadrà* (*It's Happening Tomorrow*, 1988) and *Il portaborse* (*The Yes Man*, 1990), Moretti's own *Palombella rossa* (*Red Wood Pigeon*, 1989) and *Caro diario* (*Dear Diary*, 1993), and **Mimmo Calopresti**'s *La seconda volta* (*The Second Time*, 1995). In 1989 the company set up the Premio Sacher (Sacher Prize), with the first Sacher d'oro (Golden Sacher) being awarded that year to **Marco Risi**'s *Mery per sempre* (*Forever Mary*, 1989). In 1991 the company also opened an independent art house cinema in Rome, Nuovo Sacher, screening films in the original language, and in 1996 initiated the annual Sacher Film Festival.

Since 1997 the company has also operated as a distributor under the name of Tandem. Among the company's biggest successes in recent years have been **Marco Tullio Giordana**'s *La meglio gioventù* (*The Best of Youth*, 2003) and Moretti's own *Il caimano* (*The Caiman*, 2006), both recipients of the **David di Donatello** prize.

SALCE, LUCIANO (1922–1989). Actor, playwright, screenwriter, film and theater director. After graduating from the National Academy of Dramatic Art in 1947, Salce established a strong reputation as a stage actor, working with directors such as Giorgio Strehler and **Luchino Visconti**. In the early 1950s he spent several years in Brazil, where he became artistic director of the Teatro Brasileiro da Comédia and directed two films for the Vera Cruz film company, *Uma pulga na balança* (*A Flea on the Scales*, 1953) and *Floradas na serra* (1954). Having returned to Italy, he resumed his extensive involvement with the theater while also frequently appearing on the screen in small roles in many of the light comedies directed by **Steno** (**Stefano Vanzina**). In 1960 he directed his first film, *Le pillole di Ercole* (*Hercules' Pills*, 1960), which was soon followed by what many still regard as his two best films, *Il federale* (*The Fascist*, 1961) and *La voglia matta* (*Crazy Desire*, 1962), both of which helped to reveal the considerable acting range of **Ugo Tognazzi**, until then largely regarded as a television comic.

In the following years, while continuing to work in theater, radio, and television, Salce also directed another dozen ebulient, but often uneven, comedies in the satirical vein of the ***commedia all'italiana***. In the mid-1970s, however, he managed to achieve a huge box office success with the first two films featuring the hapless character of Fantozzi, *Fantozzi* (*White Collar Blues*, 1975) and *Il secondo tragico Fantozzi* (*The Second Tragic Fantozzi*, 1976). Unfortunately, this success was not repeated in any of the handful of comedies he made subsequently, including those in which he worked with Fantozzi actor Paolo Villaggio. His last film was the lackluster romantic comedy *Quelli del casco* (*Those with the Helmets*, 1987).

SALVATORES, GABRIELE (1950–). Screenwriter, theater and film director. One of the most promising of the younger generation of filmmakers who emerged as part of the **New Italian Cinema** in the 1980s, Salvatores came to the cinema after a long and fruitful experience in theater. Indeed, his first film, *Sogno di una notte d'estate* (Dream of a Summer's Night, 1983), was a screen adaptation of a rock musical version of Shakespeare's *A Midsummer Night's Dream* that he had previously directed to great acclaim at Milan's Teatro dell'Elfo. In 1986, however, together with producer Maurizio Totti and actor **Diego Abatantuono**, he founded the **Colorado Film** production company, with which he made a number of bittersweet road movies that appeared to be giving voice to the last murmurs of the utopic aspirations of the 1968 generation. Having achieved a huge popularity in Italy with his portrayals of youthful male camaraderie in *Marrakech Express* (1989) and *Turnè* (Tour, 1990), he then scored his greatest triumph with *Mediterraneo* (1991), for which he received not only a **David di Donatello** and a **Nastro d'argento** at home but also the American Academy Award for Best Foreign Film.

After a less successful reworking of many of the same elements in *Puerto Escondido* (1992), he began to experiment with more openly political themes in *Sud* (*South*, 1993), with digital imagery and computer games in the futuristic *Nirvana* (1997), and with split-screen narration in *Amnèsia* (2002). His filmmaking reached a new level of maturity, however, with his luminous adaptation of Niccolò Ammaniti's best-selling novel *Io non ho paura* (*I'm Not Scared*, 2003), which was nominated for six David awards as well as for the Golden Bear at Berlin. His *Quo vadis, baby* (2005) is an impressive experiment in using a mixture of digital, video, and filmic formats to create an effective neo-noir featuring a middle-aged female private detective.

SALVATORI, RENATO (1933–1988). Actor. A handsome, athletic lifeguard with no previous acting experience, Salvatori was discovered in his teens by director **Luciano Emmer**, who promptly cast him as **Lucia Bosé**'s jealous fiancé in *Le ragazze di Piazza di Spagna* (*Three Girls from Rome*, 1952). After playing supporting roles in a number of relatively minor films, he came to national attention as one of the two male leads in **Dino Risi**'s extraordinarily popular *Poveri ma belli* (*Poor, but Handsome*, 1956) and its equally successful sequel, *Belle ma povere* (*Pretty but Poor*, 1957), both of which topped the box office in their respective years. He subsequently appeared as one of the misguided petty thieves in **Mario Monicelli**'s *I soliti ignoti* (*Big Deal on Madonna Street*, 1958) and in **Francesco Rosi**'s *I magliari* (*The Magliari*, 1959) before giving what is generally regarded as the most impressive performance of his entire career playing Simone in **Luchino Visconti**'s *Rocco e i suoi fratelli* (*Rocco and His Brothers*, 1960). For the next 20 years he continued to appear, although for the most part in supporting roles, in films by major Italian and international directors, among them Monicelli's *I Compagni* (*The Organizer*, 1963), **Giulio Pontecorvo**'s *Queimada* (*Burn!* 1969),

Costa-Gavras's Z (1968) and *État de siège* (*State of Siege*, 1972), and **Francesco Rosi**'s *Cadaveri eccellenti* (*Illustrious Corpses*, 1976). In the early 1980s, however, he abandoned his acting career in order to work in politics. His last appearance on the screen was in **Bernardo Bertolucci**'s *La tragedia d'un uomo ridicolo* (*Tragedy of a Ridiculous Man*, 1981).

SANDRELLI, STEFANIA (1946–). Actress. One of the most accomplished actresses of Italian postwar cinema, Sandrelli graduated to the screen after winning the Miss Cinema Viareggio beauty contest in 1960. Following a small part in **Luciano Salce**'s *Il federale* (*The Fascist*, 1961), she played her first significant role as the beautiful young cousin for whom Baron Cefalù (**Marcello Mastroianni**) kills his wife in **Pietro Germi**'s *Divorzio all'italiana* (*Divorce Italian Style*, 1961). She subsequently gave impressive performances as the victimized teenager in Germi's *Sedotta e abbandonata* (*Seduced and Abandoned*, 1964) and the defenseless Adriana in **Antonio Pietrangeli**'s *Io la conoscevo bene* (*I Knew Her Well*, 1965). In the following years she played Clerici's wife in **Bernardo Bertolucci**'s *Il conformista* (*The Conformist*, 1970), a much less malleable wife in Germi's *Alfredo, Alfredo* (1972), where she was pitted against Dustin Hoffman, and then gave one of her finest performances in **Ettore Scola**'s *C'eravamo tanto amati* (*We All Loved Each Other So Much*, 1974). After a host of other films in the late 1970s she displayed her versatility but also caused something of a scandal when she starred in **Tinto Brass**'s adaptation of Junichiro Tanizaki's explicitly erotic novel *La chiave* (*The Key*, 1983). In subsequent years she alternated between playing similar strongly erotic roles as in Paolo Quaregna's *Una donna allo specchio* (*A Woman in the Mirror*, 1984) and *L'attenzione* (*Attention*, 1984), directed by her husband, Giovanni Soldati, and much more demure and vulnerable characters such as the cheerful mother but suffering wife in **Francesca Archibugi**'s *Mignon è partita* (*Mignon Has Come to Stay*, 1988), for which she received both a **Nastro d'argento** and a **David di Donatello**. After a host of other awards, especially for her performances in Scola's *La cena* (*The Dinner*, 1998) and **Gabriele Muccino**'s *L'ultimo bacio* (*One Last Kiss*, 2001), in 2005 she was awarded a Golden Lion at the **Venice Festival** in recognition of her outstanding career.

SANSON, YVONNE (1926–2003). Actress. Greek-born Sanson moved to Italy in her teens in order to study but within a few years had embarked on a career in films. After a small part in Giuseppe Maria Scotese's *La grande aurora* (*The Great Dawn*, 1946), she played her first major role as the mistress-become-wife in **Alberto Lattuada**'s *Il delitto di Giovanni Episcopo* (*Flesh Will Surrender*, 1947). She then achieved an extraordinary popularity as the female lead in a series of hugely successful melodramas directed by **Raffaello Matarazzo**, beginning with *Catene* (*Chains*, 1949) and continuing with *Figli di Nessuno* (*Nobody's Children*, 1951), *Chi è senza peccato* (*Whomever Is without Sin*, 1952), *Angelo Bianco* (*The White Angel*, 1955), and *Malinconico autunno* (*Melancholic Autumn*, 1959), in all of which she was paired with male heartthrob **Amedeo Nazzari**. She also acquitted herself well in supporting roles in films such as Lattuada's *Il cappotto* (*The Overcoat*, 1952), **Mario Camerini**'s *La bella mugnaia* (*The Miller's Beautiful Wife*, 1955) and René Clément's *La diga sul Pacifico* (*This Angry Age*, 1956). By the beginning of the 1960s, however, her career was in decline. She appeared as Olga Manfredi, **Vittorio Gassman**'s faded ex-lover, in **Roberto Rossellini**'s *Anima nera* (Black Soul, 1962) but subsequently made few other films until **Bernardo Bertolucci**, perhaps in homage to her earlier popularity, cast her as Giulia's petit bourgeois mother in *Il conformista* (*The Conformist*, 1970).

SCACCIANOCE, LUIGI (1914–1981). Art director and production designer. Scaccianoce studied design at the **Centro Sperimentale di Cinematografia** and worked with a number of minor directors before collaborating on Orson Welles's *Othello* (1951). His meticulous attention to historical detail earned him a **Nastro d'Argento** for Best Production Design on **Mauro Bolognini**'s *Senilità* (*Careless*, 1962), an award repeated two years later for his design of **Francesco Maselli**'s *Gli indifferenti* (*A Time of Indifference*, 1964). He worked extensively with **Pier Paolo Pasolini** on *Il Vangelo secondo Matteo* (*The Gospel According to St. Matthew*, 1964), *Uccellacci e uccellini* (*Hawks and Sparrows*, 1966), and *Edipo Re* (*Oedipus Rex*, 1967), and collaborated closely with costume designer **Danilo Donati** to achieve the eerie and almost surreal atmosphere of **Federico Fellini**'s

Satyricon (1969). He subsequently worked with **Vittorio De Sica** on the latter's last two films, *Una breve vacanza* (*A Brief Vacation*, 1973) and *Il viaggio* (*The Voyage*, 1974). Scaccianoce's last film was *La cage aux folles II*, directed in 1980 by Edouard Molinaro.

SCARPELLI, FURIO (1919–). Screenwriter. One half of the famous **Age e Scarpelli** screenwriting team, Scarpelli worked regularly with Agenore Incrocci for almost four decades to create many of the great classics of Italian screen comedy. Their partnership began with a collaboration on **Mario Monicelli**'s *Totò cerca casa* (*Toto Looks for an Apartment*, 1949), the first of over a dozen films they would help to write for master comic actor Totò. After working together on a host of films ranging from romantic comedies to action adventures, in 1958 they laid the foundations for the so-called *commedia all'italiana* with their screenplay for Monicelli's *I soliti ignoti* (*Big Deal on Madonna Street*, 1958), for which they shared their first **Nastro d'argento**. They subsequently wrote many of the great classics of the genre together, including *La grande guerra* (*The Great War*, 1960), *Tutti a casa* (*Everybody Go Home*, 1960), *Il sorpasso* (*The Easy Life*, 1962), *I mostri* (*15 from Rome*, 1963), and *C'eravamo tanto amati* (*We All Loved Each Other So Much*, 1974). In 1965 they shared an Oscar nomination for their work on Monicelli's *I compagni* (*The Organizer*, 1963), and in 1980 their script for **Ettore Scola**'s *La terrazza* (*The Terrace*) earned them the award for Best Screenplay at Cannes. They were both also credited with helping to write **Sergio Leone**'s *Il buono, il brutto, il cattivo* (*The Good, the Bad and the Ugly*, 1966), although it appears that much of what they wrote was ultimately judged to be too comic and so not included in the final shooting script.

Following his amicable professional separation from Incrocci in the mid-1980s, Scarpelli continued his prolific activity as a screenwriter, collaborating in particular on many of Ettore Scola's later films. He also frequently ventured into more dramatic territory with films such as Renzo Martinelli's *Porzus* (1997) and **Carlo Lizzani**'s *Celluloide* (*Celluloid*, 1996). In 1996, after having already shared two Oscar nominations with Incrocci for earlier films, Scarpelli was nominated a third time for his work on Michael Radford's *Il postino* (*The Postman*, 1994).

SCOLA, ETTORE (1931–). Cartoonist, screenwriter, director. Although he enrolled first in medicine and then in law at the University of Rome, Scola's talent for comic sketches and cartoons drew him from an early age to the satirical magazine *Marc'Aurelio*. There he met a host of other comic writers who would later also figure prominently in the Italian film industry, including **Steno (Stefano Vanzina)**, **Cesare Zavattini**, **Federico Fellini**, **Mario Monicelli**, **Ruggero Maccari**, and **Furio Scarpelli**. After serving an apprenticeship as uncredited gag writer on a host of made-to-order comedies such as *Totò Tarzan* (1950), he earned his first screenwriting credit on Sergio Grieco's *Fermo tutti, arrivo io* (Hold Everything, I'm Coming, 1953). He next teamed up with the more established screenwriter Ruggero Maccari, to write **Mario Mattoli**'s *Due notti con Cleopatra* (*Two Nights with Cleopatra*, 1953), which initiated a screenwriting partnership that would see Scola and Maccari work together on more than a dozen films and share the **Nastro d'argento** for screenwriting four times. At the same time, beginning with *Lo scapolo* (*The Bachelor*, 1955), Scola began a close professional relationship with writer-director **Antonio Pietrangeli**, subsequently writing or cowriting all of Pietrangeli's major films. He also began to work extensively with **Dino Risi**, collaborating on the screenplays of *Il sorpasso* (*The Easy Life*, 1962) and *I mostri* (*The Monsters*, 1963, but known in the United States as *15 from Rome*) before making his own directorial debut with *Se permettete parliamo di donne* (*Let's Talk About Women*, 1964), a series of mordant comic sketches highlighting the defects of the Italian male, all starring Scola's favorite actor, **Vittorio Gassman**.

After directing several more satirical comedies in the late 1960s, among them *L'arcidiavolo* (*The Devil in Love*, 1966), which saw Gassman teamed up with Mickey Rooney, *Riusciranno i nostri eroi a ritrovare l'amico misteriosamente scomparso in Africa?* (*Will Our Heroes Be Able to Find Their Friend Who Has Mysteriously Disappeared in Africa?* 1968), and *Dramma della gelosia: tutti i particolari in cronaca* (*The Pizza Triangle*, 1970), which was not only popular in Italy but also nominated for the Palme d'or at Cannes, Scola began the 1970s with two more politically engaged films, *Permettete? Rocco Papaleo* (*My Name Is Rocco Papaleo*, 1972), shot in the United States and highlighting the dark underside of the American dream, and *Trevico-Torino, viaggio nel Fiat-Nam* (*From Trevico to Turin*, 1973), a self-financed quasi **documentary** about the exploitation of southern Italian migrant workers who had become factory fodder in northern cities like Turin. Scola then returned to comedy to make what many regard as his most accomplished film. Undoubtedly one of the high points of the *commedia all'italiana*, *C'eravamo tanto amati* (*We All Loved Each Other So Much*, 1974) traces the trajectory of both the hopes and the disappointments of Italian postwar history through the intersecting and diverging lives of three men and the woman with whom they all at some time fall in love. Ingeniously dovetailing social and political history with cinema history, the film also carries out an affectionate homage to the great achievements of Italian postwar cinema and is dedicated, rather appropriately, to **Vittorio De Sica**, who also appears briefly in the film as himself.

Following *Brutti, sporchi e cattivi* (*Down and Dirty*, 1976), a funny but merciless portrait of subproletarian life in a shantytown reminiscent of the early films of **Pier Paolo Pasolini**, Scola produced what has been his most critically acclaimed film to date, *Una giornata particolare* (*A Special Day*, 1977). Bringing **Marcello Mastroianni** and **Sophia Loren** together again in a moving story of a chance encounter between a harried housewife and a homosexual radio journalist on a rather particular day in Fascist Italy, the film was nominated for two Oscars and the Palme d'or at Cannes, in the event winning the César Award in France, a Golden Globe, two **David di Donatello** awards, and three Nastri d'argento. *I nuovi mostri* (*The New Monsters*, 1978), directed collaboratively with Dino Risi and **Mario Monicelli** and providing an update on the social malaise uncovered 15 years earlier, was followed by *La terrazza* (*The Terrace*, 1980), *Passione d'amore* (*Passion of Love*, 1981), and *Il mondo nuovo* (*That Night in Varennes*, 1982). The charming (and silent) *Ballando ballando* (also known as *Le Bal*, 1983) proved to be another critical triumph, receiving an Oscar nomination, the Silver Bear at Berlin, the César in France, and five David di Donatello awards in Italy.

Generally unaffected by the crisis that debilitated the Italian film industry in the following years, Scola directed another dozen fine films. Among them *La famiglia* (*The Family*, 1987) stands out as a remarkably detailed portrait of an Italian middle-class family seen over a period of three generations and *Concorrenza Sleale* (*Unfair Competition*, 2001) for the way in which the director is able to explore the consequences of the 1938 anti-Jewish laws in Italy through their effects on the daily lives of two neighboring shopkeepers. Scola's most recent work, *Gente di Roma* (*People of Rome*, 2003), written in collaboration with his two daughters, Paola and Silvia, and shot entirely on digital film, is an affectionate portrait of Rome and its disparate, and often zany, inhabitants.

SEGRE, DANIELE (1952–). Screenwriter, producer, director. One of Italy's most socially committed and independent filmmakers, Segre began making documentaries in the mid-1970s, the first being *Perchè droga* (*Why Drugs?* 1976). In the following years, having set up his own independent production company, I cammelli, he devoted himself to a cinema that blurred the line between fiction and reality in order to draw attention to a whole range of social problems and marginalities. After shorts such as *Ritratto di un piccolo spacciatore* (Portrait of a Small-Time Dealer, 1982), he directed his first full-length feature, *Testadura* (Hardhead, 1983), which was shown at the **Venice Festival**. He continued to explore social marginalization in works such as *Vite di ballatoio* (Balcony Lives, 1984), which highlighted the precarious existence of transvestites and transsexuals on the streets of Turin, and in 1989 he established a school to train young people to use video for social purposes.

After *Partitura per volti e voci* (Score for Faces and Voices, 1991), an intimate and layered portrait of workers and union delegates, he produced his second feature film, *Manila Paloma Blanca* (1992), the story of the difficult encounter between a young and wealthy Jewish woman and a mentally disturbed out-of-work actor. This was followed by *Come prima, più di prima, ti amerò* (I'll Love You More Than Ever, 1995), a **documentary** on HIV-positive sufferers, and *A proposito di sentimenti* (A Propos Feelings, 1999), dealing with the affective life of Down syndrome sufferers. In 2002 his second feature, *Vecchie* (*Old Women*, 2000), was a provocative exploration of the theme of old age through the heated exchanges of two elderly women trapped in a seaside one-room apartment. His most recent film, *Mitraglia e il Verme* (*Machinegun and the Worm*, 2004), is a powerful exploration of human suffering and endurance, completely set in the lavatories of the vegetable market of a large city.

Segre has also taught at the **Centro Sperimentale di Cinematografia** and since 2002 has been codirector of the Festival of Bellario, which seeks to showcase new socially conscious films by young directors.

SERANDREI, MARIO (1907–1966). Editor. Although working at various times as a journalist, assistant director, supervisor of dubbing, and screenwriter, Serandrei is remembered mostly for his film editing. After a period of writing for *Cinematografo*, the film journal edited by **Alessandro Blasetti**, Serandrei came to edit many of Blasetti's films of the early 1940s: *La corona di ferro* (*The Iron Crown*, 1941), *La cena delle beffe* (*The Jester's Supper*, 1941), and *Quattro passi fra le nuvole* (*A Stroll through the Clouds*, 1942). He edited **Luchino Visconti**'s *Ossessione* in 1943 and continued to work with Visconti after the war, on *Bellissima* (1951), *Senso* (1954), *Rocco e i suoi fratelli* (*Rocco and His Brothers*, 1960), *Il Gattopardo* (*The Leopard*, 1963), and *Vaghe stelle dell'orsa*. In 1945, together with Visconti and **Giuseppe De Santis**, he codirected and edited *Giorni di gloria* (*Days of Glory*), a **documentary** on the wartime **Resistance** movement. After collaborating on the screenplay of **Mario Bava**'s groundbreaking **horror** film, *La maschera del demonio* (*Black Sunday*, 1960), Serandrei worked with **Francesco Rosi** on *Le mani sulla città* (*Hands over the City*, 1963). He subsequently edited Giuseppe De Santis's epic *Italiani, brava gente* (*Attack and Retreat*, 1964) and **Giulio Pontecorvo**'s *La Battaglia di Algeri* (*The Battle of Algiers*, 1965). His last film was Pasquale Festa Campanile's *Il soldato di ventura* (*The Soldier of Fortune*, 1975).

SERENA, GUSTAVO (1881–1970). Actor and director. A Roman marquis with a passion for the stage, Serena approached the silver screen with an extensive theatrical background. Beginning in 1911 with appearances in a number of films for the Film D'Arte Italiana, which specialized in theatrical adaptations, he acted and directed for a number of production houses (**Cines**, Cinegraph, Pasquali) before joining the Roman Caesar Film in 1915. Here, for the next three years, he acted in and directed many of his best films, frequently in collaboration with diva **Francesca Bertini**, whom he first directed in the highly acclaimed *Assunta Spina* (1915). He worked sporadically through the crisis years of the early 1920s, producing, directing, and acting in *La perla nera* (*The Black Pearl*, 1922) and *Coscienza* (Conscience, 1923) and appeared in, among others, *The White Sister*, a Metro production starring Lillian Gish and Ronald Coleman, filmed in Italy in 1923. In 1927 he assembled a small theatrical company that experimented with staging plays by utilizing a film sequence to set the theatrical scene. In the sound years he directed *Zaganella e il cavaliere* (Zaganella and the Honorable Gentleman, 1932), the adaptation of a play by Luigi Capuana, and played one of the leading roles in *Naufraghi* (*Shipwrecked*, 1939). In the postwar years he continued to play small supporting roles in a number of unremarkable films, his last appearance being a walk-on part in *Don Camillo Monsignore ma non troppo* (*Don Camillo, Monsignor*, 1961), directed by fellow veteran of the Italian silent era **Carmine Gallone**.

SIMI, CARLO (1924–2000). Costume, set, art, and production designer. After graduating in architecture from the University of Rome, Simi began working in the film industry as a set decorator, originally on a number of genre films directed by **Sergio Corbucci**. In 1964, under the pseudonym Charles Simons, he designed the sets and costumes for **Sergio Leone**'s *Per un pugno di dollari* (*For a Fistful of Dollars,* 1964) and continued to work with Leone on the latter's subsequent Westerns, receiving special praise for his production and costume design for *C'era una volta il West* (*Once upon a Time in the West*, 1968). He then abandoned the cinema for several years in order to work as an architect, designing, among other things, the offices of **Alberto Grimaldi**'s Produzioni Europee Associate (PEA). He returned to the industry in the mid-1970s, working as art director on Sergio Sollima's action thriller *Revolver* (*Blood in the Streets*, 1973) and collaborating with comic actor-director **Carlo Verdone**, for whom he designed the sets and costumes of *Un sacco bello* (*Fun Is Beautiful*, 1980). In 1985, having teamed up once again with Leone, Simi received a **Nastro d'argento** for his production design for *C'era una volta l'America* (*Once upon a Time in America*, 1984). His last contribution to Italian cinema was the art direction on **Pupi Avati**'s *La via degli angeli* (*A Midsummer's Night Dance*, 1999).

SINDACATO NAZIONALE CRITICI CINEMATOGRAFICI ITALIANI (SNCCI). (National Union of Italian Film Critics.) Association. Founded in 1971, the SNCCI is the association that brings together film critics in Italy. Partly funded by the Ministry for Culture, it carries out a series of activities aimed at promoting Italian cinema, which include the publication of the prestigious quarterly journal *Cinecritica*, the organization of a special week of screenings and critical discussion of films during the **Venice Festival**, and a number of conferences and round tables held throughout the year in all the major Italian cities. Since 2003 it maintains a very active website at www.sncci.it.

SOLDATI, MARIO (1906–1999). Writer, director, screenwriter, literary critic, academic, actor. Perhaps better known as a writer than a filmmaker, Soldati always claimed to have become involved in cinema merely in order to make money. Nevertheless, he was obviously attracted by the medium and joined the revamped **Cines** studios during **Emilio Cecchi**'s period as artistic director there in 1932. He began working as a screenwriter, collaborating on the screenplays of many of **Mario Camerini**'s best-known films, including *Gli uomini che mascalzoni* (*What Scoundrels Men Are*, 1932), *Il cappello a tre punte* (*The Three-Cornered Hat*, 1935), and *Il signor Max* (*Mister Max*, 1940), as well as on **Alessandro Blasetti**'s *Contessa di Parma* (*The Countess of Parma*, 1937) and **Renato Castellani**'s debut feature, *Un colpo di pistola* (*A Pistol Shot*, 1942). From the late 1930s he tried his hand at directing, beginning with *Dora Nelson* (1939), a **white telephone** comedy set in the film industry itself, which he followed with the two "calligraphic" films for which he would become best known: *Piccolo mondo antico* (*Old-Fashioned World*, 1941) and *Malombra* (1942), both elegant and atmospheric adaptations of novels by 19th-century writer Antonio Fogazzaro.

After the war, while intensifying his literary output, he also continued to direct films, moving effortlessly between stylish literary adaptations such as *Eugenia Grandet* (*Eugenie Grandet*, 1946) and *La provinciale* (*The Wayward Wife*, 1952) to swashbuckling adventure fantasies such *Il sogno di Zorro* (*Zorro's Dream*, 1952) and *Jolanda la figlia del corsaro Nero* (*Jolanda, the Daughter of the Black Pirate*, 1953). After the erotic melodrama *La donna del fiume* (*The River Girl*, 1955), which showcased both the body and the acting talents of a very young **Sophia Loren**, Soldati became intensely interested in television and produced a number of travel documentaries for the RAI, including *Viaggio nella valle del Po* (*Travels along* *the Po Valley*, 1957) and *Viaggio lungo il Tirreno* (*Travels along the Tyrrean Coast*, 1961), which he made in collaboration with **Cesare Zavattini**. The last film he directed, before devoting himself almost completely to writing, was the light ironic comedy *Policarpo*, *"ufficiale di scrittura"* (*Policarpo*, 1959).

SOLDINI, SILVIO (1958–). Screenwriter and director. One of the most impressive of the younger filmmakers to emerge in the mid-1980s, Soldini was born in Milan but studied film and television at New York University. It was there that he produced his first prize-winning short, *Drimage* (1982). After returning to Italy he worked as a translator and assistant director before making the evocative *Paesaggio con figure* (*Figures in a Landscape*, 1983) and *Giulia in ottobre* (*Giulia in October*, 1984), the latter winning the Jury Prize at the Annecy Italian Film Festival. In 1984 he founded his own production company, Monogatari, and began making documentaries. *Voci celate* (*Hidden Voices*, 1986), a one-hour video filmed in a psychiatric day hospital, won the Salsomaggiore Festival competition. He made several more shorts before directing his first full-length commercial feature, *L'aria serena dell'ovest* (*The Peaceful Air of the West*, 1990). A sharply observed portrait of tangentially touching lives in contemporary Milan, the film was nominated for the Golden Leopard at the Festival of Locarno. After several more shorts and documentaries he directed his second feature, *Un'anima divisa in due* (*A Soul Split in Two*, 1993). Presented in competition at the **Venice Festival**, the film earned **Fabrizio Bentivoglio** the Volpi Cup for his performance as the young Milanese who falls in love with a gypsy girl. Soldini's third feature, *Le acrobate* (*The Thread*, 1997), another social drama about lives that touch each other by chance, won first prize at the Paris Rencontres Internationales de Cinéma. Soldini would score his greatest commercial and critical triumph, however, with *Pane e tulipani* (*Bread and Tulips*, 2001), which achieved record worldwide sales and received nine **David di Donatello** awards, five **Nastri d'Argento**, the Flaiano Prize, and three European Academy Awards nominations. After *Brucio nel vento* (*Burning in the Wind*, 2002), a brooding study of broken lives and an impossible love, Soldini returned to brighter themes with the sparkling comedy *Agata e la tempesta* (*Agatha and the Storm*, 2004), nominated for eight David di Donatello awards.

SOLINAS, FRANCO (1927–1982). Screenwriter. Born in Sardinia, Solinas participated actively in the **Resistance** movement during World War II. After the war he joined the Italian Communist Party and, turning his back on a law degree, began writing. Following minor contributions to films by **Luigi Comencini** and **Mario Camerini**, he initiated a fruitful partnership with **Gillo Pontecorvo** by adapting his own novel, *Squarciò*, into what would become Pontecorvo's first feature film, *La grande strada azzurra* (*The Wide Blue Road*, 1957). He subsequently scripted Pontecorvo's *Kapò* (1960), the moving story of a Jewish girl in the death camp of Treblinka, before collaborating with **Francesco Rosi** on the screenplay of *Salvatore Giuliano* (1963). In 1966 he wrote Pontecorvo's *La battaglia di Algeri* (*The Battle of Algiers*), a landmark film that won the Golden Lion for Best Film at the **Venice Festival** as well as an Academy Award nomination for Best Screenplay.

Solinas's strong social commitment was responsible for the political dimension of a number of **spaghetti Westerns** of the late 1960s, in particular **Damiano Damiani**'s *Quién sabe?* (*A Bullet for the General*, 1967) and Sergio Corbucci's *Il mercenario* (*A Professional Gun*, 1968). There followed his last collaboration with Pontecorvo, *Queimada* (*Burn!* 1969), a powerful indictment of colonialism that starred Marlon Brando. In the 1970s Solinas worked with Costantin Costa-Gavras on *État de siège* (*State of Siege*, 1973), a political thriller that explored American involvement in the Chilean coup d'état, and **Francesco Maselli**, for whom he wrote the screenplay of *Il sospetto* (*The Suspect*, 1975), another taut political thriller set in Fascist Italy. During this period he also worked with Joseph Losey, coscripting both *The Assassination of Trotsky* (1972) and *Monsieur Kline* (*Mr. Klein*, 1976). Solinas's last screenplay was for Costa-Gavras's *Hanna K.* (1983), a film that dealt with the Jewish-Palestinian question. Following Solinas's untimely death in 1982, an annual prize was instituted in his name to encourage young screenwriters and to recognize their generally undervalued contribution to Italian cinema.

SONEGO, RODOLFO (1921–2000). Screenwriter. One of the most respected screenwriters in postwar Italian cinema, Sonego studied drawing at the Turin Academy of Fine Arts before taking part in the **Resistance** movement during World War II. Following the war he moved to Rome where he wrote and directed a number of documentaries on scientific and art-historical subjects for the **Lux Film** company. After earning his first screenwriting credit on Giorgio Ferroni's *Tombolo, paradiso nero* (*Tombolo*, 1947), he worked with **Carlo Lizzani** on *Achtung! Banditi!* (*Attention! Bandits!* 1951) and helped to write **Alberto Lattuada**'s *Anna* (1951) and *La spiaggia* (*Riviera*, 1953). Having met actor **Alberto Sordi** on the set of Franco Rossi's *Il seduttore* (The Seducer, 1954), Sonego initiated what would become a lifelong personal and professional relationship that would see him as a regular screenwriter on practically all of the films in which Sordi either acted or directed, thus allowing him an opportunity to modulate Sordi's characters as time went on so as to present a composite portrait of the changing face of the ordinary Italian male. Among the host of films he penned for Sordi were *Il vedovo* (The Widower, 1959) and *Una vita difficile* (*A Difficult Life*, 1961), directed by **Dino Risi**; *Il vigile* (*The Traffic Policeman*, 1960) and *Bello, onesto, emigrato in Australia sposerebbe compaesana illibata* (*A Girl in Australia*, 1971), directed by **Luigi Zampa**; *Un eroe dei nostri tempi* (*A Hero of Our Times*, 1955), directed by **Mario Monicelli**; and, directed by Sordi himself, *Un italiano in America* (*An Italian in America*, 1967), *In viaggio con papa* (*Journey with Papa*, 1982), *Un tassinaro a New York* (*A Taxi Driver in New York*, 1987), and *Il comune senso del pudore* (*A Common Sense of Modesty*, 1976). His numerous other screenwriting credits include collaborations with **Mario Camerini** on *I briganti italiani* (*The Italian Brigands*, 1962), with **Tinto Brass** on *Il disco volante* (*The Flying Saucer*, 1964), and with **Vittorio De Sica** on *Una breve vacanza* (*A Brief Vacation*, 1973).

SORDI, ALBERTO (1920–2003). Actor and director. Probably the most prolific and certainly one of the most popular actors of the Italian silver screen, Sordi (or Albertone, as he was affectionately known) appeared in close to 150 films in a career that spanned over 60 years.

Frustrated by the limited success of his precocious attempts to establish himself on the stage, Sordi moved to the cinema and was appearing in films as an extra in his late teens. A first break came in 1937 when he was chosen to dub the voice of Oliver Hardy in Italian versions of the popular MGM Laurel and Hardy films. He took on minor parts in Fyodor Otsep's *La principessa Tarakanova* (*Princess Tarakanova*, 1938) and **Carlo Campogalliani**'s *La notte delle beffe* (*The Night of Tricks*, 1939) before being offered his first significant role as an idealistic young pilot in **Mario Mattoli**'s war film, *I tre aquilotti* (*The Three Pilots*, 1942). In the immediate postwar period he began working again as a dubber of Hollywood films, lending his voice to many first-rank American actors, among them Victor Mature, Robert Mitchum, and Anthony Quinn. He also performed character sketches in stage revues but achieved his first real success on the radio, through his creation of a number of fictional characters who anticipated in many ways those he would play in later films. After appearing in a strong supporting role in **Renato Castellani**'s *Sotto il sole di Roma* (*Under the Sun of Rome*, 1948), he finally began to make his mark in two of **Federico Fellini**'s early films, in the title role of *Lo sceicco bianco* (*The White Sheik*, 1952) and as Alberto, perhaps the most woeful of the five layabouts in *I vitelloni* (*Spivs*, 1953), an intepretation that brought him his first **Nastro d'argento**.

From this point his film career really took off in earnest as he furiously set about creating that gallery of fundamentally flawed but amiable characters with whom he would come to be so closely identified. In 1954 alone he appeared in over a dozen films, which included **Mario Mattoli**'s farcical *Due notti con Cleopatra* (*Two Nights with Cleopatra*, 1954), in which he played the male lead opposite **Sophia Loren** in one of her first substantial roles, and **Steno**'s *Un americano a Roma* (*An American in Rome*, 1954), in which he gave life to one of the most typical of his early characters, the ebullient, if rather misguided, Nando Moriconi. In the same year, while acting the title role of Franco Rossi's *Il seduttore* (The Seducer, 1954), he met screenwriter **Rodolfo Sonego** and initiated what would become a lifelong partnership between them, with Sonego subsequently working on the screenplay of practically every film in which Sordi appeared from then on. With over 60 films already to his credit by the late 1950s, Sordi came to occupy a central position in the development of the ***commedia all'italiana***, contributing with his ever more mature acting style and nuanced character delineation to creating many of the great classics of the genre and giving particularly memorable performances in films such as **Dino Risi**'s *Una vita* *difficile* (*A Difficult Life*, 1961) and **Mario Monicelli**'s *La grande guerra* (*The Great War*, 1959), for which he received both a Nastro d'argento and a **David di Donatello**. After apppearing in a host of other *commedie* and as the Italian count, Emilio Ponticelli, in Ken Annakin's *Those Magnificent Men in Their Flying Machines* (1965), Sordi made his own directorial debut with *Fumo di Londra* (*Smoke over London*, 1966), a witty comedy of manners set in the London of the swinging '60s. Throughout the 1960s and 1970s he continued to appear in films where the most dramatic subjects were inflected in a comic vein, alternating between playing figures like the appalling Doctor Tersilli in **Luigi Zampa**'s satire on greedy doctors who abuse the health system in *Il medico della mutua* (*Be Sick . . . It's Free*, 1968) and the hapless husband and father, Giuseppe Di Noi, abruptly imprisoned without recourse in **Nanni Loy**'s Kafkaesque parable *Detenuto in attesa di giudizio* (*Why*, 1971). Then, after directing himself again in a comic but caustic denunciation of the arms trade in *Finché c'è guerra c'è speranza* (*While There's War There's Hope*, 1974), Sordi provided what many regard as the most outstanding performance of his entire career playing a meek and mild father who becomes a torturer in avenging the death of his son in Monicelli's *Un borghese piccolo piccolo* (*An Average Little Man*, 1977), a tour de force of inspired acting for which he again received both a David and a Nastro d'argento. While he may seldom have reached such an intensity again, he continued to perform brilliantly in a host of subsequent films, whether as the prankster nobleman in Monicelli's historical costume drama, *Il Marchese del Grillo* (*Marquis Del Grillo*, 1981), or as Arpagon, the great miser, in Tonino Cervi's adaptation of Molière's classic *L'avaro* (*The Miser*, 1990). In addition to a plethora of prizes he received for his role in specific films, Sordi was awarded three special Davids for Lifetime Achievement and a posthumous Nastro d'argento for all his work. Underscoring his contribution not only to Italian cinema but to Italian culture generally, in 2002 he was invested with an honorary degree from the University of Salerno.

SORRENTINO, PAOLO (1970–). Director and screenwriter. Widely hailed as one of the most promising young directors of the new millennium, Sorrentino first began to make his mark as a film writer, winning the 1997 Solinas screenwriting prize for his original script,

Dragoncelli di fuoco (*Little Fire Dragons*). After collaborating on the screenplay of **Antonio Capuano**'s *Polvere di Napoli* (*Dust of Naples*, 1998), he made the short *L'amore non ha confini* (*Love Has No Limits*, 1998), before writing and directing his first full feature, *L'uomo in più* (*One Man Up*, 2001). The intriguing story of two men with the same name whose destinies cross by chance, the film was screened in competition at the **Venice Festival** and won wide acclaim, with Sorrentino subsequently being awarded the **Nastro d'argento** for Best New Director. Three years later his similarly impressive second feature, *Le consequenze dell'amore* (*The Consequences of Love*, 2004), was nominated for the Palme d'or at Cannes and at home received five **David di Donatello**, including Best Film, Best Director, and Best Screenplay, and three Nastri d'argento. Following a highly praised adaptation of **Eduardo De Filippo**'s play *Sabato, domenica e lunedì* (*Saturday, Sunday and Monday*, 2005), made for RAI television, and appearing in a supporting role in **Nanni Moretti**'s *Il caimano* (*The Caiman*, 2006), Sorrentino wrote and directed *L'amico di famiglia* (*The Family Friend*, 2006), the unsettling story of a repulsive but oddly fascinating neighborhood loan shark, which was again nominated for the Golden Palm at Cannes. His fourth feature, *Il divo*, an ironic portrait of Italian Christian Democrat leader and seven-time prime minister Giulio Andreotti, received the Jury Prize at Cannes in 2008.

SPAGHETTI WESTERN. *See* WESTERN *ALL'ITALIANA*.

SPENCER, BUD. *See* PEDERSOLI, CARLO.

SQUITIERI, PASQUALE (1938–). Screenwriter and director. After graduating in law in his native Naples, Squitieri moved to Rome, where he began acting in the theater. Attracted by the lure of cinema, he was soon working as assistant director to **Francesco Rosi**. He made his directorial debut with *Io e Dio* (*God and I*, 1969), a film about a priest in southern Italy, encouraged and produced for him by **Vittorio De Sica**. There followed two forays into the **Western all'italiana** under the pseudonym William Redford, *Django sfida Sartana* (Django Defies Sartana, 1970) and *La vendetta è un piatto che si serve freddo* (*Vengeance Is a Dish Served Cold*, 1971), before *Camorra*

(*Gang War in Naples*, 1972), the first of a number of films exploring the issue of organized crime in southern Italy, which included what many still regard as Squitieri's best film, *Il prefetto di ferro* (*The Iron Prefect*, 1977). A heroic portrait of Cesare Mori, the police prefect from northern Italy who was sent to Sicily in 1925 in order to subdue the Mafia, *Il prefetto* was awarded the **David di Donatello** for Best Film and its film score by **Ennio Morricone** was nominated for an Academy Award. Following another film on the Mafia, *Corleone* (*Father of the Godfathers*, 1978), Squitieri changed direction to make *Claretta* (*Claretta Petacci*, 1984), a film about Mussolini's mistress, Clara Petacci, which starred the actress with whom he most often worked and had married, **Claudia Cardinale**. The film was critically acclaimed, earning Cardinale a **Nastro d'argento** for her powerful interpretation of the role, but Squitieri was also fiercely attacked for what appeared to many to be an indulgence in Fascist sympathies.

Squitieri subsequently worked for a period in television before returning to the big screen with several strongly socially committed films, *Gli invisibili* (The Invisible Ones, 1988), which tackled the theme of political terrorism, and *Atto di dolore* (*Act of Sorrow*, 1990), the moving story of a mother struggling to save her son from a heroin addiction. He also returned to the theme of criminality in southern Italy, and to the style of his earlier spaghetti Westerns, in *Li chiamarono briganti* (*Brigands*, 1999). His most recent film, *L'avvocato de Gregorio* (*Counselor de Gregorio*, 2003), is about an elderly lawyer in straitened circumstances who manages to reassert his sense of dignity by taking a stance for justice.

STENO. *See* VANZINA, STEFANO.

STOPPA, PAOLO (1906–1988). Actor. After studying acting at the Academy of Santa Cecilia in Rome, Stoppa made his professional stage debut in 1927 with the Capodaglio-Racca-Olivieri company. In the 1930s, while becoming better known for his work on stage, he also began to work as a film dubber and to take on small parts in films, his first appearance being in a tiny role in **Enrico Guazzoni**'s *Re burlone* (*The Joker King*, 1935).

In the postwar period he continued to pursue a career on both the stage and the screen. Beginning in 1945 he distinguished himself in a host of productions of both classic and contemporary plays, frequently under the direction of **Luchino Visconti**. At the same time, he took on minor roles in dozens of otherwise unremarkable films before playing one of his first significant parts as Rappi, the turncoat hobo, in **Vittorio De Sica**'s *Miracolo a Milano* (*Miracle in Milan*, 1951). He subsequently appeared as Don Peppino, the hysterically distraught widower in the "Pizze a credito" episode of De Sica's *L'oro di Napoli* (*The Gold of Naples*, 1954); as Cecchi, the boxing impressario, in Visconti's *Rocco e i suoi fratelli* (*Rocco and His Brothers*, 1960); and in **Roberto Rossellini**'s *Viva l'Italia* (*Garibaldi*, 1960), in which he played the role of Nino Bixio. Perhaps his most memorable role, however, was as the upstart mayor and father of Angelica in Visconti's *Il gattopardo* (*The Leopard*, 1963). Although generally cast in supporting roles, Stoppa appeared in over 150 films. One of his last interpretations, that of Pope Pius VIII in **Mario Monicelli**'s *Il Marchese del Grillo* (*Marquis Del Grillo*, 1981), brought him the third **Nastro d'argento** of his career.

STORARO, VITTORIO (1940–). Cinematographer. Son of a projectionist for the **Lux Film** studios in Rome, Storaro developed an early passionate interest in photography, which he pursued privately at the Italian Cinemagraphic Training Center, and then professionally at the **Centro Sperimentale di Cinematografia**. After an apprenticeship as assistant cameraman on **Bernardo Bertolucci**'s *Prima della rivoluzione* (*Before the Revolution*, 1966), Storaro graduated to director of photography on Franco Rossi's *Giovinezza, Giovinezza* (*Youth, Oh Youth*, 1969). A year later with *La strategia del ragno* (*The Spider's Stratagem*) and *Il conformista* (*The Conformist*) there began a long partnership with Bernardo Bertolucci that would see Storaro as regular cinematographer on all of Bertolucci's major films, from *Ultimo Tango a Parigi* (*Last Tango in Paris*, 1972) and *Novecento* (*1900*, 1976) to *The Sheltering Sky* (1990) and *The Little Buddha* (1993). In between, Francis Ford Coppola would lure Storaro to the Philippines to photograph *Apocalypse Now* (1979), for which Storaro would receive his first Academy Award, an achievement repeated two years later with his work on Warren Beatty's *Reds*. He would receive a third Oscar for his work on Bertolucci's *The Last Emperor* (1987). Considered by many to be the leading cinematographer of his

generation—*Moviemaker* once called him "the high priest of light"—
Storaro has been honored with numerous awards and prizes including the Lifetime Achievement Award by the American Society of
Cinematographers (2001) and the Coolidge Award for Cinematography in 2005. Currently, Storaro teaches cinematography at the Centro Sperimentale di Cinematografia.

– T –

TAVIANI, PAOLO (1931–) AND VITTORIO (1929–). Directors and
screenwriters. In one of the most remarkable partnerships in the history of Italian cinema, brothers Paolo and Vittorio Taviani have always written and directed their films in harmonious collaboration,
with no distinction ever made between what each has contributed.

According to their own account, the brothers were inspired to become filmmakers during their student days at the University of Pisa
when they first saw **Roberto Rossellini**'s *Paisà* (*Paisan*, 1946). They
were thus drawn from the very beginning to a socially committed and
political cinema. Their first film, made in 1954 with the help of **Cesare Zavattini** and **Valentino Orsini**, was *San Miniato, luglio '44*
(San Miniato, July 1944), a **documentary** that attempted to recon-
struct a massacre carried out by the Germans in the church of their
native town, San Miniato, during World War II. The film was
awarded second prize at the Documentary Festival of Pisa and encouraged the brothers, always in partnership with Orsini, to continue
making documentaries for the next five years. The experience culminated in a collaboration with Dutch documentarist Joris Ivens on
L'Italia non è un paese povero (*Italy Is Not a Poor Country*, 1960), a
wide-ranging documentary produced for Italian television. Two years
later, together with Orsini, they directed their first feature, *Un uomo
da bruciare* (*A Man for Burning*, 1962), a stark and dramatic recounting of the last days of Sicilian union organizer and social activist Salvatore Carnevale before he was brutally murdered by the
Mafia. The following year, again with Orsini, the brothers made *I
fuorilegge del matrimonio* (*The Marriage Outlaws*, 1963), a film that
attempted to dramatize in six separate episodes many of the issues relating to the absence of divorce in Italy at that time.

In spite of the film's reasonable box office success, the brothers were unable to finance another project until 1967 when, in a climate of growing social unrest, they made *I sovversivi* (*The Subversives*, 1967). Shot in cinema verité style, the film explored the profound effect of the death of Italian Communist Party leader Palmiro Togliatti on the personal lives of a number of party members. The dark and violent utopian allegory in the Tavianis' next film, *Sotto il segno dello scorpione* (*Under the Sign of Scorpio*, 1969), made in direct response to the explosion of political protest of 1968, confounded the critics when it was first shown at the **Venice Festival** but confirmed the Tavianis' status as committed political filmmakers. The brothers continued to explore the tension between aspirations to a political utopia and its unachievability in the two films that followed, *San Michele aveva un gallo* (*Saint Michael Had a Rooster*, 1971) and *Allonsanfan* (1973), both set in the context of failed revolutionary movements of the 19th century. However, it would be the more contemporary and personal struggle for freedom recounted in *Padre padrone* (*My Father My Master*, 1977) that would finally bring the brothers international recognition. Financed by RAI state television and originally shot on 16 mm film, the story of an illiterate Sardinian shepherd struggling to liberate himself from the tyranny of his father proved to be an overwhelming success at Cannes, where it was championed by no less than Rossellini himself and awarded both the Palme d'or and the International Federation of Film Critics prize. At home the film received both a **Nastro d'argento** and a special **David di Donatello**, but a cooler reception greeted their next film, *Il prato* (*The Meadow*, 1979).

The brothers returned to form, however, and to the grand operatic style of their earlier work, in what remains perhaps their most accomplished and acclaimed film, *La notte di San Lorenzo* (*Night of the Shooting Stars*, 1982). Structured as a bedtime story told by a mother to her infant child, the film revisits the history of the massacre at San Miniato, which had been the subject of the Tavianis' first documentary, but this time in the style of an epic and poetic fable. A work of stunning visual beauty, complemented by a stirring musical score by **Nicola Piovani**, the film was awarded six Davids and two Nastri d'argento at home and both the Ecumenical and the Grand Jury Prize at Cannes, where it was also nominated for the Palme d'or. This tour de force of filmmaking was followed by the equally impressive *Kaos*

(*Chaos*, 1984), a masterful retelling of four stories by Luigi Pirandello in the Tavianis' now characteristic poetic style. Three years later, *Good morning Babilonia* (*Good Morning, Babylon*, 1987), the invented story of two Italian brothers trained as art restorators called to work on the set of D. W. Griffith's *Intolerance* (1916), was essentially the Taviani brothers' own hymn to the art of cinema.

While not excluding political themes altogether, from the early 1990s the brothers largely concentrated their efforts on literary adaptations, providing elegant transcriptions of novels by Leo Tolstoy in *Il sole anche di notte* (*Night Sun*, 1990), *Anna Karenina* (2000), and *Resurrezione* (*Resurrection*, 2002), and by Johann Wolfgang Goethe in *Le affinità elettive* (*The Elective Affinities*, 1996).

TERZANO, MASSIMO (1892–1947). Cinematographer. Having begun in the industry as a cameraman in 1913, Terzano graduated to director of photography in the last generation of the **Maciste** films, most notably *Maciste imperatore* (*Emperor Maciste*, 1924) and *Maciste all'inferno* (*Maciste in Hell*, 1926). With the advent of the sound era, he worked as cinematographer on **Goffredo Alessandrini**'s *La segretaria privata* (*The Private Secretary*, 1931) and then on several of **Mario Camerini**'s most renowned films, including *Gli uomini che mascalzoni* (*What Scoundrels Men Are!* 1932) and *Il cappello a tre punte* (*The Three-Cornered Hat*, 1935). One of his greatest achievements during this period was his work on Walter Ruttman's *Acciaio* (*Steel*, 1933), much of which had to be shot under extremely difficult conditions inside a steel foundry. He subsequently served as director of photography on **Carmine Gallone**'s *Casta diva* (1935) and *Giuseppe Verdi* (*The Life of Giuseppe Verdi*, 1938) and in the early 1940s became closely associated with so-called calligraphers such as **Mario Soldati**, for whom he produced the stunning photography of *Malombra* (1942) and *La miserie del Signor Travet* (*His Young Wife*, 1945), and **Renato Castellani**, with whom he worked on *Un colpo di pistola* (*A Pistol Shot*, 1941) and *Zazà* (1944).

In the immediate postwar period he contributed to the ensemble partisan film *Giorni di gloria* (*Days of Glory*, 1945) and renewed his collaboration with Camerini as cinematographer for *Due lettere anonime* (*Two Anonymous Letters*, 1945) before his promising career was cut short by his untimely death in 1947.

TOGNAZZI, RICKY (1955–). Actor and director. Son of veteran actor **Ugo Tognazzi**, Ricky made his first appearance in films at the age of eight, playing his father's son in one of the episodes of **Dino Risi**'s *I mostri* (*15 from Rome*, 1963). He subsequently studied at the DAMS (Faculty of Communication) in Bologna before serving as an assistant on a number of films directed by, among others, **Pupi Avati**, **Luigi Comencini**, and **Maurizio Ponzi**. He also worked as an actor, playing his first significant part as a young nobleman in Ponzi's *Qualcosa di biondo* (*Aurora by Night*, 1984), for which he received the **David di Donatello** award for best supporting role. After appearing in **Ettore Scola**'s *La famiglia* (*The Family*, 1987) he made his directorial debut with the light social comedy *Piccoli equivoci* (*Little Misunderstandings*, 1988), for which he received both the David and the **Nastro d'argento** for Best New Director. He then turned to more socially committed themes with *Ultrà* (*Hooligans*, 1991), a powerful portrayal of the phenomenon of soccer hooliganism that was awarded both a David and the Silver Bear at Berlin; *La scorta* (*The Escort*, 1993), a film about an honest judge trying unsuccessfully to break the hold of the Sicilian Mafia; and *Vite strozzate* (*Strangled Lives*, 1996), a thriller centered on the new social scourge of usury in Italy in the 1990s, the latter earning him another nomination for the Golden Bear at Berlin. After *Excellent Cadavers* (1999), a fictional portrait of the Mafia-fighting judges Giovanni Falcone and Paolo Borsellino, made entirely in English for American television, Tognazzi changed direction somewhat with *Canone inverso—making love* (2000), the adaptation of a Holocaust novel by Paolo Maurensig. His most recent directorial effort has been the much-praised *Il Papa buono* (*John XXIII: The Good Pope*, 2003), a fictional biography of Pope Roncalli, with English actor Bob Hoskins in the title role.

TOGNAZZI, UGO (1922–1990). Actor. A popular actor who appeared in over 140 films in a career that spanned three decades, Tognazzi began working in amateur theater in his teens and continued to hone his stage skills by entertaining troops while doing his military service during World War II. After the war he embarked on a professional career in show business and began touring in numerous vaudeville shows and musical revues. Over the next decade he became enormously popular with his comic sketches and routines, initially only onstage and on the radio but eventually also on television, where for almost five years he performed regularly with fellow comic actor Raimondo Vianello in the long-running variety program *Uno due tre* (One Two Three, 1955–1959). During this time he also appeared on the big screen in a host of lightweight comedies, but his film career only really took off in the early 1960s, due largely to the much more complex characters he was able to create in two films directed by **Luciano Salce**, *Il federale* (*The Fascist*, 1961) and *La voglia matta* (*The Crazy Urge*, 1962). From then on, usually playing some variation on a cynical, self-serving, womanizing scoundrel, he became one of the fixtures of the Italian silver screen, starring in films such as **Dino Risi**'s *I mostri* (The Monsters, 1963, also known in the United States as *15 from Rome*), **Antonio Pietrangeli**'s *Il magnifico cornuto* (*The Magnificent Cuckold*, 1964), **Alberto Lattuada**'s *Venga a prendere il caffè da noi* (*Come Have Coffee with Us*, 1970), and **Mario Monicelli**'s *Vogliamo i colonnelli* (*We Want the Colonels*, 1973). He contributed significantly in his sardonic supporting role to **Pier Paolo Pasolini**'s *Porcile* (*Pigpen*, 1969) but undoubtedly provided his most memorable performances in the many films in which he worked with **Marco Ferreri**, which included *L'ape regina* (*The Conjugal Bed*, 1963), *La donna scimmia* (*The Ape Woman*, 1964), *Marcia nuziale* (*Wedding March*, 1965), *L'udienza* (*The Audience*, 1972), and *La grande abbuffata* (*The Grande Bouffe*, 1973). After playing so many dubious characters, his performance as the morally questionable father willing to exploit his own son's kidnapping for business reasons in **Bernardo Bertolucci**'s *La tragedia di un uomo ridicolo* (*Tragedy of a Ridiculous Man*, 1981) earned him the Palme d'or at Cannes and his fourth **Nastro d'argento**.

Outside of Italy, Tognazzi is probably best remembered as Renato Baldi, the gay character he played in the three *Cage aux folles* films (1978, 1980, 1985), all directed by Edouard Molinaro and Georges Lautner. Tognazzi also tried his hand at directing himself in three films, *Il mantenuto* (*His Women*, 1961), *Il fischio al naso* (*The Seventh Floor*, 1967), and *Sissignore* (*Yes Sir*, 1968).

TONTI, ALDO (1910–1988). Cinematographer. Having worked for a number of years as a news photographer, Tonti moved to **Cinecittà** in the mid-1930s, originally employed as a still photographer and cameraman. His first film as director of photography was Flavio Calzavara's *Piccoli naufraghi* (*Young Castaways*, 1938), followed by several films directed by **Goffredo Alessandrini** including *Abuna Messias* (*Cardinal Messias*, 1939), *Caravaggio, il pittore maledetto* (*Caravaggio, the Cursed Painter*, 1941), and *Nozze di Sangue* (*Blood Wedding*, 1941). After working with **Augusto Genina** on *Bengasi* (1942), Tonti collaborated with fellow cinematographer Domenico Scala to create the extraordinary visual style of **Luchino Visconti**'s landmark *Ossessione* (*Obsession*, 1943).

In the immediate postwar period Tonti worked on **Aldo Vergano**'s *Il sole sorge ancora* (*Outcry*, 1946) and **Alberto Lattuada**'s *Il bandito* (*The Bandit*, 1946), *Senza pietà* (*Without Pity*, 1948), and *Il mulino del Po* (*The Mill on the Po*, 1948). Having photographed *Il miracolo* (The Miracle), the second episode of **Roberto Rossellini**'s *L'amore* (*Ways of Love*, 1948), he returned to work with Rossellini on *Europa '51* (*The Greatest Love*, 1952), *Dov'è la libertà* (*Where Is Freedom?* 1954), and *India: Matri Bhumi* (*India*, 1959), while also serving as cinematographer on **Federico Fellini**'s *Le notti di Cabiria* (*Nights of Cabiria*, 1957). In the 1960s he filmed **Carlo Lizzani**'s *Il gobbo* (*The Hunchback of Rome*, 1960) and **Marco Ferreri**'s *La donna scimia* (*The Ape Woman*, 1964), and was also the cinematographer on John Huston's *Reflections in a Golden Eye* (1967).

With over 120 films to his credit, Tonti retired from the industry after directing photography on the big-budget action adventure *Ashanti* (1979), directed by Richard Fleisher.

TORNATORE, GIUSEPPE (1956–). Photographer, screenwriter, director. Later to become one of the leading names of the so-called **New Italian Cinema**, Tornatore achieved early success as a still photographer and a prize-winning **documentary** filmmaker. After a number of television documentaries produced for RAI, he collaborated on the script and served as second unit director for **Giuseppe Ferrara**'s *Cento giorni a Palermo* (*A Hundred Days in Palermo*, 1984), a film about General Dalla Chiesa's ill-fated attempt to destroy the Sicilian Mafia. His own feature directorial debut came two years later with another film on the Mafia, *Il camorrista* (*The Professor*, 1986), which earned him a **Nastro d'argento** as Best New Director. He would, however, achieve both national and international renown with *Nuovo cinema Paradiso* (*Cinema Paradiso*, 1989), a nostalgic and loving celebration of the golden days of cinema that won, among many other awards, the Grand Jury Prize at Cannes, a Golden Globe, and an Academy Award for Best Foreign Language Film. His next film, *Stanno tutti bene* (*Everybody's Fine*, 1990), was a less celebratory look at the social degradation in Italy in the late 1980s, but was followed by the more whimsical *Il cane blu* (*The Blue Dog*), one segment of the four-episode film *La domenica special-mente* (*Especially on Sunday*, 1992). *Una pura formalità* (*A Pure Formality*, 1994), a sort of metaphysical whodunit located almost entirely in one dark, rain-sodden room and starring Roman Polanski and Gérard Depardieu, is probably Tornatore's best and most complex film to date. This was followed by *L'uomo dalle stelle* (*The Star Maker*, 1995), another film that celebrated cinema, and then *La leggenda del pianista sull'oceano* (*The Legend of 1900*, 1998), a big-budget adaptation of a theatrical monologue by Alessandro Baricco that attracted a host of prizes including six **David di Donatello** awards and a special Nastro d'argento for **Ennio Morricone**'s score. Tornatore returned to the Sicily of his childhood again with *Malèna* (2000), an erotic coming-of-age film set during World War II and featuring the stunning looks of **Monica Bellucci**.

Putting plans for a major film on the Battle of Stalingrad on hold for the moment due to lack of finances, Tornatore has most recently directed *La sconosciuta* (*The Unknown Woman*, 2006), a neo-noir set in the northern Italian city of Trieste that earned him both the 2007 Nastro d'argento and the David di Donatello award for Best Director.

TOSI, PIERO (1927–). Costume designer. Widely regarded as Italy's leading film costume designer, Tosi first made his mark by dressing **Luchino Visconti's** *Bellissima* (1951). He went on to design the costumes for all of Visconti's subsequent films, including all the elegant period costumes of *Il gattopardo* (*The Leopard*, 1963), for which he received his first nomination for an Academy Award. Much in demand, he was called to work with all the other major Italian directors including **Vittorio De Sica**, for whom he designed the costumes of *Ieri, oggi e domani* (*Yesterday, Today and Tomorrow*, 1963) and *Matrimonio all'Italiana* (*Marriage Italian Style*, 1964), and with **Mauro Bolognini**, with whom he collaborated on a host of films from the early *Il bell'Antonio* (*Bell'Antonio*, 1960) to *La storia vera della signora delle camelie* (*The True Story of the Lady of the Camelias*, 1981). An extremely imaginative and versatile artist, Tosi was also responsible for the makeup and hairstyles of **Federico Fellini**'s *Satyricon* (*Fellini Satyricon*, 1969) as well as the overall production design of *Toby Dammit*, Fellini's contribution to the compilation film *Tre passi nel delirio* (*Spirits of the Dead*, 1968). In the 1980s he worked most often with **Franco Zeffirelli**, his designs for Zeffirelli's production of *La traviata* (1982) earning him his fifth Oscar nomination. After collaborating one last time with Zeffirelli on *Storia di una capinera* (*Sparrow*, 1994), Tosi officially retired from the film industry to continue teaching costume design at the **Centro Sperimentale di Cinematografia**.

TOTÒ (1898–1967). Actor and writer. Antonio De Curtis, known from his earliest years simply as Totò, was undoubtedly the most popular and prolific comic actor in the history of Italian cinema. As well as performing in innumerable stage shows and theatrical reviews, he appeared in over 100 films and at the time of his death had achieved such popularity as to have become a national legend.

Born illegitimately in one of the poorer quarters of Naples and baptized under his mother's maiden name of Clemente, he achieved both respectability and nobility when his father, the Marquis Giuseppe De Curtis, finally married his mother in 1921 and, several years later, officially acknowledged paternity. By another quirk of fate, in 1933 he was also legally adopted by the Marquis Francesco Maria Gagliardi Focas, all of which served to invest him with a long series of aristocratic titles that he always displayed with great pride. Ironically, while on the stage or screen he frequently played lower-class characters who were invariably poor and hungry, on the set or in the dressing room he displayed a distinct preference for being addressed as "Principe" ("Highness").

After serving as a volunteer in the army during World War I, Totò returned to Naples and began performing as an amateur, doing comic sketches and *commedia dell'arte* in many of the city's smaller theaters. In 1922 he moved to Rome, where, in what would become his trademark stage costume of bowler hat, frock coat, baggy pants, and flat shoes, he made a triumphal acting debut at the prestigious Teatro

Umberto I. From then on his reputation continued to grow as he appeared with many of the major theatrical companies of the day in prestigious theaters throughout Italy. By 1932 he had formed his own company and achieved a huge popularity touring the country with a variety of vaudeville shows and musical revues. Thus, by the mid-1930s, he had become the most renowned stage comedian in all of Italy when he was recruited to the cinema by veteran film producer **Gustavo Lombardo**.

In spite of the reputation he had built up on the stage, however, his first two films, *Fermo con le mani* (*Hands Off Me!* 1937) and *Animali pazzi* (*Mad Animals*, 1939), failed to impress, both seen by the waiting critics as little more than a stringing together of disparate comic sketches. His third film, *San Giovanni decollato* (*St. John, the Beheaded*, 1940), directed by Amleto Palermi from a well-known play by Neapolitan writer and director **Nino Martoglio**, displayed greater narrative coherence and depth of character and was considerably better received. Nevertheless, it is probably true to say that Totò's film career only really came into its own in the immediate postwar period when the unexpected but overwhelming box office success of **Mario Mattoli**'s *I due orfanelli* (*The Two Orphans*, 1947) initiated a frenetic production schedule for the next decade and a half that saw him appear in up to seven films a year, allowing *Il comandante* (*The Commandant*), made in 1963, to be billed as the comedian's 100th film.

It is undeniable that many of these were flimsy farces that, like *I due orfanelli* itself, utilized a thin narrative thread to hold together what was basically a series of inspired comic sketches, and some were also clearly hastily thrown-together parodies of other films that had achieved their own success, such as *Totò le moko* (1949), *Totò Tarzan* (1949), *Totò, Peppino e la dolce vita* (*Toto, Peppino and La dolce vita*, 1961), and *Che fine ha fatto Totò Baby?* (*What Ever Happened to Baby Toto?* 1964). Yet a number also engaged, albeit always in a comic vein, with some of the most pressing social problems of the day, as with the issue of the shortage of housing that was strongly foregrounded in films such as *Totò cerca casa* (*Toto Looks for an Apartment*, 1949) and *Arrangiatevi!* (*You're on Your Own*, 1959). But what was present in all the films, especially the ones that featured his name in the title, such as *Totò cerca moglie* (Toto Looks for a Wife, 1950), *Totò a colori* (*Toto in Color*, 1952), *Totò all'in-*

ferno (Toto in Hell, 1955), *Totò, Peppino e la malafemmina* (*Toto, Peppino, and the Hussy*, 1956), was an exceptional comic bravura that united the most extraordinary physical ability to use the body like a marionette with a verbal dexterity and linguistic inventiveness that frequently bordered on performance poetry. Indeed, certain invented phrases from the films entered the language and became common currency.

Yet in spite of their immense popularity and undeniable box office success, Totò's films continued to be generally dismissed by serious film critics, and the only critical recognition he received for the greater part of his career was the **Nastro d'argento** for his role in **Steno** and **Mario Monicelli**'s *Guardie e ladri* (*Cops and Robbers*, 1951). Then, only a year before his death, his inspired performance in **Pier Paolo Pasolini**'s *Uccellacci e uccellini* (*Hawks and Sparrows*, 1966) was recognized with a special mention at Cannes and a second Nastro d'argento. In 1995, on the occasion of the centenary of the birth of cinema, a postage stamp of Totò was issued to honor his place in Italian popular culture.

TROISI, MASSIMO (1953–1994). Actor, screenwriter, director. One of the most genial and popular directors of the so-called **New Italian Cinema**, Troisi came to films after many years of cabaret and amateur theater. He began his brief career in the late 1960s performing stand-up comedy and cabaret in Naples with the group *La smorfia* (*The Grimace*), eventually gaining a national notoriety via appearances on television programs such as *Nonstop* (1976) and *Luna Park* (1979). Deciding to branch out on his own, in 1981 he wrote, directed, and acted in his first feature film, *Ricomincio da tre* (*I'm Starting from Three*, 1981), which earned him the immediate recognition of two **David di Donatello** awards, including Best Film, and three **Nastri d'argento**. He subsequently wrote and directed himself in *Scusate il ritardo* (Sorry I'm Late, 1982) before pairing up with **Roberto Benigni** to codirect and act in the hilarious road movie through Italian history, *Non ci resta che piangere* (Nothing Left to Do but Cry, 1985). After acting in Cinzia Th. Torrini's *Hotel Colonial* (1987), he directed himself again in *Le vie del signore sono finite* (The Ways of the Lord Have Ended, 1987) before appearing in **Ettore Scola**'s *Splendor* (1988); *Che ora è* (*What Time Is It?* 1989), for which he shared the Volpi Cup for Best Actor at the **Venice Festival** with **Marcello Mastroianni**; and *Il viaggio di Capitan Fracassa* (*The Voyage of Captain Fracassa*, 1990). He directed himself again in *Pensavo fosse amore, invece era un calesse* (*I Thought It Was Love*, 1991) before making his last appearance, when already quite ill from a congenital heart ailment, in Michael Radford's *Il Postino* (*The Postman*, 1994), for which he received a posthumous Oscar nomination. His tragic early death was widely mourned by many who thought he was just reaching his artistic maturity.

TROVAJOLI, ARMANDO (1917–). Musician and composer. After learning to play the violin at home as a child, Trovajoli graduated in piano at the Conservatory of Saint Cecilia in Rome before undertaking further studies in composition under Angelo Francesco Lavagnino. He was, however, most attracted to jazz, and by the age of 20 was playing with some of the best Italian jazz ensembles of the period. After the war he continued his career as a jazz pianist and had occasion to perform with such internationally renowned musicians as Duke Ellington, Louis Armstrong, Miles Davis, Chet Baker, and Django Reinhardt. In the early 1950s he began an extensive series of recordings while at the same time working with **Piero Piccioni**, presenting regular jazz programs on national radio.

Although already introduced to composing for film by Lavagnino himself, Trovajoli's first real foray into music for cinema was the song "El Negro Zumbón," which **Silvana Mangano** sang in **Alberto Lattuada**'s *Anna* (1951) and which subsequently became a huge international hit when released as a single. From this point on, Trovajoli's crowded career alternated between performing and directing music himself, writing highly popular musical revues such as the legendary *Rugantino* (1962), and composing the soundtrack of literally hundreds of films. He worked at various times with practically all the major directors (with the notable exeption of **Federico Fellini**), including **Vittorio De Sica**, for whom he scored *La ciociara* (*Two Women*, 1960), *Ieri, oggi, domani* (*Yesterday, Today and Tomorrow*, 1963), and *Matrimonio all'italiana* (*Marriage Italian Style*, 1964), and **Giuseppe De Santis**, with whom he collaborated on the war epic *Italiani brava gente* (*Attack and Retreat*, 1964). He established an especially close relationship with both **Dino Risi**, for whom he scored over 30 films, and with **Ettore Scola**, contributing the music to all of Scola's films and winning the **Nastro d'argento** for *Una giornata particolare* (*A Special Day*, 1977) and *La famiglia* (*The Family*, 1987) and the **David di Donatello** for *Ballando ballando* (also known as *Le Bal*, 1983). At the same time he also embraced all the popular genres, writing the music for everything from **Totò** and **peplum** films to **horror** and **Western** *all'italiana* movies.

With over 300 film scores to his credit, Trovajoli continues to be one of Italy's most acclaimed film composers. His international popularity was underscored by Quentin Tarantino's decision to incorporate a section of Trovajoli's score for the **spaghetti Western** *I lunghi giorni della vendetta* (*Long Days of Vengeance*, 1966) in his *Kill Bill, Vol. I* (2003).

– U –

UMILIANI, PIERO (1926–2001). Musician and film composer. A passionate jazz enthusiast from his earliest years, Umiliani nevertheless graduated in law before going on to study at the Luigi Cherubini Conservatory in Florence, where he majored in fugue and counterpoint. In 1952 he moved from his native Florence to Rome, where he worked as an arranger for **Armando Trovajoli** and soon thereafter recorded his first album for RCA, *Dixieland in Naples*. In 1955 he was hired by the RAI studios as resident pianist, conductor, and arranger. His first composition for film was the groundbreaking jazz score he provided for **Mario Monicelli**'s *I soliti ignoti* (*Big Deal on Madonna Street*, 1958), on which he featured the legendary American trumpeter Chet Baker. He subsequently worked with many of the major Italian directors and across all the popular film genres, from the *commedia all'italiana* and spy films to **Western** *all'italiana* and the *giallo*. One of his most highly regarded film scores was the orchestral jazz soundtrack for Siro Marcellini's crime thriller *La legge dei gangsters* (*Gangsters' Law*, 1969). At the other end of the scale, his simple but catchy "Mahna Mahna" theme, originally written for the mondo-style documentary *Svezia, Inferno e Paradiso* (*Sweden Heaven and Hell*, 1968), received a new lease on life when performed by the Muppets in 1977 and has been revived in countless versions ever since. After penning the music for some 150 feature films, documentaries, and television programs, in the early 1980s Umiliani suffered a severe brain hemorrhage and only recovered the ability to play music a few years before his death.

UNIONE CINEMATOGRAFICA ITALIANA (UCI). (Italian Cinematographic Union.) In January 1919, in response to the declining fortunes of the film industry at home and increased competition from abroad, 11 of the major Italian studios, together with their actors, directors, and financial underwriters, united under the leadership of Baron Alberto Fassini, formerly head of **Cines**, to create the Unione Cinematografica Italiana. While the consortium initially had some success in increasing production, poor management practices and disagreements between a number of the major players prevented it from functioning smoothly from the very start. By February 1920 Baron Fassini had left to join the board of an Italian American shipping line. Then in 1921, with productions proliferating, costs soaring, and box office earnings continuing to fall, the collapse of one of the trust's principal backers, the Banca Italiana di Sconto, dealt it a mortal blow. Recklessly, however, more large-scale productions were financed and executed but most failed dismally at the box office. Furthermore, the trust's poor distribution network meant that many of the films that were produced were not properly exhibited and sometimes never released. With an expensive remake of *Quo vadis?* still in production in 1923, the consortium was declared legally bankrupt, although it was not officially wound up until 1926 when all its assets were liquidated, most being bought up by the enterprising **Stefano Pittaluga**.

– V –

VALERI, FRANCA (1920–). (Real name Franca Maria Norsa.) Actress and playwright. One of Italy's most celebrated comediennes, Milanese-born Valeri came to popular notice in the late 1940s for her comic characterizations on the radio, achieving particular notoriety for her impersonation of the snobbish and opinionated young northerner *signorina Cesira* (*Miss Cesira*). Her characters soon migrated to the stage as part of the Teatro dei Gobbi, which Valeri helped to found and with which she toured Europe, and for the next two decades she also reappeared in various guises on many of the most watched television comedy and variety shows.

From the early 1950s she also began to appear in films, making her debut as a Hungarian choreographer in *Luci del varietà* (*Variety Lights*, 1950) and continuing as the rich and spoiled Giulia Sofia in *Totò a colori* (*Toto in Color*, 1952); as Lady Eva, the pseudoaristocratic heart-to-heart columnist in **Steno**'s *Piccola posta* (1955); and as the plainer cousin of **Sophia Loren** in **Dino Risi**'s *Il segno di Venere* (*The Sign of Venus*, 1955), which she also helped to write. One of her most memorable incarnations from this period was as the shrewish wife and nemesis of **Alberto Sordi** in Risi's *Il vedovo* (*The Widower*, 1959). Although she continued to appear in films in the following years, most frequently in supporting roles but also starring at times, as in several comedies directed by her husband, Vittorio Caprioli, her first love remained the theater, and from the mid-1980s she worked mostly onstage, frequently writing and acting in her own plays. She returned to television in the mid-1990s as a regular in a number of popular situation comedies and miniseries such as *Norma e Felice* (1995), *Caro maestro* (Dear Teacher, 1996), and *Linda e il brigadiere* (*Linda and the Sergeant,* 1999). In 2003, while continuing to perform a number of her own plays on stage, she also returned to the big screen in an adaptation of her play *Tosca e altre due* (*Tosca and the Women*, 2003), an amusing take on the well-known opera, directed by Giorgio Ferrara.

VALLI, ALIDA (1921–2006). Actress. Born Baroness Alida Maria Altenburger in Pola (then Istria, now part of Croatia), Valli moved to Rome in 1935 to become one of the first students at the **Centro Sperimentale di Cinematografia**. She abandoned the Centro after only a year in order to take a small part in **Enrico Guazzoni**'s *I due sergenti* (*The Two Sergeants*, 1936) and then a more substantial role in **Mario Bonnard**'s *Il feroce saladino* (The Fierce Sultan, 1937), for which she first assumed the stage name of Alida Valli. In the following years she gained wide popularity playing the young innocent in a number of the so-called **white telephone films** and by the end of the 1930s had achieved star status. Her reputation as a serious actress was then consolidated by her moving interpretation of Luisa in **Mario Soldati**'s *Piccolo mondo antico* (*Old-Fashioned World*, 1941), for which she received the Best Actress award at the **Venice Festival**, and her stirring performance as Kira in **Goffredo Alessandrini**'s *Noi vivi* (*We the Living*, 1942).

Immediately after the war, Valli appeared in **Mario Mattoli**'s *La vita ricomincia* (*Life Begins Anew*, 1945) and was again chosen by Soldati to play the lead in *Eugenia Grandet* (*Eugenie Grandet*, 1947), a performance that brought her a **Nastro d'argento** and also to the attention of David O. Selznick, who lured her to Hollywood to play opposite Gregory Peck in Alfred Hitchcock's *The Paradine Case* (1947). After again playing the female lead opposite Fred MacMurray and a very young Frank Sinatra in Irving Pichel's *The Miracle of the Bells* (1948), she was called to England to play Anna Schmidt in Carol Reed's *The Third Man* (1949).

Having returned to Europe in the early 1950s, she made a number of minor films, both in Italy and in France, before providing one of the best performances of her career as the Countess Livia Serpieri in **Luchino Visconti**'s *Senso* (*The Wanton Countess*, 1954). She was subsequently the protagonist's wife, Rosetta, in **Gillo Pontecorvo**'s debut film, *La grande strada azzurra* (*The Wide Blue Road*, 1957), Irma in **Michelangelo Antonioni**'s *Il grido* (*The Outcry*, 1957), Queen Merope in **Pier Paolo Pasolini**'s *Edipo Re* (*Oedipus Rex*, 1967), and then Draifa, the enigmatic former mistress of the protagonist's father, in **Bernardo Bertolucci**'s *La strategia del ragno* (*The Spider's Stratagem*, 1970). In the following years, while continuing to work with auteurs like **Valerio Zurlini**—she was Vanina's mother in *La prima notte di quiete* (*The Professor*, 1972)—and with Bertolucci again in *Novecento* (*1900*, 1976) and *La luna* (Luna, 1979), she also took on cameo roles in a number of B-grade **horror** thrillers such as **Mario Bava**'s *La casa dell'esorcismo* (*The House of Exorcism*, 1973), Pierre Grunstein's *Tendre Dracula* (*Tender Dracula*, 1974), and Giulio Berruti's *Suor omicidi* (*Killer Nun*, 1978). She is particularly remembered by horror buffs for her part as Miss Tanner in **Dario Argento**'s horror classic *Suspiria* (1977). From the mid-1950s onward she alternated between film and theater and often appeared on television, both in Italy and abroad. After hosting the television music show *Music Rama* (1966), she also tried her hand at producing and codirecting the **documentary** *L'amore in tutte le sue espressioni* (*Love in All Its Manifestations*, 1968). She continued to work throughout the 1980s and 1990s, although mostly in supporting roles, earning a **David di Donatello** for Best Supporting Actress in **Marco Tullio Giordana**'s *La Caduta degli angeli ribelli* (*The Fall of the Rebellious Angels*, 1981), and a year later the Italian theater critics' Ennio Flaiano Award for her performance onstage in the Renaissance comedy *La Venexiana*. After a host of other prizes and recognitions, including the honorific title of Cavaliere della Repubblica, she was awarded a **David di Donatello** for her career achievements in 1991 and in 1997 a Golden Lion at the **Venice Festival** for her contribution to world cinema.

VALLONE, RAF (1916–2002). Actor. Endowed with handsome good looks and a strong athletic build, Raffaele (shortened to Raf) Vallone was one of the leading male actors of the postwar period.

Having tried unsuccessfully to pursue a career as a professional soccer player, Vallone studied law and literature at the University of Turin, graduating in both. Before joining the ranks of the **Resistance** movement, he landed a small walk-on role in **Goffredo Alessandrini**'s *Noi vivi* (*We the Living*, 1942). After the war he worked as a sports and cultural writer for the Communist daily *L'Unità* before playing a strong supporting role in **Giuseppe De Santis**'s runaway success, *Riso amaro* (*Bitter Rice*, 1949). His acting career was assured as he was called to play the lead roles in De Santis's *Non c'è pace fra gli ulivi* (*Under the Olive Tree*, 1950), **Pietro Germi**'s *Il cammino della speranza* (*Path of Hope*, 1950), and the powerful, even if at times excessively melodramatic, part of Bruno in Curzio Malaparte's *Il Cristo proibito* (*The Forbidden Christ*, 1951). **Alberto Lattuada** gave him the very sympathetic role of Andrea in *Anna* (1951), after which he played Giuseppe Garibaldi in Alessandrini's historical drama, *Camicie Rosse* (*Red Shirts*, 1952). Having by now begun to acquire an international reputation, he was called to France to play the male lead opposite Simone Signoret in Marcel Carné's *Thérèse Raquin* (1953), following which Lattuada provided him with more positive roles as the progressive Communist mayor in *La spiaggia* (*The Beach*, 1954) and the father in *Guendalina* (1957). In the late 1950s he extended himself further by taking to the stage, receiving particular acclaim for his portrayal of Eddie Carbone in Peter Brook's Parisian production of Arthur Miller's *A View from the Bridge*, a role that he reprised in Sidney Lumet's 1961 screen adaptation of the play. After playing **Sophia Loren**'s sometime lover in **Vittorio De Sica**'s *La ciociara* (*Two Women*, 1960), he was lured to Hollywood, where he gave many creditable performances including that of Count Ordóñez in Anthony Mann's *El Cid* (1961) and Cardinal Quarenghi in Otto Preminger's *The Cardinal* (1963), the first of many clerics he would play from then on.

He subsequently appeared in a wide variety of films, from political thrillers such as John Huston's *The Kremlin Letter* (1970) and Otto Preminger's *Rosebud* (1975) to B-grade **horror** films like William M. Rose's *The Girl in Room 2a* (1973). At the same time he worked extensively for television in Italian miniseries such as *Il mulino del Po* (*The Mill on the Po*, 1971) and *Marco Visconti* (1975) and in American telefilms such as *Honor Thy Father* (1973), in which he played New York gangster Joe Bonanno. Fittingly, perhaps, one of his last on-screen roles was the part of the honest Cardinal Lamberto in Francis Ford Coppola's *The Godfather: Part III* (1990). In 2001 Vallone recounted his long and interesting career in his autobiographical *Alfabeto della memoria* (*An Alphabet of Memory*).

VANCINI, FLORESTANO (1926–). Director and screenwriter. Beginning in 1949, Vancini directed some 40 documentaries and worked as assistant director to **Mario Soldati** and **Valerio Zurlini** before making an impressive directorial debut in 1960 with *La lunga notte del '43* (*Long Night in 1943*). Adapted from a novel by Giorgio Bassani that recounted the events surrounding a massacre by the Fascists in Ferrara during World War II, *La lunga notte* was awarded the prize for Best First Film at the **Venice Festival**. Then, following the crime drama *La banda Casaroli* (The Casaroli Gang, 1962) and *La calda vita* (*The Warm Life*, 1963), Vancini used the pseudonym Stan Vance to make a foray into the **Western** *all'italiana* with *I lunghi giorni della vendetta* (*Long Days of Vengeance*, 1967). He returned to a more socially committed cinema with *La violenza: Quinto potere* (*The Sicilian Checkmate*, 1972), which used the format of the courtroom drama to investigate the links between illegal power networks in Sicily, and *Bronte, cronaca di un mas-*

sacro che i libri di storia non hanno raccontato (*Liberty*, 1972), a fictional re-creation of a brutal reprisal carried out by the northern Italian forces during the **Risorgimento** period. This was followed by another attempted historical reconstruction in *Il delitto Matteotti* (*The Assassination of Matteotti*, 1973) before a turn to an exploration of familial and interpersonal relationships in *Amore amaro* (*Bitter Love*, 1974) and *Un dramma borghese* (*Mimi*, 1979). Vancini subsequently worked mostly for television, directing, among others, the second run of the very popular long-running series on the Mafia, *La Piovra* (*Octopus*, 1985), and the miniseries *Piazza di Spagna* (1993).

VANZINA, STEFANO (1917–1988). Screenwriter and director. Although probably best remembered for a string of delightful comedies that he directed during the early 1950s, Vanzina, better known as Steno, was a professional and versatile director who could work comfortably in a variety of genres.

While studying law at the University of Rome, Vanzina became one of the animators of the satirical magazine *Marc'Aurelio*. In the late 1930s, together with a number of other writers from the magazine, he began to work as a screenwriter, helping to pen a series of films directed by **Mario Mattoli** and featuring popular comic actor **Erminio Macario**. In the immediate postwar period he continued to work as a screenwriter before making his own directorial debut in 1949 with *Al diavolo la celebrità* (*A Night of Fame*, 1949), the first of nine films that he would direct in partnership with **Mario Monicelli**. In the same year, together with Monicelli, he directed *Totò cerca casa* (*Toto Looks for an Apartment*, 1949), the first of thirteen films he would make with master comic actor **Totò**, which would include the much-acclaimed *Guardie e ladri* (*Cops and Robbers*, 1951), nominated for the Grand Prize at Cannes, as well as *Totò a colori* (*Toto in Color*, 1952), the first Italian film to be made in color. After *L'uomo, la bestia e la virtù* (*Man, Beast and Virtue*, 1953), an adaptation of a play by Luigi Pirandello that featured Orson Welles in one of the major roles, Vanzina directed the now-legendary *Un americano a Roma* (*An American in Rome*, 1954), the film that first showcased the comic talents of **Alberto Sordi**.

While he continued to show a marked propensity for the comic genre throughout his career, in the early 1970s Vanzina also made a foray into the gangster genre with *Cose di Cosa Nostra* (*Gang War*, 1971) and directed several tense police thrillers, the best known being *La polizia ringrazia* (*Execution Squad*, 1972). He scored one of his biggest successes of the 1970s with *Febbre da cavallo* (Horse Fever, 1976), a film set in the world of horse racing. In the late 1980s he returned to the police thriller with six films made for television, featuring the maverick police commissioner Jack Clementi, also known as the Professor.

VENICE FESTIVAL. Now regarded as the most important event in the Italian film calendar, the Venice Festival was inaugurated in 1932 when the screening of films was first incorporated into the Venice Biennial Exhibition of the Arts. Although initiated by private tourist operators as a stratagem for attracting more visitors to Venice, it was also strongly supported by the Fascist government through its Institute of Educational Cinema (Istituto del Cinema Educatore) as a way of demonstrating the regime's modern outlook and its openness to the international exchange of ideas.

Indeed, in its early years the festival was relatively liberal and included not only Hollywood fare such as Rouben Mamoulian's *Dr. Jekyll and Mr. Hyde* (1931) and *Becky Sharp* (1935) but also films of ideological persuasion in contrast with that of the regime, such as René Clair's *À nous la liberté* (*Liberty for Us*, 1932) and Jean Renoir's antiwar masterpiece, *La grande illusion* (*The Grand Illusion*, 1937). The festival proved so popular that in 1935 it was transformed from a biennial to an annual event. However, the regime had been gradually assuming tighter control of the organizational reins and in the wake of Italy's invasion of Ethiopia and the ensuing international boycotts, the festival was reduced to a local and largely European affair, screening and rewarding only films that promulgated the ideology of the German-Italian alliance.

The festival was discontinued in 1943 due to the war but reinstated in 1946 when it hosted, among others, **Roberto Rossellini**'s *Paisà* (*Paisan*, 1946) and Marcel Carné's *Les enfants du paradis* (*Children of Paradise*, 1945), with the prize for best film going to Jean Renoir's *The Southerner* (1945). In 1949 the festival's major prize was officially designated as the Golden Lion and the program was expanded to include special sessions for children's films, short films, and documentaries. In the following years, although often riven with political controversy, it continued to host some of the best national and international films, to highlight and champion particular themes, and to create new categories of award. However, in 1968, echoing what was happening elsewhere in the country, violent protests and demonstrations disrupted the festival, leading organizers to continue the screening of films for the next decade but, with the exception of Golden Lions recognizing the careers of a number of major international directors in 1971–1972, to discontinue the award of prizes.

The practice of recognizing particular films was resumed in 1980 and new awards recognizing lifetime achievement as well as other categories continued to be introduced in the following years. In 1992 filmmaker **Giulio Pontecorvo** was installed as artistic director and under his energetic leadership the festival flourished and expanded, confirming its status as one of the great manifestations of world cinema. (A full listing of festival winners is given in the appendix.)

VERDONE, CARLO (1950–). Actor and director. Son of film historian and critic Mario Verdone, Carlo studied directing at the **Centro Sperimentale di Cinematografia**. While serving his apprenticeship as assistant director on several minor films, he also worked extensively in cabaret theater and on radio. In 1977 he wrote, directed, and acted in *Tali e quali* (*Just So!*), a stage show in which he played a dozen different comic characters and which displayed his remarkable talent for accurate impersonation. He was soon parading his characters on television in the popular long-running comedy series *Non stop*.

After a minor role in **Bernardo Bertolucci**'s *La luna* (*Luna*, 1979), Verdone met **Sergio Leone**, who agreed to produce his first feature, *Un sacco bello* (*Fun Is Beautiful*, 1980). The film again amply displayed Verdone's talent for playing multiple character types and earned him a special **David di Donatello** and a **Nastro d'argento**. There followed *Bianco, Rosso e Verdone* (White, Red and Green, 1981) and *Borotalco* (Talcum Powder, 1982), which won five Davids, including Best Film and Best Actor for Verdone himself. His popularity and critical acclaim continued unabated in the following years as the character types he created in films such as *Acqua e sapone* (*Soap and Water*, 1983), *Troppo forte* (*Great!* 1985), *Io e mia sorella* (*Me and My Sister*, 1987), *Compagni di scuola* (School Friends, 1988), *Maledetto il giorno che t'ho incontrato* (*Damned the Day I Met You*, 1992), *Al lupo, al lupo* (*Wolf! Wolf!* 1992), and *Perdiamoci di vista* (*Let's Not Keep in Touch*, 1994) searingly satirized many aspects of young Italian males in perpetual personal crisis. As well as directing himself in his own films, Verdone appeared as **Alberto Sordi**'s *In viaggio con papà* (*Journey with Papa*, 1982), in which he played Sordi's son, and more recently in one of the stories of Giovanni Veronesi's *Manuale d'amore* (*Manual of Love*, 2005), for which he won another David di Donatello for Best Supporting Actor. His most recent film, the bittersweet generational comedy *Il mio miglior nemico* (*My Best Enemy*, 2006), has been critically acclaimed and nominated for five Davids.

VERGANO, ALDO (1891–1957). Screenwriter and director. After fighting as a volunteer in World War I, Vergano became a militant left-wing journalist and wrote for a number of radical newspapers. In 1925 he was associated with the unsuccessful Zaniboni plot to kill Benito Mussolini but miraculously escaped prosecution. He became a traveling salesman for a period until he met **Alessandro Blasetti** and was drawn to writing for Blasetti's film journal, *Cinematografo*. He then worked with Blasetti on *Sole* (*Sun*, 1929), for which he wrote both the story and the screenplay, and soon followed Blasetti to the new **Cines** studios where he directed the **documentary** *I fori imperiali* (*The Imperial Forums*, 1932). Thereafter he worked extensively as writer, cowriter, and sometimes production manager on a wide variety of films including **Goffredo Alessandrini**'s *Don Bosco* (1935) and *Cavalleria* (Cavalry, 1936) and **Mario Bonnard**'s *L'albero di Adamo* (*Adam's Tree*, 1937) while also directing two features, *Pietro Micca* (1938) and *Quelli della montagna* (*Mountain People*, 1943).

An active member of the Partito d'azione (Action Party), Vergano fought in the **Resistance** movement and in the immediate postwar period directed what is widely regarded as the great classic Resistance film, *Il sole sorge ancora* (*Outcry*, 1946), which was financed by the National Partisan Association (ANPI) and enlisted the collaboration of a number of later directors such as **Carlo Lizzani**, **Giulio Pontecorvo**, and **Giuseppe De Santis** in key acting roles. Although schematic and rather one sided, the film was widely praised, receiving the **Centro Sperimentale di Cinematografia** prize at the **Venice Festival** that year and earning Vergano a special **Nastro d'argento** in 1947 for his direction. However, none of the handful of films he made subsequently received any praise or critical attention and he is reputed to have died lonely and disappointed after having drafted his aptly titled memoirs, *Cronache di anni perduti* (*Chronicles of Wasted Years*), published posthumously in 1958.

VINCENZONI, LUCIANO (1926–). Screenwriter and producer. Having graduated with a degree in law from university, Vincenzoni nevertheless turned his back on a legal career in order to work in cinema. His first collaboration was with **Pietro Germi** on the screenplay of *Il Ferroviere* (1955). After a number of less-distinguished films, such as Angelo Dorigo's *Amore e guai* (*Love and Troubles*, 1958), he established his reputation as a first-rate screenwriter by writing the story and the screenplay for **Mario Monicelli**'s *La grande guerra* (*The Great War*, 1959). Having collaborated with **Carlo Lizzani** on the script for *Il gobbo* (*The Hunchback of Rome*, 1960), and with **Mario Camerini** on *Crimen* (*And Suddenly It's Murder!* 1960) and *I briganti italiani* (*The Italian Brigands*, 1961), he worked again with Germi on *Sedotta e abbandonata* (*A Matter of Honor*, 1963) and *Signori e signore* (*The Birds, the Bees and the Italians*, 1965), both of which earned him a **Nastro d'argento**. Greater financial success came from his sometimes stormy collaboration with **Sergio Leone**, with whom he worked on *Per qualche dollaro in più* (*For a Few Dollars More*, 1965), *Il buono, il brutto, il cattivo* (*The Good, the Bad, and the Ugly*, 1966) and *Giù la testa* (*Duck, You Sucker*, 1971).

He subsequently worked on a wide range of both Italian and international films, including the unsuccessful *Jaws* imitation, *Orca* (*The Killer Whale*, 1977), directed by Michael Anderson, which Vicenzoni produced as well as scripted, and Duccio Tessari's CIA thriller *Beyond Justice* (1992). In 1996 he was awarded the Flaiano International Prize for his career achievement. In 2000 his short story "Ma l'amore no" ("But Not Love") was used by **Giuseppe Tornatore** as the basis for the screenplay of *Malèna* (2000).

VIRZÌ, PAOLO (1964–). Director and screenwriter. One of the most interesting young directors to emerge as part of the **New Italian Cinema**, Virzì graduated from the **Centro Sperimentale di Cinematografia**, where he specialized in screenwriting. After collaborating on the screenplays of **Giuliano Montaldo**'s *Tempo di uccidere* (*Time to Kill*, 1989) and **Gabriele Salvatores**'s *Turnè* (Tour, 1990), he made his own directorial debut with *La bella vita* (*Living It Up*, 1994), an ironic portrait of working-class life in provincial Italy that earned him both the **David di Donatello** and the **Nastro d'argento** for Best New Director. His second feature, *Ferie d'agosto* (Summer Holidays, 1996), a caustic social comedy in the best tradition of the *commedia all'italiana*, received similar acclaim and was awarded that year's David for Best Film. A year later the heartwarming working-class, coming-of-age tale *Ovosodo* (*Hardboiled Egg*, 1997) was both a commercial and critical success and won the Special Grand Jury Prize at the **Venice Festival**. There followed *Baci e abbracci* (*Kisses and Hugs*, 1999), a quirky story revolving around the attempt by three retrenched workers to establish their own ostrich farm in Tuscany, and *My Name Is Tanino* (2001), a bemused portrayal of the misadventures of a Sicilian boy attempting to follow his American dream. Virzì then scored his biggest national and international success with *Caterina va in città* (*Caterina in the Big City*, 2003), a biting critique of contemporary Italian foibles carried out in the form of another coming-of-age movie. After also appearing in a small role in **Nanni Moretti**'s *Il caimano* (*The Caiman*, 2006), Virzì directed *N: Io e Napoleone* (*N.: Napoleon & Me*, 2006), a historical costume drama that uses Napoleon's period of exile on the island of Elba as a way to reflect on contemporary Italian mores.

VISCONTI, LUCHINO (1906–1976). Screenwriter and director of opera, theater, and film. Acknowledged as one of the foremost directors of the Italian cinema, Visconti was born into a rich and noble family that traced its ancestry to the rulers of Milan during the Renaissance period. The family had always had an extremely close association with the Teatro alla Scala and Visconti's most passionate interests in his youth were music, opera, literature, and theater. After studying in the finest private schools in northern Italy, he joined the Royal Cavalry Regiment and was quickly promoted to the rank of officer. On his release from military service, having become an excellent rider and a passionate horse lover, he established himself successfully as a trainer and breeder of racehorses.

In the early 1930s, during frequent stays in Paris, he became closely acquainted with many of the leading French artists and intellectuals and through his friendship with Coco Chanel was introduced to French director Jean Renoir. With cinema now added to his passionate interests, Visconti began working with Renoir, initially as an uncredited properties master on *Toni* (1935) and then hired officially as costume designer and third assistant director on *Une partie de campagne* (*A Day in the Country*, 1936). The experience of working with Renoir in France not only introduced Visconti to filmmaking but also left him deeply and permanently influenced by Renoir's left-wing politics and by the ideology of the Popular Front.

After extensive travels in Europe and America, Visconti returned to Italy and in 1939 moved to Rome, where Renoir and his assistant, Carl Koch, had arrived to direct a version of *Tosca* at the Scalera studios. Given their earlier experience and the friendship that had developed between them, Renoir invited Visconti to collaborate on the screenplay and to serve as second assistant director for the film. When the outbreak of the war forced Renoir to abandon Italy, Visconti helped Koch to complete the film, although the relative contribution of each to the final product has always remained unclear. During this time he also met, and became part of, a group of militant young critics writing for the prestigious film journal *Cinema* that included **Giuseppe De Santis**, Mario Alicata, and **Gianni Puccini**. It was with this group that Visconti would produce his first film, an adaptation of James M. Cain's *The Postman Always Rings Twice* that, beginning as *Palude* (Swamp), eventually became *Ossessione* (*Obsession*, 1943).

A steamy noir narrative in which a handsome drifter helps a beautiful woman to murder her older husband, effectively transposed from heartland America to northern Italy, *Ossessione* was stunningly innovative in both content and style and unlike anything previously produced in Italian cinema. The film was warmly acclaimed when first screened to an invited audience in 1943, but its morally questionable content and its powerful realism provoked a generally hostile reaction from conservative authorities in many places where it was subsequently shown. Consequently, the film, later acknowledged as a milestone in the history of Italian cinema, was not seen again in Italy until after the war. Meanwhile, as the war itself intensified, Visconti took an ever more active part in the **Resistance** movement. In April 1944 he was arrested and imprisoned, and was released only with the arrival of the Allied forces. Immediately following the war Visconti collaborated with **Mario Serandrei** and others on the making of *Giorni di Gloria* (*Days of Glory*, 1945), a **documentary** on the Resistance financed by the National Partisan Association, before devoting himself almost exclusively to the theater, soon becoming renowned for his superb productions of contemporary plays, among them Jean Cocteau's *Les parents terribles* and Tennessee Williams's *The Glass Menagerie*. A documentary about Sicilian fishermen commissioned by the Italian Communist Party expanded greatly to become Visconti's second feature film, *La terra trema* (*The Earth Trembles*, 1948). Based on Giovanni Verga's 19th-century novel, *I Malavoglia*, the three-hour film was largely improvised on location in the Sicilian fishing village of Aci Trezza, using as actors only the local people, who spoke in their own dialect. Although the film thus thoroughly exemplified what by now had become established as the major tenets of **neorealism**, it was received very poorly, in part because its all-too-genuine dialect was largely incomprehensible to non-Sicilians. A subsequent version dubbed into standard Italian fared little better at the box office. A disappointed Visconti returned to the theater and for the next decade and a half continued to divide his energies between the stage and the screen.

After more theatrical triumphs, which included a production of Shakespeare's *As You Like It* designed by Salvador Dalí, Visconti returned to the cinema with *Bellissima* (1951), the story of a Roman working-class mother obsessively trying to get her young daughter into the movies. By contrast with Visconti's previous film, *Bellissima* was warmly received and earned **Anna Magnani**, as the misguided mother, her fourth **Nastro d'argento**. Theater and screen began to come closer together in Visconti's next film, *Senso* (*The Wanton Countess*, 1954), an operatic melodrama that attracted much praise for its sumptuous elegance and pictorial style but which was also criticized for what appeared to some to be a negative portrayal of the **Risorgimento**. A more modest film, *Le notti bianche* (*White Nights*,

1957), adapted from a novel by Fyodor Dostoyevsky, was better received and awarded the Silver Lion at the **Venice Festival**. With *Rocco e i suoi fratelli* (*Rocco and His Brothers*, 1960) Visconti returned to his neorealist roots to recount the tragic story of a southern Italian family disintegrating when transplanted into a northern city. Fiercely attacked for what conservatives saw as its left-wing political leanings and censored for some of its graphic violence, the film was nevertheless hailed as a major cinematic achievement, confirmed by the award of three Nastri d'argento, a **David di Donatello**, and the Special Prize at Venice, where political lobbying deprived it of the Golden Lion for which it had been nominated.

After *Il lavoro* (Work), an episode of the compilation film *Boccaccio '70* (1962), Visconti directed what remains one of his most celebrated films, *Il gattopardo* (*The Leopard*, 1963). A near-perfect adaptation of the novel by Giuseppe Tomasi di Lampedusa, set once again in the Risorgimento period, the film was a huge critical and box office success, although its budget overrun also contributed to bankrupting its production company, Titanus. Then, after more work in the theater, including a memorable production of Giuseppe Verdi's *Il trovatore* at Covent Garden in London, Visconti returned to the screen with *Vaghe stelle dell'orsa* (*Sandra of a Thousand Delights*, 1965), an intense family drama that finally brought him the Golden Lion at Venice. There followed the short *La strega bruciata viva* (*The Witch Burned Alive*), made as an episode for the compilation film *Le streghe* (*The Witches*, 1967), and *Lo straniero* (*The Stranger*, 1967), adapted from Albert Camus' popular novel of the same name, before the monumental *La caduta degli dei* (*The Damned*, 1970). Portraying the violent disintegration of a powerful German family as a mirror for the social dissolution of Germany itself under the onslaught of Nazism, *The Damned* was greater in scope and spectacle than any of Visconti's previous films, and proved to be an unqualified success, both critically and at the box office. A year later, *Morte a Venezia* (*Death in Venice*, 1971) adapted a novella by Thomas Mann to paint the elegiac portrait of another dissolution, this time of an aging composer identifiable with Gustav Mahler but with undeniable allusions to Visconti himself.

A year later with his next film, *Ludwig* (1973), shot but still unedited, Visconti suffered a minor stroke that left him partially paralyzed on his left side. Nevertheless, in the next few months, with great will and determination, he struggled back to the point of not only being able to edit the film but also to accept an invitation to return to the theater and direct a much-acclaimed version of *Manon Lescaut* at the 1973 Spoleto Festival. Although this would be his theatrical swan song, he would manage, even if from a wheelchair, to direct two further films, *Ritratto di una famigla in un interno* (*Conversation Piece*, 1974) and *L'innocente* (*The Innocent*, 1976), passing away in March 1976 as this final film was still in the process of postproduction.

VITROTTI, GIOVANNI (1882–1966). Cameraman and documentarist. A pioneer of the Italian cinema, Vitrotti worked for **Arturo Ambrosio** and his companies from 1905 to 1913 (and again between 1918 and 1920), often in collaboration with fellow cameraman and passionate documentarist **Roberto Omegna**. After shooting a huge number of both documentaries and feature films for Ambrosio Film in Turin, Vitrotti made several trips to Russia and central Europe in 1909 and 1911 as part of Ambrosio's partnership with German and Russian film companies, contributing, among other things, his technical knowledge and experience to the development of the fledgling Russian film industry. On his return to Italy in 1914 Vitrotti founded his own company, Leonardo Film, which, however, folded within a year. He subsequently worked for Musical Film and the Neapolitan Polifilm company before being conscripted into the army and serving as a documentarist for the Italian armed forces for the duration of World War I. From 1921 to 1931 he worked mostly in Germany before returning to Italy, where he continued to make quality documentaries.

VITTI, MONICA (1931–). (Born Maria Luisa Ceciarelli.) Actress. Although outside Italy Vitti is probably best remembered for her intensely dramatic roles in the films of **Michelangelo Antonioni**, in Italy she has always been better known as a comic actress, a talent that quickly came to the fore at the Rome Academy of Dramatic Art, from which she graduated in 1953. Her first (uncredited) film role was in *Ridere, Ridere, Ridere* (*Laugh, Laugh, Laugh*, 1954), a series of comic sketches directed by Edoardo Anton. While pursuing her career on the stage with the Sbragia-Lisi-Ronconi company she met

Antonioni, who used her voice to dub **Alida Valli** in his *Il grido* (*The Cry*, 1957). There followed the major Antonioni films *L'avventura* (*The Adventure*, 1960), *La notte* (*The Night*, 1961), *L'eclisse* (*The Eclipse*, 1962), and *Il deserto rosso* (*The Red Desert*, 1964), intense portraits of ennui and alienation in which Vitti became the perfect mouthpiece for Antonioni himself.

After more stage work, which included a 1964 production of Arthur Miller's *After the Fall*, directed by **Franco Zeffirelli**, she moved decisively to film comedy, from then on starring in a host of *commedie all'italiana* including **Mario Monicelli**'s *La ragazza con la pistola* (*Girl with a Pistol*, 1968), *Amore mio aiutami* (*Help Me My Love*, 1969), in which she acted with and was directed by **Alberto Sordi**, and **Dino Risi**'s *Noi donne siamo fatte così* (*That's How We Women Are*, 1971). At the same time she worked with international directors, appearing in, among others, Joseph Losey's *Modesty Blaise* (1966), Miklós Jancsó's *La pacifista* (*The Pacifist*, 1970), and Luis Buñuel's *Le fantôme de la liberté* (*The Phantom of Liberty*, 1974).

After returning briefly to work with Antonioni in *Il mistero di Oberwald* (*The Oberwald Mystery*, 1981), she retired from cinema during the 1980s except for two films directed by her then partner, Roberto Russo, *Flirt* (1983) and *Francesca è mia* (*Francesca Is Mine*, 1986), preferring during this period to concentrate on theater, which included appearing in a female version of Neil Simon's *The Odd Couple* (1987), directed by **Franca Valeri**. In 1990 she turned to directing herself in *Scandalo segreto* (*Secret Scandal*, 1990), for which she won Golden Globes for both acting and direction. Soon thereafter she published an autobiography, *Sette sottane* (Seven Underskirts, 1993), which won the Fregene Prize for biography, and a novel, *Il letto è una rosa* (*The Bed Is a Rose*, 1995).

During a long and distinguished career Vitti won five **David di Donatello** awards and three **Nastri d'argento**. In 1995 she received a Golden Lion at the **Venice Festival** for her lifetime achievement.

VOLONTÈ, GIAN MARIA (1933–1994). Actor. One of the most accomplished and distinctive actors in Italy in the postwar period, Volonté was also the foremost representative of a cinema of political commitment and social denunciation.

Having graduated from the National Academy of Dramatic Art in 1957, Volontè soon began to draw attention for the intensity of his acting, both in classics on the stage and on television, where he came to particular notice in a much-praised production of Fyodor Dostoyevsky's *The Idiot*. His film career began in a minor key with a small part in Duilio Coletti's war drama, *Sotto dieci bandiere* (*Under Ten Flags*, 1961), and an appearance as the King of Sparta in **Vittorio Cottafavi**'s **peplum** *Ercole alla conquista di Atlantide* (*Hercules and the Conquest of Atlantis*, 1961). His participation in genre cinema continued with the villains he played in two of **Sergio Leone**'s Westerns, *Per un pugno di dollari* (*A Fistful of Dollars*, 1964) and *Per qualche dollaro in più* (*For a Few Dollars More*, 1965), and the part of El Chuco in **Damiano Damiani**'s *Quién sabe?* (*A Bullet for the General*, 1967). At the same time, his appearance as Salvatore, the union activist who dares to challenge the power of the Mafia in **Paolo and Vittorio Taviani**'s *Un uomo da bruciare* (*A Man for Burning*, 1962), had opened the way to what would be a long line of much more socially conscious and politically committed roles, particularly in the films of **Elio Petri** and **Francesco Rosi**. His interpretation of Paolo Laurana in *A ciascuno il suo* (*We Still Kill the Old Way*, 1967), Petri's adaptation of Leonardo Sciascia's novel about politics and the Mafia in contemporary Sicily, earned Volontè both a **Nastro d'argento** in Italy and a nomination for the Palme d'or at Cannes. After appearing as Lieutenant Ottolenghi in *Uomini contro* (*Many Wars Ago*, 1970), the first of many films he would make with Rosi, which would include *Il caso Mattei* (*The Mattei Affair*, 1972), *Lucky Luciano* (1973), and *Cristo si è fermato a Eboli* (*Christ Stopped at Eboli*, 1979), he provided what remains perhaps his most stunning and engaging performance in Petri's ***Indagine su un cittadino al di sopra di ogni sospetto*** (*Investigation of a Citizen Above Suspicion*, 1970), which brought him his second Nastro d'argento and a **David di Donatello**.

Highly respected internationally, Volontè was also called to work with a number of non-Italian directors, including Jean-Luc Godard on *Le vent d'est* (*Wind from the East*, 1970), André Delvaux on his adaptation of Marguerite Yourcenar's novel, *L'oeuvre au noir* (*The Abyss*, 1988), and Swiss director Bernard Fontana on *La mort de Mario Ricci* (*The Death of Mario Ricci*, 1983) in an intepretation that was widely praised and for which he received the Best Actor award at Cannes. In 1991 his three decades of achievement were recognized with a career Golden Lion at the **Venice Festival**. After an extraordinarily thoughtful performance as Judge Vito Di Francesco in **Gianni Amelio**'s *Porte aperte* (*Open Doors*, 1990), for which he received both another David and the Special Prize of the Jury at the European Film Awards, Volontè died suddenly of a heart attack while filming Theodoros Angelopoulos's *Ulysses' Gaze* (1995).

– W –

WERTMÜLLER, LINA (1928–). Born Arcangela Felice Assunta Wertmüller von Elgg Spanol von Braucich, a factor that probably conditioned her later taste for long and extravagant titles, Wertmüller trained as a theater director at the Pietro Sharoff Academy before working extensively in a variety of theatrical forms including musical revues and puppet theater. At the same time she also worked in radio and television, where she achieved her greatest success with *Il giornalino di Gian Burrasca* (*Gian Burrasca's Diary*, 1964), an eight-part series adapted from a famous children's novel and revealing the considerable acting talents of the young pop singer Rita Pavone.

By Wertmüller's own admission, her most formative film experience was as one of the assistant directors on **Federico Fellini**'s *Otto e mezzo* (*8½*, 1963), which prompted her to make her first feature, *I basilischi* (*The Lizards*, 1963), a sort of southern Italian version of Fellini's *I vitelloni* (*Vitelloni*, 1963). Two years later, in response to **Ettore Scola**'s male-centered *Se permettete parliamo di donne* (*Let's Talk about Women*, 1964), she directed *Questa volta parliamo di uomini* (*This Time Let's Talk about Men*, 1965), a multiepisode film satirizing male-female relations, all episodes featuring **Nino Manfredi**. Under the pseudonym George Brown, Wertmüller then directed *Rita la zanzara* (*Rita the Mosquito*, 1966) and *Non stuzzicate la zanzara* (*Don't Sting the Mosquito*, 1967), two lightweight teen musicals, essentially vehicles for Rita Pavone. Having already established something of a reputation in Italy, Wertmüller then soared to international renown with a series of mordant but rather grotesque social farces featuring the duo of **Mariangela Melato** and **Giancarlo Giannini**, beginning with *Mimì metallurgico ferito nell'onore* (*The Seduction of Mimi*, 1972), nominated for the Palme d'or at Cannes that year, and followed by *Film d'amore e anarchia ovvero stamattina alle 10 in via dei Fiori nella nota casa di tolleranza* (*Love and Anarchy*, 1973), *Travolto da un insolito destino nell'azzurro mare d'agosto* (*Swept Away*, 1974), and *Pasqualino Settebellezze* (*Seven Beauties*, 1975), which achieved strong box office success and was nominated for two Oscars, making Wertmüller the first female to receive the Academy Award nomination for Best Director.

Many of her subsequent films continued to display a baroque tendency to visual and emotional excess, although she was able to achieve more nuanced results in films such as the made-for-television *Sabato, domenica e lunedì* (*Saturday, Sunday and Monday*, 1990), an adaptation of an Edoardo De Filippo play that featured **Sophia Loren** in her best role in years, and *Io speriamo che me la cavo* (*Ciao, Professore!* 1992), from the best-selling novel by Marcello D'Orta. After the elegant and relatively restrained historical costume drama *Ferdinando e Carolina* (*Ferdinand and Caroline*, 1999), she returned to something of her old form with *Peperoni ripieni e pesci in faccia* (*Too Much Romance . . . It's Time for Stuffed Peppers*, 2004), a comic family drama starring Sophia Loren and F. Murray Abraham.

In addition to her films, Wertmüller has continued to direct for the theater and has also published a number of novels, among them *Essere e avere ma per essere devo avere la testa di Alvise su un piatto d'argento* (*The Head of Alvise*, 1982) and *Avrei voluto uno zio esibizionista* (I Would Have Liked an Exhibitionist Uncle, 1990).

WESTERN *ALL'ITALIANA*. Film genre. The Western Italian style, more commonly known outside Italy as the "spaghetti Western," was a prolific genre that flourished in the mid-1960s, largely replacing the **peplum**, which had held the field in the previous decade. Some 450 such Westerns were made in Italy between 1964 and 1978, mostly as low-budget European or American coproductions and shot, for the most part, at the **Cinecittà** studios in Rome and on external locations in southern Italy and Spain.

Although quite a number of B-grade Westerns had been made in Italy in the early 1960s—and indeed something of a forerunner of the genre had already appeared 20 years earlier in Giorgio Ferroni's *Il fanciullo del West* (*The Boy in the West*, 1943)—the film that definitively launched the genre and defined its general characteristics was **Sergio Leone**'s *Per un pugno di dollari* (*A Fistful of Dollars*, 1964). Stylishly filmed and dramatically punctuated by a stirring musical score composed by **Ennio Morricone**, the film was made on a shoestring budget but soon broke all box office records. Its enormous and unexpected commercial success led Leone to make four more of what came to be regarded as classics of the genre: *Per qualche dollaro in più* (*For a Few Dollars More*, 1965), *Il buono, il brutto, il cattivo* (*The Good, the Bad and the Ugly*, 1966), *C'era una volta il west* (*Once upon a Time in the West*, 1968), and *Giù la testa* (*Duck, You Sucker*, 1971, also known as *A Fistful of Dynamite*). Departing conspicuously from the formula of the classic American Western, which clearly distinguished good and evil and ultimately reasserted the values of society and civilization, in these films Leone delighted in creating a more cynical and self-serving anti-hero who inhabited a violent and amoral universe in which only the clever and the ruthless survived. The new formula was immediately embraced by a host of other directors, often using Anglo-Saxon pseudonyms for themselves and their actors in an effort to make the films appear more genuinely American. Directors such as **Sergio Corbucci**, Enzo Barboni, Duccio Tessari, and Gianfranco Parolini created new but recognizable versions of Leone's gunslinger with no name who, under the guise of Django, Ringo, Sabata, and Sartana, reappeared in so many films as to create subgenres of their own.

   Although generally regarded as popular escapist fantasy, and in some of its later versions drawing the ire of the censors for its indulgence in extreme and explicit violence, the genre also developed a more politically conscious strand as in Sergio Sollima's *La resa dei conti* (*The Big Gundown*, 1966); **Damiano Damiani**'s *Quien sabe?* (*A Bullet for the General*, 1967), written by Marxist screenwriter **Franco Solinas**; and **Carlo Lizzani**'s *Requiescant* (*Kill and Pray*, 1966), in which director **Pier Paolo Pasolini** appears in a supporting role as a revolutionary Mexican priest. After dominating the popular film market for a decade, the genre faded away in the later 1970s, although the slapstick *My Name Is Trinity* version, starring the comic duo **Terence Hill** and **Bud Spencer**, continued to reappear sporadically into the late 1980s.

WHITE TELEPHONE FILMS. (*Telefoni bianchi.*) Genre. A generic characterization applied, usually with pejorative connotations, to a large number of light comedies and melodramas made in Italy during the Fascist period. Frequently set in elegant upper-class environments, these sophisticated comedies often featured white telephones as part of their decor, hence the name. The majority were produced at **Cinecittà** between 1938 and 1943, made largely in response to a heightened demand for films for the home market following the withdrawal of the American majors from Italy in the wake of the state monopoly on film distribution introduced by the Alfieri law (1938).

Modeled in part on the Hollywood screwball comedy and in part on a form of situational social comedy that was flourishing in Hungary in the 1920s—indeed, a large number of them were nominally set in (a largely fictitious) Budapest—these flighty films were extremely popular with audiences but came under fire from serious critics for their frivolousness and unreality. The call for a more realistic and socially conscious cinema that emerged from the pages of film journals such as *Cinema* was in large part a reaction to the proliferation of the genre. That such films actually served the interests of the Fascist regime in distracting the populace from the harsh realities of the time came to be a widely held view in the immediate postwar period, especially within the context of the advent of **neorealism**. However, the extent to which the films may have functioned as a form of indirect propaganda for the regime has continued to be a matter of debate. Although the genre is generally associated with many minor directors, the first three films directed by **Vittorio De Sica**, *Rose scarlatte* (*Red Roses*, 1940), *Maddalena zero in condotta* (*Maddalena, Zero for Conduct*, 1940), and *Teresa Venerdì* (*Mademoiselle Friday*, 1941), are usually listed under the white telephone rubric as are **Mario Camerini**'s *Batticuore* (*Heartbeat*, 1939) and **Alessandro Blasetti**'s *La Contessa di Parma* (*The Duchess of Parma*, 1937). Among the other directors who came to be associated with the genre were **Carmine Gallone, Mario Mattoli, Raffaello Matarazzo, Carlo Ludovico Bragaglia**, Nunzio Malasomma, Camillo Mastrocinque, Giacomo Gentilomo, and several central European directors also working in Italy at the time, including Max (or Massimiliano) Neufeld, László Vajda, and László Kish.

– Z –

ZA-LA-MORT. Character. Created by **Emilio Ghione** and modeled on the French mystery crime films of Victorin Jasset and Louis Feuillade, Za-la-Mort was a ruthless master criminal with a haggard face but a noble heart. Ghione appears to have derived the name from a battle cry intoned in Jasset's *Zigomar* trilogy (1911–1913), meaning "Long Live Death." The character's first appearance was in *Nelly la gigolette* (*Nelly, the Fast Girl*, 1914), but Ghione went on to develop the character through more than a dozen feature films as well as several multiepisode series. After 1915 Za was usually flanked by his faithful female sidekick, Za-la-Vie, played by Kelly Sambucini. Gaunt faced but photogenic and moving with feline grace, Ghione's "sentimental Apache" threaded his way through loosely constructed serial plots that, although not always logical, held cinema audiences spellbound. A tough criminal, capable of violence and murder in the earlier films, Za became more of an investigator and defender of the law in the later ones. In *Za-la-Mort contro Za-la-Mort* (Za-la-Mort versus Za-la-Mort, 1922) Za is forced to track down a real thief who is impersonating him but whose crimes are soiling Za's reputation. In one of the last films, *Ultimissime della notte* (Latest Night News, 1924), Za abandons his usual criminal attitude to take on the role of investigative journalist. By this time, however, Za's popularity had begun to wane and so the films were discontinued. One attempt to revive the character was made in 1947 by director **Raffaele Matarazzo**. The film, titled *Fumatori d'oppio o il ritorno di Za La Mort* (*The Opium Smokers or the Return of Za La Mort*), starred Ghione's son, Emilio Jr., but it received little notice and sank without a trace.

ZAMPA, LUIGI (1905–1991). Director, novelist, playwright, screenwriter. Coming from a poor background, Zampa began studying architecture and engineering at university but gravitated toward the theater and wrote a number of stage plays before enrolling at the newly formed **Centro Sperimentale di Cinematografia** in 1935. He then worked extensively as a screenwriter on a host of the so-called **white telephone films** before directing his first feature, a light theatrical comedy titled *L'attore scomparso* (The Actor Who Disappeared, 1941). This was followed by the historical costume drama *Fra' Diavolo* (*The Adventures of Fra Diavolo*, 1942) and *Un americano in vacanza* (*A Yank in Rome*, 1945), a love story set in the context of the American liberation of Italy.

In the immediate postwar period Zampa achieved a great deal of popularity with a number of films that were regarded, especially outside Italy, as part of the neorealist movement, in particular *Vivere in pace* (*To Live in Peace*, 1946), which was hugely successful both in Italy, where it won a **Nastro d'argento** for best story, and abroad, where it received, among others, the New York Film Critics award for Best Foreign Film. A year later *L'onorevole Angelina* (*Angelina, MP*, 1947), the story of a working-class woman who almost becomes a politician, similarly successful at the box office, was nominated for the Golden Lion at the **Venice Festival** and earned its star, **Anna Magnani**, both the Volpi Cup and a Nastro d'argento for her feisty interpretation. There followed a fruitful collaboration between Zampa and Sicilian novelist Vitaliano Brancati, with Brancati adapting his own novels for Zampa's *Anni difficili* (*Difficult Years*, 1948), *Anni facili* (*Easy Years*, 1953), and *L'arte di arrangiarsi* (*The Art of Getting Along*, 1954), biting satirical comedies that foregrounded the Italian knack for political and social compromise. During this time Zampa also made what many regard as his most accomplished film, *Processo alla città* (*The City Stands Trial*, 1952), a dramatic revisiting of the Cuocolo murders and the struggle for control of Naples by the camorra in the early 1900s.

Following Brancati's untimely death, Zampa filmed an adaptation of Alberto Maravia's novel *La romana* (*Woman of Rome*, 1954), with the screenplay written by Moravia himself, before going on to make a handful of only moderately successful films, which included *Il magistrato* (*The Magistrate*, 1959), *Il vigile* (*The Traffic Policeman*, 1960), and *Anni ruggenti* (*Roaring Years*, 1963). He achieved huge box office success again with *Il medico della mutua* (*Be Sick! It's Free*, 1968), a satirical take on the Italian health-care system starring **Alberto Sordi**, who by this stage had become a regular in Zampa's films, and then, again with Sordi playing the lead, *Bello, onesto, emigrato Australia sposerebbe compaesana illibata* (*A Girl in Australia*, 1971).

Zampa continued to address contemporary social problems in a comic vein in *Contestazione generale* (*Let's Have a Riot*, 1970), a satire on the student uprisings at the time that included stock footage of the student demonstrations. This was followed by *Bisturi, la mafia bianca* (*Hospitals: The White Mafia*, 1973), a caustic critique of corrupt doctors in the Italian medical system, and *Gente di rispetto* (*The Flower in His Mouth*, 1975), which took aim at the Mafia itself. After the psychological thriller *Il mostro* (*The Monster*, 1977) and *Letti selvaggi* (*Tigers in Lipstick*, 1979), an erotic escapade in eight episodes, Zampa retired from the cinema. In retirement he published several novels, including *Il primo giro della manovella* (The First Take, 1980) and *Pianeta nudo* (Naked Planet, 1987).

ZAVATTINI, CESARE (1902–1989). Novelist, screenwriter, director. Having worked for many years as a journalist, a novelist, a painter, and a cultural organizer, in 1935 Zavattini also embraced the cinema by writing the story and screenplay for **Mario Camerini**'s *Darò un milione* (*I'll Give a Million*, 1936). He then worked on the screenplay of **Alessandro Blasetti**'s *Quattro passi fra le nuvole* (*A Stroll through the Clouds*, 1942) before initiating what would be his very long and fruitful collaboration with **Vittorio De Sica** with his screenplay for *I bambini ci guardano* (*The Children Are Watching Us*, 1943).

In the immediate postwar period he wrote, alone or in collaboration, the screenplays of many of the great neorealist classics, as well as becoming the most prominent theoretical voice of the neorealist movement itself by championing the notion of cinema as a *pedinamento* (tailing or following) of everyday life in an unremitting search for truth. Although his theoretical ideas were often judged utopian and many of his projects frequently remained unrealized, he continued to be an important presence in Italian postwar culture and accrued an impressive list of screenwriting credits: he wrote *Sciuscià* (*Shoe-Shine*, 1946), *Ladri di biciclette* (*Bicycle Thieves*, 1948), *Miracolo a Milano* (*Miracle in Milan*, 1951), *Umberto D* (1952), *La ciociara* (*Two Women*, 1960), *Ieri, oggi, domani* (*Yesterday, Today, Tomorrow*, 1963), and *Il giardino dei Finzi-Contini* (*The Garden of the Finzi-Continis*, 1972), all for De Sica. He also collaborated again with Blasetti on *Prima comunione* (*First Communion*, 1950), with **Luciano Emmer** on *Domenica d'agosto* (*Sunday in August*, 1950), and with **Luchino Visconti** on *Bellissima* (1951). Widely respected both by his fellow writers and by the many filmmakers with whom he worked, he served for many years as president of the Associazione Nazionale Autori Cinematografici (ANAC, National Film Writers Association). In 1976 he received the American Screenwriters Association Award and in 1982 both the Luchino Visconti Award and a career Golden Lion at the **Venice Festival**. Curiously, for someone so involved in the production of cinema, he directed only one film on his own, *La veritaaaà* (*The Truuuuth*, 1981), a fairly transparent autobiographical work in which an energetic 80-year-old man escapes from his nursing home in order to exhort people in the street to think more independently and to realize themselves through social responsibility.

ZEFFIRELLI, FRANCO (1923–). (Born Gianfranco Corsi.) Art director, costume designer, director of theater, opera, and film. Zeffirelli became active in student theater while studying architecture at the University of Florence. In the immediate postwar period he abandoned his architectural studies and embarked on a career as a theatrical set and costume designer, working onstage with **Luchino Visconti** before serving as one of the assistant directors on Visconti's ill-fated *La terra trema* (*The Earth Trembles*, 1948). After serving a further apprenticeship with Visconti on *Bellissima* (1951) and *Senso* (*The Wanton Countess*, 1954), Zeffirelli directed his first feature, the light comedy *Camping* (1957). After this foray into film he returned to work extensively on the stage, designing and directing a number of acclaimed theatrical productions in London and New York. In 1962 he received the Tony Award for his design and direction of a much-lauded production of Shakespeare's *Romeo and Juliet* at the Old Vic in London.

In the late 1960s Zeffirelli achieved international renown for his innovative Shakespearean film adaptations, beginning in 1967 with a flamboyant version of *The Taming of the Shrew* that starred Richard Burton and Elizabeth Taylor and was nominated for two Oscars. A year later he cast two unknown teenage actors in a youthful version of *Romeo and Juliet* that was nominated for four Academy Awards, in the event winning two of them, as well as five **David di Donatello**.

Zeffirelli subsequently alternated between directing theater and opera on stage, and films such as *Brother Sun, Sister Moon* (1973), but he also often managed to combine stage and screen, as in the filmed versions of *La traviata* (1982), *Cavalleria rusticana* (1982), and *Otello* (1986). In 1990 he returned to Shakespeare with his screen adaptation of *Hamlet* (1990), with Mel Gibson playing the lead. In the following years he filmed a creditable adaptation of Charlotte Brontë's *Jane Eyre* (1996), effectively re-created the Florence of his youth in *Un thé con Mussolini* (*Tea with Mussolini*, 1999), and created a tribute to one of the divas he often worked with on the stage in *Callas Forever* (2002).

In 2004, having been elected to the Italian Senate in the ranks of *Forza Italia*, Zeffirelli was recognized for his services to the performing arts in Britain with the award of an honorary British knighthood.

ZINGARETTI, LUCA (1961–). Actor. After graduating from the National Academy of Dramatic Art in 1984, Zingaretti dedicated himself to the stage, working frequently with directors Luca Ronconi and Peter Stein. His first film appearance was in a small role in **Giuliano Montaldo**'s *Gli occhiali d'oro* (*The Gold Rimmed Glasses*, 1987). In the 1990s he began to appear more prominently in films such as **Marco Risi**'s *Il branco* (*The Pack*, 1994) and **Ricky Tognazzi**'s *Vite strozzate* (*Strangled Lives*, 1996), in both of which he played villains. After another supporting role in **Paolo and Vittorio Taviani**'s *Tu ridi* (*You Laugh*, 1998) and a great deal of television work, he gave a very powerful performance in two films directed by **Roberto Faenza**, *Alla Luce del Sole* (*Come into the Light*, 2005), where he played the priest Don Pino Puglisi, murdered by the camorra in 1993, and *I giorni dell'abbandono* (*The Days of Abandonment*, 2005), the heartwrenching story of a marriage breakup, both roles earning him nominations for the **Nastro d'argento**.

In spite of a long line of acting achievements and other activities—in 2004 he also directed *Gulu*, a moving **documentary** on the plight of war-torn Uganda—Zingaretti is undoubtedly best known, both in Italy and abroad, for his portrayal of Inspector Montalbano in the popular and long-running television adaptations of the detective novels of Andrea Camilleri.

ZURLINI, VALERIO (1926–1982). Art critic, screenwriter, director. After graduating in law from the University of Rome, Zurlini began his film career in the late 1940s with a series of short documentaries on urban life. His first feature, *Le ragazze di San Frediano* (*The Girls of San Frediano*, 1955), based on a novel by Vasco Pratolini, was the first of several fine adaptations of literary works that would mark his relatively short but distinguished career and which would include *Cronaca familiare* (*Family Diary*, 1962), with which he shared the Golden Lion at the **Venice Festival**, and *Le soldatesse* (*The Camp Followers*, 1965), the adaptation of a wartime novel by **Ugo Pirro**. After a profound but melancholic exploration of the doomed nature of love in both *Estate violenta* (*Violent Summer*, 1959) and *La ragazza con la valigia* (*The Girl with a Suitcase*, 1960), he made *Seduto alla sua destra* (*Black Jesus*, 1968), a fierce indictment of white colonialism in Africa but also a more general parable of man's inhumanity to man. He returned to explore further the precarious nature of love and interpersonal relationships in what was perhaps his most personal film, *La prima notte di quiete* (*Indian Summer*, 1972). Zurlini is probably best remembered, however, for his final film, a delicately wrought and intellectually complex adaptation of Dino Buzzati's novel *Il deserto dei Tartari* (*The Desert of the Tartars*, 1976).

Appendix
Winners at the Venice Festival and of the David di Donatello and Nastri d'argento

VENICE FESTIVAL

1932

Public voting only

Best Director: Nikolai Ekk, *Putjowka v zizn* (*The Road to Life*) (USSR)

Most Enjoyable Film: *À nous la liberté* (*Liberty for Us*), dir. René Clair (France)

Most Original Fantasy Film: *Dr. Jekyll and Mr. Hyde*, dir. Rouben Mamoulian (U.S.)

Most Moving Film: *The Sin of Madelon Claudet*, dir. Edgar Selwyn (U.S.)

Best Actress: Helen Hayes, *The Sin of Madelon Claudet*

Best Actor: Fredric March, *Dr. Jekyll and Mr. Hyde*

1934

Coppa Mussolini for Best Italian Film: *Teresa Confalonieri* (*Loyalty of Love*), dir. Guido Brignone

Prize for Best Foreign Film: *The Man of Aran*, dir. Robert Flaherty (UK)

Gold Medal, Best Actress: Katharine Hepburn, *Little Women*, dir. George Cukor (U.S.)

Gold Medal, Best Actor: Wallace Beery, *Viva Villa!* dir. Jack Conway (U.S.)

1935

Coppa Mussolini for Best Italian Film: *Casta diva*, dir. Carmine Gallone

Prize for Best Foreign Film: *Anna Karenina*, dir. Clarence Brown (U.S.)

Coppa Volpi, Best Director: King Vidor, *The Wedding Night* (U.S.)

Coppa Volpi, Best Actress: Paula Wessely, *Episode*, dir. Walter Reisch (Austria)

Coppa Volpi, Best Actor: Pierre Blanchar, *Crime et châtiment* (*Crime and Punishment*), dir. Pierre Chenal (France)

1936

Coppa Mussolini for Best Italian Film: *Squadrone bianco* (*White Squadron*), dir. Augusto Genina

Coppa Mussolini for Best Foreign Film: *Der Kaiser von Kalifornien* (*The Emperor of California*), dir. Luis Trenker (Germany)

Coppa Volpi, Best Actor: Paul Muni, *The Story of Louis Pasteur*, dir. William Dieterle (U.S.)

Coppa Volpi, Best Actress: Annabella, *Veille d'armes* (*Sacrifice of Honor*), dir. Marcel l'Herbier (France)

Coppa Volpi, Best Director: Jacques Feyder, *La Kermesse Héroïque* (*Carnival in Flanders*) (France)

1937

Coppa Mussolini for Best Italian Film: *Scipione l'Africano* (*Scipio the African*), dir. Carmine Gallone

Prize for Best Foreign Film: *Un carnet de bal* (*Christine/Dance of Life*), dir. Julien Duvivier (France)

Coppa Volpi, Best Actor: Emil Jannings, *Der Herrscher* (*The Ruler*), dir. Veit Harlan (Germany)

Coppa Volpi, Best Actress: Bette Davis, *Kid Galahad*, dir. Michael Curtiz (U.S.), and *Marked Woman*, dir. Lloyd Bacon (U.S.)

Prize for Best Director: Robert Flaherty and Zoltan Korda, *Elephant Boy* (UK)

1938

Coppa Mussolini for Best Film: *Olympia*, dir. Leni Riefensthal (Germany), and *Luciano Serra pilota* (*Luciano Serra, Pilot*), dir. Goffredo Alessandrini (Italy)

Coppa Volpi, Best Actor: Leslie Howard, *Pygmalion*, dir. Anthony Asquith and Leslie Howard (UK)

Coppa Volpi, Best Actress: Norma Shearer, *Marie Antoniette*, dir. W. S. Van Dyke II (U.S.)

Best Director: Carl Froelich, *Heimat* (*Homeland*) (Germany)

1939

Coppa Mussolini for Best Film: *Abuna Messias* (*Cardinal Messias*), dir. Goffredo Alessandrini (Italy)

1940

Coppa Mussolini for Best Italian Film: *L'assedio dell'Alcazar* (*The Siege of the Alcazar*), dir. Augusto Genina

Coppa Mussolini for Best Foreign Film: *Der Postmeister* (*The Stationmaster*), dir. Gustav Ucicky (Germany)

1941

Coppa Mussolini for Best Italian Film: *La corona di ferro* (*The Iron Crown*), dir. Alessandro Blasetti

Coppa Mussolini for Best Foreign Film: *Ohm Krüger*, dir. Hans Steinhoff (Germany)

Gold Medal for Best Director: G. W. Pabst, *Komödianten* (*The Comedians*)

Coppa Volpi, Best Actress: Luise Ullrich, *Annelie* (*"Die Geschichte eines Lebens"*), dir. Josef von Baky (Germany)

Coppa Volpi, Best Actor: Ermete Zacconi, *Don Buonaparte*, dir. Flavio Calzavara (Italy)

1942

Coppa Mussolini for Best Italian Film: *Bengasi*, dir. Augusto Genina

Coppa Mussolini for Best Foreign Film: *Der große König* (*The Great King*), dir. Veit Harlan (Germany)

Coppa Volpi, Best Actress: Kristina Söderbaum, *Die goldene Stadt*, dir. Veit Harlan (Germany)

Coppa Volpi, Best Actor: Fosco Giachetti, *Bengasi*

1943–1945

The festival is suspended because of the war.

1946

Best Film (selected by the Journalists' Association): *The Southerner*, dir. Jean Renoir (U.S.)
Coppa dell'ANICA: *Paisà* (*Paisan*), dir. Roberto Rossellini (Italy)
Prize of the Centro Sperimentale di Cinematografia: *Il sole sorge ancora* (*Outcry*), dir. Aldo Vergano (Italy)

1947

Grand International Prize for Best Film: *Siréna*, dir. Karel Stekly (Czechoslovakia)
International Prize for Best Actress: Anna Magnani, *L'Onorevole Angelina* (*Angelina, MP*), dir. Luigi Zampa (Italy)
International Prize for Best Actor: Pierre Fresnay, *Monsieur Vincent*, dir. Maurice Cloche (France)
International Prize for Best Director: Henri-Georges Clouzot, *Quai des Orfèvres* (*Jenny Lamour*) (France)

1948

Grand International Prize for Best Film: *Hamlet*, dir. Laurence Olivier (UK)
Prime Minister's Prize for Best Italian Film: *Sotto il sole di Roma* (*Under the Sun of Rome*), dir. Renato Castellani
International Prize for Best Actress: Jean Simmons, *Hamlet*
International Prize for Best Actor: Ernst Deutsch, *Der Prozess* (*The Trial*), dir. George Wilhelm Pabst (Austria)
International Prize for Best Director: G. W. Pabst, *Der Prozess*

1949

Leone di San Marco for Best Film: *Manon*, dir. Henri-Georges Clouzot (France)

Prime Minister's Prize for Best Italian Film: *Cielo sulla palude* (*Heaven over the Marshes*), dir. Augusto Genina

International Prize for Best Director: Augusto Genina, *Cielo sulla palude*

International Prize for Best Actress: Olivia de Havilland, *The Snake Pit*, dir. Anatole Litvak (U.S.)

International Prize for Best Actor: Joseph Cotten, *Portrait of Jennie*, dir. William Dieterle (U.S.)

1950

Leone di San Marco: *Justice est faite* (*Justice Is Done*), dir. André Cayatte (France)

Prime Minister's Prize for Best Italian Film: *Domani è troppo tardi* (*Tomorrow Is Too Late*), dir. Léonide Moguy

International Prize for Best Actress: Eleanor Parker, *Caged*, dir. John Cromwell (U.S.)

International Prize for Best Actor: Sam Jaffe, *The Asphalt Jungle*, dir. John Huston (U.S.)

1951

Leone di San Marco: *Rashômon*, dir. Akira Kurosawa (Japan)

Prime Minister's Prize for Best Italian Film: *La città si difende* (*Four Ways Out*), dir. Pietro Germi

Special Jury Prize: *A Streetcar Named Desire*, dir. Elia Kazan (U.S.)

Coppa Volpi, Best Actress: Vivien Leigh, *A Streetcar Named Desire*

Coppa Volpi, Best Actor: Jean Gabin, *La nuit est mon royaume* (*The Night Is My Kingdom*), dir. Georges Lacombe (France)

International Prize: *Ace in the Hole*, dir. Billy Wilder (U.S.)

1952

Leone di San Marco: *Jeux interdits* (*Forbidden Games*), dir. René Clément (France)

International Prize: *Saichaku ichidai onna* (*Diary of Oharu*), dir. Kenji Mizoguchi (Japan), and *Europa '51*, dir. Roberto Rossellini

Coppa Volpi, Best Actor: Fredric March, *Death of a Salesman*, dir. Lásló Benedek (U.S.)

1953

Leone di San Marco not awarded.

Leone d'argento: *Ugetsu Monogatari* (*Tales of Ugetsu*), dir. Kenji Mizoguchi (Japan); *I vitelloni*, dir. Federico Fellini (Italy); *Little Fugitive*, dir. Ray Ashley, Morris Engel, and Ruth Orkin (U.S.); *Moulin Rouge*, dir. John Huston (UK); *Thérèse Raquin*, dir. Marcel Carné (France); *Sadko*, dir. Aleksandt Prusko (USSR)

Coppa Volpi, Best Actor: Henri Vilbert, *Le bon Dieu sans confession*, dir. Claude Autant-Lara (France)

Coppa Volpi, Best Actress: Lilli Palmer, *The Fourposter*, dir. Irving Reis (U.S.)

1954

Leone d'oro for Best Film: *Romeo and Juliet*, dir. Renato Castellani (UK/Italy)

Leone d'argento: *Shichinin no samurai* (*Seven Samurai*), dir. Akira Kurosawa (Japan); *La strada*, dir. Federico Fellini; *On the Waterfront*, dir. Elia Kazan (U.S.); *Sanshô dayû* (*The Legend of Bailiff Sansho*), dir. Kenji Mizoguchi (Japan)

Coppa Volpi, Best Actor: Jean Gabin, *L'air de Paris* (*Air of Paris*), dir. Marcel Carné (France/Italy); *Touchez pas au Grisbi* (*Grisbi*), dir. Jacques Becker (France)

1955

Leone d'oro: *Ordet* (*The Word*), dir. Carl Theodor Dreyer (Denmark)

Leone d'argento: *Le amiche* (*The Girlfriends*), dir. Michelangelo Antonioni; *Ciske de rat*, dir. Wolfgang Staudte (Holland); *Poprygun' ja* (*The Grasshopper*), dir. Samson Samsonov (USSR); *The Big Knife*, dir. Robert Aldrich (U.S.)

Coppa Volpi, Best Actor: Kenneth More, *The Deep Blue Sea*, dir. Anatole Litvak (UK); Curd Jürgens, *Les héros sont fatigués* (*Heroes and Sinners*), dir. Yves Ciampi (France/West Germany)

1956

Leone d'oro not awarded.

Coppa Volpi, Best Actress: Maria Schell, *Gervaise*, dir. René Clément (France)

Coppa Volpi, Best Actor: *Bourvil, La traversée de Paris* (*Four Bags Full*), dir. Claude Autant-Lara (France)

1957

Leone d'oro: *Aparajito* (*The Unvanquished*), dir. Satyajit Ray (India)
Leone d'argento: *Le notti bianche* (*White Nights*), dir. Luchino Visconti
Coppa Volpi, Best Actress: Zita Ritenbergs, *Malva*, dir. Vladimir Braun (USSR)
Coppa Volpi, Best Actor: Anthony Franciosa, *A Hatful of Rain*, dir. Fred Zinnemann (U.S.)

1958

Leone d'oro: *Muhomatsu No Isshô* (*Muhomatsu the Rickshaw Man*), dir. Iroshi Inagaki (Japan)
Special Jury Prize: *Les amants* (*The Lovers*), dir. Louis Malle (France); *La sfida* (*The Challenge*), dir. Francesco Rosi
Coppa Volpi, Best Actor: Alec Guinness, *The Horse's Mouth*, dir. Ronald Neame (UK)
Coppa Volpi, Best Actress: Sophia Loren, *Black Orchid*, dir. Martin Ritt (U.S.)

1959

Leone d'oro: *Il Generale della Rovere* (*General della Rovere*), dir. Roberto Rossellini (Italy); *La grande guerra* (*The Great War*), dir. Mario Monicelli (Italy)
Special Jury Prize: *Ansiktet* (*The Magician/The Face*), dir. Ingmar Bergman (Sweden)
Coppa Volpi, Best Actor: James Stewart, *Anatomy of a Murder*, dir. Otto Preminger (U.S.)
Coppa Volpi, Best Actress: Madeleine Robinson, *À double tour* (*Leda*), dir. Claude Chabrol (France)

1960

Leone d'oro: *Le passage du Rhin* (*The Crossing of the Rhine*), dir. André Cayatte (France)

Special Prize: *Rocco e i suoi fratelli* (*Rocco and His Brothers*), dir. Luchino Visconti (Italy)
Coppa Volpi, Best Actress: Shirley MacLaine, *The Apartment*, dir. Billy Wilder (U.S.)
Coppa Volpi, Best Actor: John Mills, *Tunes of Glory*, dir. Ronald Neame (UK)

1961

Leone d'oro: *L'année dernière à Marienbad* (*Last Year at Marienbad*), dir. Alain Resnais (France)
Special Jury Prize: *Mir Vchodyashchemu* (*Peace to Him Who Enters*), dir. Aleksandr Alov and Vladimir Naumov (USSR)
Coppa Volpi, Best Actor: Toshirô Mifune, *Yojimbo*, dir. Akira Kurosawa (Japan)
Coppa Volpi, Best Actress: Suzanne Flon, *Tu ne tueras point* (*Thou Shalt Not Kill*), dir. Claude Aurant-Lara (Liechtenstein)

1962

Leone d'oro: *Cronaca familiare* (*Family Diary*), dir. Valerio Zurlini (Italy); *Ivanovo Detstvo* (*Ivan's Childhood/My Name Is Ivan*), dir. Andrei Tarkovsky (USSR)
Special Jury Prize: *Vivre sa vie* (*My Life to Live*), dir. Jean-Luc Godard (France)
Coppa Volpi, Best Actor: Burt Lancaster, *Birdman of Alcatraz*, dir. John Frankenheimer (U.S.)
Coppa Volpi, Best Actress: Emanuelle Riva, *Thérèse Desqueyroux*, dir. Georges Franju (France)

1963

Leone d'oro: *Le mani sulla città* (*Hands over the City*), dir. Francesco Rosi (Italy)
Special Jury Prize: *Le feu follet* (The Fire Within), dir. Louis Malle (France); *Vstuplenie* (*Introduction*), dir. Igor Talankin (USSR)
Coppa Volpi, Best Actor: Albert Finney, *Tom Jones*, dir. Tony Richardson (UK)

Coppa Volpi, Best Actress: Delphine Seyrig, *Muriel, ou le temps d'un retour* (*Muriel, or the Time of Return*), dir. Alain Resnais (France)

1964

Leone d'oro: *Deserto rosso* (*The Red Desert*), dir. Michelangelo Antonioni (Italy)

Special Jury Prize: *Il Vangelo secondo Matteo* (*The Gospel According to St. Matthew*), dir. Pier Paolo Pasolini; *Gamlet* (*Hamlet*), dir. Grigorii Kozintsev (USSR)

Coppa Volpi, Best Actor: Tom Courtenay, *King and Country*, dir. Joseph Losey (UK)

Coppa Volpi, Best Actress: Herriet Andersson, *Att Älska* (*To Love*), dir. Jörn Donner (Sweden)

1965

Leone d'oro: *Vaghe stelle dell'Orsa* (*Sandra of a Thousand Delights*), dir. Luchino Visconti (Italy)

Special Jury Prize: *Simón del desierto* (*Simon of the Desert*), dir. Luis Buñuel (Mexico); *Mne Dvadtsat' let* (*I Am Twenty*), dir. Marlen Khutsiev (USSR); *Modiga Mindre Män*, dir. Leif Krantz (Sweden)

Coppa Volpi, Best Actress: Annie Girardot, *Trois chambres à Manhattan* (*Three Rooms in Manhattan*), dir. Marcel Carné (France)

Coppa Volpi, Best Actor: Toshirô Mifune, *Akahige* (*Red Beard*), dir. Akira Kurosawa (Japan)

1966

Leone d'oro: *La battaglia di Algeri* (*The Battle of Algiers*), dir. Gillo Pontecorvo (Italy/Algeria)

Special Jury Prize: *Chappaqua*, dir. Conrad Rooks (U.S.), *Abschied von gestern* (*Yesterday Girl*), dir. Alexander Kluge (West Germany)

Coppa Volpi, Best Actor: Jacques Perrin, *Un uomo a metà* (*Half a Man*), dir. Vittorio De Seta (Italy)

Coppa Volpi, Best Actress: Natalia Arinbasarova, *Pervyi uchitel'* (*The First Teacher*), dir. Andrei Mikhalkov-Konchalovsky (USSR)

1967

Leone d'oro: *Belle de jour*, dir. Luis Buñuel (France)
Special Jury Prize: *La Cina è vicina* (*China Is Near*), dir. Marco Bellocchio (Italy); *La Chinoise*, dir. Jean-Luc Godard (France)
Coppa Volpi, Best Actor: Ljubisa Samardzic, *Jutro* (*The Morning*), dir. Purisa Djordjevic (Yugoslavia)
Coppa Volpi, Best Actress: Shirley Knight, *Dutchman*, dir. Anthony Harvey (UK)

1968

Leone d'oro: *Die Artisten in der Zirkuskuppel: Ratlos* (*Artists under the Big Top: Perplexed*), dir. Alexander Kluge (West Germany)
Special Jury Prize: *Nostra Signora dei Turchi* (*Our Lady of the Turks*), dir. Carmelo Bene (Italy); *Le Socrate* (*Socrates*), dir. Robert Lapojade (France)
Coppa Volpi, Best Actor: John Marley, *Faces*, dir. John Cassavetes (U.S.)
Coppa Volpi, Best Actress: Laura Betti, *Teorema* (*Theorem*), dir. Pier Paolo Pasolini (Italy)

1969–1979

The festival is held but no prizes are awarded.

1980

Leone d'oro: *Atlantic City*, dir. Louis Malle (Canada); *Gloria*, dir. John Cassavetes (U.S.)
Leone d'oro for New Cinema: *O Megalèxandros* (*Alexander the Great*), dir. Theo Angelopoulos (Greece/Italy)

1981

Leone d'oro: *Die bleierne Zeit* (*Marianne and Juliane/The German Sisters*), dir. Margarethe von Trotta (West Germany)
Special Jury Prize: *Sogni d'oro*, dir. Nanni Moretti; *Eles não usam black tie* (*They Don't Wear Black Tie*), dir. Leon Hirszman (Brazil)

1982

Leone d'oro: *Der Stand der Dinge* (*The State of Things*), dir. Wim Wenders (West Germany)

Special Jury Prize: *Imperativ* (*Imperative*), dir. Krzysztof Zanussi (West Germany)

Leone d'oro for Lifetime Achievement: Alessandro Blasetti, Frank Capra, George Cukor, Jean-Luc Godard, Sergej Jutkevic, Alexander Kluge, Akira Kurosawa, Michael Powell, Satyajit Ray, King Vidor, Cesare Zavattini, Luis Buñuel

1983

Leone d'oro: *Prénom Carmen* (*First Name: Carmen*), dir. Jean-Luc Godard (France)

Special Jury Prize: *Biguefarre*, dir. Georges Rouquier (France)

Prize for Best Actress: Darling Legitimus, *Rue cases nègres* (*Black Shack Alley*), dir. Euzhan Palcy (France)

Prize for Best Actor: Matthew Modine, Michael Wright, Mitchell Lichtenstein, David Alan Grier, Guy Boyd, George Dundza, *Streamers*, dir. Robert Altman (U.S.)

Leone d'oro for Lifetime Achievement: Michelangelo Antonioni

1984

Leone d'oro: *Rok Spokojnego Slonca* (*The Year of the Quiet Sun*), dir. Krzysztof Zanussi (Poland)

Leone d'argento: *Sonatine*, dir. Micheline Lanctôt (Canada)

Special Jury Prize: *Les favoris de la lune* (*Favorites of the Moon*), dir. Otar Iosseliani (France)

Special Prize for Best Actress: Pascale Ogier, *Le nuits de la pleine lune* (*Full Moon in Paris*), dir. Eric Rohmer (France)

Prize for Best Actor: Nasceruddin Shah, *Paar* (*The Crossing*), dir. Goutam Ghosh (India)

1985

Leone d'oro: *Sans toit ni loi* (*Vagabond*), dir. Agnès Varda (France)

Leone d'argento: *Dust*, dir. Marion Hansel (Belgium)

Special Grand Jury Prize: *Tangos: El exilio de Gardel* (*Tangos: The Exile of Gardel*), dir. Fernando E. Solanas (Argentina)
Special Prize: *The Lightship*, dir. Jerzy Skolimowski (U.S.)
Special Leone d'oro for Lifetime Achievement: Manoel de Oliveira
John Huston Prize for Best Actor: Gérard Depardieu, *Police*, dir. Maurice Pialat (France)
Leone d'oro for Lifetime Achievement: Federico Fellini

1986

Leone d'oro: *Le rayon vert* (*The Green Ray*), dir. Eric Rohmer (France)
Special Grand Jury Prize: *Chuzhaya, belaya i ryaboi* (*Wild Pigeon*), dir. Sergei Soloviev (USSR); *Storia d'amore*, dir. Francesco Maselli (Italy)
Best Actor: Carlo delle Piane, *Regalo di Natale* (*Christmas Present*), dir. Pupi Avati (Italy)
Best Actress: Valeria Golino, *Storia d'amore*
Leone d'oro for Lifetime Achievement: Paolo and Vittorio Taviani

1987

Leone d'oro: *Au revoir les enfants* (*Goodbye Children*), dir. Louis Malle (France)
Leone d'argento: *Lunga vita alla signora* (*Long Live the Lady!*), dir. Ermanno Olmi (Italy); *Maurice*, dir. James Ivory (UK)
Special Grand Jury Prize: *Hip, Hip, Hurra!* dir. Kjell Grede (Sweden/Denmark/Norway)
Best Actress: Kang Soo-Yeon, *Sibajî*, dir. Kwon-Taek Im (South Korea)
Best Actor: James Wilby and Hugh Grant, *Maurice*, dir. James Ivory (UK)
Leone d'oro for Lifetime Achievement: Luigi Comencini, Joseph L. Mankiewicz

1988

Leone d'oro: *La leggenda del santo bevitore* (*The Legend of the Holy Drinker*), dir. Ermanno Olmi (Italy)
Leone d'argento: *Topío stín omíhli* (*Landscape in the Mist*), dir. Theo Angelopoulos (Greece)

Special Grand Jury Prize: *Camp de Thiaroye* (*The Camp at Thiaroye*), dir. Sembène Ousmane and Thierno Faty Sow (Senegal)

Coppa Volpi, Best Actress: Isabelle Huppert, *Une affaire de femmes* (*Story of Women*), dir. Claude Chabrol (France); Shirley MacLaine, *Madame Souzatzka*, dir. John Schlesinger (UK)

Coppa Volpi, Best Actor: Don Ameche and Joe Mantegna, *Things Change*, dir. David Mamet (U.S.)

Leone d'oro for Lifetime Achievement: Joris Ivens

1989

Leone d'oro: *Beiqing chengshi* (*City of Sadness*), dir. Hou Xiaoxian (Taiwan)

Special Jury Prize: *Et la lumière fut* (*And Then There Was Light*), dir. Otar Iosseliani (Germany/France)

Leone d'argento: *Recordaçoes da casa amarela* (*Recollections of the Yellow House*), dir. João César Monteiro (Portugal); *Sen no Rikyu* (*Death of a Tea Master*), dir. Kei Kumai (Japan)

Coppa Volpi, Best Actor: Marcello Mastroianni and Massimo Troisi, *Che ora è?* (*What Time Is It?*), dir. Ettore Scola (Italy)

Coppa Volpi, Best Actress: Peggy Ashcroft and Geraldine James, *She's Been Away*, dir. Peter Hall (UK)

President of the Senate's Gold Medal: *Scugnizzi* (*Streetkids*), dir. Nanni Loy (Italy)

Leone d'oro for Lifetime Achievement: Robert Bresson (France)

1990

Leone d'oro: *Rosencrantz and Guildenstern Are Dead*, dir. Tom Stoppard (UK)

Special Jury Prize: *An Angel at My Table*, dir. Jane Campion (New Zealand)

Leone d'argento for Best Director: Martin Scorsese, *Goodfellas* (U.S.)

Coppa Volpi, Best Actor: Oleg Borisov, *Edinstvenijat Svidetel* (*The Only Witness*), dir. Michail Pandurski (Bulgaria)

Coppa Volpi, Best Actress: Gloria Munchmeyer, *La luna en el espejo* (*The Moon in the Mirror*), dir. Silvio Caiozzi (Chile)

Leone d'oro for Lifetime Achievement: Miklós Jancsó, Marcello Mastroianni

1991

Leone d'oro: *Urga* (*Close to Eden*), dir. Nikita Mikhalkov (France/USSR)
Special Grand Jury Prize: *A Divina Comédia* (*Divine Comedy*), dir. Manoel de Oliveira (Portugal/France)
Leone d'argento: *Da hong deng long gao gao gua* (*Raise the Red Lantern*), dir. Zhang Yimou (China); *J'entends plus la guitare* (*I Can No Longer Hear the Guitar*), dir. Philippe Garrel (France); *The Fisher King*, dir. Terry Gilliam (U.S.)
Coppa Volpi, Best Actor: River Phoenix, *My Own Private Idaho*, dir. Gus Van Sant (U.S.)
Coppa Volpi, Best Actress: Tilda Swinton, *Edward II*, dir. Derek Jarman (UK)
President of the Senate's Gold Medal: *Allemagne 90 neuf zero* (*Germany Year 90 Nine Zero*), dir. Jean-Luc Godard (France)
Leone d'oro for Lifetime Achievement: Gian Maria Volontè

1992

Leone d'oro: *Qiu Ju da guansi* (*Qiu Ju Goes to Court*), dir. Zhang Yimou (China)
Leone d'argento: *Hôtel de Lux* (*Luxury Hotel*), dir. Dan Pita (Romania); *Jamón Jamón*, dir. Juan José Bigas Luna (Spain); *Un coeur en hiver* (*A Heart in Winter*), dir. Claude Sautet (France)
Grand Jury Prize: *Morte di un matematico napoletano* (*Death of a Neapolitan Mathematician*), dir. Mario Martone (Italy)
Coppa Volpi, Best Actress: Gong Li, *Qiu Ju da guansi*
Coppa Volpi, Best Actor: Jack Lemmon, *Glengarry Glen Ross*, dir. James Foley (U.S.)
Leone d'oro for Lifetime Achievement: Francis Ford Coppola, Jeanne Moreau, Paolo Villaggio

1993

Leone d'oro: *Trois couleurs: Bleu* (*Three Colors: Blue*), dir. Krzysztof Kieslowski (France/Poland); *Short Cuts*, dir. Robert Altman (U.S.)
Leone d'argento: *Kosh ba kosh*, dir. Bakhtiyar Khudojnazarov (Tajikistan)
Grand Jury Prize: *Bad Boy Bubby*, dir. Rolf De Heer (Australia)

Coppa Volpi, Best Actress: Juliette Binoche, *Trois couleurs: Bleu*
Coppa Volpi, Best Actor: Fabrizio Bentivoglio, *Un'anima divisa in due* (*A Soul Split in Two*), dir. Silvio Soldini (Italy)
Premio CIAK d'oro for Best Italian Film: *Mille bolle blu*, dir. Leone Pompucci
Leone d'oro for Lifetime Achievement: Steven Spielberg, Claudia Cardinale, Robert De Niro, Roman Polanski

1994

Leone d'oro: *Before the Rain*, dir. Milcho Manchevski (UK/Macedonia); *Aiqing Wansui* (*Vive l'amour*), dir. Tsai Ming-Liang (Taiwan)
Leone d'argento: *Little Odessa*, dir. James Gray (U.S.); *Heavenly Creatures*, dir. Peter Jackson (Germany/New Zealand/UK); *Il Toro* (*The Bull*), dir. Carlo Mazzacurati (Italy)
Special Grand Jury Prize: *Natural Born Killers*, dir. Oliver Stone (U.S.)
Premio CIAK d'oro for Best Italian Film: *La bella vita* (*Living It Up*), dir. Paolo Virzì
President of the Senate's Gold Medal: Jirì Menzel, *Zivot a neobycejna dobrodruzstvi vojaka Ivana Conkina* (*The Life and Extraordinary Adventures of Private Ivan Chonkin*) (Czech Republic)
Coppa Volpi, Best Actress: Maria de Medeiros, *Três Irmãos* (*Two Brothers, My Sister*), dir. Teresa Villaverde (Portugal/France)
Coppa Volpi, Best Actor: Xia Yu, *Yangguang canlan de rizi* (*In the Heat of the Sun*), dir. Jiang Wen (China/Hong Kong)
Leone d'oro for Lifetime Achievement: Ken Loach, Suso Cecchi D'Amico, Al Pacino

1995

Leone d'oro: *Xich-lô* (*Cyclo*), dir. Tran Ahn Hung (Vietnam/France)
Special Grand Jury Prize: *A Comédia de Deus* (*God's Comedy*), dir. João César Monteiro (Portugal); *L'uomo delle stelle* (*The Star Maker*), dir. Giuseppe Tornatore (Italy)
President of the Senate's Gold Medal: *Pasolini: Un delitto italiano* (*Pasolini, An Italian Crime*), dir. Marco Tullio Giordana (Italy)
Coppa Volpi, Best Actress: Isabelle Huppert and Sandrine Bonnaire, *La Cérémonie* (*A Judgement in Stone*), dir. Claude Chabrol (France/Germany)

Coppa Volpi, Best Actor: George Göetz, *Der Totmacher* (*Deathmaker*), dir. Romuald Karmakar (Germany)

Leone d'oro for Lifetime Achievement: Woody Allen, Alain Resnais, Martin Scorsese, Giuseppe De Santis, Goffredo Lombardo, Ennio Morricone, Alberto Sordi, Monica Vitti

1996

Leone d'oro: *Michael Collins*, dir. Neil Jordan (Ireland/UK/U.S.)

Special Grand Jury Prize: *Brigands, chapitre VII* (*Brigands, Chapter VII*), dir. Otar Iosseliani (France/Russia/Italy/Switzerland)

Coppa Volpi, Best Actress: Victoire Thivisol, *Ponette*, dir. Jacques Doillon (France)

Coppa Volpi, Best Actor: Liam Neeson, *Michael Collins*

Leone d'oro for Lifetime Achievement: Vittorio Gassman, Michele Morgan, Robert Altman, Dustin Hoffman

1997

Leone d'oro: *Hana-Bi* (*Fireworks*), dir. Takeshi Kitano (Japan)

Special Grand Jury Prize: *Ovosodo* (*Hardboiled Egg*), dir. Paolo Virzì (Italy)

Coppa Volpi, Best Actress: Robin Tunney, *Niagara Niagara*, dir. Bob Gosse (U.S./Canada)

Coppa Volpi, Best Actor: Wesley Snipes, *One Night Stand*, dir. Mike Figgis (U.S.)

Leone d'oro for Lifetime Achievement: Gérard Depardieu, Stanley Kubrick, Alida Valli

1998

Leone d'oro: *Così ridevano* (*The Way We Laughed*), dir. Gianni Amelio (Italy)

Special Grand Jury Prize: *Terminus paradis* (*Next Stop Paradise*), dir. Lucian Pintilie (France/Romania)

Leone d'argento for Best Director: Emir Kusturica, *Crna macka, beli macor* (*Black Cat, White Cat*) (Germany/Serbia/France)

Coppa Volpi, Best Actress: Catherine Deneuve, *Place Vendôme*, dir. Nicole Garcia (France)

Coppa Volpi, Best Actor: Sean Penn, *Hurlyburly*, dir. Anthony Drazan (U.S.)

Leone d'oro for Lifetime Achievement: Sophia Loren, Andrzej Wajda, Warren Beatty

1999

Leone d'oro: *Yi ge dou bu neng shao* (*Not One Less*), dir. Zhang Yimou (China)

Grand Jury Prize: *Bad ma ra khahad bord* (*The Wind Will Carry Us*), dir. Abbas Kiarostami (France/Iran)

Special Prize for Directing: Zhang Yuan, *Guo Nian Hui Jia* (*Seventeen Years*) (China/Italy)

Coppa Volpi, Best Actress: Nathalie Baye, *Une liaison pornographique* (*A Pornographic Affair*), dir. Frédéric Fontane (France)

Coppa Volpi, Best Actor: Jim Broadbent, *Topsy-Turvy*, dir. Mike Leigh (UK)

Leone d'oro for Lifetime Achievement: Jerry Lewis

2000

Leone d'oro: *Dayereh* (*The Circle*), dir. Jafar Panahi (Iran/Italy)

Grand Jury Prize: *Before Night Falls*, dir. Julian Schnabel (U.S.)

Special Prize for Directing: Buddhadeb Dasgupta, *Uttara* (*The Wrestlers*) (India)

Coppa Volpi, Best Actress: Rose Byrne, *The Goddess of 1967*, dir. Clara Law (Australia)

Coppa Volpi, Best Actor: Javier Bardem, *Before Night Falls*

Leone d'oro for Lifetime Achievement: Clint Eastwood

2001

Leone d'oro: *Monsoon Wedding*, dir. Mira Nair (India)

Grand Jury Prize: *Hundstage* (*Dog Days*), dir. Ulrich Seidl (Austria)

Special Prize for Directing: Babak Payami, *Raye Makhfi* (*Secret Ballot*) (Italy/Iran)

Coppa Volpi, Best Actor: Luigi Lo Cascio, *Luce dei miei occhi* (*Light of My Eyes*), dir. Giuseppe Piccioni (Italy)

Coppa Volpi, Best Actress: Sandra Ceccarelli, *Luce dei miei occhi*
Leone d'oro for Lifetime Achievement: Eric Rohmer

2002

Leone d'oro: *The Magdalene Sisters*, dir. Peter Mullan (UK/Ireland)
Grand Jury Prize: *Dom durakov* (*House of Fools*), dir. Andrei Konchalovsky (Russia/France)
Special Prize for Directing: Lee Chang-Dong, *Oasis* (South Korea)
Coppa Volpi, Best Actor: Stefano Accorsi, *Un viaggio chiamato amore* (*A Journey Called Love*), dir. Michele Placido (Italy)
Coppa Volpi, Best Actress: Julianne Moore, *Far from Heaven*, dir. Todd Haynes (U.S./France)
Leone d'oro for Lifetime Achievement: Dino Risi

2003

Leone d'oro: *Vozvrašcenie* (*The Return*), dir. Andrei Zvyagintsev (Russsia)
Grand Jury Prize, Leone d'argento: *Le cerf-volant* (*The Kite*), dir. Randa Chahal Sabbag (Lebanon/France)
Special Prize for Directing, Leone d'argento: Takeshi Kitano, *Zatoichi* (Japan)
Coppa Volpi, Best Actor: Sean Penn, *21 Grams*, dir. Alejandro Gonzàlez Iñárritu (U.S.)
Coppa Volpi, Best Actress: Katja Riemann, *Rosenstrasse* (*The Women of Rosenstrasse*), dir. Margarethe von Trotta (Germany)
Leone d'oro for Lifetime Achievement: Dino De Laurentiis, Omar Sharif

2004

Leone d'oro: *Vera Drake*, dir. Mike Leigh (UK)
Grand Jury Prize, Leone d'argento: *Mar adentro* (*The Sea Inside*), dir. Alejandro Amenábar (Spain)
Special Prize for Directing, Leone d'argento: Kim Ki-duk, *Bin jip* (*3-Iron*) (South Korea)
Coppa Volpi, Best Actor: Javier Bardem, *Mar adentro*

Coppa Volpi, Best Actress: Imelda Staunton, *Vera Drake*
Leone d'oro for Lifetime Achievement: Manoel de Oliveria, Stanley Donen

2005

Leone d'oro: *Brokeback Mountain*, dir. Ang Lee (U.S.)
Grand Jury Prize, Leone d'argento: *Mary*, dir. Abel Ferrara (Italy/France/U.S.)
Special Prize for Directing, Leone d'argento: Philippe Garrel, *Les amants réguliers* (*Regular Lovers*) (France)
Coppa Volpi, Best Actor: David Strathairn, *Good Night, and Good Luck*, dir. George Clooney (U.S.)
Coppa Volpi, Best Actress: Giovanna Mezzogiorno, *La bestia nel cuore* (*The Beast in the Heart/Don't Tell*), dir. Cristina Comencini (Italy)
Leone d'oro for Lifetime Achievement: Hayao Miyazaki, Stefania Sandrelli

2006

Leone d'oro: *Sanxia Haoren* (*Still Life*), dir. Jia Zhangke (China/Hong Kong)
Grand Jury Prize, Leone d'argento: *Daratt* (*Dry Season*), dir. Mahamat-Saleh Haroun (Chad/France/Belgium/Austria)
Special Prize for Directing, Leone d'argento: Alain Resnais, *Coeurs* (*Private Fears in Public Places*) (France/Italy)
Coppa Volpi, Best Actor: Ben Affleck, *Hollywoodland*, dir. Allen Coulter (U.S.)
Coppa Volpi, Best Actress: Helen Mirren, *The Queen*, dir. Stephen Frears (UK/France/Italy)
Leone d'oro for Lifetime Achievement: David Lynch

2007

Leone d'oro: *Se, jie* (*Lust, Caution*), dir. Ang Lee (U.S./Taiwan)
Grand Jury Prize, Leone d'argento: *La graine et le mulet* (*The Dream of the Grain*), dir. Abdellatif Kechiche (France); *I'm Not There*, dir. Todd Haynes (U.S.)

Special Prize for Directing, Leone d'argento: Brian De Palma, *Redacted* (U.S.)

Coppa Volpi, Best Actor: Brad Pitt, *The Assassination of Jesse James by the Coward Robert Ford*, dir. Andrew Dominik (U.S.)

Coppa Volpi, Best Actress: Cate Blanchett, *I'm Not There*

Leone d'oro for Lifetime Achievement: Tim Burton

Leone d'oro for the festival's 75th Anniversary: Bernardo Bertolucci

DAVID DI DONATELLO

1956

Best Film: *Racconti romani* (*Roman Tales*), dir. Gianni Franciolini, prod. Nicolò Theodoli; *Pane, amore e . . .* (*Scandal in Sorrento*), dir. Dino Risi, prod. Goffredo Lombardo

Best Director: Gianni Franciolini, *Racconti romani*

Best Actor: Vittorio De Sica, *Pane, amore e . . .*

Best Actress: Gina Lollobrigida, *La donna più bella del mondo* (*The World's Most Beautiful Woman*), dir. Alberto Leonardi

1957

Best Film: *Le notti di Cabiria* (*Nights of Cabiria*), dir. Federico Fellini, prod. Dino De Laurentiis; *L'impero del sole* (*Empire in the Sun*), dir. Enrico Gras and Mario Craveri, prod. Renato Gualino

Best Director: Federico Fellini, *Le notti di Cabiria*

1958

Best Film: *La muraglia cinese* (*Behind the Great Wall*), dir. Carlo Lizzani, prod. Leonardo Bonzi; *Anna di Brooklyn* (*Anna of Brooklyn*), dir. Carlo Lastricati, prod. Milko Skofic

Best Actress: Anna Magnani, *Wild Is the Wind*, dir. George Cukor

1959

Best Film: *La tempesta* (*Tempest*), dir. Alberto Lattuada, prod. Dino De Laurentiis; *Maja desnuda* (*Naked Maja*), dir. Hermann Kosterlitz and Mario Russo, prod. Titanus

Best Director: Alberto Lattuada, *La tempesta*
Best Actress: Anna Magnani, *Nella città l'inferno* (*Wild Wild Women*),
dir. Renato Castellani

1960

Best Film: *La grande guerra* (*The Great War*), dir. Mario Monicelli,
prod. Dino De Laurentiis; *Il Generale della Rovere* (*General della
Rovere*), dir. Roberto Rossellini, prod. Zebra Film
Best Director: Federico Fellini, *La dolce vita*
Best Actor: Vittorio Gassman and Alberto Sordi, *La grande guerra*

1961

Best Film: *Tutti a casa* (*Everybody Home!*), dir. Luigi Comencini, prod.
Dino De Laurentiis; *Rocco e i suoi fratelli* (*Rocco and His Brothers*),
dir. Luchino Visconti, prod. Goffredo Lombardo
Best Director: Michelangelo Antonioni, *La notte* (*The Night*)
Best Actor: Alberto Sordi, *Tutti a casa*
Best Actress: Sophia Loren, *La ciociara* (*Two Women*), dir. Vittorio De
Sica

1962

Best Film: *Mondo cane*, dir. Paolo Cavara, Gualtiero Jacopetti, and
Franco Prosperi, prod. Angelo Rizzoli's Cineriz; *Una vita difficile* (*A
Difficult Life*), dir. Dino Risi, prod. Dino De Laurentiis
Best Director: Ermanno Olmi, *Il posto* (*The Job*)
Best Actor: Raf Vallone, *A View from the Bridge*, dir. Sidney Lumet

1963

Best Film: *Il gattopardo* (*The Leopard*), dir. Luchino Visconti, prod.
Goffredo Lombardo; *Uno dei tre* (*The Sword and the Balance*), dir.
André Cayatte, prod. Ultra Film
Best Director: Luchino Visconti, *I sequestrati di Altona* (*The Condemned of Altona*)
Best Actor: Vittorio Gassman, *Il sorpasso* (*The Easy Life*), dir. Dino
Risi

Best Actress : Gina Lollobrigida, *Venere imperiale* (*Imperial Venus*), dir. Jean Delannoy; Silvana Mangano, *Il processo di Verona* (*The Verona Trial*), dir. Carlo Lizzani

1964

Best Film: *Ieri, oggi, domani* (*Yesterday, Today and Tomorrow*), dir. Vittorio De Sica, prod. Carlo Ponti; *Sedotta e abbandonata* (*Seduced and Abandoned*), dir. Pietro Germi, prod. Franco Cristaldi; *La ragazza di Bube* (*Bebo's Girl*), dir. Luigi Comencini, prod. Franco Cristaldi
Best Director: Pietro Germi, *Sedotta e abbandonata*
Best Actor: Marcello Mastroianni, *Ieri, oggi, domani*
Best Actress: Sophia Loren, *Ieri, oggi, domani*

1965

Best Film: *Matrimonio all'italiana* (*Marriage Italian Style*), dir. Vittorio De Sica, prod. Carlo Ponti
Best Director: Francesco Rosi, *Il momento della verità* (*The Moment of Truth*), and Vittorio De Sica, *Matrimonio all'italiana*
Best Actor: Vittorio Gassman, *La congiuntura* (*Hard Time for Princes*), dir. Ettore Scola; Marcello Mastroianni, *Matrimonio all'italiana*
Best Actress: Sophia Loren, *Matrimonio all'italiana*

1966

Best Film: *The Bible . . . in the Beginning*, dir. John Huston, prod. Dino De Laurentiis; *Signore e signori* (*The Birds, the Bees and the Italians*), dir. Pietro Germi, prod. Robert Haggiag and Pietro Germi; *Africa addio* (*Farewell Africa*), dir. Gualtiero Jacopetti and Franco Prosperi, prod. Rizzoli Film
Best Director: Alessandro Blasetti, *Io, io, io . . . e gli altri* (*Me, Me, Me . . . and the Others*); Pietro Germi, *Signore e signori*
Best Actor: Alberto Sordi, *Fumo di Londra* (*Smoke over London*), dir. Alberto Sordi
Best Actress: Giulietta Masina, *Giulietta degli spiriti* (*Juliet of the Spirits*), dir. Federico Fellini

1967

Best Film: *Il tigre* (*The Tiger and the Pussycat*), dir. Dino Risi, prod. Mario Cecchi Gori; *La bisbetica domata* (*The Taming of the Shrew*), dir. Franco Zeffirelli, prod. FAI Films
Best Director: Luigi Comencini, *Incompreso* (*Misunderstood*)
Best Actor: Vittorio Gassman, *Il tigre*; Ugo Tognazzi, *L'immorale* (*Too Much for One Man*), dir. Pietro Germi
Best Actress: Silvana Mangano, *Le streghe* (*The Witches*), dir. Pier Paolo Pasolini, Vittorio De Sica, Franco Rossi, Mauro Bolognini, and Luchino Visconti

1968

Best Film: *Banditi a Milano* (*Bandits in Milan*), dir. Carlo Lizzani, prod. Dino De Laurentiis; *Il giorno della civetta* (*The Day of the Owl*), dir. Damiano Damiani, prod. Ermanno Donati and Luigi Carpentieri
Best Director: Carlo Lizzani, *Banditi a Milano*
Best Actor: Franco Nero, *Il giorno della civetta*
Best Actress: Claudia Cardinale, *Il giorno della civetta*

1969

Best Film: *La ragazza con la pistola* (*Girl with a Pistol*), dir. Mario Monicelli, prod. Gianni Hecht Lucari; *C'era una volta il west* (*Once upon a Time in the West*), dir. Sergio Leone, prod. Bino Cicogna
Best Director: Franco Zeffirelli, *Romeo e Giulietta* (*Romeo and Juliet*)
Best Actor: Nino Manfredi, *Vedo nudo* (*I See Naked*), dir. Dino Risi; Alberto Sordi, *Il medico della mutua* (*The Family Doctor*), dir. Luigi Zampa
Best Actress: Gina Lollobrigida, *Buona sera, Signora Campbell* (*Buona Sera, Mrs. Campbell*), dir. Melvin Frank; Monica Vitti, *La ragazza con la pistola*

1970

Best Film: *Indagine su un cittadino al di sopra di ogni sospetto* (*Investigation of a Citizen above Suspicion*), dir. Elio Petri, prod. Daniele

Senatore and Marina Cicogna; *Metello*, dir. Mauro Bolognini, prod. Gianni Hecht Lucari

Best Director: Gillo Pontecorvo, *Queimada (Burn!)*

Best Actor: Gian Maria Volontè, *Indagine su un cittadino al di sopra di ogni sospetto*; Nino Manfredi, *Nell'anno del signore (The Conspirators)*, dir. Luigi Magni

Best Actress: Sophia Loren, *I girasoli (Sunflower)*, dir. Vittorio De Sica

1971

Best Film: *Il giardino dei Finzi-Contini (The Garden of the Finzi-Continis)*, dir. Vittorio De Sica, prod. Gianni Hecht Lucari; *Il conformista (The Conformist)*, dir. Bernardo Bertolucci, prod. Maurizio Lodi Fé; *Waterloo*, dir. Sergei Bondarchuk, prod. Dino De Laurentiis

Best Director: Luchino Visconti, *Morte a Venezia (Death in Venice)*

Best Actor: Ugo Tognazzi, *La califfa (Lady Caliph)*, dir. Alberto Bevilacqua

Best Actress: Florinda Bolkan, *Anonimo veneziano (The Anonymous Venetian)*, dir. Enrico Maria Salerno; Monica Vitti, *Ninì Tirabusciò: La donna che inventò la mossa (Ninì Tirabusciò)*, dir. Marcello Fondato

1972

Best Film: *La classe operaia va in paradiso (The Working Class Goes to Heaven)*, dir. Elio Petri, prod. Euro International Film; *Questa specie d'amore (This Kind of Love)*, dir. Alberto Bevilacqua, prod. Mario Cecchi Gori

Best Director: Sergio Leone, *Giù la testa (Duck, You Sucker)*; Franco Zeffirelli, *Fratello Sole, Sorella Luna (Brother Sun, Sister Moon)*

Best Actor: Giancarlo Giannini, *Mimì metallurgico ferito nell'onore (The Seduction of Mimì)*, dir. Lina Wertmüller; Alberto Sordi, *Detenuto in attesa di giudizio (Why)*, dir. Nanni Loy

Best Actress: Claudia Cardinale, *Bello onesto emigrato Australia sposerebbe compaesana illibata (A Girl in Australia)*, dir. Luigi Zampa

1973

Best Film: *Ludwig*, dir. Luchino Visconti, prod. Ugo Santalucia; *Alfredo, Alfredo*, dir. Pietro Germi, prod. Andrea Rizzoli
Best Director: Luchino Visconti, *Ludwig*
Best Actor: Alberto Sordi, *Lo scopone scientifico* (*The Scientific Cardplayer*), dir. Luigi Comencini
Best Actress: Florinda Bolkan, *Cari genitori* (*Dear Parents*), dir. Enrico Maria Salerno; Silvana Mangano, *Lo scopone scientifico*

1974

Best Film: *Amarcord*, dir. Federico Fellini, prod. Franco Cristaldi; *Pane e cioccolata* (*Bread and Chocolate*), dir. Franco Brusati, prod. Maurizio Lodi Fè
Best Director: Federico Fellini, *Amarcord*
Best Actor: Nino Manfredi, *Pane e cioccolata*
Best Actress: Sophia Loren, *Il viaggio* (*The Journey*), dir. Vittorio De Sica; Monica Vitti, *Polvere di stelle* (*Stardust*), dir. Alberto Sordi

1975

Best Film: *Gruppo di famiglia in un interno* (*Conversation Piece*), dir. Luchino Visconti, prod. Rusconi Film; *Fatti di gente per bene* (*Drama of the Rich*), dir. Mauro Bolognini, prod. Filmarpa and Lira Films
Best Director: Dino Risi, *Profumo di donna* (*Scent of a Woman*)
Best Actor: Vittorio Gassman, *Profumo di donna*
Best Actress: Mariangela Melato, *La poliziotta* (*Policewoman*), dir. Steno

1976

Best Film: *Cadaveri eccellenti* (*Illustrious Corpses*), dir. Francesco Rosi, prod. Alberto Grimaldi; *Amici miei* (*My Friends*), dir. Mario Monicelli, prod. Andrea Rizzoli
Best Director: Francesco Rosi, *Cadaveri eccellenti*

Best Actor: Adriano Celentano, *Bluff*, dir. Sergio Corbucci; Ugo Tognazzi, *Amici miei*; Ugo Tognazzi, *L'anatra all'arancia* (*Duck in Orange Sauce*), dir. Luciano Salce
Best Actress: Monica Vitti, *L'anatra all'arancia*
Premio David "Luchino Visconti": Michelangelo Antonioni

1977

Best Film: *Il deserto dei tartari* (*The Desert of the Tartars*), dir. Valerio Zurlini, prod. Italnoleggio; *Un borghese piccolo piccolo* (*An Average Little Man*), dir. Mario Monicelli, prod. Luigi and Aurelio De Laurentiis
Best Director: Valerio Zurlini, *Il deserto dei tartari*; Mario Monicelli, *Un borghese piccolo piccolo*
Best Actor: Alberto Sordi, *Un borghese piccolo piccolo*
Best Actress: Mariangela Melato, *Caro Michele* (*Dear Michael*), dir. Mario Monicelli
Premio David "Luchino Visconti": Robert Bresson

1978

Best Film: *In nome del Papa Re* (*In the Name of the Pope King*), dir. Luigi Magni, prod. Franco Committeri; *Il prefetto di ferro* (*The Iron Prefect*), dir. Pasquale Squitieri, prod. Gianni Hecht Lucari
Best Director: Ettore Scola, *Una giornata particolare* (*A Special Day*)
Best Actor: Nino Manfredi, *In nome del Papa Re*
Best Actress: Mariangela Melato, *Il gatto* (*The Cat*), dir. Luigi Comencini; Sophia Loren, *Una giornata particolare*
Premio David "Luchino Visconti": Andrzej Wajda

1979

Best Film: *L'albero degli zoccoli* (*The Tree of Wooden Clogs*), dir. Ermanno Olmi, prod. Italnoleggio and RAI; *Cristo si è fermato a Eboli* (*Christ Stopped at Eboli*), dir. Francesco Rosi, prod. Franco Cristaldi; *Dimenticare Venezia* (*To Forget Venice*), dir. Franco Brusati, prod. Angelo Rizzoli

Best Director: Francesco Rosi, *Cristo si è fermato a Eboli*
Best Actor: Vittorio Gassman, *Caro Papà* (*Dear Father*), dir. Dino Risi
Best Actress: Monica Vitti, *Amori miei* (*My Loves*), dir. Steno
Premio David "Luchino Visconti": Rainer Werner Fassbinder

1980

Best Film: *Mani di velluto* (*Velvet Hands*), dir. Castellano and Pipolo,
  prod. Mario Cecchi Gori; *Don Giovanni*, dir. Joseph Losey, prod.
  Opera Film and Gaumont
Best Director: Gillo Pontecorvo, *Ogro* (*Operation Ogre*); Marco Bel-
  locchio, *Salto nel vuoto* (*A Leap in the Dark*)
Best Actor: Adriano Celentano, *Mani di velluto*
Best Actress: Virna Lisi, *La cicala* (*The Cricket*), dir. Alberto Lattuada
Premio David "Luchino Visconti": Andrei Tarkovsky

1981

Best Film: *Ricomincio da tre* (*I'm Starting from Three*), dir. Massimo
  Troisi, prod. Fulvio Lucisano
Best Director: Francesco Rosi, *Tre fratelli* (*Three Brothers*)
Best Actor: Massimo Troisi, *Ricomincio da tre*
Best Actress: Valeria D'Obici, *Passione d'amore* (*Passion of Love*), dir.
  Ettore Scola; Mariangela Melato, *Aiutami a sognare* (*Help Me
  Dream*), dir. Pupi Avati
Premio David "Luchino Visconti": François Truffaut

1982

Best Film: *Borotalco* (*Talcum Powder*), dir. Carlo Verdone, prod. Mario
  and Vittorio Cecchi Gori
Best Director: Marco Ferreri, *Storie di ordinaria follia* (*Tales of Ordi-
  nary Madness*)
Best Emerging Director: Luciano Manuzzi, *Fuori stagione* (*Off Season*)
Best Actor: Carlo Verdone, *Borotalco*
Best Actress: Eleonora Giorgi, *Borotalco*
Premio David "Luchino Visconti": Cesare Zavattini

1983

Best Film: *La notte di San Lorenzo* (*Night of the Shooting Stars*), dir. Paolo and Vittorio Taviani, prod. Giuliani G. De Negri
Best Director: Paolo and Vittorio Taviani, *La notte di San Lorenzo*
Best Emerging Director: Francesco Laudadio, *Grog*
Best Actor: Francesco Nuti, *Io, Chiara, e lo scuro* (*The Pool Hustlers*), dir. Maurizio Ponzi
Best Actress: Giuliana De Sio, *Io, Chiara, e lo scuro*
Premio David "Luchino Visconti": Orson Welles

1984

Best Film: *Ballando Ballando* (*Le bal*), dir. Ettore Scola, prod. Franco Committeri and Giorgio Silvagni; *E la nave va* (*And the Ship Sails On*), dir. Federico Fellini, prod. Franco Cristaldi, Aldo Nemni, and Renzo Rossellini
Best Director: Ettore Scola, *Ballando Ballando*
Best Emerging Director: Roberto Russo, *Flirt*
Best Actor: Giancarlo Giannini, *Mi manda Picone* (*Picone Sent Me*), dir. Nanni Loy
Best Actress: Lina Sastri, *Mi manda Picone*
Premio David "Luchino Visconti": Federico Fellini

1985

Best film: *Carmen*, dir. Francesco Rosi, prod. Patrice Ledoux, Renzo Rossellini, and Daniel Toscan du Plantier
Best director: Francesco Rosi, *Carmen*
Best Emerging Director: Luciano De Crescenzo, *Così parlò Bellavista* (*Thus Spake Bellavista*)
Best Actor: Francesco Nuti, *Casablanca, Casablanca*, dir. Francesco Nuti
Best Actress: Lina Sastri, *Segreti Segreti* (*Secrets Secrets*), dir. Giuseppe Bertolucci
Premio David "Luchino Visconti": Istvan Szabo

1986

Best Film: *Speriamo che sia femmina* (*Let's Hope It's a Girl*), dir. Mario Monicelli, prod. Giovanni di Clemente
Best Director: Mario Monicelli, *Speriamo che sia femmina*
Best Emerging Director: Enrico Montesano, *A me mi piace* (*I Like It*)
Best Actor: Marcello Mastroianni, *Ginger e Fred* (*Ginger and Fred*), dir. Federico Fellini
Best Actress: Angela Molina, *Un complicato intrigo di donne, vicoli e delitti* (*Camorra: A Story of Streets, Women and Crime*), dir. Lina Wertmüller
Premio David "Luchino Visconti": Ingmar Bergman

1987

Best Film: *La famiglia* (*The Family*), dir. Ettore Scola, prod. Franco Committeri
Best Director: Ettore Scola, *La famiglia*
Best Emerging Director: Giorgio Treves, *La coda del diavolo* (*The Malady of Love*)
Best Actor: Vittorio Gassman, *La famiglia*
Best Actress: Liv Ullmann, *Mosca addio* (*Farewell Moscow*), dir. Mauro Bolognini
Premio David "Luchino Visconti": Alain Resnais

1988

Best Film: *L'ultimo imperatore* (*The Last Emperor*), dir. Bernardo Bertolucci, prod. John Daly, Franco Giovale, Joyce Herlihy, and Jeremy Thomas
Best Director: Bernardo Bertolucci, *L'ultimo imperatore*
Best Emerging Director: Daniele Luchetti, *Domani accadrà* (*It's Happening Tomorrow*)
Best Actor: Marcello Mastroianni, *Oci Ciornie* (*Dark Eyes*), dir. Nikita Mikhalkov
Best Actress: Elena Safonova, *Oci Ciornie*
Premio David "Luchino Visconti": Stanley Kubrick

1989

Best Film: *La leggenda del Santo Bevitore* (*The Legend of the Holy Drinker*), dir. Ermanno Olmi, prod. Mario and Vittorio Cecchi Gori, Roberto Cicutto, and Marcello Siene
Best Director: Ermanno Olmi, *La leggenda del Santo Bevitore*
Best Emerging Director: Francesca Archibugi, *Mignon è partita* (*Mignon Has Come to Stay*)
Best Actor: Roberto Benigni, *Il piccolo diavolo* (*The Little Devil*), dir. Roberto Benigni
Best Actress: Stefania Sandrelli, *Mignon è partita*
Premio David "Luchino Visconti": Paolo and Vittorio Taviani

1990

Best Film: *Porte aperte* (*Open Doors*), dir. Gianni Amelio, prod. Conchita Airoldi, Dino Di Dionisio, and Angelo Rizzoli Jr.
Best Director: Mario Monicelli, *Il male oscuro* (*Dark Illness*)
Best Emerging Director: Ricky Tognazzi, *Piccoli equivoci* (*Little Misunderstandings*)
Best Actor: Gian Maria Volontè, *Porte aperte*; Paolo Villaggio, *La voce della luna* (*The Voice of the Moon*), dir. Federico Fellini
Best Actress: Elena Sofia Ricci, *Ne parliamo lunedì* (*We'll Talk About It on Monday*), dir. Luciano Odorisio
Premio David "Luchino Visconti": Eric Rohmer

1991

Best Film: *Mediterraneo*, dir. Gabriele Salvatores, prod. Mario and Vittorio Cecchi Gori, Silvio Berlusconi, and Gianni Minervini; *Verso Sera* (*Towards Evening*), dir. Francesca Archibugi, prod. Leo Pesacarolo and Guido De Laurentiis
Best Director: Ricky Tognazzi, *Ultrà*; Marco Risi, *Ragazzi fuori* (*Boys on the Outside*)
Best Emerging Director: Sergio Rubini, *La stazione* (*The Station*); Alessandro D'Alatri, *Americano rosso* (*Red American*)
Best Actor: Nanni Moretti, *Il portaborse* (*The Yes Man*), dir. Daniele Luchetti

Best Actress: Margherita Buy, *La stazione*
Premio David "Luchino Visconti": Marcel Carné

1992

Best Film: *Il ladro di bambini* (*The Stolen Children*), dir. Gianni Amelio, prod. Enzo Porcelli, Angelo Rizzoli Jr.
Best Director: Gianni Amelio, *Il ladro di bambini*
Best Emerging Director: Maurizio Zaccaro, *Dove comincia la notte* (*Where Night Begins*)
Best Actor: Carlo Verdone, *Maledetto il giorno che t'ho incontrato* (*Damned the Day I Met You*), dir. Carlo Verdone
Best Actress: Giuliana De Sio, *Cattiva* (*The Wicked*), dir. Carlo Lizzani
Premio David "Luchino Visconti": Ermanno Olmi

1993

Best Film: *Il grande cocomero* (*The Great Pumpkin*), dir. Francesca Archibugi, prod. Leo Pescarolo, Giudo De Laurentiis, and Fulvio Lucisano
Best Director: Roberto Faenza, *Jona che visse nella balena* (*Jonah Who Lived in the Whale*); Ricky Tognazzi, *La scorta* (*The Escort*)
Best Emerging Director: Mario Martone, *Morte di un matematico napoletano* (*Death of a Neapolitan Mathematician*)
Best Actor: Sergio Castellitto, *Il grande cocomero*
Best Actress: Antonella Ponziani, *Verso sud* (*Towards the South*), dir. Pasquale Pozzessere
Premio David "Luchino Visconti": Edgar Reitz

1994

Best Film: *Caro diario*, dir. Nanni Moretti, prod. Nella Banfi, Angelo Barbagallo, and Nanni Moretti
Best Director: Carlo Verdone, *Perdiamoci di vista* (*Let's Not Keep in Touch*)
Best Emerging Director: Simona Izzo, *Maniaci sentimentali* (*Sentimental Maniacs*); Francesco Martinotti, *Abissinia* (*Abyssinia*); Leone Pompucci, *Mille bolle blu* (*A Thousand Blue Bubbles*)

Best Actor: Giulio Scarpati, *Il giudice ragazzino* (*The Boy Judge*), dir. Alessandro Di Robilant

Best Actress: Asia Argento, *Perdiamoci di vista*

Premio David "Luchino Visconti": Manoel de Oliveira

1995

Best Film: *La scuola* (*School*), dir. Daniele Luchetti, prod. Rita Cecchi Gori

Best Director: Mario Martone, *L'amore molesto* (*Nasty Love*)

Best Emerging Director: Paolo Virzì, *La bella vita* (*Living It Up*)

Best Actor: Marcello Mastroianni, *Sostiene Pereira* (*Pereira Declares*), dir. Roberto Faenza

Best Actress: Anna Bonaiuto, *L'amore molesto*

Premio David "Luchino Visconti": Pupi Avati

1996

Best Film: *Ferie d'agosto* (*Summer Holidays*), dir. Paolo Virzì, prod. Rita Cecchi Gori

Best Director: Giuseppe Tornatore, *L'uomo delle stelle* (*The Star Maker*)

Best Emerging Director: Stefano Incerti, *Il verificatore* (*The Gas Inspector*)

Best Actor: Giancarlo Giannini, *Celluloide* (*Celluloid*), dir. Carlo Lizzani

Best Actress: Valeria Bruni Tedeschi, *La seconda volta* (*The Second Time*), dir. Mimmo Calopresti

1997

Best Film: *La tregua* (*The Truce*), dir. Francesco Rosi, prod. Leo Pescarolo and Guido De Laurentiis

Best Director: Francesco Rosi, *La tregua*

Best Emerging Director: Fulvio Ottaviani, *Cresceranno i carciofi a Mimongo* (*Artichokes Will Grow at Mimongo*)

Best Actor: Fabrizio Bentivoglio, *Testimone a rischio* (*An Eyewitness Account*), dir. Pasquale Pozzessere

Best Actress: Asia Argento, *Compagna di viaggio* (*Travelling Companion*), dir. Peter Del Monte

1998

Best Film: *La vita è bella* (*Life Is Beautiful*), dir. Roberto Benigni, prod. Elda Ferri and Gianluigi Braschi
Best Director: Roberto Benigni, *La vita è bella*
Best Emerging Director: Roberta Torre, *Tano da morire* (*To Die for Tano*)
Best Actor: Roberto Benigni, *La vita è bella*
Best Actress: Valeria Bruni Tedeschi, *La parola amore esiste* (*Notes of Love*), dir. Mimmo Calopresti

1999

Best Film: *Fuori dal mondo* (*Not of This World*), dir. Giuseppe Piccioni, prod. Lionello Cerri
Best Director: Giuseppe Tornatore, *La leggenda del pianista sull'oceano* (*The Legend of 1900*)
Best Emerging Director: Luciano Ligabue, *Radiofreccia* (*Radio Arrow*)
Best Actor: Stefano Accorsi, *Radiofreccia*
Best Actress: Margherita Buy, *Fuori dal mondo*

2000

Best Film: *Pane e tulipani* (*Bread and Tulips*), dir. Silvio Soldini, prod. Daniele Maggioni
Best Director: Silvio Soldini, *Pane e tulipani*
Best Emerging Director: Alessandro Piva, *La Capagira* (*My Head Is Spinning*)
Best Actor: Bruno Ganz, *Pane e tulipani*
Best Actress: Licia Maglietta, *Pane e tulipani*

2001

Best Film: *La stanza del figlio* (*The Son's Room*), dir. Nanni Moretti, prod. Angelo Barbagallo and Nanni Moretti

Best Director: Gabriele Muccino, *L'ultimo bacio* (*The Last Kiss*)
Best Emerging Director: Alex Infascelli, *Almost Blue*
Best Actor: Luigi Lo Cascio, *I cento passi* (*The Hundred Steps*), dir. Marco Tullio Giordana
Best Actress: Laura Morante, *La stanza del figlio*

2002

Best Film: *Il mestiere delle armi* (*The Profession of Arms*), dir. Ermanno Olmi, prod. Luigi Musini, Roberto Cicutto, and Ermanno Olmi
Best Director: Ermanno Olmi, *Il mestiere delle armi*
Best Emerging Director: Marco Ponti, *Santa Maradona* (*Holy Maradona*)
Best Actor: Giancarlo Giannini, *Ti voglio bene Eugenio* (*I Love You, Eugenio*), dir. Francisco Josè Fernandez
Best Actress: Marina Confalone, *Incantesimo napoletano* (*A Neapolitan Spell*), dir. Paolo Genovese and Luca Miniero

2003

Best Film: *La finestra di fronte* (*Facing Windows*), dir. Ferzan Ozpetek, prod. Gianni Romoli and Tilde Corsi
Best Director: Pupi Avati, *Il cuore altrove* (*The Heart Is Elsewhere*)
Best Emerging Director: Daniele Vicari, *Velocità massima* (*Maximum Velocity*)
Best Actor: Massimo Girotti, *La finestra di fronte*
Best Actress: Giovanna Mezzogiorno, *La finestra di fronte*

2004

Best Film: *La meglio gioventù* (*The Best of Youth*), dir. Marco Tullio Giordana, prod. Angelo Barbagallo
Best Director: Marco Tullio Giordana, *La meglio gioventù*
Best Emerging Director: Salvatore Mereu, *Ballo a tre passi* (*Three-Step Dancing*)
Best Actor: Sergio Castellitto, *Non ti muovere* (*Don't Move*), dir. Sergio Castellitto
Best Actress: Penélope Cruz, *Non ti muovere*

2005

Best Film: *Le conseguenze dell'amore* (*The Consequences of Love*), dir. Paolo Sorrentino, prod. Domenico Procacci and Nicola Giuliano
Best Director: Paolo Sorrentino, *Le conseguenze dell'amore*
Best Emerging Director: Saverio Costanzo, *Private*
Best Actor: Toni Servillo, *Le conseguenze dell'amore*
Best Actress: Barbora Bobulova, *Cuore sacro* (*Sacred Heart*), dir. Ferzan Ozpetek

2006

Best Film: *Il caimano* (*The Caiman*), dir. Nanni Moretti, prod. Angelo Barbagallo and Nanni Moretti
Best Director: Nanni Moretti, *Il caimano*
Best Emerging Director: Fausto Brizzi, *Notte prima degli esami* (*Night Before the Exams*)
Best Actor: Silvio Orlando, *Il caimano*
Best Actress: Valeria Golino, *La guerra di Mario* (*Mario's War*), dir. Antonio Capuano

2007

Best Film: *La sconosciuta* (*The Unknown*), dir. Giuseppe Tornatore, prod. Medusa
Best Director: Giuseppe Tornatore, *La sconosciuta*
Best Emerging Director: Kim Rossi Stuart, *Anche libero va bene* (*Along the Ridge*)
Best Actor: Elio Germano, *Mio fratello è figlio unico* (*My Brother Is an Only Child*), dir. Daniele Luchetti
Best Actress: Kseniya Rappoport, *La sconosciuta*

NASTRI D'ARGENTO

1945–1946

Best Film: *Roma città aperta* (*Open City*), dir. Roberto Rossellini
Best Director: Alessandro Blasetti, *Un giorno nella vita* (*A Day in the Life*); Vittorio De Sica, *Sciuscià* (*Shoe-Shine*)

Best Actress in a Leading Role: Clara Calamai, *L'adultera* (*The Adulteress*), dir. Duilio Coletti

Best Actor in a Leading Role: Andrea Checchi, *Due lettere anonime* (*Two Anonymous Letters*), dir. Mario Camerini

Best Actress in a Character Role: Anna Magnani, *Roma città aperta*

Best Actor in a Character Role: Gino Cervi, *Le miserie del signor Travet* (*His Young Wife*), dir. Mario Soldati

1946–1947

Best Film: *Paisà* (*Paisan*), dir. Roberto Rossellini

Best Director: Roberto Rossellini, *Paisà*

Best Actress: Alida Valli, *Eugenia Grandet* (*Eugenie Grandet*), dir. Mario Soldati

Best Actor: Amedeo Nazzari, *Il bandito* (*The Bandit*), dir. Alberto Lattuada

1947–1948

Best Film: *Gioventù perduta* (*Lost Youth*), dir. Pietro Germi

Best Director: Alberto Lattuada, *Il delitto di Giovanni Episcopo* (*Flesh Will Surrender*); Giuseppe De Santis, *Caccia tragica* (*The Tragic Hunt*)

Best Actress: Anna Magnani, *L'onorevole Angelina* (*Angelina, MP*), dir. Luigi Zampa

Best Actor: Vittorio De Sica, *Cuore* (*Heart*), dir. Duilio Coletti

1948–1949

Best Film: *Ladri di biciclette* (*Bicycle Thieves*), dir. Vittorio De Sica

Best Director: Vittorio De Sica, *Ladri di biciclette*

Best Actress: Anna Magnani, *L'amore* (*Ways of Love*), dir. Roberto Rossellini

Best Actor: Massimo Girotti, *In nome della legge* (*In the Name of the Law*), dir. Pietro Germi

1949–1950

Director of Best Film: Augusto Genina, *Cielo sulla palude* (*Heaven over the Marshes*)

1950–1951

Director of Best Film: Alessandro Blasetti, *Prima comunione* (*Father's Dilemma*)
Best Actress: Anna Maria Pierangeli, *Domani è troppo tardi* (*Tomorrow Is Too Late*), dir. Leonida Moguy
Best Actor: Aldo Fabrizi, *Prima comunione*

1951–1952

Director of Best Film: Renato Castellani, *Due soldi di speranza* (*Two Cents' Worth of Hope*)
Best Actress: Anna Magnani, *Bellissima*, dir. Luchino Visconti
Best Actor: Totò, *Guardie e ladri* (*Cops and Robbers*), dir. Mario Monicelli and Steno

1952–1953

Director of Best Film: Luigi Zampa, *Processo alla città* (*The City Stands Trial*); Claudio Gora, *La febbre di vivere* (*Eager to Live*)
Best Actress: Ingrid Bergman, *Europa '51*, dir. Roberto Rossellini
Best Actor: Gabriele Ferzetti, *La provinciale* (*The Wayward Wife*), dir. Mario Soldati

1953–1954

Producer of Best Film: Peg-Film and Cité Films, *I vitelloni* (*Spivs*), dir. Federico Fellini
Best Director: Federico Fellini, *I vitelloni*
Best Actress: Gina Lollobrigida, *Pane, amore e fantasia* (*Bread, Love and Dreams*), dir. Luigi Comencini
Best Actor: Nino Taranto, *Anni facili* (*Easy Years*), dir. Luigi Zampa

1954–1955

Producer of Best Film: Ponti-De Laurentiis, *La strada*, dir. Federico Fellini

Best Director: Federico Fellini, *La strada*

Best Actress: Silvana Mangano, *L'oro di Napoli* (*The Gold of Naples*), dir. Vittorio De Sica

Best Actor: Marcello Mastroianni, *Giorni d'amore* (*Days of Love*), dir. Giuseppe De Santis

1955–1956

Producer of Best Film: Cines, *Amici per la pelle* (*Friends for Life*), dir. Franco Rossi

Best Director: Michelangelo Antonioni, *Le amiche* (*The Girlfriends*)

Best Actor: Alberto Sordi, *Lo scapolo* (*The Bachelor*), dir. Antonio Pietrangeli

1957

Producer of Best Film: ENIC-Ponti-De Laurentiis, *Il ferroviere* (*The Railroad Man*), dir. Pietro Germi

Best Director: Pietro Germi, *Il ferroviere*

Best Actress: Anna Magnani, *Suor Letizia* (*The Awakening*), dir. Mario Camerini

1958

Producer of Best Film: Dino De Laurentiis, *Le notti di Cabiria* (*Nights of Cabiria*), dir. Federico Fellini

Best Director: Federico Fellini, *Le notti di Cabiria*

Best Actress: Giulietta Masina, *Le notti di Cabiria*

Best Actor: Marcello Mastroianni, *Le notti bianche* (*White Nights*), dir. Luchino Visconti

1959

Best Producer: Franco Cristaldi

Director of Best Film: Pietro Germi, *L'uomo di paglia* (*A Man of Straw*)

Best Actor: Vittorio Gassman, *I soliti ignoti* (*Big Deal on Madonna Street*), dir. Mario Monicelli

1960

Director of Best Film: Roberto Rossellini, *Il Generale della Rovere* (*General della Rovere*)
Best Producer: Goffredo Lombardo
Best Actress: Eleonora Rossi Drago, *Estate violenta* (*Violent Summer*), dir. Valerio Zurlini
Best Actor: Alberto Sordi, *La grande guerra* (*The Great War*), dir. Mario Monicelli

1961

Director of Best Film: Luchino Visconti, *Rocco e i suoi fratelli* (*Rocco and His Brothers*)
Best Producer: Dino De Laurentiis
Best Actress: Sophia Loren, *La ciociara* (*Two Women*), dir. Vittorio De Sica
Best Actor: Marcello Mastroianni, *La dolce vita*, dir. Federico Fellini

1962

Director of Best Film: Michelangelo Antonioni, *La notte* (*The Night*)
Best Producer: Alfredo Bini
Best Actor: Marcello Mastroianni, *Divorzio all'italiana* (*Divorce Italian Style*), dir. Pietro Germi

1963

Director of Best Film: Nanni Loy, *Le quattro giornate di Napoli* (*The Four Days of Naples*); Francesco Rosi, *Salvatore Giuliano*
Best Producer: Goffredo Lombardo
Best Actress: Gina Lollobrigida, *Venere imperiale* (*Imperial Venus*), dir. Jean Delannoy
Best Actor: Vittorio Gassman, *Il sorpasso* (*The Easy Life*), dir. Dino Risi

1964

Director of Best Film: Federico Fellini, *Otto e mezzo* (8½)
Best Producer: Angelo Rizzoli, *Otto e mezzo*
Best Actress: Silvana Mangano, *Il processo di Verona* (*The Verona Trial*), dir. Carlo Lizzani
Best Actor: Ugo Tognazzi, *Una storia moderna—L'ape regina* (*The Conjugal Bed*), dir. Marco Ferreri

1965

Director of Best Film: Pier Paolo Pasolini, *Il Vangelo secondo Matteo* (*The Gospel According to St. Matthew*)
Best Producer: Franco Cristaldi
Best Actress: Claudia Cardinale, *La ragazza di Bube* (*Bebo's Girl*), dir. Luigi Comencini
Best Actor: Saro Urzì, *Sedotta e abbandonata* (*Seduced and Abandoned*), dir. Pietro Germi

1966

Director of Best Film: Antonio Pietrangeli, *Io la conoscevo bene* (*I Knew Her Well*)
Best Producer: Marco Vicario, *Sette uomini d'oro* (*Seven Golden Men*), Marco Vicario
Best Actress: Giovanna Ralli, *La fuga* (*The Escape*), dir. Paolo Spinola
Best Actor: Nino Manfredi, *Questa volta parliamo di uomini* (*Let's Talk About Men*), dir. Lina Wertmüller

1967

Director of Best Film: Gillo Pontecorvo, *La battaglia di Algeri* (*The Battle of Algiers*)
Best Producer: Antonio Musu, *La battaglia di Algeri*
Best Actress: Lisa Gastoni, *Svegliati e uccidi* (*Wake Up and Die*), dir. Carlo Lizzani
Best Actor: Totò, *Uccellacci e uccellini* (*Hawks and Sparrows*), dir. Pier Paolo Pasolini

1968

Director of Best Film: Elio Petri, *A ciascuno il suo* (*We Still Kill the Old Way*)
Best Producer: Alfredo Bini, *Edipo Re* (*Oedipus Rex*), dir. Pier Paolo Pasolini
Best Actor: Gian Maria Volontè, *A ciascuno il suo*

1969

Director of Best Film: Franco Zeffirelli, *Romeo e Giulietta* (*Romeo and Juliet*)
Best Producer: Ermanno Donati and Luigi Carpentieri, *Il giorno della civetta* (*The Day of the Owl*), dir. Damiano Damiani
Best Actress: Monica Vitti, *La ragazza con la pistola* (*Girl with a Pistol*), dir. Mario Monicelli
Best Actor: Ugo Tognazzi, *La bambolona* (*Baby Doll*), dir. Franco Giraldi

1970

Director of Best Film: Luchino Visconti, *La caduta degli dei* (*The Damned*)
Best Producer: Alberto Grimaldi
Best Actress: Paola Pitagora, *Senza sapere niente di lei* (*Without Knowing Anything about Her*), dir. Luigi Comencini
Best Actor: Nino Manfredi, *Nell'anno del Signore* (*The Conspirators*), dir. Luigi Magni

1971

Director of Best Film: Elio Petri, *Indagine su un cittadino al di sopra di ogni sospetto* (*Investigation of a Citizen above Suspicion*)
Best Producer: Silvio Clementelli, *Gott mit uns* (*God with Us*), dir. Giuliano Montaldo
Best Actress: Ottavia Piccolo, *Metello*, dir. Mauro Bolognini
Best Actor: Gian Maria Volontè, *Indagine su un cittadino al di sopra di ogni sospetto*

1972

Director of Best Film: Luchino Visconti, *Morte a Venezia* (*Death in Venice*)

Best Emerging Director: Alberto Bevilacqua, *La califfa* (*Lady Caliph*)

Best Producer: Mario Cecchi Gori

Best Actress: Mariangela Melato, *La classe operaia va in paradiso* (*The Working Class Goes to Heaven*), dir. Elio Petri

Best Actor: Riccardo Cucciolla, *Sacco e Vanzetti* (*Sacco and Vanzetti*), dir. Giuliano Montaldo

1973

Director of Best Film: Bernardo Bertolucci, *Ultimo tango a Parigi* (*Last Tango in Paris*)

Best Producer: Alberto Grimaldi

Best Actress: Mariangela Melato, *Mimì metallurgico ferito nell'onore* (*The Seduction of Mimi*), dir. Lina Wertmüller

Best Actor: Giancarlo Giannini, *Mimì metallurgico ferito nell'onore*

1974

Director of Best Film: Federico Fellini, *Amarcord*

Best Emerging Director: Marco Leto, *La villeggiatura* (*Black Holiday*)

Best Producer: Franco Cristaldi

Best Actress: Laura Antonelli, *Malizia* (*Malice*), dir. Salvatore Samperi

1975

Director of Best Film: Luchino Visconti, *Gruppo di famiglia in un interno* (*Conversation Piece*)

Best Emerging Director: Luigi Di Gianni, *Il tempo dell'inizio* (*The Time of the Beginning*)

Best Producer: Rusconi Film, *Gruppo di famiglia in un interno*

Best Actress: Lisa Gastoni, *Amore amaro* (*Bitter Love*), dir. Florestano Vancini

Best Actor: Vittorio Gassman, *Profumo di donna* (*Scent of a Woman*), dir. Dino Risi

1976

Director of Best Film: Michelangelo Antonioni, *Professione reporter* (*The Passenger*)

Best Emerging Director: Ennio Lorenzini, *Quanto è bello lu murire acciso* (*How Wonderful to Die Assassinated*)

Best Producer: Andrea Rizzoli, *Amici miei* (*My Friends*), dir. Mario Monicelli

Best Actress: Monica Vitti, *L'anatra all'arancia* (*Duck in Orange Sauce*), dir. Luciano Salce

Best Actor: Michele Placido, *Marcia trionfale* (*Victory March*), dir. Marco Bellocchio

1977

Director of Best Film: Valerio Zurlini, *Il deserto dei Tartari* (*The Desert of the Tartars*)

Best Emerging Director: Giorgio Ferrara, *Un cuore semplice* (*A Simple Heart*)

Best Producer: Edmondo Amati

Best Actress: Mariangela Melato, *Caro Michele* (*Dear Michael*), dir. Mario Monicelli

Best Actor: Alberto Sordi, *Un borghese piccolo piccolo* (*An Average Little Man*), dir. Mario Monicelli

1978

Director of Best Film: Paolo and Vittorio Taviani, *Padre padrone* (*My Father My Master*)

Best Emerging Director: Sergio Nuti, *Non contate su di noi* (*Don't Count on Us*)

Best Producer: RAI-TV

Best Actress: Sophia Loren, *Una giornata particolare* (*A Special Day*), dir. Ettore Scola

Best Actor: Nino Manfredi, *In nome del papa re* (*In the Name of the Pope King*), dir. Luigi Magni

1979

Director of Best Film: Ermanno Olmi, *L'albero degli zoccoli* (*The Tree of Wooden Clogs*)
Best Emerging Director: Salvatore Nocita, *Ligabue*
Best Producer: RAI-TV
Best Actress: Mariangela Melato, *Dimenticare Venezia* (*To Forget Venice*), dir. Franco Brusati
Best Actor: Flavio Bucci, *Ligabue*

1980

Director of Best Film: Federico Fellini, *La città delle donne* (*City of Women*)
Best Emerging Director: Maurizio Nichetti, *Ratataplan*
Best Producer: Franco Cristaldi and Nicola Carraro
Best Actress: Ida Di Benedetto, *Immacolata e Concetta* (*Immacolata and Concetta: The Other Jealousy*), dir. Salvatore Piscicelli
Best Actor: Nino Manfredi, *Café express*, dir. Nanni Loy

1981

Director of Best Film: Francesco Rosi, *Tre fratelli* (*Three Brothers*)
Best Emerging Director: Massimo Troisi, *Ricomincio da tre* (*I'm Starting from Three*)
Best Producer: Fulvio Lucisano and Mauro Berardi, *Ricomincio da tre*
Best Actress: Mariangela Melato, *Aiutami a sognare* (*Help Me Dream*), dir. Pupi Avati
Best Actor: Vittorio Mezzogiorno, *Tre fratelli*

1982

Director of Best Film: Marco Ferreri, *Storie di ordinaria follia* (*Tales of Ordinary Madness*)
Best Emerging Director: Alessandro Benvenuti, *Ad ovest di Paperino* (*West of Paperino*)
Best Producer: Mario and Vittorio Cecchi Gori
Best Actress: Eleonora Giorgi, *Borotalco*, dir. Carlo Verdone

Best Actor: Ugo Tognazzi, *Tragedia di un uomo ridicolo* (*Tragedy of a Ridiculous Man*), dir. Bernardo Bertolucci

1983

Director of Best Film: Paolo and Vittorio Taviani, *La notte di San Lorenzo* (*Night of the Shooting Stars*)
Best Emerging Director: Franco Piavoli, *Il pianeta azzurro* (*The Blue Planet*)
Best Producer: RAI-TV
Best Actress: Giuliana De Sio, *Io, Chiara e lo scuro* (*The Pool Hustlers*), dir. Maurizio Ponzi
Best Actor: Francesco Nuti, *Io, Chiara e lo scuro*

1984

Director of Best Film: Federico Fellini, *E la nave va* (*And the Ship Sails On*); Pupi Avati, *Una gita scolastica* (*A School Outing*)
Best Emerging Director: Gabriele Lavia, *Il principe di Homburg*
Best Producer: Gianni Minervini, *Mi manda Picone* (*Picone Sent Me*), dir. Nanni Loy
Best Actress: Lina Sastri, *Mi manda Picone*
Best Actor: Carlo Delle Piane, *Una gita scolastica*

1985

Director of Best Film: Sergio Leone, *C'era una volta in America* (*Once upon a Time in America*)
Best Emerging Director: Luciano Da Crescenzo, *Così parlò Bellavista* (*Thus Spake Bellavista*)
Best Producer: Fulvio Lucisano
Best Actress: Claudia Cardinale, *Claretta* (*Claretta Petacci*), dir. Pasquale Squitieri
Best Actor: Michele Placido, *Pizza Connection*, dir. Damiano Damiani

1986

Director of Best Film: Mario Monicelli, *Speriamo che sia femmina* (*Let's Hope It's a Girl*)

Best Emerging Director: Enrico Montesano, *A me mi piace* (*I Like It*)
Best Producer: Fulvio Lucisano
Best Actress: Giulietta Masina, *Ginger e Fred* (*Ginger and Fred*), dir. Federico Fellini
Best Actor: Marcello Mastroianni, *Ginger e Fred*

1987

Director of Best Film: Ettore Scola, *La famiglia* (*The Family*)
Best Emerging Director: Giuseppe Tornatore, *Il camorrista* (*The Professor*)
Best Producer: Franco Committeri, *La famiglia*
Best Actress: Valeria Golino, *Storia d'amore* (*Love Story*), dir. Francesco Maselli
Best Actor: Roberto Benigni, *Down by Law*, dir. Jim Jarmusch

1988

Director of Best Film: Bernardo Bertolucci, *L'ultimo imperatore* (*The Last Emperor*)
Best Emerging Director: Carlo Mazzacurati, *Notte italiana* (*Italian Night*)
Best Producer: Nanni Moretti and Angelo Barbagallo
Best Actress: Ornella Muti, *Io e mia sorella* (*Me and My Sister*), dir. Carlo Verdone
Best Actor: Marcello Mastroianni, *Oci Ciornie* (*Dark Eyes*), dir. Nikita Mikhalkov

1989

Director of Best Film: Ermanno Olmi, *La leggenda del Santo Bevitore* (*The Legend of the Holy Drinker*)
Best Emerging Director: Francesca Archibugi, *Mignon è partita* (*Mignon Has Come to Stay*)
Best Producer: Mario and Vittorio Cecchi Gori
Best Actress: Ornella Muti, *Codice privato* (*Private Access*), dir. Francesco Maselli
Best Actor: Gian Maria Volontè, *L'oeuvre au noir* (*The Abyss*), dir. André Delvaux

1990

Director of Best Film: Pupi Avati, *Storia di ragazzi e di ragazze* (*The Story of Boys and Girls*)

Best Emerging Director: Ricky Tognazzi, *Piccoli equivoci* (*Little Misunderstandings*)

Best Producer: Claudio Bonivento, *Mery per sempre* (*Forever Mary*), dir. Marco Risi

Best Actress: Virna Lisi, *Buon Natale, Buon Anno* (*Merry Christmas . . . Happy New Year*), dir. Luigi Comencini

Best Actor: Vittorio Gassman, *Lo zio indegno* (*The Sleazy Uncle*), dir. Franco Brusati

1991

Director of Best Film: Gianni Amelio, *Porte aperte* (*Open Doors*)

Best Emerging Director: Sergio Rubini, *La stazione* (*The Station*)

Best Producer: Mario and Vittorio Cecchi Gori

Best Actress: Margherita Buy, *La stazione*

Best Actor: Marcello Mastroianni, *Verso sera* (*Towards Evening*), dir. Francesca Archibugi

1992

Director of Best Film: Gabriele Salvatores, *Mediterraneo*

Best Emerging Director: Antonio Capuano, *Vito e gli altri* (*Vito and the Others*)

Best Producer: Nanni Moretti and Angelo Barbagallo, *Il Portaborse* (*The Yes Man*), dir. Daniele Luchetti

Best Actress: Francesca Neri, *Pensavo fosse amore invece era un calesse* (*I Thought It Was Love*), dir. Massimo Troisi

Best Actor: Roberto Benigni, *Johnny Stecchino*, dir. Roberto Benigni

1993

Director of Best Film: Gianni Amelio, *Il ladro di bambini* (*The Stolen Children*)

Best Emerging Director: Mario Martone, *Morte di un matematico napoletano* (*Death of a Neapolitan Mathematician*)

Best Producer: Angelo Rizzoli
Best Actress: Antonella Ponziani, *Verso Sud (Towards the South)*, dir.
Pasquale Pozzessere
Best Actor: Diego Abatantuono, *Puerto Escondido*, dir. Gabriele Salvatores

1994

Director of Best Italian Film: Nanni Moretti, *Caro Diario (Dear Diary)*
Best Emerging Director: Pappi Corsicato, *Libera*
Best Italian Producer: Leo Pescarolo, Fulvio Lucisano, and Guido De
Laurentiis, *Il grande cocomero (The Great Pumpkin)*, dir. Francesca
Archibugi
Best Actress: Chiara Caselli, *Dove siete? Io sono qui (Where Are You?
I'm Here)*, dir. Liliana Cavani
Best Actor: Paolo Villaggio, *Il segreto del bosco vecchio (The Secret of
the Old Woods)*, dir. Ermanno Olmi

1995

Director of Best Italian Film: Gianni Amelio, *Lamerica*
Best Emerging Director: Paolo Virzì, *La bella vita (Living It Up)*
Best Producer: Mario and Vittorio Cecchi Gori
Best Actress: Sabrina Ferilli, *La bella vita*
Best Actor: Alessandro Haber, *La vera vita di Antonio H (The True Life
of Antonio H.)*, dir. Enzo Monteleone

1996

Director of Best Italian Film: Giuseppe Tornatore, *L'uomo delle stelle
(The Star Maker)*
Best Emerging Director: Sandro Baldoni, *Strane storie (Weird Tales)*
Best Producer: Nanni Moretti and Angelo Barbagallo, *La seconda volta
(The Second Time)*, dir. Mimmo Calopresti
Best Actress: Anna Bonaiuto, *L'amore molesto (Nasty Love)*, dir. Mario
Martone
Best Actor: Sergio Castellitto, *L'uomo delle stelle*

1997

Director of Best Italian Film: Maurizio Nichetti, *Luna e l'altra* (*Luna and the Other*)
Best Emerging Director: Roberto Cimpanelli, *Un inverno freddo freddo* (*A Cold, Cold Winter*)
Best Italian Producer: Antonio and Pupi Avati and Aurelio De Laurentiis, *Festival*, dir. Pupi Avati
Best Actress: Virna Lisi, *Va' dove ti porta il cuore* (*Follow Your Heart*), dir. Cristina Comencini; Iaia Forte, *Luna e l'altra*
Best Actor: Leonardo Pieraccioni, *Il ciclone* (*The Cyclone*), dir. Leonardo Pieraccioni

1998

Director of Best Italian Film: Roberto Benigni, *La vita è bella* (*Life Is Beautiful*)
Best Emerging Director: Roberta Torre, *Tano da morire* (*To Die for Tano*)
Best Italian Producer: Marco Risi-Maurizio Tedesco, *Il bagno turco* (*Hamam: The Turkish Bath*), dir. Ferzan Ozpetek
Best Actress: Francesca Neri, *Carne trémula* (*Live Flesh*), dir. Pedro Almodóvar
Best Actor: Roberto Benigni, *La vita è bella*, dir. Roberto Benigni

1999

Director of Best Italian Film: Giuseppe Tornatore, *La leggenda del pianista sull'oceano* (*The Legend of 1900*)
Best Emerging Director: Luciano Ligabue, *Radiofreccia* (*Radio Arrow*)
Best Producer: Medusa film, *La leggenda del pianista sull'oceano*
Best Actress: Giovanna Mezzogiorno, *Del perduto amore* (*Of Lost Love*), dir. Michele Placido
Best Actor: Giancarlo Giannini, *La stanza dello scirocco* (*The Room of the Scirocco*), dir. Maurizio Sciarrra

2000

Director of Best Italian Film: Silvio Soldini, *Pane e tulipani* (*Bread and Tulips*)
Best Emerging Director: Alessandro Piva, *La Capagira* (*My Head Is Spinning*)
Best Producer: Sciarlò, *Il manoscritto del principe* (*The Prince's Manuscript*), dir. Roberto Andò
Best Actress: Licia Maglietta, *Pane e tulipani*
Best Actor: Silvio Orlando, *Preferisco il rumore del mare* (*I Prefer the Sound of the Sea*), dir. Mimmo Calopresti

2001

Director of Best Italian Film: Nanni Moretti, *La stanza del figlio* (*The Son's Room*)
Best Emerging Director: Alex Infascelli, *Almost Blue*
Best Producer: Tilde Corsi and Gianni Romoli, *Le fate ignoranti* (*His Secret Life*), dir. Ferzan Ozpetek; Michel Propper, Amos Gitai, and Laurent Truchot, *Kippur*, dir. Amos Gitai
Best Actress: Margherita Buy, *Le fate ignoranti*
Best Actor: Stefano Accorsi, *Le fate ignoranti*

2002

Director of Best Italian Film: Marco Bellocchio, *L'ora di religione* (*The Religion Hour—My Mother's Smile*)
Best Emerging Director: Paolo Sorrentino, *L'uomo in più* (*One Man Up*)
Best Producer: Fandango, *L'ora di religione*
Best Actress: Valeria Golino, *Respiro* (*Respiro: Grazia's Island*), dir. Emanuele Crialese
Best Actor: Sergio Castellitto, *L'ora di religione*

2003

Director of Best Italian Film: Gabriele Salvatores, *Io non ho paura* (*I'm Not Scared*)

Best Emerging Director: Maria Sole Tognazzi, *Passato prossimo* (*Past Perfect*)

Best Producer: Fandango, *L'imbalsamatore* (*The Embalmer*), dir. Matteo Garrone; *Ricordati di me* (*Remember Me, My Love*), dir. Gabriele Muccino; *Velocità massima* (*Maximum Velocity*), dir. Daniele Vicari

Best Actress: Giovanna Mezzogiorno, *Ilaria Alpi, il più crudele dei giorni* (*The Cruelest Day*), dir. Ferdinando Vicentini Orgnani; *La finestra di fronte* (*Facing Windows*), dir. Ferzan Ozpetek

Best Actor: Neri Marcorè, *Il cuore altrove* (*The Heart Is Elsewhere*), dir. Pupi Avati; Gigi Proietti, *Febbre da cavallo—la Mandrakata* (*Horse Fever: The Mandrake Sting*), dir. Carlo Vanzina

2004

Director of Best Italian Film: Marco Tullio Giordana, *La meglio gioventù* (*The Best of Youth*)

Best Emerging Director: Franco Battiato, *Perduto amor* (*Lost Love*)

Best Producer: Angelo Barbagallo, *La meglio gioventù*

Best Actress: Adriana Asti, *La meglio gioventù*; Sonia Bergamasco, *La meglio gioventù*; Maya Sansa, *La meglio gioventù*; Jasmine Trinca, *La meglio gioventù*

Best Actor: Roberto Herlitzka, *Buongiorno, notte* (*Good Morning, Night*), dir. Marco Bellocchio; Alessio Boni, *La meglio gioventù*; Fabrizio Gifuni, *La meglio gioventù*; Luigi Lo Cascio, *La meglio gioventù*; and Andrea Tidona, *La meglio gioventù*

2005

Director of Best Italian Film: Gianni Amelio, *Le chiavi di casa* (*The House Keys*)

Best Emerging Director: Saverio Costanzo, *Private*

Best Producer: Aurelio De Laurentiis, *Che ne sarà di noi* (*What Will Happen to Us*), dir. Giovanni Veronesi, and *Tutto in quella notte* (*Everything That Night*), dir. Franco Bertini

Best Actress: Laura Morante, *L'amore è eterno finché dura* (*Love Is Eternal, as Long as It Lasts*), dir. Carlo Verdone

Best Actor: Toni Servillo, *Le conseguenze dell'amore* (*The Consequences of Love*), dir. Paolo Sorrentino

2006

Director of Best Italian Film: Michele Placido, *Romanzo criminale* (*Crime Novel*)

Best Emerging Director: Francesco Munzi, *Saimir*

Best Producer: Marco Chimenz, Riccardo Tozzi, and Giovanni Stabilini, *La bestia nel cuore* (*The Beast in the Heart/Don't Tell*), dir. Cristina Comencini, *Quando sei nato non puoi più nasconderti* (*Once You're Born You Can No Longer Hide*), dir. Marco Tullio Giordana, and *Romanzo criminale*

Best Actress: Katia Ricciarelli, *La seconda notte di nozze* (*The Second Wedding Night*), dir. Pupi Avati

Best Actor: Stefano Accorsi, *Provincia meccanica* (*Mechanical Province*), dir. Stefano Mordini; Pierfrancesco Favino, *Romanzo criminale*; Claudio Santamario, *Romanzo criminale*; Kim Rossi Stuart, *Romanzo criminale*

2007

Director of Best Italian Film: Giuseppe Tornatore, *La sconosciuta* (*The Unknown*)

Best Emerging Director: Kim Rossi Stuart, *Anche libero va bene* (*Along the Ridge*)

Best Producer: Nanni Moretti and Angelo Barbagallo, *Il caimano* (*The Caiman*), dir. Nanni Moretti

Best Actress: Margherita Buy, *Saturno contro* (*Saturn in Opposition*), dir. Ferzan Ozpetek, and *Il caimano*

Best Actor: Silvio Orlando, *Il caimano*

Bibliography

CONTENTS

INTRODUCTION

So much has been, and continues to be, published on all aspects of Italian cinema that it would be impossible to offer anything like an exhaustive bibliography here. What follows is a selected bibliography chosen with the aim of indicating a first port of call for the reader who may want to explore further any of the films, directors, topics, or issues encountered in the dictionary. Of necessity the greater part of the material listed here is in Italian, but with an eye to serving the interests of the non-Italian reader, relevant English works have been included wherever possible.

As one might expect, there exist a large number of excellent historical overviews of the Italian cinema in Italian, ranging from the more concise pocket-book treatments of Paolo Russo's *Breve storia del cinema italiano* to the extremely comprehensive and lavishly illustrated *La città del cinema*, produced under the auspices of the Prime Minister's Department to celebrate the centennial of cinema in Italy. Undoubtedly the most authoritative and comprehensive mapping of the Italian cinema in Italian has been carried out by Gian Piero Brunetta in the various multivolume histories he has been publishing since the 1980s but which have now been conveniently synthesized for a more popular audience in his one-volume *Guida alla storia del cinema italiano 1905–2003*. An even more thorough coverage of the Italian cinema since the 1930s is now available in Italian in the monumental multivolume *Storia del cinema italiano* recently produced by a team of film scholars under the auspices of the National Film School. For the English reader, one of the best general and most accessible overviews of the cinema in the postwar period continues to be Peter Bondanella's originally groundbreaking *Italian Cinema from Neorealism to the Present*, now revised and updated in its third edition. Although slightly limited by their date of publication, Mira Liehm's *Film in Italy from 1942 to the Present* and Pierre Leprohon's *The Italian Cinema* also retain their usefulness as entry points to a general history of the cinema in Italy. Despite being marred by a number of factual errors, Pierre Sorlin's *Italian National Cinema* also provides a good sociologically based account of the history of cinema in Italy organized as a discussion of five generations of filmgoing and filmmaking. Angela Dalle Vacche's *The Body in the Mirror* and Marcia Landy's *Italian Film* are two extremely stimulating and theoretically sophisticated attempts to draw together strands of Italian cinema using a thematic rather than chronological approach, with both also succeeding in providing overarching views of Italian cinema. Carlo Celli and Marga Cottino-Jones's more recent *A New Guide to Italian Cinema* takes a largely historical and didactic approach to providing a very solid manual furnished with a number of useful appendixes, including a full list of all the top ten grossing films in Italy since 1945. On the other hand, Mary P. Wood's similarly recent *Italian Cinema* adopts a more multifaceted thematic approach to explore and exemplify what she rightly calls "the richness of an incredibly productive national cinema," ranging widely from a consideration of popular cinema and successes at the box office to discussions of cinematic space and visual style. Embracing a different strategy, the volume edited by Giorgio Bertellini, *The Cinema of Italy*, attempts to present an overview of the Italian cinema via specially commissioned essays on 24 historically significant films, ranging from Mario Camerini's 1932 classic *Gli Uomini che mascalzoni (Men, What Rascals!)* to Gianni Amelio's *Lamerica* (1994). An engaging personal overview of Italian cinema, limited in large part to films and directors of the immediate postwar period but including long excerpts from the films themseves, has also now been provided by Italian American director Martin Scorsese, with his *My Voyage to Italy*. Widely available on DVD, it is particularly suitable for anyone just beginning to explore the richness of Italian films.

Italian readers with a general interest in the cinema are also well served by a number of excellent encyclopedic reference works, the most comprehensive being the multivolume *Dizionario del cinema italiano* published by Gremese and edited by a variety of authors including Roberto Chiti, Roberto Poppi, and Enrico Lancia. Few similar quick and reliable reference works exist in English, but the British Film Institute *Companion to Italian Cinema* is excellent in this regard, limited only by its brevity.

For much of the postwar period, with the exception of the pioneering works of Maria Prolo and Roberto Paolella, Italian silent cinema remained something of an unknown continent. Since the early 1980s, however, there has been an enormous and growing amount of both interest and research in the cinema of the silent period, much of it generated by, and revolving around, the now-legendary Le giornate del cinema muto held at Pordenone. Unfortunately, very little of the voluminous and groundbreaking research that has been done by scholars such as Aldo Bernardini and Vittorio Martinelli has made it into English. More recently, however, thanks to an issue of the journal *Film History* that was partly dedicated to Italian silent cinema, there now exist brief but informative accounts in English of at least four of the major film studios of the early silent period (see the articles by Silvio Alovisio, Raffaele De Berti, Claudia Gianetto, and Kimberly Tomadjoglou). Aldo Bernardini's analysis of the recession in the Italian film industry in 1908–1909, published in the same journal a decade earlier, also provides a fascinating glimpse into the workings of the Italian studios during those very early days of film production.

The question of whether and to what extent the cinema itself became Fascist during the years of the regime has continued to excite much debate. The triumph of neorealism in the period immediately following the war prompted a general and wholesale denigration by Italian film historians of the films produced during the Fascist period, which, largely without being seen, came to be summarily dismissed as either propagandistic and party political or mindlessly evasive (white telephone films). In 1975, however, following a historic retrospective and a major conference on neorealism held at Pesaro the previous year, the Mostra del Nuovo Cinema Internazionale also held a retrospective of Italian cinema before neorealism, of films made between 1929 and 1943. The screenings and the large-scale conference that followed, the proceedings of which were published as *Cinema italiano sotto il fascismo*, edited by Riccardo Redi, initiated a profound rethinking and reexamination of what were discovered to be the quite complex and sometimes contradictory relations between Fascism and the cinema that was produced under it. A review of all this rethinking has recently been carried out by Vito Zagarrio in his *Cinema e fascismo: Film, modelli, immaginari*, which provides not only a historical and theoretical reflection on the question but also informative interviews with a large number of writers, actors, and directors who worked in the Italian film industry during the interwar period, among them Cesare Zavattini, Luigi Comencini, and Giuseppe De Santis. Written two decades earlier but still fundamental to any attempt to understand the Italian cinema under Fascism is Jean A. Gili's *Stato fascista e cinematografia: Repressione e promozione*. In English, Geoffrey Nowell-Smith has supplied a brief but illuminating account in his article "The Italian Cinema under Fascism," while James Hay and Marcia Landy have closely studied many of the films of the period in some detail in their *Popular Film Culture in Fascist Italy* and *Fascism in Film: The Italian Commercial Cinema 1931–1943*. Both Hay and Landy have also contributed further perceptive analyses to the excellent and wide-ranging anthology *Re-viewing Fascism: Italian Cinema 1922–1943*, edited by Jacqueline Reich and Piero Garofalo. An engrossing and informative firsthand account of the cinema under Fascism is provided by the person most responsible for it from 1934 to 1943, Luigi Freddi, in his *Il cinema: Il governo dell'immagine*, although, regretfully, the work remains untranslated. Also untranslated but an invaluable resource for the Italian reader is the collection of personal and professional reminiscences of those who worked in the film industry between 1930 and 1943, collected by Francesco Savio and edited by Tullio Kezich in the three-volume *Cinecittà anni trenta: Parlano 116 protagonisti del secondo cinema italiano*.

The Resistance to Fascism featured frequently as a theme in many films of the immediate postwar period, especially those styled as neorealist, but disappeared almost completely from sight during the 1950s, due largely to the ostracism of successive center-right governments. The reasons for this hostility and the problematic nature of the Resistance as a theme, in the cinema and in the media generally during this period, are discussed by Philip Cooke in his article "The Italian State and the Resistance Legacy in the 1950s and 1960s." The Resistance reappeared on Italian screens during the early 1960s and in successive stages thereafter. In 1970 a major conference on the Resistance in postwar cinema was held under the auspices of the Venice Biennale with the proceedings being published in full as *Atti del convegno di studi sulla Resistenza nel cinema italiano del dopoguerra*, edited by Camillo Bassotto. A more systematic attempt at listing and commenting all the films in which the Resistance features as setting or major theme was made in 1995 with the publication of *La Resistenza nel cinema italiano 1945–1995*, edited by Mauro Manciotti and Aldo Viganò. More accessible and better illustrated is the section on the Resistance in Gianfranco Casadio's *La guerra al cinema*, which divides the films into four separate historical periods with an introduction to each discussing their differing interpretations. In English, where the appearance of the Resistance in Italian films has been studied, it has been done largely within the context of an attempt to analyze how cinema deals with historical themes, as in Pierre Sorlin's "The Italian Resistance in the Second World War" and "*The Night of the Shooting Stars*: Fascism, Resistance and the Liberation of Italy."

Neorealism is, without doubt, the seminal theme in Italian postwar cinema and, as Pierre Leprohon has suggested, has had more written about it than any other film movement in history. Discussions in Italian are legion, but fundamental for understanding the multifaceted nature of the movement and the variety of interpretations are the proceedings of the historic conference held at

Pesaro in 1974 and edited by Lino Miccichè as *Il neorealismo cinematografico italiano*. Bert Cardullo's reasoned bibliography provides a useful tool for navigating the mass of material published in English until the late 1980s. In addition to Bondanella's already mentioned *Italian Cinema from Neorealism to the Present* and Liehm's *Passion and Defiance: Film in Italy from 1942 to the Present*, both of which contain excellent extended discussions of neorealism, two of the best introductions to the movement in English remain Roy Armes's *Patterns of Realism* and Paul Monaco's *Realism, Italian Style*. Among the texts regarded as canonical in any discussion of neorealism are the many short essays in which André Bazin defined the movement and defended its films, now ranged under the rubric of "An Aesthetic of Reality: Cinematic Realism and the Italian School of Liberation" in his *What Is Cinema?* David Overbey's anthology, *Springtime in Italy: A Reader on Neorealism*, provides an excellent selection of primary sources, which includes comments or writings by Rossellini, Zavattini, De Sica, and De Santis, while Christopher Wagstaff's "The Place of Neorealism in Italian Cinema from 1945 to 1954" concisely but effectively contextualizes the movement within postwar Italian cinema generally. One of the most illuminating works in English on the movement and its subsequent influence on Italian cinema is Millicent Marcus's *Italian Film in the Light of Neorealism*. The importance of the movement globally and its significant influence on other national cinemas is now well explored in the anthology *Italian Neorealism and Global Cinema*, edited by Laura E. Ruberto and Kristi M. Wilson. Mention should also be made of Vincent F. Rocchio's *Cinema of Anxiety: A Psychoanalysis of Italian Neorealism*, an interesting and, in many ways, convincing attempt to read neorealism in a psychoanalytic key. Rocchio's tendency to dismiss the value of all other previous and different approaches to the movement, however, is something of a limitation.

In the wake of neorealism, Italian cinema has been probably more consistently socially reflexive and politically engaged than any other national cinema. This may explain why film censorship has continued to be a bigger issue in Italy and for longer, perhaps, than in other comparable countries. While few extended studies exist in English, Mino Argentieri's *La censura nel cinema italiano* remains the classic history of film censorship in Italy from its beginnings to the 1970s. Domenico Liggieri's *Mani di forbice: La censura cinematografica in Italia* retraces some of Argenteri's steps but also updates the discussion to the 1990s. While both these authors tend to evoke a ubiquitous and suffocating censorial presence hovering over all Italian films for almost a century, David Forgacs's countercurrent article "Sex in the Cinema: Regulation and Trangression in Italian Films, 1930–1943" suggests that there was probably quite a bit more sex and transgression in Italian films during the Fascist period than critics have previously either noticed or been willing to admit.

If Italian cinema has been to a large extent a cinema of auteurs, it has also been a very literary cinema and a cinema of literary adaptations. Italian readers have available a remarkably exhaustive catalogue raisonné of film adaptations of Italian literary works in Cristina Bragaglia's *Il piacere del racconto: Narrativa italiana e cinema (1895–1990)*. A good introduction to the problematics of adaptation and a study of literary adaptation in the cinema of Pier Paolo Pasolini and Luchino Visconti is Antonio Costa's *Immagine di un'immagine: Cinema e letteratura*. An illustration of the successive adaptations of one particular work, the classic Italian 19th-century novel by Alessandro Manzoni, is provided by Vittorio Martinelli and Matilde Tortora in their *I promessi sposi nel cinema*. In English, however, one of the best works on Italian film adaptations remains Millicent Marcus's *Filmmaking by the Book: Italian Cinema and Literary Adaptation*, which offers a complex and illuminating analysis of 10 significant films by five major Italian directors. More recently, Carlo Testa has also supplied a wide-ranging discussion of Italian filmmakers' adaptations of non-Italian, and more specifically European, literary texts in his *Italian Cinema and Modern European Literatures, 1945–2000* and *Masters of Two Arts: Recreation of European Literatures in Italian Cinema*.

Even when adapting literary texts, postwar Italian cinema has inevitably tended toward the political. An overarching survey of the persistence of a political cinema in the postwar period is provided by Maurizio Fantoni Minella in his *Non riconciliati: Politica e società nel cinema italiano dal neorealismo a oggi*, while in their *Destra e sinistra nel cinema italiano: Film e immaginario politico dagli anni '60 al nuovo millennio*, Christian Uva and Michele Picchi uncover a strong political dimension even in many of the popular genre and B-grade films from the 1960s to the 1990s. In English, one of the best overall works in the field remains John J. Michalczyk's *The Italian Political Filmmakers*, which closely analyzes and contextualizes the major works of Francesco Rosi, Pier Paolo Pasolini, Bernardo Bertolucci, Marco Bellocchio, Giulio Pontecorvo, Elio Petri, and Lina Wertmüller.

The perceived threat to the cinema posed by television from the mid-1970s onward is palpable in Enza Troianelli's article "Il cinema, fiore all'occhiello del palinsesto televisivo" and Ansano Giannarelli's "Cinema e TV: Un nodo da sciogliere," both from the militant journal *Cinemasessanta*. However, in the long run, as Luisa Cigognetti and Pierre Sorlin demonstrate in their "Italy. Cinema and Television: Collaborators and Threat," the relation eventually developed in a positive direction, from rivalry to collaboration and to the mutual advantage of both.

Surprisingly, perhaps, while the Mafia as a phenomenon has been studied extensively both in Italy and abroad, the massive appearance of the Mafia in Italian cinema, in both auteur and genre films, has received much less attention in the literature. A systematic attempt to look at films dealing with the Sicilian Mafia has been made by Vittorio Albano in his *La mafia nel cinema siciliano: Da "In nome della legge" a "Placido Rizzotto."* In English, analysis has generally been limited to specific films by particular directors. Claudio Mazzolla has offered a close reading of the neorealist style of Francesco Rosi's *Lucky Luciano* while Millicent Marcus has provided a discussion of the parodic portrayal of the Mafia in Roberta Torre's hilarious film *Tano da morire* (1997) in her "Postmodern Pastiche, the *Sceneggiata*, and the View of the Mafia from Below in Roberta Torre's *To Die for Tano.*"

Although given the right to vote in 1945 and exercising a greater independence and autonomy than ever before, women continued to occupy an ambivalent and often subaltern position in Italy immediately after the war, at least until the coming of Italian feminism in the early 1970s, and this was strongly reflected in the cinema. Leandra Negro's "Le donne del secondo dopoguerra nel cinema italiano (1949–1955)" and Anna Maria Caso's "L'immagine della donna nel cinema del boom economico (1955–1963)" trace the slow evolution of a more modern role for women in the films of this period. Giovanna Grignaffini's "Il femminile nel cinema italiano. Racconti di nascita," however, convincingly argues that the entire renewal of Italian cinema, and with it Italian society, in the immediate postwar period occurs precisely under the sign of the feminine, a notion similarly explored by Millicent Marcus in "The Italian Body Politic Is a Woman: Feminized National Identity in Postwar Italian Cinema." Nevertheless, and in spite of the definitive changes wrought by feminism in Italy in the 1970s, Giovanni Grazzini's *Eva dopo Eva* concludes from its review of almost 150 films made from 1962 to 1980 that in many ways the stereotypes remained. Maria Ossi's *Donne e cinema nell'Europa duemila: Fra immaginario e quotidianità* discusses the more varied images of women presented in Italian films in the 1990s and provides a European context for comparison. Tiziano Sossi's *Dizionario delle registe: L'altra metà del cinema* attempts to give female Italian directors their due, alongside female directors worldwide. By far one of the most engaging works on the presence of women in the Italian film industry is Giuliana Bruno's *Streetwalking on a Ruined Map*, which provides not only a much-needed rehabilitation of Elvira Notari, one of the great but largely neglected Italian female directors of the silent period, but also a profound meditation on the nature and function of the cinema in the silent era. The actresses of the silent period have now also been given their due in Vittorio Martinelli's *Le dive del silenzio* and, at a more popular level, the lives and careers of over 80 major female stars of the Italian cinema have been documented in Stefano Masi and Enrico Landa's very readable and well-illustrated *Italian Movie Goddesses: Over 80 of the Greatest Women in Italian Cinema.* An admirably wide ranging and perceptive study of the appearance of both genders in the Italian cinema has now been provided by Maggie Günsberg in her *Italian Cinema: Gender and Genre.*

While long devalued by serious critics as an inferior form of cinema, the Italian genres have in fact contributed substantially to both the economic viability of the Italian film industry over the years and to the popularity of Italian cinema throughout the world. While a great deal has now also been written in Italy about the major genres, some of the best works on genres such as Italian horror, the *giallo*, and the spaghetti Western have appeared in English. Adrian Luther Smith's *Blood and Black Lace* is, indeed, as it claims, the definitive guide to Italian sex and horror films, and Christopher Frayling's *Spaghetti Westerns: Cowboys and Europeans from Karl May to Sergio Leone* is also one of the best contextualized introductions to the study of the Italian Western. Gary Needham's "Playing with Genre: Defining the Italian *Giallo*" is particularly helpful for English readers still puzzled about the exact parameters of this popular but elusive genre.

If not exclusively, Italian cinema is overwhelmingly a cinema of auteurs, of directors who approach their filmmaking as, first and foremost, a form of artistic expression. Forced by necessity and reasons of space, we have limited our bibliographies to writings on 14 major directors. Our selection of materials has aimed at utility and accessibility rather than mere inclusiveness and, always with an eye to the non-Italian reader, we have attempted, wherever possible, to indicate relevant works in English. It is regrettable that almost nothing has appeared in English on a major figure such as Dino Risi, although the volume dedicated to him by the Centro Sperimentale di Cinematografia and edited by Angela Prudenzi and Cristina Scogliamiglio, *Dino Risi: Maestro dell'equilibrio e della leggerezza*, amply indicates his status as one of the great Italian directors.

But filmmaking is an industry as well as an art and while this area has tended to receive less attention from film scholars, Enrico Magrelli's edited anthology, *Sull'industria cinematografica italiana*, provides the Italian reader with a remarkably wide range of analyses of the more commercial aspects of making films in Italy. In English, Cristina Degli-Esposti Reinhert offers a brief overview of the history of the Italian film industry in her article in Gorham Kindem's anthology *The International Movie Industry*, but an even richer source of historical and personal reminiscences regarding Italian film production is the lavishly illustrated English and Italian parallel text *Capitani Coraggiosi: Produttori Italiani 1945–1975/Captains Courageous: Italian Producers 1945–1975*, edited by Stefano Della Casa.

Continuing passion and enthusiasm for Italian cinema have inevitably led to a huge number of websites supplying a great deal of information on all aspects of the cinema. The major state film institutions, the Centro Sperimentale di

Cinematografia, Cinecittà, and LUCE all have very informative and user-friendly sites, with LUCE actually offering a searchable archive of materials that can be viewed online (in Italian only and registration required). One of the richest sources of factual information about Italian cinema for Italian users is *Cinematografo.it*, a searchable database maintained by the governmental Fondazione Ente dello Spettacolo. For the English reader interested in consulting more printed material on Italian cinema, one of the best sites is the bibliography of books and articles in the University of California, Berkeley, library, also available online.

GENERAL OVERVIEWS

Argentieri, Mino. *Il cinema italiano dal dopoguerra a oggi.* Rome: Editori Riuniti, 1998.

Bertellini, Giorgio. *The Cinema of Italy.* London: Wallflower Press, 2004.

Bolzoni, Francesco, Mario Foglietti, and Soveria Mannelli (eds.). *Le stagioni del cinema: Trenta registi si raccontano.* Catanzaro: Rubbettino, 2000.

Bondanella, Peter. "Recent Work on Italian Cinema." *Journal of Modern Italian Studies* 1, no. 1 (1995): 101–123.

——. "Italian Cinema from the 1950s to the Present." In *Italy: Fiction, Theatre, Poetry, Film Since 1950,* ed. Robert S. Dombroski. New York: Griffin House, 2000.

——. *Italian Cinema from Neorealism to the Present.* 3rd ed. New York: Continuum, 2001.

Brunetta, Gian Piero. *Cent'anni di cinema italiano.* 2 vols. Rome: Laterza, 1995.

——. *Guida alla storia del cinema italiano: 1905–2003.* Turin: Einaudi, 2003.

Buss, Robin. *Italian Films.* New York: Holmes & Meier, 1989.

Celli, Carlo, and Marga Cottino-Jones. *A New Guide to Italian Cinema.* New York: Palgrave Macmillan, 2006.

Dalle Vacche, Angela. *The Body in the Mirror: Shapes of History in Italian Cinema.* Princeton, NJ: Princeton University Press, 1992.

Della Casa, Stefano. *Storia e storie del cinema popolare italiano.* Turin: La Stampa, 2001.

Di Giammatteo, Fernaldo. *Lo sguardo inquieto: Storia del cinema italiano: 1940–1990.* Florence: La Nuova Italia, 1994.

Dipartimento per l'informazione e l'editoria. *L'arte di tutte le arti: Il centenario del cinema in Italia.* Rome: Dipartimento per l'Informazione e l'Editoria, 1995.

Ente Cinema, Cinecittà, and Istituto LUCE. *La città del cinema: I primi cento anni del cinema italiano*. Milan: Skira, 1995.

Giacovelli, Enrico. *Un secolo di cinema italiano 1900–1999*. 2 vols. Turin: Lindau, 2002.

Gundle, Stephen. "From Neorealism to *Luci Rosse*: Cinema, Politics, Society, 1945–85." In *Culture and Conflict in Postwar Italy: Essays on Mass and Popular Culture*, ed. Zygmunt G. Baranski and Robert Lumley. New York: St. Martin's Press, 1990.

Landy, Marcia. *Italian Film*. Cambridge: Cambridge University Press, 2000.

Leprohon, Pierre. *The Italian Cinema*. Trans. Roger Greaves and Oliver Stallybrass. London: Secker and Warburg, 1972.

Liehm, Mira. *Passion and Defiance: Film in Italy from 1942 to the Present*. Berkeley: University of California Press, 1984.

Livolsi, Marino (ed.). *Schermi e ombre: Gli italiani e il cinema nel dopoguerra*. Florence: La Nuova Italia, 1988.

Lizzani, Carlo. *Il cinema italiano dalle origini agli anni ottanta*. Rome: Editori Riuniti, 1992.

Mariotti, Franco (ed.). *Cinecittà tra cronaca e storia, 1937–1989*. Rome: Presidenza del Consiglio dei Ministri, Dipartimento per l'Informazione e l'Editoria, 1992.

Pintus, Pietro. *Storia e film: Trent'anni di cinema italiano (1945–1975)*. Rome: Bulzoni, 1980.

Reteuna, Dario. *Cinema di carta: Storia fotografica del cinema italiano*. Alessandria: Falsopiano, 2000.

Rohdie, Sam. "A Brief History of the Italian Cinema." *Metro* 121/122 (2000): 101–112.

Russo, Paolo. *Breve storia del cinema italiano*. Turin: Lindau, 2002.

Scorsese, Martin. *My Voyage to Italy*. DVD. California: Miramax, 2003.

Scuola Nazionale di Cinema (ed.). *Storia del cinema italiano*. Vols. 7–13. Venice: Marsilio; Rome: Edizioni Bianco & Nero, 2001–2004.

Sorlin, Pierre. *Italian National Cinema 1896–1996*. New York: Routledge, 1996.

Verdone, Mario. *Storia del cinema italiano*. Rome: Tascabili Economici Newton, 1995.

Wagstaff, Christopher. "Cinema." In *Italian Cultural Studies: An Introduction*, ed. David Forgacs and Robert Lumley. Oxford: Oxford University Press, 1996.

Witcombe, R. T. *The New Italian Cinema: Studies in Dance and Despair*. London: Secker and Warburg, 1982.

Wood, Mary P. *Italian Cinema*. Oxford: Berg, 2005.

DICTIONARIES, COMPANIONS, AND BIBLIOGRAPHIES

Canova, Gianni (ed.). *Enciclopedia del cinema Garzanti*. Milan: Garzanti, 2002.
Di Giammatteo, Fernaldo, with Cristina Bragaglia. *Dizionario del cinema italiano: Dagli inizi del secolo a oggi, i film che hanno segnato la storia del nostro cinema*. Rome: Editori Riuniti, 1995.
Fulgheri, Ennio. *Manuale del cinema italiano*. Milan: Swan, 1998.
Gremese (various editors). *Dizionario del cinema italiano*. 6 vols. Rome: Gremese, 1991–2000.
Mereghetti, Paolo, with Alberto Pezzotta. *Il Mereghetti: Dizionario dei film 2006*. 2 vols. Milan: Baldini, Castoldi, Dalai, 2005.
Nowell-Smith, Geoffrey, with James Hay and Gianni Volpi. *The Companion to Italian Cinema*. London: Cassell, 1996.
Stewart, John. *Italian Film: A Who's Who*. Jefferson, NC: McFarland, 1994.

SILENT CINEMA

Alovisio, Silvio. "The 'Pastrone System': Itala Films from the Origins to World War I." *Film History* 12, no. 3 (2000): 250–261.
Bernardini, Aldo. *Il cinema muto italiano*. 3 vols. Rome: Laterza, 1980–1982.
———. "An Industry in Recession: The Italian Film Industry 1908–1909." *Film History* 3 (1989): 341–368.
———. *Cinema italiano delle origini: Gli ambulanti*. Gemona: La Cineteca del Friuli, 2001.
———. *Il cinema muto italiano. I film dal vero, 1895–1914*. Gemona: La Cineteca del Friuli, 2002.
Bernardini, Aldo, and Vittorio Martinelli. *Il cinema muto italiano. I film degli anni d'oro, 1911*. Turin: Nuova ERI, 1995.
———. *Il cinema muto italiano. I film dei primi anni, 1910*. Turin: Nuova ERI, 1996.
Bertetto, Paolo, and Gianni Rondolino (eds.). *Cabiria e il suo tempo*. Milan: Il Castoro, 1998.
Brunetta, Gian Piero. "Le origini del cinema in Italia." *Italian Quarterly* (Winter 1980): 65–75.
———. *Il cinema muto 1895–1929*. Rome: Editori Riuniti, 1993.
Bruscolini, Elisabetta, Angela Prudenzi, and Sergio Toffetti. *La fiamma del peccato: L'eros nel cinema muto*. Turin: Lindau, 1997.
Centro Culturale dell'Immagine Il Fotogramma (ed.). *Dive e divi del cinema muto italiano: Accademia delle arti e nuove tecnologie*. Rome: Sintesi Grafica, 1995.

Chiti, Roberto. *Dizionario dei registi del cinema muto italiano*. Rome: MICS, 1997.

De Berti, Raffaele. "Milano Films: The Exemplary History of a Film Company of the 1910s." *Film History* 12, no. 3 (2000): 276–287.

Ente Autonomo di Gestione per il Cinema (ed.). *Mito e realtà del cinema muto italiano*. Rome: SIAT, 1987.

Gianetto, Claudia. "The Giant Ambrosio, or Italy's Most Prolific Silent Film Company." *Film History* 12, no. 3 (2000): 240–249.

Martinelli, Vittorio. *Il cinema muto italiano: I film degli anni d'oro, 1914.* Turin: Nuova ERI, 1993.

——. *Le dive del silenzio.* Genoa: Le Mani, 2001.

Paolella, Roberto. *Storia del cinema muto.* Naples: Giannini, 1956.

Prolo, Maria Adriana. *Storia del cinema muto italiano.* Milan: Poligono Società Editrice di Milano, 1951.

Redi, Riccardo. *Cinema muto italiano (1896–1930).* Turin: Fondazione Scuola Nazionale di Cinema, 1999.

Renzi, Renzo (ed.). *Sperduto nel buio: Il cinema muto italiano e il suo tempo, 1905–1930.* Bologna: Cappelli, 1991.

Rondolino, Gianni. *Il cinema muto.* Turin: UTET, 1996.

Tomadjoglou, Kimberly. "Rome's Premiere Film Studio: Società Italiana Cines." *Film History* 12, no. 3 (2000): 262–275.

Tortora, Matilde. *Lo schermo in tasca.* Catanzaro: Abramo, 2000.

SOUND CINEMA

Fascism

Aprà, Adriano, and Patrizia Pistagnesi (eds.). *I favolosi anni trenta: Cinema italiano, 1929–1944.* Milan: Electa, 1979.

Argentieri, Mino. *L'occhio del regime.* Rome: Bulzoni, 2003.

——. (ed.). *Risate di regime: La commedia italiana 1930–1944.* Venice: Marsilio, 1991.

——. (ed.). *Schermi di guerra: Cinema italiano 1939–1945.* Rome: Bulzoni, 1995.

Aristarco, Guido. *Il cinema fascista: Il prima e il dopo.* Bari: Dedalo, 1996.

Ben-Ghiat, Ruth. "Visioni della modernità." In *La cultura fascista.* Bologna: Il Mulino, 2000.

Bernagozzi, Giampaolo. "Il cinema nel ventennio fascista." In *Storia del cinema: Dall'affermazione del sonoro al neorealismo*, ed. Adelio Ferrero. Venice: Marsilio, 1978.

——. *Il mito dell'immagine*. Bologna: CLUEB, 1983.

Bolzoni, Francesco. *Il progetto imperiale: Cinema e cultura nell'Italia del 1936*. Venice: Edizioni de la Biennale di Venezia, 1976.

Bosworth, R. J. B. "The Traces of Fascism in Music, Film, Literature and Memory: A Fascist Cultural Legacy?" In *The Italian Dictatorship: Problems and Perspectives in the Interpretation of Mussolini and Fascism*. London: Arnold, 1998.

——. "Film Memories of Fascism." In *Italian Fascism: History, Memory and Representation*, ed. R. J. B. Bosworth and Patrizia Dogliani. Basingstoke: Macmillan, St. Martin's Press, 1999.

Brunetta, Gian Piero. *Intellettuali, cinema e propaganda tra le due guerre*. Bologna: R. Patron, 1972.

——. *Cinema italiano tra le due guerre: Fascismo e politica cinematografica*. Milan: Mursia, 1975.

——. *Storia del cinema italiano: Il cinema del regime, 1929–1945*. Rome: Editori Riuniti, 2001.

Brusaporco, Ugo. *I monelli di Verona: Cinema e fascismo in città*. Verona: Bonato, 1997.

Cannistraro, Philip V. "Il cinema." In *La fabbrica del consenso: Fascismo e mass media*. Rome: Laterza, 1975.

Carabba, Claudio. *Il cinema del ventennio nero*. Florence: Vallecchi, 1974.

Casadio, Gianfranco. *Il grigio e il nero: Spettacolo e propaganda nel cinema italiano degli anni trenta (1931–1943)*. Ravenna: Longo, 1989.

Casadio, Gianfranco, Ernesto G. Laura, and Filippo Cristiano. *Telefoni bianchi: Realtà e finzione nella società e nel cinema italiano degli anni quaranta*. Ravenna: Longo, 1991.

Freddi, Luigi. *Il cinema: Il governo dell'immagine*. Rome: Gremese, 1994.

Gili, Jean A. *Stato fascista e cinematografia: Repressione e promozione*. Rome: Bulzoni, 1981.

——. *L'Italie de Mussolini et son cinéma*. Paris: H. Veyrier, 1985.

Gori, Gianfranco Miro. *Patria diva: La storia d'Italia nei film del ventennio*. Florence: La Casa Usher, 1988.

Hay, James. *Popular Film Culture in Fascist Italy: The Passing of the Rex*. Bloomington: Indiana University Press, 1987.

Lacalamita, Michele. *Fascismo e antifascismo nel cinema del ventennio*. Florence: Tip. Commerciale Fiorentina, 1959.

Landy, Marcia. *Fascism in Film: The Italian Commercial Cinema, 1931–1943*. Princeton, NJ: Princeton University Press, 1986.

——. *The Folklore of Consensus: Theatricality in the Italian Cinema, 1930–1943*. Albany: State University of New York Press, 1998.

Mancini, Elaine. *Struggles of the Italian Film Industry during Fascism, 1930–1935*. Ann Arbor, MI: UMI Research Press, 1985.

Marino, Natalia, and Emanuele Valerio Marino. *L'ovra a Cinecittà: Polizia politica e spie in camicia nera.* Turin: Bollati Boringhieri, 2005.

Messina, Nunzia. *Le donne del fascismo: Massaie rurali e dive del cinema nel ventennio.* Rome: Ellemme, 1987.

Nowell-Smith, Geoffrey. "The Italian Cinema under Fascism." In *Rethinking Italian Fascism: Capitalism, Populism and Culture,* ed. David Forgacs. London: Lawrence and Wishart, 1986.

Redi, Riccardo (ed.). *Cinema italiano sotto il fascismo.* Venice: Marsilio, 1979.

Reich, Jacqueline, and Piero Garofalo (eds.). *Re-viewing Fascism: Italian Cinema, 1922–1943.* Bloomington: Indiana University Press, 2001.

Renzi, Renzo. *Il cinema dei dittatori: Mussolini, Stalin, Hitler.* Bologna: Grafis, 1992.

Ruffin, Valentina, and Patrizia D'Agostino. *Dialoghi di regime: La lingua del cinema degli anni trenta.* Rome: Bulzoni, 1997.

Savio, Francesco. *Cinecitta anni trenta: Parlano 116 protagonisti del secondo cinema italiano (1930–1943).* Ed. Tullio Kezich. Rome: Bulzoni, 1979.

Tinazzi, Giorgio (ed.). *Il cinema italiano dal fascismo all'antifascismo.* Padua: Marsilio, 1966.

Zagarrio, Vito. "Ideology Elsewhere: The Contradictory Models of Italian Cinema." In *Resisting Images: Essays on Cinema and History,* ed. Robert Sklar and Charles Musser. Philadelphia: Temple University Press, 1990.

———. *Cinema e fascismo: Film, modelli, immaginari.* Venice: Marsilio, 2004.

War and the Resistance

Argentieri, Mino. *Il cinema in guerra: Arte, comunicazione e propaganda in Italia, 1940–1944.* Rome: Editori Riuniti, 1998.

Bassotto, Camillo (ed.). *Atti del convegno di studi sulla Resistenza nel cinema italiano del dopoguerra.* Venice: Stamperia di Venezia, 1970.

Brunetta, Gian Piero, et al. *Cinema, storia, resistenza: 1944–1985.* Milan: F. Angeli, 1987.

Casadio, Gianfranco. "La Resistenza." In *La guerra al cinema: I film di guerra nel cinema italiano.* Vol. 2. Ravenna: Longo, 1997.

Cinema italiano e Resistenza. Quaderni di agora 7 (April 1995). Zurich: Federazione Colonie Libere Italiane in Svizzera, 1995.

Cooke, Philip. "The Italian State and the Resistance Legacy in the 1950s and 1960s." In *Culture, Censorship and the State in Twentieth-Century Italy,* ed. Guido Bonsaver and Robert S. C. Gordon. London: Legenda, 2005.

Gili, Jean A. (ed.). *Fascisme et résistance dans le cinéma italien (1922–1968).* Paris: Lettres Modernes Minard, 1970.

Gobetti, Paolo. "La résistance dans les films italiens (1945–1955)." In *Fascisme et résistance dans le cinéma italien (1922–1968),* ed. Jean A. Gili. Paris: Lettres Modernes Minard, 1970.

Il sole sorge ancora: 50 anni di Resistenza nel cinema italiano. 2 vols. Turin: ANCR (Archivio Nazionale Cinematografico della Resistenza), 1994.

Manciotti, Mauro, and Aldo Viganò (eds.). *La Resistenza nel cinema italiano: 1945–1995.* Genoa: Istituto Storico della Resistenza in Liguria, 1995.

Meldini, Piero. "Interpretazioni della Resistenza nei film sulla Resistenza." In *Passato ridotto: Gli anni del dibattito su cinema e storia,* ed. Gianfranco Gori. Florence: La Casa Usher, 1982.

Sorlin, Pierre. "The Italian Resistance in the Second World War." In *The Film in History: Restaging the Past.* Totowa, NJ: Barnes and Noble, 1980.

———. "*The Night of the Shooting Stars:* Fascism, Resistance and the Liberation of Italy." In *Revisioning History: Film and the Construction of a New Past,* ed. Robert A. Rosenstone. Princeton, NJ: Princeton University Press, 1995.

Ufficio per la Storia della Resistenza e della Società Contemporanea del Vittoriese (ed.). *Dal fascismo alla Resistenza: Un percorso dialettico attraverso il cinema.* Treviso: H. Kellerman, 1996.

Neorealism

Aitken, Ian. "Post-war Italian and Spanish Realist Cinema." In *European Film Theory and Cinema: A Critical Introduction.* Edinburgh: Edinburgh University Press, 2001.

Archivio Nazionale Cinematografico della Resistenza. *Neorealismo D.O.C.: I film del 1948.* Turin: Archivio Nazionale Cinematografico della Resistenza, 1995.

Aristarco, Guido. *Neorealismo e nuova critica cinematografica: Cinematografia e vita nazionale negli anni quaranta e cinquanta tra rotture e tradizioni.* Florence: Nuova Guaraldi, 1980.

Armes, Roy. *Patterns of Realism.* New York: Garland, 1986.

Bazin, André. "An Aesthetic of Reality: Cinematic realism and the Italian School of the Liberation." In *What Is Cinema?* vol 2, trans. Hugh Gray. Berkeley: University of California Press, 1971.

Cannella, Mario. "Ideology and Aesthetic Hypotheses in the Criticism of Neo-Realism." *Screen* 14, no. 4 (1973–74): 5–60.

Canziani, Alfonso. *Gli anni del neorealismo.* Florence: La Nuova Italia, 1977.

Canziani, Alfonso, and Cristina Bragaglia. *La stagione neorealista.* Bologna: Cooperativa Libraria Universitaria Editrice, 1976.

Cardullo, Bert. *What Is Neorealism? A Critical English-Language Bibliography of Italian Cinematic Neorealism.* Lanham, MD: University Press of America, 1991.

Casadio, Gianfranco. *Adultere, fedifraghe, innocenti: La donna del "neorealismo popolare" nel cinema italiano degli anni cinquanta.* Ravenna: Longo, 1990.

Cassac, Michel. *Littérature et cinéma néoréalistes: Réalisme, réel et represen-tation*. Paris: L'Harmattan, 2004.

De Nicola, Francesco. *Neorealismo*. Milan: Editrice Bibliografica, 1996.

Di Nolfo, Ennio. "Intimations of Neorealism in the Fascist *Ventennio*." In *Re-viewing Fascism: Italian Cinema, 1922–1943*, ed. Jacqueline Reich and Piero Garofalo. Bloomington: Indiana University Press, 2002.

Fanara, Giulia. *Pensare il neorealismo: Percorsi attraverso il neorealismo cin-ematografico italiano*. Rome: Lithos, 2000.

Farassino, Umberto (ed.). *Neorealismo: Cinema italiano 1945–1949*. Turin: EDT, 1989.

Furno, Mariello, and Renzo Renzi (eds.). *Il neorealismo nel fascismo: Giuseppe De Santis e la critica cinematografica 1941–1943*. Bologna: Ti-pografia Compositori, 1984.

Gallagher, Tag. "NR = MC^2: Rossellini, Neorealism, and Croce." *Film History* 2 (1988): 87–97.

Hillier, Jim. *Cahiers du cinéma, the 1950s: Neo-realism, Hollywood, New Wave*. Cambridge, MA: Harvard University Press, 1985.

Keohane, Robert O. (ed.). *Neorealism and Its Critics*. New York: Columbia University Press, 1986.

Kinder, Marsha, and Beverle Houston. "Neo-realism." In *Patterns of Italian Cin-ema*, ed. Giose Rimanelli. Albany: State University of New York Press, 1980.

Lawton, Ben. "Italian Neorealism: A Mirror Construction of Reality." *Film Criticism* 3, no. 2 (1979): 8–23.

Marcus, Millicent. *Italian Film in the Light of Neorealism*. Princeton, NJ: Princeton University Press, 1986.

Miccichè, Lino. *Il neorealismo cinematografico italiano*. Venice: Marsilio, 1999.

Milanini, Claudio (ed.). *Neorealismo: Poetiche e polemiche*. Milan: Il Saggia-tore, 1980.

Monaco, Paul. "Realism, Italian Style." In *Ribbons in Time: Movies and Soci-ety Since 1945*. Bloomington: Indiana University Press, 1987.

Moneti, Guglielmo. *Neorealismo fra tradizione e rivoluzione: Visconti, De Sica e Zavattini: Verso nuove esperienze cinematografiche della realtà*. Siena: Nuova Immagine, 1999.

Monticelli, Simona. "Italian Post-war Cinema and Neo-realism." In *The Oxford Guide to Film Studies*, ed. John Hill and Pamela Church Gibson. Oxford: Oxford University Press, 1998.

Overbey, David (ed.). *Springtime in Italy: A Reader on Neo-realism*. London: Talisman Books, 1978.

Pinto, Francesco. "Progetto neorealista e politica culturale cattolica." In *Storia del cinema: Dall'affermazione del sonoro al neorealismo*, ed. Adelio Fer-rero. Venice: Marsilio, 1978.

Reeves, Nicholas. "Italian Neo-Realist Films: Fascism, War and Liberation." In *The Power of Film Propaganda: Myth or Reality?* London: Cassell, 1999.

Rhode, Eric. "Why Neo-realism Failed." *Sight and Sound* 30, no. 1 (1960–1961): 27–32.

Rocchio, Vincent F. *Cinema of Anxiety: A Psychoanalysis of Italian Neorealism.* Austin: University of Texas Press, 1999.

Ruberto, Laura E., and Kristi M. Wilson (eds.). *Italian Neorealism and Global Cinema.* Detroit: Wayne State University Press, 2007.

Shiel, Mark. *Italian Neorealism: Rebuilding the Cinematic City.* London: Wallflower Press, 2006.

Sitney, P. Adams. *Vital Crises in Italian Cinema: Iconography, Stylistics, Politics.* Austin: University of Texas Press, 1995.

Sorlin, Pierre. "Tradition and Social Change in the French and Italian Cinemas of the Reconstruction." In *The Culture of Reconstruction: European Literature, Thought and Film, 1945–50*, ed. Nicholas Hewitt. Basingstoke: Macmillan, 1989.

Tinazzi, Giorgio, and Maria Zancan. *Cinema e letteratura del neorealismo.* Venice: Marsilio, 1990.

Verdone, Mario. "A Discussion of Neo-realism: Interview with Rossellini." *Screen* 14, no. 4 (1973–1974): 69–77.

———. *Il cinema neorealista: Da Rossellini a Pasolini.* Trapani: Celebes, 1977.

Wagstaff, Christopher. "The Place of Neorealism in Italian Cinema from 1945 to 1954." In *The Culture of Reconstruction: European Literature, Thought and Film, 1945–50*, ed. Nicholas Hewitt. Basingstoke: Macmillan, 1989.

Zavattini, Cesare. "Some Ideas on the Cinema: Neorealism." In *Patterns of Italian Cinema*, ed. Giose Rimanelli. Albany: State University of New York Press, 1980.

———. *Cinema: Diario cinematografico, neorealismo ecc.* Ed. Valentina Fortichiari and Mino Argentieri. Milan: Bompiani, 2002.

1950s

Aristarco, Guido. *Sciolti dal giuramento: Il dibattito critico-ideologico sul cinema negli anni cinquanta.* Bari: Dedalo Libri, 1981.

Brunetta, Gian Piero (ed.). *Identità italiana e identità europea nel cinema italiano dal 1945 al miracolo economico.* Turin: Edizioni della Fondazione Giovanni Agnelli, 1996.

Capussotti, Enrica. *Gioventù perduta: Gli anni cinquanta dei giovani e del cinema in Italia.* Florence: Giunti, 2004.

Carlini, Fabio, and Maurizio Gusso. *I sogni nel cassetto: Il cinema mette in scena la societa italiana della ricostruzione, 1945–1957.* Milan: Franco Angeli, 2002.

Casetti, Francesco. "Cinema in the Cinema in Italian films of the Fifties: *Bellissima* and *La signora senza camelie*." *Screen* 33, no. 4 (1992): 375–393.

Dalla Casa, Stefano (ed.). *Il cinema ricomincia: I film italiani del 1945 e del 1946*. Turin: Archivio Nazionale Cinematografico della Resistenza, 1992.

Ferrero, Adelio. *Storia del cinema: Autori e tendenze negli anni cinquanta e sessanta*. Venice: Marsilio, 1978.

Mughini, Giampiero. *Ma che belle le ragazze di via Margutta: I registi, i pittori e gli scrittori che fecero della Roma degli anni cinquanta la capitale del mondo*. Milan: Mondadori, 2004.

Pellizzari, Lorenzo. *Cineromanzo: Il cinema italiano, 1945–1953*. Milan: Longanesi, 1978.

Phillips, John. *Italian Films: Il dopoguerra*. Spilimbergo (Pordenone): CRAF, 1995.

Rondi, Gian Luigi. *Italian Cinema Today, 1952–1965*. New York: Hill and Wang, 1966.

Spinazzola, Vittorio. *Cinema e pubblico: Lo spettacolo filmico in Italia 1945–1965*. Rome: Bulzoni, 1984.

Tinazzi, Giorgio (ed.). *Il cinema italiano degli anni '50*. Venice: Marsilio, 1979.

1960s

Attolini, Giovanni. *Il cinema italiano degli anni sessanta: Tra commedia e impegno*. Bari: Edizioni B.A. Graphis, 1998.

Camerino, Vincenzo. *Cinema e il 68: Le sfide dell'immaginario*. Manduria (Taranto): Barbieri, 1998.

Canziani, Alfonso. *I migliori anni del nostro cinema*. Rome: Bulzoni, 1992.

Di Marino, Bruno. *Sguardo inconscio azione: Cinema sperimentale e underground a Roma: 1965–1975*. Rome: Lithos, 1999.

Ferrero, A., G. Grignaffini, and L. Quaresima. *Il cinema italiano degli anni '60*. Florence: Guaraldi, 1977.

Miccichè, Lino. *Cinema italiano: Gli anni '60 e oltre*. Venice: Marsilio, 1995.

Moscati, Italo. *1969, un anno bomba: Quando il cinema scese in piazza*. Venice: Marsilio, 1998.

Pirro, Ugo. *Soltanto un nome nei titoli di testa: I felici anni sessanta del cinema italiano*. Turin: Einaudi, 1998.

Restivo, Angelo. *The Cinema of Economic Miracles: Visuality and Modernization in the Italian Art Film*. Durham, NC: Duke University Press, 2002.

1970s

Faldini, Franca, and Goffredo Fofi. *Il cinema italiano d'oggi 1970–1984: Raccontato dai suoi protagonisti*. Milan: Mondadori, 1984.

Miccicchè, Lino. *Cinema italiano degli anni '70: Cronache 1969–78*. Expanded ed. Venice: Marsilio, 1989.

———. (ed.). *Il cinema del riflusso: Film e cineasti italiani degli anni '70*. Venice: Marsilio, 1997.

Monicelli, Mino. *Cinema italiano: Ma cos'è questa crisi?* Rome: Laterza, 1979.

1980s

Camerino, Vincenzo (ed.). *Il cinema italiano degli anni ottanta . . . ed emozioni registiche*. Lecce: P. Manni, 1992.

Fofi, Goffredo. "Registi." In his *Prima il pane: Cinema, teatro, letteratura, fumetto e altro nella cultura italiana tra anni ottanta e novanta*. Rome: Edizione e/o, 1990.

Kezich, Tullio. *Il film '80: Cinque anni al cinema, 1982–1986*. Milan: Mondadori, 1986.

Marianacci, Dante. *La cultura degli anni 80: Interviste: Letteratura, arte, teatro, cinema, televisione, giornalismo, storia*. Foggia: Bastogi, 1984.

Micciche, Lino. *Schermi opachi: Il cinema italiano degli anni '80*. Venice: Marsilio, 1998.

Montini, Franco. *I novissimi: Gli esordienti nel cinema italiano degli anni '80*. Turin: Nuova ERI, 1988.

1990s and Beyond

Brunetta, Gian Piero. *Identikit del cinema italiano oggi*. Venice: Marsilio, 2000.

Gieri, Manuela. *Contemporary Italian Filmmaking. Strategies of Subversion*. Toronto: University of Toronto Press, 1995.

Hope, William (ed.). *Italian Cinema: New Directions*. Bern: Peter Lang, 2005.

Marcus, Millicent. *After Fellini: National Cinema in the Postmodern Age*. Baltimore: Johns Hopkins University Press, 2002.

Marrone, Gaetana (ed.). *New Landscapes in Contemporary Italian Cinema*. Chapel Hill, NC: Annali d'Italianistica, 1999.

Montini, Franco. *Il cinema italiano del terzo millennio: I protagonisti della rinascita*. Turin: Lindau, 2002.

Repetto, Monica, and Carlo Tagliabue (eds.). *La vita è bella? Il cinema italiano alla fine degli anni novanta e il suo pubblico*. Milan: Il Castoro, 2000.

Sesti, Mario. *Nuovo cinema italiano: Gli autori, i film, le idee*. Rome: Theoria, 1994.

———. (ed.). *La "scuola" italiana: Storia, strutture, e immaginario di un altro cinema, 1988–1996*. Venice: Marsilio, 1996.

Vitti, Antonio (ed.). *Incontri con il cinema italiano*. Caltanissetta: S. Sciascia, 2003.

Zagarrio, Vito. *Cinema italiano anni novanta*. Venice: Marsilio, 2001.

———. (ed.). *Il cinema della transizione: Scenari italiani degli anni novanta*. Venice: Marsilio, 2000.

———. (ed.). *La meglio gioventù: Nuovo Cinema Italiano 2000–2006*. Venice: Marsilio, 2006.

SOCIAL AND CULTURAL THEMES

General

Bouchard, Norma (ed.). *Risorgimento in Modern Italian Culture: Revisiting the 19th Century Past in History, Narrative, and Cinema*. Madison, NJ: Fairleigh Dickinson University Press, 2005.

Cacucci, Francesco. *Il prete nel cinema italiano dal 1945 a oggi*. Bari: Ecumenica Editrice, 1980.

Carotti, Carlo. *Alla ricerca del Paradiso: L'operaio nel cinema italiano, 1945–1990*. Genoa: Graphos, 1992.

Cigognetti, Luisa, and Lorenza Servetti. *Migranti in celluloide: Storici, cinema ed emigrazione*. Foligno, Perugia: Editoriale Umbra, 2003.

Fantuzzi, Virgilio. *Cinema sacro e profano*. Rome: Civiltà Cattolica, 1983.

Lapertosa, Viviana. *Dalla fame all'abbondanza: Gli italiani e il cibo nel cinema italiano dal dopoguerra a oggi*. Turin: Lindau, 2002.

Liguori, Guido, and Antonio Smargiasse. *Ciak, si gioca! Calcio e tifo nel cinema italiano*. Milan: Baldini & Castoldi, 2000.

Repetto, Monica, and Carlo Tagliabue. *Vecchio Cinema Paradiso: Il cinema italiano all'estero*. Milan: Il Castoro, 2001.

Censorship

Argentieri, Mino. *La censura nel cinema italiano*. Rome: Editori Riuniti, 1974.

Bonsaver, Guido, and Robert S. C. Gordon (eds.). *Culture, Censorship and the State in Twentieth-Century Italy*. London: Legenda, 2005.

Cesari, Maurizio. *La censura nel periodo fascista*. Naples: Liguori, 1978.

———. *La censura in Italia oggi (1944–1980)*. Naples: Liguori, 1982.

Forgacs, David. "Sex in the Cinema: Regulation and Transgression in Italian Films, 1930–1943." In *Re-viewing Fascism: Italian Cinema, 1922-1943*, ed. Jacqueline Reich and Piero Garofalo. Bloomington: Indiana University Press, 2001.

Liggeri, Domenico. *Mani di forbice: La censura cinematografica in Italia.* Alessandria: Edizioni Falsopiano, 1997.

Quargnolo, Mario. *La censura ieri e oggi nel cinema e nel teatro.* Milan: Pan Editrice, 1982.

Literature

Autelitano, Alice, and Valentina Re (eds.). *Il racconto del film: La novellizzazione, dal catalogo al trailer: XII convegno internazionale di studi sul cinema. Narrating the Film: Novelization, from the Catalogue to the Trailer: XII International Film Studies Conference.* Udine: Forum, 2006.

Bragaglia, Cristina. *Il piacere del racconto: Narrativa italiana e cinema, 1895–1990.* Florence: Nuova Italia, 1993.

Brunetta, Gian Piero. *Spari nel buio: La letteratura contro il cinema italiano: Settant'anni di stroncature memorabili.* Venice: Marsilio, 1994.

Bussi, G. Elisa, and Laura Salmon Kovarski (eds.). *Letteratura e cinema: La trasposizione. Atti del Convegno su letteratura e cinema, Forlì, dicembre 1995.* Bologna: CLUEB, 1996.

Cavalluzzi, Raffaelle. *Cinema e letteratura.* Bari: B. A. Graphis, 1997.

Costa, Antonio. *Immagine di un'immagine: Cinema e letteratura.* Turin: UTET, 1993.

Dotoli, Giovanni (ed.). *Musica, cinema e letteratura: Atti del convegno internazionale, Martina Franca, 29–30 luglio 1996.* Fasano (Brindisi): Schena, 1997.

Grignani, Antonietta (ed.). *Il cinema e Pirandello: Atti del convegno di Pavia 8–10 novembre 1990.* Florence: La Nuova Italia, 1992.

Guidorizzi, Ernesto. *La narrativa italiana e il cinema.* Florence: Sansoni, 1973.

Marcus, Millicent Joy. *Filmmaking by the Book: Italian Cinema and Literary Adaptation.* Baltimore: Johns Hopkins University Press, 1993.

Marlia, Giulio (ed.). *L'immagine della parola: Incontri fra cinema e letteratura nella storia del Premio letterario Viareggio-Rèpaci.* Viareggio (Lucca): M. Baroni, 2000.

Martinelli, Vittorio, and Matilde Tortora. *I promessi sposi nel cinema.* Doria (Cosenza): La Mongolfiera, 2004.

Raya, Gino. *Verga e il cinema.* Rome: Herder, 1984.

Testa, Carlo. *Italian Cinema and Modern European Literatures, 1945–2000.* Westport, CT: Praeger, 2002.

———. *Masters of Two Arts: Re-creation of European Literatures in Italian Cinema.* Toronto: University of Toronto Press, 2002.

Verdone, Mario. "Gabriele D'Annunzio nel cinema italiano." *Bianco e nero* 24, no. 7–8 (1963): 1–21.

Politics

Fantoni, Minnella. *Non riconciliati: Politica e società nel cinema italiano dal neorealismo a oggi*. Turin: UTET Libreria, 2004.

Michalczyk, John J. *The Italian Political Filmmakers*. Rutherford, NJ: Fairleigh Dickinson University Press, 1986.

Pellitteri, Paolo. *Cinema come politica: Una commedia all'italiana*. Milan: F. Angeli, 1992.

Quaglietti, Lorenzo. *Storia economico-politica del cinema italiano, 1945–1980*. Rome: Editori Riuniti, 1980.

Uva, Christian, and Michele Picchi. *Destra e sinistra nel cinema italiano: Film e immaginario politico dagli anni '60 al nuovo millennio*. Rome: Edizioni Interculturali, 2006.

Television

Barbera, Alberto (ed.). *Cavalcarono insieme: 50 anni di cinema e televisione in Italia*. Milan: Electa, 2004.

Cereda, Giuseppe. "Piccoli schermi e grandi antenne. Cinema e televisione ieri oggi e domani." In *La "scuola" italiana: Storia, strutture, e immaginario di un altro cinema, 1988–1996,* ed. Mario Sesti. Venice: Marsilio, 1996.

Cigognetti, Luisa, and Pierre Sorlin. "Italy: Cinema and Television: Collaborators and Threat." In *European Cinemas in the Television Age*, ed. Dorota Ostrowska and Graham Roberts. Edinburgh: Edinburgh University Press, 2007.

Giannarelli, Ansano. "Cinema e TV: Un nodo da sciogliere." *Cinemasessanta* 142 (November–December 1981): 6–14.

Grasso, Aldo. "Cinema e televisione: Breve storia di un rapporto difficile." In *Schermi e ombre: Gli italiani e il cinema nel dopoguerra*, ed. Marino Livolsi. Florence: La Nuova Italia, 1988.

Mitchell, T. "Berlusconi, Italian Television and Recent Italian Cinema: Reviewing *The Icicle Thief*." *Film Criticism* 21, no. 1 (1996): 13–33.

Somaschini, Ambra. "Il film e il piccolo schermo." *Cinemasessanta* 133–134 (May–August 1980).

Troianelli, Enza. "Il cinema, fiore all'occhiello del palinsesto televisivo." *Cinemasessanta* 127 (May–June 1979): 17–22.

Vaime, Enrico. "Cinema e TV: odio o amore?" In *L'arte di tutte le arti: Il centenario del cinema in Italia*, [no ed.]. Rome: Dipartimento per l'Informazione e l'Editoria, 1995.

Zagarrio, Vito. *L'anello mancante: Storia e teoria del rapporto cinema-televisione*. Torino: Lindau, 2004.

Mafia

Adornato, Francesco (ed.). *Le letture della mafia*. Vibo Valentia: Jaca Book, 1991.

Albano, Vittorio. *La mafia nel cinema siciliano: Da "In nome della legge" a "Placido Rizzotto."* Manduria (Taranto): Barbieri, 2003.

Marangi, Michele, and Paolo Rossi. *La mafia è cosa nostra: 10 film sull'onorata societa*. Turin: Gruppo Abele, 1993.

Marcus, Millicent. "Postmodern Pastiche, the *Sceneggiata*, and the View of the Mafia from Below in Roberta Torre's *To Die for Tano*." In *After Fellini: National Cinema in the Postmodern Age*. Baltimore: Johns Hopkins University Press, 2002.

Mazzola, Claudio. "The Other Side of Glamorous Killings: *Lucky Luciano*, Rosi's Neo-realistic Approach to the Mafia." In *Poet of Civic Courage: The Films of Francesco Rosi*, ed. Carlo Testa. Wiltshire, UK: Flicks Books, 1996.

Women

Bruno, Giuliana. *Streetwalking on a Ruined Map: Cultural Theory and the City Films of Elvira Notari*. Princeton, NJ: Princeton University Press, 1993.

Bruno, Giuliana, and Maria Nadotti (eds.). *Off Screen: Women and Film in Italy*. London: Routledge, 1988.

Casadio, Gianfranco. *Adultere, fedifraghe, innocenti: La donna del "neorealismo popolare" nel cinema italiano degli anni cinquanta*. Ravenna: Longo, 1990.

Caso, Anna Maria. "L'immagine della donna nel cinema del boom economico (1955–1963)." In *Le linee d'ombra dell'identità repubblicana: Comunicazione, media e società in Italia nel secondo novecento*, ed. Pietro Cavallo and Gino Frezza. Naples: Liguori, 2004.

Cortellazzo, Sara, and Massimo Quaglia (eds.). *Donne sullo schermo*. Turin: CELID, 2003.

Detassis, Piera, and Giovanna Grignaffini (eds.). *Sequenza segreta: Le donne e il cinema*. Milan: Feltrinelli Economica, 1981.

Grazzini, Giovanni. *Eva dopo Eva: La donna nel cinema italiano dagli anni sessanta a oggi*. Rome: Laterza, 1980.

Grignaffini, Giovanna. "Il femminile nel cinema italiano. Racconti di rinascita." In *Identità italiana e identità europea nel cinema italiano dal 1945 al miracolo economico*, ed. Gian Piero Brunetta. Turin: Edizioni della Fondazione Giovanni Agnelli, 1996.

Günsberg, Maggie. "Domestic Space in Italian Cinema: *Ossessione*, *Ladri di biciclette* and *Ladri di saponette*." In *Women and Market Societies: Crisis and Opportunity*, ed. Barbara Einhorn and Eileen James Yeo. Aldershot, UK: E. Elgar, 1995.

——. *Italian Cinema: Gender and Genre*. Houndmills, UK: Palgrave Macmillan, 2005.

Marcus, Millicent. "The Italian Body Politic Is a Woman: Feminized National Identity in Postwar Italian Film." In *Sparks and Seeds: Medieval Literature and Its Afterlife: Essays in Honor of John Freccero*, ed. Dana E. Stewart and Alison Cornish. Turnhout, Belgium: Brepols, 2000.

Martinelli, Vittorio. *Le dive del silenzio*. Genoa: Le Mani/Cineteca di Bologna, 2001.

Masi, Stefano, and Enrico Landa. *Italian Movie Goddesses: Over 80 of the Greatest Women in Italian Cinema*. Rome: Gremese, 1997.

Negro, Leandra. "Le donne nel secondo dopoguerra nel cinema italiano (1949–1955)." In *Le linee d'ombra dell'identità repubblicana: Comunicazione, media e società in Italia nel secondo novecento*, ed. Pietro Cavallo and Gino Frezza. Naples: Liguori, 2004.

O'Healy, Aine. "Theatre and Cinema, 1945–2000." In *A History of Women's Writing in Italy*, ed. Letizia Panizza and Sharon Wood. Cambridge: Cambridge University Press, 2001.

Ossi, Maria. *Donna e cinema nell'Europa duemila: Fra immaginario e quotidianità*. Terano: Demian, 1994.

Pagliano, Graziella (ed.). *Presenze femminili nel novecento italiano: Letteratura, teatro, cinema*. Naples: Liguori, 2003.

Riviello, Tonia Caterina (ed.). *Women in Italian Cinema—La donna nel cinema italiano*. Rome: Libreria Croce, 2001.

Sossi, Tiziano. *Dizionario delle registe: L'altra metà del cinema*. Rome: Gremese, 2000.

GENRES

Comedy

D'Amico, Masolino. *La commedia all'italiana: Il cinema comico in Italia dal 1945 al 1975*. Milan: Mondadori, 1985.

Giacovelli, Enrico. *La commedia all'italiana: La storia, i luoghi, gli autori, gli attori, i film*. Rome: Gremese, 1995.

——. *Non ci resta che ridere: Una storia del cinema comico italiano*. Turin: Lindau, 1999.

Grande, Maurizio. *La commedia all'italiana*. Ed. Orio Caldiron. Rome: Bulzoni, 2003.

Marlia, Giulio (ed.). *Non ci resta che ridere: Testimonianze sul cinema comico italiano*. Montepulciano, Siena: Editori del Grifo, 1988.

Pergolari, Andrea. *Verso la commedia: Momenti del cinema di Steno, Salce, Festa Campanile*. Florence: Firenze Libri, 2002.

———. *Dizionario dei protagonisti del cinema comico e della commedia italiana*. Rome: Un Mondo a Parte, 2003.

Giallo

Gallant, Chris. *Art of Darkness: The Cinema of Dario Argento*. Guildford, UK: FAB, 2000.

Joisten, Bernard. *Crime Designer: Dario Argento et le cinéma*. Broché: Éditions Inculte, 2007.

Koven, Mikel J. *La dolce morte: Vernacular cinema and the Italian Giallo Film*. Lanham, MD: Scarecrow Press, 2006.

Lancia, Enrico, and Roberto Poppi. *Gialli, polizieschi, thriller: Tutti i film italiani dal 1930 al 2000*. Rome: Gremese, 2004.

Luther Smith, Adrian. *Blood and Black Lace: The Definitive Guide to Italian Sex and Horror Movies*. Liskeard, UK: Stray Cat Publishing, 1999.

Needham, Gary. "Playing with Genre: Defining the Italian *Giallo*." In *Fear without Frontiers: Horror Cinema across the Globe*, ed. Steven Jay Schneider. Godalming, UK: FAB, 2003.

Horror

Colombo, Maurizio, and Antonio Tentori. *Lo schermo insanguinato: Il cinema italiano del terrore 1957–1989*. Chieti: Marino Solfanelli, 1990.

De Gaetano, Roberto. *Il corpo e la maschera: Il grottesco nel cinema italiano*. Rome: Bulzoni, 1999.

Harper, Jim. *Italian Horror*. Baltimore: Luminary Press, 2005.

Howarth, Troy. *The Haunted World of Mario Bava*. Guildford, UK: FAB, 2002.

Jenks, Carol. "The Other Face of Death: Barbara Steele and *La maschera del demonio*." In *Popular European Cinema*, ed. Richard Dyer and Ginette Vincendeau. London: Routledge, 1992.

Mangravite, Andrew. "Once upon a Time in the Crypt." *Film Comment* 29, no. 1 (1993): 50–54.

McCallum, Lawrence. *Italian Horror Films of the 1960s: A Critical Catalog of 62 Chillers*. Jefferson, NC: McFarland, 1998.

McDonagh, Maitland. "The Elegant Brutality of Dario Argento." *Film Comment* 29, no. 1 (1993): 55–58.

Mora, Teo. "Elegia per una donna vampiro: Il cinema fantastico italia no 1957–1966." *Storia del cinema dell'orrore,* vol. 2, chap. 12. Rome: Fanucci, 1978.

Morsiani, Alberto (ed.). *Rosso italiano (1977–1987): Dieci anni di horror con Argento, Bava, Fulci e . . . gli altri.* Verona: Nuova Grafica Cierre, 1988.

Palmerini, Luca M., and Gaetano Mistretta. *Spaghetti Nightmares: Italian Fantasy-Horrors as Seen through the Eyes of Their Protagonists.* Trans. Gilliam M. A. Kirkpatrick. Key West, FL: Fantasma Books, 1996.

Paul, Louis. *Italian Horror Film Directors.* Jefferson, NC: McFarland, 2004.

Pilo, Gianni. *Dizionario dell'orrore: Una guida fondamentale.* Rome: Newton & Compton, 2004.

Peplum

Lagny, Michèle. "Popular Taste: The Peplum." In *Popular European Cinema,* ed. Richard Dyer and Ginette Vincendeau. London: Routledge, 1992.

Lucanio, Patrick. *With Fire and Sword: Italian Spectacles on American Screens 1958–1968.* London: Scarecrow, 1994.

Salotti, Marco. "Note sul cinema mitologico italiano: 1957–1964." In *Il mito classico e il cinema,* [no ed.], introd. Ferruccio Bertini. Genoa: Dipartimento di Archeologia, Filologia Classica e Loro Tradizioni, 1997.

Schenk, Irmbert. "The Cinematic Support to National(istic) Mythology: The Italian Peplum 1910–1930." In *Globalization, Cultural Identities, and Media Representations,* ed. Natascha Gentz and Stefan Kramer. Albany: State University of New York Press, 2006.

Solomon, Jon. *The Ancient World in the Cinema.* Rev. and expanded ed. New Haven, CT: Yale University Press, 2001.

Wyke, Maria. *Projecting the Past: Ancient Rome, Cinema and History.* New York: Routledge, 1997.

Western

Beatrice, Luca. *Al cuore, Ramon, al cuore: La leggenda del western all'italiana.* Florence: Tarab, 1996.

De Luca, Lorenzo. *C'era una volta il western italiano.* Rome: Istituto Bibliografico Napoleone, 1987.

Eleftheriotis, Dimitris. "Genre Criticism and the Spaghetti Western." In *Popular Cinemas of Europe: Studies of Texts, Contexts, and Frameworks.* New York: Continuum, 2001.

Frayling, Christopher. *Spaghetti Westerns: Cowboys and Europeans from Karl May to Sergio Leone.* London: I. B. Tauris, 1998.

Moscati, Massimo. *Western all'italiana*. Milan: Pan, 1978.

Papadimitriou, Lydia. "Spaghetti Western, Genre Criticism and National Cinema: Re-defining the Frame of Reference." In *Action and Adventure Cinema*, ed. Yvonne Tasker. London: Routledge, 2004.

Piselli, Stefano, and Riccardo Morrochi. *Western all'italiana*. Florence: Glittering Images, 1998.

Staig, Laurence, and Tony Williams. *Italian Western: The Opera of Violence*. London: Lorrimer, 1975.

Wagstaff, Christopher. "A Forkful of Westerns: Industry, Audiences and the Italian Western." In *Popular European Cinema*, ed. Richard Dyer and Ginette Vincendeau. London: Routledge, 1992

Weisser, Thomas. *Spaghetti Westerns: The Good, the Bad, and the Violent. A Comprehensive, Illustrated Filmography of 558 Eurowesterns and Their Personnel, 1961–1977*. Jefferson, NC: McFarland, 1992.

DIRECTORS

Antonioni, Michelangelo

Achilli, Alberto, Alberto Boschi, and Gianfranco Casadio. *Le sonorità del visibile: Immagini, suoni e musica nel cinema di Michelangelo Antonioni*. Ravenna: Longo, 1999.

Antonioni, Michelangelo. *That Bowling Alley on the Tiber: Tales of a Director*. Trans. William Arrowsmith. New York: Oxford University Press, 1986.

———. *Fare un film e per me vivere: Scritti sul cinema*. Ed. Carlo Di Carlo and Giorgio Tinazzi. Venice: Marsilio, 1994.

———. *The Architecture of Vision: Writings and Interviews on Cinema*. Ed. Carlo di Carlo and Giorgio Tinazzi. New York: Marsilio, 1996.

———. *Comincio a capire*. Valverde (Catania): Il Girasole, 1999.

Aristarco, Guido. *Su Antonioni: Materiali per una analisi critica*. Rome: La Zattera di Babele, 1988.

Aristarco, Guido, and Luciana Bohne. "Notes on Michelangelo Antonioni." *Film Criticism* 9, no. 1 (1984): 4–7.

Arrowsmith, William. *Antonioni: The Poet of Images*. New York: Oxford University Press, 1995.

Bachmann, Gideon. "Antonioni after China: Art versus Science." *Film Quarterly* 28, no. 4 (1975): 26–30.

———. "Love of Today: An Interview with Michelangelo Antonioni." *Film Quarterly* 36, no. 4 (1983): 1–4.

Biarese, Cesare, and Aldo Tassone. *I film di Michelangelo Antonioni*. Rome: Gremese, 1985.

Bonfand, Alain. *Cinéma de Michelangelo Antonioni*. Paris: Images Modernes, 2003.

Brunette, Peter. *The Films of Michelangelo Antonioni*. Cambridge: Cambridge University Press, 1998.

Cameron, Ian. *Michelangelo Antonioni: A Study*. London: Movie Magazine, 1963.

———. (ed.). "Special Issue: Antonioni." *Film Quarterly* 16, no. 1 (1962).

Cameron, Ian, and Robin Wood. *Antonioni*. New York: Praeger, 1971.

Casetti, Francesco. "Antonioni and Hitchcock: Two Strategies of Narrative Investment." *SubStance: A Review of Theory and Literary Criticism* 15:3, no. 51 (1986): 69–86.

Chatman, Seymour. *Antonioni, or, the Surface of the World*. Berkeley: University of California Press, 1985.

———. "Antonioni in 1980: An Interview." *Film Quarterly* 51, no. 1 (1997): 2–10.

———. *Michelangelo Antonioni: The Complete Films*. Cologne: Taschen, 2004.

Chatman, Seymour, and Paul Duncan. *Michelangelo Antonioni: The Investigation*. Cologne: Taschen, 2004.

Comune di Ferrara (ed.). *Michelangelo Antonioni: Identificazione di un autore*. 2 vols. Parma: Pratiche, 1983–1985.

Cuccu, Lorenzo. *La visione come problema: Forme e svolgimento del cinema di Antonioni*. Rome: Bulzoni, 1973.

———. *Antonioni, il discorso dello sguardo: Da "Blow up" a "Identificazione di una donna."* Pisa: ETS, 1990.

Di Carlo, Carlo (ed.). *Il cinema di Michelangelo Antonioni*. Milan: Il Castoro, 2002.

Farina, M. Debora. *Eros is sick: Il cinema di Michelangelo Antonioni*. Italy: Cinetecnica, 2005.

Forgacs, David. "Antonioni: Space, Place, Sexuality." In *Spaces in European Cinema*, ed. Myrto Konstantarakos. Exeter, UK: Intellect, 2000.

Giacci, Vittorio (ed.). *L'avventura, ovvero l'isola che c'è. Lipari* (Messina): Edizioni del Centro Studi e Ricerche di Storia e Problemi Eoliani, 2000.

Giacomelli, Annamaria, and I. Saitta. *Crisi dell'uomo e della società nei film di Visconti e di Antonioni*. Alba: Edizioni Paoline, 1972.

Gianetti, David. *Invito al cinema di Michelangelo Antonioni*. Milan: Mursia, 1999.

Godard, Jean-Luc. "Night, Eclipse, Dawn: An Interview with Michelangelo Antonioni." *Cahiers du Cinéma* 1 (January 1966): 19–29.

Godmann, Annie. *Cinéma et société moderne: Le cinéma de 1958 à 1968: Godard, Antonioni, Resnais, Robbe-Grillet*. Paris: Éditions Anthropos, 1971.

Graham, Alison. "The Phantom Self." *Film Criticism* 9, no.1 (1984): 47–62.

Huss, Roy (ed.). *Focus on "Blow-up."* Englewood Cliffs, NJ: Prentice Hall, 1971.

Johnson, K. "The Point of View of the Wandering Camera." *Cinema Journal* 32, no. 2 (1993): 49–56.

Kezich, Tullio, and Alessandra Levantesi (eds.). *Cronaca di un amore: Un film di Michelangelo Antonioni: Quando un'opera prima è già un capolavoro.* Turin: Lindau, 2004.

Leprohon, Pierre, with Michelangelo Antonioni. *Michelangelo Antonioni: An Introduction.* Trans. Scott Sullivan. New York: Simon and Schuster, 1963.

Lyons, Robert Joseph. *Michelangelo Antonioni's Neo-realism: A World View.* New York: Arno Press, 1976.

Marcus, Millicent Joy. "Antonioni's *Red Desert*: Abstraction as the Guiding Idea." In *Italian Film in the Light of Neorealism.* Princeton, NJ: Princeton University Press, 1986.

Mayet Giaume, Joelle. *Michelangelo Antonioni: Le fil intérieur.* Crisnee, Belgium: Yellow Now, 1990.

Mazzotta, Giuseppe. "The Language of Movies and Antonioni's Double Vision." *Diacritics* 15, no. 2 (1985): 2–10.

Moore, Kevin Z. "Eclipsing the Commonplace: The Logic of Alienation in Antonioni's Cinema." *Film Quarterly* 48, no. 4 (1995): 22–34.

Moses, Gavriel. "Sleepwalking in the Snow: Antonioni and the Voice of the Canon." *RLA: Romance Languages Annual* 8 (1996): 238–244.

Nowell-Smith, Geoffrey. "Antonioni: Before and After." *Sight and Sound* 5, no. 12 (1995): 16–20.

———. *L'avventura.* London: British Film Institute, 1997.

Orsini, Maria (ed.). *Michelangelo Antonioni: I film e la critica 1943–1995.* Rome: Bulzoni, 2002.

Perez, Gilberto. "A Man Pointing: Antonioni and the Film Image." *Yale Review* 82, no. 3 (1994): 38–65.

Perry, Ted, and Rene Prieto. *Michelangelo Antonioni: A Guide to References and Resources.* Boston: G. K. Hall, 1986.

Rifkin, Ned. *Antonioni's Visual Language.* Ann Arbor, MI: UMI Research Press, 1982.

Rohdie, Sam. *Antonioni.* London: British Film Institute, 1990.

Rosenbaum, Jonathan. "A Cinema of Uncertainty: Films by Michelangelo Antonioni." In *Placing Movies.* Berkeley: University of California Press, 1995.

Rudman, Mark. "The Night: On Michelangelo Antonioni." *Raritan: A Quarterly Review* 14, no. 2 (1994): 83–108.

Schliesser, John. "Antonioni's Heideggerian Swerve." *Literature/Film Quarterly* 26, no. 4 (1998): 278–287.

Schwarzer, Mitchell. "The Consuming Landscape: Architecture in the Films of Michelangelo Antonioni." In *Architecture and Film*, ed. Mark Lamster. New York: Princeton Architectural Press, 2000.

Snyder, Stephen. "Antonioni: Cubist Vision in the *Red Desert*." In *The Transparent I: Self/Subject in European Cinema*. New York: P. Lang, 1994.

Strick, Philip. *Michelangelo Antonioni*. Loughton, UK: Motion Publications, 1963.

Tassone, Aldo. "Entretien avec Michelangelo Antonioni." *Positif* 292 (June 1985): 38–45.

Tinazzi, Giorgio. *Antonioni*. Florence: La Nuova Italia, 1974.

Tomasulo, Frank P. "The Architectonics of Alienation: Antonioni's Edifice Complex." *Wide-Angle* 15, no. 3 (1993): 3–20.

Wenders, Wim. *My Time with Antonioni: The Diary of an Extraordinary Experience*. Trans. Michael Hofmann. London: Faber, 2000.

Wuss, Peter. "Narrative Tension in Antonioni." In *Suspense: Conceptualizations, Theoretical Analyses, and Empirical Explorations*, ed. Peter Vorderer, Hans J. Wulff, and Mike Friedrichsen. Mahwah, NJ: Erlbaum, 1996.

Wyeth, Andrew. *Antonioni*. London: Continuum, 2004.

Zumbo, Saverio. *Al di la delle immagini: Michelangelo Antonioni*. Alessandria: Falsopiano, 2002.

Bertolucci, Bernardo

Amengual, Barthelemy, Paul Crinel, Joel Magny, and Bernard Oheix. *Bernardo Bertolucci*. Paris: Lettres Modernes, 1979.

Bertetto, Paolo, and Franco Prono (eds.). *Dossier Bernardo Bertolucci*. Turin: Lindau, 2002.

Burgoyne, Robert. *Bertolucci's "1900": A Narrative and Historical Analysis*. Detroit: Wayne State University Press, 1991.

Campani, Ermelinda M. *L'anticonformista: Bernardo Bertolucci e il suo cinema*. Fiesole (Florence): Cadmo, 1998.

Campari, Roberto, and Maurizio Schiaretti (eds.). *In viaggio con Bernardo: Il cinema di Bernardo Bertolucci*. Venice: Marsilio, 1994.

Carabba, Claudio, Gabriele Rizza, and Giovanni Maria Rossi (eds.). *La regola delle illusioni: Il cinema di Bernardo Bertolucci*. Florence: Aida, 2003.

Casetti, Francesco. *Bernardo Bertolucci*. Florence: La Nuova Italia, 1976.

Costa, Francesco (ed.). *Bernardo Bertolucci*. Rome: D. Audino, 1996.

Garofalo, Marcello. *Bertolucci: Images*. Lucca: M. Pacini Fazzi, 2000.

Gerard, Fabien, T. Jefferson Kline, and Bruce Sklarew (eds.). *Bernardo Bertolucci: Interviews*. Jackson: University Press of Mississippi, 2000.

Izod, John. *Screen, Culture, Psyche: A Post-Jungian Approach to Working with the Audience*. New York: Routledge, 2006. [Chaps. 3–5 on Bertolucci.]

Kinder, Marsha, and Beverle Houston. "Bertolucci and the Dance of Danger." *Sight and Sound* 42, no. 4 (1973): 186–191.

Kline, T. Jefferson. *Bertolucci's Dream Loom: A Psychoanalytic Study of Cinema*. Amherst: University of Massachusetts Press, 1987.

Kolker, Robert Phillip. *Bernardo Bertolucci*. London: British Film Institute, 1985.

Pitiot, Pierre, and Jean-Claude Mirabella. *Sur Bertolucci*. Castelnau-le-Lez: Climats, 1991.

Prono, Franco. *Bernardo Bertolucci: Il conformista*. Turin: Lindau, 1998.

Sklarew, Bruce H. (ed.). *Bertolucci's "The Last Emperor": Multiple Takes*. Detroit: Wayne State University Press, 1998.

Socci, Stefano. *Bernardo Bertolucci*. Milan: Il Castoro, 1996.

Tonetti, Claretta Micheletti. *Bernardo Bertolucci: The Cinema of Ambiguity*. New York: Twayne, 1995.

Ungari, Enzo. *Scene madri di Bernardo Bertolucci*. Milan: Ubulibri, 1987.

Ungari, Enzo, with Donald Ranvaud. *Bertolucci by Bertolucci*. London: Plexus, 1987.

Yoshitzky, Yosefa. *The Radical Faces of Godard and Bertolucci*. Detroit: Wayne State University Press, 1995.

Blasetti, Alessandro

Blasetti, Alessandro. *Il cinema che ho vissuto*. Ed. Franco Prono. Bari: Dedalo, 1982.

———. *Scritti sul cinema*. Ed. Adriano Aprà. Venice: Marsilio, 1982.

Centro Sperimentale di Cinematografia (eds.). *Per Alessandro Blasetti: Atti della tavola rotonda dell'11 marzo 1987*. Rome: Centro Sperimentale di Cinematografia, 1989.

Gori, Gianfranco. *Alessandro Blasetti*. Florence: La Nuova Italia, 1984.

Masi, Stefano. *A. Blasetti: 1900–2000*. Rome: Comitato Alessandro Blasetti, 2001.

Micheli, Paola. *Il cinema di Blasetti, parlò cosi: Un'analisi linguistica dei film (1929–1942)*. Rome: Bulzoni, 1990.

Museo di Roma in Trastevere (ed.). *Alessandro Blasetti: Il mestiere del cinema*. Rome: Gangemi, 2002.

Sette, Grazia (ed.). *Alessandro Blasetti: Un primo incontro*. Rome: Comitato Alessandro Blasetti per il Centenario della Nascita, 2001.

Verdone, Luca. *I film di Alessandro Blasetti*. Rome: Gremese, 1989.

Verdone, Mario. *Alessandro Blasetti, 1900–1987*. Rome: Strenna dei Romanisti, 1988.
——. *Alessandro Blasetti*. Rome: Edilazio, 2006.

De Sica, Vittorio

Caldiron, Orio (ed.). *Tutti i De Sica*. Rome: E. Carpintieri, 1984.
Cardullo, Bert. *Vittorio De Sica: Director, Actor, Screenwriter*. Jefferson, NC: McFarland, 2002.
Curle, Howard, and Stephen Snyder (eds.). *Vittorio De Sica: Contemporary Perspectives*. Toronto: University of Toronto Press, 2000.
Darretta, John. *Vittorio De Sica: A Guide to References and Resources*. Boston: G. K. Hall, 1983.
De Santi, Gualtiero. *Vittorio De Sica*. Milan: Il Castoro, 2003.
De Sica, Vittorio. *La porta del cielo: Memorie 1901–1952*. Introd. Gualtiero De Santi. Cava de' Tirreni (Salerno): Avagliano, 2004.
Governi, Giancarlo. *Parlami d'amore Mariù*. Rome: Gremese, 1993.
Miccichè, Lino (ed.). *De Sica: Autore, regista, attore*. Venice: Marsilio, 1992.
Moscati, Italo. *Vittorio De Sica: Vitalità, passione e talento in un'Italia dolceamara*. Rome: Ediesse, Rai-ERI, 2003.
Pecori, Franco. *Vittorio De Sica*. Florence: La Nuova Italia, 1980.

Fellini, Federico

Alpert, Hollis. *Fellini: A Life*. New York: Atheneum, 1986.
Angelini, Pietro. *Controfellini: Il fellinismo tra restaurazione e magia bianca*. Milan: Ottaviano, 1974.
Angelucci, Gianfranco (ed.). *Gli ultimi sogni di Federico Fellini*. Rimini: Associazione Federico Fellini, 1997.
Arpa, Angelo. *Fellini: Persona e personaggio*. Naples: Parresia, 1996.
——. *La dolce vita: Cronaca di una passione*. Naples: Parresia, 1996.
Bachmann, Gideon. "Federico Fellini: Beyond Neorealism: Interview." In *Patterns of Italian Cinema*, ed. Giose Rimanelli. Albany: State University of New York Press, 1980.
Baxter, John. *Fellini*. London: Fourth Estate, 1993.
Benderson, Albert Edward. *Critical Approaches to Fellini's 8½*. New York: Arno Press, 1974.
Betti, Liliana. *Fellini*. Trans. Joachim Neugroschel. Boston: Little, Brown, 1979.

Bìspuri, Ennio. *Federico Fellini, il sentimento latino della vita*. Rome: Ventaglio, 1981.

——. *Interpretare Fellini*. Rimini: Guaraldi, 2003.

Bondanella, Peter. *Federico Fellini: Essays in Criticism*. New York: Oxford University Press, 1978.

——. "Literature as Therapy: Fellini and Petronius." *Annali d'Italianistica* 6 (1988): 179–198.

——. *The Cinema of Federico Fellini*. Princeton, NJ: Princeton University Press, 1992.

——. "Beyond Neorealism: Calvino, Fellini and Fantasy." In *Italian Criticism: Literature and Culture*, ed. Gregory L. Lucente. Ann Arbor: Michigan Romance Studies, 1996.

——. *The Films of Federico Fellini*. Cambridge: Cambridge University Press, 2002.

——. (ed.). *Federico Fellini: Essays in Criticism*. New York: Oxford University Press, 1978.

Bondanella, Peter, and Cristina Degli-Esposti. *Perspectives on Federico Fellini*. New York: G. K. Hall, 1993.

Borin, Fabrizio. *Federico Fellini*. Rome: Gremese, 1999.

Burke, Frank. *Federico Fellini: Variety Lights to La Dolce Vita*. Boston: Twayne, 1984.

——. "Fellini: Changing the Subject." *Film Quarterly* 43 (Fall 1989): 36–48.

——. *Fellini's Films: From Postwar to Postmodern*. Boston: Twayne, 1996.

Burke, Frank, and Marguerite R. Waller (eds.). *Federico Fellini: Contemporary Perspectives*. Toronto: University of Toronto Press, 2002.

Cardullo, Bert (ed.). *Federico Fellini: Interviews*. Jackson: University Press of Mississippi, 2006.

Chandler, Charlotte. *I, Fellini*. New York: Random House, 1995.

Cirio, Rita. *Il mestiere di regista: Intervista con Federico Fellini*. Milan: Garzanti, 1994.

Colon, Carlos. *Rota-Fellini: La música en las películas de Federico Fellini*. Seville: Universidad de Sevilla, 1981.

Conti, Isabella. "Federico Fellini: Artist in Search of Self." *Biography: An Interdisciplinary Quarterly* 7, no. 4 (1984): 292–308.

Cordelli, Valentina, and Riccardo Costantini (eds.). *Invenzioni della memoria: Il cinema di Federico Fellini*. Udine: Centro Espressioni Cinematografiche, 2003.

Costantini, Costanzo. *Omaggio a Federico Fellini*. Rome: Edizioni Vittoria, 1993.

——. (ed.). *Conversations with Fellini*. Trans. Sohrab Sorooshian. San Diego: Harcourt Brace, 1995.

Costello, Donald P. *Fellini's Road*. Notre Dame, IN: University of Notre Dame Press, 1983.

Cro, Stelio. "Fellini's Freudian Psyche between Neo-realism and Neo-baroque." *Canadian Journal of Italian Studies* 18, no. 51 (1995): 162–183.

De Benedictis, Maurizio. *Linguaggi dell'aldilà: Fellini e Pasolini*. Rome: Lithos, 2000.

De Castro, Enzo. *Fellini in cento pagine*. Rome: Edizioni dell'Oleandro, 2003.

Fava, Claudio G., and Aldo Vigano. *The Films of Federico Fellini*. Trans. Shula Curto. Secaucus, NJ: Citadel Press, 1985.

Fellini, Federico. *Fare un film*. Turin: Einaudi, 1980.

———. *La mia Rimini*. Bologna: Cappelli, 1987.

———. *Comments on Film*. Ed. Giovanni Grazzini, trans. Joseph Henry. Fresno: Press at California State University, 1988.

———. *Cinecittà*. Trans. Graham Fawcett. London: Studio Vista, 1989.

———. *Imago: Appunti di un visionario. Conversazione-intervista di Toni Maraini*. Rome: Semar, 1994.

———. *I'm a Born Liar: A Fellini Lexicon*. Ed. Damian Pettigrew. New York: Harry N. Abrams, 2003.

Finocchiaro Chimirri, Giovanna. *Fellini a m'arcord*. Catania: C.U.E.C.M., 1994.

———. *Testimonianza per Fellini*. Catania: C.U.E.C.M., 1995.

Giacci, Vittorio (ed.). *La voce della luce: Federico Fellini*. Rome: Progetti Museali, 1995.

Giacovelli, Enrico. *Tutti i film di Federico Fellini*. Turin: Lindau, 2002.

Gieri, Manuela. "Character and Discourse from Pirandello to Fellini: Defining a Countertradition in an Italian Context." In *Contemporary Italian Filmmaking: Strategies of Subversion*. Toronto: University of Toronto Press, 1995.

———. "Fellini, Advertising and the Ineffable Objects of Desire." *Forum Italicum* 33, no. 1 (1999): 169–184.

Hughes, Eileen Lanouette. *On the Set of Fellini Satyricon: A Behind-the-Scenes Diary*. New York: Morrow, 1971.

Keel, Anna, and Christian Strich (eds.). *Fellini on Fellini*. Trans. Isabel Quigly. London: Eyre Methuen, 1976.

Ketcham, Charles B. *Fellini: The Search for a New Mythology*. New York: Paulist Press, 1976.

Kezich, Tullio. *Fellini*. Milan: Rizzoli, 1988.

———. *Su "La dolce vita" con Federico Fellini: Giorno per giorno la storia di un film che ha fatto epoca*. Venice: Marsilio, 1996.

———. *Federico Fellini: His Life and Work*. Trans. Minna Proctor with Vivianna Mazza. New York: Faber and Faber, 2006. (Translation of *Federico: Fellini, la vita e i film*. Milan: Feltrinelli, 2002.)

Levergeois, Bertrand. *Fellini: La dolce vita du maestro*. Paris: Éditions de l'Arsenal, 1994.

Mollica, Vincenzo (ed.). *Fellini sognatore: Omaggio all'arte di Federico Fellini*. Montepulciano (Siena): Editori del Grifo, 1992.

———. (ed.). *Fellini sognato*. Castiglione del Lago (Perugia): Di, 2002.

———. (ed.). *Fellini!* Milan: Skira, 2003.

Murray, Edward. *Fellini the Artist*. New York: F. Ungar, 1976.

Panicelli, Ida, and Antonella Soldaini. *Fellini: Costumes and Fashion*. Milan: Charta, 1996.

Papio, Michael. "Derailment of Closure: The Father-Son Enigma in Fellini." *Italica* 74, no. 3 (1997): 392–407.

Pasolini, Pier Paolo. "The Catholic Irrationalism of Fellini." *Film Criticism* 9, no. 1 (1984): 63–73.

Pecori, Franco. *Federico Fellini*. Florence: La Nuova Italia, 1974.

Pillitteri, Paolo. *Appunti su Fellini*. Milan: Cooperativa Libraria I.U.L.M., 1986.

Provenzano, Roberto. *Invito al cinema di Federico Fellini*. Milan: Mursia, 1995.

Reich, Jacqueline. "'Remember, It's a Comedy': Mastroianni in the Films of Federico Fellini." In *Beyond the Latin Lover: Marcello Mastroianni, Masculinity, and Italian Cinema*. Bloomington: Indiana University Press, 2004.

Renzi, Renzo. *L'ombra di Fellini: Quarant'anni di rapporti con il grande regista e uno stupidario degli anni ottanta*. Bari: Dedalo, 1994.

Risset, Jacqueline. *L'incantatore: Scritti su Fellini*. Milan: Libri Scheiwiller, 1994.

Rohdie, Sam. *Fellini Lexicon*. London: British Film Institute, 2002.

Rosenthal, Stuart. *The Cinema of Federico Fellini*. South Brunswick, NJ: A. S. Barnes, 1976.

Sciannemeo, Franco. *Nino Rota, Federico Fellini, and the Making of an Italian Cinematic Folk Opera, Amarcord*. Lewiston, NY: Edwin Mellen Press, 2005.

Snyder, Stephen. "*Fellini Satyricon*: The Self Inside Vision." In *The Transparent I: Self/Subject in European Cinema*. New York: Peter Lang, 1994.

Solomon, John. "Fellini and Ovid." *Classical and Modern Literature: A Quarterly* 3, no. 1 (1982): 39–44.

Strich, Christian (ed.). *Fellini's Films: The Four Hundred Most Memorable Stills from Federico Fellini's Fifteen and a Half Films*. New York: Putnam, 1977.

Stubbs, John C. "The Fellini Manner: Open Form and Visual Excess." *Cinema Journal* 32, no. 4 (1993): 49–64.

———. "Fellini's Portrait of the Artist as a Creative Problem Solver." *Cinema Journal* 41, no. 4 (2002): 116–131.

———. *Federico Fellini as Auteur: Seven Aspects of His Films*. Carbondale: Southern Illinois University Press, 2006.

Theall, Donald F. "The Ambivalence of the Poetic as Critique: Science Fiction and Fellini Films." In *Beyond the Word: Reconstructing Sense in the Joyce Era of Technology, Culture, and Communication*. Toronto: University of Toronto Press, 1995.

Tornabene, Francesco. *Federico Fellini: The Fantastic Visions of a Realist*. Berlin: Taschen, 1990.

Tornabuoni, Lietta (ed.). *Federico Fellini*. New York: Rizzoli, 1995.

Verdone, Mario. *Federico Fellini*. Rome: Il Castoro, 1994.

Wiegand, Chris. *Federico Fellini: Ringmaster of Dreams, 1920–1993*. Cologne: Taschen, 2003.

Zanelli, Dario. *L'inferno immaginario di Federico Fellini: Cose dette da F. F. a proposito de "Il viaggio di G. Mastorna."* Rimini: Guaraldi, 1995.

Zapponi, Bernardino. *Il mio Fellini: Massiccio e sparuto, furente e dolcissimo, vecchio e infantile: L'uomo e il regista nel racconto del suo sceneggiatore*. Venice: Marsilio, 1995.

Leone, Sergio

Aguilar, Carlos. *Sergio Leone: El hombre, el rito, la muerte*. Almería: Diputación de Almería, 2000.

Cèbe, Gilles. *Sergio Leone*. Paris: H. Veyrier, 1984.

Cumbow, Robert C. *The Films of Sergio Leone*. Lanham, MD: Scarecrow, 2008.

De Fornari, Oreste. *Sergio Leone: The Great Italian Dream of Legendary America*. Rome: Gremese International, 1997.

Di Claudio, Gianni. *Directed by Sergio Leone*. Chieti: Libreria Universitaria Editrice, 1990.

Fawell, John. *The Art of Sergio Leone's "Once upon a Time in the West": A Critical Appreciation*. Jefferson, NC: McFarland, 2005.

Frayling, Christopher. *Sergio Leone: Something to Do with Death*. London: Faber, 2000.

———. *Once upon a Time in Italy: The Westerns of Sergio Leone*. New York: Harry N. Abrams, 2005.

Garofalo, Marcello. *Tutto il cinema di Sergio Leone*. Milan: Baldini & Castoldo, 1999.

———. (ed.). *C'era una volta in America: Un film di Sergio Leone. Photographic memories*. Rome: Editalia, 1988.

Granata, Roberto. *Leone*. Catania: G. Maimone, 2002.

Lambert, Gilles. *Les bons, les sales, les méchants et les propres de Sergio Leone*. Paris: Solar, 1976.
Martin, Adrian. *Once upon a Time in America*. London: British Film Institute, 1998.
Mininni, Francesco. *Sergio Leone*. Rome: Il Castoro, 1994.
Ortoli, Philippe. *Sergio Leone: Une Amérique des légendes*. Paris: L'Harmattan, 1994.
Roth, Lane. *Film Semiotics, Metz, and Leone's Trilogy*. New York: Garland, 1983.
Saccutelli, Gianluca. *C'era una volta Sergio Leone*. Porto Sant'Elpidio (Ascoli-Piceno): Ottava Musa, 1999.
Zanello, Fabio. *C'era una volta il west di Sergio Leone*. Chieti: Libreria Universitaria, 2003.

Moretti, Nanni

Bonsaver, Guido (ed.). "Three Colours Italian—Interview with Nanni Moretti." *Sight and Sound* 12, no. 1 (2002): 28–30.
Coco, Giuseppe. *Nanni Moretti: Cinema come diario*. Milan: Mondadori, 2006.
Cordelli, Valentina, and Riccardo Costantini (eds.). *Ecce Nanni!!! Il cinema autarchico di Nanni Moretti*. Udine: Centro Espressioni Cinematografiche, 2006.
D'Aquino, Antonella. "Nanni Moretti: Intellettuale ibrido. Il cinema come specchio della crisi di un maitre a penser." *Italica* 81, no. 3 (2004): 367–397.
De Bernardinis, Flavio. *Nanni Moretti*. Rome: Il Castoro, 1993.
De Gaetano, Roberto. *La sincope dell'identità: Il cinema di Nanni Moretti*. Turin: Lindau, 2002.
Detassis, Piera (ed.). *Caro Diario*. Lipari (Messina): Edizioni del Centro Studi, 2002.
Gili, Jean A. *Nanni Moretti*. Rome: Gremese, 2001.
Giovannini, Memmo, Enrico Magrelli, and Mario Sesti. *Nanni Moretti*. Napoli: Edizioni Scientifiche Italiane, 1986.
Mascia, Gianfranco. *Qualcosa di sinistra: Intervista a Nanni Moretti*. Genoa: Flli. Frilli, 2002.
Mazierska, Ewa, and Laura Rascaroli. *The Cinema of Nanni Moretti: Dreams and Diaries*. London: Wallflower, 2004.
Menarini, Roy. *Studiare il film: Alcuni esempi di analisi del cinema di Moretti*. Porretta Terme, Bologna: I Quaderni del Battello Ebbro, 2002.
Nanni Moretti. Turin: Paravia Scriptorium, 1999.
Porton, Richard, and Lee Ellickson (eds.). "Comedy, Communism, and Pastry: An Interview with Nanni Moretti." *Cineaste* 21, nos. 1–2 (1995): 11–15.

Ugo, Paola, and Antioco Floris. *Facciamoci del male: Il cinema di Nanni Moretti*. Cagliari: CUEC/Tredicilune, 1990.

Young, Deborah. "Me, Myself and Italy." *Film Comment* 38, no. 1 (2002): 56–61.

Zagarrio, Vito. "Nanni Moretti e la Renaissance italiana." In *Incontri con il cinema italiano*, ed. Antonio Vitti. Caltanissetta: S. Sciascia, 2003.

Pasolini, Pier Paolo

Associazione "Fondo Pier Paolo Pasolini" (ed.). *Pier Paolo Pasolini: Un poeta di opposizione*. Milan: Skira, 1995.

Baranski, Zygmunt. *Pasolini Old and New: Surveys and Studies*. Dublin: Four Courts Press, 1999.

Bellezza, Dario. *Morte di Pasolini*. Milan: Mondadori, 1981.

Blandeau, Agnès. *Pasolini, Chaucer and Boccaccio: Two Medieval Texts and Their Translation to Film*. Jefferson, NC: McFarland, 2006.

Camporeale, Cosimo (ed.). *Pier Paolo Pasolini, testimone problematico del nostro tempo: Il poeta, il narratore, il regista, il giornalista*. Bari: Ladisa, 1994.

Canziani, Alfonso. "Bibliografia su Pier Paolo Pasolini." In *I migliori anni del nostro cinema*, 156–66. Rome: Bulzoni, 1992.

Caspar, Marie-Hélène (ed.). *Pasolini*. Nanterre: Université de Paris X, 1994.

Cavalluzzi, Raffaele. *Il limite oscuro: Pasolini visionario: La poesia, il cinema*. Fasano (Brindisi): Schena, 1994.

Cherubini, Laura (ed.). *Pasolini e noi: Relazioni tra arte e cinema*. Cinisello Balsamo (Milan): Silvana, 2005.

De Giusti, Luciano. *I film di Pier Paolo Pasolini*. Rome: Gremese, 1983.

Ferrero, Adelio. *Il cinema di Pier Paolo Pasolini*. Venice: Marsilio, 1986.

Ferretti, Gian Carlo. *Pasolini: L'universo orrendo*. Rome: Editori Riuniti, 1976.

Fortini, Franco. *Attraverso Pasolini*. Turin: Einaudi, 1993.

Friedrich, Pia. *Pier Paolo Pasolini*. Boston: Twayne, 1982.

Furfaro, Amedeo. *La Calabria di Pasolini*. Cosenza: Edizioni Periferie, 1990.

Gordon, Robert S. C. *Pasolini: Forms of Subjectivity*. Oxford: Clarendon Press, 1996.

Greene, Naomi. *Pier Paolo Pasolini: Cinema as Heresy*. Princeton, NJ: Princeton University Press, 1990.

Indiana, Gary. *Salò or the 120 Days of Sodom*. London: British Film Institute, 2000.

Lacoue-Labarthe, Philippe. *Pasolini, une improvisation: D'une sainteté*. Bordeaux: Pharmacie de Platon, 1995.

Magrelli, Enrico (ed.). *Con Pier Paolo Pasolini*. Rome: Bulzoni, 1977.

Martellini, Luigi. *Introduzione a Pasolini*. Rome: Laterza, 1989.

Michalczyk, J. J. "Pier Paolo Pasolini: The Epical-Religious Cinema of Political Sexuality." In *The Italian Political Filmmakers*. Rutherford, NJ: Fairleigh Dickinson University Press, 1986.

Moscati, Italo. *Pasolini e il teorema del sesso, 1968: Dalla mostra del cinema al sequestro: Un anno vissuto nello scandalo.* Milan: Il Saggiatore, 1995.

Naldini, Nico. *Pasolini: Una vita*. Turin: Einaudi, 1989.

Pasolini, Pier Paolo. *Lettere: Con una cronologia della vita e delle opere*. Ed. Nico Naldini. Turin: Einaudi, 1986.

———. *Le regole di un'illusione: I film, il cinema*. Ed. Laura Betti and Michele Gulinucci. Rome: Associazione "Fondo Pier Paolo Pasolini," 1991.

Pierangeli, Fabio, and Patrizio Barbaro. *Pasolini: Biografia per immagini*. Cavallermaggiore: Gribaudo, 1995.

Rappaport, Mark. "The Autobiography of Pier Paolo Pasolini." *Film Quarterly* 56, no. 1 (2002): 2–8.

Rhodes, John D. *Stupendous, Miserable City: Pasolini's Rome*. Minneapolis: University of Minnesota Press, 2007.

Rinaldi, Rinaldo. *L'irriconoscibile Pasolini*. Rome: Marra, 1990.

Rohdie, Sam. *The Passion of Pier Paolo Pasolini*. Bloomington: Indiana University Press, 1995.

Rumble, Patrick. *Allegories of Contamination: Pier Paolo Pasolini's Trilogy of Life*. Toronto: University of Toronto Press, 1996.

Rumble, Patrick, and Bart Testa (eds.). *Pier Paolo Pasolini: Contemporary Perspectives*. Toronto: University of Toronto Press, 1994.

Schwartz, Barth David. *Pasolini Requiem*. New York: Pantheon Books, 1992.

Siciliano, Enzo. *Pasolini: A Biography*. Trans. John Shepley. New York: Random House, 1982. (Translation of *Vita di Pasolini*. Milan: Rizzoli, 1978.)

Stack, Oswald. *Pasolini on Pasolini: Interviews with Oswald Stack*. London: Thames and Hudson, 1969.

Teatro Tenda (ed.). *Per conoscere Pasolini*. Rome: Bulzoni & Teatro Tenda, 1978.

Trombadori, Duccio (ed.). *Pier Paolo Pasolini: Figuratività e figurazione*. Rome: Edizioni Carte Segrete, 1992.

Viano, Maurizio. *A Certain Realism: Making Use of Pasolini's Film Theory and Practice*. Berkeley: University of California Press, 1993.

White, Edmund. "Movies and Poems: Pier Paolo Pasolini." In *The Burning Library: Essays*. Ed. David Bergman. New York: A. A. Knopf, 1994.

Zigaina, Giuseppe. *Pasolini e la morte: Mito alchimia e semantica del nulla lucente*. Venice: Marsilio, 1987.

Risi, Dino

Caprara, Valerio. *Dino Risi: Maestro per caso*. Rome: Gremese, 1993.
———. (ed.). *Mordi e fuggi: La commedia secondo Dino Risi*. Venice: Marsilio, 1993.
Comand, Mariapia. *Dino Risi: Il sorpasso*. Turin: Lindau, 2002.
D'Agostini, Paolo. *Dino Risi*. Rome: Il Castoro, 1995.
Miccichè, Lino. *Una vita difficile di Dino Risi: Risate amare nel lungo dopoguerra*. Venice: Marsilio, 2000.
Prudenzi, Angela, and Cristina Scognamillo (eds.). *Dino Risi: Maestro dell'equilibrio e della leggerezza*. Rome: Fondazione Scuola Nazionale di Cinema / Centro Sperimentale di Cinematografia, 2002.
Risi, Dino. *I miei mostri*. Milan: Mondadori, 2003.
Viganò, Aldo. *Dino Risi*. Milan: Moizzi, 1977.

Rosi, Francesco

Bolzoni, Francesco. *I film di Francesco Rosi*. Rome: Gremese, 1986.
Ciment, Michel. *Le dossier Rosi: Cinéma et politique*. Paris: Stock, 1976.
Crowdus, Gary. "Francesco Rosi: Italy's Postmodern Realist." *Cineaste* 20, no. 4 (1994): 19–27.
Georgakas, Dan, and Lenny Rubenstein (eds.). "Francesco Rosi: The Audience Should Not Be Just Passive Spectators." In *Art, Politics, Cinema: The Cineaste Interviews*. London: Pluto Press, 1985.
Gesù, Sebastiano (ed.). *Francesco Rosi*. Acicatena (Catania): Incontri con il Cinema, 1991.
Gili, Jean A. *Francesco Rosi: Cinéma et pouvoir*. Paris: Éditions du Cerf, 1977.
———. (ed.). *Francesco Rosi*. Paris: Lettres Modernes Minard, 2001.
Klawans, Stuart, and Howard Feinstein. "Illustrious Rosi." *Film Comment* 31, no. 1 (1995): 60–65.
Mancino, Anton Giulio, and Sandro Zambetti. *Francesco Rosi*. Rome: Il Castoro, 1998.
Marcus, Millicent. "Rosi's *Christ Stopped at Eboli*: A Tale of Two Italies." In *Italian Film in the Light of Neorealism*. Princeton, NJ: Princeton University Press, 1986.
Michalczyk, J. J. "Francesco Rosi: The Dialectical Cinema." In *The Italian Political Filmmakers*. Rutherford, NJ: Fairleigh Dickinson University Press, 1986.
Rosi, Francesco. *Cristo si è fermato a Eboli: Dal libro di Carlo Levi al film*. Turin: Testo e Immagine, 1996.

Tassone, Aldo, Gabriele Rizza, and Chiara Tognolotti. *La sfida della verità: Il cinema di Francesco Rosi*. Florence: Aida, 2005.

Testa, Carlo (ed.). *Poet of Civic Courage: The Films of Francesco Rosi*. Westport, CT: Greenwood Press, 1996.

Zambetti, Sandro. *Francesco Rosi*. Florence: La Nuova Italia, 1976.

Rossellini, Roberto

Aprà, Adriano (ed.). *Rosselliniana: Bibliografia internazionale*. Rome: Di Giacomo, 1987.

Bondanella, Peter. *The Films of Roberto Rossellini*. Cambridge: Cambridge University Press, 1993.

Brunette, Peter. *Roberto Rossellini*. New York: Oxford University Press, 1987.

Bruni, David. *Roberto Rossellini: Roma, città aperta*. Turin: Lindau, 2006.

Bruno, Edoardo (ed.). *R. R., Roberto Rossellini*. Rome: Bulzoni, 1979.

Dagrada, Elena. *Le varianti trasparenti: I film con Ingrid Bergman di Roberto Rossellini*. Milan: LED, 2005.

Di Giammatteo, Fernaldo. *Roberto Rossellini*. Scandicci (Florence): La Nuova Italia, 1990.

Forgacs, David. *Rome Open City*. London: British Film Institute, 2000.

Forgacs, David, Sarah Lutton, and Geoffrey Nowell-Smith (eds.). *Roberto Rossellini: Magician of the Real*. London: British Film Institute, 2000.

Gallagher, Tag. *The Adventures of Roberto Rossellini*. New York: Da Capo Press, 1998.

Giammusso, Maurizio. *Vita di Roberto Rossellini*. Rome: Elleu Multimedia, 2004.

Gottlieb, Sidney (ed.). *Roberto Rossellini's "Rome Open City."* Cambridge: Cambridge University Press, 2004.

Leto, Antonio. *La città di Rossellini*. Salerno: Plectica, 2004.

Masi, Stefano. *I film di Roberto Rossellini*. Rome: Gremese, 1987.

Menon, Gianni (ed.). *Dibattito su Rossellini*. Rome: Partisan, 1972.

Michelone, Guido. *Invito al cinema di Roberto Rossellini*. Milan: Mursia, 1996.

Ranvaud, Don (ed.). *Roberto Rossellini*. London: British Film Institute, 1981.

Rondolino, Gianni. *Roberto Rossellini*. Turin: UTET, 1989.

Rossellini, Isabella. *In the Name of the Father, the Daughter and the Holy Spirits: Remembering Roberto Rossellini*. London: Haus, 2006.

Rossellini, Renzo. *Chat Room Roberto Rossellini*. Rome: L. Sossella, 2002.

Rossellini, Roberto. *The War Trilogy: Open City, Paisan, Germany—Year Zero*. Ed. Stefano Roncoroni, trans. Judith Green. London: Lorrimer, 1973.

———. *Quasi un'autobiografia*. Ed. Stefano Roncoroni. Milan: Mondadori, 1987.

———. *My Method: Writings and Interviews*. Ed. Adriano Aprà, trans. Annapaola Cancogni. New York: Marsilio, 1992. (Translation of *Il mio metodo: scritti e interviste*. Venice: Marsilio, 1987.)

———. *Il mio dopoguerra*. Rome: Edizioni e/o, 1995.

Rossi, Patrizio. *Roberto Rossellini: A Guide to References and Resources*. Boston: G. K. Hall, 1988.

Seknadje-Askénazi, Enrique. *Roberto Rossellini et la Seconde Guerre mondiale: Un cinéaste entre propagande et réalisme*. Paris: L'Harmattan, 2000.

Serceau, Michel. *Roberto Rossellini*. Paris: Éditions du Cerf, 1986.

Trasatti, Sergio. *Rossellini e la televisione*. Rome: La Rassegna, 1978.

Scola, Ettore

Bìspuri, Ennio. *Ettore Scola: Un umanista nel cinema italiano*. Rome: Bulzoni, 2006.

De Santi, Pier Marco (ed.). *Ettore Scola: Immagini per un mondo nuovo*. Pisa: Giardini Editori, 1988.

De Santi, Pier Marco, and Rossano Vittori. *I film di Ettore Scola*. Rome: Gremese, 1987.

Ellero, Roberto. *Ettore Scola*. Milan: Il Castoro, 1996.

Gieri, Manuela. "Ettore Scola: A Cinematic and Social Metadiscourse." In *Contemporary Italian Filmmaking: Strategies of Subversion*. Toronto: University of Toronto Press, 1995.

Maraldi, Antonio (ed.). *Il film e le sceneggiature di Ettore Scola*. Cesena: Centro Cinema Città di Cesena, 1982.

Marinucci, Vinicio. *Ettore Scola*. Rome: Ministry of Tourism and Entertainment, 1981.

Marlia, Giulio (ed.). *Ettore Scola: Il volto amaro della commedia all'italiana*. Viareggio (Lucca): M. Baroni, 1999.

Masi, Stefano. *Ettore Scola*. Rome: Gremese, 2006.

Micheli, Paola. *Ettore Scola: I film e le parole*. Rome: Bulzoni, 1994.

Russo, Paolo (ed.). *Ettore Scola: Pesaro, 21–29 giugno 2002*. Pesaro: Fondazione Pesaro Nuovo Cinema Onlus, 2002.

Scola, Ettore. *Il cinema e io: Conversazione con Antonio Bertini*. Rome: Officina Edizioni, 1996.

Taviani, Paolo and Vittorio

Accialini, Fulvio, and Lucia Coluccelli. *Paolo e Vittorio Taviani*. Florence: La Nuova Italia, 1979.

Ambrosini, Maurizio, and Ignazio Occhipinti. *Le affinità elettive di Paolo e Vittorio Taviani: L'ideazione, la scrittura, l'avventura del set: La traduzione cinematografica di un classico della letteratura.* Milan: Sapiens, 1996.

Aristarco, Guido. *Sotto il segno dello scorpione: Il cinema dei Fratelli Taviani.* Messina: Casa Editrice G. D'Anna, 1977.

Brunette, Peter. "Vittorio Taviani: An Interview." *Film Quarterly* 36, no. 3 (1983): 2–9.

Camerino, Vincenzo, and Antonio Tarsi. *Dialettica dell'utopia: Il cinema di Paolo e Vittorio Taviani.* Manduria: Lacaita, 1978.

Crowdus, Gary. "The Taviani Brothers: We Believe in the Power of Cinema." In *The Cineaste Interviews 2: On the Art and Politics of the Cinema*, ed. Gary Crowdus and Dan Georgakas. Chicago: Lake View Press, 2002.

Cuccu, Lorenzo. *The Cinema of Paolo and Vittorio Taviani: Nature, Culture and History Revealed by Two Tuscan Masters.* Rome: Gremese, 2001. (Translation of *Il cinema di Paolo e Vittorio Taviani: Natura, cultura, storia nei film dei due registi toscani.* Rome: Gremese, 2001.)

De Poli, Marco. *Paolo e Vittorio Taviani.* Milan: Moizzi, 1977.

De Santi, Pier Marco. *I film di Paolo e Vittorio Taviani.* Rome: Gremese, 1988.

Ehrenstein, David. "Your Own Reality: An Interview with Paolo and Vittorio Taviani." *Film Quarterly* 47, no. 4 (1994): 2–6.

Ferrucci, Riccardo (ed.). *La Bottega Taviani: Un viaggio nel cinema da San Miniato a Hollywood.* Florence: La Casa Usher, 1987.

Ferrucci, Riccardo, and Patrizia Turini. *Paolo and Vittorio Taviani: Poetry of the Italian Landscape.* Rome: Gremese, 1995. (Translation of *Paolo e Vittorio Taviani: La poesia del paesaggio.* Rome: Gremese, 1995.)

Gili, Jean A. *Paolo et Vittorio Taviani: Entretien au pluriel.* Lyon: Institut Lumière, 1993.

Graham, M. "*Padre Padrone* and the Dialectics of Sound." *Film Criticism* 6, no. 1 (1981): 21–30.

Landy, Marcia. "Neorealism, Politics, and Language in the Films of the Tavianis." *Annali d'Italianistica* 6 (1988): 236–251.

———. "Language, Folklore and Politics in the Films of the Taviani Brothers." In *Film, Politics, and Gramsci.* Minneapolis: University of Minnesota Press, 1994.

Legrand, Gérard. *Paolo et Vittorio Taviani.* Paris: Éditions de l'Étoile, 1990.

Marcus, Millicent Joy. "The Taviani Brothers' *Night of the Shooting Stars*: Ambivalent Tribute to Neorealism." In *Italian Film in the Light of Neorealism.* Princeton, NJ: Princeton University Press, 1986.

Montiroli, Umberto, and Sebastiano Gesù. *La Sicilia di Pirandello nel cinema dei Taviani.* Comiso: Salarchi Immagini, 2000.

O'Healy, Aine. "Weeping for Togliatti: The Taviani Brothers' 'Optimistic Tragedy.'" *RLA: Romance Languages Annual* 8 (1996): 265–270.

Orto, Nuccio. *La notte dei desideri*. Palermo: Sellerio, 1987.

Parmeggiani, F. "Lo sguardo rivolto al passato: Storia e storie nel cinema dei Taviani (1971–1984)." *Italica* 80, no. 3 (2003): 403–421.

Setti, Raffaella. 2001. *Cinema a due voci: Il parlato nei film di Paolo e Vittorio Taviani*. Florence: F. Cesati, 2001.

Zagarrio, Vito (ed.). *Utopisti esagerati: Il cinema di Paolo e Vittorio Taviani*. Venice: Marsilio, 2004.

Visconti, Luchino

Aristarco, Guido. *Su Visconti: Materiali per una analisi critica*. Rome: La Zattera di Babele, 1986.

Aristarco, Guido, and G. Carancini (eds.). *Rocco e i suoi fratelli, di Luchino Visconti*. Bologna: Cappelli, 1960.

Bacon, Henry. *Visconti: Explorations of Beauty and Decay*. Cambridge: Cambridge University Press, 1998.

Baldelli, Pio. *Luchino Visconti*. Milan: Mazzotta, 1973.

Bencivenni, Alessandro. *Luchino Visconti*. Florence: La Nuova Italia, 1982.

Bruni, David, and Veronica Pravadelli (eds.). *Studi viscontiani*. Venice: Marsilio, 1997.

Callegari, Giuliana, and Nuccio Lodato (eds.). *Leggere Visconti: Scritti, interviste, testimonianze e documenti di e su Luchino Visconti, con una bibliografia critica generale*. Pieve del Cairo (Pavia): Arti Grafiche La Cittadella, 1977.

Cavallaro, Giovanni Battista (ed.). *Luchino Visconti: Senso*. Bologna: Cappelli, 1977.

Cecchi D'Amico, Suso. *Il film "Il gattopardo" e la regia di Luchino Visconti*. Bologna: Cappelli, 1963.

Costantini, Costanzo. *L'ultimo Visconti*. Milan: SugarCo, 1976.

D'Amico de Carvalho, Caterina. *Album Visconti*. Milan: Sonzogno, 1978.

——. (ed.). *Viscontiana: Luchino Visconti e il melodramma verdiano*. Milan: Mazzotta, 2001.

——. (ed.). *Luchino Visconti e il suo tempo*. Milan: Electa, 2006.

D'Amico de Carvalho, Caterina, Vera Marzot, and Umberto Tirelli (eds.). *Visconti e il suo lavoro*. Milan: Electa, 1995.

De Berti, Raffaele (ed.). *Il cinema di Luchino Visconti tra società e alter arti: Analisi di film*. Milan: CUEM, 2005.

De Giusti, Luciano. *I film di Luchino Visconti*. Rome: Gremese, 1985.

Di Giammatteo, Fernaldo. *La controversia Visconti*. Rome: Edizioni dell'Ateneo & Bizzarri, 1976.

Dombroski, Robert. "Giuseppe Tommasi di Lampedusa and Luchino Visconti: Substances of Form." In *Properties of Writing: Ideological Discourse in Modern Italian Fiction*. Baltimore: Johns Hopkins University Press, 1994.

Ferrero, Adelio. *Visconti, il cinema: Tavola rotonda*. Modena: Comune, Ufficio Cinema, 1978.

Fumagalli, Paola. *"Il gattopardo": Dal romanzo al film*. Florence: Firenze Libri, 1988.

Gastel Chiarelli, Cristina. *Musica e memoria nell'arte di Luchino Visconti*. Milan: Archinto, 1997.

Guillaume, Yves. *Luchino Visconti*. Paris: Éditions Universitaires, 1966.

Hillman, Roger. "Pivot Chords: Austrian Music and Visconti's *Senso* (1954)." In *Unsettling Scores: German Film, Music, and Ideology*. Bloomington: Indiana University Press, 2005.

Lagny, Michèle. *Senso, Luchino Visconti: Étude critique*. Paris: Nathan, 1992.

———. *Luchino Visconti: Vérités d'une légende*. Paris: BiFi, 2002.

Larere, Odile. *De l'imaginaire au cinéma: Violence et passion de Luchino Visconti*. Paris: Albatros, 1980.

Liandrat-Guigues, Suzanne. *Le couchant et l'aurore: Sur le cinéma de Luchino Visconti*. Paris: Méridiens Klincksieck, 1999.

Mancini, Elaine. *Luchino Visconti: A Guide to References and Resources*. Boston: G. K. Hall, 1986.

Mannino, Franco. *Visconti e la musica*. Lucca: Akademos & LIM, 1994.

Marzot, Vera, and Umberto Tirelli (eds.). *L'arte del costume nel cinema di Luchino Visconti: Documentazione dei costumi ideati da Piero Tosi per i film di Luchino Visconti*. Rome: L'Arte della Stampa, 1977.

Miccichè, Lino. *Visconti e il neorealismo: Ossessione, La terra trema, Bellissima*. Venice: Marsilio, 1990.

———. *Luchino Visconti: Un profilo critico*. Venice: Marsilio, 1996.

———. (ed.). *"La terra trema" di Luchino Visconti: Analisi di un capolavoro*. Turin: Associazione Philip Morris Progetto Cinema, 1994.

Naglia, Sandro. *Mann, Mahler, Visconti: "Morte a Venezia."* Pescara: Tracce, 1995.

Navone, Luisa (ed.). *Tutti i film di Luchino Visconti*. Siena: Amministrazione Provinciale di Siena, 1987.

Nowell-Smith, Geoffrey. *Luchino Visconti*. London: British Film Institute, 2003.

Partridge, C. J. *Senso: Visconti's Film and Boito's Novella: A Case Study in the Relation between Literature and Film*. Lewiston, NY: Edwin Mellen Press, 1992.

Petrucci, Francesco (ed.). *Visconti e "Il gattopardo": La scena del principe*. Milan: De Agostini-Rizzoli Arte & Cultura, 2001.

Pravadelli, Veronica (ed.). *Il cinema di Luchino Visconti*. Venice: Marsilio, 2000.

Renzi, Renzo. *Visconti segreto*. Rome: Laterza, 1994.

Rohdie, Sam. *Rocco and His Brothers (Rocco e i suoi fratelli)*. London: British Film Institute, 1992.

Rondolini, Gianni. *Luchino Visconti*. Turin: UTET, 1981.

Schifano, Laurence. *Luchino Visconti: The Flames of Passion*. London: Collins, 1990.

Schüler, Rolf, and Berliner Filmkunsthaus Babylon (eds.). *Visconti*. Berlin: Filmkunsthaus Babylon, 1995.

Servadio, Gaia. *Luchino Visconti: A Biography*. London: Weidenfeld and Nicholson, 1982.

Stirling, Monica. *A Screen of Time: A Study of Luchino Visconti*. New York: Harcourt Brace Jovanovich, 1979.

Tonetti, Claretta Micheletti. *Luchino Visconti*. New York: Twayne, 1997.

Tramontana, Gaetano. *Invito al cinema di Luchino Visconti*. Milan: Mursia, 2003.

Villien, Bruno. *Visconti*. Paris: Calmann-Lévy, 1987.

THE INDUSTRY

Bernardini, Aldo, and Vittorio Martinelli. *Titanus: La storia di tutti i film di una grande casa di produzione*. Milan: Coliseum, 1986.

Bizzarri, Libero, and Libero Solaroli. *L'industria cinematografica italiana*. Florence: Parenti, 1958.

Cesaro, Marco. *Italian film show: Guida ai festival del cinema italiani*. Faenza: Cinetecnica, 2004.

Cordaro, Chiara. "Censimento 1: Case di produzione e produttori." In *La "scuola" italiana: Storia, strutture, e immaginario di un altro cinema, 1988–1996*, ed. Mario Sesti. Venice: Marsilio, 1996.

Corsi, Barbara. *Con qualche dollaro in meno: Storia economica del cinema italiano*. Rome: Editori Riuniti, 2001.

Degli-Esposti Reinert, Cristina. "Italy." In *The International Movie Industry*, ed. Gorham Kindem. Carbondale: Southern Illinois University Press, 2000.

Della Casa, Stefano (ed.). *Capitani coraggiosi: Produttori italiani 1945–1975 / Captains Courageous: Italian Producers 1945–1975*. Trans. Christopher Evans. Milan: Mondadori Electa, La Biennale di Venezia, 2003.

Ghezzi, Luigi, and Luisa Zampieri. "Prima del sonoro: L'industria cinematografica italiana negli anni venti." *Bianco e Nero* 40 (March–April 1979): 2–49.

Magrelli, Enrico (ed.). *Sull'industria cinematografica italiana*. Venice: Marsilio, 1986.

Quaglietti, Lorenzo. *Storia economico-politica del cinema italiano: 1945–1980*. Rome: Editori Riuniti, 1980.
Valerio, Silvana. "La nascita della Lux film." *Cinemasessanta*, no. 144 (March–April 1982).
Wagstaff, Christopher. "Il cinema italiano nel mercato internazionale." In *Identità italiana e identità europea nel cinema italiano dal 1945 al miracolo economico*, ed. Gian Piero Brunetta. Turin: Edizioni della Fondazione Giovanni Agnelli, 1996.
———. "Italian Genre Films in the World Market." In *Hollywood and Europe: Economics, Culture, National Identity, 1945–95*, ed. Geoffrey Nowell-Smith and Stephen Ricci. London: British Film Institute, 1998.
Zanchi, Claudio. "L'industria cinematografica italiana del primo dopoguerra." In *Il neorealismo cinematografico italiano*, ed. Lino Miccichè. Venice: Marsilio, 1975.

WEBSITES

Activcinema. Rivista Attiva di Archeologia Cinematografica: www.activitaly.it/immaginicinema/ (in Italian)
ANICA: www.anica.it/ (in Italian)
Association of College and Research Libraries. "Wessweb. Italian Studies Web—Cinema": www.library.uiuc.edu/mdx/itacinwess.htm
Banca Dati del Cinema Mondiale: www.cinematografo.it/Banca_dati/00000059.html (in Italian)
Biografie Cinema: http://biografie.leonardo.it/categoria.htm?c=Cinema (in Italian)
Buio in Sala: www.mclink.it/mclink/cinema/ (in Italian)
Celluloide.it: www.celluloide.it/home/index.asp (in Italian)
Centro Sperimentale di Cinematografia: www.csc-cinematografia.it/csc/pages/homepage.php (some content available in English)
Cinecittà online: www.cinecitta.com/ (in Italian)
Cinematografo.it: www.cinematografo.it/ (in Italian)
Cinemotore: www.cinemotoreonline.net/ (in Italian)
Close-up: www.close-up.it/ (in Italian)
Comune di Reggio Emilia catalogo film: www.municipio.re.it/cinema/catfilm.nsf/web/Ctlgflm?opendocument (in Italian)
David di Donatello Awards: www.daviddidonatello.it/ (in Italian)
Dizionario Autori Cinema: www.girodivite.it/antenati/mg_aut.htm (in Italian)
Effettonotte Online: www.effettonotteonline.com/enol/index.html (in Italian)
Falso Movimento: www.altrovideo.com/wordpress/ (in Italian)

Gli Attori del Cinema Italiano: www.artemotore.com/attorita.html (in Italian)
History of Italian Horror: www.horror-wood.com/italianhorror1.htm
ilCinemante: www.ilcinemante.com/index.asp (in Italian)
ildocumentario.it: www.ildocumentario.it/ (in Italian)
Images Online Journal, "Issue 5: The Golden Age of Italian Horror, 1957–1979": www.imagesjournal.com/issue05/infocus.htm
Images Online Journal, "Issue 6: Spaghetti Westerns": www.imagesjournal.com/issue06/infocus/spaghetti.htm
Istituto LUCE—Archivio Storico: http://ricerca.archivioluce.com/h3/h3.exe/a1/fric_avanzata (in Italian)
Italica Momenti del Cinema Italiano: www.italica.rai.it/cinema/ (also in English)
Museo Nazionale del Cinema: www.museonazionaledelcinema.org/, www.ottoemezzo.com/ (in Italian)
Pezzotta, Alberto. "A Journey through Italian Cinema." Senses of Cinema: www.sensesofcinema.com/contents/03/26/journey_italian.html
Senses of Cinema: www.sensesofcinema.com/ (see especially Great Directors section, covering many Italian directors)
Sentieri Selvaggi: www.sentieriselvaggi.it/ (in Italian)
Sindacato Nazionale Giornalisti Cinematografici Italiani: www.cinegiornalisti.it (in Italian)
Tempi Moderni: http://www.tempimoderni.com/ (in Italian)
Treccani Cinema: www.treccani.it/site/Cinema/Abiografie.htm (in Italian)
UC Berkeley, "Italian Cinema: A Bibliography of Books and Articles in the UC Berkeley Libraries, 1996": www.lib.berkeley.edu/MRC/italianfilmbib.html
Venice Biennale—Mostra internazionale d'arte cinematografica: www.labiennale.org/it/cinema/ (also in English)

About the Author

Gino Moliterno was born in Italy but grew up in Sydney, Australia. He completed both his undergraduate and postgraduate studies at the University of Sydney, where he received his doctorate for a thesis on the Renaissance philosopher Giordano Bruno. He taught Italian language and literature at a number of Australian and New Zealand universities before joining the Australian National University (ANU) in Canberra, where he was for many years the convenor of the Italian Studies Program. In the mid-1990s he helped to establish the Film Studies Program at the ANU, where he has since taught and periodically heads. Among his publications are an annotated translation of Giordano Bruno's 16th-century comedy, *Candelaio,* and *Sydney and the Italian Touch*, an anthology of reminiscences of Italian Australians in Sydney, coedited with Roberto Pettini.

Dr. Moliterno in 2000 served as general editor of the *Routledge Encyclopedia of Contemporary Italian Culture*, for which he also wrote many of the film entries. He has been a contributor to the online film journals *Screening the Past* and *Senses of Cinema*, and his essay on Pier Paolo Pasolini has been included in the Facet DVD release of the documentary on the director's life and death, *Whoever Says the Truth Must Die*. More recently he has written on Francis Ford Coppola and Martin Scorsese for the Routledge *New Makers of Modern Culture* (2006).